*The
Southern
Appalachian
Region*

THE SOUTHERN APPALACHIANS

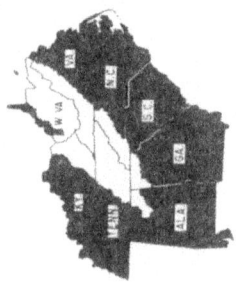

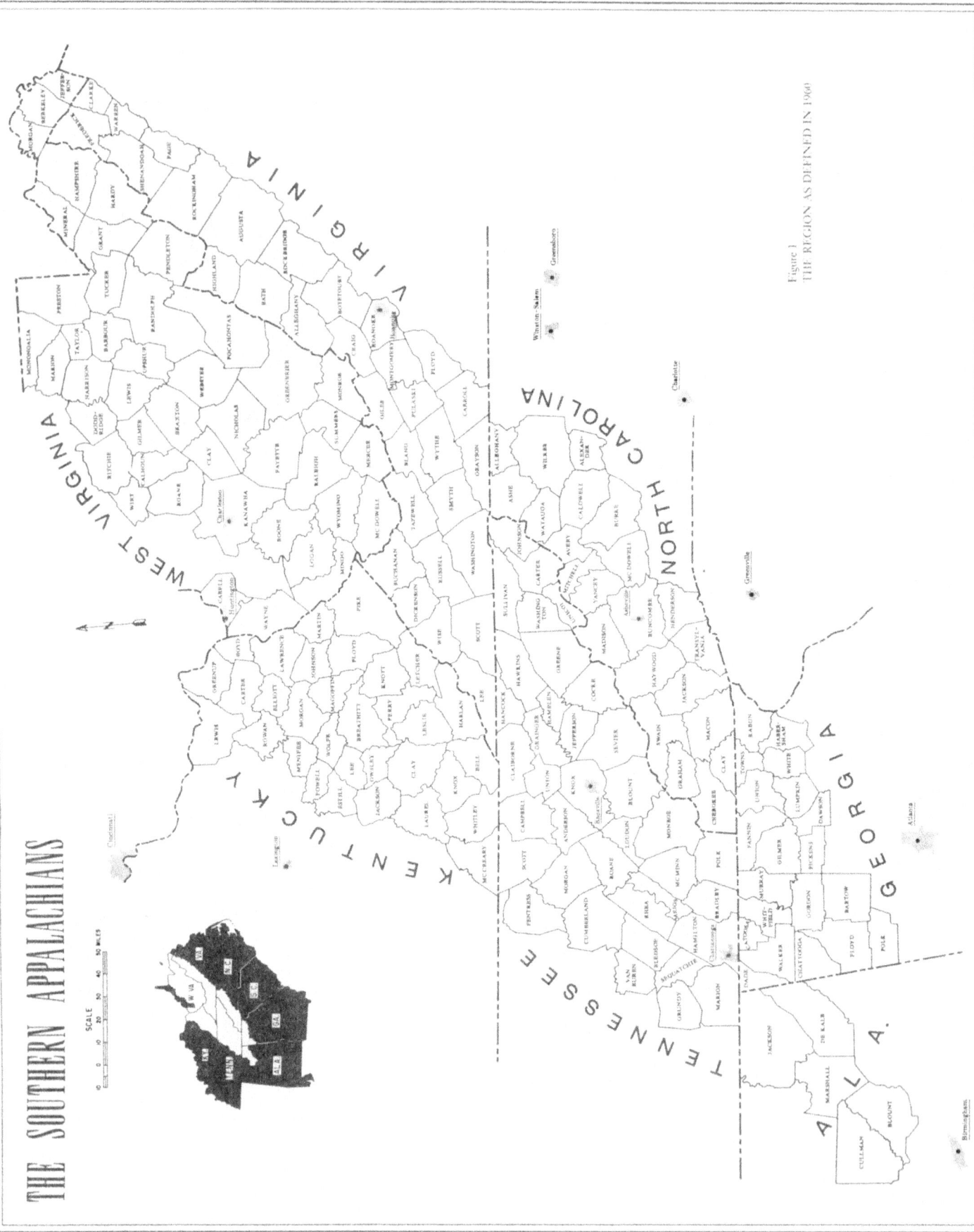

Figure 1
THE REGION AS DEFINED IN 1960

The Southern Appalachian Region

A Survey

Edited by

THOMAS R. FORD

Contributors

RUPERT B. VANCE

THOMAS R. FORD

JOHN C. BELCHER

JAMES S. BROWN

GEORGE A. HILLERY, JR.

ROSCOE GIFFIN

ROY E. PROCTOR

T. KELLEY WHITE

HAROLD A. GIBBARD

CHARLES L. QUITTMEYER

LORIN A. THOMPSON

JOHN W. MORRIS

PAUL W. WAGER

AELRED J. GRAY

ORIN B. GRAFF

EARL D. C. BREWER

C. HORACE HAMILTON

WILLIAM E. COLE

W. D. WEATHERFORD

WILMA DYKEMAN

FRANK H. SMITH

BERNICE A. STEVENS

UNIVERSITY OF KENTUCKY PRESS, LEXINGTON

Foreword

THIS VOLUME PRESENTS THE FINDINGS of the most comprehensive survey of the Southern Appalachians ever undertaken. Many smaller studies have been made in the Region during the past twenty-five years. Some of them have been studies of special subjects such as health conditions or the work of a single denomination in the mountains. Others have been limited to a single state, county, or community. Regional data which are comparable from one state to another have rarely been available. So little original field work has been done in recent years that data have been insufficient to enable any organization to set up a sound Regionwide program for progress.

The most recent regional survey of social and economic conditions in this section of America was made in the early 1930's by the United States Department of Agriculture in cooperation with the United States Office of Education and the Agricultural Experiment Stations of Tennessee, Virginia, West Virginia, and Kentucky. This study was supported by "a limited amount of field work," and has long since been outdated by the changes that have taken place in the region. Nevertheless, it has served a great purpose in identifying specific regional problems and characteristics.

The present study had its origin in a conference of delegates from a number of religious denominations who had gathered at Berea, Kentucky, in 1956 to discuss the possibilities of cooperative programs in religious education and welfare in the mountain area. Recognizing the need for current information on social, cultural, and economic conditions as a basis for sound programs, the delegates asked Berea College to be host for a survey of the Region, using as much field work as feasible. As chairman of the conference and as Vice-Chairman of the Berea College Board of Trustees, I was asked to explore the possibilities of securing adequate funds for such a study. The Ford Foundation generously furnished two hundred and fifty thousand dollars, and churches and universities added in cash and services about sixty thousand dollars.

The group which originated the study incorporated under the name "Southern Appalachian Studies," and the actual research was started in June of 1958. Eleven universities, including all but one of the state universities of the states comprising the Region, several independent colleges, the Tennessee Valley Authority, and other independent agencies released time for investigators who conducted the individual studies contributing to the comprehensive survey.

The overall direction of the survey was provided by a central committee composed of Dr. Earl D. C. Brewer, Dr. Thomas R. Ford, Dr. Rupert B. Vance, and myself.

Southern Appalachian Studies had as its objectives to find out (1) *what changes had taken place in the Region since the study published in 1935; (2) whether these changes were constructive or destructive; (3) what the actual situation of the Region was with reference to health, education, religion, economic status, and other problem areas; (4) what the people really needed to bring them up to the American standards of living and culture; and (5) whether the revealed facts would point to some practical solutions of the problems found.* A further responsibility assumed by the Studies was to find agencies to use the results of the survey in setting up constructive programs which would bring the level of Appalachian life up to national standards.

Southern Appalachian Studies is, therefore, definitely committed to an implementation of policies based on its factual findings insofar as existing agencies can be induced to carry them out. We concur with the view expressed by the President of the Ford Foundation, that its grant should not be used simply to publish a book of facts, but rather to see that the facts were actively applied to better the lives of the Region's people. There are many problems yet to be studied, but we believe this volume, and perhaps others coming later, will provide both data and guidelines for constructive work.

W. D. WEATHERFORD
Director of Administration

Contents

Figures

Tables

CHAPTER ONE

The Region: A New Survey

RUPERT B. VANCE

CITY AND COUNTRY, EAST AND WEST, the United States is a nation of many contrasts. In this pattern of unity in diversity, the Southern Appalachians stand out as a distinctive region. It bears certain resemblances to highland areas everywhere; its life and culture remained in the frontier stage longer than in most American regions; it is also a province of the American South; but, most important, it is an integral part of our national structure—a fact to be emphasized throughout.

The Southern Appalachians, with the highest peaks and the most sharply dissected plateaus east of the Rockies, consist of three roughly parallel strips (Figure 2). The Blue Ridge Mountains form the eastern rim, rising abruptly out of the rolling Piedmont, and reaching their loftiest heights in the Great Smokies and the Black Mountains. At places this mass of mountains and hills widens to a span of one hundred miles. Next comes the Great Valley, broadened and flattened as its rivers have worn valleys in the underlying limestone. Farther to the west is the Cumberland Plateau, much dissected by streams and containing one of the richest bituminous coal areas in the world. Sometimes the valleys are so narrow as to be V-shaped gorges.

F. J. Marshner made use of distinctions in forms of relief, soil types, and differences in climate to demarcate subregions that appear to be uniform. His study showed three physiographic divisions with numerous subregions. The Eastern division consists of the Blue Ridge Mountains, the highest ranges within the area. The Central division consists of four valleys with their ridges: the Central, Southern, East Tennessee, and Southwest Virginia Valleys along with the rough terrain of the Central Appalachian Ridges. The Western division consists of the Appalachian Plateau, having various degrees of dissection in the Allegheny, the Northeastern Cumberland and the Northwestern Cumberland areas. In addition Marshner listed three fringe areas on the East, the Northern, Central and Southern Piedmont Plateaus, and two on the West, the upper Ohio Hills and the Highland Rim. The inclusion of these fringe areas indicates the degree of flexibility used in drawing the boundaries of the Southern Appalachian subregions.[1]

Relatively little of the Southern Appalachian area is truly mountainous. These areas are as follows: (1) Great Smokies, Unakas, Black Mountains (north and northeast of Asheville), and associated groups; (2) the more rugged parts of the Blue Ridge; (3) the most rugged parts of the Ridge and Valley Province

THE SOUTHERN APPALACHIANS

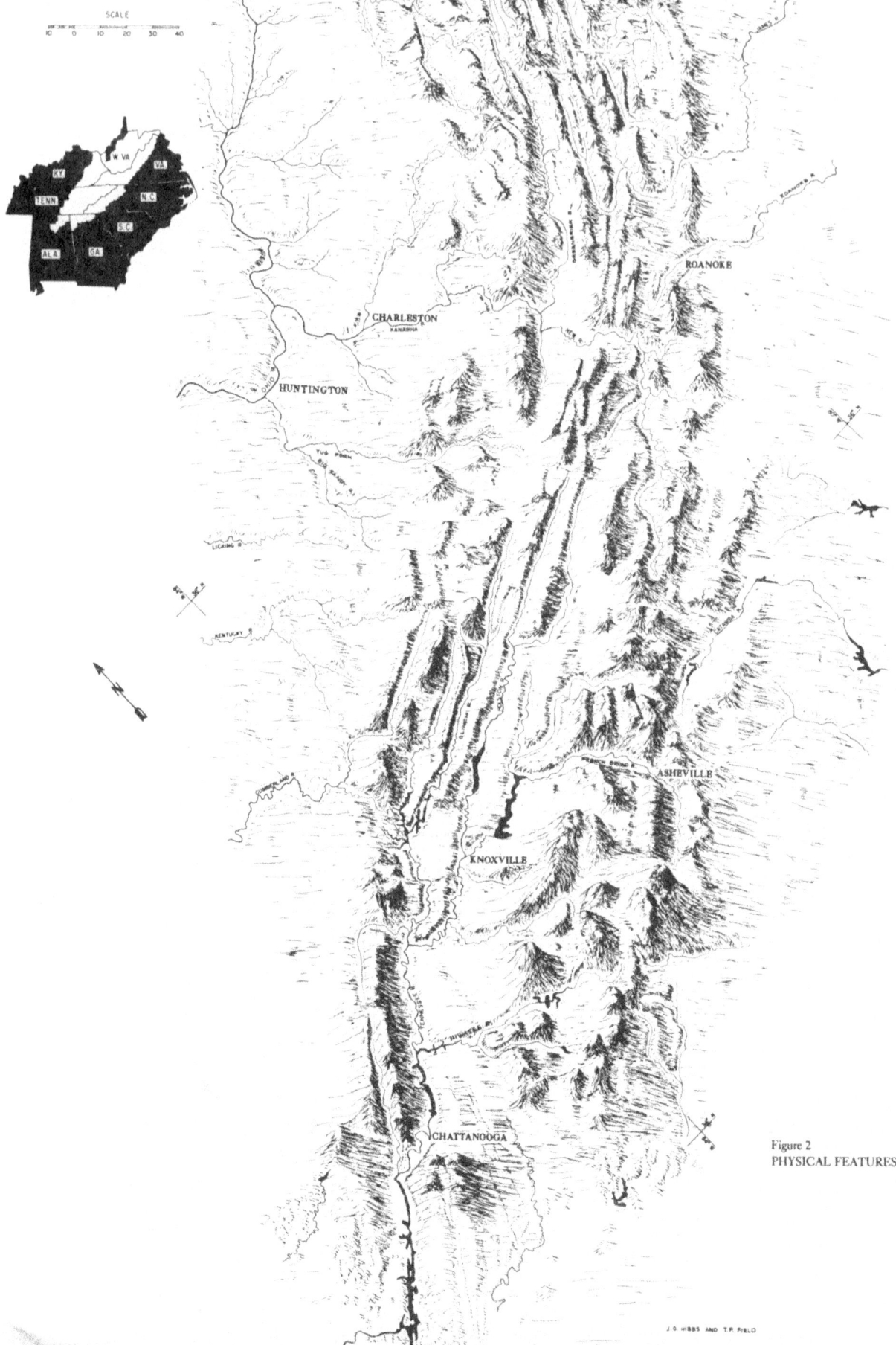

SCALE
10 0 10 20 30 40

Figure 2
PHYSICAL FEATURES

J.O. HIBBS AND T.P. FIELD

(e.g., parts of eastern and southeastern West Virginia); and (4) the most deeply dissected parts of the Allegheny and Cumberland Escarpments.

The truly mountainous areas contain little or no population and are generally heavily forested. They are important for watersheds, for forestry, and often for recreation; but the problem areas on which much of this study will focus are mainly in the hill lands (often dissected plateau areas) which make up the bulk of the Southern Appalachians.

In the first important survey of Appalachian problems, John C. Campbell (1921) selected a maximum number of counties on the basis of problems then encountered. Including fringes, he presented 210 counties in nine states—a region of some 112,000 square miles, an area almost as large as that of England, Ireland, Scotland, and Wales. In 1910, the latest census year Campbell considered, his region contained 5,300,111 people.[2] The area included in the present study, however, had that year a population of 3,513,222.

In the last full survey before the present, the U. S. Department of Agriculture (1935) reported that this region involved nine states, but contained only 109,500 square miles. This study selected 205 counties in six states with a total area of some 86,161 square miles, a region which had 3,794,794 population in 1910, the year of the Campbell survey.[3] For 1930 the region delimited by the USDA had 4,976,601 population, as compared with 4,771,813 in the area of the present survey. A 1960 report on the Appalachian Region, sponsored by the Maryland Department of Economic Development, covered an eleven-state problem area reaching from New York state to Alabama.[4] Concentrating on economic and population trends, it found an existing job deficit of 1,100,000 with 450,000 additional jobs needed by 1970. It outlined the serious problems of the area, pointed out the function of migration as a present relief, and deliberately avoided the recommendation of specific solutions.

The present definition of the Region makes use of the new concept of state economic areas, developed jointly in 1950 by the Bureau of the Census and the U. S. Department of Agriculture for the entire United States (Figure 3). Counties whose livelihood is drawn from the same economic base were grouped to form similar economic areas. Some are agricultural, based on types of crops; others are metropolitan areas containing a city of at least 50,000 inhabitants along with the counties integrated with the central city.[5]

The Appalachian subregion is accounted a portion

of the Eastern and Central Upland region. By dispensing with fringe areas, the Southern Appalachians are thus reduced to 19 state economic areas and eight metropolitan areas. The area now includes 190 counties, and no longer has any counties in Maryland or South Carolina (Figure 3). With only one economic area in Alabama, the Region does not take in the coal and iron complex centering in Birmingham. The Southern Appalachian Region as now defined remains large—more than 600 miles long and nearly 250 miles across at its widest point. This core of the Region is approximately 80,000 square miles in area. It contained 5,672,178 people by census count in 1960.

A Problem Area

While no attempt will be made in the introductory chapter to anticipate the results of the analysis to follow, the question may well be asked: Why was this Region chosen for study? There can be but one answer. *Over a period of time the Appalachians have come to be recognized as a definite problem area in the national economy.* Variations are great among communities and class groups and the majority will rank among comparable groups in the nation. Nevertheless, there remains a core problem area which can be recognized throughout a long period of regional history. The problem is defined in economic terms and the simplified definition established by the study, verified by income statistics, imputes no unworthiness to the populations involved.

The recognition of the Appalachian problem followed the development of national policy toward the general welfare. In the period of pioneer settlement, it is doubtful that the mountains were regarded as a disadvantaged area. Certainly the history of settlement offers no indication that people were shunted into the mountains nor that they were of inferior

[1] U. S. Department of Agriculture, *Economic and Social Problems and Conditions of the Southern Appalachians*, Miscellaneous Publication No. 205 (1935), pp. 7, 10-15; see also pocket map.

[2] John C. Campbell, *The Southern Highlander and His Homeland* (New York, 1921), pp. 10-18, 360-70.

[3] USDA, *Economic and Social Problems*, pp. 16, 120-21.

[4] Maryland Department of Economic Development, *The Appalachian Region: A Preliminary Analysis of Economic and Population Trends in an Eleven State Problem Area* (Annapolis, 1960).

[5] Donald J. Bogue, "Economic Areas as a Tool for Research and Planning," *American Sociological Review*, XV (1950), pp. 409-16; U. S. Department of Commerce, Bureau of the Census, *State Economic Areas* (1951), pp. 1-6; "An Outline of the Complete System of Economic Areas," *American Journal of Sociology*, LX (1954), pp. 136-39.

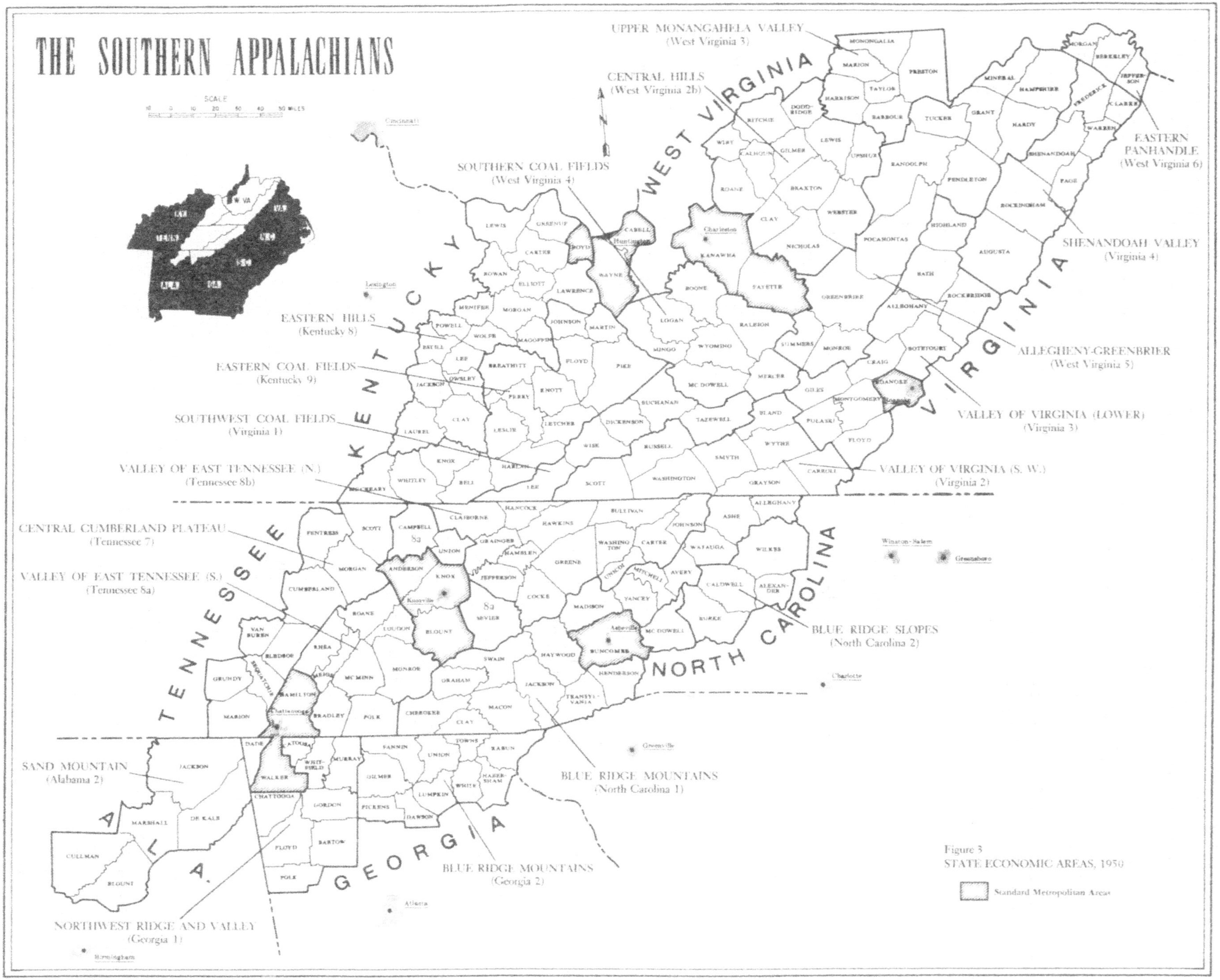

THE SOUTHERN APPALACHIANS

SCALE
0 10 20 30 40 50 MILES

EASTERN PANHANDLE (West Virginia 6)

SHENANDOAH VALLEY (Virginia 4)

ALLEGHENY-GREENBRIER (West Virginia 5)

VALLEY OF VIRGINIA (LOWER) (Virginia 3)

VALLEY OF VIRGINIA (S.W.) (Virginia 2)

BLUE RIDGE SLOPES (North Carolina 2)

UPPER MONANGAHELA VALLEY (West Virginia 3)

CENTRAL HILLS (West Virginia 2b)

SOUTHERN COAL FIELDS (West Virginia 4)

BLUE RIDGE MOUNTAINS (North Carolina 1)

BLUE RIDGE MOUNTAINS (Georgia 2)

EASTERN HILLS (Kentucky 8)

EASTERN COAL FIELDS (Kentucky 9)

SOUTHWEST COAL FIELDS (Virginia 1)

VALLEY OF EAST TENNESSEE (N.) (Tennessee 8b)

CENTRAL CUMBERLAND PLATEAU (Tennessee 7)

VALLEY OF EAST TENNESSEE (S.) (Tennessee 8a)

SAND MOUNTAIN (Alabama 2)

NORTHWEST RIDGE AND VALLEY (Georgia 1)

WEST VIRGINIA

VIRGINIA

KENTUCKY

NORTH CAROLINA

TENNESSEE

GEORGIA

ALA.

Figure 3
STATE ECONOMIC AREAS, 1950

☐ Standard Metropolitan Areas

stock. When D. H. Davis studied the Blue Grass and the Mountain Region for the State Geological Survey of Kentucky he reported: "The stock is, in all probability, in a large part the same as that of the Blue Grass, but it has been modified by long isolation in an area of lesser opportunity."[6]

In the era of private philanthropy, the region was established as a home mission field. Voluntary agencies and the churches subsidized ministers' salaries, built churches, and established academies that did the work of nonexistent public high schools. Frontier nurses on horseback delivered babies in isolated homes and pioneered in public health work.

Despite the earlier efforts of such men as John C. Campbell to call attention to the serious plight of the Region, not until the depression of the 1930's when various New Deal agencies gave full publicity to the pressure of population on limited regional resources was the problem made clear to the nation.

In 1938, a special report of the U. S. Department of Agriculture concluded from an examination of national farm conditions in 1930: "There are more than half a million farms in the United States on land so poor that it will literally starve the families living on it if they continue to try to make a living by farming."[7] Data from the 1930 census of agriculture revealed that the Appalachians held the highest concentration of low income farms in the country. Many returned less than $600 value of gross products; subsistence farms sold little in the open market; and many were part-time farms where the main operator worked off the farm 150 or more days a year for supplementary income. Every measure used served to indicate the uneconomic returns from Appalachian agriculture (Figure 4). The density of farm population was roughly 50 percent greater than in the best agricultural areas of the Middle West, where a large proportion of the land is adapted to farming and production per acre is much greater.

During the 1930's the rugged Cumberland Plateau was the subject of special analysis.[8] The people of that area stood out as the lowest income group in United States agriculture. Gross incomes per farm inhabitant averaged less than $150 in most of these counties and less than $300 in all. Six counties had more than half their population on relief during the depression while in the coal plateaus 21.8 percent of the population were on relief.

Measuring the magnitude of the problem in 84 coal plateau counties in the 1930's, the Study of Population Redistribution concluded that 350,000 people should leave that region's agriculture, that 60,000 should leave mining, and that forestry resources should be developed to support 70,000. As a minimum, accordingly, the population of the area needed to be reduced by 340,000 people, or 14.5 percent. The theoretical ceiling, in order to equalize living standards, was placed at an outward movement of 640,000 people, or a 27 percent reduction of the coal region's population.[9] This figure can be compared with the average of 500,000 persons on relief in the coal plateaus during the fiscal year 1934-1935.

The depression of the 1930's introduced relief and public works to the mountains and changed the practices of generations in one short period. Without any lowering of the customary "live-at-home" and "do-without" economy, the application of federal standards made at least half the population in certain Appalachian areas eligible for relief. Public Works, the Civilian Conservation Corps, and National Youth Administration, all introduced the people to the money economy and increased their wants. The depression, then, actually served to raise standards for many families in the region who had lacked contact with the American standard of living. But it left the region with a high rate of relief and a low basis for economic security. Self-employment and a deficit of large-scale industry left many occupations uncovered by social security, thus placing a double burden on welfare agencies in this new development. In addition, residential requirements for aid undoubtedly served to immobilize some workers and their families in problem areas.

Change from the outside came in the form of public works and the support of public education. Highway systems, financed and engineered by federal and state governments, cut through the mountains and destroyed isolation at little cost to local budgets and with little attention paid to local plans and leadership. In education, North Carolina during this depression period initiated the plan whereby it took over the state support of local schools. Elsewhere state equalization funds poured money into the local school budgets at an impressive rate.

The present paradox of the mountains is thus very

[6] D. H. Davis, *Geography of the Kentucky Mountains* (Frankfort, Ky., 1928), pp. 157-58.

[7] Carl C. Taylor, *et al.*, *Disadvantaged Classes in American Agriculture*, U. S. Department of Agriculture, Farm Security Administration, Social Research Report 8 (1939), p. 5.

[8] Carter Goodrich, *et al.*, *Migration and Economic Opportunity* (Philadelphia, 1936), pp. 59-79.

[9] Goodrich, pp. 122-23.

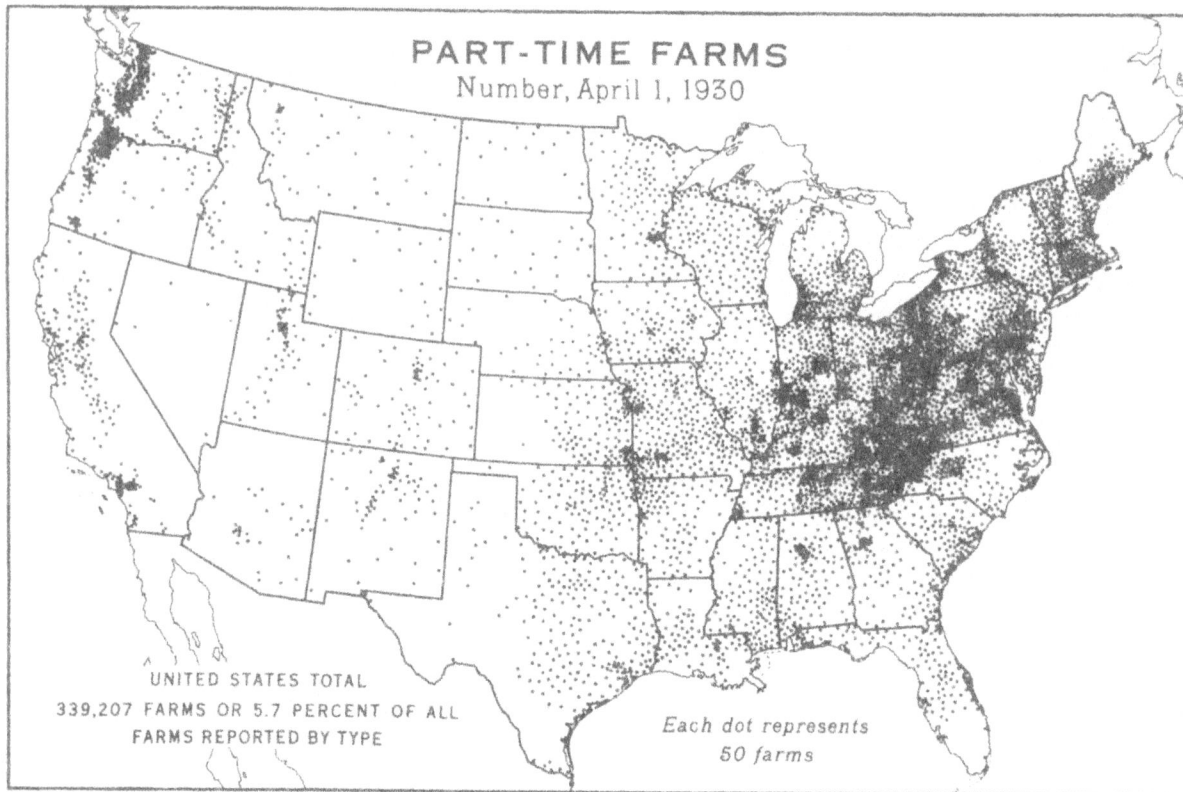

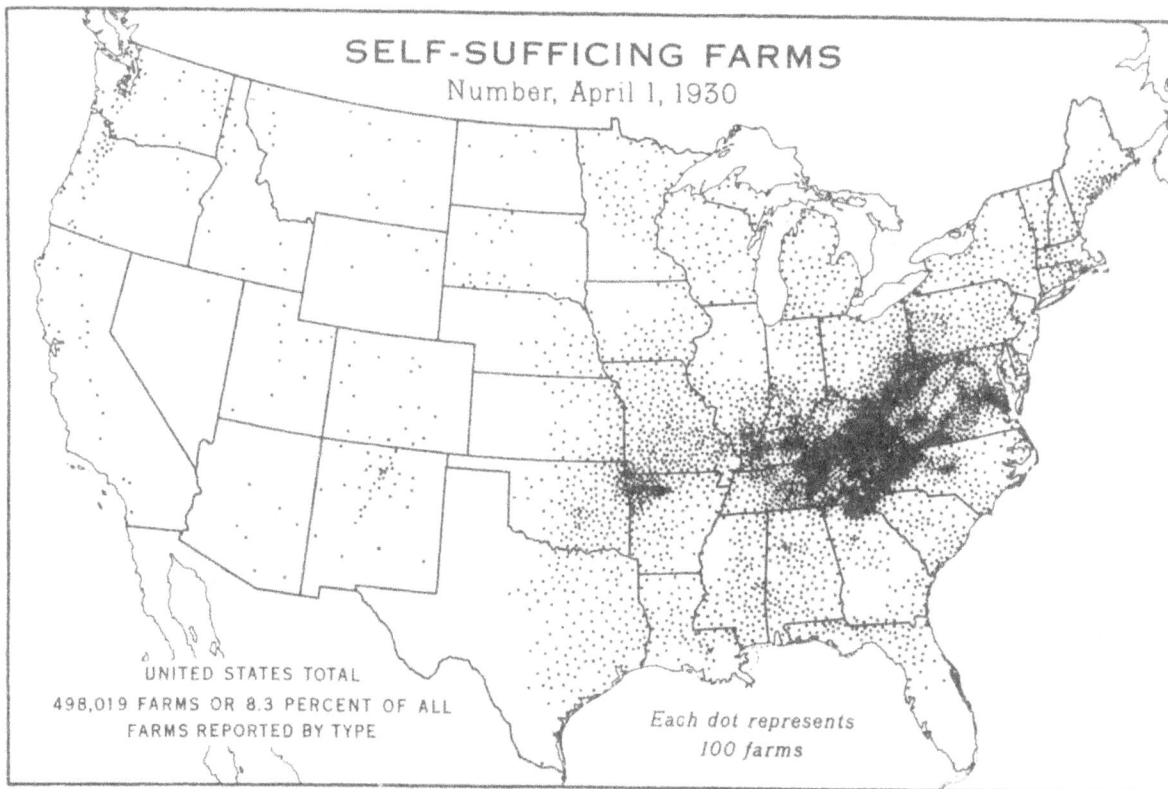

Figure 4. *Part-Time and Self-Sufficing Farms, United States, 1930*

real. Those rugged individualists, who hope to run their own affairs, now expect and receive more outside relief and subsidy from government, churches, and private agencies in proportion to their own contributions than any area of comparable size in the nation. The one exception, however, is an important one. Small subsistence farms grow few staples and cannot afford to cut back production. Accordingly, the mountain area benefits very little from the agricultural subsidies of the crop-control program.

This general position of the Region offers certain problems that will have to be faced by volunteer agencies and church bodies as well as by agencies of government.

If the problem of the Appalachians is to be met, it must be interpreted in the context of national development. We are concerned with questions as to the extent to which the Region has lagged behind in the processes of population redistribution, of economic and cultural development, and in the equalization of opportunity. Where these lags exist, the question then arises: What projects and plans can bring the area closer into line with national development?

Plans for the Region's subareas must of necessity be adjusted to the fact that urban and metropolitan areas are expanding, agricultural and rural areas shrinking. The extent to which population redistribution has put people in line with the movement toward national equalization is not generally recognized. In Oklahoma, over half the rural farm population moved off their farms in a single decade from 1940 to 1950. Close to half the people born in the state of Arkansas have migrated to other states. It has been suggested that we are tending toward the development of a single, national community in which regional, rural-urban and social class differences will become less important. This, it is apparent, will not be due entirely to the large-scale movements of our population to cities and their surrounding metropolitan districts. The spread of education makes for this type of equalization, so that now the only illiterate groups are found among the older people. This trend toward greater convergence also exists in the rising income level of the American population.

The Appalachians have not been isolated from the main trends of American life. Industries have moved into the area; cities and metropolitan areas have developed and extended the range of their influence; incomes have risen; and stranded populations have migrated outward to greater opportunities. All this is demonstrated in our report. Nevertheless, the Ap-

palachians have lagged behind the nation on all counts, including the development of resources and the industrialization of the area. And where industrialization has occurred, losses in mining, forestry, and agriculture have retarded total advance.

Pools of unemployment and poverty in stagnant economic areas are now estimated to affect about 10 percent of the nation's population. They offer the major hindrance in the trend toward greater equalization of opportunity. These areas are scattered throughout the country, and it is not contended that the Appalachian problem areas contribute anything like the major proportion. The mountain areas, however, do have more than their share of the nation's non-commercial agriculture and depressed coal mining. Like their counterparts in the nation, the Appalachian problem areas show no tendency to go away if they are simply left alone. However, since they also show little tendency to depress the normal trend line of national prosperity, it has been suggested that they can be accepted as chronic pockets of poverty and thus safely disregarded in the ordinary plans of business and government.

The fallacy of this argument, as one commentator says, "is that it ignores the enormous human and social cost of the depressed areas and the danger to national policy involved in letting them fester." The continued wastage of human resources in depressed areas has thus been called "a social crime, an economic absurdity and a political menace."[10]

Poor people have poor ways and, left undisturbed, these poor ways tend to perpetuate themselves. As John Galbraith says, if people "cannot have what the larger community regards as the minimum necessary for decency, they cannot wholly escape the judgment of the larger community that they are therefore indecent."[11] To some extent family life itself is today a kind of luxury dependent on adequate income. Cleanliness, so close to Godliness, is among other things a function of adequate plumbing, and basic morality in family life is fostered by privacy in household arrangements. While these are things that social workers of the Region know well and of which the members of our affluent society need to be occasionally reminded, they serve mainly as background for the pages to follow.

In expressing our fears lest a permanent culture of

[10] Melvin R. Levin, "What Do We Do With Depressed Areas?" *Iowa Business Digest*, April, 1960, p. 1.
[11] John Galbraith, *The Affluent Society* (Boston, 1958), pp. 323-24.

poverty emerge in certain areas, we do not commit ourselves either to a geographic or an economic determinism of the issue. Rather, we now wish to reverse the process of regional analysis: to go from the attitudes and institutions of the people to ascertain what changes these factors may make in the physical environment in which the people live. Before perusing the following chapters, we shall do well to examine the implications of the new regional approach.

The older regional study was more concerned with causation than with social change. It looked back to physical conditions and limitations; and from physical resources and crude modes of making a living, it moved forward to describe institutional adjustments and the attitudes of the people and their local leaders. Such analysis appeared static in its implications and gave but little indication of the great changes already on the way.

In a study like the present we come to a point where we find it hard to distinguish between cause and effect. If we devote attention to religion in the mountains, we find not only that it is an effect of conditions under which people have lived, but also that it operates either to change or to perpetuate those conditions. Isolation, which begins as a physical limitation enforced by distance and rugged terrain, becomes mental and cultural isolation that causes people to remain in disadvantaged areas and to resist the changes that would bring them into contact with the outside world. The effect of conditions thus becomes a new cause of conditions, but the new cause is an attitude, not a mountain. Since the mountains are not likely to be moved, we proceed on the assumption that men can be moved.

Feeling as we do that the goals and aspiration of the people will determine the future of the Region for good or ill, this study, as a departure in regional surveys, is devoting special attention to the attitudes, opinions, and stated beliefs of the people concerned. This, it should be said, is done with the express conviction that attitudes which represented virtues in the early days may become handicaps in the present.

Once named the nation's economic problem number one on highest authority, the South has made a real recovery since the 1930's—one which has not gone unnoticed. The report of the Study of Population Redistribution at this time suggested that the region would have to get out of cotton, that the tenancy system was on the verge of collapse, and that some six to seven million persons ought to leave the cotton South even if they had nowhere else to go.[12] Cotton has been reduced and tenancy all but abolished. Migration still continues; but in the main the South has mechanized its farming, increased the size of its farms, changed the type of agriculture, moved out the redunant farm population, and increased industrial and white-collar employment. As a current witticism has it, much of the South is now prosperous enough to vote Republican if the party will but have the grace to change its name.

It is feared that one great subregion—the Southern Appalachians—has not kept step with the South's advance. The present study has undertaken to examine the foundations of this judgment, to determine the status of the Region and of the component elements that determine its position, and to suggest the next steps possible in the various sectors of the Region's economy, in its public life and services, its social institutions, and its ideas and beliefs.

A region and a people are always in process of development, and many of their abilities remain potential for the future, for as the philosopher Heraclitus said: "Nothing is; everything is becoming." Back of the present study is the realization that the Southern Appalachians are rapidly coming to the next stage of development; that today's people, and these states, and this nation already hold most of the important decisions in their hands. The people can either stand back and let such changes happen as they will, or under responsible leaders they can stride forward and make changes happen. The need for determining and directing social changes in the Region is the necessity behind the present study.

Short of national reversal, there should be no reversal in the ongoing change now spreading over the Appalachians, but human losses from the transition can be reduced and the changeover facilitated if the major institutions of the Region gear their forces to this undertaking. This report appeals directly to the Region's institutions and their leaders, to the schools, the churches, local government, and the health agencies who direct their programs toward the achievements so necessary in the great transition.

[12] Goodrich, p. 162.

CHAPTER TWO

The

Passing

of

Provincialism

THOMAS R. FORD

EVEN THE MOST CASUAL OBSERVER of conditions in the Southern Appalachian Region during the past three decades cannot fail to be aware of the tremendous material changes. The sprawling growth of the Region's metropolitan areas and the abandoned cabins up narrow hollow roads provide impressive evidence of major population shifts. Brush cover and second-growth timber reclaiming mountain slopes once cultivated to the very ridges, and unfamiliar silhouettes of industrial smokestacks in the Great Appalachian Valley bear equally eloquent testimony of a transforming economy. Hard-surface highways along mountain streams which themselves a scant generation ago served as roadbeds, and television antennas clustered on mountain tops are functional symbols of the intrusion of contemporary mass culture into even the most isolated areas. That the Twentieth Century has come to the people of the Southern Appalachians is unquestionable. But whether the people of the Southern Appalachians have come to the Twentieth Century is, at least in the minds of many observers, a moot question.

To some the question may seem anomalous, even absurd. Yet sociologists and anthropologists have long recognized that all parts of culture do not change at an equal rate. As a general rule, at least in our time, the technological aspects are the first to change, followed more slowly by adaptations of social organization to new techniques. Most resistant to change are the fundamental sentiments, beliefs, and values of a people, the ways they feel their world is and should be ordered. So it is not implausible to suppose that the value heritage of the Appalachian people may still be rooted in the frontier, even though the base of their economy has shifted from subsistence agriculture to industry and commerce and the people themselves have increasingly concentrated in towns and cities.

In the early planning of the Southern Appalachian studies it was decided that some attempt should be made to probe beneath the statistics that measure social and economic changes in order to gain some insight into the relationships between those changes and the values, beliefs, and attitudes of the people affected by them. Have the Appalachian people clung to their frontier-agrarian traditions, resisting the philosophical premises of industrial society? Or are they willing to accept the social consequences of a new economy whose benefits must be purchased at the price of a radical alteration of an accustomed way of life? Are there evidences of major discrepancies between new modes of behavior and old patterns of thought? If so, what do these portend in the way of future social problems? And what implications do the beliefs and values of the Appalachian people, whatever they may be, hold for those who are actively working to promote social and economic change in the Region? For as the late Howard Odum observed a quarter of a century ago with reference to the entire South: "To attempt . . . to reconstruct its agriculture and economy without coming to grips with its folk culture and attitudes would be quite futile."[1]

The means selected for collecting information that would help to answer these questions was a survey of Appalachian residents drawn from a representative sample of households in the Region. Obviously one cannot gain from even a great many survey interviews the depth of sympathetic understanding that a John C. Campbell was able to acquire from a quarter century of living and traveling through the Region. Neither is it possible to reduce to cold statistics the subtle complexities of warm humans. Yet, despite its limitations, the survey method offered a number of advantages for a study of the type contemplated. For one thing, it could be conducted quickly, and time was at a premium. More important, it could be designed to secure information from a cross-section of the heterogeneous Appalachian population. To a considerable extent the popular but erroneous impression of a homogeneous mountain culture stems from the fact that most contemporary studies have been of relatively isolated communities, often selected because they still preserved a way of life that was rapidly disappearing from the remainder of the Region. Not only has this bias created a false impression of homogeneity, but it has also tended to obscure the tremendous cultural changes that have been taking place for many years. Even forty years ago, John C. Campbell, whose authoritative work *The Southern Highlander and His Homeland* became a classic in the field, was disturbed by "the difficulties in the way of writing of a people who, while forming a definite geographical and racial group, were by no means socially homogeneous."[2] He was particularly concerned that his readers might not realize that many of his statements "applicable to the remote rural folk who were the particular object of his study were not true of their urban and valley kinsfolk."

The survey was seen as a way to secure data for different social groups (which Campbell had seen as desirable but infeasible), although not necessarily the same groups that Campbell might have chosen. The

selection of major groups was implicit in the method used to choose the sample households. The Region was divided into residential areas of three types: (1) metropolitan, which included counties containing cities of 50,000 or more and adjacent counties within the zone of metropolitan influence; (2) smaller towns and cities with populations between 2,500 and 50,000, designated for purposes of simplicity as urban places; and (3) rural areas, containing both village and open-country population. Nearly 1,500 sample households were then selected, each type of area contributing to the sample in numbers roughly proportionate to the total population of such areas in the Region.

A primary reason for grouping the population in this manner was to see if there was any "apparent" change in values with increasing industrialization. It was not possible to measure any real change with only one survey, of course, and no comparable surveys had been made at an earlier period. It was reasoned, however, that industrialization would have its greatest impact on the metropolitan population and affect least the rural population. The difference between the beliefs and attitudes of metropolitan residents and those of rural residents would give some indication of a value shift that would be particularly significant because of the increasing concentration of the Appalachian population in metropolitan areas.

The actual interviewing of respondents from selected households took place during the summer of 1958, and 1,466 completed interview schedules were obtained. Of these, 31.5 percent were from metropolitan households, 19.1 percent from other urban households, and 49.4 percent from rural households. Some of the characteristics of these households are shown in Table 1. In addition, interviews were held with 379 individuals named as community leaders by respondents in the sampled localities. About these more will be said later.

Once the interviews were completed, it was possible to divide the residential groups into other sub-groups, or statistical categories, for purposes of comparison. All household respondents were classified on the basis of sex, age, educational level, and socioeconomic status. To measure socioeconomic status, a composite index was devised from data on household income, occupation and education of the household head, possession of various items of household equipment,

---

[1] Howard Odum, *Southern Regions of the United States* (Chapel Hill, N.C., 1936), p. 499.
[2] John C. Campbell, *The Southern Highlander and His Homeland* (New York, 1921), p. xiv.

and the respondent's identification of himself as a member of the upper, middle, or working class.[3] The population was then divided according to index score into four status categories arbitrarily labeled upper, upper middle, lower middle, and lower. This made it

Table 1. *Selected Characteristics of the Survey Households, 1958*

Characteristic	Rural	Urban	Metro-politan	All areas
Percentage of survey population	54.1	16.4	29.5	100.0
Percentage white	97.9	95.0	93.6	96.1
Average number persons per household	3.9	3.1	3.3	3.5
Median household income, 1957	$2,830	$4,478	$5,475	$3,951
Percentage incomes under:				
$ 1,000	12.9	4.8	3.1	8.3
3,000	53.2	25.4	15.8	36.2
5,000	81.6	59.6	43.4	65.4
7,000	94.2	78.5	70.2	83.6
10,000	98.0	91.9	83.6	92.3
Percentage dwellings with:				
gas or electric stove	75.3	97.5	99.8	86.4
washing machine	88.5	85.4	83.3	86.3
television set	65.6	84.6	93.9	78.2
flush toilet	48.3	100.0	93.9	72.6
deep freeze	23.9	17.5	27.5	23.8
Percentage respondents classified by socioeconomic status as:				
Upper	5.0	12.5	22.1	11.8
Upper middle	14.4	25.4	33.5	22.5
Lower middle	30.2	23.6	21.4	26.2
Lower	20.7	7.5	5.2	13.3
Unknown	29.7	31.1	17.7	26.2

possible to compare different socioeconomic groups within the same type of residential area as well as to compare equal-status groups in residential areas of different types. Similar comparisons could also be made of respondents classified by the other characteristics.

There was still the crucial issue of which specific culture traits should be examined. No culture is simply a collection of traits, of course, yet each has its distinctive attributes and emphases. The distinctive themes of Appalachian culture in an earlier day were not difficult to identify, inasmuch as they attracted the attention of practically all who wrote about life in the Region. The problem, then, was to select those which seemed most significant in view of the social changes taking place. Since a major focus of interest was in the persistence of frontier-agrarian values, the selection was largely guided by the literature on the isolated rural highlander in the late nineteenth and early twentieth centuries.

From a considerable variety of themes, a number were chosen for analysis of which four will be discussed in this essay: (1) individualism and self-reliance; (2) traditionalism; (3) fatalism; (4) fundamentalist religion containing a powerful strain of Puritanism. In examining the web of mountain life, one finds these themes intertwined and generally, though not always, mutually supporting. Most so-called "mountain traits" are to be found in one form or another throughout the nation, particularly in rural areas. At the same time, each of them has its antithesis in contemporary industrial society. The self-reliant individualist, at least as an "ideal type," stands at the far end of the scale from the much berated "organization man." Traditionalism, not only in the sense of clinging to an earlier heritage but also in the exaltation of resistance to social change, is viewed as both anachronistic and vaguely immoral by a larger society that values progress through rational, scientific endeavor. Even more reprehensible to a culture that stresses achievement, self-betterment, and mastery over nature is a passive resignation to one's situation in life, particularly if it is a situation viewed as both undesirable and remediable. Less subject to censure by the larger society, perhaps, but contrasting as sharply with its dominant values—and not immune from ridicule— is the rigid, pervasive religious ethos of the Region.

Although it may not be possible to state with any high degree of precision what the current position of Appalachian culture is with respect to any of these values, one may judge whether current attitudes and beliefs seem to reflect the values ascribed to the highlander by such men as Campbell, Horace Kephart, W. G. Frost,[4] and others who studied him in his isolated environment near the turn of the century. Or, moving to a different point of reference, one may compare the apparent values of Appalachian society with those of the encompassing national society as depicted in recent times by scholars such as Robin Williams, Clyde and Florence Kluckhohn, Robert Lynd, Lloyd Warner,[5] and others.

[3] About a fourth of the respondents were excluded from the four socioeconomic status categories (See Table 1). For the most part these were older persons—retired men, wives of retired men, and widows—from whom meaningful occupational data could not be obtained.

[4] Horace Kephart, *Our Southern Highlanders* (New York, 1913); William G. Frost, "Our Contemporary Ancestors in the Southern Mountains," *Atlantic Monthly*, March 1899, pp. 311-19.

[5] Robin Williams, *American Society—A Sociological Interpretation* (New York, 1957); Clyde Kluckhohn and Florence R. Kluckhohn, "American Culture: Generalized Orientations and Class Patterns" in *Conflicts of Power in Modern Culture*, ed. Lyman Bryson *et al.* (New York, 1948), pp. 106-28; Robert S. Lynd, *Knowledge for What?* (Princeton, N.J., 1939); Lloyd Warner, *American Life—Dream and Reality* (Chicago, 1953).

Of necessity the interpretation of the survey data as they relate to the various cultural themes reflects the judgment of the author. Because of space limitations, no attempt has been made to present all the data upon which the judgments have been made,

Table 2. *Attitudes toward Relief and Welfare: Percentage Distribution of Replies to Selected Questions*

Question and response	Rural	Urban	Metro-politan	All areas
Do you think the present relief and welfare program is a good thing?				
Yes	86.0	88.2	82.7	85.4
No	7.0	6.1	5.8	6.5
Don't know & no reply	7.0	5.7	11.5	8.0
Do you think relief payments are too high, too low, about right?				
Too high	1.8	2.5	2.8	2.3
Too low	33.7	34.3	32.5	33.4
About right	41.4	34.6	40.0	39.7
Don't know & no reply	23.1	28.6	24.7	24.6
Do you think it reflects badly on a family if they are receiving relief?				
Yes	10.2	13.9	9.7	10.8
No	64.4	63.9	68.6	65.6
In some cases	22.0	20.0	20.3	21.1
Don't know & no reply	3.4	2.2	1.4	2.5

although some of the materials are presented in graphic and tabular form to illustrate certain points. Other relevant tables are presented in the statistical supplement to the main volume. It should also be noted that a supplementary objective of the survey was to secure data, both factual and attitudinal, on specific subjects of interest to those who were making studies of special topics. Consequently, various references to the survey and analyses of question responses will be found in the chapters dealing with population, education, social welfare, local government, religion, and health. Some of the same questions are dealt with in this analysis, but with a different objective in mind. The concern of the other authors is with the topics themselves; the concern here is with tracing the warp threads of culture themes through the several topics that provided the weft of the interview schedule, or questionnaire.

Individualism and Self-Reliance

"Remote from ordered law and commerce, the Highlander learned by hard necessity to rely upon himself," John C. Campbell wrote four decades ago. "Each household in its hollow lived its own life. The man was the provider and the protector. He actually was the law, not only in the management of affairs within the home, but in relation to the home to the outside world. Circumstances forced him to depend upon his own action until he came to consider independent action not only a prerogative, but a duty."[6]

The fierce independence and proud self-reliance of the highlander, a heritage of frontier life, were viewed with mixed feelings even by so sympathetic an observer as Campbell. On the one hand they symbolized the courage and resourcefulness of the pioneer—qualities to be valued in any age. On the other hand, independence carried to its extreme became a major obstacle to the establishment of the law and order necessary for the functioning of a more complex society. And the attachment of supreme value to self-reliance was seen by Campbell as anachronistic in "a new age, one that calls for cooperative service and community spirit." Horace Kephart, writing a few years earlier than Campbell, had felt a similar conflict in his assessment of the highlander, observing that "the very quality that is his strength and charm as a man—his staunch individualism—is proving his weakness and reproach as a citizen."[7]

Individualism has many facets, and in mountain culture the aspects which received greatest emphasis were independence from social restraints or at least legal norms, and abstention from cooperative endeavors in any sustained form, with the possible exception of those that involved kin. During frontier days there were, of course, numerous cooperative ventures involving mutual aid, such as cabin raisings, corn huskings, and the like, but they were activities of special occasions, not daily routines. Complete economic independence was the mark of a successful man, and self-reliance, like many other frontier necessities, was elevated into a virtue.

Whatever their intrinsic moral virtues, independent economic operations are frequently inefficient, as many nineteenth-century craftsmen learned in their losing struggle against competing factories. In an industrial economy, purchasing power, not self-sufficiency, is the standard of success. More because of the changing standards of a nation than because of any deterioration of living conditions, the Appalachian Region came to be viewed as an economic problem area. Consequently, during the Great Depression of the 1930's, when the Federal government openly assumed as a responsibility of the state the economic welfare of its citizens, the rural highlanders found themselves eminently qualified

---

[6] Campbell, *The Southern Highlander*, p. 93.
[7] Kephart, *Our Southern Highlanders*, p. 309.

to become the recipients of public relief and welfare assistance.

If there were those who supposed that the traditional value accorded self-reliance by the highlanders would lead them to reject the welfare offerings of the

Table 3. *Attitudes toward Federal Assistance: Percentage Distribution of Replies to Selected Questions*

Question and response	Rural	Urban	Metro-politan	All areas
Do you think the government is doing enough for the people or too much or too little?				
Enough	51.5	53.2	48.5	50.9
Too much	5.7	10.7	15.1	9.6
Too little	24.9	21.1	15.1	21.1
Don't know & no reply	17.9	15.0	21.2	18.4
Are you in favor of Federal aid to help local governments provide more and better public services?				
Yes	75.4	72.1	66.0	71.8
No	10.4	23.6	23.2	16.9
Don't know & no reply	14.2	4.3	10.8	11.2
We do not at present have a program of Federal aid to education. What do you think of such a program?				
Favor	74.4	69.3	61.7	69.4
Oppose	11.3	18.9	19.5	15.3
Don't know & no reply	14.2	11.8	18.8	15.2
Do you think Federal aid to local areas makes the people less self-reliant?				
Yes	44.1	50.0	56.5	49.1
No	32.6	35.3	27.9	31.6
Don't know & no reply	23.3	14.6	15.6	19.2

national government, they were doomed to early disappointment. "Reputed to be the most individualistic of all the regions," wrote Howard Odum of the southern people, "they cooperate most fully with New Deal techniques."[8] His observation applied with equal validity to the residents of the Southern Appalachians.

There is little evidence that the acceptance of public assistance was ever seen as incompatible with the value themes of individualism and self-reliance as they were defined by the average highlander. "It is interesting to see how accepting welfare and charity has been fitted into local values of pride and independence," Marion Pearsall has observed in a recent study of an isolated mountain community in Tennessee. "It is clear that acquiring money from a welfare agency is not in itself considered degrading. Indeed, accepting welfare money seems almost as legitimate as earning it by some other method. As one woman puts it, 'It's the good Lord taking care

of me because I've worked hard all my life and prayed to Him.' "[9]

The data from the survey provide incontrovertible evidence that public assistance measures and programs are endorsed by the great majority of Southern Appalachian residents (Table 2). Six out of seven respondents gave an affirmative reply to the question, "Do you think the present relief and welfare program is a good thing?" even though no specification of "the present program" was provided. Two out of three respondents indicated there was little stigma attached to a family's being "on relief," and most of the remaining third thought that only in some cases was a family's reputation jeopardized. Despite real differences in the proportions of rural, urban, and metropolitan residents dependent upon public assistance, and presumed differences in their evaluation of individualism and self-reliance, there was surprisingly little difference in their appraisal of existing welfare philosophy and practice. Most residents in all areas believed it to be "a good thing."

It was quite conceivable, especially in this Region that has a long history of political support of the Republican Party, that government subsidies to community agencies might be regarded quite differently from welfare assistance to individuals and families. So far as the survey data are indicative, however, shifting the benefits from the individual to the community and its institutions only slightly reduced the support accorded Federal subsidization programs (Table 3).

Most respondents (51 percent) agreed that in general the government was doing "enough" for the people. Significantly, however, more than twice as many thought the government was doing "too little" (21 percent) as thought it was doing "too much." Questioned about specific kinds of government support, the enthusiasm of the respondents picked up considerably. Seventy-two percent said they were in favor of "*Federal aid to help local government provide more and better services.*" Sixty-nine percent expressed themselves in favor of Federal aid to education. The question concerning Federal aid to local government was intentionally loaded to emphasize the benefits in an effort to identify the size of the hard-core group inalterably opposed to Federal grants and subsidies, while the question concerning Federal aid to education was neutrally worded. The loading seemed to have little effect. Only 17 percent openly

[8] Odum, *Southern Regions*, p. 97.

[9] Marion Pearsall, *Little Smoky Ridge* (Tuscaloosa, Ala., 1959), p. 57.

opposed aid to local government and 15 percent opposed aid to education. The remaining respondents in both cases were either unsure or unwilling to voice an opinion.

Was the overwhelming endorsement of Federal subsidization of local institutions attributable to a failure to perceive such assistance as a threat to independence and self-reliance? Apparently not. At least, when asked, *"Do you think Federal aid to local areas makes the people less self-reliant?"* considerably more respondents said they thought it did (49 percent) than said they thought it did not (32 percent). About a fifth of the respondents said they didn't know. Apparently self-reliance is not so highly cherished as to generate a strong opposition to Federal aid programs that a great many Appalachian residents believe will ultimately weaken it.

It has already been noted that the differences in attitudes of rural, urban, and metropolitan respondents toward welfare assistance were relatively small. The differences were somewhat larger with respect to other programs of Federal aid. Strongest support for these came from rural residents, weakest from residents of metropolitan areas. It is probable that rural areas would receive the greatest benefits from programs of the type proposed, and rural residents as well as those of urban and metropolitan areas are well aware of this fact. Second, the rural population contains a considerably higher proportion of poor people than either the urban or metropolitan populations, and whether poverty breeds dependency or vice versa, the two characteristics are closely related.

The relationship between socioeconomic status and attitudes toward Federal assistance is clearly evident in the survey data. For example, in response to the question of whether the Federal government was doing enough, too much, or too little for the people, 38 percent of the upper status respondents but less than one percent of the lower status group said "too much." Federal aid to assist local government and education was endorsed by slightly more than half of the upper status respondents but by three-fourths of the lower status respondents. Finally, the percentage of respondents who said they believed Federal aid reduced local self-reliance dropped steadily and sharply from 71 percent of the upper status category to only 36 percent of the lower status group. Since schooling level was closely related to socioeconomic status, the response variation followed a roughly similar pattern. Differences between extreme groups (those with seven or fewer years of schooling and those who had gone

beyond high school) were somewhat smaller, however. In fact, there was little difference between categories with less than 12 years of schooling, but generally a relatively large gap between high school graduates and those with some college training, the latter being considerably less enthusiastic about the expansion of Federal programs. However, a majority of respondents in all categories endorsed both the existing welfare programs and the proposed Federal assistance to local government and education.

The variations of responses with age of respondent may offer one clue to the changes in values over time. So far as attitudes toward public assistance are concerned, the changes were small and inconsistent. The strong approval accorded relief and welfare activities by old and young alike suggests that either there has been little recent change or that older persons have changed their previous views about as rapidly as the younger generation has acquired its current set of beliefs. There were consistent variations with age in the responses concerning expanded Federal assistance programs, however. The proportion of respondents who thought the government was doing "too much" for the people, for example, declined from 21 percent of those 65 years old or over to only 4 percent of the respondents under 30 years of age. Furthermore, endorsement of Federal aid to local government declined from 83 percent of the youngest group to 67 percent of the oldest, while support of Federal aid to education dropped from 80 percent to 56 percent. Finally, only 40 percent of the youngest group compared with 56 percent of the oldest considered Federal assistance a threat to local self-reliance. The same pattern, it should be noted, was found in all three types of residential areas, although the actual percentages varied. While it is possible that other factors (such as increasing conservatism with age) may account for the impressive and consistent pattern of differences, the evidence at least does not contravene the conclusion that the value attached to individualism and self-reliance has been on a decline in the Region.

If there has been a weakening of these traits in mountain culture, as the evidence suggests there has, has it been accompanied by a strengthening of the spirit of cooperation and a growing realization of the advantages of organized group action? There is at least some evidence in the survey data that this has been the case.

One of the specific indicators of an increasing appreciation of social organization is to be found in the strength of organized labor in the Region. Half a century ago, when coal mining was a well-established industry in West Virginia but just getting underway in Kentucky, the organization of labor unions was a difficult business, not only because of the violent opposition of the mining companies but also because the highlanders themselves had little concept of and less taste for organization. As Kephart reported at the time, "they simply will not stick together."[10] This difficulty was not easily overcome, and the history of labor organization in the mines and mills of the Appalachian Region is one of blood and violence. Perhaps even more than the mines and industries themselves, labor unions were viewed as an intrusion of an alien way of life.

Considering the general economic character of the Region and the early difficulties of union organization, it came as a distinct surprise that 42 percent of the surveyed households reported that the male wage earner was currently or had previously been a union member. It does not necessarily follow, of course, that they were active members or strong supporters of the unions in which they held membership. Yet there can be no doubt that the general impression of unions in the Region is favorable. Questioned as to whether they thought workers in industry were better off because of unions, three out of every five respondents said they were; only one said they were not; and one said he didn't know. Union membership, past or current, was reported most frequently in metropolitan households (47 percent) compared with 34 percent in urban areas and 42 percent in rural areas. Metropolitan respondents also had the most favorable impression of unions so far as worker benefits were concerned. Seventy-one percent claimed that industrial workers were better off because of unions compared with 59 percent of the urban respondents and 56 percent of the rural respondents.

Responses to various other survey questions appeared to substantiate a growing recognition of the advantages of organized group action. For example, more than 90 percent of the respondents in all areas endorsed the idea that "people should get together and try to bring industry to the community or county" in which they lived. Parent-teacher organizations and 4-H clubs were given highest approval in the ratings of various school-related organizations and activities. And even in the ratings of church activities, substantial majorities approved most of those that implied some considerable degree of organization. One cannot fail to be impressed by the fact that in this region where

religion has traditionally stressed personal salvation and other-worldliness, four out of five respondents in rural as well as urban and metropolitan areas endorsed "community improvement programs" as a legitimate church activity. Even if this is only a token recognition, it is symbolic of a changing attitude.

If we are to accept these responses as evidence of a developing sense of cooperation, we must also note the survey evidence (further discussed in Chapter X) that most Appalachian residents appear not in favor of programs that must be supported by local taxes. As a plausible but oversimplified explanation of the conflicting attitudes of highlanders toward cooperation and taxes, it is suggested that the average highlander does not really see in government an extension of himself and his neighbors. The government is "they," not "we." He looks to a beneficent Federal government to ease his lot with little consideration that what is provided must be paid for by someone, but this realization comes sharply home when the support of local government activities is at issue. In both cases he perceives government through the eyes of the individualist—"I" or "they," one or the other, but never both. Willing to accept the benefits of tax-supported services, he is not yet ready to assume the obligation of helping to finance them. His concept of democratic government has expanded to include an expectation of economic and social assistance, if not security, but this broadening of perceived rights has not been accompanied by a commensurately developed perception of responsibilities. If this is to be regarded as a flaw in the social perspective of the Appalachian residents it is surely one that he shares with a great many of his fellow citizens in other regions.

Traditionalism and Fatalism

Turning to other aspects of the value system of the Region, there is considerable logic in examining traditionalism and fatalism together. This is not to imply that all traditionalism is attended and supported by a fatalistic philosophy for this is clearly not the case, even in the mountains. However, much of the traditionalistic thinking that is of greatest concern to those who would seek to improve mountain life is of this variety, and, as has already been noted, it is a culture trait that seems strangely out of place in a national society that so highly prizes progress, achievement, and success.

[10] Kephart, *Our Southern Highlanders*, p. 309.

It seems unlikely that fatalism and traditionalism were as closely linked in frontier days as they later came to be. The frontier settler, after all, was seeking to better his lot, and his approach to this end was one that required both high motivation and strenuous

Figure 5. *What Type of Work Would You Like to See a Son of Yours Go Into? Percentage of Respondents Naming White Collar and Blue Collar Occupations, by Sex and Socioeconomic Status*

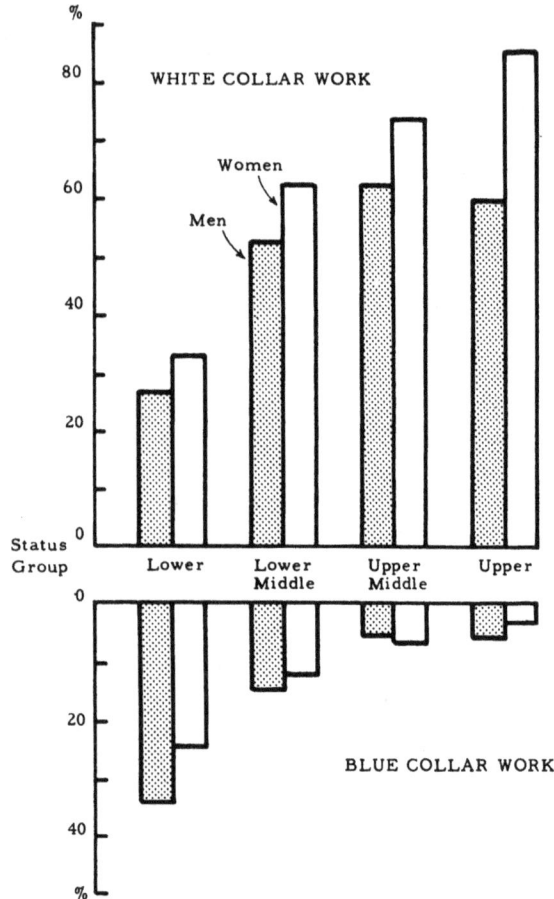

activity. Fatalism developed in response to the same circumstances that were largely responsible for the other-worldly emphasis of mountain religion. Both fatalism and other-worldliness share the premise that life is governed by external forces over which humans have little or no control, an outlook which seems peculiar only where advanced technology has given men confidence in their own ability to master nature.

If the early mountain settlers possessed such a confidence, they could not have long retained it in the face of the harsh realities of mountain life. Neither the frontiersmen nor their descendants possessed the resources necessary to gain control over an environment that at times must have seemed merciless. Under the circumstances, their development of a philosophy of fatalism appears eminently reasonable, for after generations of relatively fruitless efforts, what hope could be placed in continued strivings? To some extent one must suppose that many of those who still believed their work should be attended by rewards tempered their hopes with reason and moved on to seek more benevolent circumstances. Of those who remained, many turned to God in the faith that He would provide recompense in a future life for their earthly misery. And others, lacking both hope and faith, simply resigned themselves to fate. "Sometimes it seems that the greatest obstacle of all is lack of desire," wrote Edwin White in his *Highland Heritage*. "People in general simply do not rebel against what ought not to be, do not demand more of life; among far too large a share of the population there is no thought that things can be different. A spirit of passive resignation pervades much of the section."[11]

Not all resistance to change was in the form of passive resignation. Some highlanders, having learned to cope with their situation or at least to subsist with a minimum of effort, actively opposed all measures aimed at altering their way of life by those who sought to improve their social and economic conditions. In many instances they saw in such measures a threat to their inheritance of the Kingdom of Heaven, for which poverty was a necessary if not sufficient condition. In other cases their antagonism reflected nothing more than fear, skepticism, and distrust of strangers and unfamiliar ways.

However strong and prevalent the values of traditionalism and fatalism were a generation ago, and we have no way of measuring them, there is considerable evidence that they have weakened considerably in recent decades. The migration of hundreds of thousands of Appalachian natives to other regions is in itself indicative that at least for them the motivation to improve their lot in life outweighed whatever reasons that they may have had for remaining. At the same time, it is not an illogical proposition that migration drains off those who are energetic and highly motivated to succeed, leaving behind only those who still value tradition above change or who are too apathetic to take action even in their own behalf.

The survey data indicate that this proposition, as plausible as it may seem, is not sound. It is not possible here to review all the evidence in detail, but

[11] Edwin White, *Highland Heritage* (New York, 1937), p. 92.

responses from a few questions from various sections of the questionnaire will serve for illustrative purposes.

One technique that is frequently employed to elicit the values and attitudes of adults is to see what aspirations they hold for their children. In the survey a

Figure 6. *How Much Schooling Would You Like a Son of Yours to Get? A Daughter? Percentage of Respondents, by Residence, Indicating Four or More Years of College*

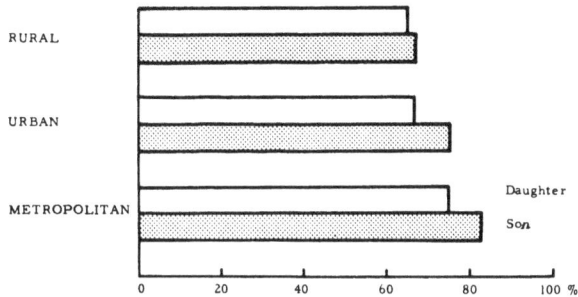

number of questions were asked concerning children, either actual or hypothetical, and the responses were in most cases quite revealing. A typical question was *"What type of work would you like to see a son of yours go into?"* One value apparently tapped by this particular question was individualism, for a fairly high proportion—almost a third—of the respondents said this matter should be left to the son and refused to give a specific reply. Of those who did reply, though, about eight out of ten named a white collar job, and seven out of ten specified a profession. Respondents of comparable status seemed to have about the same distribution of choices, white collar or blue collar, regardless of where they lived. The higher their status and the more schooling they had received, the more often respondents said they would like for a son to go into some white collar occupation, but only lower status men more often specified a blue collar job (Figure 5).

Women generally held higher aspirations for their children than did men, possibly because the accomplishments of children are more often considered to reflect credit or discredit upon the mother than upon the father. It is probably of some significance that both younger groups of respondents (under 30 years and 30-44 years) named white collar over blue collar jobs by a ratio of six to one compared with a ratio of less than three to one for the two older groups. The aspirations of the latter may have been tempered to some degree, however, by the actual jobs which their grown children held, a mitigating condition which had not yet affected the ambitions of younger parents and

prospective parents. Even so, the relatively high aspirations expressed by the younger groups in all areas indicate that they are neither tradition-bound nor lacking in hopes for a better future, at least so far as their children are concerned.

The achievement aspirations of Appalachian residents were also evident in their responses to questions about how much education they would want a son or daughter to get. Three out of four said they would like for a son to complete college and two out of three expressed a similar hope for a daughter. Less than one percent indicated that they would be satisfied for a son or daughter to have less than a high school education. More than 90 percent said they would want a son or daughter to take advantage of an opportunity to go to college in preference to remaining at home to help the family, and almost all of those said they would be willing to borrow money to help pay part of the college expenses. Such aspirations are obviously unrealistic in this Region where in 1950 only one adult in twenty-five had completed four or more years of college, but it would be a mistake to dismiss them as representing nothing more than the pathetic attempts of the respondents to win the approval of their interviewers. More likely, the responses indicate that Appalachian residents view higher education in much the same way as do people in other parts of the nation, and are cognizant of its value in an industrial society. And the fact that they believe their children *should* receive a good education, whether or not they actually believe they will, is indication not only of the willingness to accept industrial society but also of the hope that an oncoming generation will be able to participate in it effectively.

Larger proportions of metropolitan respondents expressed desires for their children to have a college education (Figure 6). Even so, about two-thirds of the rural residents stated such a desire, and the actual differences between comparable socioeconomic groups in the three residential areas were quite small. With rising socioeconomic status and educational level, increasing proportions of respondents specified a college education as the desired amount of schooling for a child. Less to be expected, perhaps, is that more than half of even the lowest status and least schooled respondents expressed the same aspiration. Even those who would argue that such expressions are merely fantasies must concede the existence of strong social and cultural forces to make this particular fantasy so prevalent.

As in the case of occupational aspirations for children, there were appreciable differences in the educational aspirations expressed by older and younger respondents. Conceivably the older respondents had adjusted their goals downward to correspond more closely with reality, although they were dealing with

Figure 7. *What Would You Say Is the Most Important Factor in a Man's Being Successful in His Work? Percentage of Respondents, by Residence, Naming Specified Factors*

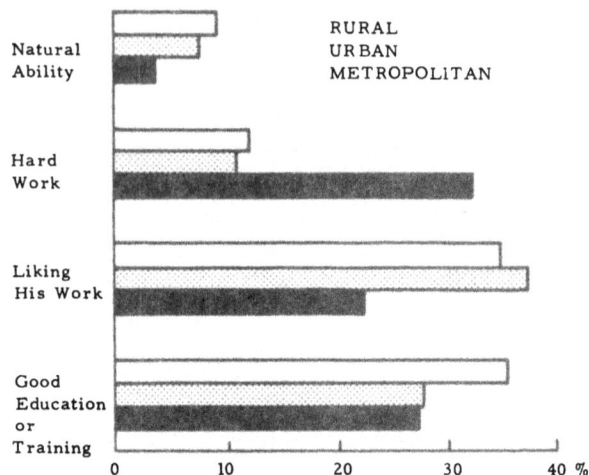

hypothetical cases and the number who said they would like for a son or daughter to get a college education was manifestly greater than the number who had actually seen such an aspiration realized. But the higher proportion of younger respondents who expressed the desire that their children go to college supports the proposition that a change in values has taken place, particularly in the rural and urban areas where the differences between age groups was the largest.

A somewhat more complex pattern of responses was obtained from a third question concerning children: *"If a child of yours was considering where to live, would you want him to stay here or go elsewhere?"* A great many considerations other than economic ones are involved in the reply to such a question, and it is not possible to determine what influence various ones may have had in shaping the pattern of replies. On purely "rational grounds" (in the economic sense) one would expect the percentage of "go elsewhere" replies to decrease with improved economic conditions. Specifically, relatively more rural residents would be expected to answer "go elsewhere" and relatively more metropolitan residents to answer "stay here." This expectation was borne out in that in both rural and urban areas the respondents who said they would wish their children to leave slightly out-

numbered those who said they would want the children to remain in the area. In contrast, metropolitan residents favored their children's remaining by a ratio of more than two to one.

More than three-fourths of those who said they would want their children to move elsewhere gave lack of economic opportunity in their home locality as the reason. In both rural and urban areas, the proportion of respondents who said they would want their children to stay at home declined with rising socio-economic status. This would seem to suggest that lower status respondents may not be as strongly interested in the achievements of their children as their replies to the questions concerning occupational and educational aspirations would indicate. However, of those who gave a definite reply, about as many lower and lower middle status respondents said they would want their children to go as to remain. Family affection was most frequently cited as the reason for desiring them to stay in the community.

In metropolitan areas the division of "stay" and "go" responses for the two lower status groups was about the same as in rural and urban areas, but this was not true of the two upper status groups. On the contrary, upper and upper middle status residents in metropolitan areas favored their children's remaining in the community by a ratio of five to one, while in rural and urban communities they clearly favored their leaving, although by a ratio of less than two to one.

But if most of the population has adopted the American norm of striving for success, there is still a significant lack of accord concerning the best means to this end. One of the more revealing questions asked in this connection was *"What would you say is the most important factor in a man's being successful in his work: natural ability, good education or training, hard work, good luck, knowing the right people, or liking his work?"* Of the six factors listed, *liking his work* and *good education or training* were most frequently named, each by 31 percent of the respondents. Eighteen percent said *hard work* and seven percent *natural ability.* Less than one percent chose either *good luck* or *knowing the right people.* The remainder named factors not listed or said they didn't know.

Several features of the distribution of replies seem significant. Relatively more rural than urban or metropolitan residents named *natural ability* (Figure 7). Metropolitan residents saw *hard work* (which is presumably subject to individual control) as the key to success far more often than did either rural or urban residents. Rural residents more frequently attributed success to good education, which, through little fault of their own, most of them lack. In their own minds, then, they are absolved of personal responsibility for their relative poverty. Urban residents, like rural residents, place little stock in hard work and, perhaps

one's associates, and when all of them are relatively well educated, other factors may seem more important in explaining differential success.

The proportion of respondents attributing primary importance to hard work declined steadily from 23

Figure 8. *Indicators of Fatalism in the Southern Appalachian Population: Percentage of Respondents, by Residence and Socioeconomic Status, Endorsing Specified Statements*

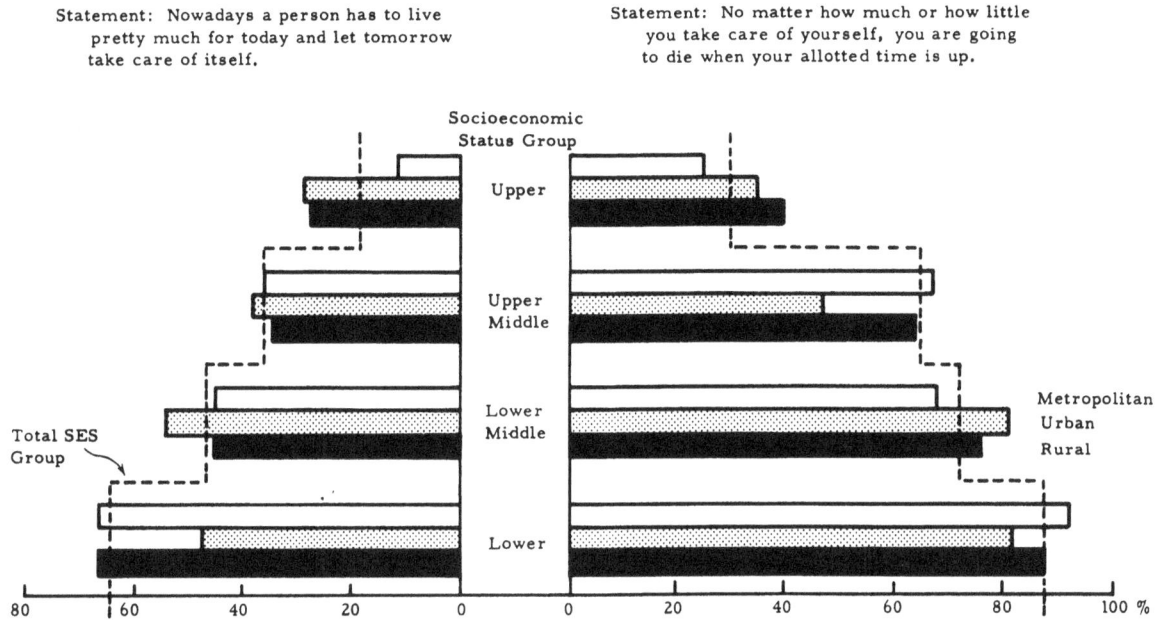

Statement: Nowadays a person has to live pretty much for today and let tomorrow take care of itself.

Statement: No matter how much or how little you take care of yourself, you are going to die when your allotted time is up.

because they are relatively well-schooled, rate liking one's work as more important than good education or training. It is difficult to say whether liking work is subject to personal control or not, and one wonders how many urban respondents who gave this reply really like their own work.

One interpretation of this pattern of responses is that the less successful tend to attribute success to factors beyond their control (but not necessarily beyond all human control) while the more successful see achievement as a product of individual effort. This interpretation is supported by the fact that upper socioeconomic status respondents named *hard work* more often than any other factor while other respondents rated *hard work* well below both *liking work* and *good education and training*, which were chosen with about equal frequency. It is equally noteworthy that respondents with less than nine years of schooling most often attributed success to *good education* while respondents with the most schooling gave less success credit to *education* and more to *hard work* than did any other category. One must take into account, however, that success is largely judged with reference to

percent of the oldest group to only 12 percent of the youngest. A reverse pattern of association was found in the selection of *liking one's work* as the most important factor. The younger the respondent group, the more often they selected it as the most important factor. Good education was considered most important by relatively more middle-aged respondents than by either older or younger ones. One could conjecture on the basis of this evidence that the value attached to honest industry has declined in recent times while the pursuit of happiness in work has become an increasingly important goal. But even among the oldest respondents, less than one in four rated hard work most important. And whatever its intrinsic worth, it must be conceded that a tremendous amount of hard work has been expended in the mountain region with very little material return or spiritual gratification.

Passive acceptance of the status quo no longer seems to be a dominant motif of Appalachian culture, if it ever was, but it probably still serves as the major adjustment mechanism for many of those less able to cope with their life circumstances. For that matter, a trace of fatalism is possessed by most of the population, to judge from responses to two statements included in a list of seven to which respondents were asked to express agreement or disagreement. The two statements designed to test the prevalence of a fatalistic outlook were:

(1) *Nowadays a person has to live pretty much for today and let tomorrow take care of itself.*

(2) *No matter how much or how little you take care of yourself, you are going to die when your allotted time is up.*

Almost half (45 percent) of the respondents agreed with the first statement, with considerably more agreement in rural areas (51 percent) than in urban (45 percent) or metropolitan (37 percent). Seventy percent agreed with the second statement, again with rural residents agreeing most often (78 percent) and metropolitan residents least (61.5 percent). In both instances, responses were closely related to socioeconomic status (Figure 8) and differences between urban, rural, and metropolitan residents of comparable status were relatively small. Thus it would appear that fatalism is not so much a direct product of rural life as it is of poverty, although in the highlands the two are highly congruent.

The apparent persistence of this fatalistic outlook, at least among the more impoverished elements, does not necessarily mean that those who profess it are committed to the course of inaction which it logically implies. Indeed, there is much evidence of illogic in their position, for while 70 percent of the respondents agreed that time of death is foreordained, more than 80 percent later claimed to have a family doctor, whose services presumably would be summoned in case of dire illness. And while one might logically suppose that endorsement of a view that tomorrow must take care of itself reflects a desperate and despondent outlook, such apparently was not the case, for three out of four respondents cheerfully agreed that *children today have a wonder future to look forward to.* Perhaps most amazing of all, the proportion of optimists was practically the same in all categories of respondents—rural and urban, rich and poor, young and old. It is strange that with all the literature devoted to the character of the mountain people, little if any attention has been paid to this spirit of almost Pollyannaish optimism.

There is other survey evidence that many Appalachian residents hold logically conflicting values as to whether they should accept or try to improve their lot in life. Certainly much of what has been reported concerning vocational and educational aspirations would indicate growing acceptance of a philosophy of success-striving that is more in harmony with national norms. Yet over the years the counter philosophy of resigned acceptance has been incorporated into the religious ethic and stamped with divine approval. "Their otherworldliness has been a gigantic obstacle to progress and has prevented wholly or in part the development of a rational control over social conditions," observed John F. Day of Kentucky mountaineers only twenty years ago. "Before each forward step can be taken—in health practices, in living conditions, in education—'The will of God' must be overcome."[12] It is therefore not entirely surprising that even at the present time when many "forward steps" are being taken, apparently with the approval of the great majority of the Appalachian population, many mountain residents still cling to the perception of God's Will that made bearable the hardships of an earlier day.

The persistence of this outlook is clearly apparent in the responses to the survey question *Do you think that God is more pleased when people try to get ahead or when they are satisfied with what they have?* The distribution of responses by residence and socioeconomic status are shown in Figure 9. Although 57.5 percent of the rural respondents replied "when people are satisfied," compared with 39 percent of the urban respondents and 38 percent of those in metropolitan areas, most of this difference is explained by the rural concentration of lower and lower middle status respondents. The striking shift in responses with changing socioeconomic status lends strong support to the common notion that religiously sanctioned passiveness is the philosophic refuge of the poor. If such passiveness has seemed to be particularly widespread in the Appalachian Region, it has probably been no more prevalent than poverty itself.

The change in interpretation of "God's Will" with varying educational status followed a pattern closely similar to that found for socioeconomic status. This relationship may be of even greater moment to those seeking ways to motivate the apparently apathetic. But the relationship between schooling and belief in striving for improvement is not a simple one in which the former is "cause" and the latter "effect." Even if it were, at least a generation of concentrated effort would be required before the educational level of the younger Appalachian population could be raised to that of the nation.

---

[12] John F. Day, *Bloody Ground* (New York, 1941), p. 104.

The survey data that have been presented, sketchy as they may be, are sufficient to illustrate the value confusion and conflict that has developed in the culture of the Region. Almost all of the people in the Region seem willing and indeed eager to accept the

their perception may not be entirely unrealistic. Even so, their apparent resignation to circumstance is not precisely the fatalism of an earlier era. Then destiny was seen as controlled almost exclusively by God; now a larger measure of control is ascribed to men, but

Figure 9. *Do You Think God Is More Pleased When People Try to Get Ahead or When They are Satisfied with What They Have? Replies by Residence and Socioeconomic Status of Respondent*

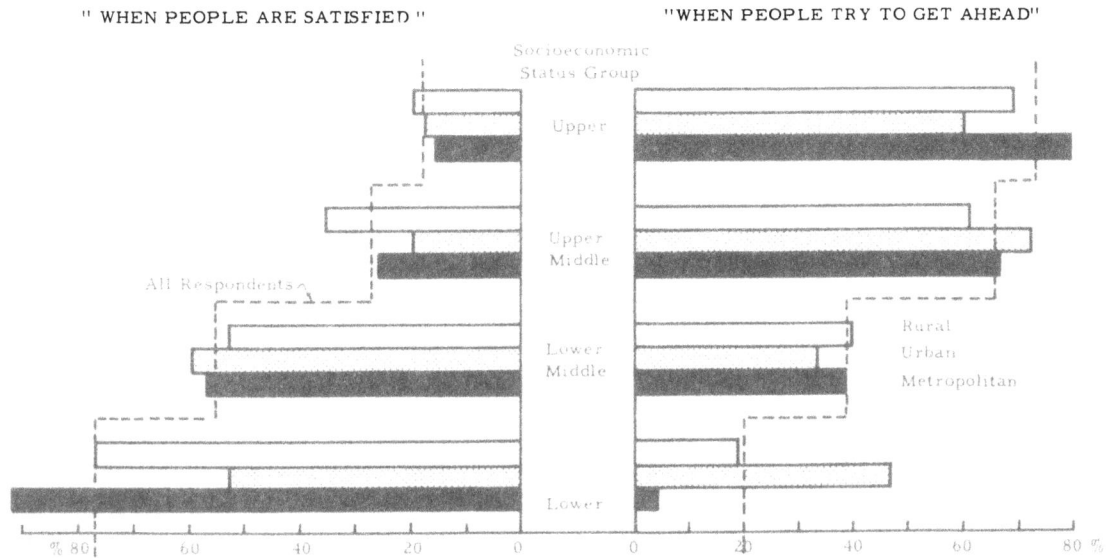

economic benefits and material comforts of urban industrial society, but they are not yet willing to abandon completely the philosophy of fatalism which has allowed them to bear hardship and destitution. There is general recognition that formal education is necessary for achievement in the new society, but many see schooling as a substitute for hard work, and for those who define work in terms of physical effort, the dissociation is understandable. It is quite possible that the value ascribed to professional jobs is traceable to the fact they do not appear to require "work." In any case it may be concluded that however traditionalistic they may be in other respects, the impoverished folk of the mountains are not so enamored of their way of life that they wish their children to follow in it. They wish them to acquire more education and to get better jobs, even if it means leaving the mountains, which in most cases it will.

But although all may hope for a better life for themselves and their children, only the economically secure seem to feel that it is within their power to direct the course of events that will lead to the realization of their hopes. Those of average and below average means still see themselves governed by forces over which they have little or no control, and

more to other men than to themselves. Thus the illiterate miner or subsistence farmer can believe that his children will have a better life if they receive a good education without blaming either himself or God because the schools are poor. He may still ask of God some heavenly recompense for his earthly suffering, but he is less likely to believe that his suffering is divinely ordained and more likely to hope that the state or federal government will do something to alleviate it. Although he views his own role in relation to society as largely passive, he is more than vaguely aware that it is not exclusively so. As a consequence his fatalism is less now than formerly a deterrent to action but rather serves as psychological insurance against failure that he half anticipates and half fears will shatter hopes and ambitions raised too high.

Religious Fundamentalism

Religious values so thoroughly permeate the culture of the Southern Appalachian Region that it is virtually impossible to treat meaningfully any aspect of life without taking them into consideration. Because they underlie so many attitudes and beliefs, they exert complex and frequently subtle influences on secular behavior which are not always apparent to outside observers or even to the people of the Region themselves. Since religious thought and behavior are treated in a separate chapter, the main concern here will be with some of the major influences of religion upon social and economic change in the Region and, to a lesser extent, the effects of change upon religious beliefs.

The basic religious tone of the Region was established during the nineteenth century, which was marked by a series of religious revivals that began with the Great Revival of 1800-1802, and continued almost uninterrupted throughout most of the century. Although the Presbyterian church was the most important religious body on the frontier in the late eighteenth century, it failed to retain its strength or popularity as the line of frontier moved westward into the mountains. Apparently more suited to frontier life were the philosophy and practices of the Baptists and Methodists. These bodies, capitalizing on the spirit of revivalism, gained tremendously in membership, although both groups lost members in turn to numerous smaller sects that sprang up incessantly. The appeal of the Baptist church, or more properly churches, lay in a simple gospel, a democratic congregational organization, and a policy of electing and utilizing lay ministers. These features, ideally suited to frontier conditions, were nearly always retained by the numerous other sects that later arose in the Region. The Methodists were less democratic than the Baptists, as evidenced by their episcopal polity, which significantly was discarded by many sects that splintered off from the Methodist church. However, the Methodists too met frontier needs through their use of circuit riders and their stress on free grace, which was much more in keeping with the democratic spirit of the frontier than was the Calvinist Presbyterians' doctrine of the elect. Most important, the Methodist church will still close enough to its sectarian origins to offer a philosophy that held a strong appeal for the simple and hard-pressed folk of the frontier. Indeed, the main determinant of whether any religious group flourished or waned on the frontier was the extent to which it could provide a plausible and emotionally satisfying explanation of the hardships and sufferings that were the common lot.

As the line of frontier moved westward, some of the religious groups in the more accessible and prosperous areas of the region began to move along the well-traveled route toward becoming formally-organized churches. As they did, they abandoned some of their sectarian traits and with them some

of the members for whom such traits held particularly strong appeal. These latter members either joined existing sectarian groups or, not uncommonly, organized a new sect. But since the greater part of the Appalachian region was neither accessible nor prosperous, the sectarian character of most religious groups remained strong throughout the nineteenth century.

Contemporary religion in the Highlands still bears the fundamentalist stamp of its sectarian origins, although only a minority of Appalachian residents could be considered true sectarians. There is no sharp dividing line between sectarian and non-sectarian fundamentalists, but if sectarianism is "a matter of spirit rather than form, organization, or size," as E. T. Clark has suggested,[13] the difference is probably one of disposition. Present day sectarianism, like that of the frontier, offers as its major appeal a psychological escape from the harsh realities of daily living. Consequently it tends to attract those for whom secular life holds few comforts, drawing its adherents predominantly from the lower economic strata. Their orientation is other-worldly, since they seek and are promised divine compensation, contingent upon salvation, for their earthly sufferings. For them as for their frontier forebears, conversion remains the "climax of human experience," while strivings for secular achievement are viewed as vain and fruitless endeavors.[14]

The survey data already presented regarding the aspirations held by Appalachian residents for their children is in itself evidence that earthly achievements are not disparaged by most of the contemporary population. It has also been noted that about as many Appalachian residents believe that striving to get ahead is divinely sanctioned as believe that passive acceptance of one's lot in life is God's will. The survey data contain other evidence of a considerable drift from sectarian practice as well as spirit, such as a surprisingly strong sentiment for a professional ministry (see Chapter XIII).

The increasing rationality of Appalachian religion implied in the predilection for professional ministers is also manifest in responses to the question: *Which is more important in leading a religious life, conversion or religious training?* Only in rural areas did more respondents attribute greater importance to conversion than to training. Conversion is still accorded primary importance by large proportions of the popu-

[13] E. T. Clark, *The Small Sects in America*, rev. ed. (Nashville, 1949), p. 20.
[14] Elizabeth R. Hooker, *Religion in the Highlands* (New York, 1933), p. 153.

lation, ranging from 47 percent in rural areas to 39 percent in urban areas, but considering that it was once viewed as the culmination of religious experience,

Figure 10. *"The Bible Is God's Word and All It Says Is True." Percentage of Respondents, by Residence and Socioeconomic Status, Endorsing Statement*

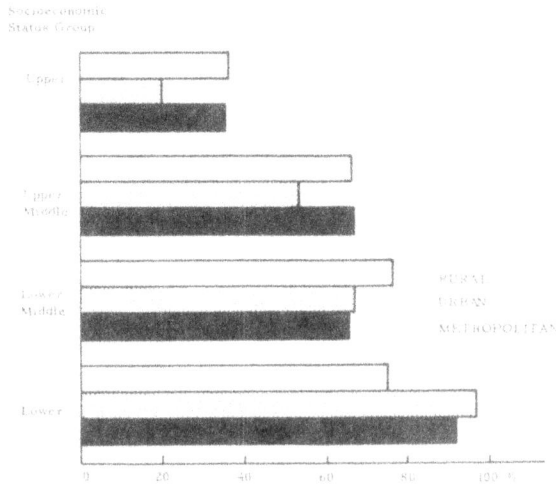

its decline in significance is striking evidence of the movement away from sectarianism.

If the main body of Appalachian religious philosophy and practice has discarded many of its sectarian attributes, it still adheres strongly to a variety of fundamentalist principles, as Brewer has documented in his chapter on religion and the churches in the Region. Most Appalachian residents still profess belief that the Bible contains the literal and infallible word of God, and the strain of Puritan morality still runs strong. Three out of four survey respondents, for example, stated the belief that drinking is always wrong, 85 percent that gambling is always wrong, and about half were of the opinion that keeping a store open on Sunday is invariably wicked. But even here there has been some adjustment to the norms of secular society, for card playing and dancing—once considered gross iniquities—were characterized as always wrong by less than a third of the respondents, although most Appalachian residents still consider them at least sometimes wrong.

As to be expected, fundamentalism as represented by Biblicism and Puritanism is much stronger in rural areas than in urban and metropolitan areas, where economic conditions are better and where there is greater exposure to the secular values of national society. The profession of fundamentalist beliefs also declined steadily with rising socioeconomic status and

educational level, but the only categories in which Biblicists constituted a minority were those of upper socioeconomic status and college-educated respondents (Figure 10).

There seems little doubt that urbanization, increasing contacts with the larger society, and improvements in education have all tended to weaken fundamentalist values in Appalachian society. Nevertheless, they remain impressively strong and it is difficult to evaluate fully their reciprocal influence on social and economic change within the Region. What would seem to be the case is that a working compromise has been effected between religious and secular values of such a nature that social changes once passively (and often actively) resisted are now passively accepted but not actively promoted. One indication of this changed outlook is found in the responses to two survey questions concerning religion and science. The raging conflicts that developed over Biblical accounts of creation and scientific teachings of evolutionary theory are still fresh in the minds of many older Appalachian residents, for it was in a Southern Appalachian county (Rhea) in Tennessee that the dramatic Scopes trial took place in 1924. Although the much publicized "Monkey Trial" was largely a contrived farce, it symbolized the lengths to which the ardent fundamentalists of the day were willing to go in order to denounce any doctrine which appeared to conflict with the revealed word of God. There is little doubt that the attitudinal climate throughout the Southern Appalachian Region at the time was one of ardent fundamentalism. A generation later the prevailing sentiment is still supportive of fundamentalism, but the militant espousal of it has largely subsided.

Responses to questions concerning disagreements between scientific and religious teachings indicate that most Appalachian residents seem to have found, or at least are searching for, some means of conciliating two essentially different systems of value and knowledge. Approximately a third of the respondents claimed that no disagreements exist between science and the teachings of their church. (The proportion is not greatly different from the proportion who had rejected the fundamentalist interpretation of the Bible.) About a fourth of the respondents claimed to be uncertain as to whether there were disagreements, and while this response may be accepted at face value for some, it probably indicated for most the avoidance of an uncomfortable confrontation of issues. A very small proportion of respondents recognized inconsistencies but were unwilling to take a stand as to which position they felt was correct. Militant, anti-scientific fundamentalism appears to be supported by only about a third of the population, and even this figure may indicate a stronger opposition to science than exists in reality. One reason for questioning its strength is that 96 percent of the respondents, when asked to rate the importance of various subjects taught in the public schools, rated science as either important or very important. In fact, science received more "very important" ratings than any other academic subject on the list. Even so, there is little evidence that scientific rationalism as a philosophy has many supporters in the Region, for of those who expressed the belief that scientific knowledge and the teachings of their church were in conflict, only about one in eighteen asserted the pre-eminence of science.

The same spirit of passive acceptance, rather than either rejection or promotion, typified the attitude which most Appalachian residents hold toward church participation in social action programs. There is still some of the older sentiment that religion should be concerned solely with the preaching of the Gospel and the salvation of souls, but it is largely confined to sectarian groups. A more common attitude at the present seems to be that the church should exercise its secular influence indirectly through the "good Christian works" of its members. Still, as has already been noted, eight out of ten survey respondents endorsed participation in community improvement programs as a legitimate activity of the church. Although this activity is not considered as vital as missionary work, revival meetings, Sunday schools, and prayer meetings, to judge by the relative number of endorsers, it was accorded about as much popular approval as fellowship suppers and church picnics, and appreciably more than bazaars, square dances, and activities directed toward raising money to pay the preacher. While it cannot be said that such endorsement is indicative of a demand for such programs or even that they would be strongly supported by most congregations, it does seem to be a tacit concession that churches may, and perhaps should, engage in secular as well as sacred activities.

The same general attitude was apparent in ratings given selected functions of ministers. There is apparently no strong opposition to ministers' engaging in community activities, but there is general belief that his pastoral and preaching functions are more important. And while there seems to be no great enthusiasm for a social gospel, most survey respondents (59 percent) said they thought ministers ought to take a public stand on public issues facing their communities.

There is no gainsaying that fundamentalism remains the main theme of religious thought in the Region, and that it shows few signs of imminent weakening. But to concentrate solely upon fundamentalist traits of Biblicism and Puritan morality as the chief characteristics of conservative Protestantism is to neglect those areas of religious belief and practice where significant changes have taken place, in particular sectarian fatalistic philosophy and exclusive concern for spiritual salvation.

In the Southern Appalachians, past and present—as indeed, in all places at all times—sectarianism has been the companion of privation and emotional insecurity. Its persistence and prevalence are ample evidence of its effectiveness as a mode of adjustment to hardship and suffering, and its decline indicates not so much a reduced efficiency as an abatement of the conditions under which it thrives. It seems almost certain that sectarianism has declined in the Region over the past decades, although it is not possible to say to what degree. In any case, only a minority of the Appalachian population—probably between a fourth and a third, although closer to a half in rural areas—seems to possess a strong sectarian spirit, even though at least two-thirds could be classified as fundamentalists.

What seems to be taking place in the main body of religious thought is a search for a consonance of values, the devising of a new philosophy that will retain the emphasis upon divine ordination of earthly affairs yet accord greater recognition to human control over life circumstances; that will continue to attach paramount importance to spiritual salvation but legitimize secular achievements. In essence the search is for the integration of traditional religious beliefs and values and at least some of the secular norms and goals of contemporary American society. Science is now rarely vilified as subversive of religion except by sectarian minorities. And though not many Appalachian residents would claim that the issues at controversy a generation ago have been resolved, even fewer are desirous of bringing them into conflict again. Most, apparently, would at the present rather consider the claims of science and religion in separate context, thus avoiding the recognition of incompatibilities in their values and beliefs drawn from the two sources. Not many Appalachian residents today view their hopes for eternal salvation and their quests for social and economic improvements as incompatible goals. In fact, to a considerable extent, particularly by those who have achieved or inherited positions of relative comfort and security, they are seen as not only harmonious but complementary.

The translation of God's will for man's earthly well-being into action is not generally perceived as a major function of the church but rather as a duty of Christian individuals. The idea that the church as an organization should undertake programs of social action is accepted, but the social reform activities are not accorded high priority.

It would seem a reasonable conclusion that the religious ethos of the Appalachians no longer poses the barrier to social and economic change that it once did, although it still operates as a restraining force among the depressed classes who continue to use religion as an escape from unpleasant reality. But although religion may no longer serve as a major deterrent to social change in the Region, it can scarcely be considered a strong influence in the promotion of social and economic development. There seems little likelihood for the immediate future that religious values will serve as the main stimulus to usher in a new age or that the churches themselves will play a major role in initiating social reform programs.

Attitudes of Community Leaders

It was earlier mentioned that a number of community leaders were interviewed in addition to the respondents from sample households. There were two major purposes in interviewing these leaders. First, if it may be assumed that leaders actually do lead, in the sense of setting the tone of future thought and action, their beliefs and values would provide an indication of the nature and direction of social and cultural change in the Region. Second, even in the event that the views of today's leaders are not those of tomorrow's masses, it is generally true that such leaders exercise greater influence than the average person in the formulation of institutional plans and in the making of community decisions.

Although the 379 leaders interviewed were selected in each locality from a list of persons named as local community leaders by respondents from sample households, it would be misleading to suggest that they were a statistically representative cross-section of local leadership in the Region. Usually the person who was interviewed as a leader was someone who had been named by several respondents in the same community, but in cases where there was no consensus,

one of the named persons was arbitrarily selected or, if there was a minister among them, he was interviewed. The latter method of choice was for the benefit of the survey sponsors, who were particularly interested in the beliefs and attitudes of minister-leaders.

The types of persons who are named as leaders in itself provides some insight into the values of a society. Four out of five persons in the Southern Appalachian group were men, and slightly more than half were between 45 and 65 years old. Only three percent were under 30 years of age compared with 16 percent aged 65 and over. The fact that only a third of the named leaders were under 45 years of age may be partly explained by the heavy migration of young people from the Region, but it is also indicative of a traditional society in which leadership is acquired with age and, presumably, wisdom. It is particularly significant that the persons named as leaders were considerably above average in education, income, and socioeconomic status. Over half of the metropolitan leaders and a third of the rural leaders had attended college. Less than a third had failed to complete high school, in contrast to 60 percent of the sample survey respondents. Total household income in 1957 reported by leaders averaged nearly $5,700, about 44 percent higher than that reported for sample households. Roughly three-fourths of the leaders were employed in professional occupations or as managers, officials, or proprietors in business or government. To some extent the professional group was inflated by the disproportionate selection of ministers, who constituted about a fourth of the named leaders. It should be remembered, however, that in Southern Appalachian society the influence of ministers is frequently community-wide, and that all of the ministers included had been named as leaders by one or more survey respondents. Since the socioeconomic status index used was based primarily on income, education, and occupation, it is not surprising but nonetheless significant that over half the leaders (51.3 percent) were classified in the upper status category, 30 percent upper middle, 15 percent lower middle, and less than 4 percent lower status. (For the sample population the distribution was 16 percent upper, 30.5 percent upper middle, 35.5 percent lower middle, and 18 percent lower.) In short, the people who were recognized as leaders by the general respondent population were on the average wealthier, better educated, and situated in positions of prestige and influence. Although named by the people, they clearly were not *of* the people in the sense of being typical representatives of the Southern Appalachian population.

To some considerable degree it is possible to infer the attitudes of the leaders from their personal and social characteristics. That is, they would be expected to think much like other residents of comparable education and status. These characteristics in themselves do not make for leadership, however, so some significance must be attached to the ways in which their views differed from those of their status peers. Of particular importance are the ways of thinking which are directly relevant to present and future change in the Region, and again we may focus upon the themes of individualism and self-reliance, traditionalism, fatalism, and religious fundamentalism.

Only leaders of the charismatic type are likely to be true individualists. The average organizational or community leader is both committed to and dependent upon group endeavor. Four out of five leaders expressed themselves, like other residents, as being in favor of current welfare and assistance programs. Only 10 percent expressed the belief that there was any stigma attached to receiving relief, a proportion that was about the same as for the general population and slightly lower than for the upper status group. Despite their relatively liberal attitudes toward public welfare, the attitudes of the leaders toward government subsidies for other purposes were relatively conservative. A fourth of the leaders, compared with less than 10 percent of the sample respondents, held that the government was doing too much for the people, and only 12 percent thought it was doing too little. On the specific issues of Federal aid to local government and to education, leaders were more conservative than the average respondent but still most of them favored such subsidies. Five out of eight expressed themselves in favor of aid to local government, two out of three in favor of Federal aid to education. Finally, five out of nine leaders compared with less than half of the general respondents but 71 percent of the upper status category said they thought such subsidies reduced local self-reliance.

It has been suggested that leaders by the very nature of the position they occupy in society are in favor of organized activities, and this seems clearly indicated by their attitudes toward organized labor. Although only about a fourth of the leaders reported any current or past union affiliation, nearly three out of four professed the belief that workers in industry were better off because of unions. This was greater support than was accorded either by the general population or by any socioeconomic status category—even the lower middle status group, in which half the men had held union membership. Practically all other organizational activities, ranging from 4-H clubs to community efforts to attract industry, were overwhelmingly endorsed by the leaders. They were nearly unanimous (97 percent) in their belief that local organized effort should be directed toward attracting industries to their communities. This would seem to indicate not only that Southern Appalachian leaders are staunch believers in "community action" (and perhaps purveyors of "booster spirit") but that as a group they are committed to a policy of economic expansion rather than to the defense of conservative agrarianism.

Nowhere was the difference in the attitudes of leaders toward community enterprises more clearly revealed than in their views toward taxation. Although they could hardly be termed eager to raise taxes, leaders were far more willing to endorse tax increases to improve or provide specified public services than was the general public. The contrast with upper status respondents was particularly striking, for the latter, who were more likely to feel the pinch of increased taxes, were especially reluctant to consider additional taxation except when they perceived some immediate resultant benefit to themselves. Undoubtedly the inclusion of a relatively high proportion of local public officials influenced the responses of the total leader group, but the number of officials was not sufficient to account for the observed differences. It seems at least plausible that leaders, being more attuned to the overall problems of the total community, are more keenly aware of the necessity of an adequate tax program if the problems are to be solved. And while their views in this regard are not likely to receive popular acclaim, their apparent willingness to subordinate class interests to community interests may be one reason why they are recognized as community leaders.

One mark of a truly traditionalistic society is that its leaders are firmly dedicated either to preserving existing patterns of belief and behavior or to restoring earlier patterns considered even more desirable. By this criterion, Southern Appalachian society could hardly be considered traditionalistic. To a far greater degree than the average resident of the Region, persons named as local leaders are devoted to the philosophy of social progress and individual achievement that is a major theme of American culture. They are nearly unanimous in their belief that industrialization would prove of major benefit to the region and, as has already been indicated, that local community efforts should be exerted to attract industry. Their dedication to a philosophy of individual striving and self-betterment is reflected in the aspirations which they hold for their children. Seven out of eight leaders who were willing to express an occupational preference for a son named a white collar job, and three out of four specified a professional occupation. This is not surprising, of course, since nearly half of the leaders were in professional occupations themselves and only about 20 percent were farmers or industrial workers. What is important is that those who were named as leaders by the population cross-section are not only relatively successful themselves by purely secular standards but also hold even higher achievement aspirations for their children.

Further evidence of this spirit of achievement is provided by the fact that nine out of ten leaders said they would want a son or daughter to complete college. Nearly a fifth of them said they would want their sons to do graduate work beyond the baccalaureate degree, and 12 percent expressed the same desire for a daughter. Only two of the 379 leaders said they would be content for their children to have less than a high school education, and only one in twenty said he would be willing for them to terminate their educations with a high school diploma. Asked whether they would want a child to stay in the community to live or go elsewhere, there was a five to four preference for remaining in the community, although about a fourth of the respondents said they didn't know. This ratio was about the same as for the total sample of survey respondents, but indicative of a greater preference for the children to seek residence elsewhere than was true of upper status respondents in the general survey.

In their evaluation of "success" factors, also, the views of leaders were somewhat closer to the total population average than to those of upper status respondents. That is, more of them rated *education* and *liking one's work* as the most important factors than rated *hard work* as most important. As was the case with the sample survey group, though, there were important differences by place of residence. Relatively more metropolitan leaders (33 percent) named *hard work* as the most important success factor, as did other metropolitan area residents, but rural leaders, like other rural residents, gave *education* top rating (40 percent), followed by *liking one's work* (33 percent), with only 10 percent giving top rating to *hard work*. Urban leaders named *hard work* more often

than *good education* but less often than *liking one's work*, the latter factor being also most frequently named by other urban respondents. It is anomalous, indeed, that hard work, so often considered to be a traditional virtue of rural Americans, is almost disparaged by Appalachian rural residents and their leaders; and that these same rural people, who reputedly have been strongly resistant to formal schooling, more often credit success to good education than do their better educated urban and metropolitan neighbors.

Considering the strong achievement drive of the leaders, one would hardly expect them to be fatalists, and this expectation is borne out by the survey results. The philosophy of "live for today and let tomorrow take care of itself" was rejected by more than three-fourths of the leader respondents. And only 42 percent endorsed the statement *no matter how much or how little you take care of yourself, you are going to die when your allotted time is up*, a statement with which seven out of ten general survey respondents agreed. Significantly, less than a third of the ministers in the leader group endorsed the latter statement, which would seem to indicate the withdrawal of religious support from the fatalistic doctrine that has so long deterred social action in the Region. This conclusion, at least so far as these particular ministers is concerned, is substantiated in the responses to the question of whether God is more pleased when people try to get ahead or when they are satisfied with what they have. Seventy percent of the minister-leaders and 72 percent of all leaders answered "when people try to get ahead." Even in rural areas, where it would be expected that ministers would be most traditionalistic in their attitudes toward secular achievement, a clear majority of the ministers (56 percent) indicated that they (and God) thought people should try to get ahead.

In summary, Southern Appalachian leaders as represented by the survey are neither fatalists nor reactionaries. Rather, they are "activists" and "progressives" for the most part, committed to a philosophy of individual achievement and social development. If they are distinctive in this regard, they are so largely with respect to the norms and values of the regional past, not those of contemporary national society. But this in itself holds considerable significance, for if their beliefs and behavior are in any way indicative of the direction in which regional values are changing, which seems surely to be the case, they portend an increasing acceptance of national culture traits.

It has been suggested that the aspect of Appalachian culture least affected by social and economic changes has been its system of religious beliefs, although even it has undergone some important modifications. The persistent conservatism that characterized the religious views of the general population was also to be found in those of the leaders, but to a slightly lesser degree, even though about a fourth of the leaders were ministers. Ministers, as to be expected, were generally more conservative than other leaders, but not as conservative as the population cross-section. This is not really surprising, since they were selected because they were considered community leaders, not because they were ministers, and religious sectarianism is by its very nature incompatible with the type of secular endeavor generally conceived of as community work. Consequently, the religious beliefs of minister-leaders would not be representative of those of most ministers in the Region and may well represent the "liberal" extreme.

In nearly all respects, including their denominational affiliations, leaders were manifestly non-sectarians. Nevertheless, relatively few of them could be considered religious liberals by most standards except those of the Region itself. Over half (53 percent) of the leaders claimed to believe in the infallibility of the Scriptures as opposed to 46 percent who took a modernist view that the Bible contained some human error. Interestingly, a smaller proportion of ministers (45 percent) than other leaders (56 percent) professed themselves Biblicists. By the criterion of Biblicism, leaders would be considered less fundamentalist than the general population, but more so than other respondents of comparable socioeconomic status and education. With respect to their acceptance of a "Puritan ethic," though, they were about as fundamentalist as the average respondent and considerably more Puritanical than most upper status and college educated respondents. For example, the percentages of leaders and general survey respondents who rated drinking and dancing as "always wrong" were almost the same, about three out of four for drinking and about one in five for dancing. But only 22 percent of the leaders, as compared with 32 percent of the general sample, rated card playing always wrong. Minister-leaders were more conservative than others but, with respect to card playing less so than the general sample.

Among leaders, as among other respondents, there was a considerable weakening of Puritan morality with increasing urbanization, but in all areas the professed beliefs of the leaders were closer to those of the middle classes than to those of upper status and college-educated respondents. Although various interpretations might be placed on this phenomenon, it does suggest that leaders are more likely to respond to the ethical norms of the "total community" rather than to those of the particular social class in which they might be placed by virtue of wealth, occupation, or education.

The closeness of the religious philosophy of leaders to that of the middle classes was also apparent in their responses to questions concerning possible conflicts between science and church teachings. Only 36 percent of the leaders (and only 27 percent of the minister-leaders) acknowledged any disagreements, at least so far as their own churches were concerned. This was very close to the comparable figure (38.5 percent) for the general survey population. Of those leaders who thought there were disagreements, only one in thirty-five said that scientific teachings were probably more nearly right, while four out of five took the side of religion. The remainder, about one in eight, claimed to be unsure as to which was right. It would thus appear that most leaders, like most of the remainder of Appalachian society, are seeking to avoid bringing to the surface any latent conflict stemming from the acceptance of both rational and sacred authority. Cognizant of the current prestige of scientific knowledge but unwilling to deny the preeminence of their religious teachings, many leaders have apparently chosen to ignore conflicting issues while focusing on areas of mutual support.

The social action philosophy of the named leaders finds expression in their beliefs concerning the proper social role of churches and ministers, but there is little evidence that they consider the promotion of social progress a major church function. Nine out of ten leaders endorsed church participation in community improvement programs, and three out of four said they thought ministers should take a public stand on important issues. But other church activities, such as revival meetings, received even more support, and 40 percent of the leaders rated the community service function of the minister as less important than any of his more traditional pastoral and priestly duties. Most leaders considered it more important than administrative duties connected with the church, however. It seems a reasonable inference that leaders, even more so than other respondents, conceive of the churches' role as being broader than mere evangelism and legitimately including the promotion of social and economic improvements. But most leaders do not identify the church as a social action agency and apparently feel that it best serves the cause of social progress through inspiring its members to engage in good works for the glory of God.

To what extent the values and beliefs of those persons identified as local community leaders may signal the future pattern of the Region there is, of course, no way of knowing. It is reasonably certain, however, that their values will figure heavily in local decisions that will shape the course of regional events for at least the near future. The evidence secured in the survey, of which it has been possible to present only fragmentary portions, indicates that the value position of these local leaders lies somewhere between that of the majority of the regional population and that of the more industrialized segment of the national population. The characteristics of the leaders themselves suggest this. They are not the bright young human dynamos that one finds in our industrial metropolises, but neither are they mossbacked rural patriarchs. For the most part they are well educated and hold responsible positions in the business, church, educational, and local governmental institutions of their communities. By national standards, their values would be considered conservative, but not reactionary; by regional standards they seem almost liberal. They have, for the most part, rejected the philosophy of passive acceptance of their social and economic circumstances. They want better conditions for themselves and for their children, and they see industrialization and improved education as primary means to this end.

Perhaps what most distinguishes those who were named as leaders from other residents of comparable education and wealth is their ability and willingness to consider issues from a community standpoint rather than as individuals or representatives of a social class. Yet this fact inevitably creates a moral dilemma which appears time and again in their responses to survey questions. Committed by culture and social position to the values of individual endeavor and free enterprise, they are painfully aware that these in themselves are inadequate to solve the problems of their local communities and of the Region. One senses their reluctance to endorse programs of Federal and state assistance which they recognize are probably necessary to the solution of their community problems but simultaneously feel will undermine the traditional virtues of individualism and self-reliance. Forced to a choice, which is already being made through numer-

ous small daily decisions and a few major ones, there is little doubt that community leaders will accept government aid in lieu of a more desirable and less likely economic prosperity created by industrial development. In choosing to tread this unhappy path, they may have whatever solace there is in knowing they have the support of the vast majority of their fellow citizens whom they seek to serve.

Tradition, Change, and the Future

At the beginning of this essay, some of the questions that prompted the exploration of values, beliefs, and attitudes of Southern Appalachian people were posed: Have the people clung to their frontier-agrarian traditions, resisting the philosophical premise of industrial society? Are they willing to accept the social consequences of a new economy? Are there evidences of discrepancies between new modes of behavior and old patterns of thought, and, if so, what do they portend in the way of future social problems? And what implications do the current beliefs and values of the Appalachian people hold for those who are actively working to promote social and economic change in the Region? To conclude the chapter, it seems appropriate to return to these questions and attempt to answer them, even though the answers of necessity must be incomplete and to some considerable extent impressionistic. It is to be re-emphasized that the very attempt to present conclusions about the values and beliefs of Southern Appalachian people may create an impression of homogeneity that does not in fact exist.

The question of whether the people of the Region have clung to their earlier heritage, steadfastly resisting the secular philosophy of an industrial society, can be answered simply and categorically. The answer is no. But there is some danger both in asking the question and in answering it categorically of perpetuating the widely accepted but misleading assumption of a relatively stable pattern of regional culture introduced at the time of settlement and persisting well up into the current century. It is the same false assumption that finds currency in reference to the Highlands as an "arrested frontier." In truth the regional way of life has always been in some flux, and there is considerable evidence that there was a rapid decline in so-called "frontier spirit" not long after settlement of the Region was completed.

It is self-evident that the early settlers were not passively resigned to their life circumstances or they would not have exposed themselves to the hardships of frontier life in the first place. Quite possibly, as has been suggested, they were not the doughty pioneers of legend who moved into the mountains undaunted by foreknowledge of the hazardous and rigorous conditions they would encounter, but rather naive romanticists expecting to find a new Garden of Eden or at least a land of milk and honey.[15] In any case, they were actively searching for a better life, which meant in part freedom from the social restraints of the settled seaboard and piedmont and the opportunity to acquire farm land of their own. It is also quite probable that they brought with them and were motivated by the "fundamental pathos of American culture [the belief] that virtue should and will be rewarded—and more particularly that such economic virtues as hard work, frugality, and prudence should receive a proportionate reward."[16]

If such was their belief, they were soon disillusioned. Hard work, frugality, and prudence proved to be not guarantees of prosperity but necessities for sheer survival. Yet they could not accept the harsh verdict that virtue is its own, and often only, reward. Even less willing were they to accept the smug Calvinistic doctrine that prosperity was a sign of the divinely "elect" while poverty was the lot of the uncalled and unchosen. Thus it was no mere coincidence that the gratifying philosophy of sectarian Protestantism found unprecedented acceptance (in the New World) in the mountains. For it defined as virtue not hard work and secular striving but suffering and privation, which the mountain people had in abundance, and offered as reward not mere earthly riches but the inheritance of the Kingdom of God itself. The retreat into fatalism and sectarian religion was not evidence of some peculiar and innate character flaw, but a concession of inadequate skill and resources to control the unyielding forces of nature. Nor was their failure to master the environment, at least during the nineteenth century, because their technical skills were markedly inferior to those of other rural people. Rather, it was because the technology of the age was not adequate to cope with the conditions of their habitat. Once they adjusted psychologically to their situation, though, there was little motivation for many residents to resume the struggle against nature even when an advancing technology was able to provide them with better weapons.

But it was not the lack of motivation alone that prevented the mountain people from taking full advantage of technological advances. There was also their high degree of individualism, a frontier value strengthened by years of relative isolation. The individualism of the frontier, as many historians have pointed out, was not the individualism of nonconformity but of personal liberty and freedom from civil restraints. Inclined to be suspicious of all extra-familial social liaisons, the mountain people had little enthusiasm for or experience with the forms of social organization required for the successful functioning of an industrial economy and an urban society. A companion virtue to self-reliance, individualism was easily and often perverted to the cause of social irresponsibility and remained in active force even when the independence which it was supposed to sustain had all but disappeared.

It is difficult to say when the prevailing philosophy of resignation began to be supplanted by a philosophy more in tune with that of the national culture that emphasized work, achievement, and progress. In any event, the transition was not marked by any radical reorientation of values but rather by a gradual shifting of beliefs and sentiments. There were always "activist" individuals and groups in Appalachian society just as there are "passivist" individuals and groups today, but no one has adequately described when or why the activist element began to predominate. The relief program of the New Deal was probably one major force in bringing about the change, but not because it radically affected the value premises of regional society. (Indeed, it challenged those of the national society to a much greater degree.) Many if not most Appalachian residents who received public assistance payments under the New Deal program viewed their relief benefits as *manna*, a direct gift of God disbursed by a beneficent government. For much of the Appalachian Region the Great Depression was a period of relative prosperity, and although there was little in the emergency relief program to spur the people to greater industry, many came to experience for the first time the pleasures of having adequate food, clothing, and housing.

Probably far more effective and enduring in reorienting the value system were the forces and events that served to break down regional isolation. The growth and improvement of public education was one such force, for the schools served as a major communication channel through which the values and norms of national society were introduced into the Region. Rural electrification, too, played an important

---

[15] Arthur K. Moore, *The Frontier Mind—A Cultural Analysis of the Kentucky Frontiersman* (Lexington, Ky., 1957).

[16] Williams, *American Society*, p. 416.

role, for it made possible material comforts such as electric lights and washing machines that could be afforded by all save the poorest, and even they could aspire to their possession. Perhaps even more important, radios were also widely introduced and by this means the isolated as well as the illiterate residents not only learned more about conditions in other parts of the nation and world but were also exposed to the potent stimuli of mass advertising. Other agents of mass communication also served to arouse acquisitive desires and develop emulative tastes —the motion pictures, mail order catalogs, weekly newspapers, and farm journals. The movies were considered particularly threatening to fundamentalist values and were denounced from many pulpits with epithets earlier reserved for drinking, dancing, card playing and other sinful activities. Quite probably such denunciation exaggerated the actual influence of the cinema, but at least in the censure there was recognition that provincial values were at odds with those thought accepted by a more sophisticated society.

Education, mass communication, and improved roads that linked more closely hollows and cities, all contributed to the weakening of traditional values, a process that was greatly accelerated by World War II. Where the other forces had aroused yearnings for new ways, the war provided numerous opportunities to fulfill these desires and created yet others. Even those who did not go into the armed forces were affected by the war. Some migrated to northern cities to find employment in expanded industries at wages earlier undreamed of, and learned to cope with the conditions of urban living. Within the Region itself there were new industries and construction work, while older industries, such as the coal mines, provided employment that was gratifyingly regular and profitable. In short, it was a period of novel experiences, new opportunities, and unprecedented prosperity, and after it was all over there could be no complete return to the old ways. Literally hundreds of thousands left the Region during the post-war period, seeing little opportunity to continue to live as well so long as they remained. But of equal or greater moment, so far as the culture of the Region itself is concerned, is that the great majority of those who did remain, having once experienced flush times, could no longer view poverty as the natural condition of man. Many have since seen poverty return, but they have not, as yet, been able to accept it with the resignation of their forebears, not so much because their faith in God is less but because their faith in man is greater.

The question of whether the mountain people are prepared to accept the social consequences of industrial society along with its economic benefits is more difficult to answer. At least it cannot be answered categorically, for there are many consequences and they cannot be considered as a body.

One obvious social consequence of industrial society is urban living. That this is acceptable to many Appalachian residents is obvious from the patterns of migration that have developed in recent years. But willingness to live in cities is not the same as willingness to adopt the modes of social and civic behavior that urban living implies. Mountain residents who have moved into industrial centers, especially those outside the Region, have frequently been charged with creating a variety of social problems. In this respect, however, they do not differ greatly from European immigrants who settled in many of the same cities in the latter part of the nineteenth century. To a great extent, as Giffin has pointed out in his discussion of the urban adjustment of Appalachian migrants (Chapter V), the behavioral characteristics that create social problems in the cities are attributes of social class rather than of regional culture. If the past history of immigrant assimilation provides a useful guide, the solution of such problems depends in considerable measure upon the types of jobs the migrants are able to fill. Inasmuch as many of them lack the educational or technical qualifications to compete successfully for better paid positions, it seems unlikely that they will be easily absorbed, and complete assimilation will probably not be accomplished within a single generation.

Within the Region itself the adjustment problems are of a somewhat different order. Probably the most serious from the standpoint of regional development are those that stem from the failure to develop a strong sense of civic responsibility. This is evident in the shortage of effective community action organization and in the steadfast reluctance to increase local taxes for purposes that are generally conceded to be worthy. The reasons for this apparent unwillingness to assume social responsibilities are numerous and varied. They include the persistence of individualism as a value, which has already been discussed, and the inherent difficulty of changing from familistic to associational society. To some degree the development of a "relief philosophy" may also have served as a deterrent to community self-reliance, although there has been more emotional assertion than objective evidence to support this case. The growing recognition that the fundamental economic problems of the Region are not likely to be solved by local community action alone and that their deleterious consequences are felt far beyond the Region has also provided for some a rationale for shifting to the national level the total responsibility for seeking effective solution. There seems little doubt that even among the more conservative elements of the Region there is an increasing tendency to view Federal assistance as an alternative rather than as a supplement to local efforts to solve community problems. At the same time it must be recognized that numerous towns and cities within the Region have outstanding records of civic enterprise and that many counties have organized effective rural development programs coordinating the services of state and federal agencies and local citizen groups. The question, therefore, is not whether the people of the Region are capable of initiating and organizing local action programs but whether they are yet willing to accept and sustain the fundamental premise that furtherance of the commonweal in a democratic society requires a common effort.

The course of social transition is never smooth, for the adoption of new ways always carries the implication of the inferiority of older ways and the values that have sustained them. It is therefore inevitable that some conflict should develop between the accepters of the new and the defenders of the old. But the people of a society undergoing transition are rarely divided into two sharply distinct categories. More commonly than not, the individuals who compose such a society are internally at odds, accepting some of the new, retaining some of the old, and seeking to resolve or repress whatever logical inconsistencies may arise as a consequence.

Evidence that many members of Appalachian society are faced with internal and unresolved conflicts of various sorts has already been presented and need not be reviewed in detail. Parents with high aspirations for their children frequently do not exert the necessary effort to see that they receive the schooling that the realization of their aspirations requires. Residents of local communities concede the desirability of having better schools, better health facilities, and better government, but reject tax measures needed to provide them. Similarly, there is general recognition that organized social action is more effective than individual efforts, but attempts to organize action groups for purposes that have received popular endorsement often die a-borning. The goals and benefits of industrial society are accepted; the methods of

achieving them are endorsed but not supported; and the failure to support them is rooted in the values of agrarian society.

All of these problems of conflicting values, though, have a familiar ring, and one recognizes that they are the same problems that have attended the transition from agrarian to industrial society in other parts of the nation and, indeed, throughout the world. There is little to suggest that the problems of conflicting values, whether the conflict is between groups or within individuals, are radically different in the Southern Appalachian Region. If there is a difference, it is probably more attributable to the greater intensity and persistence of agrarian values in the Region rather than to their nature.

The final question to be considered of those that prompted the attitude survey is *What implications do the current beliefs and values of the Appalachian people hold for those who are actively working to promote social and economic change in the Region?* A major difficulty in handling such a question is that there is not really any general objective or overall program for systematic social change in the Region. Rather, there are many small relatively autonomous programs, with different aspects of social and economic organization and activity, geographically restricted, and each with its own limited objectives. If there is any common thread, it is that of seeking to change the particular local conditions with which each program is concerned to correspond more closely to some real or assumed national standard. That is, the direction in which change is being urged, whether it be in the field of health, education, economics, welfare, or almost any other with the possible exception of religion, is toward the national norm.

It is a generally (although by no means invariably) valid assumption that before the members of a society will move toward the achievement of a specific objective, they must first accept it as legitimate. Most of the people of the Region, according to the evidence of the survey data, have adopted the major goals and standards typical of American society. They, like other people throughout the nation, wish to have larger incomes, greater material comforts, and more prestigeful status. And if it seems unlikely that they will realize these aspirations for themselves, they would at least like to see them realized by their children. In short, the people of the Region have become "progressive-minded" and "achievement-oriented" to a surprisingly high degree, and a large amount of motivation effort, like the preaching, in the Southern Appalachians is expended on the already converted.

In part the continued preoccupation with motivation at the basic value level stems from the value assumptions of the promoters themselves. They believe that acceptance of goals is not only a necessary but a sufficient condition for achieving them. Firmly believing that "where there's a will, there's a way," they persistently attribute lack of achievement to lack of motivation. To support their inference, they can point both to the traditional passivist philosophy of the Region and to not a few contemporary groups and individuals whose lives are still guided by it. Yet the evidence from the attitude survey would indicate that these groups and individuals today constitute a minority of the Appalachian population; but the Region itself continues to lag in its social and economic development. It hardly seems reasonable to ascribe all the backwardness or even most of it to inadequate motivation. While this is not to suggest that motivation efforts are no longer necessary, which is obviously not the case, it is to suggest that the same energies might be more efficiently applied to other tasks.

What might some of these tasks be? Apart from the purely technological considerations of resource development, there are a number of areas of social life that would appear to benefit from rational and concerted action. One of the most obvious deficiencies that has already been discussed is the lack of a strong sense of social responsibility. In large measure this deficiency is a logical consequence of the traditional social organization of Appalachian society based on familism and the cultivation of individualism as a value. There has been a growing acceptance of the necessity of interdependence for the functioning of an industrial economy and urban society, but it has been viewed as little more than a necessity. There has been little concession that such interdependence entails any greater obligation to or responsibility for one's fellow citizens than what is absolutely necessary to maintain a specific activity. The bonds of loyalty to group or community are often so tenuous as to appear lacking altogether. Not uncommonly projects such as new schools or hospitals that apparently have widespread and even enthusiastic approval fail to receive support when presented as bond issues. Nor can this failure be traced to any belief on the part of the majority of the citizens that education and health are not desirable or that good schools and hospitals do not contribute to their improvement. True, in most such instances numerous rationalizations are

offered for the failure—taxes are already too high or the ventures are being promoted by individuals with vested interests or countless others—but the underlying reason is generally the lack of a sense of social responsibility. Certainly the development of this trait would seem to be a worthwhile task for those who are concerned with the improvement of life in the Region. There would appear to be a ready-made basis for such development in the religious ethos, but so far there have been relatively few efforts to establish an explicit linkage between Christ's precept to love one's neighbor as oneself and the solving of community problems. While the appeal to religious values might be considered a hypocritical expediency in some parts of the nation, it need not necessarily be so in the Southern Appalachians, for as our survey data have shown, the leaders themselves seem to be of the same religious persuasion as most of the general population.

Another area in which concerted action could help develop a broader consciousness of social obligations is in the teaching of the techniques of group organization and action. In the criticism of Appalachian residents for their failure to support and participate in organized activities, sight has often been lost of the fact that the social skills required for such participation are not automatically acquired. It is difficult for proud and sensitive people to enter into unaccustomed activities that they feel will reveal them as gauche and inadequate. Consequently many would rather foresake the benefits of group endeavor than endure the humiliation of being considered ignorant and inept. The survey data indicate that the value of organized action is more widely recognized that the low participation rates would indicate. The diffidence that underlies much, although by no means all, of the reluctance to engage in cooperative activities can probably be overcome to some degree through small-scale programs, involving limited numbers of people, that are designed to provide training in the skills and conventions of group action. Many agencies, such as the agricultural extension services of the various states, already incorporate this objective in their programs. But more typically, existing agencies and new organizations concentrate exclusively on the attainment of some concrete program objective and call repeatedly on the services of the overburdened few who are already familiar with the techniques and processes of carrying out group programs. And while most agency and community leaders are aware that program involvement itself generates support, under the pressures of time and circumstance they seldom undertake to broaden the base of support through systematic, long-range plans to train potential participants and develop future leaders.

A third task implicit in the survey findings is in the area of reducing the social conflict and personal confusion arising from the confrontation of different value systems. In recent times the major arena of social conflict arising from the contact of disparate value systems has been in the industrial cities of the north to which Appalachian migrants have flocked by the hundreds of thousands. More often than not the problem has been defined as the inability of the "hill-billies" to adjust to the ways of urban and industrial life. There has been less recognition that the rural provincialism of the mountain migrants is matched by the urban provincialism of city dwellers, and that this latter also figures in the maladjustment.

The most promising approach to the solution of this problem would seem to be one of education. Certainly there is a need to familiarize the mountain migrants, preferably before they migrate, with the requirements and expectations of urban life and the conditions they are likely to face. There is also a need to acquaint the officials, agency workers, teachers, and ordinary citizens of industrial cities with some valid knowledge of the ways and problems of the migrants. Some beginning steps toward meeting this latter need have already been taken through a series of workshops on adjustment problems of Appalachian migrants held at Berea College, Kentucky, under the direction of the Council of the Southern Mountains. As a direct outgrowth of these workshops, a number of groups have been organized in major cities north of the Ohio River to deal with the great variety of complex adjustment problems faced by mountain migrants. No comparable programs have been undertaken within cities of the Region itself to help in the adjustment of rural migrants, however, and there are appreciable adjustment problems there, also, even though the cultural gap is not so great as it is in northern cities. Neither has there been any systematic effort to prepare potential migrants in rural areas for city life, either within or outside the Region, except through the normal educational programs of the public schools.

But of all the implications that may be drawn from the survey of attitudes, values, and beliefs of the Southern Appalachian people, the most important is this: that the old stereotypes that have so long guided social action in the Region no longer apply to the great majority of the residents. The Southern Appalachian people, although they may lag in their social and economic development, are living in the Twentieth Century. To be sure, they retain the impress of their rural cultural heritage, but for the most part their way of life, their beliefs, their fears, and their aspirations are not radically different from those of most other Americans. If they do not share fully in the larger culture of the nation, which in truth they do not as yet (and, indeed, some of their champions hope they will not), it can hardly be attributed to their lack of willingness to do so. To an appreciable measure their distinctiveness as a people is vested in characteristics that have persisted only because of restricted social and economic opportunities. The economic development of the Region is not so much dependent upon their cultural integration as their cultural integration is dependent upon economic development. Whether or not it is considered desirable, it seems almost certain that as the economic problems are solved, the provincialism of the Region itself will fade.

The Changing
Population

NEARLY *thirty years ago the survey published under the title* Economic
and Social Problems and Conditions of the Southern Appalachians *diagnosed the basic problems of the Region as a maladjustment between population and resources. Since then, there have been changes in both population and resource development, but the continued definition of the Southern Appalachians as a problem area is evidence of the failure to achieve a satisfactory balance thus far.*

In the first of the three essays in this section, John C. Belcher describes the major changes in the growth, distribution, and characteristics of the Region's population. He notes the significance of the declining birth rate and the decrease in the population between 1950 and 1960—the first such decrease recorded. The author analyzes some of the causes of recent population changes and conjectures on the future population characteristics of the Region.

A frequent result of imbalance between population and available resources is the removal of part of the population through migration. James S. Brown and George A. Hillery, Jr., point out in the second essay that such migration from the Southern Appalachians has been almost continuous. In recent years, however, it has risen to flood proportions, and during the 1950-1960 decade there was a net migration loss of more than a million persons from the Region. The authors discuss not only the extent of migration but also the destinations of the migrants, their characteristics, and the reasons for their leaving. Throughout their essay they emphasize the wide variation of areas within the Region with regard both to the extent of migration and the direction of migration streams.

The migration of southern highlanders is of consequence not only to the Region but also to the areas to which they move. The adjustment problems of these migrants in northern cities have received in recent years considerable national publicity, much of it of a sensational nature. In the third essay of the section, Roscoe Giffin reports the findings of an objective investigation of one of the more frequent complaints against mountain migrants—that they fail to participate in the social organizations of the cities. Since such organizations form the connective tissue of urban life, the implication of this charge is that the migrants remain a foreign—and often irritative—element in the social body of the city. Although Giffin's study is of migrants in Cincinnati, his findings probably are applicable to most of the other industrial cities to which the mountain people have flocked in increasing numbers.

CHAPTER THREE

Population

Growth

and

Characteristics

JOHN C. BELCHER

MOST INTEREST IN THE SOUTHERN Appalachians is not in physical resources, climate, and topography of the area but rather in the people of the region and their social institutions. The stereotype of the "mountaineer" which is so firmly fixed in many minds bears little resemblance to the reality of today —or, indeed, of any other time.

Tremendous changes have taken place in the Appalachians during the twentieth century and change continues today at an accelerated pace. Birth rates in the area, long higher than in other regions, are rapidly declining and today appear to be lower than for the nation as a whole. Death rates are not significantly different from those of the rest of the United States. A great interchange of population with other sections is taking place. Many more leave the Region than come to it, but even so, no longer can the Appalachians be considered isolated. The residents watch the same television programs and, perhaps less often, read the same books as do people elsewhere.

Even though the population of the nation experienced a tremendous upsurge between 1950 and 1960, the number of people dwelling in the Southern Appalachians declined for the first time since the Region was settled. No longer is livelihood based primarily upon a self-sufficient agrarianism. An increased percentage of the inhabitants live in cities, especially in the Great Valley, and engage in nonagricultural occupations. Large proportions of women work outside the home.

Although there is still a great deal of poverty in the Region, the level of living has greatly increased in recent years. Most families have modern conveniences such as radios, refrigerators, electric lights, and automobiles. The level of educational attainment is rapidly rising. In summary, the population of the Southern Appalachians today is in a period of rapid transition, reflecting the economic and social changes taking place in the Region.

From the establishment of the first Atlantic Seaboard Colonies it took approximately 150 years for the English to extend their settlement of this country to the Appalachians. The Appalachian Mountains, extending 1,300 miles from Vermont to North Alabama, long provided an effectual barrier to westward settlement. Toward the middle of the eighteenth century, some of the residents of Pennsylvania moved into the Great Appalachian Valley through a break in the Blue Ridge Mountains. A road was blazed down the Appalachian Valley and, finally, through the Cumberland Gap in the mountains to the west. This fabled wilderness road opened the lands west of the Appalachians to settlement by whites. Many thousands of migrants moved down the Great Appalachian Valley, through the Cumberland Gap, and

ley and along the valleys and coves of the streams flowing into the Valley. The settlement of the mountainous sections took place in the early 1800's, but it was not until the Cherokees were evicted from their homes in North Georgia in 1836, and gold was dis-

Table 4. *Population of the Southern Appalachian Region, 1790-1960*

Year	Total, the Region	Alabama	Georgia	Kentucky	North Carolina	Tennessee	Virginia	West Virginia
1960	5,672,178	197,137	378,012	666,572	583,775	1,406,462	956,488	1,483,732
1950	5,833,263	207,157	353,525	795,016	572,776	1,320,679	934,336	1,649,774
1940	5,408,886	204,105	318,432	820,115	533,155	1,131,120	855,631	1,546,328
1930	4,771,813	185,858	275,471	711,613	460,161	984,402	671,175	1,393,133
1920	4,063,761	161,531	248,273	588,116	383,032	837,487	678,662	1,166,660
1910	3,513,222	139,509	240,146	477,838	339,880	751,111	624,336	940,402
1900	2,965,500	118,323	230,015	400,410	306,205	657,323	547,626	705,598
1890	2,452,988	103,433	207,311	308,545	253,904	552,751	472,042	555,002
1880	1,965,006	74,098	180,087	241,801	199,319	437,208	396,178	436,315
1870	1,463,771	46,352	140,923	170,635	144,023	343,265	307,722	310,851
1860	1,334,791	51,325	134,608	136,866	125,279	311,784	294,590	380,339
1850	1,092,948	38,546	100,498	99,429	95,162	270,298	262,600	226,415
1840	828,691	34,767	51,132	66,625	70,289	227,809	208,318	169,751
1830	680,211	16,933	12,847	49,614	63,035	199,049	201,501	137,232
1820	497,669	11,166	3,669	32,353	42,328	135,312	164,888	107,953
1810	385,533	------	------	18,566	35,812	101,367	143,364	86,424
1800	293,584	------	------	1,587	25,771	73,419	124,878	67,929
1790	175,189	------	------	------	16,261	28,649	87,798	42,490

Source: U. S. Census of Population

settled in the Blue Grass country of Kentucky during the last quarter of the eighteenth century. By 1790 there was a concentration of population south of the Ohio in Kentucky. Some settlers remained in the Appalachian Valley, especially the section of the Great Valley in Virginia, but many moved on through the mountains. The total population of the Southern Appalachians when the first census of the United States was made in 1790 was only 175,189 or approximately two people per square mile. Over half of these individuals resided in what is now the state of Virginia. As migrants flowed into other sections of the mountains, the population increased rapidly for many decades (see Table 4).

Meanwhile, the old national road (Cumberland Turnpike) was opened between Baltimore and the West in 1818. This road permitted a more direct route to the west down the Ohio River, and the stream of migrants through the mountains slowed to a trickle. John C. Campbell[1] saw the rise of three great reservoirs of population: first, the Piedmont of North and South Carolina; second, Eastern Pennsylvania; and third, Western Pennsylvania. As settlement was completed in these three areas and the line of the frontier moved westward to the Mississippi River, the surplus population from these three reservoirs gradually moved into and settled the mountains. The earlier settlements were in the Appalachian Val-

covered in the North Georgia mountains about the same time, that settlement throughout the Appalachians was completed. Even at this time, however, the population was sparse and there were few residents in the more mountainous areas. Slowly, and largely as a result of natural increase, the population expanded, but throughout the nineteenth century and well into the twentieth the major arteries of transportation bypassed the Appalachian Region. One result of this isolation was the perpetuation of a folk culture based in large part upon traditions that existed when the area was first settled in the eighteenth and early nineteenth centuries.

Many writers have commented on the pure Scotch-Irish or pure Anglo-Saxon population residing in the Appalachians at the present time. The impression is left that a distinct racial group settled the Appalachians and has remained racially pure for many generations.[2] Actually no reliable evidence is available as to the origin of those settling the Appalachian area. Attempts to identify their origin have been based on such questionable approaches as a study of surnames, or of the dialect of the region. Actually, the names

[1] John C. Campbell, *The Southern Highlander and His Homeland* (New York, 1921), pp. 24-26.
[2] Ellen Churchill Semple, "The Anglo-Saxons of the Kentucky Mountains," *Bulletin American Geographical Society,* XLII (1910), pp. 561.

of many people were changed through the years, so it is impossible to make a valid study of the origins of the people through the use of surnames. And as far as the language is concerned, the dialect can be considered essentially the form of English spoken at the

Figure 11. *Growth of Population in the Southern Appalachian Region Compared with That of the United States, 1900-1960*

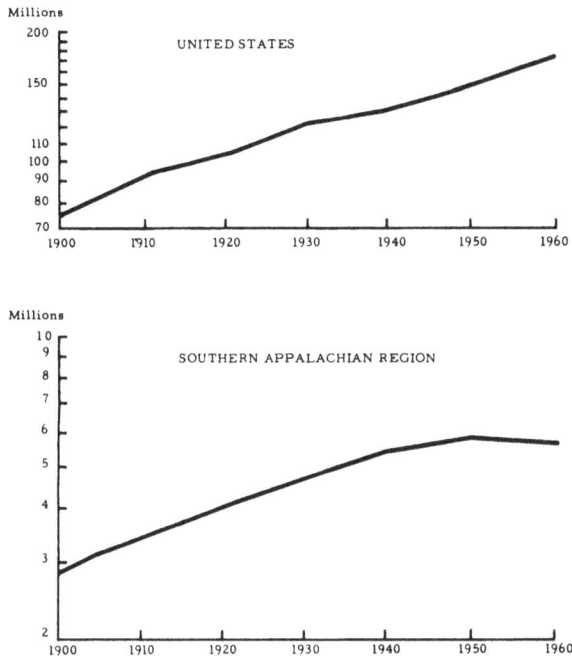

Source: U. S. Census of Population, 1900-1960

time the area was settled and relatively cut off from the world. The probability is that the settlers of the mountains were representative of the population of the nation in the early nineteenth century.

Population Growth and Distribution

Until the last very few years, the Southern Appalachians have been characterized by a steadily increasing population (see Table 4). With the exception of the Civil War period, throughout the 1800's the rate of growth for each decade was above 20 percent. The last half of the nineteenth century brought about almost a three-fold increase in the population from 1,092,948 in 1850 to 2,965,500 in 1900.

Population increase continued through the first half of the twentieth century, but at a reduced rate (Figure 11). The number of inhabitants almost doubled between 1900 and 1950, reaching 5,833,263 at the latter date. During the first half of the twentieth century the population of the Southern Appalachians

grew at approximately the same rate as that of the nation. In those five decades the number of residents of the region increased 97 percent and those of the nation 98 percent.

The growth of regional population might not have kept pace with that of the nation if it had not been for the depression of the 1930's, which slowed down out-migration from the Appalachians. As a consequence, the population of the region increased rapidly at a time when lowered birth rates reduced the growth rate of the national population. During World War II, opportunities for employment outside the area brought about a great wave of out-migration. Between 1940 and 1950 the population increased only 7.8 percent compared with 14.5 percent in the nation as a whole. (At no other time since the first United States census in 1790 had the rate of increase for the region been as low as ten percent in a decade, except for the Civil War period when it was 9.7 percent.)

In general those areas which are prospering have an increasing population and those which are depressed lose population. In this nation people tend to move where employment may be found. In the Southern Appalachians, a relatively large percentage of those moving go outside the region. The importance of the economic factor in population change is shown by comparing Figure 13, which shows the median family income by county in 1950, with Figure 12 on population change between 1950 and 1960.

For several decades, coal mining in Eastern Kentucky and West Virginia provided employment for many and brought relative population stability. The recent revolutions in mining techniques plus growing competition from other fuels have forced a tremendous decline in employment in the coal fields. Many have been compelled to move elsewhere for a livelihood. Consequently, the population of Eastern Kentucky and West Virginia has declined in the last quarter century and especially since World War II. Thousands of individuals from these areas have migrated to northern cities in search of employment.

A glance at Figure 12 shows a line of counties with population increases following the Appalachian Valley. This great valley is where industrialization is taking place and cities are developing (Figures 42, 48), and it contains an increasing percentage of the Region's inhabitants. The future of the entire Region is likely to be determined by the developments in the Appalachian Valley.

Probably the most pervasive trend in population over the past 150 years has been urbanization. Many

THE SOUTHERN APPALACHIANS

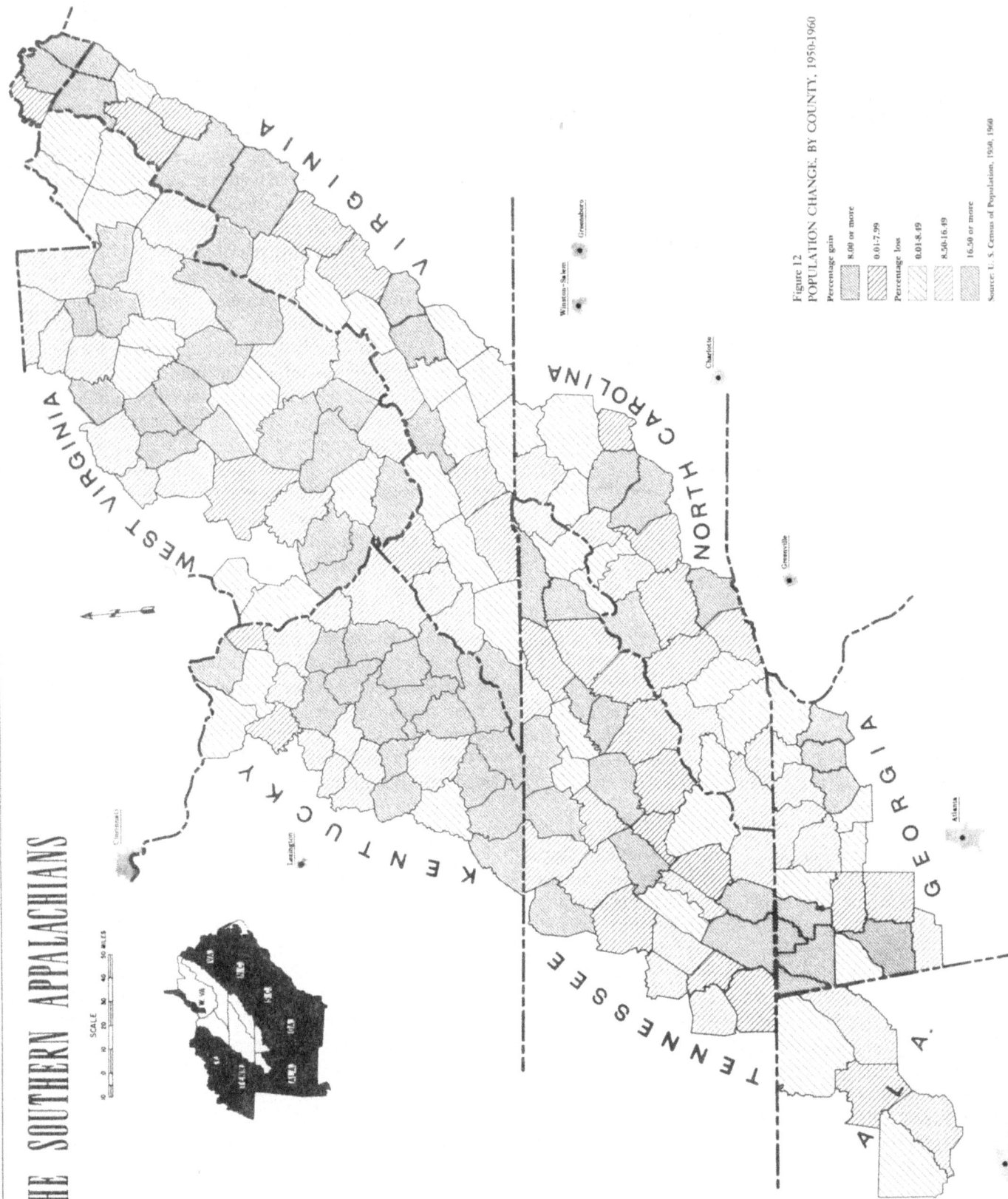

Figure 12
POPULATION CHANGE, BY COUNTY, 1950-1960

Percentage gain
8.00 or more
0.01-7.99

Percentage loss
0.01-8.49
8.50-16.49
16.50 or more

Source: U. S. Census of Population, 1950, 1960

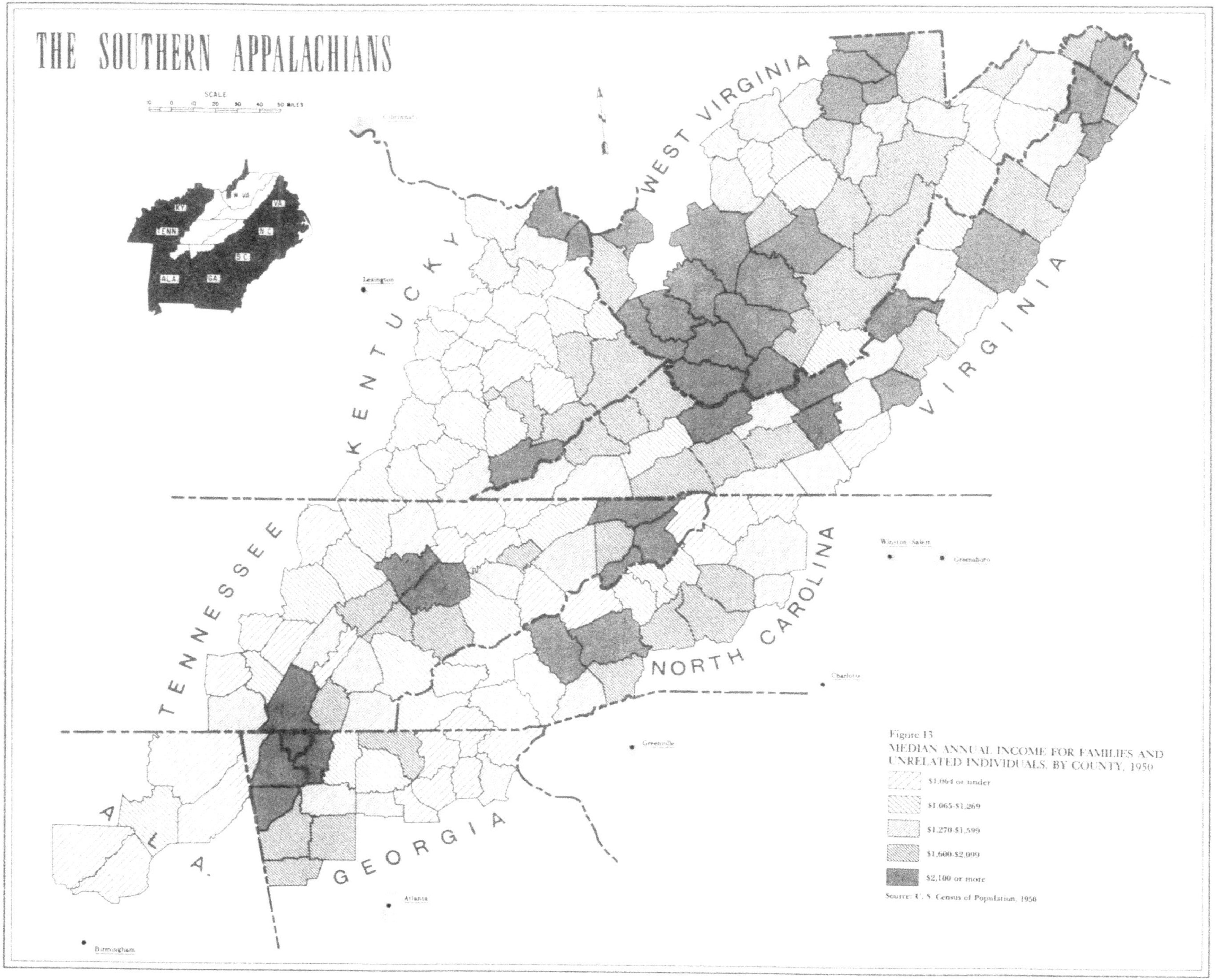

THE SOUTHERN APPALACHIANS

Figure 13
MEDIAN ANNUAL INCOME FOR FAMILIES AND
UNRELATED INDIVIDUALS, BY COUNTY, 1950

$1,064 or under
$1,065-$1,269
$1,270-$1,599
$1,600-$2,099
$2,100 or more

Source: U. S. Census of Population, 1950

VIRGINIA

WEST VIRGINIA

KENTUCKY

TENNESSEE

NORTH CAROLINA

GEORGIA

ALA.

SCALE

Lexington

Winston-Salem

Greensboro

Charlotte

Greenville

Atlanta

Birmingham

of the changes in the Appalachians in recent years are direct effects of this phenomenon. As the nation was settled, city growth steadily increased until in 1960 about 70 percent of the population of the United States lived in cities. Urbanization through-

Table 5. *Number of Urban Centers and Percentage of Population Urban, Southern Appalachian Region and United States, 1900-1960*

Year	Number of urban places		Percentage of population urban	
	SAR	US	SAR	US
1960	157	5445	33.4	69.9
1950	158	4741	29.5	64.0
1940	118	3464	23.3	56.5
1930	99	3165	23.4	56.2
1920	82	2722	17.8	51.2
1910	56	2262	12.6	45.7
1900	38	1737	8.6	39.7

Source: U. S. Census of Population, 1900-1960.

out the South has rather closely paralleled the process in the nation with a lag of some fifty years.[3] Not until 1840 did the census report any Southern Appalachian town large enough to be classified as urban. This city, Winchester, Virginia, had a population of 3,454 in 1840 and remained the only urban center in the Appalachians in 1850, when it had a population of 3,857. By 1860 there were only four centers that could be classified as urban, and they contained only slightly over one percent of the total population of the area.

It was not until 1890 that the Appalachians had as large a population classified as urban as had the nation as a whole when the first census was taken in 1790. Since 1900 the urban population of the Appalachians has grown much more rapidly than has the total population of the area, and this rate of growth was very much accelerated during the decade of the forties. During the 1950-1960 years, the urban population of the Region increased 9.4 percent while the total population declined 3.4 percent. Even so, only a third of the inhabitants of the Appalachians were classified as urban in 1950; the urban population of the nation reached 35 percent of the total in 1890. The increase since 1900 in the number of urban centers and proportion of population residing in them is shown in Table 5.

Urbanization, then, is a much more recent development in the Region than in the nation, and is less advanced in the Appalachians than in the South as a whole (Figure 14).

Numerous studies have demonstrated that cities tend to locate near breaks in transportation. Until the middle of the nineteenth century, large cities were located at seaports. With the appearance of the railroad many large inland cities developed either at the termini of railroads or where several railroads intersected. Few railroads, of course, penetrated the mountain areas, but the cities that did develop in the Appalachians during the later nineteenth century were located along the railroads that traversed the Great Appalachian Valley. Several large cities also came into existence on the periphery of the Region, including such metropolitan centers as Atlanta, Georgia, and Birmingham, Alabama. Since 1920, with the expansion of highways through the Appalachian area and the increasing importance of motor transportation, the growth of cities in the Region has been greatly enhanced. The location of cities is an important determinant of new highway location, also, as may be seen in the regional map of the proposed interstate highway system (Figure 45). The new highways will, in turn, stimulate the growth of the cities they serve. It is to be anticipated that the growth of cities will continue at a rapid rate, and that this urbanization will be accompanied by significant commercial, industrial, and agricultural changes. Even so, at the present time none of the great cities of the United States are located in the area.

With modern transportation and communication it is no longer necessary to live near the central business district of a large city to be employed there. For years large numbers of people have been moving to the edge of larger cities. This suburbanization trend is a major factor is population redistribution at the present time. The United States Census Bureau classes all cities of 50,000, together with the county or counties which are economically a part of them, as Standard Metropolitan Statistical Areas. There are six such areas within the Southern Appalachians. These metropolitan areas have experienced rapid growth in recent years. In 1900 they had a combined population of 433,913 or 14.6 percent of the population of the region. In 1960, 25.6 percent of all those living in the Southern Appalachians resided within 12 Standard Metropolitan counties (this figure includes Fayette County, which was a part of the Charleston, West Virginia area before 1960). The trend of suburbanization has had another result, the impact of which is yet unfelt. The central cities of the Standard

[3] See chapter by T. Lynn Smith in Rupert B. Vance and Nicholas J. Demerath, *The Urban South* (Chapel Hill, 1954), p. 33.

Metropolitan Statistical Areas grew very rapidly until the 1930's. Since 1930, the counties in which central cities are located have grown more rapidly than the cities themselves. For example, between 1930 and 1940 the population of these cities increased but 5.2

Figure 14. Growth of Population in Standard Metropolitan Areas of the Southern Appalachian Region Compared with Those of the United States, 1900-1960

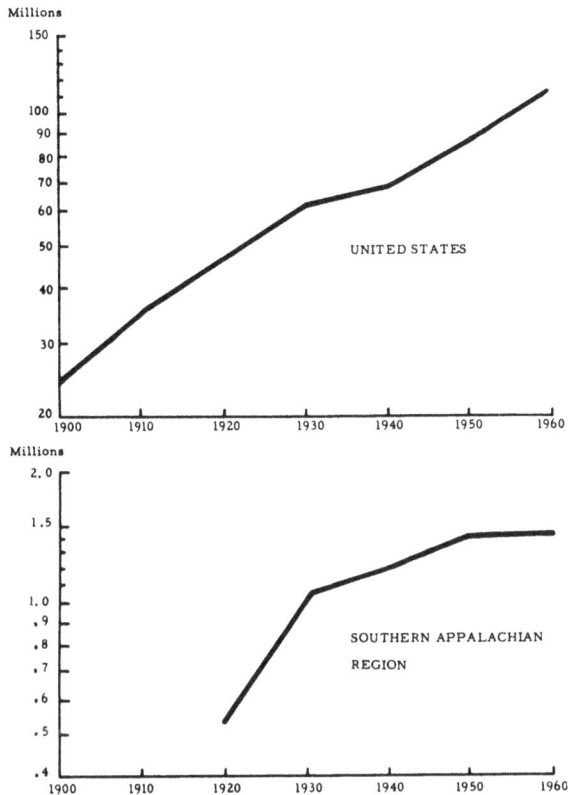

Source: U. S. Census of Population, 1900-1960

percent whereas the population of counties outside the cities increased 14.6 percent. This trend was slowed during the 1940's because of the rationing of gasoline and shortage of building materials during the war years. The 1950's brought an actual decline, although slight, in the percentage of the population in the central cities (see Table 6). At the same time the suburban areas about the cities continued to increase. The prospects are that the dominance of the largest cities in the Appalachians will continue to expand through suburbanization, although the central cities themselves may experience even greater declines.

With some of the changes taking place it seems quite possible that the suburban areas of urban centers may merge and a type of strip city develop. This trend is occurring elsewhere in the nation, and in the

distant future the Great Appalachian Valley may become one huge strip city stretching from Northern Alabama through Virginia.

Closely related to the growth of cities in the Southern Appalachians has been the recent decline of the farm population. Starting in 1930, the United States Census classified rural residences as farm or nonfarm. In 1930, 41.3 percent of those living in the Region were on farms. Because of the slowdown of out-migration during the great depression, the farm population increased to 41.6 percent in 1940. Since 1940 the number of farm residents has declined rapidly, and in 1950 only 30.4 percent of the residents of the area lived on farms. The 1960 census figures on farm population are not available at the time of writing, but no doubt will show a substantial further decline from this figure. Many of those previously classed as rural farm residents had small acreages and produced little in the way of agricultural products. They lived on the land while getting most of their incomes from nonagricultural employment. Many of these people have now completely given up farming operations. Also, a new definition of farm used by the United States Census in 1960 will eliminate large numbers of people from the rural farm category. An expected 25 percent reduction of the national farm population as a result of using the new definition will probably be exceeded in the Southern Appalachian Region because of the small size of farms (see Figures 31, 36).

Nevertheless, the Region is considerably more "rural" than the rest of the nation (Figure 15). Two out of three residents of the Region were classed as rural in the 1960 census, compared with less than a third of the residents of the nation. It is to be expected that population distribution within the Region will tend to become more like that of the rest of the nation—more urban, less rural. At the present time, however, all portions of the Region have heavy concentrations of rural dwellers (Figure 16).

The Southern Appalachians have long been an area of high human birth rates; yet, recent statistics show fertility rates in the Region to be steadily declining. It needs to be emphasized that there have always been great variations in the birth rates from one section of the Region to another. These variations are evident in Figures 17 and 18 in which counties are classified by fertility ratios (the number of children under five per 1,000 women in the ages 15 through 44 in 1930 and 15 through 49 in 1960). In both figures the counties are divided into quartiles on the basis of fertility ratios. In 1930 low fertility counties were concentrated in the Great Valley of Virginia and high fertility counties in Eastern Kentucky. Some counties differ considerably from adjacent counties. Those counties containing, or adjacent to, a large city tended to have low fertility. In general, as the dis-

Table 6. *Population of Areas Now Designated Standard Metropolitan Statistical Areas, Southern Appalachian Region, 1900-1960*

Year	Population	Percentage of regional pop. in SMSA's	Percentage of SMSA pop. in central cities
1960[a]	1,447,831	25.5	41.6
1950	1,360,120	23.3	43.5
1940	1,133,739	21.0	47.3
1930	993,306	20.8	51.3
1920	737,799	18.2	43.3
1910	577,747	16.4	34.2
1900	433,913	14.6	29.7

Source: U. S. Census of Population, 1900-1960.

[a]Fayette County, West Virginia, removed from Charleston SMSA in 1960 but included in earlier totals shown.

tance from a large urban center increased so did the birth rates. Fertility in the Appalachians was high compared with the nation, but the degree of variation among the counties was striking, the number of children under five for every thousand females ranging from 352 to 915.

For 1960 the map shows a concentration of counties with relatively low fertility throughout the greater Appalachian Valley. The section of highest fertility appeared to be concentrated along the Cumberland Plateau, with the Blue Ridge dropping to an intermediate from the high position of 1930.

The decade of the fifties brought a general decline of birth rates in the Southern Appalachians, but fertility continued to vary widely from county to county. If past trends continue, it may be expected that the lowest fertility will be concentrated more and more in the greater Appalachian Valley but with pockets of low fertility in urban counties outside the valley; that fertility in the Blue Ridge outside the cities will be intermediate; and that the highest fertility of the Region will continue to be in the Cumberland Plateau, perhaps increasingly concentrated toward the southern limit of the Cumberlands.

A somewhat more intensive analysis of county variation in fertility brings out numerous factors associated with these differences. Fertility drops rapidly as the percentage of population that is urban increases. Birth rates rise as median family incomes decline and the percentage of the labor force engaged in agriculture increases. Fertility goes down as the

percentage of women working outside the home increases and median years of school completed by adults go up. The higher the proportion of white population in a county, the larger the fertility ratios. This last result is different from that observed in the nation as a whole, and probably can be attributed to the fact that Negroes in the Appalachians are concentrated in cities, where their birth rates tend to be low.

In 1940, birth rates in the Appalachians were much higher than the national rate, but during the following decade there was a considerable narrowing of the differential (Figure 19). Because many births were not registered, especially in the early 1940's, the crude birth rates probably underrepresent the actual level of reproduction. The birth rate remained high during the early forties but fell sharply in 1945 as a result of the disruptive influence of World War II on family life. With the termination of hostilities, normal family life was reestablished and birth rates increased very rapidly in 1947. Since then, despite more complete birth registration, the crude birth rate in the Region has steadily declined. By 1952 it was lower than the national rate, and the gap between the two has since widened.

Though the crude birth rate has declined below the level of the national rate, the number of children per family may still be higher than for the rest of the nation. Because the crude birth rate measures the number of births per 1,000 total population, it tends to be low in populations that have small proportions of women in the child-bearing ages. This proportion of young women in the Region has been reduced by out-migration. Women in the age group 15 to 44 years constituted 47.7 percent of the total female population in 1940, 45.1 percent in 1950, and probably an even smaller percentage in 1960. Even so, there is no question that the actual number of births in the Region has declined—which will, of course, slow the rate of population increase.

Not all of the dramatic decline in regional birth rates should be attributed to the migration of young people. Evidence from the 1958 attitude survey seems to indicate an important shift in values with regard to family size. One question asked of married informants was "How many children did you hope to have when you were married?" The most frequent answer (by 36 percent of the respondents) was two. Eighty-two percent of all those answering the questions said they hoped to have two, three, or four children. Less than 8 percent said fewer than two children, but only slightly more than 10 percent answered five or more. When asked, "What do you think is the ideal number of children for a young couple starting out today?" about 95 percent of the respondents again replied two, three, or four children.

Figure 15. *Rural-Urban Distribution of Population of the Southern Appalachian Region and the United States, 1930-1960*

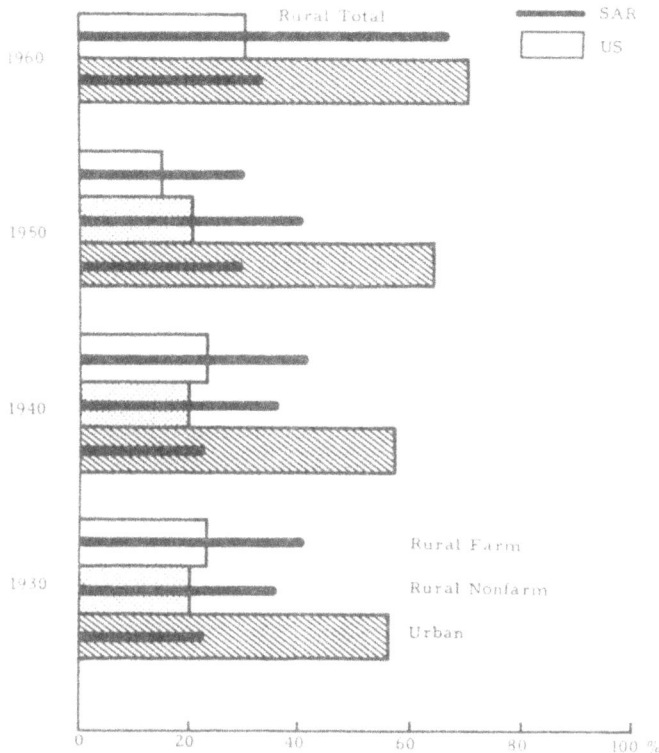

Source: U. S. Census of Population, 1930-1960
ªFarm-nonfarm distribution unavailable for 1960.

Such responses clearly indicate that the value system of Appalachian residents now supports a small family.

That these responses reflect economic considerations is shown by the reply to the question "What do you think is the ideal number of children for a couple that is well-off?" In this case very few informants mentioned two or fewer children and the modal answer was four children. Twenty-seven percent of those interviewed said that six or more children would be the ideal size for a couple that was well-off. In contrast, when asked the ideal number for a couple that was *not* well-off, only 7 percent of the informants mentioned any number above two and nearly 26 percent of the respondents expressed the belief that those not well-off should have no children.

In spite of the fact that almost all informants felt there should be some limit to the size of families,

there is still strong feeling that fate or nature should determine family size. For example, when asked "Do you think it is always wrong, sometimes wrong, or never wrong for married people to use birth control practices?" over 27 percent of the respondents indicated that birth control was always wrong, and 43 percent said that birth control was sometimes wrong. In general, however, the change in birth rates in the Southern Appalachians indicates that families have discarded the large-family ideal that apparently existed in the past. Further, those in the childbearing ages probably practice birth control, although opposition is quite prevalent among those above the childbearing ages. A considerably higher percentage of older people than of the younger thought birth control practices "always wrong."

Migration is often a more important factor in population change than fertility. Between 1940 and 1960 nearly 2,000,000 more people moved out of the Southern Highlands than moved in. With the exception of a handful of urban areas, all sections of the Region have lost population through migration. Two-thirds of the counties of the Region experienced total population declines between 1950 and 1960. Yet, if the numbers of births and deaths were the only factors, all would have shown population growth.

The Appalachians remain a principal reservoir of population for several places outside the Region, and there is a great deal of movement within the area itself. Because of the great importance of migration as a factor influencing population and social change in the Region, it has been accorded a separate chapter in this volume.

The crude death rates in the Region have consistently been under those of the nation as a whole. The probable reason for this is that a greater percentage of the population of the Southern Appalachians is in the age groups where the death rates are low, since there is little evidence that they enjoy better health. Although there have been yearly fluctuations in the recent death rates, there are no obvious trends in these variations. For the nation, on the other hand, death rates steadily declined from 1940 to 1954. For both the Region and the nation these rates have slightly increased since 1954. This change is not great, however, and probably reflects an increasing number of people in the advanced ages where death rates rapidly increase. It is to be anticipated that the crude death rates will continue to increase as a greater percentage of the population reaches fifty years of age or more.

THE SOUTHERN APPALACHIANS

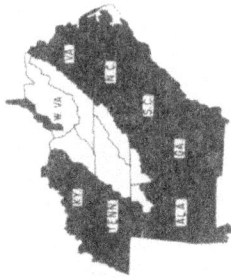

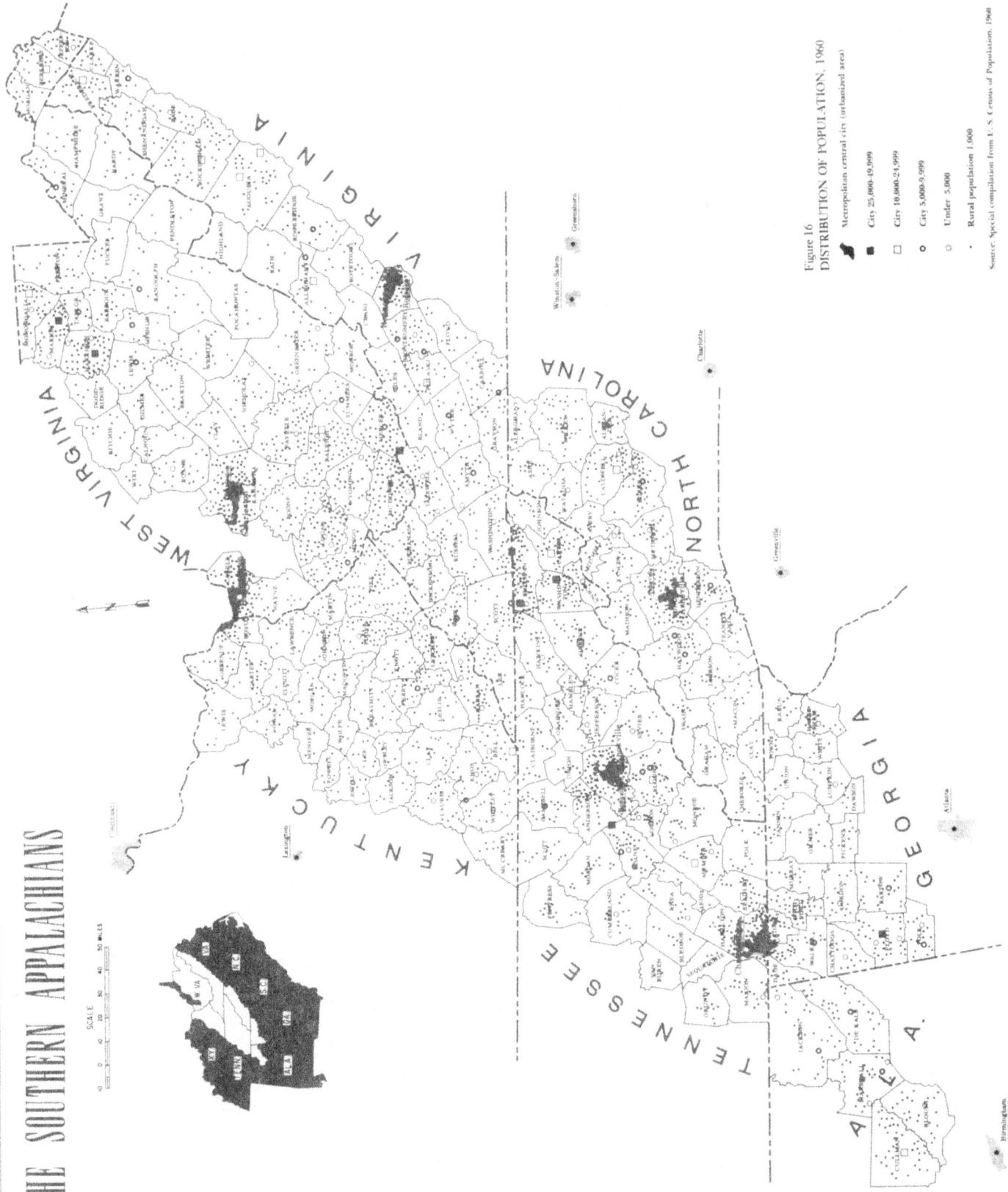

Figure 16
DISTRIBUTION OF POPULATION, 1960

	Metropolitan central city (urbanized area)
	City 25,000-49,999
	City 10,000-24,999
	City 5,000-9,999
	Under 5,000
	Rural population 1,960

Source: Special compilation from U. S. Census of Population, 1960

Though there have not been great changes in the crude death rates of the Region in recent years, there have been striking changes in the causes of death. There have been sharp reductions in mortality from communicable diseases such as tuberculosis, polio, syphilis, and influenza and pneumonia. There has also been a sharp decline in deaths of mothers at childbirth. At the other extreme, there have been rapid increases in deaths from cerebral hemorrhage, cancer, and diseases of the heart. These are the degenerative diseases characteristic of old age. Now that the communicable diseases have largely been brought under control, more and more people are surviving to adulthood and eventually succumb to one of the diseases of old age. Infant mortality is only a fraction of what it was a few decades ago. Consequently, it may be expected that heart disease, cancer and the like will account for increasingly higher proportions of the deaths in the Region as they do in the remainder of the nation.

Population Composition

In several characteristics the Southern Appalachian population differs strikingly from that of the rest of the nation. In particular may be noted the low proportions of non-white and foreign-born residents and the relatively high proportion of individuals in the dependent ages, especially children.

In 1950 nearly 94 percent of the inhabitants of the Region were classified as white. Data on racial distribution from the 1960 census are not available at the time of writing, but no radical changes in proportions are expected. From 1930 to 1940 the proportion of non-whites declined from 7.6 percent to 6.7 percent, but in 1950 the proportion was 6.2 percent. It is doubtful that the migration rate of non-whites greatly exceeded that of the white population during the fifties, if it exceeded it at all. The numerical change in the non-white population from 1930 to 1950 was relatively small. In 1930 there were 337,463 non-whites; in 1950 there were 338,158. During the same period the white population increased from 4,428,114 to 5,495,105.

In recent years, large numbers of non-whites have moved to urban centers, especially Chattanooga. In 1950, 12.6 percent of all non-whites in the Southern Appalachians resided in Hamilton County, Tennessee, where Chattanooga is located. The city of Chattanooga alone had 11.6 percent of all the non-whites in the Region. There was another heavy concentration of Negroes around Charleston, West Virginia, and a large group in McDowell County, West Virginia, where the vast majority were employed in the coal mines.

Although almost all of the non-whites in the Southern Appalachians are Negroes (99 percent), there is a small concentration of American Indians (3,927 in 1950). A majority (67 percent) of these are located in two counties of North Carolina—Jackson and Transylvania—and are Eastern Cherokees.

Because the Region was for many decades isolated from the major paths of immigration to the United States, over 99 percent of Southern Appalachian residents were born in this country. In 1950 there were only 38,490 foreign-born people living in the entire Region, and 60 percent of these individuals were in West Virginia. Although recent census tabulations are not available on the places of birth of the foreign-born in the area, the 1940 census figures do show nativity. Migration to the United States has been at a low rate in recent years, so these older data should indicate roughly the nativity of the foreign-born now living in the Region. Most of the foreign-born in West Virginia came from Italy, Poland, Hungary, and other nations in Central and Southern Europe. One-fourth of all foreign-born in West Virginia came from Italy alone.

Undoubtedly the number of foreign-born in the Region is declining. The bulk of foreign-born in the nation and probably in the Southern Appalachians came here before 1920, and death is now taking a heavy toll as they reach old age. Between 1940 and 1950, there was an increase in the number of foreign-born females in the Region, which can probably be accounted for by servicemen's bringing home "war brides." But, the number of males dropped so much that the total number of foreign-born decreased between 1940 and 1950 and without doubt will show much greater declines between 1950 and 1960.

In all societies age is of prime importance in determining the contribution of various members of the group. In the Western world, with its greatly increased specialization of labor, the young and the old make little contribution to the economic productivity of the group. In the Southern Appalachians during the days of self-sufficient agriculture, nearly all, regardless of age, would have been economically productive. Today, we more frequently find that the young are in school and the old are retired and are not members of the labor force.

Demographers often consider the relationship of those in the productive ages, say between 15 and 65,

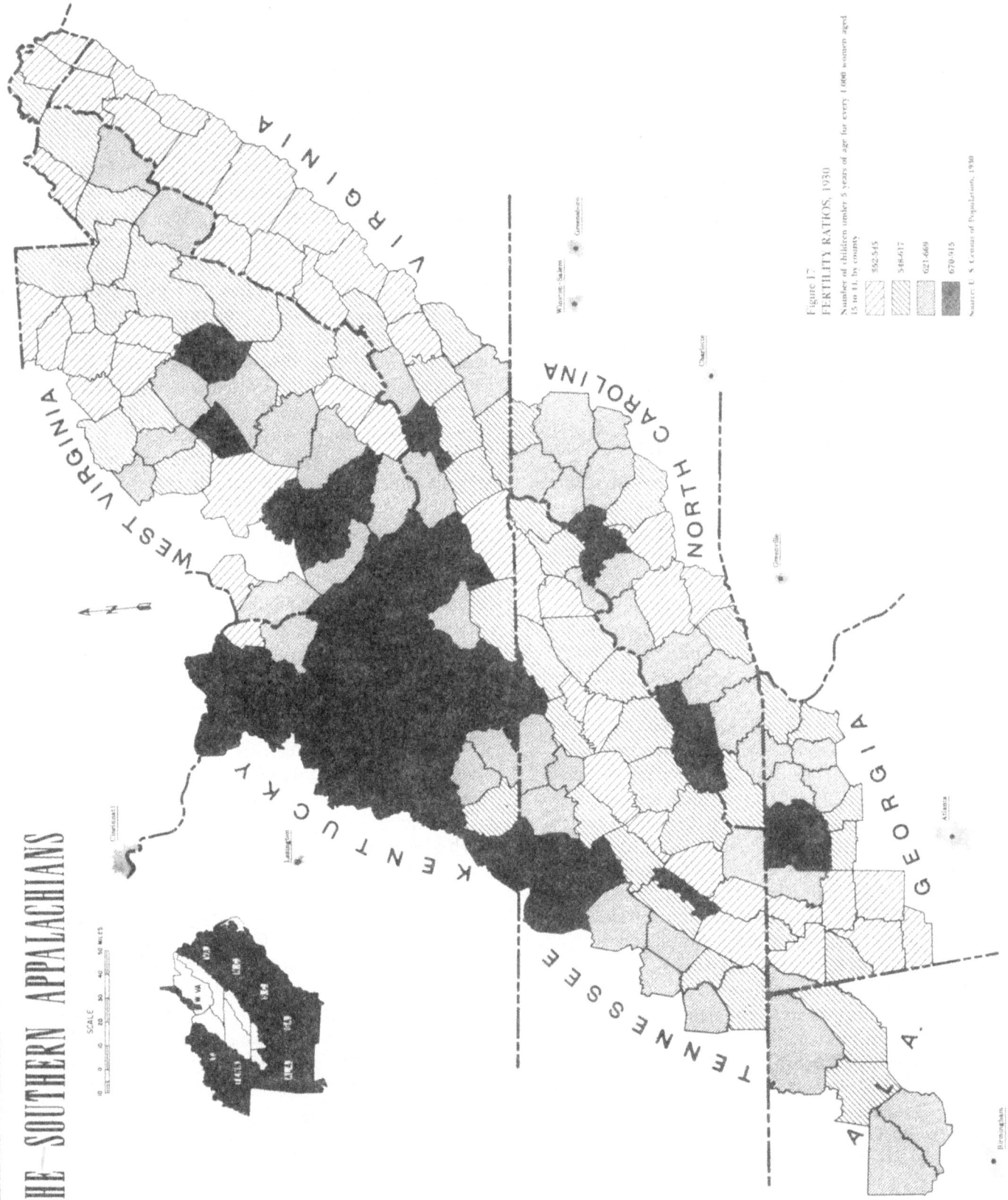

THE SOUTHERN APPALACHIANS

Figure 17.
FERTILITY RATIOS, 1930

Number of children under 5 years of age for every 1,000 women aged
15 to 44, by county.

352-545

546-617

621-669

670-915

Source: U. S. Census of Population, 1930.

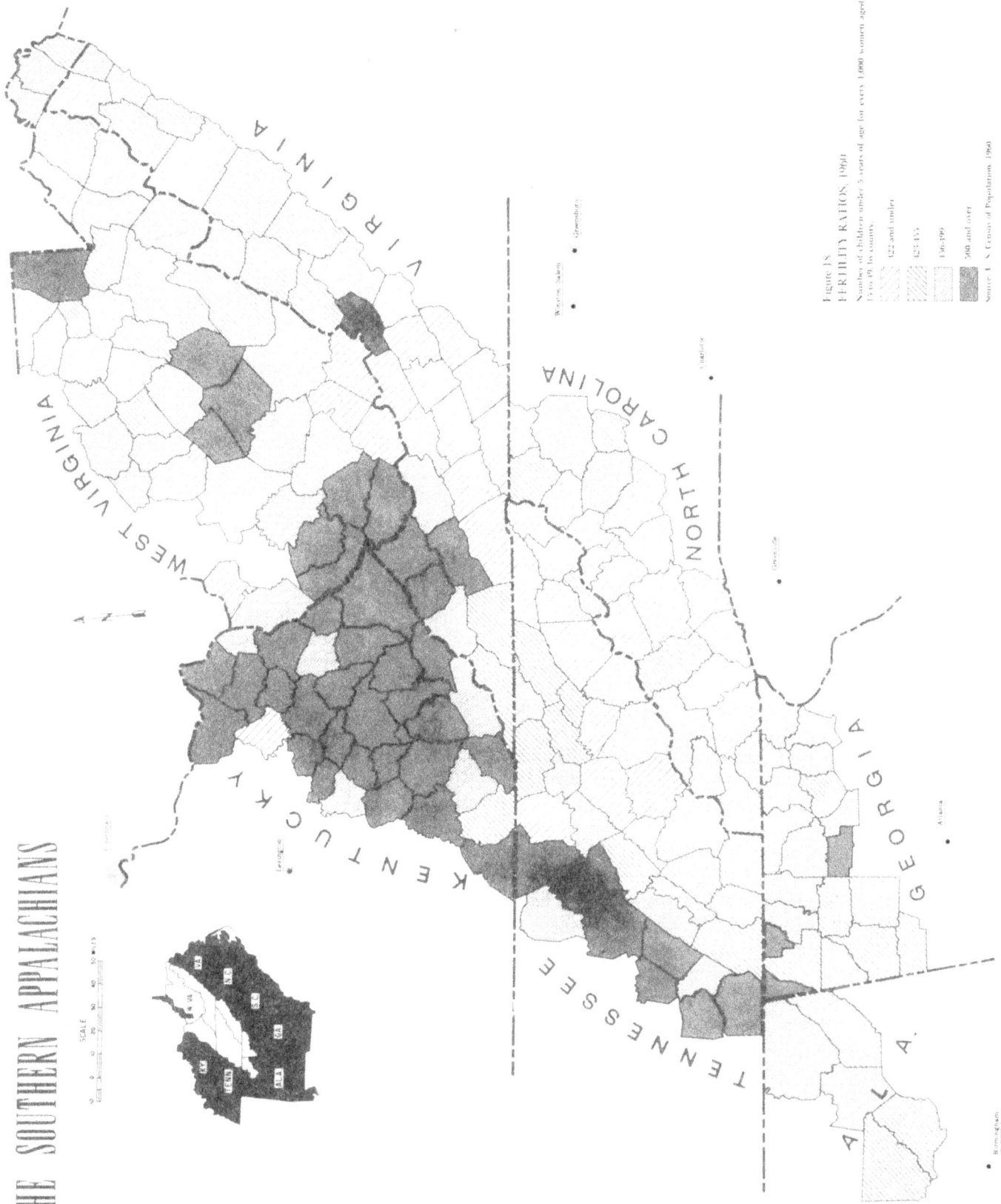

THE SOUTHERN APPALACHIANS

Figure 18.
FERTILITY RATIOS, 1960

Number of children under 5 years of age for every 1,000 women aged 15 to 49, by county.

	422 and under
	423-455
	456-599
	560 and over

Source: U.S. Census of Population, 1960

to those under 15 and those above 65. Figure 20 shows that the percentage of the population of the Southern Appalachian counties above the age of 65 is increasing. In 1930 only 4 percent of the population was 65 or older, compared with 6.3 percent in 1950. During the

Expressed as the number of males per 100 females, the decline was from 103 to 99.6. Nationally the number of males per 100 females declined during the twenty-year period from 102.5 to 98.6, and further declined to 97 in 1960. It is anticipated that the

Figure 19. *Number of Births per 1,000 Residents, Southern Appalachian Region and the United States, 1940-1957*

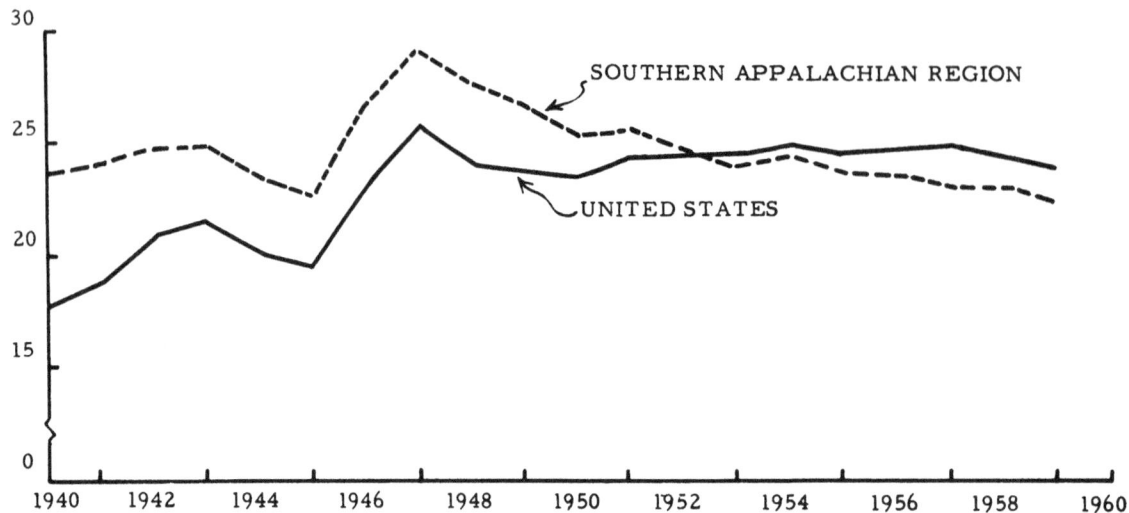

Source: Vital Statistics of the United States, 1940-1957

same twenty-year period the percentage of the population under 15 years of age had dropped from 37.5 to 33.2. The proportion in the productive ages rose from 58.5 percent in 1930 to 61.7 percent in 1940 but then declined to 60.5 percent in 1950. The percentage of the population in the economically productive ages in the Region was not as greatly different from the national percentage in 1950 as in 1940.

The population of the Region is aging and it may be anticipated that an even smaller percentage will be in the economically productive ages in the future. The migration of older youth and young adults has also served to reduce the proportion of economically productive members of the society, and only a radical and improbable reversal of the migration flow is likely to change the existing trend. Indeed, the trend may well be accelerated by the attraction of people of retirement age to the Region, as has already occurred in several places, such as Asheville, in the southern portion. While such persons may not be productive in the usual sense, their retirement income could add substantially to the economy of the Region.

The percentage of the population of the Southern Appalachians that is male has been slowly declining through the years. In 1930, 50.7 percent of the population was male compared with 49.9 percent in 1950.

trend of a decreasing sex ratio will continue in the Region as in the nation.

Migration plays a major role in changing the balance between the sexes (see Chapter IV). Women tend to migrate from rural areas more than men, but migrant males tend to move greater distances. Women outnumbered men in all the metropolitan areas of the Region in 1950, but in two out of three nonmetropolitan areas men outnumbered women. As a general rule the more remote rural areas have the highest proportions of males while the most highly urbanized areas have high proportions of females.

Family income in the Southern Appalachians was quite low in 1949 in comparison with the rest of the nation. According to the 1950 census, 36 percent of the families in the Southern Appalachians had incomes under $1,500, only 10 percent had incomes above $5,000, and the median income was $2,115. At that time the median family income for the nation as a whole was $3,073; almost 22 percent of the nation's families had incomes under $1,500 but the incomes of 20 percent exceeded $5,000.

The 1958 survey of households in the Southern Appalachians indicates that there have been very substantial increases in income since 1949. Only 23 percent of all households reported incomes under

$2,000 and 33 percent had incomes above $5,000. Median income had increased to $3,949. Of course, during the same period the national median family income had climbed to nearly $5,000.

Even though incomes in the Region are still significantly under those of the nation, the level of

Figure 20. *Percentage Distribution of the Population of the Southern Appalachian Region and the United States into Younger Dependent, Older Dependent, and Economically Productive Age Groups, 1930-1960*

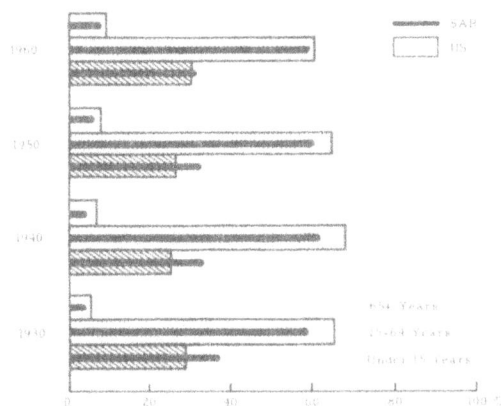

Source: U. S. Census of Population, 1930-1960

living in the Region has been drastically altered in recent decades, as the results of the 1940 and 1950 censuses of housing show. The vast majority of the Region's people continue to live in single-family dwelling units. In other sections of the nation, especially in the large cities, a substantial percentage of the population resides in multiple-family dwellings. In 1950, 84 percent of the homes in the Appalachians were the single detached type. In comparison with the rest of the nation, fewer of the dwelling units have hot and cold running water, flush toilets, bathing facilities and refrigeration; but more Southern Appalachian homes have electric lights (99 percent as compared with 94 percent for the nation in 1950). TVA and RECC electric power is now available at low rates throughout much of the Region and accounts for the high percentage of homes with electricity. Only 7 percent of the units in 1950 used piped steam or hot water for heating compared with 24 percent in the nation, and only 12 percent had warm air furnaces as contrasted with 27 percent in the nation. Radios were reported in 94 percent of the dwelling units in the Region in 1950, only slightly less than the 96 percent for the nation. The considerable extent to which the Appalachian people have contact with

the channels of mass communication was further indicated by the 1958 survey, which revealed that three-fourths of all sample households and two-thirds of the rural households had television sets.

Prior to the present century, the vast majority of those employed in the Region gained their livelihood from agriculture, but there has been a definite trend of declining agricultural employment for many years. By 1930 only one employed person in five was a farmer or farm manager; by 1950, only one in nine. Farm residence is not a sure guide to occupation, for in 1950 almost half (45 percent) of the employed farm population gained their major income from nonagricultural occupations. Current trends clearly indicate a further decline in the labor force engaged in agriculture and increases in a variety of nonagricultural industries. More persons were employed in manufacturing than in any other single major industry in the region in 1950, but manufacturing accounted for only 21 percent of all employment.

One significant change taking place is the increasing entrance of women into the labor force. In 1930 only 16 percent of all workers were women, but this figure had risen to 22 percent by 1950. The changing balance is also partly explained by the retirement of older men in nonagricultural occupations. In general, farmers in the past never "retired," which meant that the percentage of men employed was greater then than more recently. As an increasing percentage of women, especially married women, find employment outside the home, the traditional family pattern is altered. (Wives of farmers have generally not been counted as employed even though their work in the home was indispensable.) It is logical to expect that the employed wife will tend to have fewer children than those who remain at home, and continued increase in the employment of women could have a considerable impact on the future birth rates of the Region.

For both men and women, but especially for women, in the Appalachians there have been significant changes in occupations in recent years (see Table 7). There was a great drop between 1940 and 1950 in the percentage of women employed as private household workers with a large increase in the percentage engaged in clerical and sales work and a high number employed as operatives, generally in manufacturing establishments.

Although the rise of nonagricultural employment and the increased employment of women in the Region are bringing about great changes in the roles of husband and wife, the 1958 survey of households reveals that the family—not the simple nuclear family of husband, wife, and children, but the extended family including grandparents, aunts, uncles, cousins and other kin—is still basic to the social structure.

of all those above 25 in the Region had never attended school, but by 1950 this figure had dropped to 3.1 percent. Meanwhile the median years of school completed by those above 25 years of age increased from 7.5 in 1940 to 8.1 in 1950. The median years of school

Table 7. *Percentage Distribution by Occupation of Employed Persons, Southern Appalachian Region, 1940 and 1950*

Major occupation group	1950			1940		
	Male	Female	Total	Male	Female	Total
Professional, semiprofessional, technical, & kindred	4.7	14.1	6.8	3.7	14.7	5.8
Farmers & farm managers	15.1	1.0	12.0	21.1	2.6	17.6
Managers, officials & proprietors, except farm	7.4	4.3	6.7	6.4	3.6	5.9
Clerical & kindred workers & sales workers	8.4	28.4	12.8	7.3	18.7	9.5
Craftsmen, foremen & kindred workers	15.6	1.2	12.5	11.3	.6	9.3
Operatives & kindred workers	29.0	22.9	27.7	26.2	22.9	25.6
Private household workers	.2	9.7	2.3	.3	22.5	4.5
Service workers except private household workers	3.6	12.4	5.5	3.5	9.5	4.6
Farm laborers, unpaid family workers	3.2	2.3	3.0	5.1	.3	5.5
Farm laborers except unpaid & farm foremen	3.8	.5	3.1	6.2	2.3	4.2
Laborers except farm & mines	7.6	.7	6.1	8.1	.9	6.7
Occupation not reported	1.4	2.5	1.5	.8	1.4	.8

Source: U. S. Census of Population, 1940 and 1950.

When asked "do you have any relatives who live nearby?" 78 percent of all respondents replied "yes." This response was considerably higher in the rural areas, where 85 percent of all individuals stated that they had relatives living in the vicinity. Further, the family ties are strong. When asked "do you and your relatives call on each other for help?" 95 percent of all individuals responded "yes"; 83 percent answered "yes" when asked, "do you think a person has an obligation to help relatives even though he does not feel real close to them?" An additional question was "if you were in trouble, would you be more likely to turn to your close friends or your relatives for help?" Two-thirds said they would call their relatives first and but 26 percent would turn to close friends.

The educational characteristics of the population are also changing rapidly, but perhaps not as rapidly as might be hoped. In 1930, 6.9 percent of the Region's residents over the age of 10 were illiterate, compared with only 4.3 percent for the nation as a whole. Isolation is a major factor in low educational attainment. In 1930, 3.8 percent of city dwellers of the Southern Appalachians were illiterate, which is not greatly different from the 3.2 percent in all the cities of the nation. In the rural-farm areas of the Region, the illiteracy rate was 8.3 percent, compared with 6.9 in the rural-farm sections of the nation.

Since 1930, the United States Census has discontinued tabulating the number of illiterates but rather presents information on years of school completed for all persons above the age of 25. In 1940, 4.7 percent

completed by adults of the nation was 8.6 in 1940 and 9.3 in 1950. The Region still lags behind the nation and at the present rate of change does not seem to be catching up (Figure 54).

Future Population

What the population characteristics of the Southern Appalachians will be ten or fifteen years from now is impossible to say with any certainty. All population projections are based to a considerable degree upon conjecture, and estimates of the regional population even for 1970 vary from 4.5 million to 8 million as different assumptions are made and different projection procedures are used. Wars, fluctuations in the business cycle, technological changes and many other conditions that only slightly change birth, death, or migration rates may cause predictions to miss by a wide margin.

Just such social, political, and especially economic changes are likely to be the main determinants of the future population of the Appalachian Region. If nonagricultural employment opportunities at high wages are greatly developed within the Region, its population may be expected to grow rapidly, concentrating in those localities where the opportunities are. On the other hand, if few new industries are developed and others, like agriculture and mining today, decline, the population will also continue to decline. If residents continue to desire a higher level of living than can be found in the Region, they will continue to migrate to places where it is available. If the ideal of a small family pattern becomes more generally accepted, birth rates will further decline. None of these contingencies can be predicted with certainty, but the most logical basis for estimating the future would seem to be the assumption that recent trends will continue.

Certainly there is every reason to believe that some of the current trends which affect the entire nation as well as the Region will continue into the immediate future. For example, knowing the present age structure of the population and current rates, we can predict with reasonable confidence that the number of old people will continue to increase. A rapid decline in the farm population can also be anticipated during the next decade, along with continued increases in the number of people living in towns and cities. Quite probably an increasing percentage of the regional population will live in the Great Appalachian Valley, while more isolated areas of the Cumberland and Blue Ridge highlands will continue to lose population. A second possible area of population increase is the transitional zone where the southeastern fringe of the Blue Ridge Mountains breaks into the Piedmont.

Inasmuch as the Region is rapidly losing its isolation, the residents are exposed to the same mass communication media as the other people of the nation and are becoming more and more members of mass society. The size of the population of the Region will be largely governed by the degree to which the economic resources can provide a level of living desired and expected by contemporary mass society. There tends to be an equilibrium established at the point where the economy provides the desired level of living. The large number of migrants from the Region over a long period of time is evidence of the limited capacity of the economy to support a population at the desired level. If various forms of urban industry were to develop in the Region, it *could* support several times its present population. However, such development is unlikely over the next few years.

If the imbalance of population and economic opportunities continues to result in out-migration, the migrant stream will be composed largely of young adults, to judge from past experience. The declining number of people of child-bearing age should lead to a further reduction in the birth rate until, as an equilibrium is reached, migration decreases. Of course, the provision of greater opportunities for employment would probably lead to the retention of more younger people and to a rise in the crude birth rate. In either case, though, the changing value system portends smaller families than have characterized the region in the past.

Continued improvements in health care and medical services should serve to lower death rates at any given age during the coming decade. As an increasing percentage of the population reaches advanced years, however, a slight rise in the total number of deaths per thousand population can be anticipated.

The average number of years of school completed by the adult population should continue to rise for many years as an increasing proportion of young people complete high school and college and death takes older people who had little opportunity for education.

The number of Negroes and foreign-born in the Region may continue to decline for at least the next few years, but since they constitute such a small proportion of the total population, the social consequences are not likely to be of any great moment. Of possibly greater significance will be the movement into the Region of persons from other parts of the nation, especially if industry and commerce requiring specialized talents continue to develop. Certainly the increasing mobility of our society suggests that the future population of the Region will become more heterogeneous.

The decline of agricultural and mining employment may be expected to continue and a much higher proportion of the people will be employed in nonagricultural industries. Further, the trend of modern industry is such that the number of unskilled laborers and others in low-paying occupations will diminish. If this trend does materialize in the Region, it can be expected that incomes will increase substantially, at least for the employed population. The presence of large numbers of persons who are poorly educated and either unskilled workers or displaced miners, many of whom are too old for vocational retraining, suggests that a rapid rise in the regional level of living is not to be immediately expected. Indeed, the employment situation may well get worse before it improves. In the long run, though, provided that adequate measures are taken to equip young people for participation in our industrial economy, the level-of-living gap between Region and nation should gradually close.

CHAPTER FOUR

The Great Migration, 1940-1960

JAMES S. BROWN

GEORGE A. HILLERY, JR.

DURING THE TEN YEARS BETWEEN 1950 and 1960, the Southern Appalachian Region had a net loss through migration of more than one million persons, a number equal to nearly a fifth of the total population in 1950. So many more people left the Region than came into it that the rate of natural increase (excess of births over deaths) could not offset the net loss due to migration. Consequently, the 1960 census revealed a regional population decrease for the first time since the Appalachians were settled.

Since before the turn of the century, the American people have been moving from rural, low-income areas to cities, where industrial and commercial development have increasingly offered greater economic opportunities. Like other Americans, the people of the Southern Appalachians have for decades been moving out of the Region's rural areas to share more fully in the social and economic benefits of American life. Although the general public has only recently become aware of this movement, during every decade since 1900 the Region has lost more people by migration than it has gained. But, because of the great excess of births over deaths, the Region's total population increased steadily during the first half of this century. The rate of increase, however, gradually diminished as migration losses became greater and greater. Finally, during the 1950's the migration loss exceeded the natural increase.

There were, of course, ups and downs during these decades as the social and economic situation of the Region and nation changed. For example, in the decade of the twenties the rate of loss from the rural population of the Southern Appalachians was much greater than during the thirties, a period of depression in both farm and urban areas. With the coming of World War II and the accompanying industrial prosperity and demand for labor, the rate of migration loss from the Appalachians rose. During the fifties, as we have indicated, the loss increased markedly, even exceeding that of the 1940's.

In actuality, Appalachian people desiring higher levels of living have had few alternatives to migration. The prospects for commercial farming have not been bright, industry has been reluctant to settle in the Region, and coal mining has proved to be an undependable and inadequate source of employment even in the areas richest in coal resources. For many, migration offers the only alternative to a life of material and cultural poverty.

Unfortunately for the migrants, the American

scene, too, has been changing rapidly, and the economic and cultural integration of Appalachian migrants into the national life presents serious problems for the migrants themselves, for the areas in which they must settle, and ultimately for the nation as a whole. There are further consequences for the areas being depopulated, requiring adjustment in social and economic institutions to correspond with the losses—sometimes catastrophic losses—in population.

At the same time, all of these consequences are feeding back upon each other, so that there is no situation where one part simply adjusts to the other. Rather, multitudinous parts must adjust to multitudinous other parts, each of which is also adjusting, adjustments must be made to the adjustments, and so on.

In this chapter's discussion of migration, four questions are involved: How many migrants were there? Where did they go? What were they like? Why did they move? One might add a fifth question, which runs as an undercurrent through each of the other four: What implications does this great migratory movement hold for the Region, for the nation, and for the migrants themselves?—What does it mean?

The five questions cannot all be answered with equal adequacy. There are more data pertaining to the first question than to any of the others. Direction of migration is known with some completeness only for the periods 1935-1940 and 1949-1950. The data on characteristics of the migrants are scanty, and pertain mainly to the year 1949-1950. Answers to the fourth question, of course, depend heavily on those preceding.

Extent of Migration, 1940-1960

So far we have been speaking of the Appalachians as a whole. The "Southern Appalachian Region," however, is not an entirely homogeneous area. In many ways, the people lack the common cultural and social patterns and the sense of unity and cohesion which would differentiate them from inhabitants of other regions. Rather, the Region is a somewhat arbitrary grouping of diverse and heterogeneous areas which are not closely interrelated and interdependent parts of a functional social system. Furthermore, the economy of the Region is increasingly segmented; many of the Region's subareas, including some of the more populous ones, have closer economic ties outside the Region than within it. In seeking to understand the tremendous population changes of the past two decades, attention therefore must focus on the separate parts; for when the parts are summed to arrive at a regional picture, we tend to blur what has

really happened and even miss completely some of the most important developments and trends. Obviously the specific situations of 190 Appalachian counties[1] cannot be discussed in such a short chapter as this. Instead, several groupings of counties will be used to indicate the major population developments and the possible explanations of these trends.

The most striking general trend during the past two decades has been the increase in number of persons leaving the Region. Figures 21 and 22 impressively document the greater migration loss in the more recent years. Most apparent are the decline in the number of areas gaining through net migration and the complementary increase in the number of areas losing by migration during the 1950-1960 period as compared with 1940-1950. The gains were few and widely scattered in both decades, but there were several counties with sizeable rates of net increase in both periods, notably Roanoke and Frederick Counties in Virginia, Catoosa and Whitfield in Georgia, and Hamblen in Tennessee. Both Virginia counties contain cities (Roanoke and Winchester), and those in Georgia are adjacent to the Chattanooga metropolitan area. The eastern section of the Southern Appalachians had the smallest losses during both the 1940's and the 1950's, except for a group of counties southeast of Knoxville. On the other hand, the northwestern part of the Region, particularly the Kentucky and West Virginia counties, sustained the heaviest losses in the two periods.

The increasing influence of migration on the size of the Appalachian population is apparent in the comparison of population changes in the 1940-1950 and 1950-1960 decades. From 1940 to 1950 all three of the major physiographic divisions—the Blue Ridge,

The writers wish to express their appreciation especially to Gordon F. DeJong and K. M. George for their assistance at several stages in the analysis of the data and to Thomas R. Ford for penetrating and constructive criticisms. Numerous other persons and organizations have contributed materially to this chapter, in particular, Howard W. Beers, Gladys K. Bowles, Ormond Corry, C. Horace Hamilton, Charles E. Lively, Henry S. Shryock, Jr., Leonard M. Sizer, Lorin Thompson, and Rupert B. Vance; the Departments of Health of Alabama, Kentucky, Virginia, and West Virginia; the Departments of Public Health of Georgia and Tennessee, and the State Board of Health of North Carolina. Much of the writers' time has been made available through the Agricultural Experiment Station of the University of Kentucky. Of course, the sole responsibility for the use and interpretation of these materials rests with the present writers.

[1] Data on the components of population change (births, deaths, net migration) for individual counties may be obtained from the Department of Rural Sociology, University of Kentucky.

THE SOUTHERN APPALACHIANS

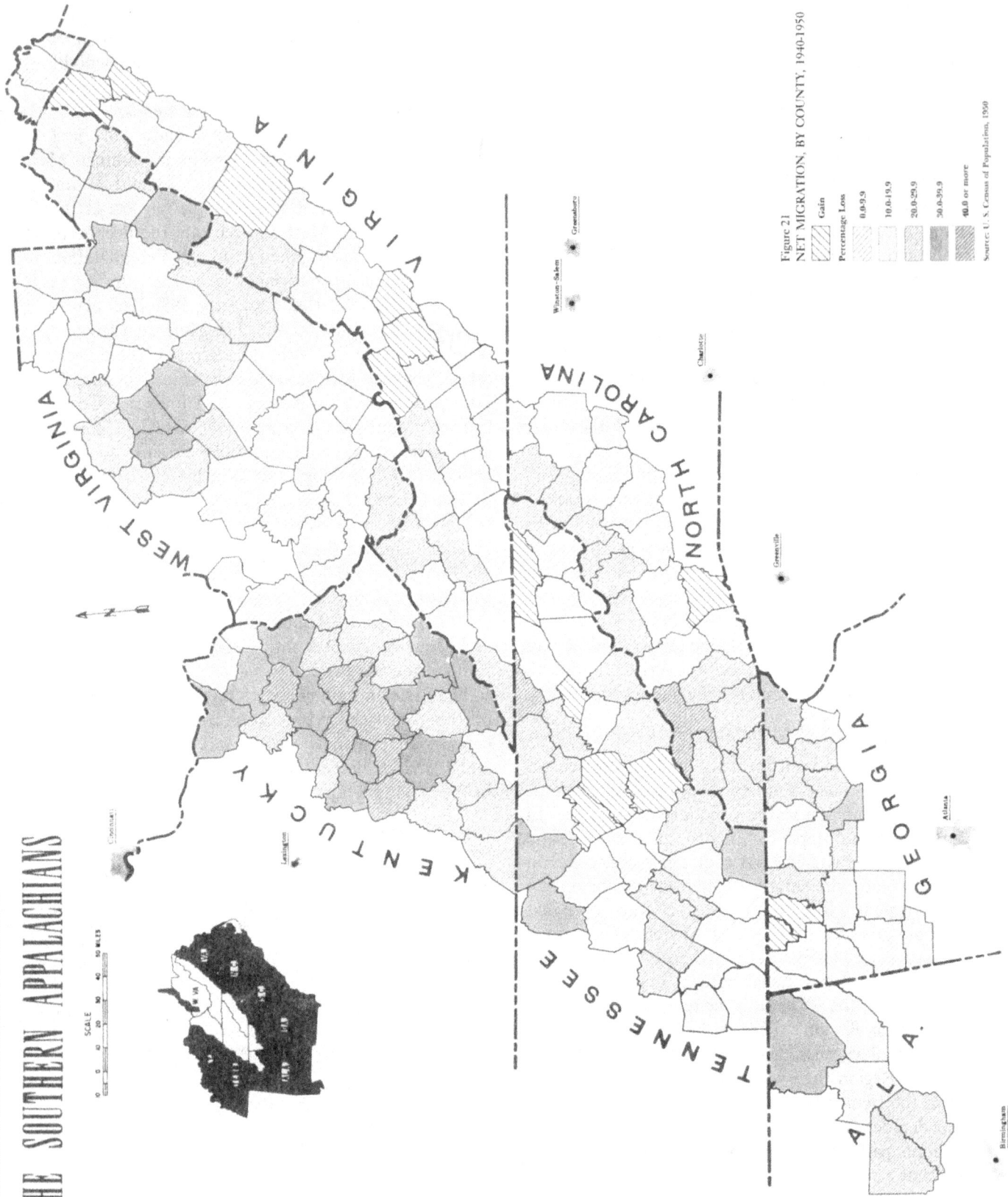

Figure 21
NET MIGRATION, BY COUNTY, 1940-1950

Gain

Percentage Loss

0.0-9.9
10.0-19.9
20.0-29.9
30.0-39.9
40.0 or more

Source: U. S. Census of Population, 1950

THE SOUTHERN APPALACHIANS

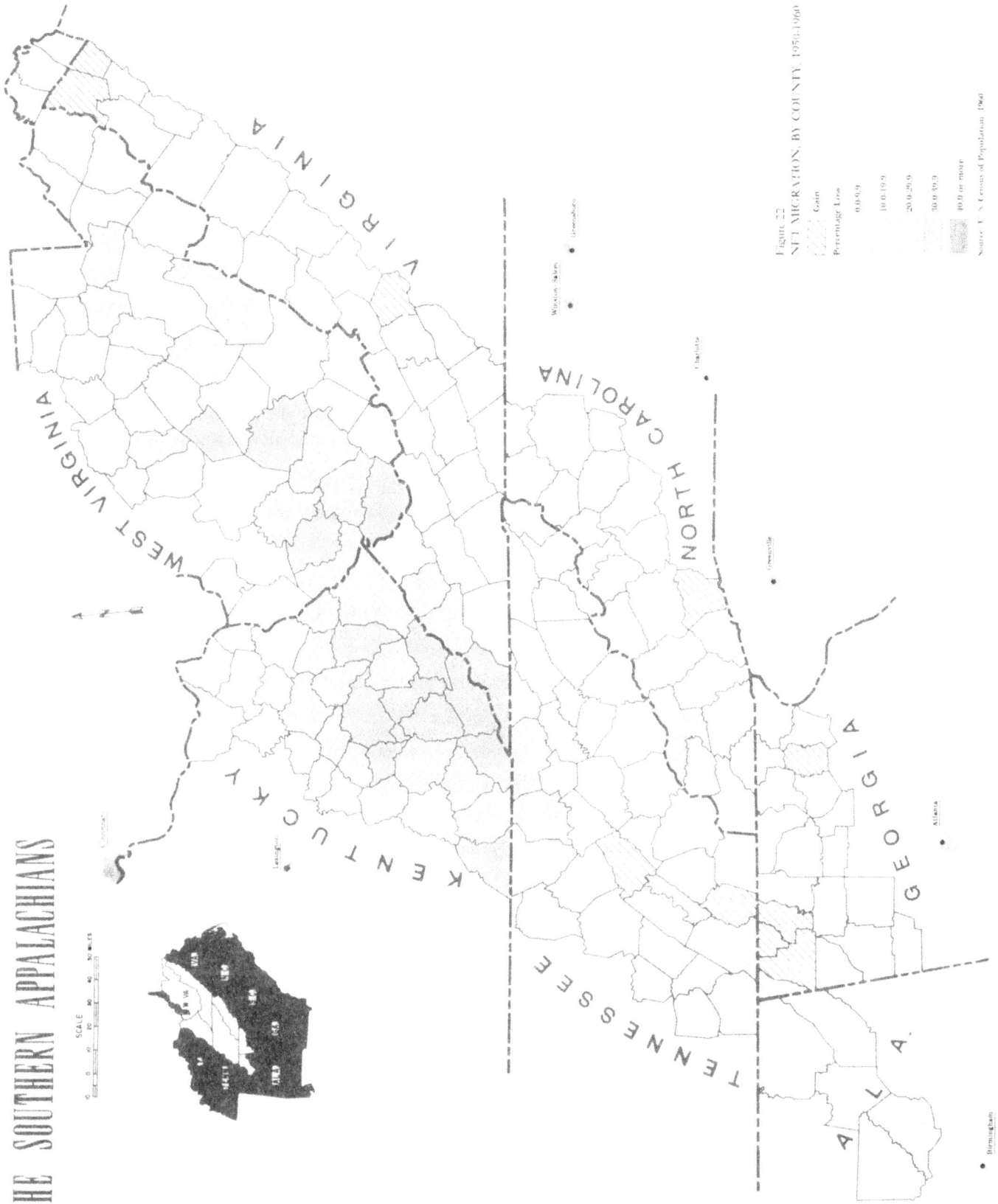

SCALE

0   10   20   30   40   50 MILES

THE SOUTHERN APPALACHIANS

WEST VIRGINIA

VIRGINIA

KENTUCKY

TENNESSEE

NORTH CAROLINA

GEORGIA

A L A.

Winston-Salem

Greensboro

Charlotte

Greenville

Atlanta

Birmingham

Lexington

Figure 22
NET MIGRATION, BY COUNTY, 1950-1960

Gain

Percentage Loss

0.0-9.9

10.0-19.9

20.0-29.9

30.0-39.9

40.0 or more

Source: U.S. Census of Population, 1960

the Great Valley, and Alleghany and Cumberland Plateaus—gained population. The population of the Blue Ridge grew from 846,000 to 906,000; the Great Valley from 1,885,000 to 2,145,000; and finally, the Alleghany and Cumberland Plateaus from 2,674,000

The population of the Appalachian parts of each of the seven Appalachian States increased from 1940 to 1950 with the single exception of the Kentucky counties which decreased 2.8 percent. The Appalachian counties of Tennessee, because of the great

Table 8. *Components of Population Change, Southern Appalachian Region, by Physiographic Divisions, 1940-1950 and 1950-1960*

| | Number | | | | Rate | | | |
| | Natural increase | | Net migration | | Natural increase | | Net migration | |
Physiographic division	1940-50	1950-60	1940-50	1950-60	1940-50	1950-60	1940-50	1950-60
Cumberland and Allegheny Plateaus	597,233	464,319	-488,983	- 787,913	22.3	16.7	-18.3	-28.3
Great Valley	355,430	344,770	- 97,066	- 187,033	18.9	16.1	- 5.1	- 8.7
Blue Ridge	179,216	137,960	-119,800	- 133,188	21.2	15.2	-14.2	-14.7
The Region	1,131,879	947,049	-705,849	-1,108,134	20.9	16.2	-13.1	-19.0

Source: Vital Statistics of the United States, 1940-1960; U. S. Census of Population, 1950 and 1960.

to 2,783,000. The Great Valley had the largest percentage gain (13.7) followed by the Blue Ridge (7.1) and the Plateaus (4.1).

For the entire Region, the population count of 5,672,178 in April, 1960, was about 160,000 less than in April, 1950, a decline of 2.8 percent. All three divisions lost population through migration, but the rate of loss was substantially lower in the Great Valley than in the other two. The rates of natural increase were lower in all three divisions than in the previous decade, and did not vary greatly between divisions. The lower migration loss in the Great Valley resulted in a net gain of population here, while population dropped in both the Blue Ridge and the Plateaus (see Table 8).

The Great Valley grew during the two periods because the Region's cities, industries, and better farming areas all tend to be concentrated there. The population of the Blue Ridge remained virtually stationary during the fifties; here the development of industry and tourism undoubtedly served to retard out-migration, which was substantially lower than in the Plateau areas. The Cumberland and the Alleghany Plateaus, with their mining, subsistence agriculture, and relatively few employment opportunities in industry, had a very heavy out-migration, the net migration loss being 18.3 percent in 1940-1950 and 28.3 percent for the period 1950-1960. The rate of natural increase in the Plateaus continued to be the highest among the three physiographic divisions but was not sufficient in the latter decade to prevent a population decline.

increase in the Knoxville metropolitan area as well as the general economic development of Eastern Tennessee, had the highest increase, 16.7 percent. The pattern during the 1950-1960 decade was somewhat different. Population gains were made by the Appalachian counties of Georgia (7 percent), Tennessee (7 percent), Virginia (2 percent), and North Carolina (2 percent). These are modest increases compared with the growth of the national population (about 18 percent). Greater economic opportunities and higher levels of living in these four states than in the rest of the Southern Appalachians account for their population gains.

There were also populations which showed a decrease from 1950 to 1960 in the Appalachian counties of Alabama (—5 percent), West Virginia (—10 percent), and Kentucky (—16 percent). The great decline in the number of men employed in mining had a heavy impact on many of the Kentucky and West Virginia counties and led to tremendous out-migration. In other Appalachian counties of these two states and Alabama, thousands left the subsistence farms characteristic of these areas to seek jobs in industrial centers.

When attention is focused directly on migration, the pattern is seen as one of a heavy loss for Appalachian sections in all of the states (Table 9). Although some counties gained through migration, the gains were few and the net result was one of decrease. In terms of absolute numbers, the 20-year losses from the Southern Appalachian parts of each state ranged from tens of thousands to hundreds of thousands of migrants. In each case, the losses were greater from 1950 to 1960 than from 1940 to 1950. Georgia had the smallest net loss of migrants in the 1940-1950 decade (35,000), and its loss was not much greater in the later decade. The biggest loser during the forties was

seven of the 19 nonmetropolitan areas *gained* a total of 93,245 persons; the other 12 areas had a total population *loss* of 348,334. Except for a gain of less than one percent in the Shenandoah Valley (Virginia 4) in 1940-1950, each of the 19 areas showed a net

Table 9. *Components of Population Change, Southern Appalachian Region, by States, 1940-1950 and 1950-1960*

| | Number | | | | Rate | | | |
| | Natural increase | | Net migration | | Natural increase | | Net migration | |
State	1940-50	1950-60	1940-50	1950-60	1940-50	1950-60	1940-50	1950-60
Alabama	45,683	32,165	- 42,144	- 42,185	22.4	15.5	-20.7	-20.4
Georgia	69,187	60,239	- 34,647	- 35,752	21.7	17.0	-10.9	-10.1
Kentucky	206,362	146,632	-229,394	- 275,076	25.2	18.4	-28.0	-34.6
North Carolina	110,031	87,385	- 71,446	- 76,386	20.6	15.3	-13.4	-13.3
Tennessee	246,803	225,518	- 58,434	- 139,735	21.8	17.1	- 5.2	-10.6
Virginia	160,317	143,959	- 75,402	- 121,807	18.9	15.4	- 8.9	-13.0
West Virginia	293,496	251,151	-194,382	- 417,193	18.9	15.2	-12.5	-25.3
The Region	1,131,879	947,049	-705,849	-1,108,134	20.9	16.2	-13.1	-19.0

Source: Vital Statistics of the United States, 1940-1960; U. S. Census of Population, 1950 and 1960.

Kentucky, with a net loss of almost a quarter of a million migrants. West Virginia exceeded this number during the fifties with a net loss of more than four hundred thousand.

The picture is not greatly changed if loss rates rather than absolute numbers of migrants are considered. Tennessee had the lowest loss rate in the earlier decade (—5.2 per 100 residents in 1940), whereas Georgia had the lowest rates during the following ten years. The Kentucky part of the Region was the greatest loser of migrants for both decades, with rates of —28.0 percent for 1940-1950 and —34.6 percent for 1950-1960.

Nonmetropolitan areas of the Region, although containing four-fifths of the 1940 population, accounted for less than half of the 1940-1950 population growth. The total population of the nineteen nonmetropolitan areas of the Region increased by 204,000 or 4.8 percent from 1940 to 1950, compared with a gain of about 20 percent in the metropolitan areas. As a group the nonmetropolitan areas had a total net migration loss of about 715,000 people during the 1940-1950 decade (Table 10). Expressed as a percentage of the 1940 population, this is a net migration rate of —16.8. Only a high rate of natural increase, 21.5 percent, enabled these areas to make the observed modest gain in population. From 1950 to 1960, the nonmetropolitan population declined 255,000, or 6 percent, compared with a gain of 7 percent in the metropolitan areas.

There were important differences in growth rates within these areas (Table 10). From 1950 to 1960,

deficit of migrants for both the decades under study, the loss rates going as high as 34 percent in the 1940's and 41 percent in the 1950's (Figures 21 and 22).

The differences in rates of population growth among the metropolitan areas of the region are also significant, but even more striking is the failure of these metropolitan areas during the 1950-1960 decade to keep pace with the metropolitan areas of the nation as a whole. As a group, the Standard Metropolitan Statistical Areas (SMSA's) of the Region have increased in population every decade since 1900, and at rates far higher than the nonmetropolitan areas, except during the 1930's, when the rates of growth were about the same. The greatest rates of growth were in the first three decades of the century: 1900-1910, 33 percent; 1910-1920, 28 percent; and 1920-1930, 35 percent. In the depression 1930's, the rate of increase dropped precipitously to 14 percent; it went up to 20 percent in the 1940's (compared with 22 percent for all U. S. metropolitan areas) and then again declined sharply from 1950 to 1960, to only 7 percent—less than in any previous decade since 1900—while the population of all U. S. SMSA's increased 26 percent. Only 30 of the 212 SMSA's in the nation had population losses or increases of less than 10 percent in the decade 1950-1960; four of the six metropolitan areas of the Region (Huntington-Ashland, Charleston, Asheville, and Knoxville) were among these. The rates of increase of the other two (Chattanooga 13.3 percent and Roanoke 18.1 percent) were both well below the median increase of all U.S. SMSA's.

Southern Appalachian metropolitan areas have

Table 10. *Population and Components of Population Change, Southern Appalachian Nonmetropolitan Areas, 1940-1950 and 1950-1960*

		Number				Rate			
		Natural increase		Net migration		Natural increase		Net migration	
State economic area	Population 1960	1940-50	1950-60	1940-50	1950-60	1940-50	1950-60	1940-50	1950-60
ALABAMA									
2. Sand Mountain	197,137	45,683	32,165	- 42,144	- 42,185	22.2	15.5	-20.7	-20.4
GEORGIA									
1. N. W. Ridge & Valley	246,917	43,117	40,009	- 16,134	- 22,074	20.0	18.3	- 8.0	- 9.6
2. Blue Ridge Mountains	85,831	18,681	13,223	- 18,468	- 13,737	21.7	15.3	-21.4	-15.9
TENNESSEE									
7. Central Cumberland Plateau	112,085	31,988	20,107	- 22,324	- 26,214	28.2	17.0	-20.6	-22.2
8. Valley of East Tennessee (S.)	252,060	53,679	40,541	- 39,376	- 34,812	22.5	16.5	-17.0	-14.1
Valley of East Tennessee (N.)	436,332	77,114	65,133	- 28,440	- 39,597	20.0	15.9	- 7.9	- 9.6
NORTH CAROLINA									
1. Blue Ridge Mountains	263,812	59,875	40,365	- 58,149	- 50,539	21.9	14.7	-21.4	-18.4
2. Blue Ridge Slopes	189,889	33,760	31,158	- 12,822	- 15,656	20.6	17.9	- 8.4	- 9.0
KENTUCKY									
8. Eastern Hills	215,719	58,021	41,345	- 89,410	- 60,245	23.2	17.6	-33.6	-25.7
9. Eastern Coal Fields	398,690	139,996	96,559	-135,805	-208,317	27.5	18.9	-26.8	-40.8
VIRGINIA									
1. Southwest Coal Fields	176,125	49,107	38,330	- 34,621	- 61,300	25.6	19.3	-18.8	-30.8
2. Valley of Virginia S. W.	212,168	40,391	31,758	- 31,185	- 35,562	19.1	14.7	-15.1	-16.5
3. Valley of Virginia	184,657	29,631	25,807	- 15,230	- 25,111	16.8	14.0	- 9.0	-13.7
4. Shenandoah Valley	224,735	26,194	27,980	- 1,348	- 5,146	13.8	13.9	- 0.8	- 2.5
WEST VIRGINIA									
2. Central Hills	158,186	28,436	22,297	- 42,112	- 48,147	14.9	12.1	-21.3	-26.2
3. Upper Monongahela Valley	254,907	39,737	32,315	- 29,170	- 64,588	14.1	11.3	-10.5	-22.5
4. Southern Coal Fields	382,303	106,226	86,960	- 56,515	-170,343	24.1	18.7	-13.6	-36.6
5. Allegheny-Greenbrier	165,669	31,280	22,010	- 37,725	- 44,591	16.3	11.7	-19.4	-23.7
6. Eastern Panhandle	60,832	6,506	7,299	- 5,389	- 2,286	11.8	13.1	- 9.9	- 4.1
The Region	4,218,054	919,422	715,361	-716,367	-970,450	20.9	16.2	-13.1	-19.0

Source: Vital Statistics of the United States, 1940-1960; U. S. Census of Population, 1950 and 1960.

Table 11. *Population and Components of Population Change, Southern Appalachian Metropolitan Areas, 1940-1950 and 1950-1960*

		Number				Rate			
		Natural increase		Net migration		Natural increase		Net migration	
State economic area	Population 1960	1940-50	1950-60	1940-50	1950-60	1940-50	1950-60	1940-50	1950-60
Asheville	130,074	16,396	15,862	- 475	- 10,191	15.1	12.8	- 0.4	- 8.2
Charleston	314,656	60,958	59,562	-15,978	- 66,978	22.0	18.5	- 5.8	-20.8
Chattanooga	283,169	38,353	44,928	- 2,579	- 8,212	18.2	18.2	- 1.2	- 3.3
Huntington-Ashland	199,342	28,698	29,436	-11,672	- 26,774	16.0	15.0	- 6.5	-13.6
Knoxville	368,080	53,058	61,816	34,240	- 30,841	21.3	18.3	13.7	- 9.1
Roanoke	158,803	14,994	20,084	6,982	5,312	13.5	15.1	6.3	4.0
Total	1,454,124	212,457	231,688	10,518	-137,684	18.7	17.0	0.9	-10.1

Source: Vital Statistics of the United States, 1900-1960; U. S. Census of Population, 1950 and 1960

failed to grow because they have not been as attractive to migrants as most metropolitan areas in the nation. During the 1940's, only Knoxville and Roanoke gained through migration, and the total net migration rate of the six areas was 0.9 percent compared with a national rate for metropolitan areas of 9.2 percent (Table 11). Practically all of the growth during the decade stemmed from the excess of births over deaths, the natural increase rate for regional metropolitan areas being 19 percent compared with 11 percent for all metropolitan areas in the nation. During the 1950-1960 decade, the combined metropolitan areas of the Region actually lost population through migration (the net migration rate being —10.1 percent), even though natural increase was great enough to bring about a seven percent population gain. All SMSA's except Roanoke lost through net migration, four of them (Asheville, Charleston, Huntington-Ashland, and Knoxville) at relatively high rates.

The growth of the Knoxville area in the 1940's was due primarily to the development of the Atomic Energy Commission plants at Oak Ridge. In the 1950's, as the number employed there decreased, the rate of growth dropped and the area suffered a net loss through migration. Chattanooga has been growing steadily, but not spectacularly. The Charleston and Huntington-Ashland SMSA's have been growing very slowly, especially in the 1950's. Though there has been much industrial development in these cities, chiefly in chemical industries based on coal, it has been at such a high technological level that large numbers of additional workers, and especially unskilled laborers, were not needed.

Migration from the Southern Appalachian Region, as we have pointed out, is by no means a new development. Nor is it an isolated phenomenon, but part of a national pattern. In the decade 1950-1960, the shift of population from farm to city appears to have been dramatically accelerated throughout the nation, and marginal farming areas, where poverty is chronic, have contributed heavily to the flow of migrants. Mechanization of the mining industry, together with a decline in the market for coal, have brought about severe unemployment in the nation's mining communities—and the Region has a large share of these. Evidence of the part played in Appalachian migration by marginal farming areas and depressed mining communities will be examined in detail in a later section. But poverty—which is not new to the Region—cannot alone account for the accelerated out-movement of the population. An increased awareness of the oppor-

tunities and benefits offered by the urban-industrial society has a significant role here (see Chapter II)

But though the Appalachian people, like other Americans, are concentrating in cities, the Region's own cities have actually lost population through migration. A large proportion of the migrants from rural areas are moving to cities outside the Region. This, too, is a point to which we shall return, for it has significant implications for the Region's future.

Direction of Migration

In the analysis of migration streams, we are dealing for the first time with data on both in- and out-migration. The data are limited to 1935-1940 and 1949-1950, for the census did not include questions directly concerning migration before 1940, and migration data from the 1960 census were not available at the time of writing. The available data are sufficient to reveal the tremendous complexity of the migration currents of the Southern Appalachians, though the major existing patterns can be readily determined.

Perhaps the most striking feature revealed by a comparison of these two migration periods is the stability of the patterns of migration. Whether attention is focused on the proportion of migrants moving within the various state economic areas, the proportion moving to nearby areas, or the proportion to distant areas—whether within or outside of the Region—the ratios for the two periods are remarkably close and at times are practically identical.

Yet, within this stability, there are differences. For one, the volume of migration increased tremendously. In 1935-1940, a total of 624,349 migrants left the state subregions,[2] a rate of 124,800 migrants per year. In 1949-1950, a one-year period, 306,640 persons moved from the state economic areas, a yearly volume almost two and one-half times that of the earlier period. A second major difference between the two periods was an increase in proportions of migrants who moved longer distances: of those who left the Appalachians, a much greater proportion of the 1949-1950 migrants than of the 1935-1940 group moved to nonadjacent areas.[3] Still, the patterns in 1935-1940 and 1949-1950 are so similar that concentration on the later period is warranted.

One of the most impressive patterns for the 1949-

---

[2] Subregions are divisions roughly comparable to the state economic areas used in the more recent decades.

[3] It should be noted that both 1935-40 and 1949-50 were periods of depressed economic activity. Although it would be difficult to compare the conditions in these years with those of other years, they are nevertheless "abnormal" situations.

THE SOUTHERN APPALACHIANS

Figure 23

CONTIGUOUS MIGRATION, 1950

Percentage of out-migrants from state economic areas going to contiguous areas

Under 25.0

25.0-34.9

35.0-44.9

45.0-54.9

55.0 or more

Source: Special tabulations from U. S. Census of Population, 1950

VIRGINIA

WEST VIRGINIA

KENTUCKY

TENNESSEE

NORTH CAROLINA

GEORGIA

A.

A.

Winston-Salem

Greensboro

Charlotte

Greenville

Atlanta

Birmingham

Louisville

Lexington

SCALE

0   10   20   30   40   50 MILES

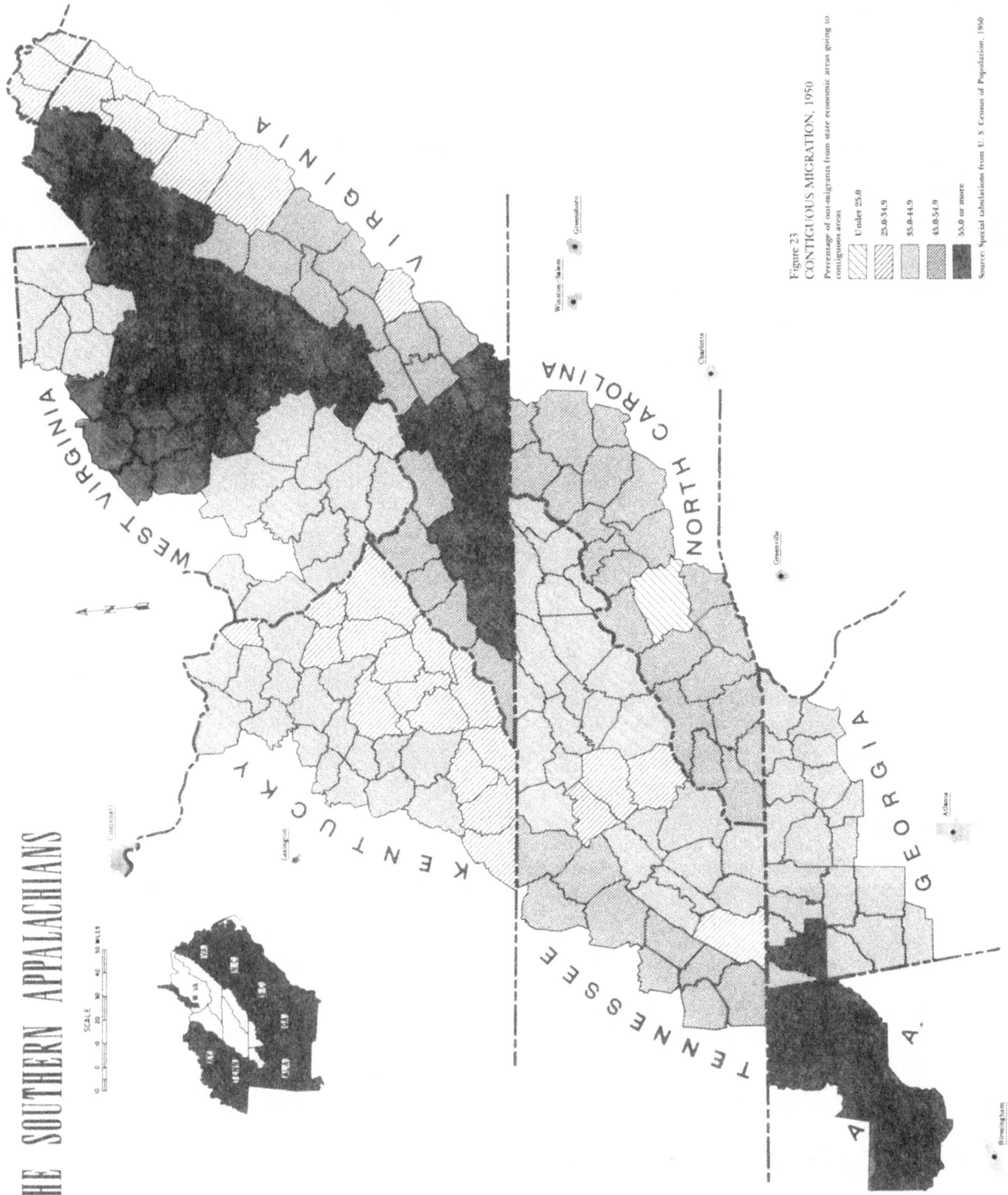

1950 data is the close correspondence between in- and out-migration streams, illustrating the well-established principle that each migration current is accompanied by a counter-current. Without exception, the proportion of people going to any destination from any

the northern areas in the Region swap migrants with each other. In some cases neighboring areas take more than 55 percent of each other's migrants. To a large extent this local movement is associated with the coal mining portions of the Region. In most parts of the

Table 12. *Percentage of Southern Appalachian Interarea Migrants Going to Specified Destinations, 1949-1950*

State economic area of origin	Remain in state of origin	Other App. states	D. C. & Maryland	Florida, Miss., & S. C.	East North Central states	Other states
ALABAMA						
2. Sand Mountain	55.4	23.3	0.2	7.6	3.9	9.6
GEORGIA						
1. N. W. Ridge & Valley	41.9	28.9	0.6	8.0	5.1	15.5
2. Blue Ridge Mountains	57.3	18.6	0.6	8.2	5.2	10.1
A. Chattanooga SMA	37.4	47.1	1.0	7.7	1.3	5.5
TENNESSEE						
7. Central Cumberland Plateau	53.4	16.9	0.2	4.0	16.7	8.8
8. Valley of East Tennessee	33.1	35.1	2.3	6.9	11.3	11.3
C. Chattanooga SMA	23.5	42.4	1.2	9.2	9.0	14.7
D. Knoxville SMA	45.5	22.0	1.7	6.7	10.2	13.9
NORTH CAROLINA						
1. Blue Ridge Mountains	42.6	24.8	3.5	11.9	4.6	12.6
2. Blue Ridge Slopes	67.6	14.2	2.6	6.9	1.9	6.8
A. Asheville SMA	44.0	17.8	3.8	16.4	4.9	13.1
KENTUCKY						
8. Eastern Hills	40.2	8.2	0.6	1.6	42.8	6.6
9. Eastern Coal Fields	26.9	30.5	1.3	3.1	28.7	9.4
C. Huntington-Ashland SMA	32.8	20.3	1.0	2.0	30.7	13.3
VIRGINIA						
1. Southwest Coal Fields	25.2	48.6	5.4	3.6	8.7	8.5
2. Valley of Virginia S. W.	35.6	48.7	5.2	3.0	4.9	1.6
3. Valley of Virginia	51.6	22.8	6.2	2.9	4.7	11.8
4. Shenandoah Valley	41.8	17.2	14.9	4.7	4.2	17.2
A. Roanoke SMA	51.9	17.8	6.4	5.6	4.8	13.5
WEST VIRGINIA						
2. Central Hills	59.7	6.6	2.3	1.7	19.1	10.6
3. Upper Monongahela Valley	37.2	8.4	8.3	3.2	16.8	26.1
4. Southern Coal Fields	32.1	38.7	3.4	3.0	11.7	11.1
5. Allegheny-Greenbrier	34.3	22.8	20.3	3.0	7.8	11.9
6. Eastern Panhandle	39.8	20.4	14.4	1.7	8.3	15.4
B. Huntington-Ashland SMA	33.7	15.9	2.8	4.9	28.5	14.2
C. Charleston SMA	50.3	13.3	3.3	4.2	13.4	15.5

Source: Special tabulations provided by U. S. Bureau of Census; U. S. Census of Population, 1950.

state economic area during the 1949-1950 period was practically identical to the proportion of area in-migrants from that place. Of the migrants leaving the Kentucky state economic areas, for example, 29.9, 14.1, and 24.2 percent left the Coal Fields, the Hills, and the Huntington-Ashland areas, respectively, to go to Ohio; 27.5, 12.0, and 20.8 percent of the in-migrants to these areas came from Ohio. This pattern can be repeated for each of the state economic areas of the Region.

Most migration is short-distance; county-to-county movements within the various economic areas are eliminated from the total statistics . The most obvious pattern revealed in Figure 23 is the extent to which

Region where there were significant numbers of miners, such as the Southwest Virginia Coal Fields (Virginia 1) and parts of the West Virginia Hills (West Virginia 2b) and Allegheny-Greenbrier (West Virginia 5) areas, a high degree of migrant "swapping" could be observed, at least in 1950.

Much of this movement to contiguous areas, of course, is intra-state migration, for migrants tend to remain within their home states. Even when migration to contiguous areas was omitted, it was still apparent that many more migrants remained within their own state than went to adjacent states. Twenty percent or more of the migrants from all areas remained in the state in which they were originally

THE SOUTHERN APPALACHIANS

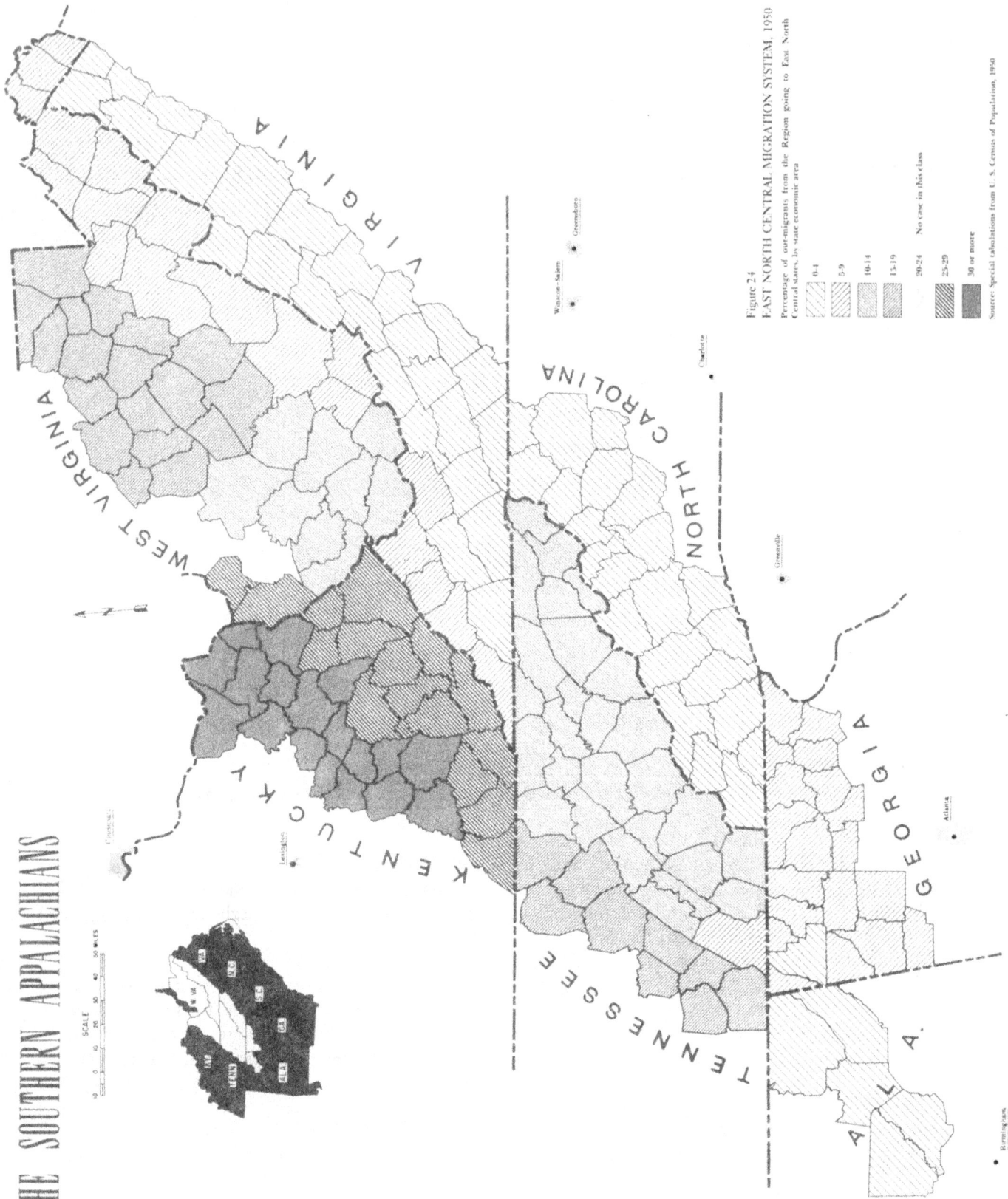

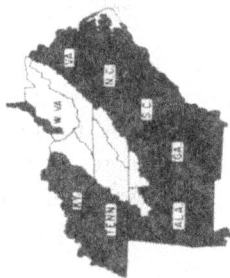

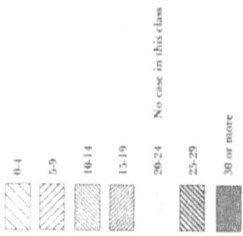

Figure 24
EAST NORTH CENTRAL MIGRATION SYSTEM, 1950

Percentage of out-migrants from the Region going to East North
Central states, by state economic area

0-4

5-9

10-14

15-19

20-24   No case in this class

25-29

30 or more

Source: Special tabulations from U. S. Census of Population, 1950

THE SOUTHERN APPALACHIANS

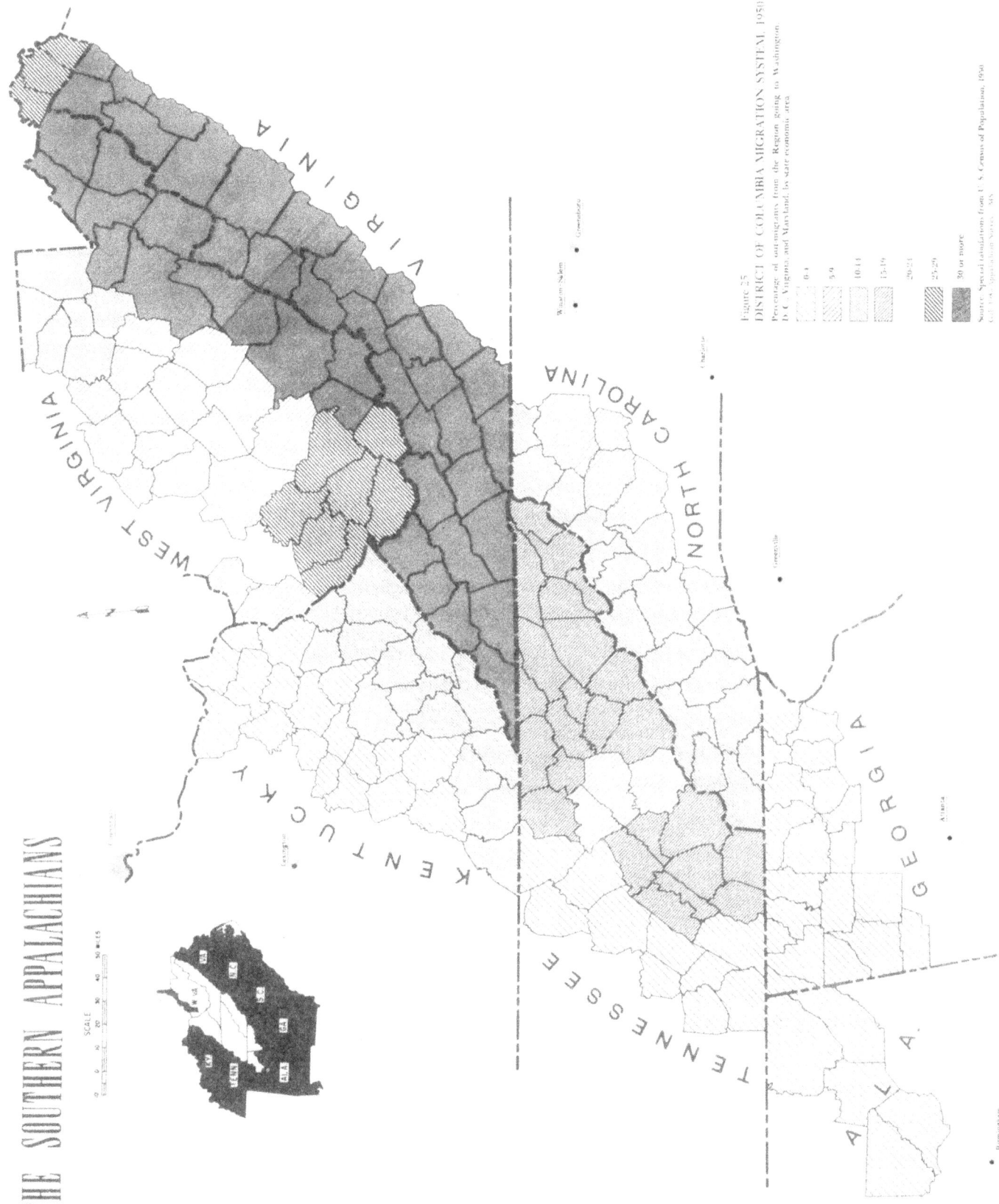

SCALE

Figure 25

DISTRICT OF COLUMBIA MIGRATION SYSTEM, 1950

Percentage of out-migrants from the Region going to Washington, D. C., Virginia, and Maryland, by state economic area

0-4
5-9
10-14
15-19
20-24
25-29
30 or more

Source: Special tabulations from U. S. Census of Population, 1950. Office of Population Studies, W.Va.

VIRGINIA

WEST VIRGINIA

KENTUCKY

TENNESSEE

NORTH CAROLINA

GEORGIA

ALA.

located, and for more than 90 percent of the areas, 30 percent of their migrants remained in the state. On the other hand, practically none of the areas sent 30 percent of their migrants to another state with which they shared boundaries.[4] Most of the areas (more than 80 percent) sent less than 20 percent to these adjoining states. These data demonstrate the important effect of state boundaries on migration streams.

Examination of in-state migration also serves to explain the high incidences of contiguous migration in certain areas. For example, the Sand Mountain Area (Alabama 2) is contiguous to the Birmingham Metropolitan Area, to which it sends 15.5 percent of its migrants. About 40 percent of the Sand Mountain migrants go to Birmingham and two areas immediately adjacent to it. North Carolina has in the Piedmont Industrial Crescent one of the most extended and spatially diffused urban areas in the Southeast. Perhaps the presence of such an area explains why the Blue Ridge Slopes (North Carolina 2) leads all of the Region's state economic areas in the proportion of in-state migrants (67.6 percent). Both of the two Georgia areas are low in percentage of contiguous migration, but the Georgia Blue Ridge Mountain Area (Georgia 2) is quite high with respect to its in-state migration. About 40 percent of its migrants go to Atlanta and the adjacent economic areas (excluding Georgia 1).

When in-state migration is excluded, the patterns presented in Figures 24 and 25 emerge, though these show only the simplest streams of migration. Most of the areas on the western side of the Appalachians send their migrants to the East North Central Region. Proportions range from 16.7 percent in the Central Cumberland Plateau (Tennessee 7) to 42.8 percent in the Eastern Kentucky Hills Area (Kentucky 8). But no other Appalachian area sends as much as 15 percent of its migrants to the East North Central Region. The migrants from the northeastern state economic areas go primarily to the District of Columbia, Maryland, and Virginia. Again, no other area in the Region sends as much as 15 percent of its migrants to this general region. Briefly, then, migrants from the western portion of the Region tend to go primarily to the East North Central Area, whereas migrants from the northern part of the Region journey toward the District of Columbia and the adjoining states.

Virginia stands as an area which is involved in several of these migration patterns. It, of course, has

a high degree of in-state migration, as does any state. It also is part of the heavy swapping in the coal mining areas. But, as Figure 24 indicates, it is also part of the migration system which contains the District of Columbia and Maryland.

Relatively stable relationships have developed between certain areas within the Region and areas of destination outside of the Region. As a consequence of this relationship, conditions in either the area of destination or the area of origin are bound to affect the other. Education in the area of origin, for example, will have its effects in the area to which the migrants go. An industrial lay-off in Detroit or Cleveland not only retards migration from Eastern Kentucky but in many instances sends laid-off employees back to the Region. Specific areas of destination, then, are influenced by specific areas of origin, and vice versa.[5] The Midwest, for example, is influenced more by Eastern Kentucky than by Western North Carolina, and the Sand Mountain Area in Alabama is of more importance to Birmingham than is the Pine Mountain area in southeastern Kentucky.

Characteristics of Migrants

To show more than the extent and direction of migration with the available data on Southern Appalachian migrants is difficult. For one thing there are only two periods when the characteristics of migrants could be measured with any exactitude: 1935-1940 and 1949-1950. Furthermore, these periods are not comparable in many ways and the 1935-1940 data available for this study contain characteristics only of in-migrants. For these reasons this analysis will be restricted to the later period. But even the 1949-1950 data present problems: (1) few of the characteristics are classified by age of migrants; (2) data are provided only on an individual basis, and thus there is no information on family moves; (3) characteristics of migrants are known only at the end of the period,

---

[4] Chattanooga was the sole exception. Walker County in Georgia, which falls within the Chattanooga Metropolitan Area, sent 41.8 percent of its inter-area migrants to Tennessee and only 37.8 percent of its migrants to Georgia. Conversely, the Tennessee side (Hamilton County) sent 28.6 percent of its inter-area migrants to Georgia and only 23.5 percent to Tennessee. Most of this migration was, of course, an interchange *within* the Chattanooga metropolitan area.

[5] In George A. Hillery, Jr. and James S. Brown, "Some Conclusions on Migratory Streams from a Study of the Southern Appalachians," a paper read at the 1961 meeting of the Population Association of America, the authors have called these clusterings of closely related "donor" and "recipient" areas "migration systems," thus emphasizing the functional interdependence of these areas.

which obscures changes—in occupation and marital status, for instance—that could be either results or causes of migration; (4) and, finally, a one-year period is an uncomfortably short span upon which to base generalizations. Because of these limitations, the basic

Figure 26. *Age Distribution of Southern Appalachian Out-Migrants and In-Migrants Compared to That of the Total United States Population, 1949-1950*

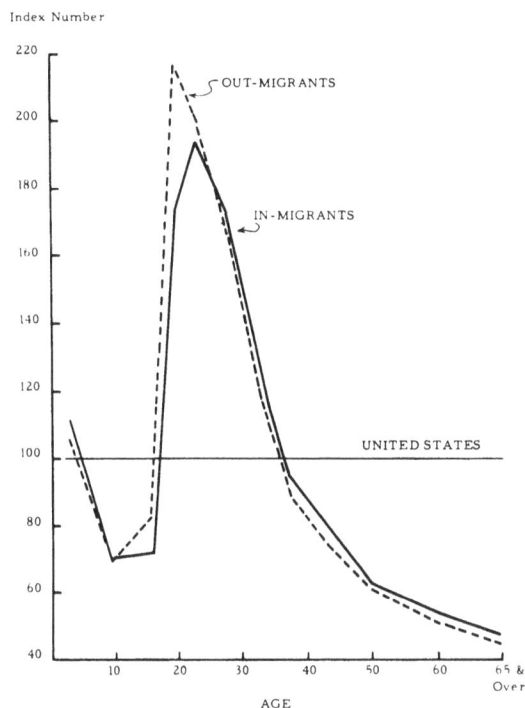

Source: U. S. Census of Population, 1950

comparisons will be confined primarily to those between the Region's migrant population and the total population and between in-migrants and out-migrants.

Almost 95 percent of the Region's 1950 resident population was white, and the migrant streams both to and from the Region were overwhelmingly white. The proportion of Negroes in the 1949-1950 migrant stream was smaller, however, for both sexes than their proportion in the total population (approximately 4 percent for both out-migrants and in-migrants and for both males and females, as contrasted with approximately 6 percent for each sex in the total population).

The migrant population is made up primarily of young adults. The age-group 18-34 years, alone, comprised almost half (49.8 percent) of the in-migrants and more than half (51.7 percent) of the out-migrants. On the other hand, this group formed only a third (33.7 percent) of the total population. Proportion-

ately twice as many persons in the total population were 65 years and over as in the migrant population. When the age distribution of migrants is graphically compared to that of the total regional population, the association of age and migration becomes especially clear (Figure 26). The obvious reason for the greater concentration of children under six years of age in the migrant population is that the adult migrants are relatively young.

In every age category the outward flow of migrants exceeded the inward one. There were interesting differences also in the age composition of the two migrant groups. Migrants from the Region were more narrowly concentrated in the teenages and young adult years than were migrants into the Region. Persons leaving their state economic areas or the Region were significantly younger than those entering, though adults who moved in either direction were younger on the average than those in the total population.

Two important consequences arise from this relation between migration and age. First, the proportion of persons in the dependent ages (less than 15 and over 65) can be expected to rise, as the young adults continue to move out. A second consequence is the decline of the number of births in the Region, brought about in part by the loss of women in the reproductive years. The implications for the future growth of the Region's population are thus clear. As the Region's most reproductive women leave (reproductive at least potentially), one can expect further declines in the population, not only from the loss of women but from the loss of their children as well.

Male migrants outnumbered the females in both outgoing and incoming streams, there being among the out-migrants 107.1 males for every 100 females. The comparable ratio for in-migrants was 106.9. Metropolitan areas, like the others, lost more men in the outward streams, and the incoming streams did not balance the deficit. But nonmetropolitan areas lost more men, both absolutely and proportionately, than did the metropolitan areas. Metropolitan areas gained relatively more females than did the nonmetropolitan areas. One result of the sex composition of the migrant streams is that a surplus of females has developed in all of the Region's metropolitan areas. On the other hand, more than half of the nonmetropolitan areas have a surplus of males (see Table 13).

The sex ratio, alone, has few social implications. The lack of a balance between males and females becomes important only in relation to such things as the ages of the people involved, the family and marital status, and so forth. Nevertheless, one may probably assume that the Region's larger cities witness a relatively sharper competition for available males than

employment. The needs of single adult migrants—because they tend to be concentrated in the same ages—will tend to be more uniform and thus more easily met by the communities in which they settle.

Table 13. *Distribution of Metropolitan and Nonmetropolitan State Economic Areas by Sex Ratios in Migrant and Total Populations, Southern Appalachian Region, 1949-1950*

Males per 100 females	Total population		Out-migrants		In-migrants	
	Metropolitan	Nonmetropolitan	Metropolitan	Nonmetropolitan	Metropolitan	Nonmetropolitan
Under 94.0	2	-	1	-	-	2
94.0 - 99.9	6	6	1	1	3	1
100.0 - 105.9	-	11	5	9	1	7
106.0 - 111.9	-	-	1	4	2	4
112.0 and over	-	-	-	3	2	3
Total[a]	8	17	8	17	8	17

Source: U. S. Census of Population, 1950.

[a]There are 8 metropolitan areas because West Virginia B and Kentucky C are considered separately, as are Tennessee C and Georgia A. In most of the other tabulations in this chapter, these areas are combined. West Virginia 2b was excluded from this analysis (sex ratio of 102.9) because tabulations are not returned separately in the Census publication. Tennessee 8a and 8b are also combined, for the same reason. Thus, there are only 17 nonmetropolitan areas instead of 19.

the other areas. Until recent years, the Appalachian Region resembled the frontier of a century ago in many ways, one of which was the presence of a surplus of males. But the continued out-pouring of males from the Region will certainly bring the balance between the sexes closer to the national pattern than has been true in the past. Already, the balance has shifted to the females, though there are still relatively more males in comparison with the country as a whole. This difference is not likely to continue.

Most adult migrants were married, as is true of the total adult population of the Southern Appalachians. There was a greater proportion of single men among the migrant males, however, than among the non-migrant, and male migrants are more often single than are female migrants (Figure 27). But among females, relatively more migrants than nonmigrants were married. Although it is plausible to believe that most of these women were married before migrating, some undoubtedly married after migrating but before the 1950 census was taken.

The concentration of children under six in the migrant population, noted above, indicates that many of the migrants are young couples with children. The consequences of migration of family units for the adjustment processes are significant. The family as a social unit carries with it a built-in psychological cushioning against the shocks of transition for the many migrants who move from rural to urban environments. There are, however, negative consequences as well. The individuals composing the family will have diverse needs, particularly for schooling, housing,

There is another implication of "family" migration, reminiscent of the problems encountered by foreign-born children. In urban areas, particularly those in the Midwest, the status of the Appalachian migrant is an inferior one. The names of "briar-hopper," "hill-billy," etc., bear their own testimony. Thus, in addition to problems stemming from the migration process itself, not to mention the usual problems of lower socioeconomic status, the children of Appalachian migrants must cope with an added burden of inferior social status. Family migration also partially accounts for the tendency of Appalachian newcomers in northern cities to flock together—a characteristic which slows the assimilation of migrants into their new communities. Such a self-imposed segregation can only accentuate their inferior status.

The adult migrants (25 years old and over) have completed more years of schooling than is true of the total Appalachian population. This was true both of migrants moving into and out of the various areas (see Table 14). Generally, the two streams were very similar in educational attainment. Out-migrants outnumbered in-migrants at all educational levels except the highest. For 1949-1950, the Region had a net migration gain of 15 persons who had completed four or more years of college.

Out-migrants and in-migrants are better educated than the Southern Appalachian population as a whole, but since out-migration has exceeded in-migration for many years, the net result has been to retard the rise in the educational level of the Region's population. On the one hand, the higher educational status of the migrants in comparison with the population they leave serves as a drain on the social resources of the Appalachian Region as a whole. But, on the other hand, the migrants have a lower average education

Figure 27. *Marital Status of Migrant and Total Populations, 14 Years Old and Over, Southern Appalachian Region, 1949-1950*

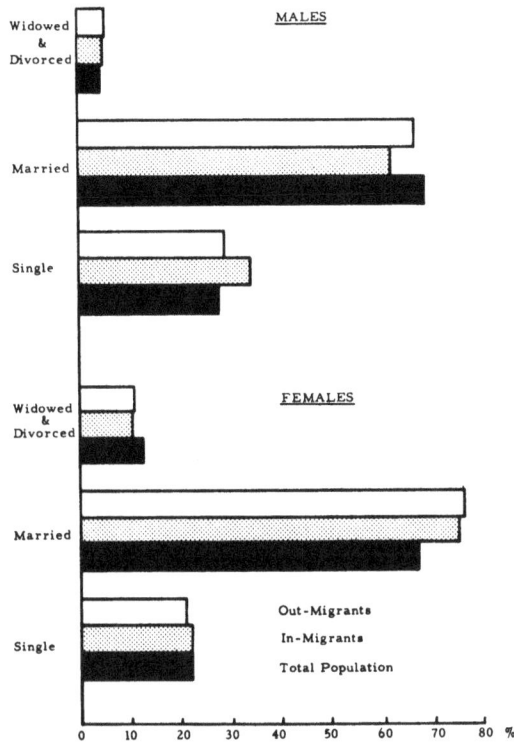

Source: U. S. Census of Population, 1950

than the population at their destination, should migration be out of the Region. For example, as measured by median number of years of schooling completed, none of the states in the Appalachians had an average educational attainment as high as any state in the East North Central region. (West Virginia had the highest median in the Appalachians, 8.5 years, as opposed to Wisconsin's median of 8.9 years, the lowest of the East North Central states.) Consequently, Appalachian outmigration tends to lower the level of education both in and out of the Region.

An accompaniment of the relatively low level of education received by Appalachian people (migrants included) is a lack of vocational training (other than agricultural). Large proportions of migrants are obliged to enter the occupational structure at its lowest level. This level is the most vulnerable to economic fluctuations. Even those who have been absorbed into the industrial structure as operatives

face the imminent prospect of being displaced as technological change occurs. In the future, untrained migrants will be less likely than in the past to be absorbed into the manufacturing system as operatives. Such a condition must be taken into account by those charged with preparing the young people of the Region to participate in the various phases of the national economy.

A comparison of the occupations of migrants with those of the total Southern Appalachian population shows that the greatest differences were in the categories of professional, technical, and kindred workers; and farmers, including farm managers (see Table 15). The proportions in the other occupations are fairly close to those in the total population. Somewhat higher proportions of the migrants were clerks and kindred workers; sales workers; craftsmen, foremen and kindred workers; service workers; farm laborers (excluding unpaid laborers); and other laborers. On the other hand, lower proportions of the migrant population were managers, officials and proprietors; operatives and kindred workers; and unpaid farm laborers.

There are two serious difficulties in any interpretation of these figures. The first is that the occupations of the migrants are known only at the end of the migration period, and of course many individuals change jobs or enter the labor market for the first time after migrating. It is impossible to tell, for example, whether farm operators are counted less often as migrants because they changed their jobs when they went to the city (or elsewhere) or whether farm operators are actually less migratory than are persons in other occupational categories. Most probably, both things are true—farm operators move less *and* they change their jobs when they move.

The second handicap is that of having figures for a migration period of only one year, which may or may not be representative. For instance, during that year the Region had net gains of professionals, farm managers, unpaid farm laborers, and managerial personnel but net losses from the other occupational groups. If 1949-1950 was a recession year, as seems to have been the case, many farmers and their families may have been returning to the Region after unsuccessful economic experiences elsewhere. It should be remembered, however, that though farmers were returning, they did not constitute a large stream, especially relative to their numbers in the total population. The same was true of managers. The net gain of professionals is somewhat puzzling. Many speculations could be offered but valid answers must await further research.

It is possible that the technological revolution of automation may have the same effect of damming

conclusions is quite strong, most of these conclusions must nevertheless be considered tentative.

The factors to be considered can be viewed from a number of different perspectives. We will here con-

Table 14. *Schooling of Migrants and Total Population, 25 Years Old and Over, Southern Appalachian Region, 1949-1950*

Years of school completed		Number			Percentage		
		Out-migrants	In-migrants	Population	Out-migrants	In-migrants	Population
Elementary	Under 5	14,325	13,755	563,895	13.1	13.3	19.1
	5-7	22,470	21,545	816,440	20.6	21.0	27.7
	8	16,500	15,515	517,505	15.1	15.1	17.5
High school	1-3	17,135	16,315	399,915	15.7	15.9	13.6
	4	18,095	15,895	327,985	16.6	15.5	11.1
College	1-3	9,140	8,595	157,115	8.4	8.4	5.3
	4 or more	9,180	9,195	113,050	8.4	8.9	3.8
No report		2,375	1,915	56,985	2.1	1.9	1.9
Total		109,220	102,730	2,952,890	100.0	100.0	100.0

Source: Special tabulations provided by U. S. Bureau of Census; U. S. Census of Population, 1950.

up the migrant stream as did the depression of the thirties. Increasingly, we can expect a greater emphasis on service production as contrasted with goods or physical production in the national economy. The educational and occupational experience of the migrants would make them best suited for employment in physical-production industries, particularly as unskilled labor. But these are the very positions that are receiving less emphasis in the national economy with the passage of time. Thus, should the Appalachians continue to produce a labor surplus and continue to give this surplus inadequate training, this surplus will face a problem that in the past has only been temporary—the problem of no place to go.

Factors Related to Migration

Paradoxically, we have both the most and the least information concerning factors associated with migration. In a sense, all of the data pertain to this question. And yet, in studying migration, one is quickly brought to the realization that little in the realm of causation can be pinned down with certainty. Though one can draw plausible inferences as to the reasons why people migrate, such inferences do not represent clearly established relationships of cause and effect. Also, since migration is usually a product of multiple economic, social, and psychological forces operating upon individuals and groups, singling out any two or three factors as "the" causes of migration is in almost every case a gross distortion of reality. Consequently, even though the inferential basis for many of our

sider geographic, socioeconomic, and sociocultural factors, and the process of metropolitanization. This process is used as a bridge between the socioeconomic and sociocultural factors.

The Region's topography has played two chief roles in migration patterns: it has acted as a barrier on the one hand and as an isolator on the other. As a barrier, the Region imposed an obstacle to those who wanted to go through it. And those who did eventually settle within it found that the topography isolated them to some degree from the rest of the world. The mountains impeded transverse movement and communication, but many parts of the region were linked by longitudinal valleys. The Great Valley, in particular, formed a natural communication artery. Until well into the twentieth century, transportation from the Region to other parts of the nation was slow and difficult, and a relatively small number of railroads provided the main connecting links. Today, there are few areas which are more than ten miles from an all-weather road, although many of the roads are still narrow and tortuous.

Sheer lack of transportation no longer ranks as a major deterrent to migration, though certain patterns of movement established when the topography was a force to be reckoned with still prevail. For example, it is easier in most places to travel with the ridges than across them, and this may partly explain why even today not many people south and east of the Great Valley migrate to the Midwest, and few migrants from Eastern Kentucky go to the Piedmont

Crescent of North Carolina, or to Atlanta or Birmingham. These journeys were once very difficult, and the migration streams were therefore established in other directions. Thus, although topography is not now a

nation has been influenced by the effects of topography on the location and development of cities. Metropolitan areas tended to grow up around the Appalachians rather than in them, and they developed

Table 15. *Occupations of Employed Males in Migrant and Total Populations, Southern Appalachian Region, 1949-1950*

Occupation group	Number			Percentage		
	Out-migrants	In-migrants	Population	Out-migrants	In-migrants	Population
Professional, technical, and kindred	5,535	6,515	67,291	9.3	11.8	4.7
Farmers and farm managers	3,355	3,665	219,881	5.6	6.6	15.2
Managers, officials, and proprietors, except farm	4,265	4,325	105,844	7.1	7.8	7.3
Clerical and kindred	2,950	2,235	56,853	4.9	4.0	3.9
Sales	3,735	3,455	64,512	6.3	6.2	4.5
Craftsmen, foremen, and kindred	10,590	8,975	225,386	17.7	16.3	15.6
Operators and kindred	16,095	14,455	417,289	27.0	26.2	28.9
Service	2,730	2,300	53,894	4.6	4.2	3.7
Farm laborers, unpaid family workers	930	1,305	46,933	1.6	2.4	3.2
Farm laborers, except unpaid and foremen	2,920	2,335	55,858	4.9	4.2	3.9
Laborers, except farm and mine	5,775	4,685	110,605	9.7	8.5	7.7
Not reported	795	970	19,701	1.3	1.8	1.4
Total	59,675	55,220	1,444,047	100.0	100.0	100.0

Source: Special tabulations provided by U. S. Bureau of Census; U. S. Census of Population, 1950.

practical determinant of migration streams, its influence can still be seen.

The shape of the Region is important to Appalachian migration in two ways. The area is very elongated, stretching diagonally southeast-northwest for approximately 640 miles. In this great length is to be found one of the causes of its diversity, not only geographically but culturally as well. This diversity is reflected in the streams of migration. Migrants from the Sand Mountain area of Alabama at the Region's southern extreme, as indicated earlier in the chapter, go more often to Birmingham, while migration streams from the Shenandoah Valley of Virginia at the northern extreme flow toward the Baltimore-Washington metropolitan area. Since the Region's boundaries are long in proportion to the total area of land, its interior is less remote from the boundaries than it would be if the area were more circular. Consequently one would expect a greater proportion of the population to cross the edges of the area than would be the case in a more compact region. It is difficult, of course, to evaluate the extent to which such a factor is important; certainly it is not a primary cause of the extensive migratory *depopulation* that has occurred.

The relation of the Region to the rest of the

within the Region on its fringes or in the Great Valley, at places which could provide easy passage through or around the mountain chain. Thus, Charleston and Huntington are on the margin of the Region; Chattanooga, Knoxville and Roanoke are all in the Great Valley. The Region is surrounded by other areas in which the topography has been more conducive to city development, and these cities have traditionally been destinations for migrants.

As metropolitan centers have become more important in national life, the incapacity of the Appalachian Region to develop and sustain many large metropolitan areas has resulted in a decline of its national significance. Furthermore, various parts of the area have tended to fall into the spheres of influence of the cities that have developed outside the Region. Consequently, it is less meaningful today to consider the Appalachians as a region in itself, since it is becoming increasingly segmented so far as its economic ties are concerned.

One influence of socioeconomic factors on migration may be seen in the relationship of net migration loss or gain to the percentage of the labor force employed in various industries of the Region's economic areas. For the 1940-1950 decade as well as for the period 1950-1957, employment in agriculture and mining was highly and consistently associated with migration loss. That is, the higher the percentage of the combined labor force employed in agriculture and mining in 1940 and 1950 the greater the loss from

Table 16. *Net Migration from Nonmetropolitan Areas, by Residence Categories, Southern Appalachian Region, 1949-1950*

Residence category[a]	Number		Rate	
	1940-50	1950-60	1940-50	1950-60
Farm	-281,468	-250,415	-22.8	-20.8
Rural nonfarm	-299,872	-526,421	-19.2	-31.8
Mixed	-135,087	-193,614	- 9.2	-12.0

Source: U. S. Census of Population, 1950.

[a]The state economic areas in the <u>farm</u> residence category in 1950 had 46 to 63 percent of their population classified as rural farm, 20 to 45 percent rural nonfarm, and 0-19 percent urban. They are Alabama 2, Kentucky 8, North Carolina 1, West Virginia 2b, Georgia 2, and Virginia 2.

In the <u>rural nonfarm</u> areas, 12 to 46 percent of the population was classified as rural farm, 48 to 71 percent rural nonfarm, and 2 to 17 percent urban. They are Tennessee 7, West Virginia 4 and 5, North Carolina 2, Kentucky 9, and Virginia 1.

The areas in the <u>mixed</u> residence category had populations 19 to .40 percent rural farm, 34 to 46 percent rural nonfarm, and 23 to 38 percent urban. They are Tennessee 8a and 8b, Virginia 3, Georgia 1, West Virginia 3 and 6.

migration during the following years. Statistical correlations also verified the expected relation between income and migration, i.e., the higher the income the less net migration loss. However, income alone was not as good a predictor of migration as was combined employment in agriculture and mining.[6]

Space limitations do not allow detailed examination of the migration rates of each of the areas, but it is particularly informative to look at one major segment of the nonmetropolitan population—the farm population. For the 1940's, data are available for the net changes due to migration in both the total and rural farm populations. These data indicate quite clearly that the heavy losses of the Southern Appalachians were primarily from the farm population. In the Southern Appalachians as a whole the net loss in the rural farm population due to migration was estimated at −595,000 people or a rate of −28.7 percent.[7]

All state economic areas of the Southern Appalachians had heavy losses of farm population during the forties, but there were some significant variations. The Kentucky areas lost at the highest rates (about 37 percent); the lowest loss rates were in West Virginia 3 (11.8 percent) followed by Tennessee 7 (17.1 percent). In most areas the loss of farm population during the 1940's was at rates three or four times those of the 1920's. No doubt a part of this

"great rush" out of the rural farm areas was a draining off of an accumulation of farm people who had been held there during the depression thirties by the lack of off-farm employment.

Data on the migration of the farm population in the 1950-1960 decade are not available in a form comparable to those for 1940-1950. In an attempt to measure the influence of farming on migration trends during the more recent period, however, the nonmetropolitan economic areas have been classified according to the proportions of their population appearing in various residence categories in 1950 (Table 16). Those areas in which the bulk of the population (46-63 percent) was classified as farm population in 1950 had the greatest migration loss during the forties (−22.8). The rate of loss from these areas was slightly lower in the fifties (−20.8). In areas where the rural nonfarm residence category was most important (representing 48-71 percent of the total population) the migration loss rose from −19.2 percent in the forties to −31.8 percent in the fifties. The dramatic increase in the migration losses of the coal mining areas was primarily responsible for this reversal. (The "rural nonfarm" category, which at present includes a sizeable component of the Southern Appalachian population, is a statistical rather than a sociological classification. Most of the rural nonfarm population is probably to be found either in the mining centers or adjacent to the metropolitan areas.) For both decades, the lightest losses appear in the "mixed" group, where the urban population attained its highest representation.

In the belief that the industrial composition of the various Southern Appalachian areas had much to do with migration gains and losses, the areas have been classified into seven groups on the basis of their industrial composition in 1950. The rates of total change and change due to net migration in these industrial groupings are shown in Table 17. During the 1940's, only those groups had losses in total population which

[6] K. M. George, "Association of Selected Economic Factors with Net Migration Rates in the Southern Appalachian Region, 1935-1957." Unpublished M.A. thesis, University of Kentucky, 1961.

[7] These rates for 1940-1950 are changes due to net migration expressed as a percentage of that part of the rural farm population which was alive at the beginning of the decade and was still surviving at the end of the decade. The data on which these rates are based are from Gladys K. Bowles, *Farm Population: Net Migration from the Rural-Farm Population, 1940-50*, U. S. Department of Agriculture, Agricultural Marketing Service, Statistical Bulletin No. 176, June 1956, and from special tabulations for the Appalachian areas furnished by Dr. Bowles.

were classified as agricultural and as agricultural with the presence of other industries. As would be expected, the manufacturing areas increased most (13.5 percent), followed by those agricultural areas which also possessed substantial manufacturing (10.4 percent).

There were very wide deviations in net migration rates. The heaviest losses were those of the agri-

even manufacturing, had net losses through migration.

The data in Table 18 provide a historical perspective of change for different industrial groupings. It was first in the 1940's that the stream of migration became so heavy from the agricultural areas that even the large natural increase was exceeded, resulting in the decline of the areas' population. In the 1950's,

Table 17. *Rates of Population Change, Net Migration, and Natural Increase for Nonmetropolitan Areas, by Industrial Classification, Southern Appalachian Region, 1940-1950 and 1950-1960*

Industrial classification[a]	Population change		Net migration		Natural increase	
	1940-50	1950-60	1940-50	1950-60	1940-50	1950-60
1. Agriculture	- 5.9	- 6.5	-28.0	-23.2	22.1	16.6
2. Agriculture with manufacturing	2.0	- 2.5	-19.1	-17.3	21.1	14.8
3. Agriculture with mining and manufacturing	- 2.1	-11.1	-20.4	-24.3	18.3	13.1
4. Mining	6.2	-18.6	-20.5	-37.4	26.7	18.9
5. Mining with manufacturing and commerce	3.8	-11.2	-10.5	-22.5	14.4	11.3
6. Manufacturing	13.5	8.3	- 8.1	- 9.4	21.6	17.6
7. Varied (agriculture, manufacturing, and commerce)	10.4	5.4	- 9.0	- 9.7	19.4	15.2

Source: Vital Statistics of the United States, 1940-1960; U. S. Census of Population, 1950 and 1960.

[a]The state economic areas were assigned to industrial classifications on the basis of employment in 1950, as follows: 1. Alabama 2, Kentucky 8; 2. Georgia 2, North Carolina 1, Virginia 2; 3. West Virginia 2b and 5, Tennessee 7; 4. West Virginia 4, Virginia 1, Kentucky 9; 5. West Virginia 3; 6. Georgia 1, North Carolina 2; 7. Virginia 3 and 4, West Virginia 6, Tennessee 8a and 8b.

cultural areas (—28.0 percent) and the mining areas (—20.5 percent), followed closely by the agricultural areas with mining and manufacturing (—20.4 percent). The lowest rates of net migration loss were from the manufacturing areas (—8.1 percent) and the varied areas (agriculture; manufacturing; trade, business, and finance: —9.0 percent).

During the 1950-1960 decade, the chief trends were as follows: Where manufacturing was the chief industry the population increased slightly (8 percent); where agriculture was the chief industry the population decreased slightly (7 percent); where mining was the chief industry the population decreased greatly (19 percent).

Rates of population change of the other areas during the 1950's fell between the extremes of the manufacturing and mining areas, depending upon the relative importance of the three major industries (see Table 17). As the importance of manufacturing increased, the rate of gain increased (or the rate of loss decreased). On the other hand, as the importance of coal mining increased, the rate of population loss increased.

Net migration losses were closely associated with these patterns. Losses were generally greatest where mining was important and lowest where there was a significant amount of manufacturing. Agricultural areas also lost heavily. But the areas in every category,

most of the remaining areas joined the agricultural areas in losing population, the two exceptions being areas in which employment in manufacturing was significant.

By far the greatest loss in the 1950's was from the mining areas. From 1950 to 1960, the population of these areas dropped from 1,175,000 to 957,000, a decrease of 218,000 (19 percent). There was a net loss through migration of 440,000 persons, a number equal to 37 percent of the total population in 1950. Primarily because of the very heavy outmigration of young people, the excess of births over deaths dropped from 295,000 in the 1940's to 222,000 in the 1950's. Indeed, the mining counties had such great population losses that with only 26.3 percent of the total population of the nonmetropolitan counties in 1950, they accounted for 45.3 percent of their total 1950-1960 loss through migration.

The data in Figure 28 show that the counties in which farm families had high levels of living lost much less through migration. The striking regularity with which migration decreased as the level-of-living scores increased is a clear indication of the great role that economic factors played in migration during both the 1940's and the 1950's.

Appalachian people, then, were moving to places where economic, social, cultural and educational opportunities were better, where higher levels of living could be attained, and where they could take their places in the main streams of American life. The parts of the Region with the highest economic and social levels had the greatest holding power. As a result, the Appalachian population was being redis-

ness or inability to accept certain notions of desirable status or achievements. Some of the poorest areas are also those in which there is a tradition of stable residence, of family solidarity, of an unwillingness to move and an extremely low regard for the traditional

Table 18. *Decennial Rates of Population Change, 1900-1960, in Southern Appalachian Nonmetropolitan Areas, by Industrial Classification*

Industrial classification[a]	1900-10	1910-20	1920-30	1930-40	1940-50	1950-60
1. Agriculture	12.1	7.5	6.0	12.5	- 5.9	- 6.5
2. Agriculture with manufacturing	6.0	6.0	6.8	13.5	2.0	- 2.5
3. Agriculture with mining and manufacturing	14.6	3.8	2.0	10.0	- 2.1	-11.1
4. Mining	45.6	43.1	32.4	17.5	6.2	-18.6
5. Mining with manufacturing and commerce	33.0	30.7	15.1	4.1	3.8	-11.2
6. Manufacturing	13.9	5.1	16.7	18.0	13.5	8.3
7. Varied (agriculture, manufacturing, and commerce)	7.6	5.0	9.1	11.2	10.4	5.4

Source: U. S. Census of Population, 1900-1960.

[a]For the state economic areas assigned to each industrial classification, see Table 17.

tributed at the same time that it was declining. Increasingly, the population has become concentrated in the metropolitan areas, the few nonmetropolitan areas in which manufacturing and trade are important, and in the better farming areas.

The association of migration with economic factors is not a perfect one-to-one relationship, but it is high enough to support the view that regional migration is increasingly influenced by extra-regional economic conditions. The Southern Appalachian Region is becoming more and more integrated with national society. One of the more significant changes occurring on the national level is the urbanization of American society, and this movement has been reflected in the tremendous loss of population from the agricultural portion of the area. The picture is complicated by the fact that a substantial proportion of the regional population has, in years past, been located in the mining areas which are still rural for the most part. Economic conditions in these latter areas are extremely sensitive to economic and technological fluctuations at the national level. Consequently, the Region is simultaneously losing its agricultural character and making a very drastic adjustment in a sector of the economy which has already become highly integrated into the national economy.

Another major aspect of the merging of regional with national society is the growing awareness of national economic opportunities and acceptance of national cultural standards. Lively and Taeuber, writing about the area in 1939, maintained: "Not only does lack of knowledge of opportunity interfere with ready adjustments but there is also an unwilling-

canons of material success."[8] There may still be areas of this sort, but the increase in migration during the past two decades, and the fact that the poorest counties are losing most heavily through net migration suggest that this is no longer the general situation. The net migration loss has been steadily increasing over the last two decades because there have been greater economic opportunities outside the area coupled with greater desire to take advantage of them.

The process of metropolitanization and its effect on migration involve a combination of socioeconomic and sociocultural factors. An analysis of the role played by metropolitan areas and farm areas (to emphasize the extremes of residential differences) thus acts as a bridge between economic and noneconomic considerations.

The Appalachian population is following the national pattern of concentrating its population in metropolitan areas. But the metropolitan areas in which Appalachian migrants are concentrating are primarily outside the Region. The Region's metropolitan areas are not attracting migrants to the extent that other such areas do, and most of the area's cities apparently are contributing to the outflow of migrants.

Rupert Vance has remarked that the South "has been understaffed with cities, and its metropolitan functions of organization and management have heretofore been performed outside the region."[9] If this

[8] C. E. Lively and Conrad Taeuber, *Rural Migration in the United States*, W. P. A. Research Monograph 19, 1939, p. 83.

[9] Rupert B. Vance, "The Sociological Implications of Southern Regionalism," *The Journal of Southern History*, XXVI, No. 1 (Feb., 1960), p. 50.

statement is true of the South as a whole, it is even more true of the Southern Appalachians. In all this vast expanse of territory only the Knoxville metropolitan area contains more than 300,000 people.

If one looks at a map showing metropolitan areas of the United States, the scarcity of such areas within

Figure 28. *Net Migration Rates, 1940-1950 and 1950-1960, for Groups of Southern Appalachian Counties Classified According to Farm Operator Level-of-Living Index, 1945 and 1954*

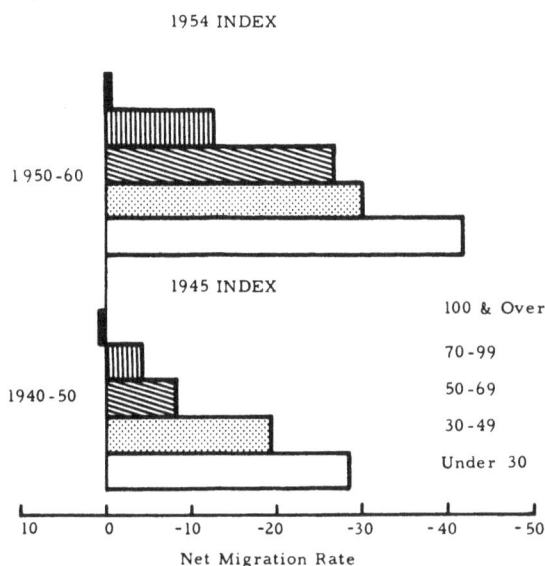

Source: Margaret Jarman Hagood, Gladys K. Bowles, and Robert R. Mount, Farm-Operator Family Level-of-Living Indexes for Counties of the United States 1945, 1950, 1954. U. S. Department of Agriculture, Agricultural Marketing Service Statistical Bulletin 204 (March, 1957).

the Southern Appalachian Region is immediately apparent, as is the "edging in" of surrounding urban areas toward the Region. This encroachment is particularly evident in the Piedmont Crescent of North Carolina, in Charlotte, in Birmingham, and even in Atlanta. Particularly important is the fact that the mountain migrants are moving out into the nearby metropolitan areas at the same time that these areas are literally moving to them. Such movements, of course, illustrate the observation—so often stressed in these pages—that the Southern Appalachian Region is a collection of fringes. The fringes are those of the metropolitan regions to which many Appalachian migrants go.

Only a few words are needed on the other aspect of rural-urban residence, since much of the migration of the farm population has been considered under socioeconomic factors. With the shift of population from rural to urban areas, the nation has experienced

a decrease in the farm population. This trend, also, is visible in the Region, but is less advanced than in the nation. The proportion of Appalachian population residing on farms was still approximately twice the national proportion in 1950 (30.4 percent as compared with 15.3 percent), despite a decline of almost half a million farm residents from the 2.2 million persons in the rural-farm category in 1940. As farm population decreases, farm residence inevitably will become less important as a determinant of migratory fluctuations. That it still exerts an influence has already been noted, but a careful examination of the evidence shows the growing importance of other influences.

The impact of national culture patterns on the Region has been cumulative. For example, the drop in births in the rural parts of the Region reflects both a trend toward smaller families and the migration of young adults. Migration thus has a double effect. It immediately removes a large number of persons, mostly in the young adult years, and it reduces the future population by the number of children such migrants would have had if they had not left.

The implications of such trends are plain, not only for the Region but for the cities to whose growth the Region has so generously contributed. To the extent that neighboring urban areas have "depended" for their population gains on Appalachian migrants, they will experience slower growth in the future. The rural seedbeds elsewhere in the nation, and particularly in the South, are also becoming depleted.[10] Urban birth trends are likely to be erratic in their fluctuations. Unless the cities develop radically different fertility patterns (which, incidentally, they are showing some signs of doing), the rate of urbanization will become markedly slower as rural population declines.

The first of the sociocultural factors, which may be treated rather briefly, is race. From the earliest settlement, almost all of the rural inhabitants of the Region have been white. The migration pattern of Negroes has differed fundamentally from that of whites, but since the Negro population constitutes so small a proportion of the total, discussion will be concerned with the white population.

A second factor to be considered is familism—a type of social organization in which the family is considered more important than either other social groups or the individual. Although familism is de-

[10] See T. Lynn Smith, *Fundamentals of Population Study* (New York, 1960), p. 461.

clining in the Region, its influence is still important. One aspect of this familism which is characteristic of the Southern Appalachians has been its very high fertility. The area is notable for the large proportion of children under fifteen in the total population. If many of them were to remain in the Region as adults, the population burden would rapidly become too great for the limited resources at the present level of economic development. Associated with, and perhaps a consequence of, this tendency toward overpopulation is the expectation that each person will leave the parental home and start his own family. This is, of course, the standard American pattern, but the fact that some sort of mobility is expected is one of the reasons why migration has been so heavy. When a strong population pressure already exists in such a system, a steady stream of out-migrants is to be expected.

The high degree of family solidarity and loyalty connected with the complex of familism have had considerable influence on migration in that the potential insecurity associated with leaving the area is lessened by the prospect of joining family members who have moved out earlier. Migration involves more than just a movement of people across the surface of the land. The integration of the migrants at the receiving end of the stream must also be considered. Much of the migration over the years has been the movement of younger members of the family to join older brothers and sisters or other relatives. Such a movement of family members joining other family members is undoubtedly one of the major reasons for the stability of the migration streams—for example, the stream from Eastern Kentucky to Southern Ohio.

The family promotes and facilitates migration, but it is chiefly through the educational system that young people become aware of opportunities in the outside world. The data show very clearly that migrants have completed relatively more years of schooling than is true for the Southern Appalachian population as a whole. Education via the schools has become a cultural bridge—and apparently the most effective bridge —between the mountain people and the national society.[11] One can expect a change in the migration pattern, however, as the educational level increases. Fewer migrants will be guided to destination areas primarily because family members are already located there, and migration will become more sensitive to the job market.

Another consideration which deserves more adequate treatment than can be given here is the influ-ence World Wars I and II and the Korean War have had in moving young men out of the region and in introducing them in many cases not only to American society but to the world at large. Of course, the heightened industrial activity of these periods probably increased the velocity of the migratory streams in general, but these recent wars not only increased movements in normal channels but also exerted a pull of more than usual force on the Region's young male population.

Summary and Conclusions

Regardless of the extent to which the Appalachians appear to have been separated from the main stream of American social and cultural development, they have become increasingly integrated—possibly re-integrated—into that stream. In this process of integration, migration has played an important role, and today the residents of the Region, in increasing numbers, are leaving their communities for places outside the Region. Furthermore, an increasing proportion of such persons are moving from mining and subsistence agricultural areas where the old social and cultural patterns have been especially persistent.

In attaining a summary view of this condition, one may conveniently return to the five basic questions asked at the beginning of the chapter: How many migrants were there? Where did they go? What were they like? Why did they move? And what does their migration mean? Our concern, however, is not as much with the first four questions as it is with the last. We will want to place most emphasis on the meaning behind the detailed observations that have been offered.

How many persons migrated? The basic answer is that more left than have been replaced, whether by in-migration or natural increase, and from all appearances this trend is likely to continue. This rather simple fact sets the stage for the remaining discussion.

Where did the migrants go? Many moved about within the Region, but significant numbers left. In general, the migrants both within the Region and outside it have gone to places, usually urban, where better opportunities were available—or at least where opportunities were thought to be better. Migrants from different parts of the Region went to different areas and to areas so widely scattered that much of

---

[11] Harry K. Schwarzweller and James S. Brown, "Education as a Cultural Bridge Between Rural and Urban Society," paper read before the annual meeting of the Rural Sociological Society, August, 1960.

the nation's population has been affected. (Almost 90 percent of the migrants went to states containing approximately 40 percent of the nation's population in 1950.) Thus, in the most immediate sense, the "Region's" problems are really local ones, in that its diverse parts are "back yards" to other regions. But in view of this involvement of other regions and because of the extensiveness of the Southern Appalachian Region itself, in a gross sense, the area's problems become national ones.

Who were the migrants? Single persons and young families, most of whom were better educated than those they left behind and not as well educated as those they settled among. Associated with these characteristics is a lack of technical skills.

The most apparent reason, the most obvious "why" of Appalachian migration has been economic. But there are other factors which appear with but little probing beneath the economic surface—factors of urbanization, family structure, education, and probably not least, mass communication. These other factors, by their influence on the people's interpretation of economic conditions, have made standards of living an important motivating factor for migration.

What does this migration mean for the future of the Region? A quarter of a century ago, another study of the Region maintained categorically that, in order to raise the level of living in the area, "appreciably large scale migration is necessary."[12] In effect, this is the course which the Appalachian peoples have taken since that time. The adjustment between the forces of sociocultural conditions, economic factors and population displacement will doubtless proceed. As time passes and the adjustment continues, the problems which have made the adjustment so apparent may well diminish, if only in the sense that there will probably be fewer persons to migrate. But until that state is reached, any damming of the migrant flow will have serious repercussions.

Throughout this chapter we have attempted to show the importance of differences among the Region's parts. We have indicated, for example, that the industrial variation among the areas was reflected clearly in net migration gains or losses. Any consideration of what will happen in the future must, then, take this Regional diversity into account. In the near future, the mining areas seem certain to have heavy losses through migration. With the present level of technological development in coal mining, the number of persons employed will not increase markedly even should there be unexpectedly great increases in

the demand for coal. These areas, however, are probably past the peak of greatest loss, both in numbers and rates. Here (primarily in West Virginia and Kentucky), acute distress is greatest now and will continue to be greatest for the foreseeable future.

These are, then, the prime "problem areas." This does not, however, mean that the average level of living of people in mining counties is the lowest in the Region. The families in the subsistence agriculture areas still have the lowest levels of living. And people from these areas will continue to move out as they have been doing for several decades, at varying but rather high rates, the fluctuation of the rate of loss being largely determined by the employment situation in industrial centers outside the Region.

The movement from the mining and subsistence agriculture areas has been great enough to be called depopulation. Such areas face serious consequences of adjustment as a result: how are local governmental services and school systems to be maintained and supported; how can the total institutional structure of these areas be reorganized so that people living there can have what Americans consider to be a good life? Indeed, it may even be pertinent to ask whether some counties can continue to be counties as they are now organized and whether some communities will continue to exist. There is nothing to indicate that there will be sufficient growth in industrial and service jobs to occupy even the present greatly reduced population, if we assume the goal of a level of living approximating the national average.

As has been said repeatedly, the Appalachian Region is not a system of closely interdependent parts but a collection of fringes of other systems which have some more or less common characteristics. More and more each of these fringes is being integrated into the particular system of which it is a part—for example, the Eastern Kentucky and the West Virginia counties with various metropolitan areas of the Midwest, the North Carolina counties with the Piedmont Crescent, etc. The patterns discussed in the section on directions of migration point to some of the systems to which Appalachian areas belong. If the population is being significantly depleted in certain areas (as in Kentucky and West Virginia), then one of the reservoirs for the population growth of the major metropolitan centers to which these areas are tied (e.g., Cincinnati, Colum-

[12] Carter Goodrich, et al., *Migration and Economic Opportunity: The Report of the Study of Population Redistribution* (Philadelphia, 1936), p. 77.

bus, Akron) is being drained and obviously this may affect the future growth of these centers. Further, the future composition of the population in these cities will continue to be affected by the composition of their migrant streams. Consequently, if the number of jobs for unskilled labor is declining in these metropolises, their dependent areas are going to be significantly affected, damming up the potential migration. The need for unskilled labor is decreasing and seems likely to decrease even more in the future. Accordingly, this makes the training of persons in these feeder-areas a crucial problem.

The problems arising from migration thus differ now in various parts of the Region and they can be expected to differ in the future. To a large extent, the focal points of change within the Region will be the metropolitan areas. These are among the few places to which migrants will go if they move to any great distance within the Region. Though the Region's metropolitan areas can be expected to grow in the future, their growth rate will be determined to a large extent by the effectiveness with which they compete with the more vigorous urban centers which surround it. The slowing of the growth rate of the Region's metropolitan areas over the last two decades is sug-

gestive in this connection. On the other hand, neither the subsistence farming areas nor the mining areas can hope to hold their natural increase, much less attract persons in large numbers from the outside. For these areas, a program of guided migration might well be a more realistic solution than an attempt to maintain an economic base compounded chiefly of large numbers in relative poverty.

In the final analysis, what needs to be developed is not the Region but the Region's people. Specifically, programs are needed to help the people prepare themselves for the modern world wherever they may live. And if they are like most Americans, they will move about a great deal. Indeed, the information in this chapter indicates that migrants from the Appalachians already move long distances and are moving further as time goes on. Preparing people for modern living of course means not merely putting opportunities for health and education in their reach but motivating them to take advantage of these opportunities. Certainly creative, experimental programs in these areas are essential, and, incidentally, such programs should teach us a good many things about the problems of the so-called underdeveloped countries of the world at large.

CHAPTER FIVE

Appalachian

Newcomers

in

Cincinnati

ROSCOE GIFFIN

ONE WAY OF EVALUATING HOW WELL families have adjusted to the demands of urban life is to study their participation in social activities. The accelerated flow of migrants from the Southern Appalachians—especially from rural areas—to northern cities within the past decade has made the experience of these newcomers in relation to schools, churches, industries, social welfare agencies, and other institutions a matter of increasing concern. Professional persons who work with new residents in such cities as Cincinnati, Cleveland, Chicago, Dayton, and Baltimore, have manifested their interest in numerous meetings and conferences held in recent years.

The present study was designed to determine by empirical means whether or not Southern Appalachian newcomers participate in the organizations of Cincinnati more or less frequently than do their neighbors of comparable social class. With the assistance of school officials, social workers, and police, five school districts were chosen which were believed to have fairly high concentrations of families from the Southern Appalachian Region. The districts were also selected with particular care to reflect a rather wide range of differences in social class. School officials provided access to the enrollment records of four elementary schools and one junior high school, from which the names of families to compose the sampling list were selected at random. The sample was limited, therefore, to families with at least one child in a grade below high school.

Information about each family was obtained through an interview, usually lasting about one hour, employing a questionnaire designed for the project. In classifying the families as to origin, we defined the Southern Appalachian Region in the same manner as for the other studies in this volume, except that a group of Kentucky counties on the western fringe of the region was included. Persons from these counties tend to think of themselves as being from the mountains and are so thought of in Cincinnati. Each household was assigned to the origin of its head, as determined by the state and county in which he spent most of the years before his sixteenth birthday. (In 75 percent of the couples, husband and wife were of the same origin.)

It is commonly said in Cincinnati that most of its newcomers are from the Southern Appalachian Region and that most of these come from Eastern Kentucky. This supposition seems substantiated by the present sample. Two-thirds of the husbands and an even larger proportion of wives came from the Region.

Of the 221 husbands and wives who came from the Southern Appalachian Region, 192 (87 percent) were from the mountains of Eastern Kentucky; only 73 of the 303 newcomer parents came from states other than Kentucky. The largest number of Eastern Ken-

Figure 29. *Selected Comparisons of Southern Appalachian Migrants and Other Residents of Three Sampling Areas of Cincinnati*

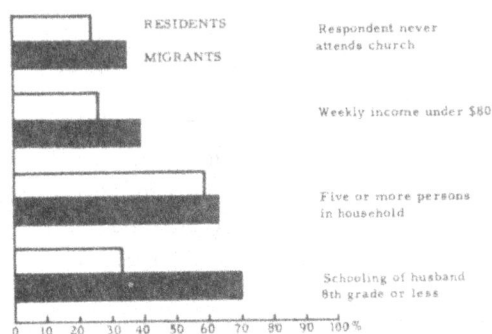

tuckians came from those counties which are not only the most populous but have been occupationally dominated by the coal mining industry. Eighty-four of the 192 Eastern Kentucky migrants were from Bell, Harlan, McCreary, Whitley, and Perry Counties. In only 61 (29 percent) of the 211 households was the husband a native of Cincinnati. Of the families who were not from the Southern Appalachians, the majority were natives of the Cincinnati area. The remainder were newcomers, most of them from the South.

An index of social class, based on the occupation of the head of the family, his schooling, and the quality of the family's housing as judged by the interviewer, was assigned to each household.[1] Seven social classes were thus identified; the Southern Appalachian families were found in smaller proportions at the upper class levels and in larger proportions at the lower levels than was true for the others. Among the Southern Appalachian families, only 28 percent were in the three highest status groups, but these three groups included 57 percent of the other families. The Southern Appalachian families, however, were more concentrated (72 percent) in the three middle groups than were the other families (56 percent). About 19 percent of the Southern Appalachian households and about 13 percent of other households were in the two lowest classes. Because of the small size of the sample, and in order to simplify reporting, the three highest status groups were combined as "higher class," and the four remaining groups were lumped together as

"lower class." Because none of the respondents in the present sample would be classified as "upper class" in a study which covered the entire range of variation in income, education, and housing to be found in Cincinnati, it should be understood that the terms "higher class" and "lower class" in this study refer only to comparative status within the sampling areas. Eighty of the 115 Southern Appalachian households were in the resulting lower-class group, and 33 in the higher class. Of the other 96 households, 40 were in the lower-class category and 55 in the upper-class. (Three families were omitted because of insufficient information.) The comparisons illustrated in Figure 29 confirm the impression that in terms of the dominant values in our society the Southern Appalachian migrants rank relatively low.

Since our sample was limited to families with school children, it clearly is not representative of persons in any other sort of family status. (Statistics in the foregoing chapter indicate, however, that families with young children are an important component of the migrant population.) Moreover, we deliberately sought to obtain a sizable proportion of higher-class families. It is probable that a larger proportion of the Southern Appalachian migrants than of the present sample are of lower-class status.

In the 211 households there were 1,141 persons. Five hundred lived in 121 households composed of three to five persons; 528 lived in 78 households of six to eight persons; the remaining 12 households of nine or more persons accounted for 113. The average of 5.4 persons per household is almost double that for the population of the corresponding census tracts in 1950.[2] This is not surprising, since all of the sample households had children in school—a selective factor which also accounts for the fact that there were only two women under 25 among the respondents, and that less than five percent of the adults were over 54. For those 25 or older, the median age was 36.9 as compared with 45.6 in the census tracts.

Other contrasts between the sample population and that of the census tracts may point to changes in the

[1] In constructing this system I have been guided primarily by: C. C. North and P. K. Hatt, "Jobs and Occupations: A Popular Evaluation" in Logan Wilson and W. L. Kolb, *Sociological Analysis* (New York, 1949), pp. 464-73; and J. A. Kahl and J. A. Davis, "A Comparison of Indexes of Socio-Economic Status," *American Sociological Review*, XX (1955), 317-325.

[2] All Census Tract data from: *Cincinnati, Ohio, Census Tracts*, 1950 U.S. Census of Population, Bulletin P-D11, U.S. Department of Commerce, Bureau of the Census, U.S. Government Printing Office, Washington (1952).

class composition of these areas of the city between 1950 and 1959. Although the adults of the sample average nearly nine years younger, the median of school years completed by the husbands and wives 25 and over in our sample exceeds by very little that of the whole population 25 and over in the 1950 census tracts: 9.0 years compared to 8.6. The Southern Appalachian migrants in the sample are better educated on the average than is characteristic of Eastern Kentucky adults. (As statistics in the foregoing chapter indicate, out-migrants from the region are somewhat better schooled than those they leave behind.) The median schooling for the Southern Appalachian migrants was 8.6 years, but none of the Eastern Kentucky counties, and only a few counties in the entire Region, registered medians as high as this in 1950. The occupational distributions for males in the sample and in the census tracts also appear to indicate a change in class composition: of those in the 1950 population 27 percent were professionals, managers, proprietors, clerks, or sales people; only 11 percent of the males in the sample were in these groups. Sixty-three percent of the sample group were craftsmen, foremen, and operatives, as against 58 percent in the 1950 census tracts. It is possible that professional, managerial, and proprietor males average so much older that many of them were excluded from the sample by the selection of families with school children.

In gathering data for our study, we found that a good way to open up an interview was to begin with questions about the children. Our first inquiry was as to the number of children in the family old enough to be in such organized activities as Boy Scouts, Girl Scouts, Boys' Club, city parks and playgrounds, community centers, church, and Sunday school. Then we sought to learn how frequently each child had participated in the programs of any of these agencies in the past year.

The differences between Southern Appalachian and other children within the two social-class divisions were too small to be considered significant.[3] Apparently there were no important cultural differences in the backgrounds of parents of the same social class such as to cause their children to differ in their frequency of participation in organized activities.

However, when the participation frequencies for the children were regrouped into the two social classes without regard to origin, we found the differences to be highly significant. A noticeably larger proportion (91 percent) of higher-class children were reported to participate "frequently" or "regularly" than was true of lower-class children (76 percent).

Respondents were next asked to choose among five statements indicating varying degrees of approval or disapproval of the organized programs in which their children might participate. Here again the responses showed no significant differences between the Appalachian migrants and the others. But when the data were grouped according to social class without consideration of origin it was evident that higher-class parents approve much more highly of organized activities for their children than do lower-class parents. More than half (52 percent) of the higher-class parents "strongly approve" such activities for their children, as compared with less than a third (32 percent) of lower-class parents. Fewer than one in ten (9 percent) of the higher-class parents, but 16 percent of the lower-class, "don't care" or "disapprove."

One further question on this subject did reveal significant differences between the Appalachian migrants and their neighbors of comparable status. We asked the parents, "Do you think your children would like to participate in programs of more organizations?" A large majority of the parents thought their children did not participate in as many programs as the children themselves would like, but considerably fewer Southern Appalachian than other parents thought their children wanted to participate more. The class differences on this question were appreciable, but within the lower-class group there was no significant difference between the Appalachian parents and the others. Appalachian parents of the higher classes, however, estimated much less interest on the part of their children in organized activities than did other parents of similar status—a judgment which possibly reflects the low levels of social participation among the adults of Southern Appalachian origin.

Tentative opinions based on personal observations and on the research of others suggested the next line of inquiry: Are Southern Appalachian parents more inclined than others to let their children go and come as they please? Do they tend to have a rather easy-going, permissive view about their children's

---

[3] To prepare the participation rate score for children of each family, we weighted the frequency responses on a scale from 5 to 0, multiplied each of the weights by the number of children indicated to have participated at a given frequency level, added the family's weighted frequencies and divided by the number of children in the household between ages of 5 and 18. We have used the chi-square method of testing for significant differences.

activities? Are they willing and able to help their children form contacts with external social groups by attending with them?

In roaming through the areas of Cincinnati in which many of the lower-status Appalachian migrants live, I have repeatedly noticed children of all ages out on the streets at almost any hour of day or night. For information on this subject, we asked the respondents what they knew about their children's activities when they were not at home, at school, or working. Within the lower class 75 percent of the parents of non-Appalachian origin stated that they always knew where their children were; but among Southern Appalachian newcomers of the same class, only 57 percent gave this answer, while 40 percent indicated they usually knew their children's whereabouts. Although this difference is significant, the higher-class parents were very much alike in the responses as to their knowledge of the whereabouts of their children. We are left, however, with some statistical support for the observation that lower-class parents are somewhat prone to let their children wander about the streets as they please. This is very probably a carryover from rural environments, where liberty to roam through the woods and fields is undoubtedly a source of considerable satisfaction and pleasurable experience for children. But such permissiveness may become dangerous neglect in a lower-status area of a modern city.

To determine whether this permissiveness might be manifested in other ways, several other questions were asked. One such question was how often in the past year a parent had taken any of the children to some city park, the zoo, or other outdoor area. For comparable social class groups, there was no evidence of any difference between Southern Appalachian newcomers and others in regard to these activities of parents and children. However, lower-class parents accompany their children to such places as parks considerably less often than do those of the higher classes. Fifty percent of the parents in the lower class stated that they had taken their children to the park four times or more in the previous year; but 68 percent of the higher-class parents had taken their children on such excursions as often as that in the previous year.

As another indicator of joint parent-child activities, we asked how often parents and children attended church together. No significant differences were found between Southern Appalachian newcomers and others within the two social class groups, but there was

a marked difference between social classes. Well over half (55 percent) of the higher-class parents reported that they often attended church with their children; of the lower-class parents 61 percent said they seldom or never did so.

Because of the strong emphasis laid on formal education today, it was thought likely that many Southern Appalachian migrants would voice high ambitions for their children's educational achievement (as was true in the attitude survey made within the Region, see Chapter II). We asked respondents to indicate the level of education at which they would be satisfied to have a son quit school, and followed this by the same question for a daughter. The responses did not differ noticeably between the origin categories, but there were distinct contrasts on the basis of social class. For example, 36 percent of the lower-class parents with sons would accept high school graduation or less for a son, but among the higher-class group only 17 percent would be satisfied with that accomplishment. On the average, higher levels are desired for boys than girls, and here also lower-class parents hold distinctly lower expectations. One might note parenthetically that, at present, educational statistics give little reason to believe that the desires of these parents will be achieved, for 70 percent of the parents desired more than a high-school education for the sons, though nationally little more than half of those who begin school finish high school.[4]

To get some indication as to how active an interest parents take in schools, we asked how frequently either parent had visited the school or discussed the school situation of a child with his teacher. Of the entire sample about 45 percent had visited twice or less during the past year. None of the differences among class or origin groups were significant. Teachers in northern urban schools have often reported their difficulties in getting Southern Appalachian newcomer parents interested in Parent-Teachers' Association activities. This we found to be true, but it was also true of other parents: more than half the parents of lower-class status, whether of Appalachian or other origin, indicated that neither husband nor wife ever attended PTA. Among parents of higher status, about a third of the Appalachian newcomers and about a fourth of the others never attended.

Asked how often they helped their children with school work, about two-thirds of the parents in all classifications indicated that they helped "often." An

4 U.S. Department of Commerce, *Statistical Abstract of the U.S.*, 1958, p. 125.

unexpected finding here was that there were no significant differences in response either by origin or social class.

It is common knowledge that the customs we follow and the choices we prefer are products to a great extent of early experiences. Among people of the Southern Appalachian Region early experience with organized groups have generally been very limited, so we would expect the Southern Appalachian migrants of Cincinnati to participate little in such activities. Interviewers asked each respondent to indicate how frequently during the previous year the husband or wife had attended meetings of such organizations as lodges, fraternities, veteran groups, labor unions, business or professional associations, women's clubs, neighborhood clubs, community centers, PTA, and recreation clubs. Scoring of the responses indicated that lower-class Appalachian migrants participated significantly less than others of similar status; those of higher status also had noticeably lower participation scores than did those of similar status but of non-Appalachian origin (though the latter difference was not statistically significant). Almost 74 percent of the Southern Appalachian parents were either non-participants or participated infrequently in these activities, whereas this was true of only 53 percent of the others. The comparison by social class also reveals a sharp contrast: 77 percent of the lower-class respondents were classified in the low or non-participant categories, compared to 47 percent of the upper class. The newcomers were also asked about their participation in such organizations before moving to Cincinnati. Out of 96 Southern Appalachian respondents who were old enough before migration to have had some such experiences, only 10 had scores indicating even a moderate amount of participation. Whatever their lack of background preparation, however, Southern Appalachian parents of the upper class did not differ significantly in this respect from others of comparable status.

Such agencies as the Ohio State Employment Service, Public Health Clinics, Cincinnati General Hospital, and the Hamilton County Department of Public Welfare offer services usually of direct and immediate benefit to the family. It is not surprising, then, that the families had more frequent contact with these agencies than with the membership organizations. No important differences were found in the use of any of these agencies by Southern Appalachian families and others of comparable social class, except in the case of the Cincinnati General Hospital, which

was used considerably more by the Appalachian migrants. As one would expect, the use of the Ohio State Employment Service was quite widely diffused through the population. The Public Welfare Department and the clinics were used much more by lower-class families.

From the responses to a question about frequency of church attendance, perhaps the most striking finding is the high proportion of respondents who never attend church. This was particularly true of the lower-class group, in which 41 percent of the Southern Appalachian migrants and 51 percent of the others reported never attending. The percentage attending once a week or more among the high-class group was 46 while among the lower-class it was only 20. Attendance "rarely" or "never" was reported by only 39 percent of the higher class in contrast to 62 percent of the lower class. The frequent lament that organized religion is not reaching the lower social classes in our society is well substantiated by these data from Cincinnati.

Numerous observers believe that when rural people, especially those from the South, move to northern cities, their well-established habits of church attendance go into a sharp decline. This belief is also substantiated by our data. We found that 60 percent of all the newcomers reported a decline in their church attendance after migration, and that those from the Southern Appalachians reported a significantly greater decrease than did those from elsewhere. Attendance by those of lower class status also went down significantly more than that of the higher status group following migration.

Differences in political participation appear to be associated with social class rather than with origin. For the entire sample, 60 percent of all husbands and wives stated they were registered voters; slightly less than half of the lower-class group were registered in contrast to 71 percent of the higher class. There were no significant differences between Southern Appalachian migrants and others of similar social status, and questions as to registration before migration did not reveal any significant changes. Of those who were registered, about 60 percent reported that they always vote; for those in the lower class this percentage drops to 44 and for those in the higher class goes up to 75. The voting behavior of Southern Appalachian migrants and others of comparable status is about the same.

This study has indicated relatively few significant differences in social participation between people of

Southern Appalachian origin and those of other origins. However, one difference of considerable importance was the finding that adults from the Southern Appalachians participate much less often in voluntary organizations such as lodges, unions, neighborhood clubs, and community center activities. Such organizations can perform important functions in helping newcomers to learn the ways of urban living and avail themselves of widened opportunities as well as to discharge some community responsibilities. But until such organizations can discover how to create more interest among Southern Appalachian newcomers, this means of urbanization will continue to be underutilized. Associated with this difficulty is the additional finding, so frequently documented by our data, that people of lower social status, whether they are from the mountains or elsewhere, are not as well adjusted to urban life as are persons of higher status, and that most Southern Appalachian newcomers are of below-average social class.

Lower-class families in our sample participate little in those organized groups whose purposes are not those of meeting immediate material needs—lodges, unions, neighborhood clubs, PTA—and make heavy demands on such organizations as Cincinnati General Hospital, public welfare agencies and public health clinics. The large number of children in these families in all likelihood resulted in a disproportionate burden on another public agency, the school system. Lower-class families also voted more seldom than others, and attended church less frequently; their children

had less contact with the organized activities which help in the socialization of children beyond the home and school—scouting, playground and community center programs, and church programs; and parents and children were less likely to attend church together or to take trips to parks, zoos, and special events which would provide the children with added opportunities for development.

Since a large proportion of the numerous Southern Appalachian newcomers in Cincinnati are among those of lower social class, we must certainly conclude that professional workers associated with schools, churches, business, recreation, law enforcement, health, and welfare have not been engaging in sheer fabrication in reporting them a problem group.

It is worth repeating that families of Southern Appalachian origin who have come from a social and cultural background which prepares them reasonably well for urban living are as well adjusted as their counterparts reared elsewhere. The problem phases of this rather extensive population shift spring largely from the inadequate social and economic development of the Region, and the lack of knowledge and resources for overcoming the resulting inadequacies of these people once they arrive in the city. One may go further and suggest that the present host of unresolved problems of the city, particularly in those areas where newcomers of lower status cluster, actually multiply and complicate the all-too-numerous inadequacies for urban living of the Southern Appalachian newcomers.

The Changing Economy

*T*HE GOAL *of a desirable balance between people and resources may be achieved in a variety of ways, but all involve changes in the population, or in the development of the resources, or both. In the preceding section, emphasis was placed on population changes in the Southern Appalachians. In this section, specialists discuss the more important economic resources in the Region, the present state of their development, and their developmental potential.*

Agriculture has been a traditional economic mainstay for many areas of the Region, even when supplementary sources of income were available. But the national agricultural revolution, involving a shift from subsistence to commercial operations, has lagged in the Southern Appalachians for a variety of reasons. Whether the Region can successfully compete against other sectors of the country more favored by topography and soil fertility is an issue of vital importance. In the first essay of the section, Roy E. Proctor and T. Kelley White analyze the current agricultural situation and appraise the potential contribution of agriculture to the future regional economy.

A second traditional source of income and employment in the Southern Appalachian economy lies in its coal, other minerals, and forests. In recent years, slackened demand for coal combined with increasing mechanization have created a major employment crisis in the coal mining areas of the Region. The outlook for forestry appears more promising, but authorities are not in agreement as to its economic potential. Harold A. Gibbard in the second essay discusses both the economic and social implications of current trends in extractive industry and forestry.

As agriculture, mining, and forestry have declined in economic importance, the people of the Southern Appalachians, as elsewhere, have increasingly looked toward the development of manufacturing industry to provide economic salvation. The extent to which industrial development has already taken place is evident in the fact that more Southern Appalachian workers are now gainfully employed in manufacturing than in agriculture, forestry, and mining combined. Charles L. Quittmeyer and Lorin A. Thompson trace the past development of manufacturing in the Region and analyze the factors that appear most likely to influence its future progress.

Much of the mountain area that is lacking in other resources possesses a rare natural beauty that is likely to become an even more precious commodity as metropolitan sprawl threatens to engulf the nation. The possibility of economically exploiting this aesthetic and recreational resource has captured the imagination of nearly all who have sought to solve the problems of the Region. In the final essay of this section, John W. Morris describes many of the existing tourist attractions—and detractions—and specifies what must be done if the high hopes now held for a productive tourist industry are to be realized.

CHAPTER SIX

Agriculture: A Reassessment

ROY E. PROCTOR

T. KELLEY WHITE

SOUTHERN APPALACHIAN AGRICULTURE is describable as a situation resulting from too few resources being divided among too many people. The low income status of the average farmer of this region cannot be attributed to a low level of productivity of the resources, other than labor, used in agriculture; it must, instead, be attributed to the fact that the Region's agricultural resources are inadequate to support the present density of farm population.

The lack of agricultural resources, especially land suitable for farming, is evidenced by the average size of farms in the Appalachians. The average farm in the Appalachians, when compared with the average farm in the seven states or with the whole United States, is smaller both in total land area and in cropland and harvested cropland. Not only is there a shortage of cropland, but the uneven topography results in division of the cropland available into such small fields that efficient use of modern machinery is impossible. Though partially offset by higher yields of most crops and more emphasis on livestock production, these factors have resulted in an agriculture characterized by small, low-income farm units.

Whenever population pressure exists in an area, changes take place commensurate with the aptitudes of the people. One of the adjustments made from 1930 to 1950 was for some of the farm population to leave agriculture as an occupation. Even though total population of the Southern Appalachian Area increased approximately 18 percent during this 20 year period, the rural farm population decreased approximately 14 percent. A much greater change occurred in the United States, with the total population increasing 23.4 percent and the farm population decreasing 20.3 percent. The remaining farm population in the Appalachians has moved into off-farm employment to supplement the farm income at about the same rate as has the farm population of the seven Appalachian states. However, from 1949 to 1954 there was a much greater shift of farm operators into the classification having "other income greater than farm sales." Nearly half of the Appalachian farms were so classified in 1954; in the seven-state area the proportion of farms so classified remained at one-third.

Those farmers who have continued as full-time operators have increased the acres per farm and particularly, where feasible, the acres in intensive crops such as tobacco and vegetables. They have converted much of the more rolling land to improved pastures so as to increase greatly the income from cattle. On the well-lying cropland, improved seed selection and cultural practices, greater use of fertilizers, and more mechanization have provided increased yields per acre far exceeding that of the adjacent areas. As a consequence, the economic gap between the agriculture

Table 19. *Percentage of Land in Farmland, by Classification and Use, Southern Appalachian Region and the United States, 1954*

Land classification and use	Percentage of all land	
	SAR	US
Cropland		
Harvested	9.1	17.5
Used for pasture only	5.1	3.5
Other	3.0	3.1
	17.2	24.1
Woodland		
Pastured	7.1	6.4
Not pastured	15.0	4.0
	22.1	10.4
Other land		
Pastured	10.2	24.1
Miscellaneous	1.1	2.2
	11.3	26.3
Total Farmland	50.6	60.8

Source: U. S. Census of Agriculture, 1954.

of the Appalachians and that of the seven states seems to be narrowing somewhat.

In the following description of the Region's agriculture, changes are shown by comparing data from the agricultural censuses of 1930, 1950, and 1954. In order to give perspective to differences within the Appalachians and to changes between census years, many comparisons are made between the Appalachians and the seven states in which they are located.

Land Classification and Use

The total land area of the 190 counties comprising the Southern Appalachians is 51.5 million acres, which is less than 3 percent of the U.S. area. Approximately one-half (50.6 percent) of this land was in farms in 1954, but this does not mean that half of the land was suitable for growing crops, or even for producing livestock. As a matter of fact, only about 17 percent of the land was classified as cropland by the census in 1954. Other land in farms was classified as woodland, pasture not cropland and not woodland, and miscellaneous land (Table 19). According to census definition, cropland included orchards, vineyards, and much land actually used as pastures; woodland included wood lots, timber tracts, and cutover land with young trees which have or will have value for timber; pasture other than cropland and woodland was made up largely of rough and

brush land which was pastured. Cropland, then, included not only land used for crop production but also most of the land which was at all suitable for crop production.

Cropland totaled 8.9 million acres, or 34 percent of all land in farms. However, 30 percent of this cropland was used only for pasture, and 17 percent was idle cropland, land in soil-improvement crops, and land on which crops had failed, leaving only 53 percent of the cropland actually harvested.

The remaining 66 percent of land in farms was composed of woodland, 44 percent; pastureland other than woodland and cropland, about 20 percent; and miscellaneous land, 2 percent. Approximately one-third of the farm woodland was pastured. This woodland pasture was almost one-third of the total land pastured. Cropland used only for pasture accounted for slightly over one-fifth of all pasture, and the remaining half was land which was neither cropland nor woodland.

Topography seems to be a major factor causing differences in land classification and use. The two state economic areas of North Georgia (Figure 3) are located adjacent to each other and have approximately the same total land area. However, the western part, Area 1, is located in the limestone hills and valley region, and 62 percent of its land is in farms; Area 2, the Blue Ridge, is located in the mountainous region with a much rougher topography and has only 40 percent of its land in farms.

The land use patterns of the Southern Appalachians are more meaningful when compared with those of the seven states in which the area lies, or with the total of 48 states (Figure 30). A smaller proportion of the total land area (51 percent) is in farms in the Appalachians than in the seven states (62 percent) or in the 48 states (61 percent). This difference may be explained by the relatively larger percentage of land in the Appalachians totally unsuited by its topography for any agricultural production except forest. Not only is a smaller part of the total land area in farms, but less of the farmland is cropland and more of the farmland is used as woodland. Cropland in the Region is fertile and well watered, so that it tends to be very productive in small plots. Because much of the land is characterized by severe slope, the Region has a higher percentage of pasture than the seven-state average, but a much lower percentage of pasture than the whole United States, where so much of the area is too poorly watered for cropland.

The percentage of total land which was in farms in 1954, and the distribution of this farmland by use, varied greatly among the areas of the Appalachians. The percentage of total land in farms ranged from a low of 20.6 percent in the Southern Coal Fields (Area

Figure 30. *Percentage of Total Land Area in Farms, Showing Farmland Use, in the Southern Appalachian Region, the Seven-State Appalachian Area, and the United States, 1954*

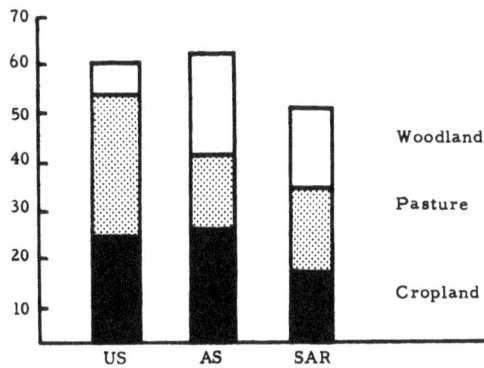

Source: U. S. Census of Agriculture, 1954

4) of West Virginia to a high of 72.3 percent in the Sand Mountain area (Area 2) of Alabama. Twelve of 21 economic areas[1] had more than one-half of the total land area in farms.

Cropland as a percentage of land in farms varied from a high of 51.2 percent in the three most eastern counties (Area 6) of West Virginia to a low of 17.6 percent in the Blue Ridge (Area 2) of Georgia. The proportion of farmland used for pasture also varied widely among the areas, from a low of 16.6 percent in the Georgia Blue Ridge to 61.0 percent in the Northwest counties (Upper Monongahela Valley) of West Virginia.

Changes in land use between 1930 and 1954 have been considerable and appear to have been fairly constant in direction while moving at an increasing rate. In general the trend has been toward using less of the total land in farms, with a smaller percentage of farmland being harvested cropland, and a larger percentage being pasture (Table 20). These changes in land use are the result of several factors, including the movement of people out of farming as more employment opportunities have become available within the Appalachians as well as outside; increased demand for land for non-agricultural uses; and shifting of poorer land into uses other than crop production.

There has been a slow change in farm sizes in the Southern Appalachians. In 1954, there were approxi-

mately 320,900 farms in the Region, 12.1 percent fewer farms than reported by the 1950 census (365,100) and 10.5 percent fewer than were reported in 1930. This is in contrast to a reduction of about 24 percent in the number of farms in the nation during the period 1930-54. All state economic areas in the Southern Appalachians showed a decrease in number of farms between 1950 and 1954, with the Central Cumberland Plateau of Tennessee (the nine counties west and north of Chattanooga) having the greatest decrease, 20.6 percent, while Eastern Panhandle of West Virginia (the three most eastern counties) had a decrease of only 2.7 percent. The latter area has had larger farms for many years. There was no appreciable difference between the relative change in number of farms in the Appalachians and in the seven contiguous states.

The average Southern Appalachian farm in 1954 was 81 acres in size and had 15 acres of harvested cropland, plus 4 acres of idle cropland; 36 acres was in pasture, and 26 acres in woodland. Farms in the U. S. averaged 242 acres in size with 40 percent (or 97 acres) of this being cropland. The average farm in the seven contiguous states was 100 acres in size and had 41 acres of cropland, 26 acres of pasture land, and 33 acres of woodland.

There was considerable variation among the counties in average farm size (Figure 31). The two extremes in average size were 164 acres per farm for a group of counties in Northeast West Virginia along the Virginia border and adjacent counties in Virginia, to a low of 55 acres in the very rugged area of Southwest West Virginia and south through Eastern Tennessee and Western North Carolina. The extremely small farms are located in areas of narrow valleys, while the larger farms tend to be associated with the broader valleys between mountains.

In contrast to the small average size of farms in the Appalachians, there were a few large farms, some of which contained more than 1,000 acres. Less than 2 percent of all farms were 500 acres or more in size, but over one-half of all farms were less than 50 acres in size.

Farm Capital and Income

Land area is only one measure of farm size; another measure which may be used is farm capital. Either of these measures is useful in itself, but the two are more meaningful when combined, just as land is more

[1] 19 state economic areas plus Cabell and Wayne counties in West Virginia, which are here treated separately.

THE SOUTHERN APPALACHIANS

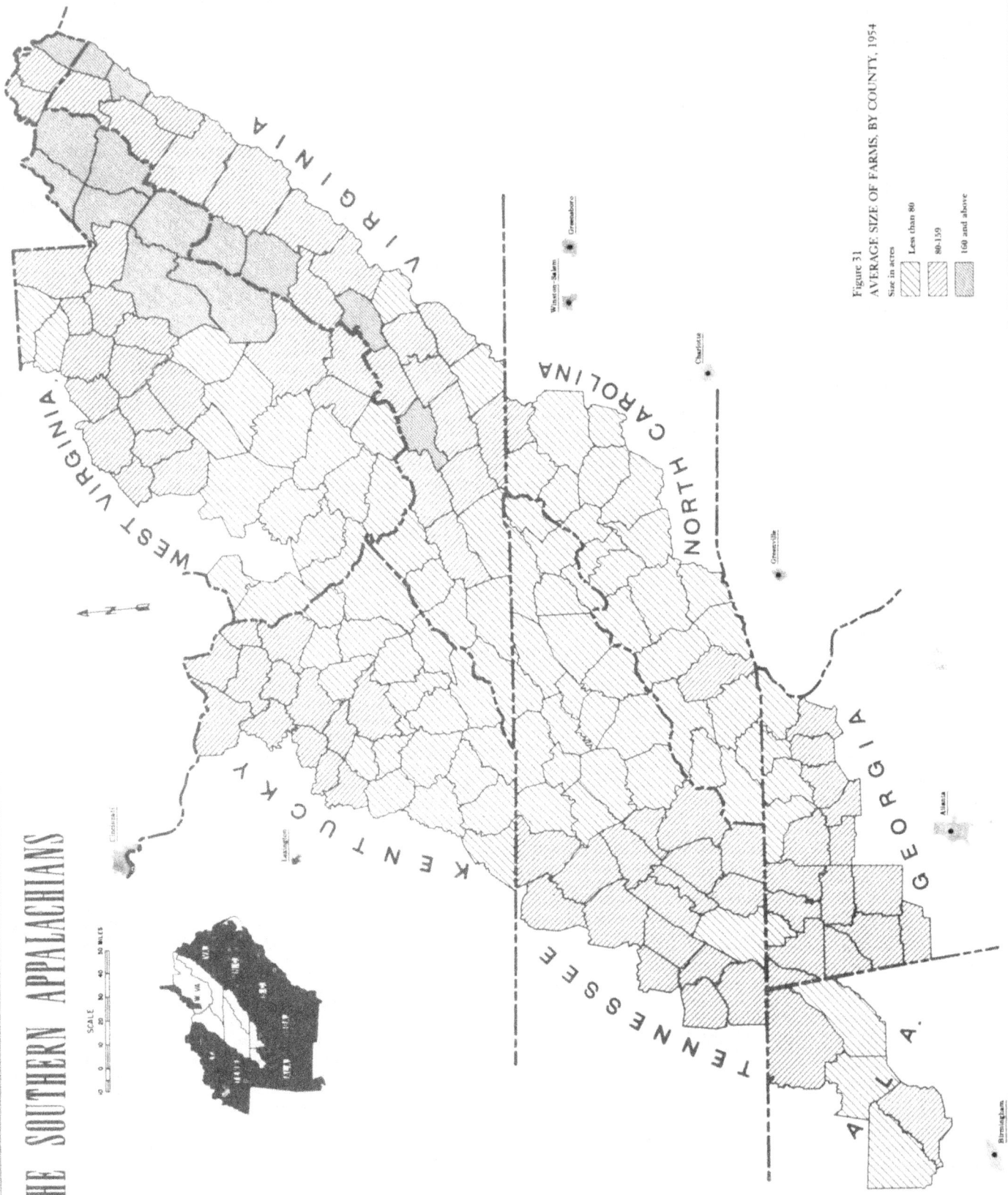

Figure 31
AVERAGE SIZE OF FARMS, BY COUNTY, 1954

Size in acres
Less than 80
80-159
160 and above

THE SOUTHERN APPALACHIANS

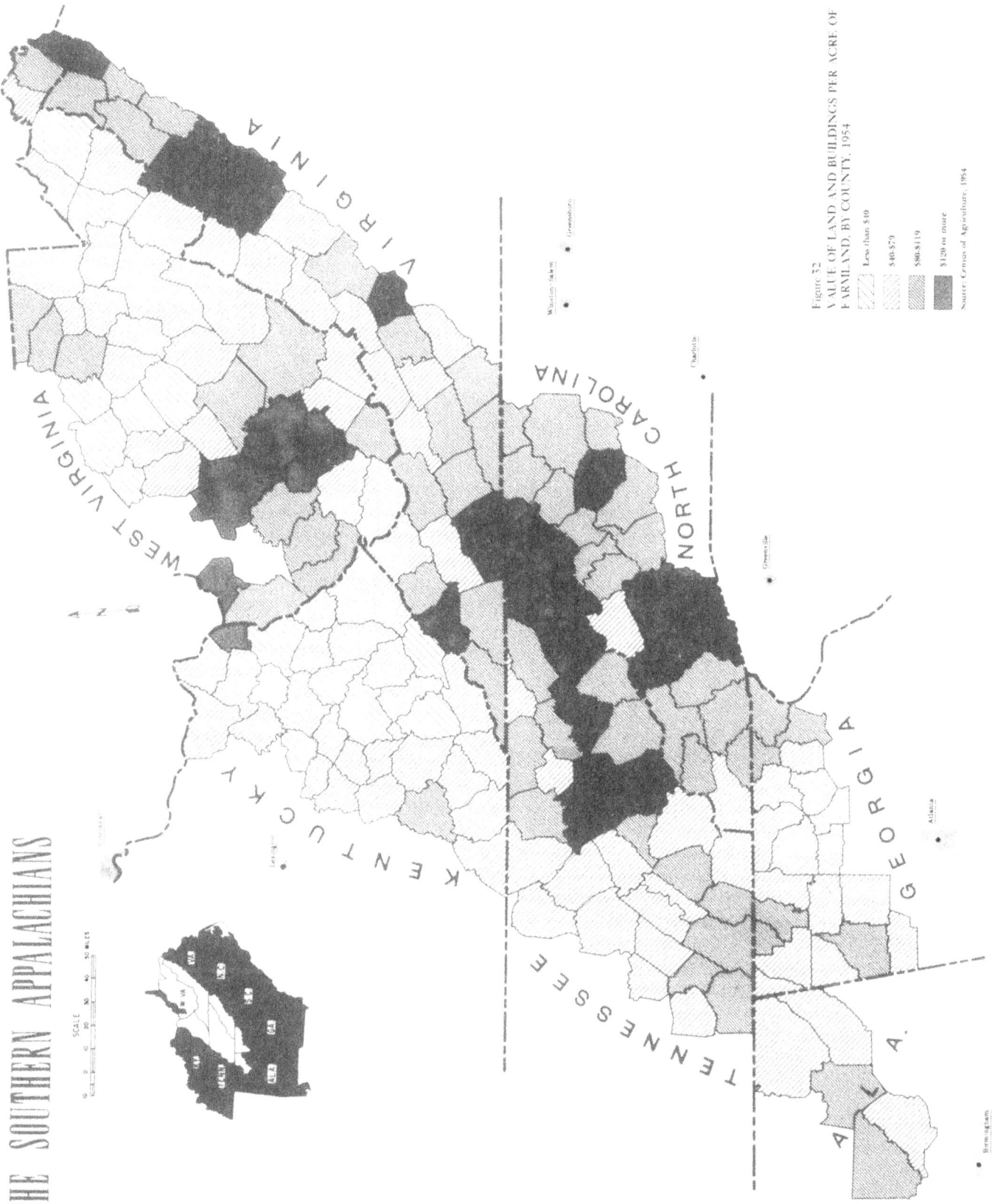

Figure 32

VALUE OF LAND AND BUILDINGS PER ACRE OF
FARMLAND, BY COUNTY, 1954

Less than $40

$40-$79

$80-$119

$120 or more

Source: Census of Agriculture, 1954

SCALE

WEST VIRGINIA

VIRGINIA

KENTUCKY

TENNESSEE

NORTH CAROLINA

GEORGIA

ALA.

useful to the farmer if he has adequate capital with which to utilize the land properly. Farm capital is defined here as the dollar value of land, buildings, equipment, livestock, and all of the other things needed in a farm business. Value of capital items

livestock, including horses and mules, cattle and calves, hogs and pigs, and chickens four months old and older.

Trucks were reported by a third of the farms in the Appalachians, making them the most frequently

Table 20. *Farmland and Farmland Use in the Southern Appalachian Region, 1930, 1950, 1954*

	Farmland		Percentage of farmland			
	Acres (thousands)	Percentage all land	Harvested	Pastured	In woodland	Other Use
1954	26,054.6	50.6	18.1	44.3	31.7	5.9
1950	28,346.6	55.1	19.9	40.8	33.9	5.4
1930	29,902.8	58.3	23.5	37.6	32.4	6.5

Source: U. S. Census of Agriculture, 1954.

was reported for land and buildings only in the 1950 and 1954 censuses of agriculture. However, numbers of other capital items on farms were reported without statement of money value, and give an indication of total farm capital and the movement toward more livestock and machinery.

The value of land and buildings *per acre* was somewhat higher in the Southern Appalachians than in the seven states. Though the buildings are somewhat better outside the mountain area, the greater number of buildings per 1000 acres of farmland raises the per acre valuation in the Southern Appalachians. In 1954, the average value per acre for land and buildings was $92.36 in the Appalachians and $85.75 in the seven states. Variation in land value within the Appalachians is shown in Figure 32. This map should be compared with Figure 31, to see that higher values per acre are related to small-farm areas. However, a few counties in the extreme northeast section of the area have high value and larger farms because of excellent crop production. The average value of land and buildings in the Appalachians was $7500 per farm as compared to $8549 for the average farm in the seven states. Value of land and buildings per farm increased 108 percent between 1930 and 1954 and 19 percent between 1950 and 1954 in the Appalachians.

Capital items possessed by farms in the Southern Appalachians can be grouped as: (1) machinery and equipment used primarily in the farm business, such as tractors, trucks, milking machines, corn pickers, pick-up balers, and combines; (2) machinery, equipment, and utilities which may be used in the farm business, but are primarily used by the farm family for use other than farm business, such as automobiles, running water, electricity, and telephones; and (3)

reported item of farm machinery (Table 21). Tractors on 22.9 percent of farms were the second most frequently reported item of machinery. Note that nearly half of the farmers had automobiles and running water. However, only a quarter had telephones and only 1 to 3 percent had specialized equipment such as milkers and harvesters. Less than 4 percent of the farms reported ownership of milking machines, corn pickers, pick-up balers, and combines. In the seven states, a larger percentage than in the Appalachians reported each of the six items of machinery.

Automobiles, running water, electric apparatus and telephones, in addition to being items of farm capital, are also considered indicators of the farm-family's level of living. The percentage of farms reporting these items in 1954 ranged from 22 percent with telephones to 92 percent reporting electric power, as shown in Table 21. The increase from 1950 to 1954 in percentage of farms reporting electricity and running water was rather impressive. Farms reporting running water increased from 17 percent in 1950 to 44 percent in 1954, and the percentage of farms reporting electricity increased from 74 percent to 92 percent during the same period.

All livestock items, except horses and mules, were reported by more than half of the farms. Two of these types of livestock (cattle and chickens) were reported by a larger percentage of farms in the Appalachians than in the seven states while for hogs and horses or mules the reverse was true.

Though horses and mules are grouped with the other types of farm livestock, they serve a distinctly different purpose and, along with tractors, should be considered farm work-power. The proportion of farms in the Appalachians and in the seven-state area possessing various combinations of work-power in 1950 and 1954 is shown in Figure 33. There has been an increase in farms without any work-power, but a great decrease in farms possessing horse power without tractors.

Farms were classified by the census on the basis of gross farm sales as "commercial farms" and "other

Table 21. *Capital Items on Southern Appalachian Farms, 1954*

Capital items	Average number per 100 farms	Percent of farms reporting
Tractors	26.3	22.9
Trucks	36.4	33.4
Milking machines	--	2.9
Corn pickers	1.1	1.1
Pick-up balers	3.2	3.2
Combines	1.8	1.8
Automobiles	51.3	45.4
Running water	--	43.7
Electricity	--	92.0
Telephones	--	22.4
Horses and mules	80.0	48.0
Cattle and calves	709.0	84.4
Hogs and pigs	276.0	60.2
Chickens 4 months old and over	4,293.0	78.7

Source: U. S. Census of Agriculture, 1954.

farms." In general, farms with gross sales valued at $1,200 or more were classified as commercial. A few farms with gross sales of $250 to $1,199 were also classified as commercial if the operator worked off the farm less than 100 days. If the operator of a farm with gross sales of $250 to $1,199 worked off the farm more than 100 days or if his nonfarm income exceeded the value of farm products sold, his farm was classified as a part-time farm. All farms with total value of farm products sold of less than $250, except abnormal farms, were classified as residential farms. (Those farms classified as abnormal include public and private institutional farms, community enterprises, experiment station farms, grazing associations, etc.)

For commercial farms, four types of tenure were reported. Full owners owned all the land they operated; part owners owned some land and rented land from others; managers operated farms owned by others and were paid wages or salaries; and tenants rented or worked on shares all the land they operated. Nearly two-thirds of all farms and all farmland in the Region were occupied by full owners (Table 22). These farms contained fewer acres than the part-owner farms. The manager-operated farms were very few but very large. Notice that for the United States more of the total farmland was occupied by part-owners, managers, and tenants and that the tenant farms were much larger in acres.

The tenure characteristics, especially tenancy, can be related to several factors, including the following: (1) the topography is not conducive to large holdings and multiple-unit operations which are usually associated with tenancy; (2) ownership of farms is usually passed down by inheritance so that few farmers have to get their start by renting; (3) farm enterprises common to the Appalachians are not well suited to cropper operation of farms; and (4) the subsistence type of agriculture, which is more common in the Appalachians, is usually associated with owner operation rather than tenant operation. Full-owner, part-owner, and manager-operated farms were larger in size in the seven states than in the Appalachians. Tenant-operated farms in the Appalachians tend to be entire farms rented as units, rather than multiple-unit operations, commonly found outside the mountains. Tenancy is rarest in the Northeastern section where no cotton or tobacco is grown. In 1930, 29.3 percent of all Appalachian farms were operated by tenants. By 1950 these had declined to 15.4 percent, and in 1954 only 13.5 percent of farms were operated by tenants. This reduction indicates a great exodus of non-owners, and shows clearly that farmers do not wish to divide a low income among many workers.

Commercial farms were further subdivided into six classes on the basis of annual farm sales. The distribution of commercial farms and land in commercial farms among these classes may be seen in Table 23. The farms in the three higher-sales classes account for a larger share of farm land than of numbers of farms, while the inverse is true of the three lower-sales classes. More than 70 percent of the farms had less than $2,500 gross sales per year in 1954. Only 58 percent of commercial farms in the seven-state area and 32 percent of the nation's commercial farms had gross sales so low.

If the class VI commercial farms are combined with the part-time and residential farms we find that 75 percent of the farms in the Southern Appalachians had gross annual sales valued at less than $1200.

Not only did 75 percent of all farms in the Appalachians have farm sales of less than $1200, but those farms classified as residential, 41.6 percent of all farms, had farm sales valued at less than $250 per farm. This is not to imply that three-fourths of the farm families had incomes of less than $1200, because all part-time farms either had operators who worked off the farm more than 100 days, or they and members of their families earned other income greater than the value of farm products sold. The distribution of farms in this low-income group, other than the part-time farms, is shown in Figure 34, which indicates the dominance of subsistence agriculture in large parts of the Region.

In contrast to these low income farms, 12.5 percent of the farms classified as commercial, or 5.1 percent

Figure 33. *Percentage of Farms by Type of Farm Work-Power in the Southern Appalachian Region and the Seven-State Appalachian Area, 1950 and 1954*

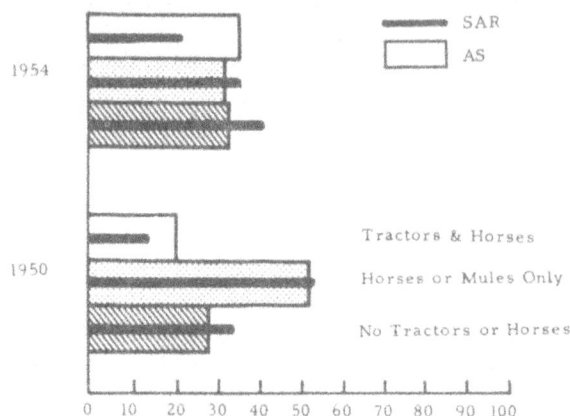

Source: U. S. Census of Agriculture, 1950 and 1954

of all farms, had farm sales which were valued at $5,000 or more.

The value of all farm products sold by farmers in the Southern Appalachians in 1954 was $1267 per farm. This was an increase of 20.6 percent over the value of gross farm sales in 1950. Not only have there been changes in total value of farm products sold, but there have been changes in the relative importance of crop, livestock, and forest production as sources of gross farm sales. The relative importance of these three sources of farm sales for three census years are shown in Figure 31. Here we find another major difference between the agriculture of the Southern Appalachians and that of the seven states. Whereas, in 1954, livestock accounted for almost two-thirds of all farm sales in the Appalachians, livestock accounted for only 30 percent in the seven-state totals. Much of the greater emphasis on livestock production in the Appalachians is due to the lack of sufficient land suitable for crop production. However, a few counties in East-Central Kentucky, North Alabama and North-East Tennessee had such emphasis on intensive row crops (mostly tobacco or cotton) that crop sales were greater than livestock sales. This is the area of high tenancy. Notice, also, in Figure 35 that sales of forest products as a proportion of all sales have declined very much since 1930. This is due to depletion of forest and addition of livestock.

The average value of all farm products sold per farm in the Appalachians ($1267) in 1954, however, was only 56.6 percent as great as the average value of all farm products sold per farm in the seven states, where the average was $2242, and was only 25 percent of the average value per farm in the United States, where the average was $5153 per farm. This difference was even greater in 1950 when the average value of gross farm sales in the Appalachians was only 54 percent of the seven-state average.

However, the difference between the Appalachians and the seven states is somewhat less per acre than per farm. In 1954 the value of all farm products sold per acre of farm land was $15.70 in the Appalachians, $22.49 in the seven states and $21 in the United States. In other words, an acre of farmland in the Appalachians produced 70 percent as much in value of farm products sold as did an acre of farmland in the seven states as a whole. Value of farm products sold per acre of farmland varied greatly within the Appalachians. The Eastern Kentucky Coal Fields (Area 9) had the lowest value per acre with $3.66 and the Shenandoah Valley of Virginia (Area 4) had the highest value with an average of $51.30 per acre. In general, the areas with high values per acre were either poultry-producing areas or areas producing specialty crops such as tobacco, truck crops, and fruits (see Figure 36). The counties near mining operations have high concentrations of subsistence farms, and counties which have intensive crops or poultry have higher sales per acre.

The value of gross farm sales is of little importance to the farm operator except as a measure of farm-business volume. The difference between gross sales and farm expenditures is what determines the economic well-being of the operator and his family.

The census of 1954 did not report total farm expenditures but did report five of the more important expenditures. These five specified expenditures provide an indication of the relationship of expenditures to gross sales. The five specified expenditures reported by the 1954 census were for hired labor, machine hire, feed for livestock and poultry, fuel and oil products, and fertilizer and liming materials. Expenditures for hired labor included only cash payments, excluding payments for hired housework, custom work, and contract construction work. Expenditures for machine hire included all custom machine work and labor involved in the cost of the machine hire. Expenditures for feed included cash expenses for pasture, salt, concentrates, and mineral supplements; as well as those for grain, hay and mill feed, and for grinding and mixing feeds. Expenditures for fuel and oil products included only those used for the farm business. Expenditures for fertilizer and lime included only commercial fertilizer or fertil-

Table 22. *Tenure of Commercial Farms and Average Size of Farms by Tenure, Southern Appalachian Region and the United States, 1954*

Tenure of operator	Percentage of farms		Percentage of land		Average size (acres)	
	SAR	US	SAR	US	SAR	US
Full owners	65.1	57.4	67.0	34.2	128	130
Part owners	17.7	18.2	20.8	40.6	144	520
Managers	0.4	0.4	2.4	8.6	736	580
Tenants	16.8	24.0	9.8	16.6	72	175

Source: U. S. Census of Agriculture, 1954.

izing material. These five expenditure items comprise a very large portion of the total production cost on most farms. They do not include costs of ownership of any capital items or land such as interest, taxes, repairs, or replacement. The proportion of total farm expenditures included in these five items is not the same for all types of farms. For example, on a poultry farm, the major items of expense are feed, fuel, and hired labor, all three of which are included; while on a feed-lot operation one of the major items of expense, purchases of livestock, is not included in the five specified items.

The cost of feed was more than half of all cash expenditures (Table 24). Hired labor and fertilizer were the next in importance. When these five major expense items of $710 were subtracted from the sale of farm products ($1,267) the net return was only $557. This amount was left for paying interest, taxes, buying replacement livestock, and for family living.

When expressed in terms of dollars per acre of farmland, net income above these specified expenditures amounted to an average of $6.86 per acre in the Appalachians in 1954, in contrast to the average gross value of products sold per acre of farmland of $15.70 in the same year. The net above specified expenditures ranged from a high of $29.47 per acre in the Eastern Panhandle of West Virginia to a low of $0.06 per acre in Wayne County of the same state. The difference between gross sales and net above specified expenditures was greatest in areas that were heavily dependent on poultry for farm sales. In contrast to the Appalachians, net returns above specified expenditures for all farms in the United States were 62 per-

cent of the gross sales. This was an average net return of $3,200 per farm or $13 per acre of farm land.

As would be expected in a region having low income from farming, the percentage of farm operators working off the farm and having income from sources

Table 23. *Commercial Farms by Economic Class, Southern Appalachian Region, 1954*

Class	Gross annual sales	Percent of all commercial farms	Percent of all land in commercial farms
I	$25,000 and over	1.3	5.7
II	10,000 - 24,999	4.1	9.4
III	5,000 - 9,999	7.1	12.5
		12.5	27.6
IV	2,500 - 4,999	15.7	20.2
V	1,200 - 2,499	33.2	28.3
VI	250 - 1,199	38.6	23.9
		87.5	72.4

Source: U. S. Census of Agriculture, 1954.

other than the farm business is high in the Appalachians (Table 25). The percentage of operators working off-farm increased from 48.7 to 53.6 between 1950 and 1954, and the percent working off-farm 100 days or more increased from 34.6 to 38.0. The percentage having income from other sources greater than farm sales decreased slightly from 48.9 to 45.7 between 1950 and 1954. This condition is mostly due to increased employment opportunities and to greater need for cash income. The percentage of operators reporting these circumstances in 1954 was higher in the Appalachians than in the seven-state area, where 33.7 percent reported other income greater than farm sales; 45.9 percent were working off the farm; and 29.2 percent working off the farm 100 days or more.

All three circumstances (other income greater than farm sales, off-farm work, and 100 days or more off-farm work) were reported by a greater percentage of part-time farm operators than of either commercial or residential farm operators. Regular commercial farms do not emphasize a great amount of work off the farm while part-time farmers and residential farmers do not emphasize farming. But almost one-third of the residential farm operators (who by definition must have gross farm sales valued at less than $250) did not have other income greater than farm sales; approximately one-third did not work off the farm at all; and only one-half worked off the farm 100 days or more. This means that at least one-third (or about 44,000) operators of Southern Appalachian residential farms had a total annual income of less than $500 each.

THE SOUTHERN APPALACHIANS

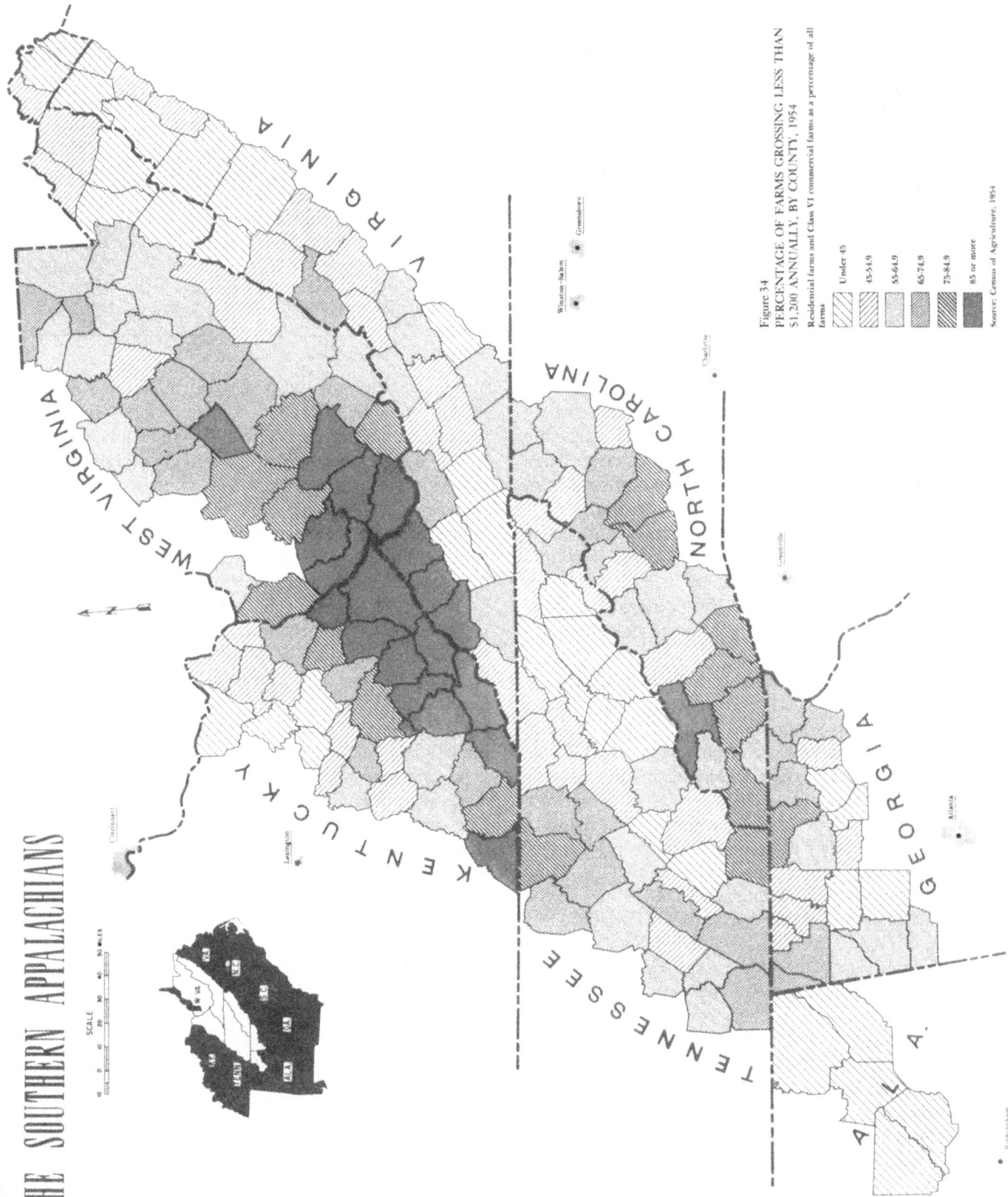

SCALE
10 0 10   20   30   40   50 MILES

Cincinnati

Lexington

K E N T U C K Y

W E S T   V I R G I N I A

V I R G I N I A

V I R G I N I A

Charleston

T E N N E S S E E

N O R T H   C A R O L I N A

Greenville

Greensboro

Winston-Salem

Charlotte

G E O R G I A

A L A.

Atlanta

Birmingham

Figure 34
PERCENTAGE OF FARMS GROSSING LESS THAN
$1,200 ANNUALLY, BY COUNTY, 1954
Residential farms and Class VI commercial farms as a percentage of all
farms

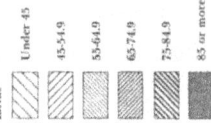

Under 45
45-54.9
55-64.9
65-74.9
75-84.9
85 or more

Source: Census of Agriculture, 1954

Livestock and Crop Production

The agriculture of the Southern Appalachians is based primarily on livestock production. Livestock and livestock products in 1954 constituted 62 percent

Figure 35. *Value Per Farm of Farm Products Sold, by Source, Southern Appalachian Region, 1954*

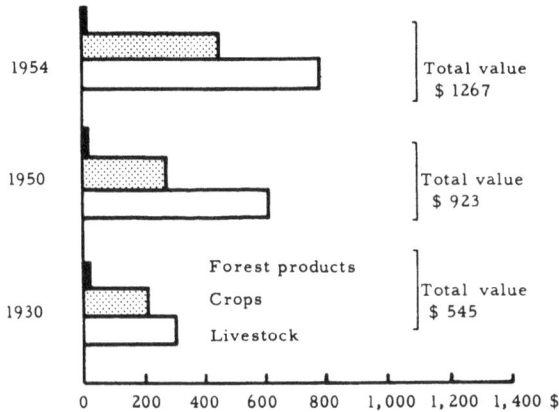

Source: U. S. Census of Agriculture, 1954

of total gross sales by farmers, and livestock and poultry feed accounted for 57 percent of specified farm expenditures reported by the census. A larger part of farmland (34 percent) was used for pasture than for any other use. In comparison, only 18 percent of all farmland was used for harvested crops as compared to 30 percent in the United States. Nearly all farms in the Region have some land which can be used only for grazing.

In 1954, 84 percent of farms in the Appalachians reported cattle and calves on hand, a larger percentage of farms than reported other types of livestock. These farms reported on hand an average of 7 cattle or calves per farm for all farms in the Appalachians or 8.4 head per farm reporting cattle and calves on hand.

The percentage of farms reporting cattle and calves on hand was much more uniform among the economic areas of the Southern Appalachians than was the average number of head per farm. Northwest Georgia, with 76.3 percent, had the smallest percentage of its farms reporting cattle and calves on hand, while that small strip of west-central Virginia from Pulaski to Bath County had 90 percent, or the largest percentage. The average number of cattle and calves per farm was much less uniform than this, ranging from 2.1 head in extreme eastern Kentucky to 21.2 head in the most eastern three counties of West Virginia.

Perhaps of more importance than the percentage of farms reporting cattle and calves on hand is the

percentage of farms reporting cattle and calves sold. In contrast to the 84.4 percent of farms reporting cattle and calves on hand in 1954, only three-fifths of these reported cattle and calves sold alive. This would seem to indicate that a considerable number of Appalachian farms kept cattle and calves primarily for home use. Only 3.3 head of cattle and calves were sold per farm in 1954. The gross income from the sale of cattle and calves averaged $216 per farm, which is approximately one-sixth of total value of farm products sold. In addition, milk sold had an average value per farm of $195. Thus the total value of cattle, calves, and milk sold per farm was $411 or approximately one-third of the total farm sales ($1,267).

Cattle and calves were reported on hand and sold by a larger percentage of farms in the Southern Appalachians than in the seven states, but the average number of cattle and calves sold per farm was greater for the whole seven states, where farms are larger, than in the Southern Appalachian segment.

Chickens were reported on hand by 78.7 percent of the Appalachian farms in 1954, but only 15 percent of the farms had poultry for sale. Poultry farming is a very specialized business and is mostly developed around a local market. For example, a few counties in North Georgia sell eggs to hatcheries which supply chicks to the broiler area just south of the Appalachians. There is, also, a concentration of poultry farms supplying commercial eggs to every city in the area, such as Chattanooga, Knoxville, Asheville, and Charleston. Almost twice as many farms (27.8 percent of all farms) reported the sale of eggs as reported chickens sold. The combined value of chickens and eggs sold was about $313 per farm, which was nearly $100 per farm less than the combined value of cattle, calves and milk sold.

The percentage of farms reporting chickens on hand, chickens sold, and eggs sold all decreased between 1950 and 1954. During the same period, the value of chickens sold more than doubled and the value of eggs sold increased by almost one-third. These changes reflect the trend toward more specialized commercial production of both broilers and eggs, and the great popularity of eggs and chicken in the diet of non-farm families.

Least important of the three types of livestock were hogs and pigs. This is an area of limited land for corn, and hogs are not generally recommended as a major enterprise. They were reported on hand by 60.2 percent of all farms in the Appalachians; but only

THE SOUTHERN APPALACHIANS

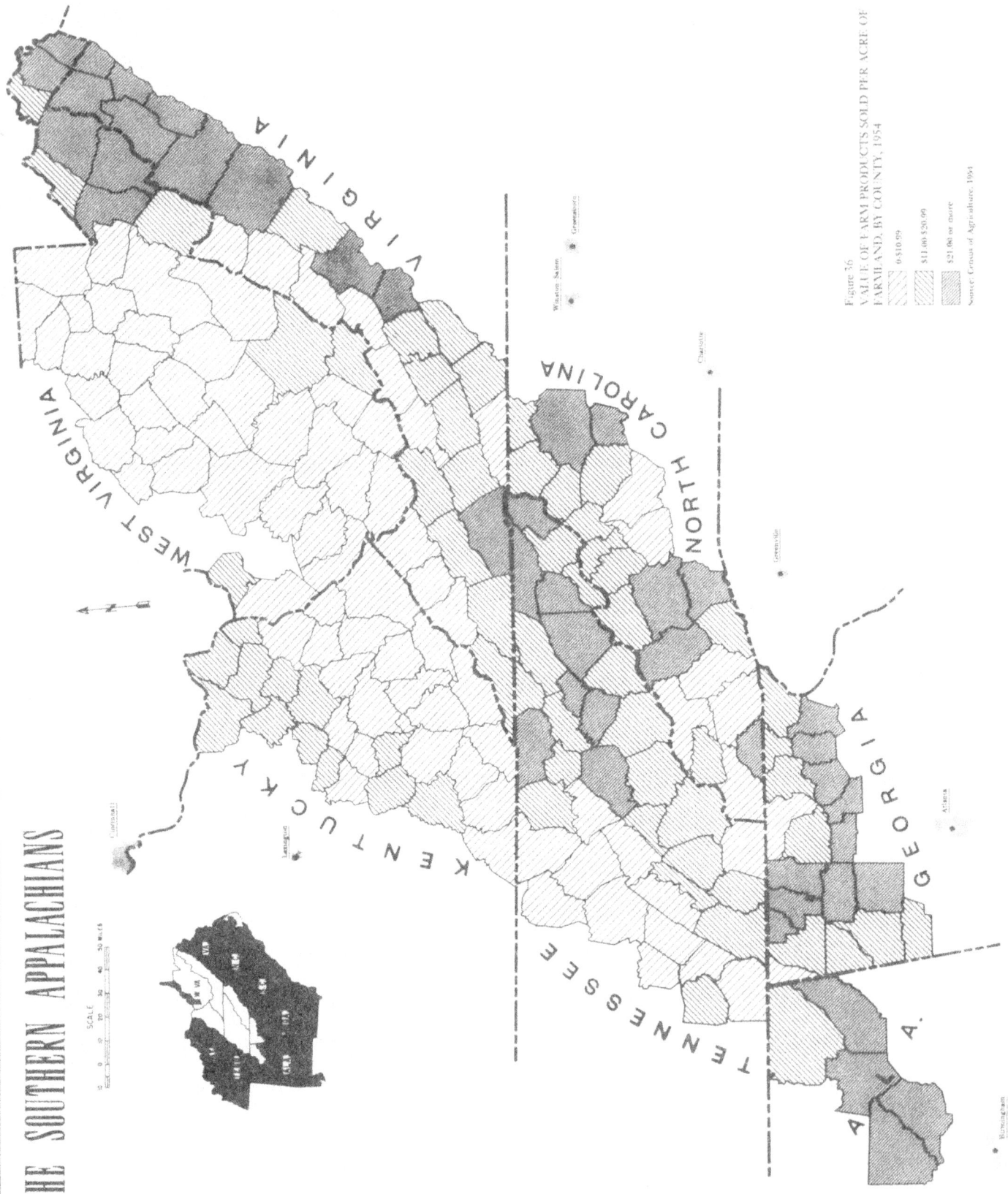

Figure 36
VALUE OF FARM PRODUCTS SOLD PER ACRE OF
FARMLAND, BY COUNTY, 1954

0-$10.99

$11.00-$20.99

$21.00 or more

Source: Census of Agriculture, 1954

16.2 percent of all Appalachian farms reported hogs and pigs sold. This is an indication of the importance of hogs raised for family consumption, which can be done partly on household and barnyard waste feeds.

The percentage of farms reporting hogs and pigs on hand was approximately the same in the Appa-

Table 24. *Reported Farm Expenditures, Southern Appalachian Region, 1954*

Reported expenditures	Average dollars per farm	Total dollars
Hired labor	$ 119	$ 38,301,291
Machine hire	31	9,966,113
Feed for livestock and poultry	406	129,949,593
Fuel and oil products	54	17,415,963
Fertilizer and lime	100	32,222,645
Total	$ 710	$ 227,855,605

Source: U. S. Census of Agriculture, 1954.

lachians as in the seven states, but only half as many farms produced hogs for sale on an average.

Crop production in the Appalachians is quite different from livestock production. Whereas all three main types of livestock are produced in all parts of the Appalachians to some extent, a crop that is of major importance in one section may not even grow in another section. Therefore, to get a picture of crop production it is necessary to study the major crop or crops in a particular section rather than comparing the production of a crop in one area with the production of the same crop in another area.

The only crop reported by the census in all counties of the Appalachians was corn. In 1954, corn was grown on almost 1.5 million acres of land, which was about one-third of all harvested cropland.

Corn was reported grown on 65.8 percent of all farms in the Appalachians in 1954. Although yields were very high in some counties, in general corn yields are low in the Appalachians, averaging only 27.3 bushels per acre in 1954. This should be compared to 37 bushels for the United States and 52 bushels for Iowa, and only 20 bushels in the seven state area. However, there is considerable variability in this regard, as indicated by the range of yields from a high of 58 bushels in North Central West Virginia and Northeast Georgia to a low of 15 bushels per acre in the Sand Mountains of Alabama. In most areas, the yields ranged between 20 and 40 bushels per acre.

Corn was planted on fewer acres in 1954 than in 1950, but the percentage of cropland on which corn was planted remained comparatively unchanged. The percentage of farms reporting corn grown decreased from 85 percent in 1930, to 66 percent in 1954. The

average yield was slightly lower in 1954 than in 1950, but was higher in both years than in 1930 when the average was 21.1 bushels per acre. This decrease in yield between 1950 and 1954 is believed to be a result of unfavorable weather conditions and not a trend. The cash sale of corn almost doubled between 1950

Table 25. *Percentage of Southern Appalachian Farm Operators Reporting Nonfarm Income and Work, 1954*

Report	Percentage of operators reporting			
	Commercial	Parttime	Residential	All operators
Other income greater than farm sales	12.3	79.5	63.2	45.7
Off-farm work	33.8	76.8	62.3	53.6
100 days or more off-farm work	12.5	66.1	50.3	38.0

Source: U. S. Census of Agriculture, 1954.

and 1954 and could indicate a shift to a more specialized type of farming in the Appalachians. Those farms with adequate bottom land for corn production may not have sufficient other resources for livestock to feed.

Wheat was an important crop only in the Appalachian areas of North Carolina, Tennessee, Virginia, and West Virginia. Some wheat was reported for Kentucky, but less than one percent of the farms in the part of Kentucky lying in the Appalachians reported growing it. Wheat production was not considered important enough in Alabama and Georgia to be reported by the census.

Wheat was harvested from less than one percent of the crop land in 1954, but the average yield was 21.7 bushels per acre, as compared to 18 bushels for the United States and 17.5 bushels per acre in Kansas, the most important wheat state. Of the wheat produced, 56.2 percent was sold. While the acreage of wheat in the Appalachians decreased by 68.4 percent between 1930 and 1954, the yield increased an average of 3.5 bushels per acre.

Tobacco was reported for all states except Alabama and West Virginia, but would not be considered an important crop from the standpoint of either acres planted or percent of farms growing it except in parts of Kentucky, North Carolina, Tennessee, and Virginia, where as many as 75 percent of the farms reported growing tobacco. The average acreage of tobacco per farm growing tobacco in 1954 was 1.2 and the average yield per acre was 1,585 pounds. In 1950 the average was 1.3 acres per farm reporting tobacco grown, with an average yield of 1,312 pounds per acre. The average farm growing tobacco in 1930 had 1.2 acres of tobacco with an average yield of only 876 pounds. Thus, we see a great increase in yield but very little change in acres. This is a crop which cannot be grown profitably unless there is a local market and adapted soils.

Cotton is an important crop in the Appalachians only in Alabama and Northwest Georgia, where it

Table 26. *Distribution of Commercial Farms by Crop Type, Southern Appalachian Region, 1930, 1950, 1954*

| | Percent of all commercial farms | | |
Type of farm[a]	1954	1950	1930
Cash grain	2.4	1.4	1.7
Cotton	12.1	15.8	27.9
Other field crops	34.9	26.8	8.8
Vegetables	1.0	1.2	1.1
Fruit and nuts	1.5	1.1	2.3
Dairy	11.2	10.3	4.0
Poultry	10.1	7.6	2.7
Other livestock	16.5	19.4	10.3
General	8.7	13.9	41.2
Miscellaneous	1.6	2.5	--

Source: U. S. Census of Agriculture, 1954.

[a]Type of farm based on product or group of products accounting for 40 percent or more of total value of all farm products sold in 1930; 50 percent in 1950 and 1954.

was reported harvested by 68.1 and 38.0 percent of farms respectively. Cotton was also grown on some farms in Western North Carolina and Southeastern Tennessee but on less than 5 percent of the farms in each area. Even in Georgia and Alabama the percentage of farms growing cotton had declined greatly. In 1930 Alabama had cotton reported on 92.9 percent of its farms; by 1950 this figure had fallen to 83.9 percent, and by 1954 to 68.1 percent The same trend has occurred in Northwest Georgia, since both areas have developed a greater interest in poultry and livestock.

Among other crops which were of some importance were oats in West Virginia and hay in West Virginia and Virginia. The combined acreage of all types of hay cut in the Southern Appalachians was 6.5 acres per farm in 1954 and 5.9 in 1950.

Vegetables were reported grown on 88 percent of all Appalachian farms in 1954, but these were largely vegetables produced for home use only. Vegetables for sale were produced only on farms near large towns or permanent mining operations. There is no indication of any chance for shipping vegetables away from the area except in extreme Northeast West Virginia and the bordering counties of Virginia. Those farms reporting vegetables grown for sale averaged 3.3 acres per farm from which the average gross sales were $106.80 per acre or $354 per farm.

The censuses of 1950 and of 1954 classified farms on the basis of relationship of the value of sales from a particular source or group of sources to the total value of all farm products sold.

The relative importance of these various types of farms in the Appalachians has changed, as can be seen from Table 26. This table tells us much about the changes taking place in agriculture during the past 25 to 30 years. Cash grain farms have increased as machines have become better adapted to rolling land, while cotton farms have declined greatly with the lower relative price of cotton and the very high cost of controlling the cotton boll weevil on land of high natural fertility. This trend is expected to continue as wage rates and job opportunities improve. Other field crops are predominantly corn, potatoes, and tobacco. Even though there has been little spread in tobacco areas, the relative price and yield have increased so much that more farms have received a greater percentage of their total farm sales from tobacco. Corn yields have increased with better varieties and farm machinery and abandonment of the former practice of topping corn before it was mature. Dairy farms have increased very greatly along with improved feed production and the demands for high quality milk in the more populous areas. Poultry farms have expanded greatly with increased demands for eggs and broilers and the fact that only small acreages are needed for employing much family labor with poultry enterprises. This is very likely to continue in an area so well adapted to this intensive enterprise as the Appalachian Area. This seems to be a further indication of the shift toward a more specialized type of agriculture.

Cash grain farms were dominant in only three counties: two in Kentucky and one in North Carolina. Cotton farms were dominant only in Alabama and Northwest Georgia. Field crops, other than cotton and cash grain (mostly tobacco with some potatoes and sweet potatoes), were the dominant type in more than one-third of all counties. The dairy type farm was dominant in nearly ten percent of the counties, mostly associated with proximity to metropolitan areas. Livestock farms, other than dairy and poultry, were the dominant type in nearly one-third of all counties, mostly in Tennessee, Virginia, and West Virginia. Poultry was the dominant type in all of Northeast Georgia, along with a few counties in Northwest Georgia, all of North Carolina, Northwest Virginia, and the counties in the adjacent area of West Virginia.

Summary

The Southern Appalachian Region is one of small farms, a high percentage of full owners, intensive enterprises in valleys, and very extensive farming on rough land. Much progress has been made toward enlarging farm businesses in the past 25 to 30 years but much more is needed. There is little evidence that total farm income can be greatly expanded by new enterprises or new methods. Farming is a business associated with reduced costs per unit of output as output per farm expands. Thus, we need to divide the total farm income among fewer persons if they are to enjoy increased net income per person or per family. There are entirely too many farm residents in the Region to be supported by the most improved agriculture.

There is no intention to discourage families from living on small farms while earning income elsewhere. There is much reason for discouraging the subdividing of small farms for complete family income. In the past, progress has been retarded by social resistance to encouraging young adults of a farm family to look for employment away from the small family farm. The subdividing of farms has gone much too far for good economy, in many instances. Rarely is it practical to ignore size of business when attempting greater efficiency.

Those areas of relatively broad valleys can enlarge their fields and whole farms to such an extent that the efficiency of production per worker can be competitive with any area. If roads and public carriers are adequate to markets, a highly developed commercial agriculture can be maintained in such communities. A few farm products, such as milk, eggs, fresh vegetables and hay tend to be produced near where they are consumed. The high cost of transportation per dollar value and high perishability place a premium on farm locations with access to population centers. The greater the urban population, the more dairymen it will support. With modern processing of milk into lower cost substitutes for fresh milk, it is no longer possible to sell milk at excessive prices. This means that successful dairymen must produce milk at low cost through selection of productive cows and balanced feeding of reasonably cheap feed. Many communities still have room for much expansion in milk production. The same general comments apply to fresh eggs and fresh vegetables.

Producers can expect a fairly low price ceiling, and production costs cannot rise greatly and leave a reward to the producer. Intensive enterprises not so restricted to nearby markets include poultry, milk for manufacturing, tobacco, and cotton. In suitable areas, these products can usually be produced on small farms without excessive costs.

The more extensive enterprises, which usually are favorable to areas of low land values, are grains, sheep, hogs, beef cattle and dairy heifers. Here again, improved technology of selection, treatment and practices must be followed for maximum gain.

Industrial and commercial development, and the expansion of urban areas will promote the migration of farm people within the whole region and increase the economic opportunities for remaining farmers to supply food and raw materials for sale. Such development can be expected, however, only in areas where adequate markets, materials, water, power, and labor are available.

Ministers, social workers, teachers, health officers, agricultural workers, elected officials, and other public servants have a definite responsibility for teaching the advantages and risks of migration. Without doubt, many farm people in congested areas would improve their well-being by moving to areas of greater productive opportunities. However, without educated leadership to see that such opportunities do exist and that the prospective migrants are suited for the migration, such movements carry great risks.

Consideration of the present agricultural situation in the Region suggests the need for a variety of educational programs. One should have as its objective the provision of a realistic assessment of the economic potential of agriculture in the various areas. Where agricultural commodities can be profitably produced, improved methods of production and marketing should be promoted. In many parts of the Region, though, farming holds little economic promise, and this fact must be squarely faced. In such areas, the people must be provided with knowledge of alternative economic opportunities, both within and outside the Region, and trained in the basic techniques and communication skills increasingly required by commercial, industrial, and service occupations. Only through such programs that will serve to reduce the pressure upon the limited agricultural resources is a balanced and prosperous regional economy likely to be achieved.

CHAPTER SEVEN

Extractive

Industries

and

Forestry

HAROLD A. GIBBARD

THE NATURAL WEALTH FOUND IN THE Southern Appalachians is in many forms. It includes the rivers that carry barge traffic and that provide hydroelectric power when dammed, as in the T.V.A. system. The soil is part of its wealth, though much of this is too poor to support a vigorous agriculture. Nearly two-thirds of the land surface is wooded, much of it in hardwoods, nearly all of it qualifying as commercial forest. The natural wealth of greatest present consequence over much of the territory, however, consists of deposits of minerals. These are of a number of sorts, but far and away the most important is bituminous coal.

The natural resource industries have certain characteristics which, when considered together, are distinctive. The location of any extractive industry is controlled by the natural distribution of the resource; extractive industries and forestry may be carried on in out-of-way places and rugged terrain not advantageous for other industries. Frequently, a single extractive industry is the sole economic base for an area (save for derivatives or service occupations), so that the well-being of the people is tied to this one industry. The typical extractive mine, quarry, or well, and the typical logging operation are relatively small enterprises if judged by manufacturing standards. Therefore, where the main support is a natural resource industry, population tends to be distributed in fairly small clusters, with cities widely scattered throughout. In the case of minerals, though not of timber, once the resource has been removed, it is gone forever. The fate of every mine is to close down ultimately for want of further materials.

Employment data give one measure of the place of mineral industries in the economy of the Southern Appalachians, and of the contributions of the Southern Appalachians to the mineral industries of the nation. According to the U.S. Census, 1950, of all persons employed in the Southern Appalachians, 12.5 percent were engaged in some form of mining employment—either metal mining, coal mining, petroleum and natural gas extraction, or nonmetal. This means that out of every eight persons employed in 1950 in the Region, one was employed in an extractive industry. If only male workers are considered, the percentage rises to 15.8; which is to say that almost one-sixth of all gainfully employed men were in an extractive industry.

In the nation as a whole, 1.7 percent of the gainfully employed reported in the 1950 census were in the mining fields. The percentage for male workers was 2.2. Thus, the Southern Appalachian percentages were about seven times as high as those for the United States. While three percent of all employed persons in 1950 were in the Southern Appalachians, 24 percent of all persons employed in mining were in this region.

A second measure of the place of mineral industries in the economy is the number of operations. In 1954, there were 4,776 of all types in the Southern Appalachians, an average of about 25 per county. In the country as a whole, there were about 12 per county. Establishments vary tremendously in size, so the national comparison is only crude.[1]

The dependence of the Southern Appalachians on mining employment is thus considerable. While the number of miners is much lower now than it was in 1950, largely as a result of fluctuations in the demand for coal and of mechanization in the coal industry, the total number is still substantial. For certain large sections of the territory, mining provides the economic base on which the entire economy rests, a base that all too often reminds the residents that their fortunes rest on a very unstable foundation.

Coal

In the Southern Appalachians, coal ranks first among the mineral industries, both in volume of employment and in value of product. It is distributed in a broad wedge, the western edge of which follows the west boundary of the Southern Appalachians through Tennessee and Kentucky, then across part of Ohio. The eastern boundary enters the Southern Appalachians at Preston County, West Virginia, cuts the western point of Virginia, enters Tennessee at Claiborne County, and from there runs to Marion County on the south and on into Alabama. This vast Appalachian coal field is one of the largest and most important continuous deposits of bituminous coal in the world.

Coal is essential to an industrial economy. It is used in the manufacture of steel, and as a raw material in products as varied as dyes, fertilizer, and aspirin. As an energy fuel, coal serves a large market, even though it has lost ground both to petroleum and natural gas. The market for coal is an unstable one. In the years of lowest production, national output is about 400 million tons, while in 1947, a peak year, nearly 631 million tons were produced.

The Southern Appalachians contribute significantly to the nation's bituminous coal supply. In most years since 1944, its annual output has exceeded 200 million

tons. At an average value of approximately five dollars per ton, the total value of this annual output is more than a billion dollars. The significance of this for the economy of the Southern Appalachians is suggested by comparing it with the value of other mineral products from this region. While the value of these latter cannot be estimated precisely—county figures being available only when releasing them would not disclose information about specific firms—a rough estimate for all minerals extracted except coal, crude oil, and natural gas for 1958 is between 70 and 100 million dollars. Beyond any doubt, the annual value of coal production in the Southern Appalachians greatly exceeds that of all other minerals combined, even in the years of low coal production.[2]

There were 3,255 coal mines in the Southern Appalachians in 1954, according to the United States Census of Mineral Industries for that year. They were distributed by states as follows: Alabama—16; Georgia—5; Kentucky—981; North Carolina—none; Tennessee—368; Virginia—607; and West Virginia—1,278. As these figures are for land areas of quite unequal sizes, they do not provide a measure of the intensity of coal mining in the several states. There is a tremendous variation within that half of the Southern Appalachian territory which is underlaid with coal. Some counties, for example Roane, West Virginia, have no current production at all. At the upper extreme, Logan County, West Virginia, produced over 22 million tons in 1957. Eight counties in all had outputs in excess of 10 million tons that year, seven in West Virginia and one in neighboring Virginia. There were two large areas of concentrated production; the southern coal fields centering in southern West Virginia, extreme western Virginia, and eastern Kentucky; and the northern fields including parts of northern West Virginia, and adjacent Pennsylvania and Ohio outside the Southern Appalachians.

Table 27 gives production for the Southern Appalachian portion of the mountain states for 1958. It points to the dominant place of West Virginia, and the high productions of Kentucky and Virginia.

Fluctuations in Southern Appalachian coal production show a tendency to follow the national pattern (Figure 37). In the United States as a whole, bituminous coal and lignite production (they are reported

---

[1] U.S. Department of Commerce, Bureau of Census, *1954 Census of Manufactures*, Vol. I, p. 203-1; and *1954 Census of Mineral Industries*, Vol. I, p. B-3.

[2] Estimate based on county data. U.S. Department of the Interior, Bureau of Mines, *Minerals Yearbook, 1958*, Vol. III, pp. 15ff, 279ff, 402ff, 690ff, 873ff, 983ff, and 1017ff.

together in the official sources) rose rapidly to a high level during World War I, then—after a postwar adjustment—continued at a high level during much of the 1920's. The years 1925 through 1929 each had production above 500 million tons. The depression

Table 27. *Bituminous Coal Production, Southern Appalachian Region, by States, 1958*

State (S. A. portion)	Million tons produced	Percentage of Southern Appalachian production
Alabama	.269	0.15
Georgia	.009	--
Kentucky	37.954	20.26
North Carolina	none	--
Tennessee	6.298	3.36
Virginia	26.826	14.32
West Virginia	115.982	61.91
Total	187.338	100.00

Source: U. S. Bureau of Mines, Minerals Yearbook, 1958.

decade saw output fall to a low of 308 million tons in 1932 and continue low until military production for World War II stimulated the economy. The years 1944 and 1947 had outputs of over 600 million tons, the only years in the history of the country when these levels were attained. Since then, tonnage has been irregular and the trend downward. Since 1951, only in 1956 did output rise above 500 million tons, and in 1954 and 1958 it fell to below 400 million tons, a rate exceeded in every non-depression year since 1910.

In the late 1920's, coal production in the Southern Appalachians was about 175 million tons per year, or a little over a third of the whole nation's output. The collapse of the national market in the 1930's resulted in a drop in output in the southern mountains. During this period, though, the proportion of the nation's coal coming from the Southern Appalachians rose to nearly 40 percent. Early in World War II, the region's production rose to over 200 million tons and continued at that level, save for the recession year 1949, until 1953. Since then it has fluctuated sharply. The recession year 1954 saw production drop to 169 million tons, a postwar low. Output was over 200 million tons again in each of the next three years, but fell to about 187 million tons in 1958. It is noteworthy that the percentage of United States production mined in the region has continued to rise. In the nine-year period 1950-1958, it was just under 45 percent.

A county by county analysis of production discloses that some counties have maintained a fairly stable production, relative to the territory as a whole, over the postwar period. Some others have suffered

a rather sharp drop in output and some, even in years of pronounced overall decline, have gained. There are several reasons for this: differences in market demand for coals of different types; differences in cost of production in different mines; nearness to markets (the average freight charge on a ton of coal in the United States is about two-thirds of its mine price).[3] More fundamental than these is the fact that from some areas the best coal has been removed and once-large mines have become exhausted, while in other areas mining is just being opened up to large-scale production. In West Virginia, where nearly two-thirds of all Southern Appalachian coal is produced, Fayette County, through which the Kanawha Valley cuts, dropped from 12.5 to 7 million tons between 1945 and 1957, while Wyoming County increased from nearly 5 to 13 million tons.[4] Since coal mining is an extractive mineral industry, the eventual decline of production in any area is certain.

In the region as a whole, there is coal for many years to come. Drawing on statewide data, in Virginia the recoverable reserves of coal are sufficient for about 175 years at the 1957 rate of production. West Virginia, with a sixth of the original reserves depleted, still has 50 billion tons to be recovered, enough for 300 years at the 1957 rate. Both Kentucky and Tennessee have coal for a thousand years at present rate of use.[5] There is not enough coal to be wasteful with it, but there is an abundant supply for the foreseeable future.

Future supply is adequate, but what of demand? Clearly, coal output has not kept pace with industrial production in the past few years; instead, it has declined while the nation's total production has risen. A major reason is that coal output has fallen behind in competition with other energy fuels.

The best available comparison is to consider the total production of the various energy fuels, though these products, including coal, are not used exclusively as fuels. Bituminous coal and lignite accounted for 70 percent of such production in 1900, and anthracite for more than half the rest. By 1940, coal's share was less than half. In 1950, it was 39.2 percent, and by 1957 it was only 30.9. Crude petroleum gained rapidly, especially in the decade 1920-1930, and has continued its advance ever since. Its per-

[3] Thomas C. Campbell, *The Bituminous Coal Freight Rate Structure: An Economic Appraisal* (West Virginia University Business and Economic Studies, June, 1954), Table 3, p. 7.

[4] *Minerals Yearbook, 1945*, p. 903 and *Minerals Yearbook, 1957*, Vol. II, p. 114.

[5] *Minerals Yearbook, 1957*, Vol. II, Table 2, p. 44-45.

centage in 1957 was 36.3. Natural gas has gained tremendously, from less than one-eighth of total mineral energy production as late as 1940 to over one-fourth in 1957.[6]

Two aspects of these percentages modify the picture somewhat. First, while energy fuels are competitive with one another in some uses, they are not in others. A major use of petroleum is as gasoline in automobiles, and coal is not so used. The bituminous coal industry claims that, when noncompetitive uses are excluded, coal is still America's prime source of energy.[7]

Second, the drop in coal's percentage has been offset in part by an overall rise in the use of mineral-energy fuels. Since the turn of the century, the rise has been sevenfold. Between 1940 and 1957, production of all fuel materials rose by two-thirds. A continued long-term rise may be confidently expected. Whether it will result eventually in an expanding market for coal, time will have to tell. There is, of course, the matter of atomic energy to be taken into account. Currently, the nation's atomic projects use more coal than they displace. In time, this new energy must be expected to take over a share of the market.

The failure of coal to keep pace with the national rise of production, or even to maintain its 1947 production level, is explained by the loss of specific

markets to other fuels. The diesel-electric locomotive has now practically everywhere replaced the coal-burning, steam-driven iron horse. The Class I railroads used 61 million tons of coal as recently as 1950, and just over 8 million in 1957, not all of that as locomotive fuel.[8] Diesel power now hauls coal from

Figure 37. *Bituminous Coal and Lignite Production, Southern Appalachian Region and the United States, Selected Years, 1925-1958*

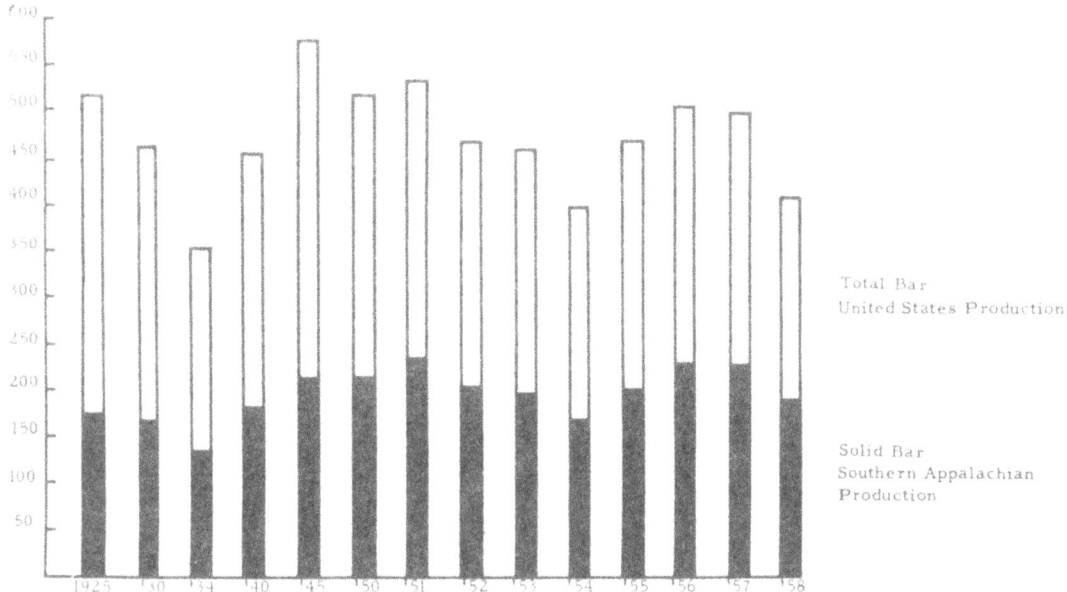

Source: U. S. Bureau of Mines, Minerals Yearbook, various issues.

the Southern Appalachian mines through the mountains toward its markets. The use of gas and oil to heat homes is now normal in the towns and cities of the whole country. Retail deliveries of coal, going largely to homes, fell from 84 million tons in 1950 to 36 million in 1957. The decline will probably continue, if only because people are moving from rural areas, where other fuels are less available, to cities and suburbs.

The industrial market continues to be a major one. About a fifth of production went to oven coke plants in 1957, to be used eventually in the making of steel. A ton of coal goes into the manufacture of a ton of steel. Other manufacturing uses accounted for another fifth of all production that year. The industrial market is apparently a fairly secure one.

Coal has yielded to both petroleum and natural gas as a source of steam in some of the nation's in-

[6] *Minerals Yearbook, 1957*, Vol. II, Table 1, p. 4.
[7] National Coal Association, *Bituminous Coal Facts, 1958* (Washington, D. C.), p. 5.
[8] *Minerals Yearbook, 1957*, Vol. II, Table 52, p. 122.

THE SOUTHERN APPALACHIANS

SCALE
10 0 20 40 60 MILES

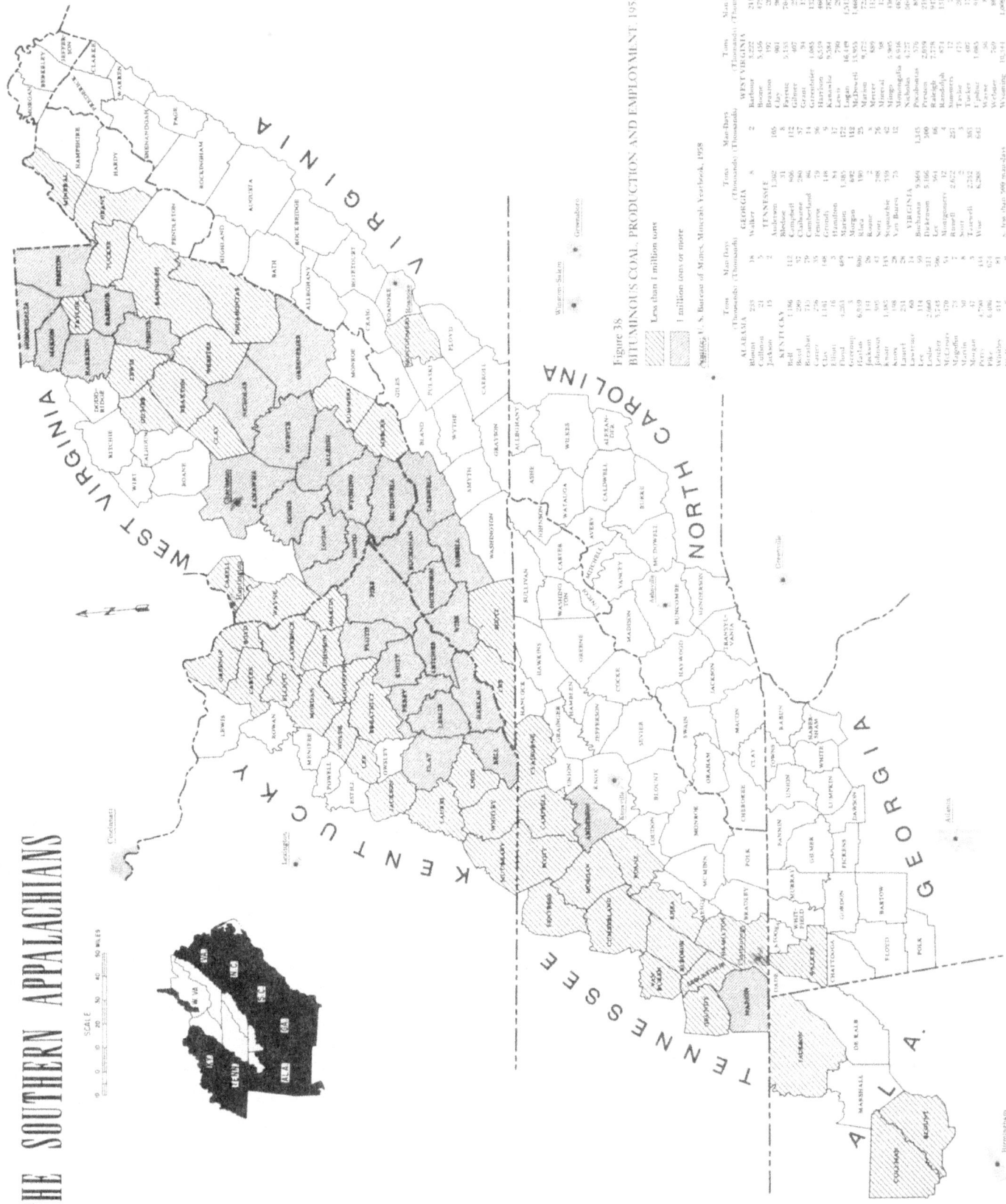

WEST VIRGINIA · VIRGINIA · KENTUCKY · TENNESSEE · NORTH CAROLINA · GEORGIA · ALA.

Figure 38
BITUMINOUS COAL PRODUCTION AND EMPLOYMENT, 1958

░ Less than 1 million tons
▒ 1 million tons or more

Source: U.S. Bureau of Mines, Minerals Yearbook, 1958

	Tons (Thousands)	Man-Days (Thousands)		Tons (Thousands)	Man-Days (Thousands)
ALABAMA			**GEORGIA**		
Blount	235	28	Walker	18	2
Calhoun	21	5	**TENNESSEE**		
Jackson	15	2	Anderson	1,162	165
KENTUCKY			Bledsoe	31	8
Bell	1,196	112	Campbell	606	112
Boyd	200	92	Claiborne	280	57
Breathitt	715	29	Cumberland	86	14
Carter	726	35	Fentress	59	36
Clay	1,161	148	Grundy	148	17
Elliott	16	3	Hamilton	34	37
Floyd	4,263	685	Marion	1,185	152
Greenup	5	1	Morgan	892	112
Harlan	6,939	836	Rhea	193	25
Jackson	113	13	Scott	298	76
Johnson	505	193	Sequatchie	559	12
Knott	1,565	28	Van Buren	75	
Knox	198	28	**VIRGINIA**		
Laurel	251		Buchanan	5,569	1,315
Lawrence	68	14	Dickenson	5,166	500
Lee	114	58	Lee	564	86
Leslie	2,660	321	Montgomery	12	4
Letcher	5,745	586	Russell	51	251
McCreary	479	54	Scott	17	
Magoffin	12		Tazewell	2,352	361
Martin	2,622	7	Wise	6,288	645
Morgan	37	7	**WEST VIRGINIA**		
Perry	4,230	361	Barbour	3,222	211
Pike	6,496		Boone	3,456	479
Whitley	511	114	Braxton	192	26
Wolfe	4	2	Clay	903	86
			Fayette	5,153	284
			Gilmer	467	25
			Grant	34	31
			Greenbrier	1,085	132
			Harrison	6,559	460
			Kanawha	9,384	282
			Lewis	780	29
			Logan	14,149	1,513
			McDowell	15,955	1,660
			Marion	4,572	722
			Mercer	685	112
			Mineral	58	12
			Mingo	5,965	436
			Monongalia	6,936	463
			Nicholas	4,257	564
			Pocahontas	370	83
			Preston	576	259
			Raleigh	7,728	947
			Randolph	871	131
			Summers	12	
			Taylor	173	
			Tucker	495	
			Upshur	1,085	
			Wayne	36	
			Webster	569	86
			Wyoming	10,341	1,099

x = less than 500 man-days

dustrial establishments. It remains a competitor for these uses, however. Many industrial installations are readily convertible from one fuel to another, so that quick advantage can be taken of any changes in their price or supply.

The brightest spot in the coal picture is its use in the electric utility industry. More than three times as much coal goes into this use now as in 1940—about twice as much as at the end of World War II. The electric generating industry is a rapidly expanding one because of the growth of electricity consumption in manufacturing plants and in homes. In 1957, about 55 percent of all electric power was produced from coal, and 70 percent of steam-generated electric power came from coal. The electric power industry is now by a large margin the largest consumer of coal in the United States. This market is of such size that it absorbs as much as ninety percent of all coal production in some of the northerly counties in the Southern Appalachians. It absorbed 157 million tons in 1957, as against only 49 million in 1940 and 80 million in 1950.[9] It is no wonder that both the coal industry and the United Mine Workers have been promoting the use of electricity!

There is no doubt but that the coal industry can supply a larger market than it now does. Using the conventional measure of coal-mine capacity—the tonnage that would be produced if the present work force, at the present rate of output, worked 280 days per year—the Southern Appalachian mines averaged 64 and 72 percent of capacity in 1950 and 1957 respectively.[10] These figures understate potential production, since there are both idle miners and idle mines.

The notion has long been current that the coal industry is overdeveloped and sick because there are too many small mines and ownership and control of them is too much dispersed. This thesis holds that the industry would be more efficient if coal production were concentrated in fewer units. The trend may now be in that direction.

There are many mines in the Southern Appalachians, 3,255 of them in 1954. Some of these are giants and others are very small. Seven had a reported production of over two million tons each in 1956; at the same time, hundreds of mines produced less than ten thousand tons each, and some reported under one thousand tons. The seven large mines are in each case the property of a company with a number of operations. Most of the small mines are individually owned.

West Virginia data illustrate the degree of concentration in the industry. In 1956, 1,382 operating coal companies accounted for 1,541 mining operations and a total production of just over 150 million tons. The average thus was about 100,000 tons per mine. Yet 27 companies each produced over a million tons, and one produced about 15 million. The three largest companies produced roughly 20 percent of the State's total, the largest sixteen about half. At the other extreme, 528 operations each employed fewer than five men, and averaged about 2,000 tons. These more than 500 mines together produced less than half as much coal as the largest single mine in the State.[11]

Besides the financial ability of the large mining company to buy out the small concern, there are several other reasons for anticipating a growing concentration in the future. It costs millions of dollars and several years to open and equip a large mechanized mine, so only large companies can undertake the venture. Large companies with mechanized equipment have a competitive advantage over smaller companies in technological efficiency and in ability to operate only their most efficient mines during periods of slack demand. As the market becomes concentrated, large firms have a sales advantage. Actually, for many years, a number of small mines have sold their coal to large companies, who then market it along with their own production. The present policy of the United Mine Workers, to remove inequalities in wage rates between large and small mines, may force the closing of some small mines.

The small mines, relying heavily on hand labor, probably account for five to ten percent of Southern Appalachian coal output and a larger percentage of mining employment. The small mines serve the socially useful function of mining the coal from small scattered acreages not suitable for mechanized mining. Occasionally, a number of mining operations, all using small-mine methods, are conducted as a single coordinated enterprise with subcontractors handling part of the work. Such operations may produce seven or eight hundred tons per day.

Heretofore, in some of the unionized mines, and still in some of the non-unionized ones, the men have been paid by the piece rate. The rate ranged from

[9] *Minerals Yearbook, 1957*, Vol. II, p. 122.
[10] *Minerals Yearbook, 1950*, p. 337ff and *1957*, Vol. II, p. 107ff. Calculation for the Southern Appalachian territory made by the author.
[11] Data Source: West Virginia Department of Mines, *Annual Report of the Coal Mining Section, 1956*, pp. 6, 11.

$1.25 to $1.75 per ton in 1958, depending on the mine, whether the miner provided his own blasting materials, and whether rock was loaded free. The men working under these conditions commonly earned $15 to $18 per day.

In some localities the smaller mines have provided more regular employment than the larger ones which adhere to the regular union pay scale. The result, in 1958 when employment was generally slack in the coal fields, was a spread of tension. The United Mine Workers of America and the operators, in the contract signed late in 1958, agreed to the "Protective Wage Clause," under which the operators agreed not to buy, process, or sell coal from mines not adhering fully to the regular contract, and the union agreed not to condone special contracts with small operators that provided for less than the full union rate of pay. The small mine operators were pressed by their union members to sign the regular United Mine Workers contract, but insisted they could not survive if forced to pay the full union scale. The result was a series of strikes, quickly settled in northern West Virginia, but protracted and violent in Kentucky and Tennessee.

The struggle for job security in the coal fields has been intensified in recent years by the replacement of men by machines in the mines. For the coal industry is undergoing a technological revolution. From the point of view of the men who mine the coal, the most important single fact about the industry is its mechanization.

Some coal is still mined by the old manual methods. In the smaller underground mines, it is still either broken from the face of the seam with picks, or by blasting without first undercutting the seam, then hand-loaded into cars to be hauled outside, in a few places by horses or mules, but more often by some motorized means.

These crude hand methods are being superseded by two types of mechanized operation. The first and earlier of these loosens and loads the coal in a series of mechanized steps. The cycle begins by undercutting the coal with a cut several inches thick. Next, holes are drilled into the face of the coal, explosives are placed in them, and the coal is shot down. The cut at the base of the seam absorbs the blast and permits the coal to fall. It is then scooped up by a loading machine that passes it back to a shuttle car or belt that carries it to mine cars for transporting to the surface. The securing of the roof, either by post and cross-timbers, or more commonly now by long roof bolts that bind the overhead strata solidly together, is fitted into the cycle. The sequence of cut, drill, blast, and load is now efficient at each stage. This method is now the most common in large underground mines.

The second method achieves in one operation the results of the four steps of the first. Continuous mining machines, of various designs, all either rip or bore the coal loose from the seam, and at the same time scoop it up and pass it back to shuttle cars or conveyor belts. These monstrous machines, costing $90,000 to $100,000 each, can mine as much as *eight tons of coal per minute*. Roofbolting equipment is now mounted on some of the machines to reduce the time when they are not removing coal. Continuous mining machines were first put into regular operation in 1948. In 1957, there were 600 in the United States, producing 17.6 percent of all deep-mined coal. The Southern Appalachian percentages were lower; none in Tennessee, 4.2 percent in Kentucky, 5.5 percent in Virginia, and 11.9 percent in West Virginia. They were on their way, however, toward a new technological order in the coal industry.

The percentage of deep-mined coal either cut by hand or "shot from solid," i.e. without undercutting, ranged from 14.7 in Virginia to 2.4 in West Virginia in 1957. The percentages hand-loaded were 2.3 in Kentucky, 1.6 in Virginia, and 5.0 in West Virginia. Thus, just a little over five percent of the coal from underground mines in the southern mountains was produced that year by essentially nonmechanical means.

The impact of the continuous miner will be felt increasingly in the future. The typical work crew, when separate machines are used for the different operations in the first method outlined above, is thirteen or fourteen. When a continuous miner is used, the full crew is six or seven, and they produce more coal.[12]

Strip mining, or surface mining as it is called, recovers coal by removing the overburden, the earth and rock covering the coal. Stripping is economical only if the coal lies near the surface. In the country as a whole, strip mining accounts for a rising percentage of all production: 1.5 percent in 1920, 9.4 percent in 1940, but 25.2 percent in 1957.

[12] For a useful report of mining methods and output see J. J. Shields, M. O. Magnuson, and J. J. Dowd, *Mechanical Mining in Some Bituminous Coal Mines, Progress Report 7: Methods of Mining with Continuous Mining Machines* (U.S. Department of the Interior, September, 1954.) Bureau of Mines Information Circular 7696.

Strip mining is relatively less important in the Southern Appalachians than in the country as a whole, because of the rugged terrain. Where the land overlying the coal is relatively flat, a large acreage can be uncovered in one continuous operation: "prairie

tion. State laws vary, but in general they provide that the operator regrade the surface to provide for good drainage, and replant the surface in trees, shrubs, and grass. The penalty for not doing so is the forfeiture of a bond ($500 per acre in West Virginia),

Figure 39. *Percentage of Total Coal Production Produced by Deep Mines, Strip Mines, and Auger Mines, Southern Appalachian Region, 1958*

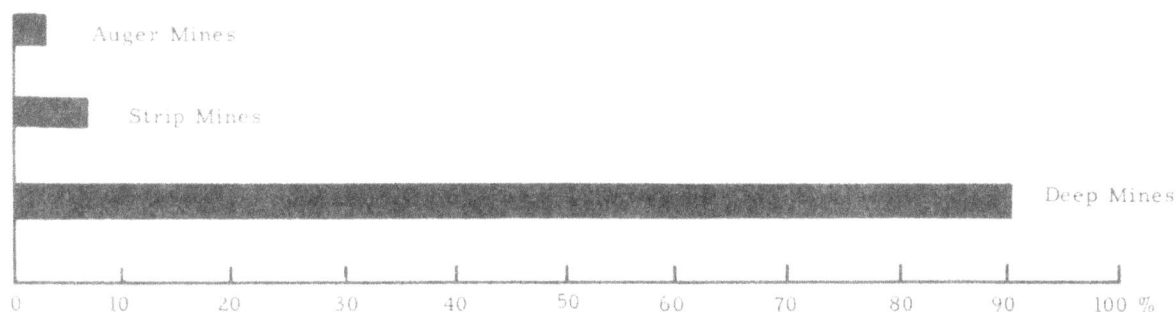

Source: U. S. Bureau of Mines, Minerals Yearbook, 1958

stripping" it is occasionally called. In the Southern Appalachians, stripping consists of uncovering coal by cutting shelves into the hillsides. This is "contour stripping." Where the hills are steep, the shelves are correspondingly narrow. Contour strip mines tend to be small, but numerous. There were 384 strip mines in the region in 1957, more than a fifth of the nation's total; but together they provided employment for fewer than 5,000 men per working day, and produced less than a twelfth of the region's tonnage. Several counties each account for more mining employment than that, and two account for more tonnage.

Stripping is efficient. In the Southern Appalachians in 1957, it produced 19.5 tons per man-day as against 8.7 tons for deep mines. This advantage is offset in part by the lower price that the coal brings. The United States average was $3.89 per ton, as against $5.52 for the deep-mine product.

Strip mining has been criticized as destructive of useful land areas. It does create ugliness. The further cost depends on the value of the surface before stripping, and the time necessary to restore it to its former use. Both of these vary widely from place to place. Much stripping occurs on territory that was not being put to economic use, but some is on agricultural land, and possibly a little on land from which trees were being harvested. It takes several years as a rule to reestablish good pasture, and much longer to restore an area to forest.

Stripping is everywhere subject to state regula-

which bond money is to be used by the state for the reclamation of the area. The law may also provide that a strip operator who has not repaired the surface within a specified time will be given no further stripping permit until he has done so. Too often it is cheaper to forfeit bond than to repair the hillside, and reclamation work proceeds slowly, if at all.

Auger mining, another postwar development, is usually a supplement to contour stripping. When the overburden is too deep for further removal, huge augers may be then used to bore into the exposed seams for further recovery of coal. These augers are commonly 16 to 20 inches in diameter, though some are much larger. They may bore into the seam for 200 feet or more. The coal flows out from the auger onto a conveyor that carries it to a truck. Auger mining is a mop-up operation. As such, it is highly productive, averaging over 26 tons per man-shift.

The revolution in coal mining has many repercussions, the most significant of which are the effects on employment and earnings. The new machines have made manpower more efficient; that, of course, is why the companies have purchased them. How much more efficient is indicated in Table 28. Note that in 1940 a miner produced, on the average, five tons of coal per shift. By 1950, his output had climbed to almost six tons. The rise steepened to 7.3 tons in 1953, up to 9.4 tons in 1957; and the steep rise is continuing. The national rate is even higher: 10.6 tons in 1957. This rise reflects the greater use of strip mining elsewhere.

At the same time as these gains in per-man-day were being registered, coal tonnage was fluctuating widely at levels much below the war and postwar periods. Employment has been affected both by wide fluctuations in the demand for coal and by

Table 28. *Bituminous Coal Production and Employment, Southern Appalachian Region, Various Years*

Year	Million tons produced	Tons per man-day	Average number of miners working daily
1934	137.1	4.51	155,860[a]
1940	181.7	5.02	170,358[a]
1950	215.6	5.94	203,114
1951	237.1	6.16	183,863
1952	208.5	6.00	168,846
1953	198.0	7.29	145,928
1954	168.8	8.32	108,902
1955	208.4	8.58	117,234
1956	233.3	9.04	122,273
1957	232.6	9.40	122,243

Source: U. S. Bureau of Mines, Minerals Yearbook, various issues.

[a]Figures for 1934 and 1940 are number of men employed.

technological displacements. Whereas the average number of men employed daily in the mines of the Southern Appalachians in 1950 was over 200,000; in the recession year 1954, the daily average was only 109,000; and in 1956 and 1957, when production ran ahead of the 1950 rate, the average number at work was only 122,000. This is a decrease of 40 percent in only six years. The drop would have been worse were it not for the fact that the proportion of all United States coal mining employment falling within the Southern Appalachians rose from 48.9 percent in 1950 to 53.5 percent in 1957.

The Southern Appalachian picture, which must be assembled from county data, cannot be carried forward statistically. It can be projected, however, from national and some state data. A preliminary figure for 1958 lists national production per man-day at 11.3 tons, with an average of only 188,500 men working daily during that year of low production, fewer than any year since 1890. In West Virginia, where 1957 employment was below that of any year since the outbreak of World War I, the April and May, 1959, figures record that about 59,000 men were employed at coal mining, about the same number as in 1908.[13]

The percentage of the region's tonnage that is produced by continuous mining machines is still small; it can hardly do other than increase. A southern West Virginia mine, mechanized according to the standards of the time in 1949, then employed an average of between 2,100 and 2,200 men. In December, 1958, getting only a part of its production

from continuous miners, it had a staff of just 749, and was almost equaling production of the earlier year. Another mine, this one in the northern coal fields, uses only continuous miners and has cut its staff to one-fourth of its previous size.[14] No matter what the market for coal—there are reasons to hope that it will rise—there can be only one basic trend in mining employment; that is downward. There are virtually no new jobs in the mines, except when a new mine is opened up or when a few carefully chosen young men are picked to be trained as supervisory personnel. It seems unlikely that the situation will change, in the large mines at least, until the rate of retirement of miners, at the end of their working span, exceeds the rate of displacement by machines.

Most of the displaced men never will be re-employed in the mines. A rapid upswing in coal output would bring a few men back, but with the average number at work in the mines falling, the prospect that many will be at all permanently rehired is so slight that none should count on it. What alternatives face these men, permanently replaced not only by continuous mining machines, but also by extensible conveyor belts and automatic tipples? Most cannot stay where they are and transfer to other kinds of employment; in the areas of most intensive mining, in the southern coal fields especially, coal is the base on which the whole economy rests. They cannot easily move into the larger manufacturing centers of the nation, for very few have transferable skills, and many are older than the large industrial concerns are willing to hire. There is an out-migration, especially of the younger men, and also real economic hardship in parts of the southern mountains that have relied heavily on mining employment.

The displacement of men, beyond that occasioned by a drop in production, is paralleled by the increased efficiency of those who remain. This efficiency has made possible a higher rate of earnings for the miners who still have jobs. Working miners are much better off than they were a few years ago.

The large mines, with very few exceptions, are organized by the United Mine Workers of America; and the wage rates prevailing in them are governed by the U.M.W. contract. The contract rate has advanced from the base rate of $13.05 per work shift in 1948 to $24.25 in the spring of 1959. Miners with special job classifications receive higher rates than

[13] Data supplied by West Virginia Department of Employment Security.

[14] Data obtained in field interviews.

this basic one. Actually, each type of position has its own rate, worked out to a fraction of a cent per hour. Most rates are above the basic rate that serves as a minimum. Outside jobs, such as those in the preparation plant, pay less than underground jobs, and also provide slightly less time per day. Fringe benefits, other than the $200 vacation pay per year, take the form of payments into the Welfare and Retirement Fund. The rate of payment has stood since 1942 at forty cents per ton mined, which amounts to a wage supplement of $3.50 to $4.00 per day. On the daily basis, the coal miner is among the most highly paid industrial workers in America. A miner, earning at the basic union rate and working 200 days per year, now receives about $5,000. If he were in one of the higher paying classifications, his earnings would be higher than that. In the larger mines of West Virginia in 1956—there have been two pay raises since then—earnings reported to the West Virginia Department of Employment Security averaged above $5,000, with supervisory personnel included.[15]

Two variables affect the earnings of the employed miners. The first is the extent to which the mines are unionized and adhere to the regular contract; the second is the number of days worked per year. Full information is not available on the first of these. The proportion of coal mined under the regular contract is known to vary a great deal. Small mines are more often non-union, or in the past have had special piece-rate contracts. Virginia has a "right to work" law. In Kentucky, Perry and Leslie Counties are reported to have relatively high proportions of non-union workers. Most of West Virginia is highly unionized.

The number of days worked per year averaged 202 in all the mines of the Southern Appalachians in 1957. The low point in the postwar period was 1949, when the average was just 155. In 1954, a depressed year for coal, it was 186. Between 1949 and 1954 there was a sharp drop in the number employed, but a rise in the days each worked.[16] There may be a tendency in the industry to concentrate employment among those who can be given fairly regular work.

Mine by mine comparisons indicate that in any one year the range is from less than 100 days worked to well over 250. There are also broad regional contrasts. All the mines in Tennessee averaged only 122 days in 1957, as against 177 in eastern Kentucky, 210 in Virginia, and 219 in West Virginia. It may also be that there are more small mines, perhaps with below-union pay scales, in the areas with the lowest number of days worked.

Coal mining has been not only a way of earning a living for thousands of men; it has also been a way of life for them and their families. The coal industry is spread in small units over a vast terrain. Some mining takes place within easy reach of large towns and cities. Most of it, however, does not. Mining has led to the establishment of communities in out-of-the-way places. The area of the most intensive coal mining in the Southern Appalachians, southern West Virginia, eastern Kentucky, and adjacent Virginia, has possibly the roughest terrain in the whole mountain territory. The hills are both steep and high; the valleys between them are tight, almost ravines. Through any one of these valleys may run a stream, a rail line, a hard-surfaced road, perhaps with buildings lining just one side, while a row or two of houses, all nearly alike, cling to the hillsides. Many miners' families live in just such settlements. Set apart from these houses may be the larger residences of the supervisory and administrative personnel. Nearby stands the tipple. There is a homogeneity to such places, if only because coal is their whole resource base. No one is there except the men who mine coal, their wives and children, and the people who sell goods or perform services, such as the gas station attendant, storekeeper, teacher, minister, and doctor. In such a settlement there is generally just one mine, and all depend on it, either directly or indirectly. The well-being of everybody has a common source.

Such communities are not fully isolated, of course. People get out to shop, to visit, to spend a vacation. Television and radio bring in the outside world. A close intimacy exists among the people in most coal communities, however, and local contacts far exceed outside ones.

Most coal communities were built as company towns. There was really no alternative. The recruited work force had to be sheltered and its basic needs met; there were no facilities for living already established, and the laborers could not be expected to erect their own. In addition to the mining properties as such, the towns included houses, a store, a church or two, and occasionally a social center or recreational hall. The houses of each settlement were nearly all built to one or two basic designs and painted

15 Unpublished data.
16 *Minerals Yearbook*, 1949, p. 319ff; 1954, Vol. II, p. 82ff; 1957, Vol. II, p. 107ff.

alike. If race practices required it, separate clusters of houses were provided for Negroes. Often these were placed in an inferior location, as along a rutted road up a "run" or "branch." The houses were simply designed and equipped with a minimum of facilities. In most communities, they were one-story detached units; in a few places, duplexes were built.

In the past twenty-five years, most coal companies have sold their houses and deeded away some of their remaining "community" properties. First in the northern coal fields, then in the southern, the ownership of the dwellings passed into the hands of the occupants. Sometimes they were sold directly. More often a town or city real estate firm bought all houses in a settlement as a single purchase, then resold them (at a higher unit price) to the occupants. In a number of communities, the new owners have added foundations, furnaces, windows, window boxes, siding, plumbing, porches, trellises, basements, paint. They made their houses their own, distinctive from their neighbors'. The basic similarity of design remains, but the old drabness has yielded to their handiwork.

The most attractive communities today appear to be those centering in large and productive mines. In a number of these, the company has removed houses no longer needed. The least attractive communities are small clusters of houses, set off by themselves away from other community facilities. Here the vacancies are most conspicuous. Besides these two types of settlements, little one-room bachelor shacks, occupied by the flotsam of the countryside, are scattered all over the coal industry.

As mining employment declines, so eventually must the population of the mining towns. In perhaps most coal communities, this has happened. A vacated house finds little market in such a place; there are no new hirings, no newcomers. Many coal communities have boarded up and abandoned houses. Some have houses that are partly razed, the job unfinished. Everything about such settlements suggests that the future is elsewhere.

Service facilities in coal communities are limited, measured by urban standards, though perhaps as extensive as the people can support. The larger coal companies operate company stores. A typical one includes a food department, appliances, hardware, work clothes and house dresses, and a lunch counter. The men are not obligated to buy there. If they do, however, they may either pay cash or "cut script," that is, charge their purchases against their earnings by endorsing a wage assignment form.

This last practice is still widespread; some store managers say they couldn't survive without it.

Churches are found in most coal communities. In all parts of the Southern Appalachians, Negroes and whites worship separately. The churches of the coal communities follow several patterns. First, there are "community" churches, once provided by the coal companies. Some of them have affiliated with one of the established denominations. By and large, as the companies gave up the ownership of houses, they deeded the church buildings to their congregations. Second, there are churches of the established denominations, with the usual range of programs. Some have their own full-time minister; others are served by a part-time or circuit minister. Third, there are "local outlook"[17] churches, given to highly emotional forms of religious expression, and dogmatically fundamentalist. Fourth, in a few localities are the "mining missions" of some of the larger denominations. They perform the usual religious functions, and also provide community centers, recreational leadership, and welfare services.

As the working miners' real wages have risen, their standards of living have risen, too. Where a larger town or city is within reach, some miners have moved in to take their places among people of various occupations. Among those who are so located that they cannot move to a more urban place, some have introduced into their standards of living practices which seem out of balance by middle-income standards. Their home appliances, television sets, and automobiles seem relatively more expensive than their houses. There are two basic reasons for this, other than taste. First, the only way they have to improve their housing (except to build afresh) is to remodel the houses they already have, for the choice of moving to successively better houses, open to city residents, is closed to them. Second, long-time purchases, such as newly built homes, would be risky at best, even if loans could be obtained. While regularly working miners have high current earnings, too many have seen their fellow workers laid off with no prospect of reemployment in coal mining. An electric washer, a television set, and a new car instead of a new house represent a compromise between the miner's high wages and his insecurity.

[17] This name is used in Mark Rich, *Some Churches in Coal Mining Communities of West Virginia* (Charleston, W. Va., 1951), p. 25ff. Rich notes that in eleven West Virginia communities, about ten percent of the churches are of the highly emotional type, but recognizes that he may have under-enumerated them.

A counterpoint to the insecurity of uncertain employment is the availability of welfare services to miners and their families through the United Mine Workers of America Welfare and Retirement Fund. This Fund receives its capital from the 40 cents per ton royalty paid on union-mined coal. The programs operated by the Fund provide pensions of $100 per month to eligible retired miners, hospital and medical care benefits for miners and their dependents, funeral expense benefits ($350), survivors' benefits ($650 paid in installments), and small amounts of help to families of miners killed or seriously injured in mine disasters.[18]

The health services are noteworthy in that they bring a quality of medical care to miners and their families that was seriously needed in the coal mining areas of the southern mountains. The Fund provides major medical service, though not "routine" home or office care, to eligible men and their dependents. These services are provided through physicians and hospitals approved by the Fund, or in the ten U.M.W. Memorial Hospitals (see Chapter XIV).[19]

Ninety-eight miners, living in three widely separated mining communities, were interviewed as part of this study. Typically, they had begun to work in the mines at 18 or 19 years of age, and had been at it for 25 or 30 years by 1958-59. By and large, they passively accept mining employment. It is what they have always done, and they are not much given to appraising it. Pressed, they say they like the high wages and dislike the danger associated with mining. Their sense of job security varies, quite realistically, with the prospect of employment at the local mine. Perhaps this is quite telling: when the ninety-eight were asked, "Would you like your son to be a miner?" eighty-seven said, "No."

What prospects actually do face the miners and their sons? Is coal mining an occupation without a future? What are the needs of those who will not again enter the mines? While the future cannot always be anticipated correctly, the prospects for the next few years seem to include the following:

The market for coal may rise, but the prospect is for less mining employment, not more. Two bases of industry optimism are the demands of the electric generating industry and the possibility that the total energy needs of the country will outgrow the production of petroleum and natural gas. But atomic energy may take over some of the market now supplied by these other fuels and by coal. Even if coal output again rises, the more widespread use of con-

tinuous mining machines is inevitable, and their use will cut employment. In the competition between small, relatively unmechanized mines and large mechanized ones, the latter seem to have the better chance. Since the small mines use more manpower, and so provide more employment per ton of coal. than do the larger mines, a larger share of production for the latter will cut employment further.

The high-wage standing of the industry should continue, and mining employment should become continually more attractive for those who have it. Work in the mines, measured by tons per manshift, should become ever more productive. Some tasks, such as the maintenance of the huge hundred-thousand-dollar continuous mining machines, are highly skilled. The levels of living of employed miners should continue to rise. There is a very limited recruiting of young men to be trained as supervisors and of mechanics. The staffing of technical and supervisory personnel appears to be neither a problem for the coal companies nor to hold out much promise for other than technically educated young men.

Because much coal mining is carried on in isolated locations, the prospect that unemployed miners may be able to get new kinds of work while staying in their present homes is not at all bright in most places. Some men have found jobs, though a number of them call for many miles of commuting daily. In northern West Virginia, where the mines are within reach of places of about 25,000 some wives have found work in the cities. While efforts must be made to attract new employers to towns that are within reach of the mining settlements, it must be remembered that the competition to attract new industries is nationwide and intense.

There has already been a substantial outmigration from the coal-mining areas of the Southern Appalachians, as another chapter of this volume attests. Young people, especially, are leaving. This out-movement should be encouraged. A very few families have moved out under special sponsorship, as that of a denomination. Any efforts to prepare the migrants for life in the cities to which they are going, and to provide them with social contacts upon arrival, are to the good. Retraining the younger men in urban

[18] United Mine Workers of America, *U.M.W.A. Welfare and Retirement Fund, Report for the Year Ending June 30, 1958,* pp. 1-32.
[19] W. A. Raleigh, Jr., "The Welfare Fund Medical Programs," *Coal Age,* LXIII (August, 1958), pp. 72-77.

skills should be undertaken. Migration is not a simple solution for the older workers, though. Few can take marketable skills with them, and many are older than the large industrial concerns are willing to hire. Some who have gone to cities have tasted defeat and returned to the mountains. Others lack the resources to move.

It is difficult to avoid the conclusion that some people are going to remain in the mining areas without work. What then? While self-help efforts such as gardening and hunting may be assumed, the need for welfare aid seems inescapable. Many families now depend largely on commodities sent as surplus foods by the federal government to the states for distribution to the needy. This program is inadequate to sustain health unless it is supplemented. The challenge to welfare services in the coal-mining areas of the southern mountains is tremendous, and must be met.

Forestry

Forestry and the primary processing of wood products make a smaller contribution than coal to the economy of the area. Altogether thirty to forty thousand people may be employed in this field in the Southern Appalachians, many of them only irregularly. They constitute about 2 percent of the employed people of the territory. Forestry activities are very widely distributed, however, occurring in virtually every county in the territory, and, in a few scattered locations, they provide substantial employment.

In the United States as a whole, 664 million acres, or 34 percent of the total land surface, is in forest, though the forest cover is quite unevenly distributed. About 70 percent of the forested area is classed as commercial, that is, capable of yielding timber and other wood for standard uses. The "non-commercial" remainder includes forest land with yields too small to enter into commerce and areas, such as national parks and other recreational areas, where logging is not permitted.[20]

The Southern Appalachian Region is fairly heavily wooded. In places the forest has given away to town and city development, and to farming, but in most areas two-thirds of the territory is still in forest, and nearly all of this forest is classed as commercial. Since less than a quarter of the nation's surface is in commercial forest, the Southern Appalachian territory has more than twice as high a proportion of land capable of supporting a forest-products industry. In only one

county, Jefferson County, West Virginia, is an appreciably lower percentage of land in commercial forest than in the nation as a whole, and only three others, two in the Great Valley of Tennessee and one in north central West Virginia, are near the national average. The remaining 186 all exceed the national mean. At the upper extreme are several counties in the most rugged portion of the Southern Appalachians, with forests covering over 90 percent of their surface.

In the United States as a whole, softwood (conifer) and hardwood (broad leaved deciduous) forests are about equal in area. The Southern Appalachian forests are largely hardwood; their boundaries correspond closely with those of the entire Appalachian hardwood region. Over 80 percent of the standing saw timber in the territory is hardwood. The range is from 57.5 percent hardwood in the five Southern Appalachian counties of Alabama and 60.5 percent for the Georgia counties to 91.3 percent in West Virginia and a high of 97.2 percent for the eight most eastern counties of Kentucky.[21] East of the mountains, the forests are largely pine. Pine is also the dominant species or appears along with hardwoods in some limited Appalachian portions of Alabama, Georgia, North Carolina, Virginia, and the Great Valley of Tennessee. Nearly everywhere else hardwoods predominate, various subspecies of oaks being the most common.

Hardwood forests are nearly everywhere of mixed species. The association of species in any one location is affected by soil, elevation, slope, and exposure. There are yellow pines and dry-site oaks on ridge tops and on upper exposed (southern and western) slopes; mixed oaks occupy lower exposed and upper protected (north and east) slopes; on sheltered slopes of moderately deep soil are several subspecies of moist-site oaks, and maple, beech, hickory, and birch; in coves there are oaks, yellow poplar, hickory, and other hardwoods, and sometimes white pine; bottom lands, poorly drained, have river birch, sycamore, and willow. Production is highest on the sheltered slopes

[20] United States Department of Agriculture, *Timber Resources for America's Future* (Forest Service Report No. 14, January, 1958), pp. 113-114.

[21] Percentages are based on data in Central States Forest Experiment Station, Northeastern Forest Experiment Station, Southeastern Forest Experiment Station, and Southern Forest Experiment Station, *Forest Survey Release*, various issues. Kentucky data are incomplete; they include only the eight eastern counties, namely Lloyd, Harlan, Knott, Leslie, Letcher, Martin, Perry, and Pike. Data for the Cumberland forest region are not available.

and coves, where the species also are in the greatest profusion.[22]

Commercial forest land is variously owned. Some of it is in public ownership; for example, municipal watershed lands and parks, state and national forests and parks, Indian reservations, and land owned by T.V.A. Of the public forest acreage, national forests include a far larger area than all other public lands combined. There are 150 such forests in the United States, with a combined acreage above 180 million acres, of which less than 85 million acres are classed as commercial forest land. The first national forests were founded in the west; none were established in the east until after 1911. That year the Weeks Law provided for the purchase of lands in watersheds of navigable streams to promote the regulation of streamflow and the production of timber. The lands purchased under the provisions of this law are administered as national forests, and include much of the publicly owned land in the Southern Appalachians (see Figure 45).

There are nine national forests either wholly or partly within the Southern Appalachians, with over 11,365,000 acres in the mountain territory. Except for the Cumberland National Forest on the western rim of the Southern Appalachian part of Kentucky and part of the Jefferson National Forest which overlaps the Virginia-Kentucky border, the land area of these forests lies on the eastern edge of the mountains, especially in the Allegheny and Blue Ridge ranges. Unlike much of the western national forest land, most of that in the Southern Appalachians has timber of commercial value.

The national forests are scientifically managed to achieve basic policy objectives. They generally include the following: First is the stocking of the forests, the cutting out of culls, setting out of seedlings in certain kinds of forests, and selective harvesting to increase forest quality. Second is harvesting so as to obtain a sustained yield. Under sound management, trees are a crop; selective cutting on a large acreage permits a yield of saw timber each year. Third, forests are administered for multiple use objectives, such as providing timber, furnishing watershed protection and sanctuary for wildlife, and for recreation. Fourth, the forests are protected against fire, insects, and disease.

The timber cut from the national forest lands in the Southern Appalachians cannot be reported precisely, since only state data are available. The national forests in the six-state area of Georgia, North Carolina, Virginia, West Virginia, Kentucky, and Tennessee lie very largely within the Southern Appalachians, however, and production data for these states do not much exaggerate the facts for the area of this study. The volume of timber cut from the national forests in these states in 1957 was more than 211 million board feet, and it was valued at 3.27 million dollars.

Approximately one-sixth of the forested area of the Southern Appalachians is in one form or another of public ownership. The rest is about equally divided between industrial holdings and farms. Much of the land in larger holdings is owned by lumber or pulp and paper companies, though some is owned by mines and some by railroads. Most of the small forest plots are on farms. In general, where the topography is too rough for agriculture, as in much of West Virginia and eastern Tennessee, industrial holdings account for much of the forest acreage; in the more open regions, farm holdings are larger, though there are few really extensive holdings. For example, in West Virginia, where industrial ownership predominates, only ten owners have over 50,000 acres. At the other extreme, forest plots under 100 acres account for 40 percent of the forest acreage and 90 percent of the ownership. Two-thirds of the acreages are under 500 acres and cover 99 percent of the owners. The prevailing pattern throughout the entire Southern Appalachians is that of a vast number of small holdings and a relatively few large ones.[23]

Most private forests, whether industrial or farm, are not well-managed. There has been an increase in the use of professional foresters since World War II, both as regular employees and on a fee-for-service basis. County foresters, serving as county agricultural agents, do provide free assistance in administering farm timber stands, though often serving a block of counties instead of a single county. Despite these, cull trees are rarely removed; young stands are seldom thinned, as they are in national forests; and the selection of trees for harvesting is scarcely ever guided by the long-term objective of a sustained yield.

The importance of forest management is pointed up in a six-county study in the Tennessee Valley. By reforesting some areas, reinforcing understocked forest

[22] For a more detailed statement see William A. Duerr, *The Economic Problems of Forestry in the Appalachian Region* (Cambridge, Harvard University Press, 1949), p. 143.

[23] West Virginia Forest Industries Committee, *West Virginia Forest Facts, 1957-58* (Huntington, W. Va.), p. 4.

land, removing culls, converting forest lands to the optimum kind of timber for each area, eliminating grazing, and controlling fires, insects, and diseases, and developing new markets, the timber growers should be able to increase their stumpage income six-fold while woods employment would increase five-fold.[24]

From the small farm plots particularly, the sale of timber is little better than haphazard. From one study, we learn that the primary reason for the sale of trees was a need for ready cash, while the next reason was to clear land for agriculture. Only 14.4 percent of sales were made because the owner considered the timber mature and ready for cutting.[25] Sales are made either of marked trees or on a "lump sum" basis which permits the buyer to take what he wants from a specified tract. With this latter type of sale, everything marketable may be removed, including first sawlogs, then pulpwood or props, then sometimes wood down to two inches in diameter for charcoal. Sales are often made on the initiative of the seller, on the basis of a single offer, for much less than their true market value.

The pulp mills, representing investments of millions of dollars, must have a regular supply of wood. Most pulp and paper companies own forest land, and it is estimated that about a third of all pulpwood comes from the company-owned tracts. These are characteristically large and well-managed. The companies rely mainly on a contract system for the rest of their supply. A mill takes its drawing area and divides it into "dealerships." In each, a wood broker is given a quota of wood to be supplied. He in turn enters into purchase contracts with woodland owners and others to supply the pulpwood and load it for shipment. The men who actually supply the wood are more often than not small operators with other sources of livelihood. The system of purchase contracts gives the suppliers the status of individual entrepreneurs, and leaves the purchasers without minimum wage or social security responsibility for them.

The range of forest products is large, even if one considers only items of primary manufacture. Lumber ranks first in the country as a whole by a large margin, while pulpwood is second, only a little ahead of firewood. The uses to which timber is put depend on location and tree species. The importance of locations is illustrated by the marketing of mine timbers, most of which are used to support mine roofs against falls. In West Virginia, with its heavy dependence on coal mining, 24.1 percent of the forest harvest by volume went into mine timbers in 1957,[26] and in Kentucky a smaller but significant percent of the total went into this use. On the other hand, the production of mine props is negligible in North Carolina, and accounts for less than one percent of Alabama's forest output.

Each type of wood use favors certain species over others. Framing materials for construction tend to be softwood. Western red cedar is preferred for wooden shingles. While white spruce is the choice stock for pulp, it is in short supply, so the southern pulp industry is built on yellow pine. White oak is used for tight cooperage and for package veneers. Certain hardwoods are used specifically for fine face veneers. Ash is used for tool handles, beech for clothespins. Locust, highly resistive to rot, is used as fence posts.

Hardwood constitutes more than half of the Southern Appalachian production. In 1942, when the demand for lumber was affected by war needs, there were 4,729 sawmills in a 164-county area in the Southern Appalachians. These mills produced 1.6 million MBF (thousand board feet) that year, about a third of which was softwood and two-thirds hardwood.[27]

Since the time of that survey, there has been a downward trend both in the number of mills and in the volume of lumber output. The territory of North Carolina that had 747 mills and produced 237,000 MBF in 1942, had 642 mills and produced 155,000 MBF in 1947, and 374 mills and 101,000 MBF in 1957. The seriousness of this drop of fifty percent in number of sawmills within fifteen years is accentuated by the fact that more than a hundred of the 1957 mills were idle. In this period the drop in production approached 60 percent.[28] The West Virginia territory, with 1,315 mills and 561,000 MBF in 1942, had 899 mills and 415,000 MBF in 1957,

[24] William H. Ogden, *The Forest Economy of a Six-County Area in the Tennessee Valley* (Tennessee Valley Authority, Division of Forestry Relations, Report No. 225-59, 1959).

[25] Wallace W. Christensen and Allen W. Goodspeed, *Marketing Forest Products in West Virginia* (West Virginia University Agricultural Experiment Station, Bulletin 421, June, 1958), p. 11.

[26] *West Virginia Forest Facts, 1957-58*, p. 9.

[27] Arthur S. Todd, Jr., *Wartime Lumber Production in the Appalachian Hardwood Region, January 1942-June 1944* (U.S. Department of Agriculture, Appalachian Experiment Station), county data, pp. 42ff.

[28] North Carolina Department of Conservation Development, Division of Forestry, *Sawmills and Lumber Production, Western North Carolina Counties, 1957* (not paged).

drops of 31 percent and 26 percent respectively.[29] If the counties for which 1942 and 1937 production data are available are representative of the whole Appalachian territory, then production in the latter was about 1.9 million MBF in 1942 and 1.2 million MBF in 1957. These are rough estimates.

Pulpwood, the nation's second-largest wood product by volume, is also one of the fastest growing products. Pulpwood consumption was 19.7 million standard cords (4' x 4' x 8') in 1947, 26.5 million cords in 1952, and according to a preliminary estimate, 35.7 million in 1957. It is projected that 56 million will be used by 1975, and 190 million by the end of the century. The southern states account for a rising percentage of the total: 44 percent in 1947 and 58 percent five years later.

In that part of the Southern Appalachians lying within the States of Alabama, Georgia, North Carolina, Tennessee, and Virginia, the production of pulpwood has risen rapidly in the postwar period. This territory produced 568 thousand cords in 1947, 788 thousand in 1952, and 1,079 thousand in 1957. The ten-year increase was thus 90 percent.[30] Pulpwood production in Kentucky and West Virginia is relatively small, being 47 thousand cords in the whole of the former state in 1947 and 52 thousand for the whole of West Virginia in 1957. There is no pulpmill in either of these states, as against ten in the mountain counties of the other states. Big mills, however, tend to be near the coast, partly so that the water pollution resulting from their operation can be quickly carried to sea.

Yellow pine has several advantages over hardwoods for the manufacture of paper. Yellow pine forests are often confined to a single species, while hardwood forests are everywhere of mixed species which have to be separated, since each species must be processed differently from the others. More fundamental, the pine is a long-fibred wood, and when treated by the sulphate or kraft process, yields high grade papers. The hardwoods are short-fibred, and quality papers are not manufactured from them. There is general consensus that hardwood pulp will be used more extensively in the future, as many present uses of paper do not require a high quality material; for example, in packing cases and utility wallboards. Also, new processes are being developed and put to use, which make the conversion of hardwood pulp bolts to paper more efficient. It seems quite likely, however, that as the consumption of pulpwood increases, the drain on the pine forests will exceed their growth, and the pulp and paper industries then will be driven to the use of the hardwoods.

The principal forms of employment provided by the primary wood industries are logging and milling. Sawmills in the Southern Appalachians have changed in a direction atypical of industry generally. Whereas there once were scattered large mills, there are now fewer large mills and many smaller ones.

The early mills were established along the rivers. The first hardwood logging may have been along the Kanawha Valley.[31] The loggers in these early operations cut over vast stretches of virgin timber, at first removing only the choicest and most accessible stock, then as methods improved, making more intensive cuttings and penetrating into less easily reached territory. Production reached its peak through the Appalachian hardwood region in 1909, with output standing at about four billion board feet of lumber. Some large operations continued well past that peak year and a number of companies, some of them controlling whole watersheds, continued high production down through the 1920's and even later. The 1930's saw the passing of most of the bandmills, which are large stationary mills. Some large mills still operate, but they no longer give the industry its dominant character.

As the original forest stands were cut and logging shifted to the sparser stands of second growth timber, small portable mills took over part of the job of sawing up the forest material. These mills, using circular saws, are usually set up under temporary shelters to cut the available sawlogs from a tract of timber, then moved on to other tracts. Small mills are scattered, literally by the hundreds, throughout the Southern Appalachian territory, converting some of the mature sawtimber into lumber, but not having access to enough raw material to be converted to stationary bandmills.

The U.S. Census of Manufacture gives county data for employment in "lumber and basic timber products" for 1954. This category includes logging camps and logging contractors, sawmills and planing mills, shingle mills, cooperage stock mills, and excelsior mills. Of the establishments fitting these categories

[29] Data from Division of Forestry, State of West Virginia Conservation Commission.

[30] J. F. McCormack, *1957 Pulpwood Production in the South* (U.S. Department of Agriculture, Forest Service, Forest Survey Release No. 53, September, 1958) county data, pp. 5-14.

[31] Todd, p. 4.

in the Southern Appalachian states, about two-thirds are sawmills or planing mills. In the Appalachian portion of these states the fraction is probably smaller, since less of the harvested hardwood than of the softwood goes into lumber.

The 1954 Census reports establishments in lumber and basic timber products in *all but two* of the 190 counties in the Southern Appalachians. Lumbering is thus widely distributed, much more so than any other manufacturing industry in the mountain area, and reaches into every section of the Southern Appalachians.

Most of these operations are very small. Of 2,732 reported for the Southern Appalachian counties in 1954, 2,458, or nine out of every ten, had fewer than twenty employees, while only 37 had a hundred or more. While county data do not provide a further refined classification, it appears that in the Southern Appalachian states as a whole, 50.1 percent of all establishments employed fewer than five workers. The vast preponderance of small units is unmistakable.

In Tennessee (the whole state) in 1946, of nearly 2,800 mills, only nineteen produced 3,000 or more MBF, and may be considered large. Together they accounted for about one-ninth of all production. Over 500 mills of medium size (500-2,999 MBF) produced more than half the state's lumber. More than a third of all output was from small mills.[32] These statewide figures exaggerate the role of the larger mills for the Southern Appalachian territory, however, for the densest scattering of small mills is in the mountain counties, while the greatest concentration of large mills is in the Memphis area. The very small mills may hold second place to medium-sized mills in the production of marketed lumber elsewhere in the Southern Appalachians, as they appear to do in Tennessee. A West Virginia sawmill study, in process at the time of this writing, appears to indicate this to be true of that state. In western North Carolina in 1957, while small mills far outnumbered all others, the proportion of mills of medium to large size (500 or more MBF per year) is increasing.[33]

Along with the emergence of small portable mills and partly as a consequence of their development has come the virtual disappearance of logging and lumber camps. As recently as 1942, there were still many in the southern mountains. In five states cut by the Southern Appalachians (Georgia and Louisiana are omitted), there were that year at least 313 camps both in and out of the mountain territory with more than 6,000 men in them. Now there are no more than three or four camps. To be sure, easier transportation and the feasibility of commuting would have reduced their number, even if the nature of logging and milling operations had not changed. It is unlikely, however, that the new ease of travel would reduce their number so quickly.

The fact that small mills are portable suggests that they provide only irregular or "casual" employment. Scattered data indicate this to be the case. The 1957 western North Carolina sawmill study reported 301 active sawmills. The average of them worked a crew of seven men 65 days during the year. The total man-days worked in the sawmills and in the woods and yards was 328,393. It is estimated that the wages paid for this work was $3,285,000, or about $10 per man-day.[34] A crew member working 65 days would thus earn about $650.

A few scattered 1956 reports of West Virginia lumber firms indicated that minimum wages—which tended to be maximum wages—were $1.00 an hour in the smaller establishments and a little higher in the larger ones. Hourly rates of $2.00 were extremely rare even for the most skilled jobs in the largest mills. The annual payrolls of the smaller operators averaged less than a thousand dollars per worker in some cases.

Low wages and temporary work, then, characterize at least a part of the basic forest products industries in sections of the Southern Appalachians. Possibly some workers have two or more forestry or lumbering employers during the year. Many of them must earn part of their livelihood at other work. The most common of these is farming. For at least some of the men who work at logging or in the mills, farming is the primary employment, and these others are supplementary.

The great social need in forestry is to increase its impact on the levels of living of the people; the route to this end is better forestry practices. The improvement of forest stands will in time serve the national interest, for while the annual sawtimber cut of hardwoods is now well below the rate of growth, the increase of population in the United States and the high rate of cut in the softwood forests across

[32] Department of Agriculture, *Tennessee's Timber Economy* (Forest Resource Report No. 9, 1955), p. 22.

[33] *Sawmills and Lumber Production, Western North Carolina, 1957.*

[34] *Sawmills and Lumber Production, Western North Carolina, 1957.*

the country may together increase the use of hardwoods.

On both large and small tracts in private ownership, better forest management is desirable. The acreages in state and national forests are professionally managed. While some public lands must serve multiple purposes, such as watershed protection and public recreation along with timber production, the forestry practices followed on them are a useful guide to private owners. Three interlocking sets of practices are needed. The quality of the forest stand should be improved by such means as removing the culls, thinning new forest stands where needed, selective harvesting, blocking erosion, and preventing grazing on timbered lands. Efforts should be intensified to prevent forest fires, especially in areas of high fire loss, and to prevent loss through blight and harmful insects. Trees should be harvested when mature; sales should be on a marked-tree basis, with competitive bidding. On many acreages harvesting can be managed so as to provide a sustained yield.

Improved forestry practices can be achieved by the land owners who want them. Professional foresters, to be employed on the large forest tracts, and forestry extension workers elsewhere, can show the way. A change away from the almost casual practices of the present to those that are technically sound should pay the owners in dollars and cents. Further, if the forest yield can be raised both in quantity and quality, forestry employment should increase, and the prospect of attracting new wood-using industries to the mountains should be enhanced.

Other Mineral Industries

No other natural resource industry has an annual output anywhere near equal in value to either coal or woodland products. A number of mineral industries, however, are locally important in that they bring purchasing power into their communities and provide employment.

All four of the generally recognized classes of minerals—metals, coal, crude petroleum and natural gas, and nonmetals—are found in the Southern Appalachians in one location or another.

The most widely distributed "mining" activity in the territory is the removal of sand and gravel. Nearly as widespread is the mining of limestone and of clay. Limestone is used structurally, most of it being in crushed form, and is a major component in cement. When burned, limestone also yields lime for agriculture. Several concentrations of plants for mining and processing limestone are to be found in the area, the chief of which are in Frederick County, Virginia, and Berkeley and Jefferson Counties, West Virginia. Clay, suitable for the manufacture of bricks and for other ceramic uses, is found at many points throughout the territory, the bricks of Carter County, Kentucky, being worthy of special mention.

Metal deposits of substantial commercial value are mined at scattered points throughout the territory. Manganese, which when found in nature is always compounded with other minerals, is a sufficiently rich element in the compounds bearing it to be of commercial value in a ribbon of counties from Unicoi, Tennessee, to Giles, Virginia. Gypsum is mined in Washington County, Virginia. Zinc, lead, and some silver are mined in two large operations in Wythe County, Virginia. Zinc is also mined in Jefferson and Knox Counties in Tennessee. The mineral cluster of Polk County, Tennessee, yields copper, pyrite, zinc, and some silver, gold, and lead. Mica is a major mineral in scattered counties of western North Carolina, where six counties account for about 85 percent of North Carolina's mica production, and also for a large proportion of all mica produced in the United States. Small amounts of brown iron ore are scattered around the southern rim of the region.

A number of nonmetals, other than those already mentioned, enter into the resource bases of certain communities. Only five mineral industries are included in this final section, and each is given only a brief summary statement. Marble, feldspar and kaolin, mica, and zinc are presented because the Southern Appalachians makes a significant contribution to the national output of each. The fifth, crude petroleum and natural gas, is included, even though Southern Appalachian production is small, because of the importance of these mineral fuels in the nation's economy.

Commercially, any rock that takes a high polish is classed as marble. True marbles result from the crystallization of limestone, and in pure form are white. Actually, nearly all marbles contain impurities, either mineral or organic, that result in veins, streaking, clouding, and coloration. Since crystallization has resulted from the pressures and heat generated by the earth, most deposits are in the mountainous regions of the country. The Appalachian marble belt, stretching from the Canadian border in Vermont to beyond Birmingham, Alabama, is the most productive of the nation. It runs close to the eastern edge of the Southern Appalachian territory across Virginia, overlaps the Tennessee-North Carolina border, and then drops into Georgia.[35]

The principal marble-quarrying areas in the southern mountain territory lie in Pickens and Gilmer Counties in Georgia, Cherokee County in North Carolina, and Blount, Grainger, Knox, and Union Counties in Tennessee.

Pickens County in Georgia is the leading marble producer in that state. Most of the marbles are of various shades of grey, and are sold for monuments, and both exterior and interior construction, depending on color and texture. Marble from the Etowah quarry in this area is characterized by green veinings and delicate shades of pink.

Commercial quarrying of marble in North Carolina is confined to a belt less than half a mile wide across Cherokee County. Two types are produced, one a dark-bluish grey which may be mottled or striated with white, the other a fairly uniform grey.

Tennessee marbles range from black through various shades of grey to pink and red, and some contain undistorted marine fossils. The State is a large producer, recently ranking second in the nation. Its principal quarries are in Blount, Knox, and Union Counties, and some black marble is quarried from Grainger County. The marbles of Tennessee, because of their great beauty and low porosity, have been widely used in both public and private structures for wainscotting, steps, floor tile, and on building exteriors, as well as for monuments. Some is crushed for terrazzo and for roof chips.

The feldspars, a group of aluminum silicate minerals containing varying proportions of potash, soda, and lime, are important raw materials for the ceramics industries. In 1957, a little over half the national production went into the manufacture of glass, more than a fourth into pottery, about four percent into enamels, and the rest into a miscellany of products. Western North Carolina is the leading source of feldspar in the United States.

Feldspar is a component of certain types of granite rocks. Currently, the most important source is a coarse-textured granite called alaskite. The development of a flotation process by which the feldspar can be separated economically from other minerals in alaskite has given the industry a new efficiency. This granite underlies much of five counties of western North Carolina. In 1957, the feldspar produced for the market was worth $2.7 million and accounted for 38 percent of the volume and 50 percent of the

value of all United States production of feldspar.

Kaolin, or china clay, is a class name for a group of clay minerals alike in chemical formula but different in crystalline structure. Kaolin is formed by the decomposition of other mineral particles, especially feldspar. North Carolina, Georgia, and South Carolina lead in production of this clay for industry. Mining is by power shovels in large open pits. The raw material is then trucked to processing plants where impurities are removed and the refined kaolin is prepared for market, to be used in making china, porcelain, mosaic and other tile, and sparkplugs.

The different varieties of mica are chemically related to feldspar. A distinctive feature of certain forms of mica is that it can be split into very thin layers. Most sheet mica is obtained from a number of small underground mines. It is separated by hand from the rock in which it is embedded, and is taken to trimming houses where it is sheeted and trimmed. In sheet or film form, it is very valuable as an insulator, and has many uses as a nonconductor in the electronics industries. Scrap or flake mica, often a waste product from sheet mica, is ground into a fine powder and used in such materials as roofing, paints, plastics, and lubricants.

North Carolina produced 84 percent of the domestic sheet mica in 1957, and 60 percent of the scrap and flake mica. Six counties accounted for 85 percent of the North Carolina production, and only very small amounts came from elsewhere in the Southern Appalachian territory.

Domestic production of sheet mica, while limited, is highly important because of its uses in electronics. The United States, the world's largest consumer of this strategic material, absorbs most of the domestic production, and imports about two-thirds of its requirement of sheet mica.

During World War II, the United States government was the sole buyer of domestic sheet mica. After the war, production fell off sharply. In the 1950's mica production was stimulated by two government programs. These government activities for procuring mica, plus the growing demand for mica in the electronics industries, have resulted in high rates of output in recent years.

Primary zinc, a bluish-white crystalline metalic element, is commercially important; first because as a corrosion inhibitor it can be used for a protective

[35] For a good, concise statement of this topic see Oliver Bowles, *Marble* (U.S. Department of the Interior, Bureau of Mines Information Circular 7829, May, 1958), pp. 1-31.

coating on steel in galvanized products, and second, because of its use in alloys. Eastern Tennessee and southwestern Virginia are large zinc producers.

The operations in Virginia accounted for about 23,000 short tons of recoverable zinc in 1957. In the same year Tennessee had a zinc production of some 58,000 tons in the nation's total of 531,000 tons. With this production, Tennessee led the South and ranked second only to New York. The zinc ore of Tennessee lies in a narrow north-south zone in the east end of the state not far from Knoxville.[36]

The share of the national mineral fuels held by petroleum remained fairly steady at around thirty-five percent during the 1950's, while natural gas rose from 19.8 to 27.7 percent between 1950 and 1957, and coal fell. While the Southern Appalachian region makes a limited contribution to the national production of crude petroleum and natural gas, it consumes more of both than it produces.

Crude petroleum and natural gas often come from the same wells, though some wells give oil but very little gas, while others produce gas but no oil. Oil and gas wells are commonly reported together, without being classified as one or the other. According to the Independent Petroleum Association of America, in 1958 either petroleum or gas (or both) was produced in 75 of the 190 counties in the Southern Appalachians: 34 in West Virginia, 30 in Kentucky, 7 in Virginia, and 4 in Tennessee.[37] In the southern mountain area the distribution of oil and gas tends to follow the location of coal resources.

The Census of Mineral Industries reported 769 crude petroleum and natural gas establishments in the Southern Appalachian counties in 1954. Of these, 585 were in West Virginia, 172 in Kentucky, 8 in Tennessee, 4 in Virginia, and none elsewhere. The counties from which they were reported are not identical with those in the 1958 report, though the differences are few. These oil and gas operations provide very little employment. In both West Virginia and Kentucky, a majority of them provide employment for no more than four people apiece, while about a sixth were listed in the Census as having no employees at all. Only seven anywhere in West Virginia and three in the whole of Kentucky employ a hundred or more.

In Kentucky, 3.58 million barrels of oil were produced in the Southern Appalachian counties in 1956.[38] This was .14 of one percent of the national output of oil for that year. West Virginia's oil production in 1957 was 2.2 million barrels for the whole state,[39]

that is, less than a tenth of one percent of the United States total for that year. Although 80 percent of the state's oil-gas wells are in the Appalachian counties, the oil production is much higher in the Ohio Valley counties of the state, so the Appalachian area accounted for no great share of the output. Petroleum production in other Southern Appalachian states is too small to be reported separately by the United States Bureau of Mines, and the same is true for natural gas.

Natural gas withdrawals in 1957 were 76 billion cubic feet in Kentucky and 206 billion cubic feet in West Virginia.[40] The proportion of these totals coming from the Southern Appalachian counties is not reported, though there are several of the larger producing fields among the Appalachian counties. Gross national withdrawals are in excess of 12,000 billion cubic feet per year; thus Kentucky and West Virginia contribute above two percent of the total.

The Present and the Future

The natural resource industries in the Southern Appalachians contribute substantially to the economic base of the territory. The two largest of them, coal and forest products, are among the most fundamental in the nation. As our industrial economy expands, so will its hunger for raw materials. What those materials will be is decided largely by the users, most of whom are outside the Region, and not by primary producers. The future of large areas in the southern mountains depends in a fundamental way on the market for their raw materials.

The forestry and lumber industries reached their peak in the southern mountains before World War I; but since sawtimber is a renewable resource, a crop, there is long-term hope for growth in timbering. The "lesser" minerals have provided local employment and tax revenues, and should continue to do so as long as these resources last. Coal, the giant among the minerals, is the principal source of economic dislocation and hunger in the most depressed sections of the Region.

The characteristics of a natural resource base, enumerated near the beginning of this chapter, take on a special significance in the light of the changes

[36] *Minerals Yearbook, 1957*, Vol. I, p. 1289.

[37] Independent Petroleum Association of America, *The Oil Producing Industry in Your State, 1958 Edition* (Tulsa), pp. 23, 53, 59, 61.

[38] Preston McGrain, *Mineral Resources for Kentucky, 1955 and 1956* (Kentucky Geological Survey, 1958), p. 22.

[39] *Minerals Yearbook, 1957*, Vol. II, p. 358.

[40] *Minerals Yearbook, 1957*, Vol. II, p. 308.

that are taking place in the mountains. Coal brought many thousands of men into the mountains. The lesser minerals have attracted people, though in much smaller numbers, to their respective localities. Miners and woodmen have gone where the exploitation of resources has afforded employment.

The specific locations of the employment have placed some of the workers in extractive industries near large settlements, for example zinc workers near Knoxville, and have put others deep in the mountains, in places that are not easily accessible even today. The most intensive coal mining in the Southern Appalachians is carried on in very rugged country. Mining and forestry range from being parts of a diversified economic base to being the sole means of subsistence, apart from welfare aid, in their localities. In either case, they have made significant contributions to their localities. Where the fortune of a people are tied to a single industry, as is true in so much of the southern coal fields, and that industry simultaneously cuts output and replaces men by machines, depression results.

Mining and forestry are both small-scale operations, when judged by manufacturing standards. When they have pulled people into otherwise unsettled areas, they have distributed them into many small clusters, a settlement pattern rarely repeated elsewhere. Each cluster has an economic reason for being only so long as the employment around which it grew persists.

Since coal mining must be expected to provide less, not more, employment in the future, a key question is *whether the settlement pattern produced by coal, in the locations and on the terrain where coal is mined, can be adapted to other kinds of economic activity.* This is the challenge, and it is folly to assume that it can be met successfully. A three-pronged attack is needed: an energetic search for new kinds of employment within accessible distance of the displaced miners, a realistic welfare program, and the redistribution of at least a part of the population. The substantial outmigration from coal mining areas that has already occurred is one type of solution.

A good life should remain for some. If the demand for the Region's basic resources stabilizes or grows, and if the population adjusts downward in response to the shrinking of jobs because of technological advance, then those who continue to draw their livelihood from the resource industries may enjoy a higher standard of living, and live with greater dignity.

CHAPTER EIGHT

The

Development

of

Manufacturing

CHARLES L. QUITTMEYER

LORIN A. THOMPSON

IN LOOKING AT THE DEVELOPMENT of manufacturing in the Southern Appalachian Region, we are faced at first with some popular preconceptions. One of these is that manufacturing would be unusual because the Region has mountains and hence must be populated with "mountain people," the very words calling up stereotyped pictures of isolation, poverty, stubborn self-reliance, poor education, and lack of communication—all characteristics unfavorable to urbanization and the development of manufacturing, which is supposed to be a part of city life. Another preconception is that there is something dehumanizing about manufacture even though it does increase incomes for its participants. The presumptive self-reliance of the mountain people thus would cause them to refuse work in manufacturing plants because of industry's oppressive nature, even if the chances to engage in such work existed for these people. A third major preconception is that industry will come to a place only if it is wanted badly enough.

Our study indicates that although there is a trace of realism in each of these preconceptions, they are largely unfounded. We have found, for example, that manufacturing has been thriving in much of the study area and plays a prominent part in the economy of the region. That the so-called "mountain people," except in isolated cases, are readily adaptable to industry and eager for manufacturing opportunities, is pointed up by a survey of industrialists' attitudes toward the Region. We have also found that much of the Region is dominated by the economic activities of the Region's cities, particularly those of the metropolitan type. For example, Roanoke has considerable economic influence northward and southward along the Great Valley of Virginia and westward into part of West Virginia. Another finding has been that the mere desire of a community or area for industrial development has little to do with obtaining factories except in a negative sense where a community may be actively hostile to the entrance of a manufacturing plant.

Data collected by the United States Bureau of the Census are very helpful in showing some of the significant developments of industry in the Southern Appalachian Region in recent years. Four subjects have been selected for illustrating the trends of Appalachian industry between 1929 and 1958: (1) number of manufacturing establishments; (2) employment in manufacturing; (3) wages paid by manufacturing industries; and (4) value added by manufacturing. Regional trends are compared with national trends, and the Appalachian parts of each state are compared with the entire state.

Figure 40 shows that Southern Appalachian manufacturing increased more rapidly than that of the tucky, North Carolina, Tennessee, and Virginia lagged behind their states on one or more measures. Regional Tennessee, regional Georgia, and regional North Carolina were ahead of their respective states on three points; regional Virginia was ahead of its

Figure 40. *Percentage Changes in Manufacturing Characteristics, 1929-1958, in the Southern Appalachian Region, the Appalachian States, and the Appalachian Parts of the States, Compared to Changes in the United States for the Same Period*

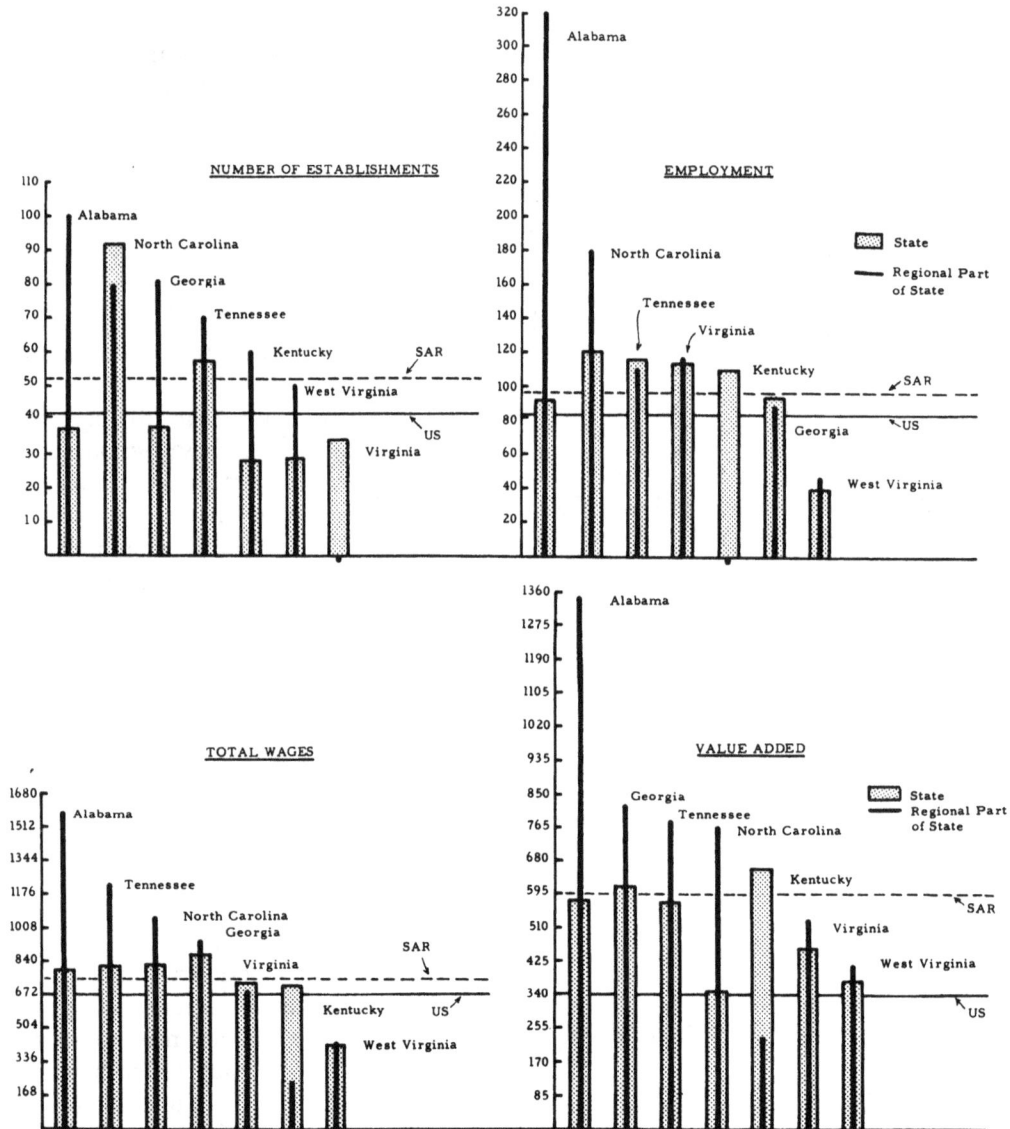

Source: U. S. Census of Manufactures, 1929 and 1958

nation as measured by all four indicators. Furthermore, manufacturing increased more rapidly on all counts in the Appalachian parts of two (Alabama and West Virginia) of the seven states during the period. The Appalachian parts of Georgia, Kentucky, North Carolina, Tennessee, and Virginia state on two points; and regional Kentucky was ahead of its state on only one measure. Table 29 supplements this by showing the number of manufacturing firms per 1,000 of population, and the rates of change during the period under review. (The population data are estimates for 1930, 1950, and 1958; the establishment data are for 1929, 1954, and 1958.)

The number of manufacturing establishments per 1,000 of population did not increase in the United States between 1929 and 1958, but during the same

Table 29. *Number of Manufacturing Establishments per 1,000 Population, United States, Appalachian States, and Southern Appalachian Region, 1929 and 1958*

Area	1929	1958	Percentage change 1929-1958
United States	1.72	1.72	0
Southern Appalachian Region	0.92	1.16	26
Alabama	1.08	1.24	15
Regional Alabama	0.59	1.13	92
Georgia	1.44	1.47	2
Regional Georgia	1.29	1.68	30
Kentucky	0.86	0.95	10
Regional Kentucky	0.42	0.70	67
North Carolina	1.20	1.64	37
Regional North Carolina	1.14	1.57	38
Tennessee	1.09	1.29	18
Regional Tennessee	1.08	1.31	21
Virginia	1.36	1.13	-17
Regional Virginia	1.39	1.18	-15
West Virginia	0.86	0.97	13
Regional West Virginia	0.72	0.95	32

Source: U. S. Census of Manufactures, 1929 and 1958; Census of Population, 1930 and 1950.

period it increased by 26 percent in the Southern Appalachian area. In number of manufacturing firms in 1958 regional Georgia ranked highest with 1.68 per 1,000 persons, and regional Kentucky lowest with 0.70 firms per 1,000. As for percentage change over 1929 on this point, regional Alabama ranked highest with an advance of 92 percent, and Virginia regional stood lowest with a decline of 15 percent.

Figure 41 shows the annual wages in manufacturing paid in 1929 and twenty-nine years later in the United States, in the Southern Appalachian Region as a whole, in each Southern Appalachian state, and in the mountain area of each state. Regional Tennessee had the greatest percentage rise in wages, regional Georgia ranking second, and regional North Carolina third. In actual annual wages in 1958 West Virginia ranked first, regional West Virginia second, and regional Kentucky third. The Appalachian regions of Tennessee, North Carolina, and Kentucky paid higher wages in 1958 than did their states; those of West Virginia, Kentucky, and Tennessee each paid a higher annual wage than the average for the whole Southern Appalachian area. The rate of change in annual wages differed greatly, regional Tennessee's rate of change being over twice that of the regional parts of West Virginia, Virginia, and Kentucky. In this twenty-nine year period, while the total wages

from manufacturing in the United States increased 673 percent, the total wages from manufactures in the Southern Appalachian Region increased 745 percent. In 1929, only Appalachian Kentucky had an annual wage above that in the nation as a whole; but in 1958 no state region was up to the national level, nor indeed were any of the seven states of which the regions were a part up to the nation's level in wages.

The lowest annual wage of those reported in 1929 was that of regional Georgia which was $561; but fortunately its percentage change between 1929 and 1958 was 452 percent, second only to that of regional Tennessee.

Each of the seven Appalachian areas of states had a higher percentage of its employed workers in manufacturing in 1950 than in 1930. In 1930 the percentage of employed persons engaged in manufacturing in regional Georgia exceeded the national percentage; in 1940 and 1950 this was true in the regional parts of North Carolina and Tennessee as well as in regional Georgia. Each of the seven Appalachian states and each of the regional parts of these states showed a larger percentage of its workers employed in agriculture than in manufacture in 1930, but by 1950 the states of Georgia, North Carolina, Virginia, and West Virginia, and the regional parts of Georgia, North Carolina, Tennessee, Virginia, and West Virginia all had a higher percentage engaged in manufacture than in agriculture. In 1930 only the state of West Virginia and its mountainous region had a higher percentage engaged in mining than in other occupations. By 1950, however, regional Kentucky could also make this claim. Of course, without abundant resources to mine, no area could have such a shift in employment.

Figure 42, in presenting changes in employment in manufacturing, speaks without the help of percentages, because statistics were incomplete for a number of counties; but even without exact percentages the trends are clear. The metropolitan areas dominate the manufacturing map of the Region. The counties around such manufacturing cities as Asheville, North Carolina, Roanoke, Virginia, and Chattanooga, Tennessee, illustrate this influence. On the other hand, Charleston, West Virginia, is hemmed in on both sides with blocks of counties of declining population. The one metropolitan area in Kentucky, Boyd County, seems to show little influence on its Kentucky neighbors. Also striking is the pattern of counties having a decrease in employment in manufactures, 1929-1954. There were, in all, 39 such counties. West Virginia had 17 such counties, 13 of which lay in two blocks, one on each side of Charleston, but Tennessee's 10 counties with decreasing manufacturing population were scattered

Figure 41. *Manufacturing Wages, 1929 and 1958, in the Southern Appalachian Region, the Appalachian States, and the United States*

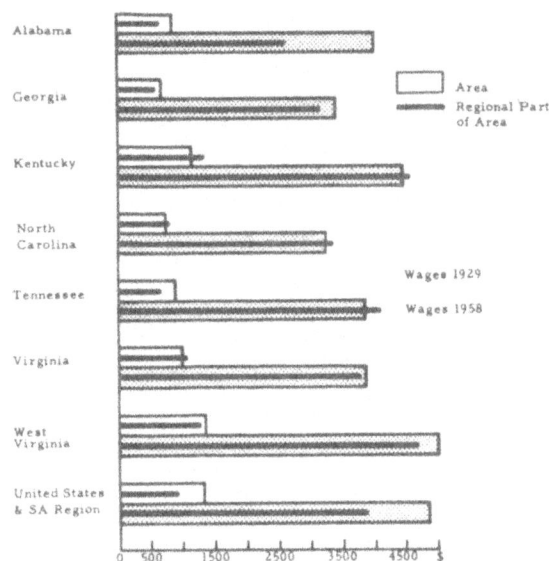

Source: U. S. Census of Manufactures, 1929 and 1958

over nonmetropolitan areas. There may be some significance in the fact that in the three states whose Southern Appalachian parts showed the greatest decrease in employment in manufactures there are also the largest number of insufficient reports.

Gains or losses between 1929 and 1954, by counties, in the value added by manufacturing are shown in Figure 43. In West Virginia 9 counties showed a decrease in value added by manufacture, in Kentucky 5 counties, in Tennessee 2, in Virginia and Georgia one each, and in Alabama and North Carolina none. Again the counties not reporting were concentrated in the same states as the counties showing a decrease in activity. This figure shows even more plainly than Figure 42 the influence of the industrial cities, flowing generally southwest to northeast in the main line of the Great Valley through Georgia, Tennessee, and Virginia, with a branch from North Carolina flowing into this main line and a tip in West Virginia.

The contrast between the western and eastern parts of Appalachian Georgia illustrates the difference between an area on the edge of an industrial center and one that has no such help. The contrast between

Virginia and West Virginia is very great, though they lie side by side.

This statistical sketch shows that manufacturing has been thriving in much of the Southern Appalachian Region. Our concern for the future leads us to examine the factors involved in the location of new plants and their implications for prosperous and nonprosperous parts of the Region.

As will be pointed out later, a survey of industrialists in the Southern Appalachian Region shows that cost advantages in materials and labor are an important factor in the location of industry in this area. Table 30 is an indication of the distribution of the kinds of manufacturing within the region according to the number of people employed. Although wage rates are also important in judging the contribution of an industry to an area, nevertheless employment itself is probably even more significant. Full employment seems to be the first economic goal of a region, rather than the height of wage rates, value added, number of plants, and the like.

Table 30 shows that the employing industries in the Southern Appalachian Region vary in their distribution from that of the United States. Textiles and apparel, industries which seek a plentiful supply of workers at low pay, ranked first and fourth in this Region in 1954; in the United States, apparel ranked fourth, and textiles were not even in the first five ranks. The ubiquitous lumber industry ranked second, food ranked third, and stone, clay, and glass ranked fifth in the Region. These industries are primarily raw-materials oriented, although they are also labor-oriented in that their wage rates are low. In the United States, transportation equipment and machinery, high-wage industries, ranked first and third, while food, apparel, and the stone group came in second, fourth, and fifth.

Textiles are important in all the Appalachian states except Kentucky and West Virginia. Not far behind in importance for these states and their Appalachian regions is apparel, a level of manufacturing one step up from textiles. Only North Carolina, regional Tennessee, West Virginia, and regional West Virginia did not show apparel within the first five ranks.

The differences among and between states and their Appalachian regions are understandable in most cases. Alabama, for instance, has primary metals in second rank because of Birmingham. But Birmingham is not in the Appalachian region. Thus regional Alabama, though fabricated metal products are ranked fifth, does not have primary metals in any of the five ranks. Primary metals ranked third in West Virginia, showing the influence of Wheeling. Since Wheeling is not included in the Appalachian region, primary metals show no rank in the regional five.

We hear a great deal about labor-oriented manufacture, materials-oriented manufacture, and market-oriented manufacture. We also hear of weight-gaining manufacture and weight-losing manufacture, and even of ubiquitous manufacturing. Each of these

Table 30. *Rank of Manufacturing Industries by Number of Employees, United States, Appalachian States, and Southern Appalachian Region, 1954*

Area	Rank				
	1	2	3	4	5
United States	Transp. equip.(A)	Food (B)	Machinery (C)	Apparel (D)	Stone, etc. (E)
Southern Appalachian Region	Textiles (F)	Lumber (G)	Food	Apparel	Stone, etc.
Alabama	Textiles	Primary metals (H)	Lumber	Apparel	Food
Regional Alabama	Textiles	Lumber	Food	Apparel	Fab. metals (I)
Georgia	Textiles	Apparel	Food	Lumber	Transp. equip.
Regional Georgia	Textiles	Apparel	Lumber	Food	Stone, etc.
Kentucky	Food	Apparel	Machinery (C)	Fab. metals	Tobacco (J)
Regional Kentucky	Lumber	Food	Stone, etc.	Apparel	Printing (K)
North Carolina	Textiles	Furniture (L)	Lumber	Tobacco	Food
Regional North Carolina	Textiles	Lumber	Furniture	Food	Apparel
Tennessee	Chemicals (M)	Textiles	Food	Apparel	Lumber
Regional Tennessee	Textiles	Food	Lumber	Chemicals	Stone, etc.
Virginia	Textiles	Chemicals	Food	Lumber	Apparel
Regional Virginia	Food	Textiles	Lumber	Apparel	Chemicals
West Virginia	Stone, etc.	Chemicals	Primary metals	Fab. metals	Food
Regional West Virginia	Stone, etc.	Food	Lumber	Printing (K)	Machinery (C)

Source: U. S. Census of Manufactures, 1954.
Note: The basic manufacturing industries classified by the U. S. Census of Manufactures number twenty. Complete titles for the manufacturing industries ranked above are:

(A)	Transportation equipment	(F)	Textile mill products	(K)	Printing and publishing
(B)	Food and kindred products	(G)	Lumber and wood products	(L)	Furniture and fixtures
(C)	Machinery, except electrical	(H)	Primary metal industries	(M)	Chemicals and products
(D)	Apparel and related products	(I)	Fabricated metal products		
(E)	Stone, clay, and glass products	(J)	Tobacco manufactures		

Specialties, such as tobacco manufactures for Kentucky and North Carolina, and furniture for North Carolina and regional North Carolina show up in the rankings.

The primary basis on which manufacturing locates and develops is the possibility of profit-making. To be sure, there are instances of governmental aids to manufacturing which on the surface might seem to put manufacturing plants in rather unprofitable locations.[1] But even in these instances the amount of profit which would favor other areas is offset by governmental subsidy or political force.

That profit maximization is the realistic underpinning of decisions on location should be kept in mind in interpreting more detailed considerations. For example, it is claimed by some that rayon manufacturing located in Virginia because of cost advantages on freight-in and freight-out. Then textile plants located near rayon manufacturing plants; and next, apparel manufacturers located near textile industrial plants.[2] Yet all these maneuvers may be related to underlying profit-making.

ideas is useful in trying to understand why plants are located in some places and not in others. But in concentrating on any one, there is a tendency to lose sight of the fundamental policy that accounting profits must be satisfactory. Other considerations such as time, effort, and capital invested are also important in maintaining a satisfactory balance between revenues and costs of operating the business.

In addition there are other factors besides those bearing directly on profit-making which affect the location of manufacturing developments. Sometimes these factors, such as "good business climate," can be shown to contribute directly to higher productivity of labor or more adequate governmental services.[3]

[1] Charles E. Marberry, "Governmental Defense Industrial Activity in Relation to the South," *Southern Economic Journal*, XXIV (1958), 458-70.
[2] Herbert A. Simon, "Theories of Decision-Making in Economics," *American Economic Review*, XLIX (1959), 262-65; Jean Gottman, *Virginia at Mid-Century* (New York, 1955), pp. 419-21, 427.
[3] General Electric Company, *Business Climate* (New York, n. d.).

THE SOUTHERN APPALACHIANS

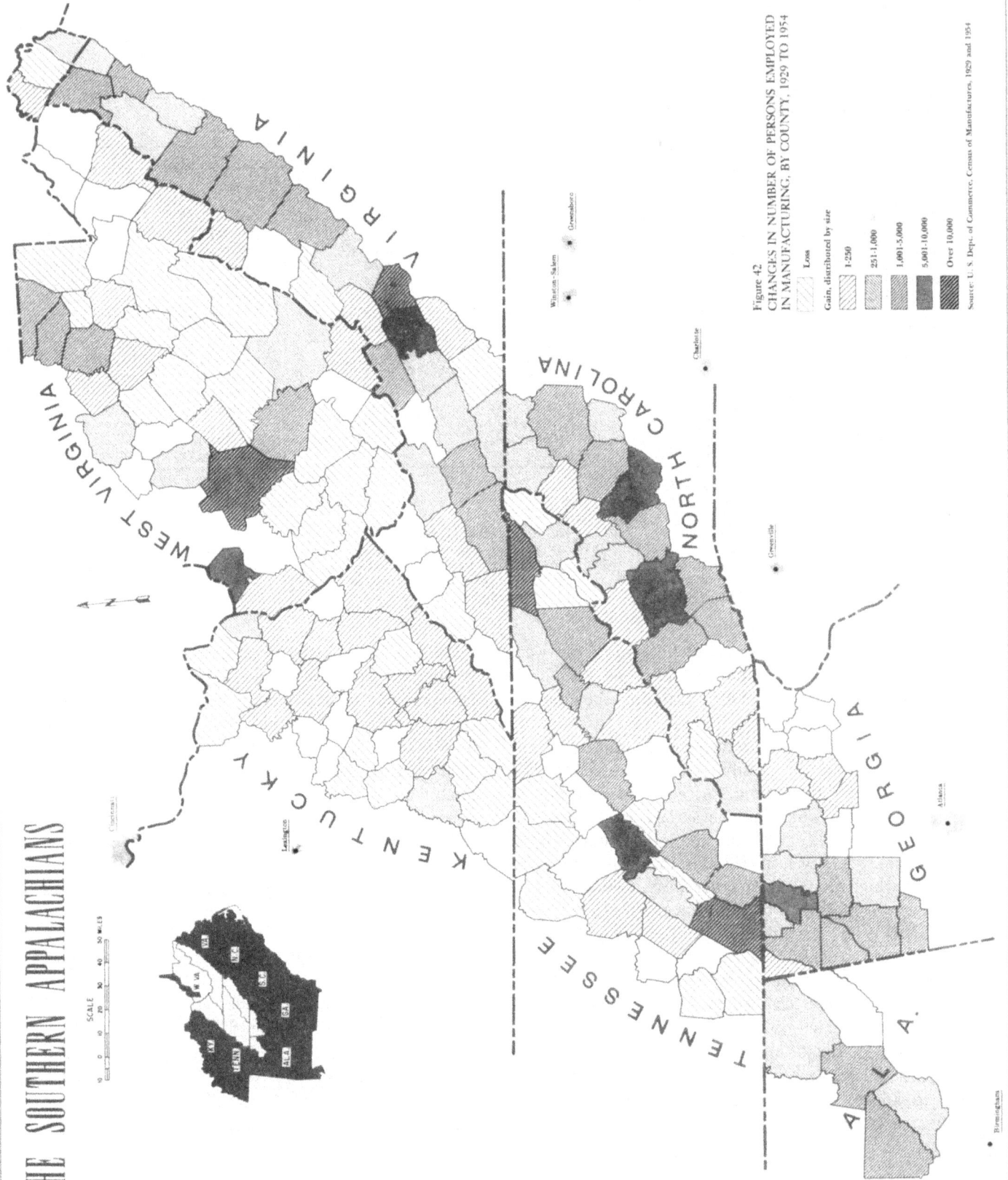

SCALE

Figure 42
CHANGES IN NUMBER OF PERSONS EMPLOYED
IN MANUFACTURING, BY COUNTY, 1929 TO 1954

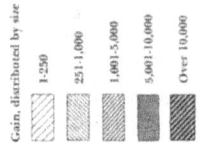

Loss

Gain, distributed by size

1-250

251-1,000

1,001-5,000

5,001-10,000

Over 10,000

Source: U. S. Dept. of Commerce, Census of Manufactures, 1929 and 1954.

VIRGINIA

WEST VIRGINIA

KENTUCKY

TENNESSEE

NORTH CAROLINA

GEORGIA

A L A.

Winston-Salem
Greensboro
Charlotte
Greenville
Atlanta
Birmingham
Chattanooga
Lexington

THE SOUTHERN APPALACHIANS

Figure 43

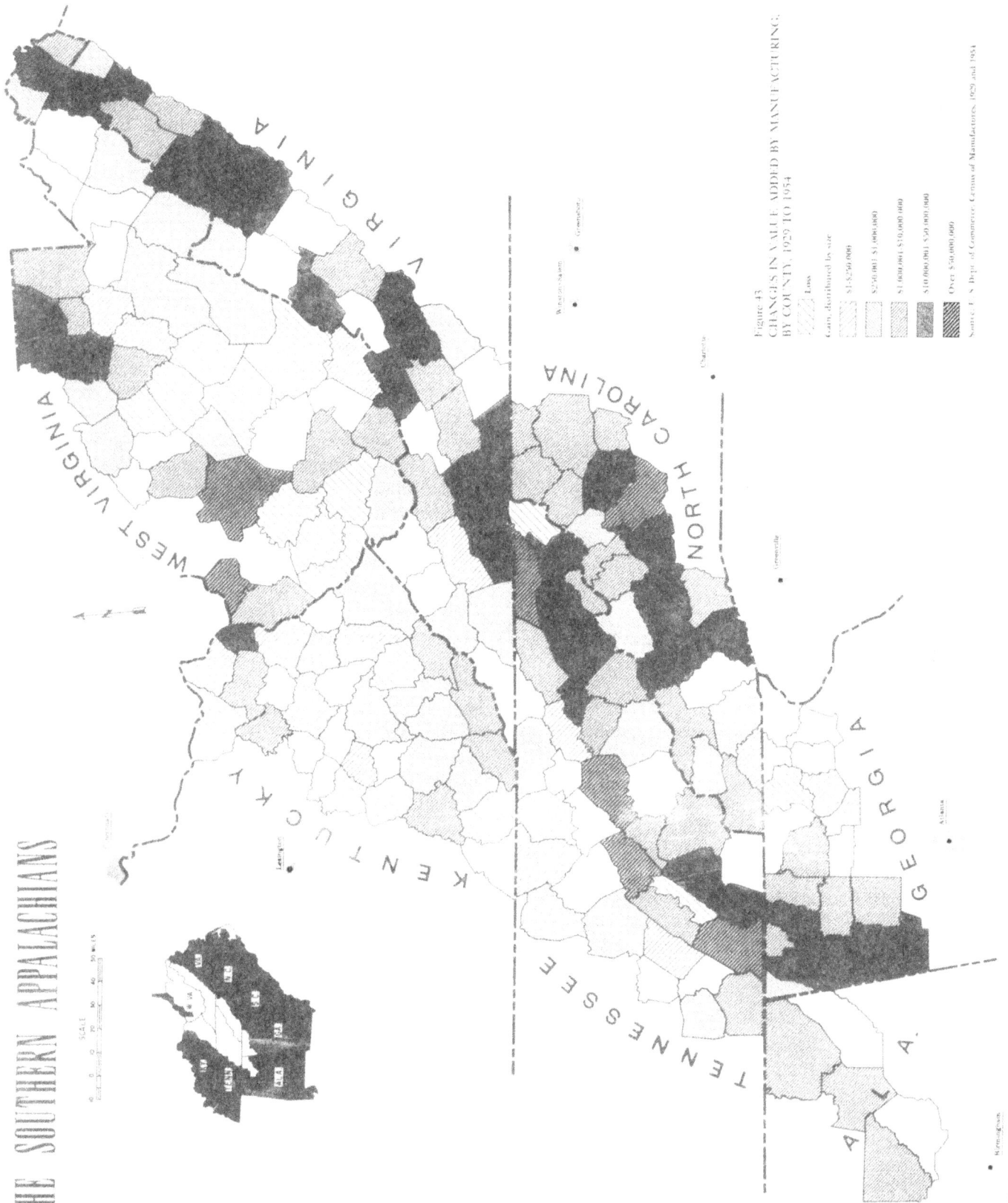

CHANGES IN VALUE ADDED BY MANUFACTURING
BY COUNTY, 1929 TO 1954

Loss

Gain, distributed by size

$1-$250,000

$250,001-$1,000,000

$1,000,001-$10,000,000

$10,000,001-$20,000,000

Over $20,000,000

Source: U.S. Dept. of Commerce, Census of Manufactures, 1929 and 1954.

VIRGINIA

WEST VIRGINIA

KENTUCKY

TENNESSEE

NORTH CAROLINA

GEORGIA

ALA.

SCALE

On the other hand, certain factors, such as the quality of education available, are less likely to bring any direct economic results except as they increase the availability of technical and communicative skills

Table 31. *Positive Factors Listed by Executives as Influencing Plant Location in the Southern Appalachian Region*

Factor	Number of favorable mentions
Labor	
Availability	47
Cost	26
Labor laws	6
	79
Raw materials	
Availability	29
Delivered cost	24
	53
Utilities (fuel, power, water)	
Availability	31
Cost	20
	51
Site	
Availability	34
Cost	12
	46
Markets	
Availability	21
Cost of reaching	17
	38
Other factors	
Community attitudes	25
Physical climate	14
Tax structure	11
Experience of other manufacturers	7
Chance	5
Public service	4
Financial facilities	3
Community accommodations	0
Other factors not listed above	10
	79

which become valuable through their influences on markets and costs.[4] Even less traceable is the effect of the supply of religious services. There are doubtless many accidental and unpredictable factors that influence the location of industries.[5]

An important implication of the "profit-satisfaction" premise of industrial development is that it throws the ultimate choice of location on the executives of the firms considering expansion, a new branch, or relocation. In effect, executives tend to *buy* a location rather than to have it *sold* to them.[6]

In order to examine industrial executives' attitudes toward location in the Region, a sample survey was undertaken in 1958. Special attention was given to plants which employ from 100 to 250 people, the twilight zone between a small plant and a large industry. Replies came from executives in various types of plants already located in each of the several states of the Region. The replies generally were

thoughtful and frank, and were deemed helpful in determining the influences affecting the location of manufacturing plants in the particular Region under study.[7] Usable replies were received for over 40 percent of the questionnaires sent out. There was nothing to indicate that the nonrespondents as a group were significantly different from the responding group.

Four salient findings emerged from the survey. First, most plants had located on their present sites since 1935, a reminder of the recent rapid development revealed by the statistical survey. Second, most were branch plants, a finding which suggests decentralization is favorable to this Region. However, it appeared that there was not yet a strong drive for training regional men for the higher positions in management. This finding implied possible problems, for absentee ownership as well as out-of-Region top management might lead toward a type of colonialism.[8] Third, since most plants indicated that expansion would be carried out within a five-year period, profitable operation might be inferred—giving evidence of good judgment in the initial choice of location. Fourth, frequent comments on the advantageous use of local raw materials and labor emphasized the importance of the cost side of business.

This study showed the reliance of the Region's larger manufacturing firms on fairly distant markets. Only about a third of the markets of the surveyed firms lay within 300 miles of the plant. On the other hand, it showed that raw materials have generally been much closer to the plant, indicating that the pull of the Region's raw materials tended to offset market distance. While 42 percent of the market was over 500 miles distant, only 14 percent of the market was within 100 miles. On the other hand, 21 percent of the raw materials came from over 500 miles away, and 41 percent of the raw materials came from within 100 miles.

Among the points suggested in this 1958 study as leading factors favorable to plant location in the

Report of the Commission to Study Industrial Development in Virginia, Senate Document No. 10 (Richmond, 1957), pp. 59-61.

[5] O. D. Turner, *Industrial Location Factors in Wyoming, A Functional Analysis* (Austin, Texas, 1958), pp. 255, 280.

[6] Lorin A. Thompson, "Factors Influencing the Industrial Development of the Southeastern States," *Social Forces*, XXV (October, 1946), 19.

[7] C. L. Quittmeyer, "Summary Report on Appalachian Questionnaire," Charlottesville, Virginia (October, 1958).

[8] S. H. Robock, "Industrialization and Economic Progress in the Southeast," *Southern Economic Journal*, XX (1954), 316-17.

Region were labor, raw materials, utilities, and markets (Table 31). While site factors had frequent mention, they were usually bunched at the middle of the favorability scale. Community attitudes were mentioned enough to warrant close attention and were

Table 32. *Negative Factors Mentioned by Executives as Influencing Plant Location in the Southern Appalachian Region*

Factor	Number of unfavorable mentions
Markets	
Distance from	27
Lack of	18
	45
Labor	
Lack of skills	11
Unionization	11
Costs	10
	32
Utilities	
Costs of fuel and power	13
Inadequate water	5
	18
Raw materials costs	17
Increased competition	9
Unfavorable tax structure	8
Lack of financial assistance	6
Unfavorable sites	5
Unfavorable physical climate	3
Unfavorable community accommodations	2
Other factors	14

evenly spread throughout the rankings. Market factors were mentioned almost as frequently as community attitudes, but tended to be weighted below average. "Other factors" such as "family home," "location in relation to other plants," and "topography," were few in number, but ranked very high. Availability of raw materials and labor ranked highest in favorability as well as in frequency of mention.

Of course, each respondent based his judgment of these factors on the experience of his present plant location. Penciled comments on the returned questionnaires sometimes indicated that a marginal factor might become critical in the light of other factors. However, in these 346 expressions of opinion on favorable factors, raw materials and labor appear to have the greatest strength. Other factors such as community accommodations, tax structure, and financial facilities appeared weaker.

Unfavorable factors (Table 32) were mentioned less than half as often as the favorable ones. However, from the answers given it seemed clear that the outstanding trouble in locating these larger firms in the Southern Appalachian Region had been markets. The distance from principal markets appeared even more disturbing than the lack of nearby markets. High cost of raw materials was mentioned unfavorably by some firms, partially offsetting the

favorable response that so many other firms gave. Fourteen ranked distance from markets as the most unfavorable factor. Three each gave first place to unfavorability to lack of markets, lack of skilled labor, and high cost of raw materials. Eight respondents simply noted that they were satisfied with their plant location. The "other factors" made up a significant number of responses. They included such weighty factors as "mediocrity in government," "poor schools," "recreational facilities," and the like. Though mentioned but once, and seeming but marginal factors, these might become critical in the aggregate of factors.

The men who make the decisions upon locations for plants are generally aware of increasing competition for their favor, and are often not at all loathe to shop around for a site after a regional study of site possibilities has been made. This attitude has strengthened the organizations of seekers after industrial development at all levels.[9] In 1957 there were in the United States some 6,700 industrial development organizations operating at local, area, state, regional, and national levels.[10]

Probably the communities are for the most part left to take the opening role of making themselves as well known and well surveyed as is possible within their limited contacts with executives who are making the ultimate decisions as to location. The need for comprehensive information about each community and the difficulties found in securing this information have been pointed out in previous articles.[11] The general information needed would include past and current data on population and income, labor wage rates, strike incidence, climate, and various other factors. Such data are often gathered by university bureaus of business and economic research, state commerce departments, area development divisions of railroads, utilities, and banks, and the state and local research bureaus of chambers of commerce. One of the difficult problems facing these various agencies is the coordination of their activities.

Each state has organizational activities which influence the development of manufacturing in its Appalachian section. The state industrial planning and development agency is usually responsible for industrial promotion and solicitation—"smokestack chasing," as it is less reverently called—which in-

[9] J. W. Clark, "State Planning and Industrial Development Agencies," *State Government*, XXIX (1956), 173-76; Leo Anderson, "How U.S. Communities Sell Themselves to Industry," *Industrial Marketing*, XLIII (March, 1958), 37-41.
[10] *Industrial Development*, XLII (October, 1957), 37-38.
[11] Thompson, pp. 19-20.

cludes advertising, mailing brochures, and direct soliciting by agency officers or others. Second, these agencies engage in research to lend some perspective to regional as well as local manufacturing objectives and plans, and to meet special needs. Studies range from those on availability of labor to chances for a specific type of firm to locate in a specific community. Third is the technical assistance given to local planning and development agencies. Community planning deals with zoning, master plans, site maps, and related matters such as urban renewal. Sometimes the financing of manufacturing is added to the state's administrative role, and there is a trend to add nuclear programming as well. All the foregoing activities are interrelated, of course.

The usual state organization for development is a "department of conservation and economic development," a carryover from the "planning board" organizational framework of the 1930s and 1940s. This department generally embraces not only industrial development, but also a host of other functions ranging from tourist promotion and recreational park administration to conservation of water resources and forests. Some of the activities, such as the forestry program, underlie parts of the industrial development of the state, whereas others, such as tourist promotion, are only indirectly related.

Within the "department of conservation and economic development" there are several ways of handling who does what. One way is for all manufacturing development and planning activities to be included within a "division of industrial development." Another is to put the advertising, promotion, and solicitation work in one group and the research and planning in another group. Sometimes the "division of industrial development" stands by itself rather than within a "department of conservation and economic development."

Whatever the organization of industrial development in the state, the agency in charge is generally considered by other developmental agencies, both private and public, statewide and local, to be the informal leader and coordinator of all developmental activities concerning manufacturing. Thus, credit redounds to the agency of the state in which manufacturing is growing, and blame is laid upon it in the reverse circumstance, regardless of the control or lack of control which the state agency may actually have had.

The positive role that a region or a community desiring industry can play is even more restricted than has already been implied, for most of them are limited in the actions they can take to get additional plants. It is much easier to exclude undesired types of industry by hostile attitudes and zoning controls than it is to attract desired types of industry. Consequently, the sometimes suggested strategy that the Southern Appalachian Region seeks to add to its industrial output by integrating more stages of the manufacturing process is much easier to propose than it is to put into effect.[12]

Much of that freedom of choice which an area or community idealizes seems to be reduced in reality simply to getting what can be got. In developed communities, for example, manufacturing will frequently be built up simply as an expansion of the type of industry already existing there, whether basic or secondary.[13] There are occasionally circumstances, however, in which a community's representative may call to the attention of manufacturers certain opportunities overlooked in the local application of manufacturing technology to indigenous raw materials. Such has been the case, for instance, with regard to apples, poultry, and feed in the Shenandoah Valley.[14]

The prospects for industrial development in any particular region or community should be examined in terms of the probability of continuing operation and of compatability within the community.

Manufacturing generally has spread out from waterways and railroad lines. Usually the big cities that have prospered and grown are located on navigable rivers, which in turn have valleys or flat places with good access to rail and highway transportation.[15] Four of the metropolitan communities of the Southern Appalachian Region—Knoxville, Chattanooga, Huntington, and Charleston—have all three transportation advantages; Asheville and Roanoke are without navigable rivers, but have the other qualifications of transportation access.

Since most of the land in the Southern Appalachian Region is characterized by severe slope, the Region as a whole is not blessed with many industrial sites of good size except in the broad valleys. Furthermore, the communities have already built up most of the land that would have been suitable for industrial sites. Hills and existing industrial plants tend to de-

[12] Alabama Research Council, *Alabama Goes Industry Hunting* (Montgomery, 1957).

[13] Alfred G. Dale, *An Economic Survey Method for Small Areas* (Bureau of Business Research, Austin, 1955), p. 10.

[14] Thompson, p. 17.

[15] Martin Mayer, "The Future of Twenty American Cities," *Esquire*, LII (June 19, 1959), 67-71.

termine further location, as cities will not ordinarily leap such barriers until there is no place else to go. The economic overhead per capita for roads, schools, churches, hospitals, and communications facilities tends to increase as the density of population de-

However, there is little reason why these desirable aims cannot be correlated with sustained flow.[18] Also, there may be opportunities while cutting roads across the hilly areas to provide fill at the same time for the development of flat sites along the new roads and

Figure 44. *Highway Mileage in the Southern Appalachian Region, by States, Various Years*

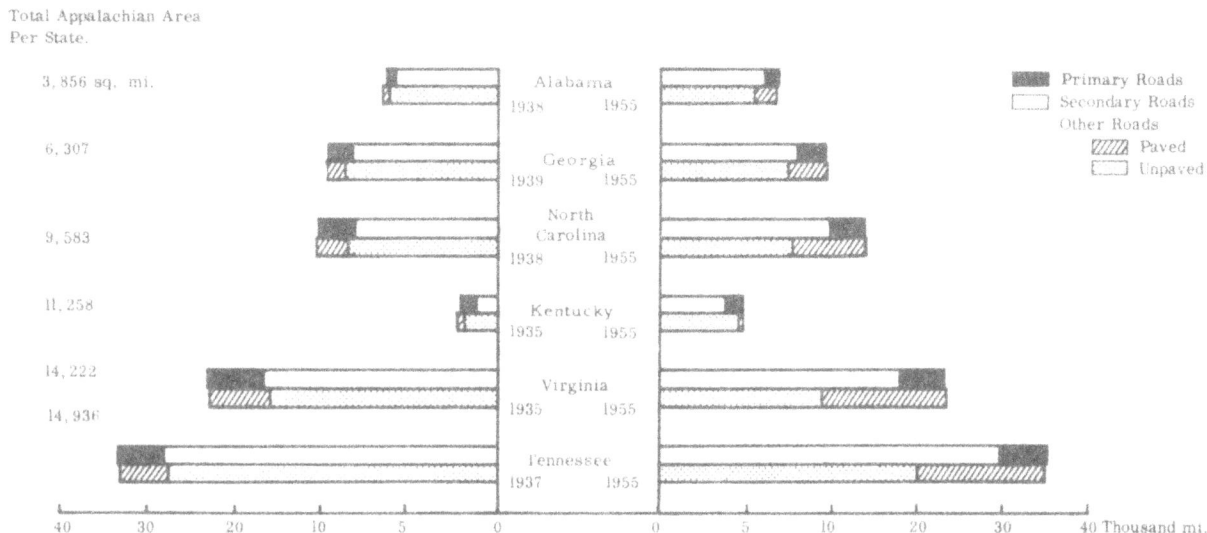

Total Appalachian Area
Per State.

Primary Roads
Secondary Roads
Other Roads
Paved
Unpaved

Source: Highway Departments of the various states.
Note: Comparable data for West Virginia was not available.

creases, a factor which is not helpful to small communities hoping to attract industry in the first place.[16] Although rural farm underemployment provides a large reservoir of potential workers, trained labor is not plentiful.[17]

Added to the shortage of site space for development and expansion is the fact that, although the water flowing through the valleys is useful, most of the numerous streams are subject to floods.

Water control is the key to greater use of the water resources of the Southern Appalachian Region. By and large the Region is well endowed with water. Control of the Tennessee River and the advantages accruing thereby for the growth of industry are readily apparent in the development of manufacturing that has already taken place in the Tennessee Valley. The major problems concerning water appear in regional Kentucky and regional West Virginia. Floods have caused severe damage in the former, and variability of stream flow has caused difficulty for industry in both areas.

The new concept of stream resources that is needed for industrial development in the mountainous areas is sustained flow. Usually the actual concept has been a combination of flood control and recreation.

to use the road embankments as dams for the impoundment of water.

Of course, since watersheds and streams pay no attention to state lines, water control is dependent on interstate and federal cooperation. In the federal sphere a promising attack on the total development of regional water resources is exemplified by the goals of the United States Study Commission on Southeast River Basins. A small part of Georgia's and North Carolina's Appalachian regions come under this commission's study. The study is an attempt to determine the benefits realizable in the Southeastern river basins from such interrelated factors as flood control, power, water quality control, water supply, drainage, pollution abatement, recreation, and soil and forest conservation. Studies of this type might be applied to other parts of the Southern Appalachian Region not already well studied.

Future growth of manufacturing in the Region will

[16] Turner, pp. 260-61.
[17] S. H. Robock, "Rural Industries and Agricultural Development," *Journal of Farm Economics*, XXXIV (April, 1952), 16-60.
[18] See Vogt, Ivers, Seaman and Associates, *Summary Report of Watershed Development Study* (West Virginia Economic Development Agency, Charleston, 1960), p. 4.

be aided by construction of the new interstate highway system.

The growth of the road system in the period from the late 1930s to 1955 for the Appalachian portions

Carolina, where in each case there was an increase. Minor hard-surfaced roads increased appreciably except in Kentucky; only in Kentucky did the non-surfaced mileage increase. Thus, the road net on the

Figure 45. *National System of Interstate and Defense Highways, Southern Appalachian Region and Adjacent South-eastern States, 1960*

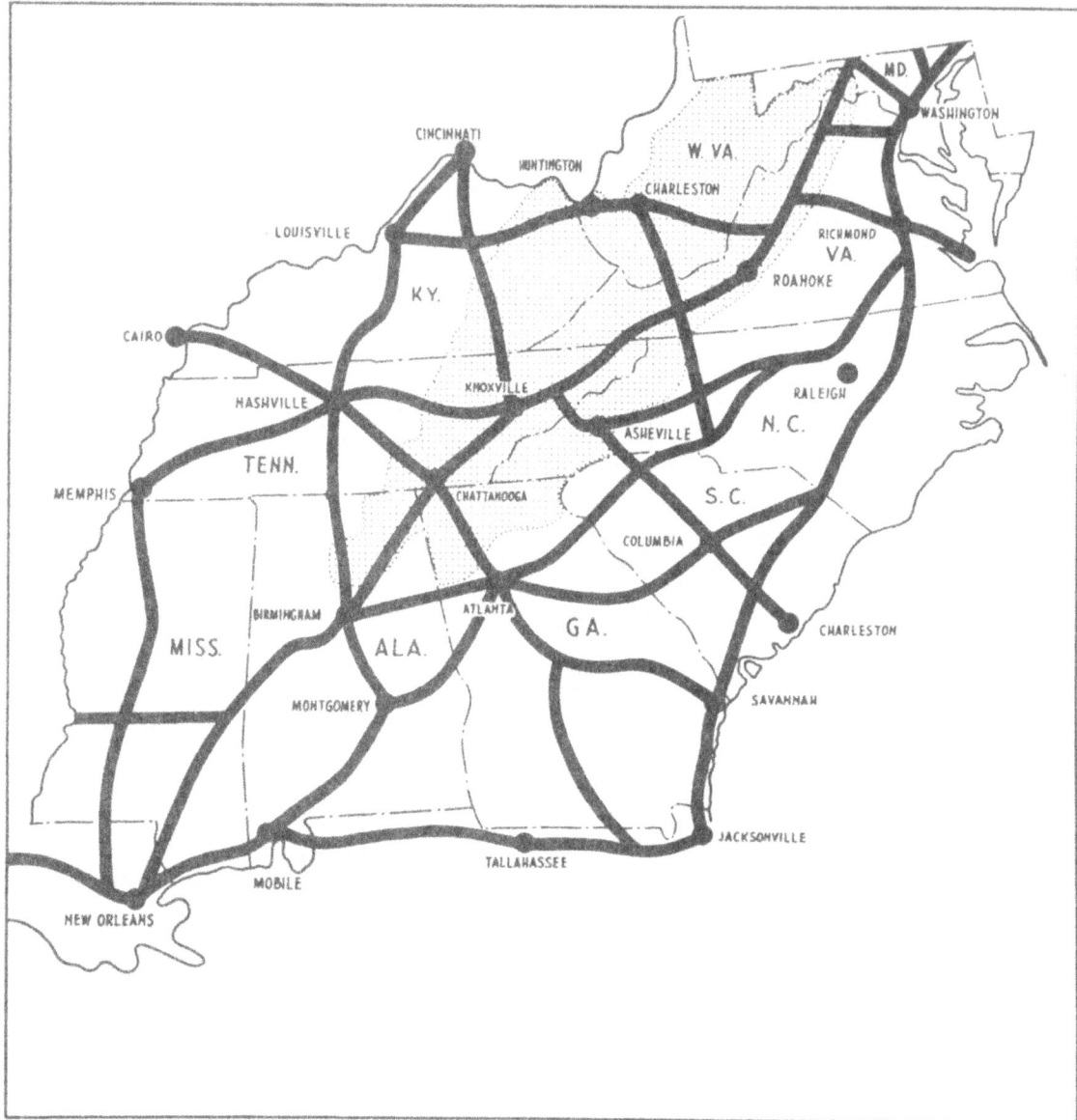

Source: Tennessee Valley Authority

of all the states except West Virginia (for which information was not available) is shown in Figure 44. The change in primary road mileage was not material for any of the sections except the small Appalachian area of Alabama. Secondary road mileage change was important only for Kentucky and North

whole has improved, but mainly with respect to surfacing.

The use of the road net has grown much faster than the road net itself, however, as indicated by the traffic changes over sample strips in each state section except in North Carolina and West Virginia.

North Carolina's evidence in gasoline consumed may indirectly tend to tell the same story. The increasing pressure on the road net has been instrumental in bringing sectional pressures for further road development.

It is clear that the six metropolitan areas of the Region will be favored by the new interstate highway system (Figure 45). Chattanooga and Knoxville in the Great Valley will each have east-west and north-south connections. Asheville and Charleston will be hubs for east-west and south routes. Roanoke is on a north-south route and a proposed east-west route. Huntington is on an east-west route.

Numerous railroads serve the Southern Appalachian Region, and although statistical information applicable just to this area or its state sections is not recorded except by a few intrastate railroads operating only in the Region, there apparently has been noticeable growth during the period under review in the rail hauling of manufactured products originating in the section. Similar evidence exists, although to a less important degree, that there is increased use of water and air transportation. The need for landing strips for aircraft, however, is acute.

We have seen that the Southern Appalachian Region as a whole has made substantial progress in the development of industry, but that there are large areas which have made little or no progress. We have also examined some of the factors which appear likely to influence future development of manufacturing in the area. Broadly, the present metropolitan areas of the Region, which have superior financial, communication, and transportation facilities, power and water supplies, and modern community life, are the most attractive to industry once the labor, materials, and market requirements are met. The whole valley which runs through the middle of the Region from northeast to southwest is favorable for industrial development largely because it has good sites, again allowing for basic labor, materials, and market requirements. Within the valley, plants may be located outside the metropolitan areas when the cities cannot offer proper sites. Otherwise, with its additional amenities, the city usually has the edge.

A realistic prognosis for future industrial development in the Region is that expansion will continue in the areas which have been growing. In the remaining areas decline may continue until such time as the advantages and resources of the area are needed.

CHAPTER NINE

The Potential of Tourism

JOHN W. MORRIS

THE UNITED STATES IS A NATION OF travelers. It has been estimated that the American people spend between 25 and 29 billion dollars yearly for travel abroad and at home. Of this amount two to three billion dollars are spent for foreign travel, five to six billion dollars for business travel, and between eighteen and twenty billion dollars for domestic tourist travel annually.

Does the Southern Appalachian area get its proportionate share of this multibillion dollar industry? Actually, nobody knows. The tourist business has grown so rapidly and become so important in the economy of the area that there is a great need for reliable facts as to its trend, size, and characteristics. Each state has a different method or no method at all, of accounting for the number of tourists that visit it. The samplings taken and the statistical reports made vary so greatly from place to place that there is little comparative reliability. For example, the number of day visitors to the state parks, as reported by the various states to the National Park Service, are by actual count for North Carolina and Tennessee, by sample and estimate for Alabama, Georgia, Virginia, and West Virginia, and by estimate only for Kentucky.[1] So inadequate and inaccurate had the counting methods of the National Park Service become that a new system was started in January, 1960, and so different is this method that the statement "Data of 1960 (new series) not comparable with previous years" now appears in the monthly reports of *Public Use National Parks and Related Areas*. Frequently the overestimates made of the size of the tourist business tend to "weaken public confidence in and support of public and private development programs. State estimates are usually so high that when added up nationally they total 50 to 100 per cent more than estimates of national travel organizations made by responsible national marketing agencies."[2]

Another question that must be answered before accurate statements about tourism in any area can be made is "Who is a tourist?" Should a family that lives in Knoxville and goes to a nearby state park for a picnic supper be classed as tourists? Should a family living in Winchester who spends a Sunday afternoon driving through Shenandoah National Park be called tourists? Is a tourist one who travels only for pleasure and recreation? The term has become so difficult to define that many surveys are now avoiding the use of the word. The National Park Service now lists those coming into its areas as visitors.

No estimates can be made as to the number of visitors to the various privately controlled areas, or of the number of tourists who drive through the Southern Appalachians but visit no tourist attraction. Even if the figures were available for all public and private areas, they would mean little unless duplications could be eliminated. (A family of four may visit four different places the same day; thus they may be counted not as four but as sixteen persons.)

approximately 2,400,000, West Virginia second with 1,700,000, and Georgia third with 1,300,000. During 1959 the TVA estimated the number of visitors to its facilities as approximately 25,000,000.

The region which attracts these numerous visitors is one of diverse natural features. The highest eleva-

Table 33. *Number of Visitors to National Park Service Areas in the Southern Appalachian Region*

Area	Visitors (thousands)					
	1940	1945	1950	1955	1958	1959
Great Smoky Mountains National Park	861.0	750.7	1,843.6	2,518.5	3,169.0	3,162.3
Shenandoah National Park	950.8	542.7	1,279.4	1,543.4	1,655.2	1,786.7
Andrew Johnson National Monument	*	16.7	26.0	34.2	37.3	37.7
Blue Ridge Parkway	*	382.9	1,996.4	4,502.2	4,989.1	5,589.4
Chickamauga-Chattanooga National Military Park	481.4	141.5	296.4	255.2	306.5	339.6
Cumberland Gap National Historical Park	*	*	*	*	78.2	165.4

Source: Attendance bulletins issued by National Park Service for years indicated.
*Not officially opened.

cations could be eliminated. (A family of four may visit four different places the same day; thus they may be counted not as four but as sixteen persons.)

Nevertheless, on the basis of available figures, the Southern Appalachians is undeniably one of the principal tourist areas of the nation. The Great Smoky Mountains National Park attracts more visitors each year than any other national park, and the Shenandoah National Park ranks among the leaders each year. The publication *Public Use National Parks and Related Areas* shows that during 1959 there were 3,162,300 visits made to the Great Smoky Mountains National Park, 1,786,700 to Shenandoah National Park, and 1,529,600 to Grand Teton National Park in Wyoming, which ranked third in the nation.[3] In visits to the related areas, the Blue Ridge Parkway far exceeds all others. During 1959 the National Park Service recorded 5,589,400 visits to the Blue Ridge Parkway as compared with the second-place Lake Mead Recreation Area of Arizona-Nevada, which reported 3,390,600 visits. Even with the new and more conservative system of counting visitors now being used, Great Smoky Mountains National Park continued to rank first during the first half of 1960. Shenandoah National Park, however, dropped to third place behind Rocky Mountain National Park in Colorado.

The number of tourists or visitors to the fifty state parks within the area is also high. For 1959 it was estimated that the number of visitors to all state parks, as shown in Table 33, totaled approximately 7,600,000. (No attempt has been made to adjust state figures.) Tennessee ranked first with

tions of the entire Appalachian system are here, with Mt. Mitchell exceeding 6,700 feet; ridges cut by water gaps and wind gaps extend for long distances in a general northeast-southwest direction; swift streams interrupted by falls and rapids have cut gorges hundreds of feet deep; valleys of all kinds—enclosed, broad, narrow, and those with wide openings—diversify the landscape.

In this region of steep hills and mountains and moderate to heavy rainfall, hundreds of small streams have developed, among them those which form the headwaters of some of the most attractive and important rivers in the nation—Potomac, Tennessee, Cumberland, Red (Kentucky), Big Sandy, Kanawha, New, and others. In those parts of the Southern Appalachians where limestone has been deposited in thick layers, many large and picturesque caves and underground rivers have formed. Water seepage and erosion have also caused the formation of natural bridges, high overlooks, and numerous springs. Natural lakes in the area, however, are few in number and small in size when compared to several areas in other parts of the nation.

In its natural state the Southern Appalachian Region was almost completely tree covered. Deciduous forests of walnut, beech, oak, hickory, and other hardwood varieties dominated, although conifers

[1] National Park Service, *State Park Statistics, 1959* (Washington, 1960), pp. 19-20.
[2] Lewis C. Copeland, *Travelers and Arkansas Business 1948 to 1956* (Arkansas Publicity and Parks Commission, Little Rock, 1958), p. 5.
[3] National Park Service, *Public Use National Park Service Areas, December 1959* (Washington, 1959), Table 3.

were sometimes located on the poorer soils. The forest areas which remain are among the recreational resources of the Region.

Climate, one of the most important physical factors influencing the development of tourism, varies within the region. The frost-free season ranges from about 235 days in the southern to approximately 120 days at the higher stations in the northern part of the Southern Appalachians. Yearly temperature averages mean little in so large an area. The average January temperature varies from about 28°F at the higher stations in northern West Virginia to about 45° in the southern part of the region in Alabama. During July, over most of the area, the average monthly temperatures range between 70° and 80°F. It should be noted, however, that extremes varying as much as 30° above the average July temperature or 60° below the average January temperature have been recorded. The average annual precipitation is greater in the southern than in the northern part of the region; no station in the Southern Appalachians records less than 35 inches during an average year. In the northern part of the region snowfall is great enough to support winter recreational activities. The usually moderate temperatures, along with a generally comfortable relative humidity, make for pleasant recreational conditions.

Tourism in the Southern Appalachians is not a new economic activity. Numerous springs in Virginia, West Virginia, and Tennessee were known and used by the various Indian tribes that inhabited the area before the coming of the white men. Many of these springs, because of their mineral content (sulphur, iron, magnesium, calcium, sodium, nitrate, etc.) early attracted the attention of the white settlers for medicinal purposes. The pioneers "held these spas in high esteem because of the curative values of the waters, hence these springs soon became natural centers for much of the social and political life of the state during the era that ended with the Civil War."[4] One of the first springs to attract national attention is located in what is now Berkeley Springs, West Virginia. The diary of George Washington records his first visit to "Ye Famed Warm Springs" on March 18, 1748. The first settler's cabin to be built at White Sulphur Springs, West Virginia, the most famous of the springs still in use as a resort, was constructed in 1774. Later, hotels, bath houses, and recreational areas were developed near many other springs. The records of Salt Sulphur Springs, West Virginia, indicate that as early as 1825 it had

466 guests and that in 1838 there were 1,439 registrations. In most instances, the greatest number of visitors came from the nearest population centers or states. Berkeley Springs, or Bath as it was then called, had numerous visitors from Philadelphia, Baltimore, and Washington. Salt Sulphur Springs was especially popular with residents of Louisiana, North Carolina, and South Carolina.

Following the Civil War many resort areas ceased functioning as such, not only for financial reasons, but also because of the changing and expanding activities of the nation. As the nation grew in size, the transportation system grew with it. At first, travel was confined to post roads and rivers. During the last half of the nineteenth century, however, railroads almost completely took over the transportation of both goods and people. By 1890 this conquest was complete, and until the 1920's the railroads dominated the passenger travel field. This domination was so complete that several railroads operated large resorts, such as White Sulphur Springs, to provide suitable destinations for vacationers served by their lines.

By the middle 1920's a great many people owned automobiles, and, although there were no suitable transcontinental highways, nevertheless they strapped camping equipment to their cars and started on their vacations. These automobile tourists could not always get to a town, an inn, or a hotel by nightfall. To take care of them, some towns established municipal tourist camps, and people camped out. As the construction of paved highways advanced, many motels were built so that the automobile tourist could find accommodations wherever nightfall overtook him. Within the twenty years from 1920 to 1940, the railroads lost their supremacy in the passenger business to the automobile, the bus, and the airplane.

To meet the increasing public demand in recent years, recreation facilities and programs have been developed by a great variety of public and private agencies. Until late in the nineteenth century, federal, state, and local governments generally considered recreation a private concern and with few exceptions spent no tax funds for it, but the last forty years have seen extensive recreational developments under government auspices. Each state in the Southern Appalachians now has a Division of Parks, usually operated as part of the Conservation Commission.

[4] Paul H. Price, John B. McCue, and Homer A. Hoskins, *Springs of West Virginia* (West Virginia Geological Survey, Morgantown, 1936), p. 3.

THE SOUTHERN APPALACHIANS

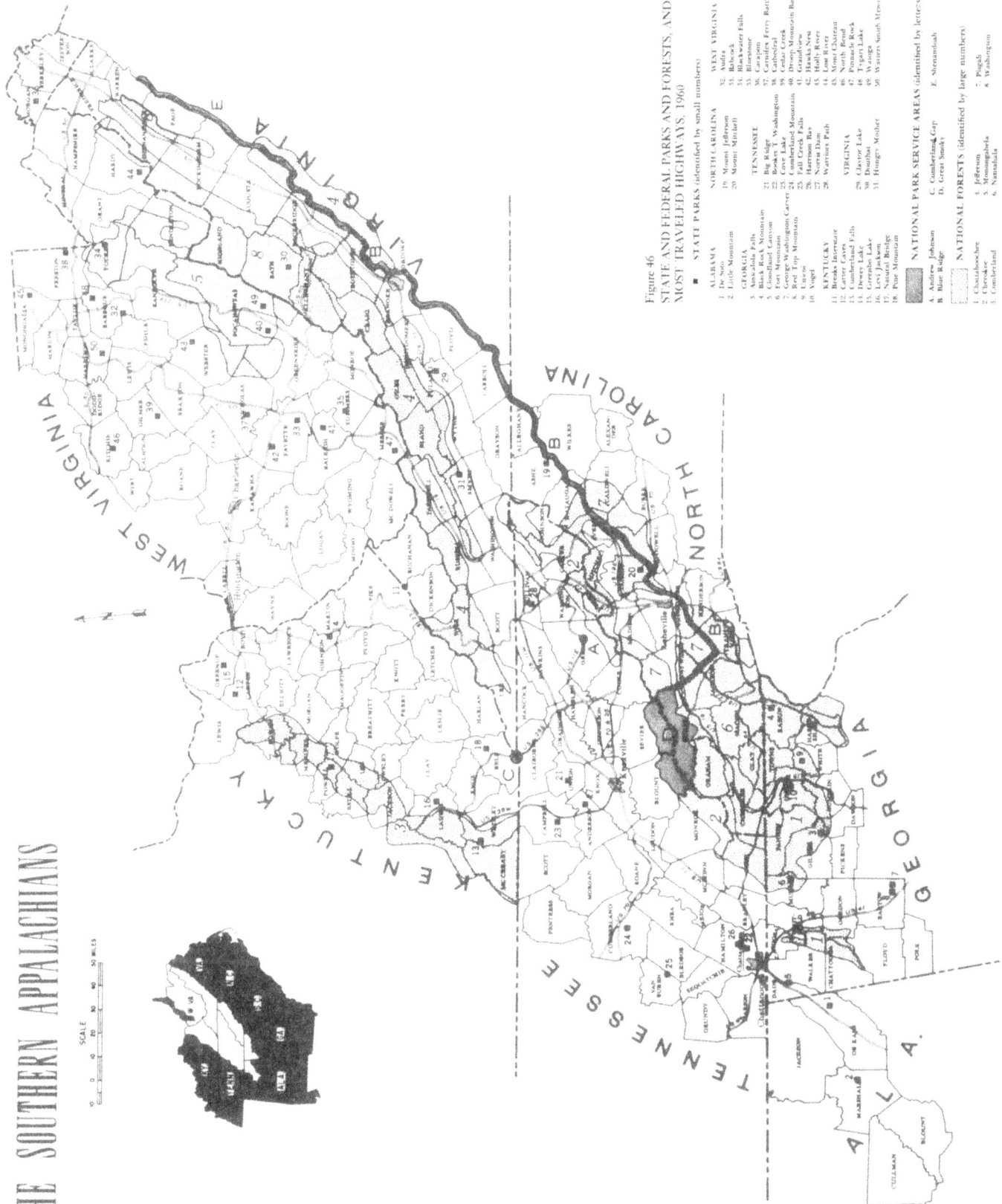

SCALE

THE SOUTHERN APPALACHIANS

WEST VIRGINIA

KENTUCKY

VIRGINIA

TENNESSEE

NORTH CAROLINA

GEORGIA

ALA.

Figure 46

STATE AND FEDERAL PARKS AND FORESTS, AND
MOST TRAVELED HIGHWAYS, 1960

■ STATE PARKS (identified by small numbers)

ALABAMA
1 De Soto
2 Little Mountain

GEORGIA
3 Amicalola Falls
4 Black Rock Mountain
5 Cloudland Canyon
6 Fort Mountain
7 George Washington Carver
8 Red Top Mountain
9 Unicoi
10 Vogel

KENTUCKY
11 Breaks Interstate
12 Carter Caves
13 Cumberland Falls
14 Dewey Lake
15 Greenbo Lake
16 Levi Jackson
17 Natural Bridge
18 Pine Mountain

NORTH CAROLINA
19 Mount Jefferson
20 Mount Mitchell

TENNESSEE
21 Big Ridge
22 Booker T. Washington
23 Cove Lake
24 Cumberland Mountain
25 Fall Creek Falls
26 Harrison Bay
27 Norris Dam
28 Warriors Path

VIRGINIA
29 Claytor Lake
30 Douthat
31 Hungry Mother

WEST VIRGINIA
32 Audra
33 Babcock
34 Blackwater Falls
35 Bluestone
36 Carnifex Ferry Battlefield
37 Cass
38 Cathedral
39 Cedar Creek
40 Droop Mountain Battlefield
41 Grandview
42 Hawks Nest
43 Holly River
44 Lost River
45 Mont Chateau
46 North Bend
47 Pinnacle Rock
48 Tygart Lake
49 Watoga
50 Watters Smith Memorial

NATIONAL PARK SERVICE AREAS (identified by letters)

A. Andrew Johnson
B. Blue Ridge
C. Cumberland Gap
D. Great Smoky
E. Shenandoah

NATIONAL FORESTS (identified by large numbers)

1 Chattahoochee
2 Cherokee
3 Cumberland
4 Jefferson
5 Monongahela
6 Nantahala
7 Pisgah
8 Washington

National Park Service Areas located in the Southern Appalachians are the Great Smoky Mountains and Shenandoah National Parks, the Blue Ridge National Parkway, Cumberland Gap National Historical Park, Andrew Johnson National Monument, and Chickamauga-Chattanooga National Military Park. The number of visitors to these areas continues to increase each year. In 1955 the total attendance in the five National Park Service Areas then organized was estimated at over 8.8 million persons. By 1959 the number of visitors had jumped to 11.0 million persons, or an increase of over 1.3 million persons in three years (Table 33). The new park at Cumberland Gap has materially increased the yearly attendance.

The Great Smoky Mountain National Park is the most popular national park in the United States. Located between the Blue Ridge and Unaka mountains and within a few hundred miles of many of the large population centers, it is easily accessible for vacations and visits of short duration. Because of its rugged topography, the park area was for many years avoided by almost all persons except the lumbermen and the mountain folk. United States Highway 441 now crosses the park through Newfound Gap, extending from Cherokee, North Carolina, to Gatlinburg, Tennessee. Other roads have been extended into some of the coves, and a paved highway has been built to the summit of Clingmans Dome. Picnic areas, places for swimming and fishing, and camping sites are numerous. Near the North Carolina entrance to the park a complete mountain farmstead has been developed. The barn is standing where it was originally built; other buildings, including a large log house, have been moved from nearby coves. Over 1,000 persons registered as visitors at the farmstead on July 4, 1959.

Two National Park Service Areas—Shenandoah National Park and the Blue Ridge Parkway—are composed largely of activities developed in conjunction with ridgetop highways. Shenandoah National Park, which follows the crest of the Blue Ridge Mountains from Front Royal, Virginia, to near Waynesboro, Virginia, is centered along the Skyline Drive. Following this paved highway one can view the scenery on either side of the Blue Ridge from numerous overlooks and trails. Two large modern lodges and several cabins offer places for overnight stops or longer visits. The Blue Ridge Parkway, when completed, will extend from the southern terminus of the Skyline Drive to the Great Smoky Mountain National Park, a distance of 470 miles. Museums, overlooks, camp sites, and other facilities have been provided for the tourist.

Cumberland Gap National Historical Park, formally opened in July, 1959, seems destined to become one of the most visited places in the Southern Appalachians. United States Highway 25E crosses through the Gap, and United States Highway 58 has a terminal there. Many people will be attracted by the historical importance of the Gap, which was traversed by Daniel Boone and the pioneers who followed the Wilderness Road. A paved highway to near the top of the Pinnacle enables tourists to view the countryside for miles around.

The two remaining areas under the control of the National Park Service are minor attractions compared to the parks, but even so the number of visitors to them extends into the thousands each year. The Andrew Johnson National Monument is composed of the tailor shop and home of the former president, two separate buildings located about two blocks apart in the business district of Greenville, Tennessee. The Chickamauga-Chattanooga National Military Park, in Tennessee and Georgia, is one of the more frequently visited Civil War battlefields.

Recreational areas developed by the federal government require vast capital investments. Since it is assumed that the provision of recreational areas is for the general public good, the federal government does not expect such areas to pay their way. In a few instances a small fee is charged. Sometimes recreation areas develop as secondary or tertiary items in a project. For example, several phases of the work of the TVA have priority over recreational activities, yet probably none serve as many people during the year.

Five of the main dams built by the Tennessee Valley Authority on the Tennessee River and sixteen dams constructed on tributaries are within the region. The dams and generating plants attract many thousands of visitors each year. Along all the TVA lakes, sandy beaches, boating, water skiing, and fishing are common. The twenty-one lakes created by the TVA in the Southern Appalachians have a total shore line of 6,245 miles and cover 314,750 acres, or an area of slightly more than 491 square miles. The largest of the lakes is Guntersville, which exceeds 69,000 acres in size and has a shore line of 962 miles; the smallest is Ocoee No. 3, located in Polk County, Tennessee, which covers 604 acres and has a shore line of twenty-four miles. Lakes of the TVA system are located in thirty-five counties of the Southern

Appalachian Region. The estimated value of the recreational facilities developed around these lakes totals over fifty-one million dollars, the largest developments being along the shore of Guntersville Lake in Alabama and on Chickamauga, Norris, and South Holston lakes in Tennessee. The 1959 estimated person-day use of TVA lakes in the Southern Appalachians exceeded twenty-four million for the year.

One of the most educational attractions in the Region is the American Museum of Atomic Energy in Oak Ridge, Tennessee, where the tourist may participate in guided tours, hear lectures, and view exhibits on the principles and uses of atomic energy. Visitors have registered from all fifty states, the District of Columbia, and eighty foreign nations. Recent attendance has been bolstered by opening the museum to the public without charge, so that now more than 100,000 persons visit the museum each year. Over half of the total attendance is in June, July, and August each year.

National and state forest areas contain large tracts of land set aside for forest conservation purposes. These areas are not of prime importance in the interstate tourist industry, since they usually occupy the most rugged parts of the mountains or plateaus and thus are not as accessible as the regular tourist areas (Figure 46). The Cumberland National Forest covers a part of the Cumberland Plateau in Kentucky; the Washington and Jefferson National Forests are in Virginia along and near the Virginia-West Virginia border; the Monongahela National Forest is in the eastern part of West Virginia; the Nantahala and Pisgah National Forests occupy large areas of western North Carolina; the Cherokee National Forest is located in Tennessee both north and south of the Great Smoky Mountain National Park; and the Chattahoochee National Forest covers large amounts of rugged land in northern Georgia.

These forests may or may not be continuous tree-covered areas. Frequently the more level land is in cultivation or used for grazing, and numerous villages and smaller cities may be located in the forest area. The best developed state forests are in West Virginia. In all forests special areas have been designated as camping sites. In many places the tourist must have permission from a ranger before making camp, and in some places it has been necessary to limit the length of the camping period. Fishing, hunting, and hiking are the chief recreational activities.

To help meet the increasing demand for recreation facilities, each state has established a system of state parks and shrines. In most instances the site selected is in an easily accessible area with a paved road or roads leading to it. Historic significance, scenic beauty, or a body of water are the chief factors considered in selecting the park location. In many instances, those parks having the largest seasonal or yearly attendance have bodies of water suitable for both swimming and boating. Cumberland Falls State Park, located in Kentucky at the Falls of the Cumberland River, has an estimated yearly attendance of 750,000 persons. Great scenic beauty, cool shallow water where children can play, deep flowing pools for swimming, and nearby fishing and boating areas make this park the most popular of all state parks in the Southern Appalachians. Warriors Path and Norris Dam State Parks, both in Tennessee, rank second and third respectively in total attendance among all the state parks. Both are located in the vicinity of TVA lakes. Fifty state parks have been or are in the process of being developed (Figure 46). Most states also have plans for additional parks or shrines when the state can provide funds for the expansion.

Facilities in the state parks range from little more than picnic areas, as in Mt. Jefferson State Park in North Carolina or Watters Smith Memorial State Park in West Virginia, to the ultramodern lodges of Blackwater Falls and Mont Chateau State Parks in West Virginia. The state park systems in the Southern Appalachian portions of West Virginia, Kentucky, Georgia, and Tennessee are better developed than those of Alabama, North Carolina, and Virginia. Certain parks in Georgia, Kentucky, and West Virginia have hotel-like accommodations, but frequently the cost of staying in such parks is beyond the means of the average tourist. These more elite parks do fill a need, however, for they often serve as meeting places for conventions or large groups. About half the parks have cabins of various sizes that can be rented by the week for reasonable rates; most have camp sites where the tourist may place his tent or trailer for a few days.

The spectacular Breaks Interstate Park, one of the latest additions to the system of state parks, is located at "a giant gorge astride the Virginia-Kentucky border where the Russell Fork River on its way westward has cut through the Cumberland Mountains."[5] Although the park was dedicated on September 5, 1955, construction has not yet been completed.

[5] Mary Bell Mapp, "The Breaks Interstate Park," *The Commonwealth* (October, 1957), 1-4.

About 70 percent of the 1,250 acres making up the park are in Dickenson County, Virginia, a few acres are in Buchanan County, Virginia, and the remainder are in Pike County, Kentucky. The Kentucky-Virginia State Highway 80 passes through the park.

Roadside parks, usually developed by the state highway departments, are found in each state along the main traveled highways, and not infrequently along the secondary roads. Tables in a small grove where one or several families may enjoy a period of relaxation or a meal are especially appreciated by parties traveling with children. During the peak period of the tourist season many roadside parks are in almost continuous use from early in the morning until late in the afternoon.

Few state parks completely pay their expenses. The maintenance of the physical plant and roads, plus the cost of labor and management, is primarily paid for by state appropriations. Parks having rental cabins are much more nearly self-supporting than others. In general their income equals from 70 to 85 percent of their operating cost. Occasionally a park, such as Big Ridge State Park in Tennessee and Amicalola Falls State Park in Georgia, will more than pay its cost and will return money to the state. In contrast, Mt. Mitchell State Park in North Carolina, one of the better known scenic attractions in the Southern Appalachians, pays only 64.8 percent of its maintenance, operating, and other costs excepting capital investments.

Many of the most successful privately developed activities are along or near United States Highway 11 in the Shenandoah Valley, within the vicinity of a national park or the Blue Ridge Parkway, or near one of the large lakes of the TVA system. Many private developments attract thousands of visitors each year. In commercially developed caves, lighted trails and steps enable the tourist to enjoy scenic tours underground. Paved roads permit driving almost to the tops of such places as Grandfather Mountain and Blowing Rock, so that a short walk will be rewarded by a view that is largely natural. Large amounts of private capital, running into the tens of thousands of dollars, have been expended in the development of such tourist attractions as Rock City near Chattanooga, Caverns of Luray, Skyline Caverns, and Endless Caverns in Virginia, Grandfather Mountain and Blowing Rock in North Carolina, and Natural Bridge in Virginia. The operators of such attractions must constantly conduct expensive advertising campaigns, in addition to paying operating expenses, and taxes. Much of the capital used to develop these private attractions came from outside the Southern Appalachians, and a large part of the profits leave the region.

Among the entirely man-made attractions are the museums. Some, like those in Cherokee and Gatlinburg, attempt to display only materials native to an earlier way of life in the Southern Appalachians. Others offer collections of some specific item, such as the early model automobiles at Luray, and some are general museums like the Southwest Virginia Museum at Big Stone Gap. The Thomas Wolfe home and the Biltmore House in Asheville, North Carolina, and the Old Castle in Berkeley Springs all attract many visitors each day.

During the tourist season three noted plays—"Unto These Hills" at Cherokee, "Horn in the West" at Boone, and "Chucky Jack" at Gatlinburg—are presented five or six nights weekly in large amphitheaters. Each portrays historical incidents directly connected with early life in the region. "Unto These Hills" has been presented during each tourist season since 1950. Up to the close of the 1959 season it had played to more than 1.2 million paid admissions.

The Cherokee Indian Reservation, adjacent to the North Carolina entrance of the Great Smoky Mountain National Park, is a distinctive tourist attraction. In and near the town of Cherokee the Indians have constructed a museum, built the Mountainside Theatre, where "Unto These Hills" is presented, and developed Oconaluftee Indian Village, where the Indian way of life of 1750 is portrayed.

Gatlinburg, at the Tennessee entrance to the Great Smoky Mountain National Park, is another tourist development. Its main street, like Cherokee's, is a continuous group of shops, motels, hotels, filling stations, and amusement centers developed for the tourist trade. Blowing Rock and Fontana Village, both in North Carolina, and White Sulphur Springs are among the better known resorts of the Southern Appalachians.

Many large industrial establishments conduct guided tours through their plants at specific times during each working day. These tours, especially those through glass, textile, and paper factories, are usually well attended. Various mineral developments are also important tourist attractions. Since the Pocahontas Coal Mine, Pocahontas, Virginia, ceased production, it has been developed as an attraction to show mining operations. Near Dahlonega, Georgia, tourists may visit the old gold workings and, if they so desire, will be shown how to pan for gold and given the opportunity to try their luck.

Some large tracts of land in the Southern Appalachians have been purchased by church organizations and developed into conference sites complete with auditoriums, hotels, buildings for numerous types of religious activities, and cabins. The three largest groups are located in North Carolina at Ridgecrest (Baptist), Montreat (Presbyterian), and Junaluska (Methodist). In a year each assembly will have between fifty and sixty-five thousand persons in attendance. Although these places have been developed primarily for religious purposes, between 60 and 75 percent of the adults attending the sessions combine their vacations with their religious activities. Field-of-the-Wood (Church of God), also in North Carolina, is just east of Turtletown, Tennessee. To see the Ten Commandments blocked out on a hillside in letters five feet high, along with other attractions, several thousand tourists visit the location each year.

No economic studies dealing with tourism have been made for the area here defined as the Southern Appalachians. Each state has made partial studies for either the whole of its domain or for some of the area included in this report. A recent study made for the Maryland Department of Economic Development includes all of the area being studied in an eleven-state report. Figures as to the exact amounts of capital invested, costs of construction, and income from the investment for recreational activities are not available. No estimate of income from tourism in the Southern Appalachians has been made, though estimates for other somewhat comparable areas place the income from over 800 million dollars to more than a billion dollars. In many parts of the Southern Appalachians tourism ranks after agriculture, mining, and manufacturing in production of income. In other places, such as Asheville and Gatlinburg, income from tourism may rank first. Generally the income from tourism is greater than that for forestry, although there are local exceptions to this, and it is apparently increasing each year.

In general about thirty-five cents from each tourist dollar is spent for food, about thirty-two cents for lodging, and fifteen cents for transportation. Although each filling station and restaurant in a tourist area has regular local customers, each is also dependent upon the tourist trade. The owner of a motel, restaurant, or filling station must make a substantial investment if he is to secure a reasonable part of the tourist dollar.

In the 1930's, a tourist cabin represented an investment of perhaps $100. It was a shelter of some type with a minimum of secondhand furniture. The unit offered a bed, a wash basin, communal toilet and shower facilities, and a parking space, at very low cost. Today the average new rental unit requires an expenditure of between $5,000 and $8,000 to build and furnish. This provides what the modern tourist wants—wall-to-wall carpeting, private toilet and bathing facilities, a telephone, a television, comfortable furniture, and air conditioning. Thus, to develop a twenty-room project, which is recommended as the minimum for best profit possibilities, requires a total outlay of $100,000 to $160,000. Many motel organizations state that the income from smaller courts, especially those with fewer than ten units, is very speculative and the turnover is high. The American Motel Association has estimated that a third of all the motels in the nation yield $3,000 per year or less after taxes.

In the tourist areas of the Southern Appalachians numerous motels have only five or six units. Generally such an enterprise is operated by a retired person, or as a sideline to some other economic activity by a man and his wife. Many of these small units are closed during the nontourist season, when the cost of fuel may be more than the income from them. Most motels in the Southern Appalachians have between fifteen and twenty units. A man and wife operating such an establishment will have a full-time job twelve months of the year, but there are some advantages for the operator in the moderate size of the business. It costs relatively little to keep the place attractive, and the small operator has the opportunity to serve his guest personally and by so doing build repeat business. To be successful in this type of operation, he must have at least 65 percent occupancy on a yearly basis.

In order to meet the motel competition, many hotels have been forced to increase their investments by adding drive-in registration windows and furnishing parking space. Both hotels and motels are now receiving competition from trailers. Small trailers that can be used by two, three, or four persons are becoming more common along the highways. Trailer sites are usually provided in state parks, national parks, and national forests as well as in many roadside parks. The trailer will also have an effect upon the restaurant business, for most people using trailers will cook their own meals.

But the economic impact of tourism goes far beyond what the tourist spends for lodging, food, transportation, and recreation. The tourist industry influences practically every business in the Southern Appalachians, and this influence will increase as the tourist industry expands.

New parks or new lakes, such as Buchanan Lake, when completed will change the life of the communities in the vicinity as have the lakes of the TVA system. As the new area becomes accessible, boat docks will be built, large and small boats will be placed on the lake, various recreational activities will develop, and nearby farms may be subdivided and lots sold for cottages or homes. Retired persons may be attracted to the community as permanent residents, and new industry will come into the Region to help supply the needs of vacation visitors. These industries, though small, provide employment for local people, and some of the small industries that start as a service for the tourist may develop natural markets. All such changes mean an increase in land values, thus an increase in tax revenue and more income for local governments. School districts usually make the greatest gains, as very few children are added to the class rolls.

Tourism is an important business that will become more important in the years ahead. The people of the United States now have more leisure time to spend than ever before and even more is promised in the future. Already the leaders of industry and labor are planning for an average work week of four days. In addition, the level of individual income is rising steadily so that there is more money available to spend for recreational purposes. Almost without exception, the more than 65 million employed persons of this nation enjoy annual paid vacations of from one to three weeks duration. They are joined on vacation by members of their families. In addition, many retired people have sufficient means to travel. Hence, it is estimated that over 100 million people take one or more vacations per year.

Although most of the tourists in any state live in that state, tourists from all the states and many foreign countries visit the Southern Appalachians each year. Some part of the Region being within a day's drive of over half the people of the nation, the Southern Appalachians should in the years to come share in the expansion of the tourist industry.

The chief physical handicaps to the continued development of tourism in the Southern Appalachians are topography and the seasonal variations in weather. Many of the principal attractions, as has already been pointed out, are the result of the ruggedness of the landscape, but most of the undeveloped areas are in their present state because of this same ruggedness.

On the other hand, many people living in the inaccessible areas want them to remain isolated. They resent the coming of the tourist, for they are afraid of this contact with the outside world even though it could help increase their standard of living.

The tourist who wants to take his vacation with as little exercise as possible will bypass any area he cannot enter on a resonably good road. In addition to good roads, the modern tourist requires a sufficient number of motels and hotels, restaurants that serve food with which he is familiar, and a variety of recreational activities. Some of the most beautiful areas in the Southern Appalachians offer none of these. There are areas of great scenic beauty in each of the 190 counties of the Region, but about a third of these counties are without any tourist activity.

State highways are often narrow and poorly paved, and have little or no embankments, and frequently no guard rails. The drive from Frenchburg to Slade along Kentucky State Highway 77 is an extremely interesting one, for the scenic views are comparable or superior to most other views in the state. The road winds through the heart of the Cumberland National Forest. Grades are steep and the curves are sharp. Near the top of one ridge a tunnel has been blasted through the mountain for about a quarter of a mile. One side of the road is bordered by a drop of several hundred feet, but there is no guard rail. In like condition, Virginia State Highway 798 that crosses Powell Mountain from the Virginia-Tennessee boundary to Jonesville provides some of the most picturesque views in the region, but probably only a lost tourist would drive such a road. The paved part of the Virginia highway is only fifteen feet wide, and in many places there is not sufficient room for two cars to pass. Similarly, the Alabama state highway following the edge of Little River Canyon near Ft. Payne is extremely dangerous although quite scenic. In some places a slip off the edge of the road could send a car over a cliff several hundred feet high. Before a large tourist industry could be developed along any of the above highways and many others like them, better and safer roads would have to be constructed.

Some areas with attractive scenery, even though the roads are good, still have little tourist trade because of the lack of sufficient accommodations. Even though there are eight state parks in the Georgian part of the Southern Appalachians, the tourist may find it necessary to drive many miles to secure suitable sleeping quarters unless he is near United States Highway 27 or 21. A tourist following Virginia State Highway 42, Kentucky State Highway 7, Tennessee State Highway 33, or United States Highway 52 between Williamson and Huntington in West Virginia may have difficulty in locating desirable overnight accommodations and restaurants. These, of course, are but examples, for similar conditions can be found along many other highways.

In these "off the beaten path" areas the tourist will be fortunate to find any of the commonly looked for recreational facilities. Most of the villages and small towns no longer have motion picture theaters, and where there is one, it may operate only on Saturdays. Even television may be lacking, since reception in some areas is either very poor or nil.

Weather is also a dominant factor in the development of tourism, especially for outdoor activities. While it is true that the major part of the nation's tourist activity takes place during the summer season, there is also considerable tourism during the winter. Weather conditions in the Southern Appalachians are almost ideal for any type of outdoor recreation from June to September. During the winter it is too cold for swimming and frequently too cool for camping and hiking. Because of these conditions the state parks of Virginia are operated on a seasonal basis, being closed from the last Monday in October to the Monday nearest to the middle of May. Many private establishments either close entirely or in part during what is called the "nontourist" season. For example, Fontana Village operates a large hotel and 300 cottages. During the winter season all cottages are closed and the hotel is only partly used. In certain sections of the northern part of the Southern Appalachians, however, winter activities have been developed. Blackwater Falls State Park in West Virginia offers a variety of winter sports and is consequently an important all-year tourist center.

Today, with the exception of a few very isolated coves, there is no such thing as a mountaineer as the tourist usually visualizes him. Nevertheless, it is in the areas most urgently in need of the economic development which tourism might provide that the conservative attitudes opposed to such development are found. It is doubtful if any except the most friendly attitude toward the tourist could be found in the great valleys that extend from northern Virginia into Alabama. From the time of the Wilderness Road to the present these valleys have been among the chief avenues of transportation for the nation. These people have been brought up with the ideas of trade and services and have no tendency to isolationism. In the eastern part of West Virginia, where many state parks have been developed, and where such famous resort areas as White Sulphur Springs are in operation, the tourist is an accepted figure. (This is the one part of the Southern Appalachians, however, where some motel operators condemn the state for developing state parks and recreational areas. These operators object particularly to publicly operated lodges and inns as competition to private industry, even though these same parks attract people who fill the motels they own.)

But attitudes toward the tourist are quite different in the most isolated parts of the Southern Appalachians which are still under the control of small landholders, in the Cumberland Plateau of Kentucky and Tennessee. Here are several small coves connected to the main highways by roads that may be impassable part of the year. Some areas, such as the one served by the Frontier Nursing Service from Hyden and Wendover, can be reached only by jeeps, on horseback, or on foot. In these places even the county seats have few tourists. Most of the older Cumberland hill people, particularly the agriculturalists, are suspicious of all strangers and especially of tourists. They realize that the coming of the tourist will eventually mean a change in their way of life, and they do not want a change in the status quo. The conservative and fundamental type of religion that has been preached to many of them for so long does not justify the styles of dress worn by numerous tourists, or the leaving of a job to "run around" for a week or two "when he ought to be working."

The breaking down of geographic isolation is relatively easy, for governments can build new roads and teach new methods of making a living; the breaking down of cultural isolation is a much more difficult task. In a small town near Cumberland Gap Historical National Park there are two restaurants, one patronized by tourists, the other almost exclusively by the natives. Reasons given by the older hill folk for not visiting the tourist cafe were: (1) too many strangers in the place, (2) cost of food too high, and (3) "we just seem out of place."

In most county seats and larger towns and villages the tendency toward segregation of tourists and natives is gradually breaking down. Most merchants will join together to attract the tourist dollar. In Jamestown, Tennessee, during a recent summer, one of the civic clubs had a booth on the Court House Square where all tourists were asked to register. On the day of the club meeting the tourist family registering nearest to noon was invited to be guests at the luncheon and given a tour of the county after the meeting. The younger editors of weekly papers are also helping, with editorials and feature articles dealing with tourist activities, to explain the importance of the tourist industry in the economy of the area.

That the hostility of isolated communities toward tourism can be overcome has been illustrated in the changes which have taken place in the Blue Ridge, Great Smokies, and Unakas. With the establishment of Great Smoky Mountains National Park, Shenandoah National Park, and the Blue Ridge National Parkway many families were forced to move, and feeling against the projects was high. Hettie Walker expressed the mountaineer attitude as follows: "We worried a sight fur awhile. We are use to it here and wouldn't want to leave from where we was born and brung up. We know how to make a livin' on our land, but we wouldn't nowheres else, I reckon."[6]

Those who were permitted to remain in the mountains soon learned that their life of individualism was nearing an end as roads slowly extended tourist activities into the most out-of-way places. Today the parks and the parkway dominate the economic activity of the Blue Ridge and Great Smoky regions. Mountain crafts and mountain arts are being revived, many young mountain people are being trained for profitable part-time or full-time work, and the willingness of the tourist to pay good prices for authentic goods is improving the standard of living for hundreds of families.

A few of the native people, naturally, do not approve of some of the rules and regulations prescribed by the National Park Service. Some object because they are not permitted to transport goods to market by using the Blue Ridge Parkway. They do not believe that a road should be built just for people "who don't do nothin' but gawk at the hills." Another group thinks that the zoning restrictions along the Parkway should not apply to those native to the area, and that they should be permitted to build stands of any type of construction they desire, where they desire, as other people do along the regular highways. One of the more common objections was that trees were being permitted to grow again in some of the meadows. This is looked upon as poor use of good grazing land. In general, however, the park agencies and private industry have developed a very successful public relations program. Almost all recreational developments or activities are accepted favorably by the natives of the area, and usually the great increase in tourism has been welcomed. Most tourist businesses employ their regular workers and about 95 percent of their seasonal help from among the people living in the area.

In addition to developing new tourist areas, more intensive use could be made of some areas already developed. Several caverns now undeveloped could be prepared for visitors, replicas of numerous historic forts or settlements might be built, and new or enlarged beaches could be formed along the lake shores. One of the prime necessities, however, is to clean up and improve the already existing facilities.

The National Park Service recognized the need for improvement when it instituted Mission 66, a ten-year development program designed to save the standards of park use, provide staffing, and furnish the physical facilities that will be required to meet the increased visitations expected. Prior to 1956, many of the physical facilities for visitor use and for park management had deteriorated to the point that some roads were unsafe, camp grounds were frequently unsightly and often overcrowded, administration buildings were somewhat outmoded and poorly equipped, and visitor centers were practically nonexistent.

The states should follow the example set by the federal government, for most state parks could serve more people than they do. For example, nine of the West Virginia state parks are classed as day parks and admission to them is prohibited from 10:00 p.m. to 8:00 a.m. Most of these have suitable sites for camping or trailer parks. In Virginia all parks are operated on a seasonal basis. Even though the lake waters become too cool for swimming, fishing and boating could continue throughout most of the year. Certainly many people would enjoy vacationing a few days in winter as well as summer. Since most state parks are relatively new, most buildings and equipment are in good condition. Access to many of the parks could be improved and better directional signs indicating routes should be installed.

[6] Elizabeth Skaggs Bowman, *Land of the High Horizons* (Kingsport, Tennessee, 1948), p. 38.

Most legitimate merchants and the state agencies having the responsibility for the development of tourism would like to see some method of control developed to check the "tourist traps" which are found along the more heavily traveled highways. It is frequently the person who travels little and has the least money who is the victim of such places. Many of the items sold in these roadside stands and stores—baskets, pottery, woven goods—are cheap imitations of various mountain crafts, generally imported and of inferior quality. A quick glance at the bottom of a basket or a piece of pottery, or at the tag on the woven goods sometimes suffices to identify an object as counterfeit, but often the name of the place in which it was made has been altered or removed.

In many respects the tourist traps are much alike. They advertise intensively with a series of gaudy signs, usually within a twenty-mile radius of their location. Their activities have little, if any, real relationship to the area in which they are located. Sometimes they have gathered a group of snakes and other "wild animals" to make a mountain zoo. Some have an old farm wagon or sled hitched to steers and advertise it as modern mountain transportation. (In one specific case the steers were Herefords to which long horns had been attached.) The unsuspecting tourist pays twenty-five or fifty cents to take a picture of such a rig or some other equally ridiculous item. Such traps usually have a souvenir shop that sells "genuine mountain goods" as well as a small "museum," cafe, or filling station.

An intensive educational program about the recreational facilities in the Southern Appalachians is needed. Especially should people working in the various service institutions be better informed about the things or places a tourist is most likely to seek. A waitress in a cafe in Greenville could not give directions to the Andrew Johnson National Monument although it was less than two blocks away; a filling station attendant in a small town ten miles from Oak Ridge, a native of the area, could not give directions to the American Museum of Atomic Energy, but thought it was in Knoxville someplace; and a worker on a state highway in North Carolina could not give directions to an entrance to the Blue Ridge Parkway even though he was less than two miles from one. Sometimes, after directions are accurately and carefully given, the informant proceeds to "knock" the area to which the tourist is going. These problems are recognized by various tourist

associations and chambers of commerce. In several places all clerks, waitresses, attendants, and their families are admitted free to local tourist attractions to get them acquainted with the activities. The National Park Service people give lectures each year about their work. Associations in numerous towns and cities are conducting schools to acquaint the local people with the assets of the community in which they live.

There is little reason to doubt that the potential of the tourist industry is much greater than has been realized to date, and that properly developed it will be a tremendous asset to the Appalachian economy. At the same time, it should be recognized that tourism is not a panacea for all the economic ills of the region, and that its full possibilities will be realized only after careful planning and much hard work.

With regard to the economic limitations of the tourist industry, some points should be reemphasized. First, the capital investments required for first-rate tourist facilities, already substantial, will probably continue to rise. It is unrealistic to suppose that a large-scale Appalachian tourist industry can be erected on a foundation consisting of numerous and uncoordinated shoestring operations. Second, the seasonal nature of tourism for most of the region is a factor with which to reckon. Although the development of year-round recreational resorts is a possibility for some few areas, it is not likely to prove generally feasible under present conditions. Consequently, supplementary forms of off-season employment for those who are primarily dependent upon tourism must be provided locally, or else a dependable supply of seasonal service workers must be developed. Third, even at best the employment opportunities provided by tourism are not as great as many people suppose. Less than half of the nation's motels, tourist courts, trailer parks, and camps in 1958 maintained a payroll, and those that did do so had less than four paid employees on the average. True, tourism increases employment in subsidiary businesses such as restaurants and service stations, but these two categories of service industries combined account for a very small percentage of the nation's employed labor force. In short, the tourist industry could not absorb the region's labor surplus in the foreseeable future even if all the latter were trained for service occupations, which of course is not the case.

Full development of the tourist industry in the region will require concentrated attention to four developmental phases. The first of these is planning.

Competent planners should be employed either by an area agency or by appropriate state agencies. On the basis of thorough studies, they should indicate the better sites for recreational expansion, determine the types of basic and supporting facilities and services that should be provided, and prepare cost estimates for development. Ideally the planning should extend beyond the specific details of the tourist facilities to take into account the relationship of the facilities to the communities in which they would be located.

A second phase of tourist development involves the indispensable element of financing. Various sources of financing are already available for promising private enterprises, including the Small Business Administration of the federal government, whose loan funds were recently increased under the provisions of the so-called Depressed Areas Bill. Some states, such as Kentucky, have appropriated special funds for low-interest loans to stimulate the development of new industry. Many of the difficulties of obtaining business loans would be overcome if an adequate prospectus of the proposed operation were presented, and this need could be filled in part by studies conducted during the planning phase.

A third phase of development would involve actual operations. One of the serious impediments to a more lucrative area tourist industry at the present time is the failure to provide the quality and variety of services that American tourists have come to expect. In part this stems from the provincial outlook of both proprietors and employees. Service that appears woefully lacking to the seasoned tourist may be viewed as well above average by local standards. The strong need to provide training in management and service operations of tourist-supported industries might be met through periodic courses offered in the vocational educational programs already provided by the various states. Such courses should provide knowledge of both the standards and techniques of good service.

Finally, as has already been indicated, the success of a tourist industry depends upon the support of the entire community in which is operates and not simply upon those directly involved in tourist-supported enterprises. Attractive facilities cannot overcome the impression created by a drab and dirty community setting nor can good service provided by a park, tourist home, or restaurant totally offset the effects of discourteous, hostile, or avaricious local citizens. The residents of local areas seeking to develop a healthy tourist trade must be adequately informed of the potential economic benefits from such a development and their own responsibilities in creating a favorable atmosphere for tourism. Such a program of public education might be carried out by a local association of commerce, a community development organization, or a service club. But who conducts such a program is of secondary importance to the recognition that community support of tourist industry is too important to leave to chance and must be cultivated as an integral part of the development process.

The key to the future success of tourism in the Southern Appalachians is the efficiency with which these four processes—planning, financing, operation, and public education—can be carried out.

The Changing Society

*M*AN IS *by nature a political animal, observed Aristotle, meaning thereby that humans live in organized societies and that their actions are in large measure the products of group influences. Thus in attempting to understand the relationship of man to his physical environment, it is necessary to take into account his social institutions—the patterns of social behavior developed to perform the basic functions of adjusting to, explaining, and, insofar as possible, controlling his life situation.*

The technological revolution of the past two centuries has been accompanied by a social revolution characterized by a general shift of basic functions from the family to larger, specialized, and highly complex organizational systems. In rural Southern Appalachian society the family has retained its traditional functions to a far greater degree than in the industrialized parts of the nation. At the same time, the factors that have led to the preservation of familism have also served to retard the development of the more highly specialized institutional forms of industrial society. In the first chapter of this section, Paul W. Wager describes the organization and functioning of local government in the Region, which he finds to be obsolescent in many respects, and discusses the problems involved in developing more effective governmental units.

In a second essay, Aelred J. Gray documents the radical changes in the distribution of the Southern Appalachian population which have rendered obsolete the traditional forms of public administration. The rapid transition from a rural to an urban society poses critical problems calling for systematic planning at the local, regional, and state levels.

Rapid change in a society imposes a particularly heavy responsibility on its institutions charged with the education of a oncoming generation. They can no longer be solely concerned with the preservation and transmission of traditional wisdom and techniques but must increasingly devote themselves to preparing the youth for new, and often uncertain, conditions of life. Failure of the schools to meet the challenge of change seriously handicaps the social and economic performance of both the individual and the society. The schools of the Southern Appalachian Region have made notable improvements in recent decades, Orin B. Graff points out in his essay on schools and education, but these changes have been insufficient to narrow the gap between the Region and the nation. In documenting the deficiencies of education in the Region, he indicates some of the requirements for bringing the regional schools up to national standards.

Prescribing the proper functions of education in our society is a difficult and provocative task, but it appears relatively simple compared with that of prescribing the functions of religion. By their very nature, religions are conservative of beliefs and values defined in absolute terms, and frequently this basic conservatism extends to other aspects of the culture. The pervasive religious heritage of the Southern Appalachian people, deeply rooted in the agrarian past, is confronted with new demands and problems of an industrial and increasingly secular society. What, then, is to be the future of the Region's religious institutions? Earl D. C. Brewer describes the present state of religious beliefs, practices, and organization, and he points out possible courses of future development.

Concepts of adequate health are rapidly changing, too, and consequently forcing continuous reassessment of health conditions and facilities. C. Horace Hamilton provides such a reassessment for the Southern Appalachian Region. His analysis indicates that the health of the people of the Region is generally as good as that of the people of the nation, although wide intraregional variations are to be found. At the same time, there exist serious deficiencies in the supply of health personnel and facilities and in provisions for the financing of health care that pose a serious threat for the future unless appropriate remedial and preventive steps are taken.

Not the least of the problems with which the people of the Region must deal is that of providing for the social and economic welfare of those who are inevitably socially dispossessed in an era of rapid change. In an earlier day, the family, the church, or the local community through such institutions as the "poor farm" were more or less adequate to handle the problems of indigency. But these have proved unequal to the new tasks imposed by social maladjustments and changing concepts of welfare adequacy. William E. Cole addresses himself to the analysis of welfare problems in the Region, their effective solution, and, above all, the need for preventive action.

CHAPTER TEN

Local

Government

PAUL W. WAGER

THIRTY YEARS AGO COUNTY AND CITY government in the Southern Appalachians was primitive and casual. The public offices were held for the most part either by petty politicians, often members of families long active politically, or by men of limited ability who were enticed by public jobs that paid quite modest salaries. No doubt the prestige, real or imagined, an easy berth, and a possible opportunity to profit by being on the "inside" were also allurements. The more important point to be made is that usually the officeholders were rank amateurs. Simple and small scale as were most operations, they demanded more skill and imagination than they generally received. Embezzlement or malfeasance on a large scale may have been rare, but legal prescriptions of many kinds were innocently or willfully violated.

A study of county government in Tennessee made in 1930 noted: "One hundred and eighty county officials checked up short in 1928 . . . the shortages ran as high as $13,000 for county funds and $3,000 for state funds. . . . They were usually the result of bad bookkeeping and inefficiency on the part of the officer . . . but in some cases officials were dishonest and took advantage of an obsolete system and local politics to cover their dishonesty."[1]

A little over thirty years ago some graduate students at the University of North Carolina made careful investigations of county government in that state. "The county buys nothing at wholesale," they reported. "Every official does his own buying. Few of the bills are itemized and the commissioners have no way of knowing whether the work was done or the material delivered." Loose financial practices prevailed. In 1925, seven months after going out of office, one sheriff owed the county $61,833, according to the auditor, who commented, "There does not appear to have been any final settlement with any sheriff in recent years."[2]

There is plenty of evidence that practices were just as crude and wasteful in other states of the Region. In fairness to North Carolina it should be stated that in 1927 the state took vigorous action to stop reckless and irresponsible spending in the counties by passing two acts known as the County Finance Act and the County Fiscal Control Act. The first set up rigid limitations on the incurring of debt and the second imposed tight budgetary controls.

In the early 1930's a study by the Kentucky Legislative Council observed that the real problem of county government in that state was one of fiscal procedure. One of the worst prevailing practices was the fee system of compensating county officials. It was noted that compensation received by officers paid on a fee basis bore little relation to the amount of work they performed. Moreover, ceilings placed on earnings of fee-compensated officers had failed to produce any considerable amount of revenue for the county; expenses tended to rise to absorb the excess earnings; or the officer, after earning the allowable maximum, remitted fees when he believed that this would help him politically.[3]

As of 1930 considerable progress had been made in the direction of a county unit plan of highway administration. In a sense, the maintenance of the roads had always been a county responsibility in the South, but actual direction of the work had been highly decentralized. In an era of dirt roads this was perhaps a practical arrangement. As late as 1930 a commentator in Tennessee reported, "Many of the small counties still rely chiefly upon the district system and require each male over eighteen years of age to work the roads a certain number of days each year with picks and shovels."[4] The demand for all-weather roads had not brought an end to small road units. This was illustrated in Virginia, where a typical county containing six magisterial districts had six separate road boards, each composed of one or two members in addition to the supervisor of that magisterial district. However, by 1930 no less than 18 Virginia counties, including 5 Appalachian counties, had county road engineers.

By that time several North Carolina counties also had county engineers, responsible either to the county board of commissioners or to a special highway commission. On the other hand, there was a multiplicity of special road districts with their own organization and their own funds. A survey made for Governor Gardner about that time revealed 150 road units in the state, most of them poorly equipped, poorly directed, overridden with politics, and utterly wasteful. These findings, along with the intense desire for lower property taxes, induced the counties to surrender the road function in its entirety to the state in 1931. Soon thereafter similar revolutions took place in Virginia and West Virginia. In the other Appalachian states, county political organizations were powerful enough to block such a transfer, still gaining local tax relief through state grants or the sharing of state taxes.

By 1930 agricultural extension work was established in all the states of the Region, though not very securely yet in many of the mountain counties. The county

appropriations were often niggardly and sometimes were cut off altogether.

In 1930 the counties in all the Southern Appalachian states still were the only public source of poor relief. Except for those afflicted persons who had been admitted to specialized state institutions, such as tuberculosis sanatoria, mental hospitals, and schools for the blind, all classes of dependents were charges of the county. Relief took the form of meager monthly allotments of cash or groceries to distressed families, or, in the case of individual dependents, commitment to the county almshouse. This institution, which was acquiring the more dignified title of "county home," though with few home attributes, existed in nearly every county as an asylum for all sorts of derelict humanity. An investigator, speaking of the situation in Virginia, reported, "With few exceptions the superintendent is a farmer. . . . The selection is sometimes made on the basis of the cheapest man; sometimes because he has been of service to the party. . . . Inmates are left largely to themselves. . . . For the most part they are housed in old, dilapidated, ill-kept buildings, surrounded by dirt and squalor, afflicted by disease, and left to themselves in despair, loneliness, and hopelessness."[5]

Recognizing that many of its county homes were too small to be properly staffed or efficiently operated, Virginia in 1926 had authorized their consolidation into district homes, and by 1930 two district homes had been established. One consolidation included a mountain county. The consolidation idea, however, never gained favor in the other states of the region.

A beginning had been made in county health services, North Carolina and Virginia being in the vanguard of this development. Even so, a contemporary observer wrote, "The distinctly rural problem remains touched only at the fringes."[6]

Deplorable conditions characterized the county jails and prison camps. The jails—sometimes nearly empty, sometimes overcrowded—were cold, austere, unsani-

[1] Carleton C. Sims, "County Government in Tennessee," unpublished dissertation (University of Tennessee, 1930).

[2] Unpublished case studies in University of North Carolina Library.

[3] "The Fee System as a Method of Compensating County Officials," Kentucky Legislative Council, Frankfort. Mimeographed.

[4] Sims, "County Government in Tennessee."

[5] Frank W. Hoffer, *Counties in Transition*, Institute for Research in the Social Sciences, University of Virginia (Charlottesville, 1929), p. 27.

[6] Wylie Kirkpatrick, *Problems in Contemporary County Government*, Institute for Research in the Social Sciences, University of Virginia (Charlottesville, 1930), p. 47.

tary, poorly equipped and unstaffed for any rehabilitation of those confined there. In 1930 there were 49 North Carolina counties, including some in the mountains, that still maintained prison camps or chain gangs, and according to the State Department of Public Welfare the management left much to be desired. The chain gangs of Georgia were notorious.

Of the Appalachian states only Virginia had taken steps to improve the administration of justice in rural areas. In that state a general act of 1926, as well as some earlier special acts, authorized the replacement of justices of the peace with a single trial justice with county-wide jurisdiction. By 1930 ten counties had instituted the plan, two being Appalachian counties.

These glimpses of county government as it operated in the Southern Appalachian region thirty years ago should be sufficient to show that it was tradition-bound, unprofessional, wasteful, and irresponsible. Probably most of the officeholders had good intentions; but they allowed themselves first to condone and then to employ the loose standards which had become customary. Nothing contributed more to this than the absence of central coordination and review. Popular election of a half dozen independent officers makes integration difficult; the lack of a full-time coordinator almost assures chaos. An investigator of county government in 1930 summed up the situation when he remarked that the chief criticism of county government was that it was headless. Surprisingly, the investigator was speaking of Tennessee, where the county judge, or full-time chairman of the county court, was supposed to supply the needed leadership. His failure to provide it was ascribed by the investigator to incompetence; but he might have added politics and the handicap of a long ballot.

In the cities, the council-manager form of government was demonstrating that local government could at the same time be alert, efficient, and responsible. Originating within the region at Staunton, Virginia in 1908, it had by 1930 been adopted in 23 other cities of the region and in hundreds of cities elsewhere.

The 1960 Census showed that the Southern Appalachian Region, as delimited for purposes of this survey, had a population of 5,672,178. Altogether it has about 1,100 units of local government. These units include 190 counties, as well as cities and other incorporated places, school districts, and a variety of special districts. The region has few large cities, but a large number of small incorporated places. Some of the incorporations which existed in 1930 have already disappeared, but a larger number of new ones have

been chartered. Between 1930 and 1960 the total number increased from 496 to 568. A majority of those units in existence throughout the period showed growth, some a substantial growth. Even so, in 1960 there were only 13 Southern Appalachian cities with a population of 25,000 or more, and only 42 with as many as 10,000 people. Appalachian Virginia alone had 11 independent cities with populations ranging from Roanoke's 97,100 to Galax's 5,200.

While only 33.6 percent of the population of the Region was classed as urban by the 1960 census, the number of people who lived in incorporated places constituted 36.5 percent of the Region's aggregate population.

As of April, 1957, these local units had 87,730 full-time employees plus numerous part-time employees, or the equivalent of 102,373 full-time employees, excluding North Carolina public school teachers, considered state employees. The importance of local government as an employer may be gained from the size of the Region's payroll as of April, 1957, when almost $25,000,000 was distributed to the local government employees.[7] About 65 percent of the total paid out in salaries that month went to teachers and other school employees. These figures do not include the entire payroll, for in North Carolina the basic salaries of teachers and other school employees are an obligation of the State. The total annual payroll in these local units amounted to over $260,000,000.

The number of employees and the size of the payrolls of the local units must be considered in light of the fact that in each state certain functions formerly local have been transferred to the state, so persons performing these functions for local units are now state employees. This is true not only of the public school teachers in North Carolina, but of workers on the secondary roads in North Carolina, Virginia, and West Virginia, public welfare workers in all states of the region except North Carolina and Virginia, and some other workers.

Functions of County Government

The counties which lie within the survey area were all established a long time ago when travel was slow and difficult. What constituted a convenient service area then has in many instances long ceased to be economically defensible. Many of the 190 counties are small in population and wealth as well as in area. Sixty-three of them have less than 15,000 population

[7] U.S. Department of Commerce, Bureau of the Census *Summary of Public Employment*, 1957, Table 23, pp. 111-28.

and 69 have less than $10,000,000 of assessed valuation.[8] Granted that assessment ratios are low, the actual value of the taxable property in most of these counties is too limited to support essential services even at minimum standards. For years the richer counties have been required through one device or another to help carry the burdens of the poorer ones. The small rural counties are so over-represented in all the state legislatures that they have been able to shift much of the cost of schools, roads, and public welfare to the larger, richer, and particularly the more urbanized, counties. This has been achieved mainly by having the state impose income, sales, and excise taxes that fall most heavily on city people, and then distribute the collection in ways which again favor the small counties.

To make the situation worse, much of the tax revenue which is assessed and collected in the small counties is dissipated in supporting needless offices and a complement of officials in near-idleness. Most county homes have been closed because they had so few occupants. Many county jails and courthouses are old and dilapidated; they should be abandoned and not replaced. Regional libraries, regional health units, and regional hospitals are proving the effectiveness of larger units, but county consolidation has made almost no headway and one cannot be sanguine that it will.

With rare exceptions, personnel practices in the courthouses of the region remain little different from what they were thirty years ago except that the hours are shorter and the pay is better. Only in the departments where a merit system is a condition for receiving federal grants is there any semblance of such a system. Almost without exception, personnel is selected on a personal or political basis. Nepotism is found everywhere, a man's wife or daughter commonly serving as his secretary. On the other hand, the "charity concept" is still strong in rural areas. Many courthouse jobs, particularly those filled by election, are occupied by widows and cripples. To be sure, county officials and employees are usually gracious and friendly, though they often have only a superficial understanding of the duties of their offices. Aware of their limitations, elected officials often retain the clerks or deputies of their predecessors, at least for awhile. One is impressed by the apparent superfluity of help in many of the offices. This is not surprising since county jobs remain the principal "pay-off" to the party faithful.

Fortunately the objectionable fee system of compensation is being discontinued or more closely regulated. In Kentucky a ceiling has been put on earnings. Yet the system persists in Kentucky, and with respect to a few offices in some counties it continues to prevail in most states of the Region. Commissions to tax collectors and treasurers seem to be the most common. For example, in a county that is just now switching over to a salary basis, the office of probate judge had been grossing about $40,000; the new salary will be $7,200.

The political institutions of the Appalachian county remain cumbersome and ineffective. Tennessee clings to the ancient quarterly court as its central governing body. It consists of a large number of justices of the peace elected by magisterial districts. The court in Blount County has 41 members. The point of view of the individual justice is often exceedingly provincial, and a small minority can block constructive programs of countywide import. The system is archaic and should be discontinued.

A Kentucky county's governing body, called the fiscal court, is also made up of magistrates elected by districts, but the number is kept small, from three to eight. Until 1957 they were paid $15 a month for service on the fiscal court, which could be supplemented by fees earned as justice of the peace. In 1957 the legislature stripped justices of their authority to try misdemeanor cases and thus of their fees. Subsequent legislation restored the right to try such cases where authorized by the county fiscal court, but justices who performed this service were placed on a salary fixed by statute and ranging from $100 to $300 per month according to the population of the county. The abolition of the fee system for misdemeanor cases, while undoubtedly serving the interest of justice, has placed a heavy burden on poor counties, where magistrates most commonly continue to try cases.

As for other Appalachian counties, Virginia's boards of supervisors range in size from three to ten and are likewise elected by districts. The individual members have no administrative or judicial responsibilities in their respective districts. West Virginia's board is called county court and its judicial functions are limited to those of a probate nature. Its three members are nominated by districts and elected at large. North Carolina counties have a board of county commissioners of three or five members, usually, but not always, elected at large. In Alabama and Georgia there is no uniformity in either the composition or

[8] Population figures are Census estimates, assessed valuations are from respective state reports.

the name of the county board, and a few Georgia counties dispense with a board altogether.

Not a single county within the Appalachian Region has a true county executive. Two Tennessee counties —Hamilton and McMinn—have county managers who have only limited appointive power, but who nevertheless can perform a valuable coordinating function. Actually, the ordinary in certain Georgia counties is the most powerful county official to be found in the Region, exercising not only executive, but legislative and judicial powers as well. He virtually runs the county. Approaching him in power and influence is the county judge in Tennessee and Kentucky. He not only presides over the nearest thing to a legislative body which a county has, but he is also its fiscal agent, budget officer, purchasing agent, custodian of county property, and often chairman of the road commission, if there is one. He is judge of the juvenile court and of a petty trial court. His official titles do not reveal his full role. Elected for a long term, often serving for several terms, involved in all aspects of the county government, he tends to become the best informed and the most heeded person in the courthouse. Simetimes he becomes the most feared, for he wields considerable political power.

North Carolina counties are required to employ a budget and fiscal control officer called a county accountant. In many cases he is also purchasing agent and the supervisor of assessments, and sometimes is given other administrative assignments. The office has made for fiscal responsibility and some of the incumbents approach the stature of managers. The lower salaries and the more pervasive political climate may explain why in some of the mountain counties the incumbents of the office do not exhibit the usual degree of professional competence.

In none of the Appalachian counties of Virginia or West Virginia is there a central administrative officer or even a fiscal control officer. A West Virginia student of local government comments, "There has been no sustained attempt to modernize county machinery. Crystallized in an era when profound distrust of centralization existed, the organization is marked by diffusion of authority. . . . The county government structure still remains the cumbersome, decentralized machine it was long prior to the establishment of the state."[9] The statement would apply generally to Virginia as well; there are five county managers or county executives in the state, but none in the mountain region.

In all the states of the Region numerous administra-

tive officers continue to be chosen by popular election, which precludes any well-integrated structure.

Despite the faulty structure of county government and the lack of a chief administrator, there has been improvement in at least some aspects of fiscal management. This is due to a greater measure of state control. In Virginia, West Virginia and Kentucky, audits are made by state auditors, and in North Carolina by private auditing firms that meet state standards. In Kentucky and West Virginia county budgets must have prior approval by a state agency, and in Kentucky counties may have the assistance of the agency in the preparation of the budget. In Virginia the state auditor prescribes the budget forms to insure uniformity of reporting. In North Carolina the Local Government Commission, a state agency, must approve that portion of the budget which covers debt service. In fact, the incurring of debt and the form it takes are tightly regulated by the agency.

While budgets are generally required of the counties in all the states of the Region, they are often that only in name. Unquestionably the mere preparation of a budget document serves to establish some balance between expected income and outgo within a fiscal year, and large deficits are less common. But there is still little accrual accounting, spending being largely governed by the current state of the treasury. Annual reports are often no more than a summary of the treasurer's receipts and disbursements. In Kentucky fees are reported to the state, and amounts collected in excess of the operating expenses of the offices are returned to the county, except in the larger counties, in which certain fees are paid to the state. If the fees are likely to be insufficient to pay respectable salaries, a county may appropriate a supplement. The state supplements the salaries of tax commissioners. The county judge may prevent exhaustion of the earnings of such offices through superfluous personnel or unduly high clerical salaries. In Virginia the salaries of all county officials, as well as the number of employees and expenses of their offices, are regulated by a state compensation board. Yet despite greater oversight by state authorities in all the states of the Region, there are occasional abuses.

The functions of county government in the Southern Appalachians have expanded in some respects in the last thirty years, and contracted in others. The expansion is due to the assumption of new functions, such as the provision of health and library services,

[9] Unpublished manuscript of Mavis Mann, University of West Virginia (Morgantown, n.d.).

the contraction to the transfer of formerly local functions to the state, as in the cases of roads and public welfare. These developments have been different in each of the seven states. However, the movements have generally been statewide, and thus not peculiar to the Appalachian counties. There is no aspect of local government that has not undergone change and none has changed more than law enforcement.

Throughout the Region the sheriff is presumed to be the chief law enforcement officer; the ultimate power to preserve the peace is legally vested in him. He is aided by a number of deputies whom he appoints. Unquestionably he has continued to play the role of a police officer more fully in the mountain counties than in the more urbanized counties. Yet even in the Appalachians he is not the robust character that he was in an earlier era, nor does he devote himself so much to police work, for in most counties there are better trained police officers. In addition to the municipal police, there is now in each state of the region a strong, mobile force of state police or highway patrolmen. Some are stationed at county seats and work closely with the sheriff's office. One West Virginia sheriff candidly stated: "I lean heavily on the state police." In five states of the region members of the state force are clothed with power to enforce all criminal laws. In Georgia and North Carolina they are primarily a highway patrol, but any crime which involves use of the highways comes within their jurisdiction. Moreover, they may on their own initiative arrest persons accused of bank robbery, murder, or other crimes of violence. Whatever the crime, they cooperate with the local law enforcement officers on invitation.

In six of the states the sheriff's term is four years; in Tennessee, two years. In West Virginia and Kentucky he is not eligible to serve for two successive terms, and in Tennessee he may not serve continuously for more than six years. Most sheriffs come into office without previous experience as law enforcement officers; rarely is a deputy elevated to the office; more often the nomination is given to someone who has been active politically, perhaps having held other courthouse jobs. Not infrequently the sheriff is primarily a politician. A newspaper of Appalachian West Virginia editorialized, "The office of sheriff is steeped in politics and it is readily admitted by all that this office is the 'prize' of the county offices."[10] Whether compensated by salary or fees, the position is one of the best paid jobs in local government, and is often sought for that very reason. In West Virginia,

Kentucky, and a few counties in North Carolina the sheriff is the county's tax collector, and the commissions for that work are a strong attraction. Evidence that the modern sheriff, even in the Southern Appalachians, is not always the strong, colorful figure of an earlier period is found in the fact that in at least one county the office was recently held by a woman.

In most respects court structure and judicial procedure are no different in the Appalachian region from what they are in other parts of the several states or from what they were thirty years ago. Whatever its name, the state court of general jurisdiction meets at stated times in each county courthouse and continues to draw the same throngs of people eager to feast on each sordid detail. There are fewer reports of shooting within the courtroom, but otherwise the same scenes are reenacted.

Below the trial court of general jurisdiction several significant developments have occurred. One is the appearance in many places of an inferior court where misdemeanors, and sometimes civil cases involving small sums, can be tried cheaply and with dispatch, for they usually meet weekly and dispense with a jury. DeKalb County, Alabama, has a so-called Superior Court with unlimited civil jurisdiction and final jurisdiction of misdemeanors; but it has also an Inferior Court which tries misdemeanors and petty civil cases, replacing justice-of-the-peace courts. Since 1934 all Virginia counties have had a county court which can try misdemeanors and civil cases involving up to $1,000. The judge, who is almost always a lawyer, is appointed by the judge of the circuit court, is paid by the state, and serves also as judge of the juvenile and domestic relations court.

A number of Tennessee counties have been permitted by special act to establish General Sessions courts similar to the Virginia courts just described, and a 1959 act makes their establishment mandatory in all except very small counties. These courts will replace the justice-of-the-peace courts in those counties. Certain of the West Virginia counties have special criminal, common pleas, or domestic relations courts. Buncombe County, North Carolina, has both a county court and a domestic relations court, and a number of North Carolina counties have within their boundaries recorders' courts with criminal jurisdiction somewhat greater than that of the justice of the peace. In Georgia, special intermediate courts, called city courts with countywide jurisdiction, have been

[10] Morgantown (West Virginia) *Post*, March 7, 1950.

established in numerous counties, and in a few counties there are so-called county courts with both civil and criminal jurisdiction more limited than that of a circuit court. In Tennessee and Kentucky the presiding officer of the county's governing body, called fiscal or quarterly court, is designated county judge. In addition to being judge of the probate court and the juvenile court, he can try petty cases, both civil and criminal, and can bind over to the higher courts.

The second significant development is the rapid decline in functions of the justice of the peace. In several of the Appalachian states, he may no longer perform marriages. His service as a trial judge is disappearing. His court has been abolished in Virginia; it has almost disappeared in Georgia, and is on the way out in Tennessee. In the other states it is rapidly declining, and was threatened with elimination in North Carolina by the 1959 legislature. The character of the office has deteriorated to the point where it is generally distrusted and in an automobile age it seems obsolete anyway.

The third significant development is the universal establishment of juvenile courts separate from the regular state courts. Except in Virginia, the judges usually hold another county office, such as clerk of the superior court in North Carolina, and serve ex officio. Though without legal training, some of these lay judges have displayed great understanding and patience, rendering a distinct service in a time when juvenile delinquency is becoming an alarming problem even in rural areas.

The county jail with all its shortcomings remains everywhere. In 1946 a survey of the county jail system of West Virginia was made by the Federal Bureau of Prisons. Its conclusions would very likely have fitted the jails in other states of the region equally well and they would be little different today. "Most jails as presently staffed, supported, and operated are anachronisms in our social order," the report said. "The majority of them are totally unfit for human habitation."[11]

Only 14 of the 55 jails in the state were found to have facilities for segregating the insane, and only 12 had separate facilities for juveniles. Six jails made no attempt to provide separate quarters for men, women, or juveniles. Bathing facilities were not available in several. The survey team attributed the deficiencies mainly to the lack of competent personnel, and the fee system of compensating the sheriff or jail. Its recommendations led the legislature to abolish the fee system of feeding prisoners in all counties, effective January 1, 1949, but two years later the system was restored in counties with populations of 30,000 or less in the interest of economy.[12] The basic recommendation of the survey was that about ten of the existing jails be retained as regional jails, a few others be designated as lockups for emergency and temporary confinement, and the rest be closed. This sensible recommendation has gained no support in West Virginia or elsewhere.

In Kentucky the jailer is elected by popular vote; elsewhere the sheriff usually makes one of his deputies jailer, with living quarters for his family in the jail building. The sheriff himself rarely serves as jailer, though sometimes he gets the fees. The salary of a jailer in Kentucky is related to the size of the county, but cannot exceed the fees earned. The allowance in the several states for "dieting" the prisoners varies from $1.25 to $1.75 a day. The turnkey fee is usually 60 cents to $1.00 each way. Reported in more than one county was the practice of rounding up "drunks" on Saturday nights, turning them loose before breakfast Sunday morning, and charging two turnkey fees and two days board. The deputy sheriff who made the arrest also got a fee, and if papers had to be served or there was a hearing a justice of the peace got his fees also. Jail population fluctuates widely. A Georgia jailer said that his jail had 40 beds but he had put up as many as 65 inmates by having them take turns sleeping. Few counties make any provision for working their prisoners, though some are confined in jail for as much as a year. An exception to this is found in North Carolina, where practically all prisoners serving more than thirty days are sent to the state road camps or prison farms.

A universal function of county government is to conduct elections, the cost of which is not trifling. Two counties selected at random will illustrate this. In 1956 elections in Madison County, North Carolina, cost $7,426, a sum equal to 9 per cent of the county's general fund.[13] In 1958 elections in Laurel County, Kentucky, cost $5,510 or 6 per cent of all that was spent from the general fund.[14] Many counties are buying voting machines, sometimes issuing bonds for the purpose.

[11] U.S. Department of Justice, Bureau of Prisons, *Survey of County Jails in West Virginia* (1946), p. 3.
[12] Harold J. Shamberger, *County Government and Administration in West Virginia*, Bureau of Government Research, West Virginia University (Morgantown, 1952), p. 27.
[13] Figures derived from county audit.
[14] Figures taken from county budget.

While an election board must legally include a representative of the minority party, registrations and elections are by no means conducted with complete impartiality. Kentucky has what is potentially an excellent permanent registration system, but the diligence displayed by the purgation boards in the respective counties to keep the lists up-to-date varies widely. One official was frank to admit that only members of the majority party were reminded that failure to vote in the last election jeopardized their qualification to vote in future elections. The supervisor of a large, well-organized county registration office in West Virginia stated that, with one exception, all of his 21 clerks were Democrats. A Virginia official explained that a long interval was needed between the primary and the general election to enable candidates to ascertain who had not paid their poll taxes. The implication was that those who promised to vote right had their poll tax paid for them. A candid and knowledgeable informant in western North Carolina stated that in his county multiple voting was common. In this same county it was reported that school teachers who did not contribute the prescribed amount to the party organization were not reappointed. In the Southern Appalachian area, regardless of the state, a great many of the people are intensely partisan and are not disposed to see their candidate defeated by their adhering closely to the rules. They reason that the opposition is resorting to equally questionable practices. Besides, honest elections are too tame.

In all seven states embraced in this study the county is the basic unit of school administration and support. The only important exception is the recognition of city units in the case of some larger cities, and even these units usually are not wholly independent of the county. The county school districts are not always separate units of government with their own tax levying power. In fact, only in West Virginia, Kentucky, and certain counties in Georgia is this the case.

Each county has a board of education which determines the location of school buildings and other matters of a policy nature. This board is chosen by the grand jury in Georgia, by a special electoral board in Virginia, and, in effect, by the Democratic county primary in North Carolina. In the four other states the members are popularly elected, though by districts in Tennessee. The county superintendent of schools is appointed by the board except in Tennessee and Georgia, where he is popularly elected. School ad-

ministration and financing is covered more fully in a separate chapter.

Early in the 1930's three states of the region—North Carolina, Virginia, and West Virginia—transferred the secondary roads from the counties to the state for maintenance. In the other four states of the region, relief took the form of financial assistance rather than transfer of the function.

Alabama counties may now choose between the alternatives, and eight counties, including one Appalachian county (DeKalb), have elected to let the state take care of their roads. In counties which have chosen to retain control, the usual arrangement has been for each member of the county governing body, not including the chairman, who is elected at large, to act as road supervisor in the district from which he was elected, the funds being divided evenly among the four commissioners regardless of relative need. Funds for road work come from three cents of the state gasoline tax and a 2.5-mill property tax levy. The revenue from two of the three cents is distributed among the 67 counties evenly; one cent is made available for matching purposes.

In Georgia the construction and maintenance of local roads remains a major county function, though with considerable financial assistance from the state. The work is under the jurisdiction of the commissioners of roads and revenue or, in the absence of such a board, the ordinary, an elected officer with a variety of administrative and judicial duties. In Appalachian Dade County, where maintenance of the county roads is under the supervision of the ordinary, the road budget in 1958 was about $40,000 with $33,000 coming from the state. By way of contrast, Appalachian Rabun County, a considerably larger county than Dade and having 500 miles of county roads, in 1958 spent some $66,000 for maintenance, deriving only $20,000 of this sum from the state. It also spent $50,000 on bridges and new construction toward which the state contributed $10,000.

In Kentucky most of the more-traveled roads have been taken into the state system. To get a road added to the state system, the county must buy the right-of-way and grade the road to meet the standards required. Then the state will take over, blacktop, and maintain. The proceeds from two cents of the gasoline tax are made available to the Division of Rural Highways for this purpose but in no year is there enough money to take over all the roads that might qualify. One county judge complained that in his county, a Republican county, only two and a half miles had been added to the state system in three years. No state money is distributed to the counties for their local road maintenance except a portion of the proceeds from the sale of truck licenses. Most counties get about $14,000 a year from this source. Any other money for maintenance of the county roads has to come from such *ad valorem* taxes as the county cares to levy. Supervision is by the individual members of the fiscal court in their respective districts.

In Tennessee, as in Georgia, the upkeep of the roads remains an important county function, though here, too, most of the money comes from the state. There are two sources of state revenue—collections from two cents of the seven-cent gasoline tax and a special appropriation for Aid to Rural Roads. One half of the amount from each source is divided equally among the counties, the other half being distributed by slightly different formulas, but with the net result that the distribution bears little relation to traffic demands. In the year which ended June 30, 1958, aid from the two sources to the 37 Appalachian counties amounted to over 12 million dollars, the least which any county received being about $206,000. Fifteen of the 37 counties had levied no property taxes for roads that year; the other 22 had levied road taxes ranging from 2 cents to 78 cents on a hundred dollars valuation. The levies aggregated some $2,000,-000. Assuming 100 percent collection, which is unrealistic, six of the larger counties provided 33 percent of their own road funds, 16 provided about 3 percent, and the other 15 furnished no local support. No uniform plan of county administration exists. A few counties have road engineers; more have only an unskilled superintendent. Sometimes the superintendent reports to a committee of the county court, sometimes to a special road commission. A reorganization effected in 1959 in Blount County provided for a road commission with one member from each of three districts into which the county is divided. The commission hires the superintendent. As in Kentucky, Tennessee will accept each year for inclusion in the state system a few miles that meet the required specifications.

Some counties have found it necessary to hire temporarily an engineer to help grade roads they seek to have accepted by the state. Otherwise county road administration generally is amateurish, wasteful, and political. In both Tennessee and Kentucky many of the back roads become virtually impassable in winter. Many streams are not bridged and when they cannot be forded, schools are closed. Improvement is slow because so much of the grant-in-aid money is dissipated.

One of the most encouraging developments in the Southern Appalachians in recent years has been the extension of public health services. Today there are only three counties not affiliated with a public health organization (see Chapter XIV).

In 1930 only 23 percent of the people in the Southern Appalachians had library service of any kind, and in many instances the service fell far below recognized standards. Only eight counties in the Southern Appalachians had countywide library service and the expenditure in those counties averaged only 34 cents per capita. Countywide service is still by no means universal, but today there are few counties in the Region that make no appropriation for libraries.

Only one of Georgia's twenty Appalachian counties is without countywide library service, and this one has within its boundaries an available municipal library. None of these 19 counties supports a county library alone. Each joins forces with neighboring counties to support a regional library. Their efforts are reinforced with a generous amount of state aid. Georgia's record of cooperative library service through regional systems is unsurpassed in the United States.

All but two of North Carolina's 22 Appalachian counties now have countywide book service. Thirteen counties have county libraries, six lie within two regional library districts, and Buncombe County helps support five city and suburban libraries. Indeed, four of the counties with county libraries also contribute to the support of town libraries. In 1957-1958 library appropriations in the 20 counties which appropriated money for this purpose aggregated $111,635, and the total income of the libraries which they helped support was $403,740.

Likewise in other states besides Georgia and North Carolina considerable progress has been made in providing library service for the county people at large.

In the Southern Appalachians far greater attention is being given today than thirty years ago to the conservation and sound use of land, water, forests, and other natural resources. Most of the conservation programs seek to enlist three-level support, federal, state, and local, with the national government being the prime mover. Agency names on courthouse doors today would appear baffling, if not disturbing, to a Rip Van Winkle aroused from a 30-year sleep, for the county seat has become an outpost of the federal government. Many are outposts of the U.S. Department of Agriculture.

The oldest program with three-level support and operating through these county outposts is the Agricultural Extension Service. County governments throughout the region are cooperating in this program. The organizational setup in all seven states is almost identical, as is also the distribution of cost. North Carolina may therefore be selected for illustration.

In 1956 there was a county agricultural agent and a home demonstration agent in every Appalachian county, and in 21 of the 22 counties one or both agents had an assistant. In fact, the 22 agricultural extension staffs consisted of 62 county agents, 42 home demonstration agents and 38 clerical workers. The cost, shared jointly by the state and the counties, was about $600,000, the counties contributing slightly over one-third of that amount.

While the county agents help farmers with all aspects of the farm enterprise, marketing as well as production, they are basically conservationists and therefore encourage practices which protect and build up the land, conserve the water, improve the forests, and restore the game. They are aided sometimes by extension foresters, hydrologists, and other specialists. Most counties make modest appropriations to aid in forest fire prevention and suppression.

Since the 1930's the work of the Extension Service has been supplemented by two other national conservation programs concerned primarily with farm lands. These are the Soil Conservation Service and the Agricultural Conservation Program. Both are almost wholly financed by the federal government, though they operate through state and county committees which have more than advisory roles.

Here and there a county is performing a function, or contributing to the support of an activity that is not the common practice. The few metropolitan counties in the Region have found it expedient to provide, or help provide, airports, auditoriums, armories, specialized institutions, correctional and educational, and other facilities and services demanded in an urbanized community; but even in the budgets of rural counties such entries are appearing as a park, a 4-H Club camp, a fair, a game warden, a community cannery, rural fire protection, an industrial commission, a Chamber of Commerce, or perhaps a subsidy to a new industry.

Financing County Functions

Though the property tax is an old tax and by far the most important local tax both in the cities and the counties, an impartial observer would concede that nearly everywhere its administration is fantastically crude and inequitable. Though the law, even the constitution, may call for assessing property at its true market value, nowhere is this done. Assessing property for tax purposes at less than true value would not be too objectionable were the same percentage applied uniformly; but fractional assessments inevitably, if not designedly, lead to a wide variation in the ratio of assessed to true value.

For example, according to studies made by the Tennessee Taxpayers' Association assessment ratios in the 37 Appalachian counties of that state ranged in 1957 from 12 to 40 percent with only ten above 20 percent.[15] There are individual properties far below these averages and many not on the books at all. The Taxpayers' Association places much of the blame on (1) the popular election of the assessor, and (2) the small amount of money spent on the assessment work. Popular election discourages vigorous and courageous performance and puts a premium on political favoritism. Low salaries attract only men of limited ability or energy. In many counties there is little actual appraising done, only a copying of the previous year's books. There is considerable sentiment in the state, particularly in the cities, for thoroughgoing revaluations, but the cost has deterred most counties. A few counties, however, have revaluations underway or projected.

What has been said about assessments in Tennessee is generally pertinent to the other states of the region. Virginia valuations have been notoriously low and uneven though there has been some improvement recently.[16] In Alabama and Georgia, the disparities which tend to flow from low valuations have been accentuated by homestead exemption, in Alabama from the state tax and in Georgia from both county and state taxes. It is obvious that if a property worth $10,000 is assessed at $3,000, and then that valuation is further pared by $2,000 if occupied by the owner, somebody else must pay higher taxes to make up the loss.

One might have expected that the constitutional limitation on property tax rates in West Virginia would have induced higher assessment ratios there, and probably it has to some extent. Even so, a special commission created to study the tax structure de-

[15] A Report upon the 1958 Annual Survey of County and Town Government, Conducted by Tennessee Taxpayers' Association, May 1, 1959.

[16] Report of Auditor of Public Accounts for year ended June 30, 1957. Also County Data Sheets prepared by Virginia Department of Conservation and Economic Development.

clared, "In West Virginia, property is valued erratically, taxed lightly, and distributed unevenly." The same commission pointed out that 37 of the 55 counties had a lower assessment in 1953 than before the tax limitation amendment of 1932.[17]

Assessment ratios are not as low in North Carolina as in some other states of the region, but they are far from uniform. A Tax Study Commission reporting to the 1959 Legislature compared the assessed value and the sales price of 4393 parcels of recently transferred real estate in 66 counties. It found the average ratio of tax value to sales price to be 36 percent, the highest county average ratio being 72 percent and the lowest 20 percent.[18]

The taxable value attached to personal property, except for a few items like automobiles, is about what the owner chooses to place on it. Even so, personal property accounts for a sizeable portion of the tax base in all states of the region except Tennessee, where almost none is required to be listed. In 1957 personal property in the state of North Carolina as a whole represented 33.4 percent of the total and in the 22 Appalachian counties of that state, 28.3 percent.

The importance of the tax on real estate and on personal property as a source of revenue not only to the counties but to other units of government as well, would seem to warrant close state supervision of its administration. Yet, except for the assessment of public utilities by a state agency, there is little oversight in the states covered by this survey. Exceptions should be noted in the case of Alabama where the State Revenue Department has powers of reassessment and equalization of assessments, and in North Carolina where the tax on intangible property is collected by the State and returned (except for a 5 percent handling charge) to the cities and counties in which the owners are domiciled.

The state governments have manifested even less interest in the collection of the tax than in its assessment. The result is a great difference among and within the states of the region in the treatment of tax delinquency. All the states appear to have adequate laws to enforce the tax liens, but the extent to which a tax levy is collected within the current year is largely a matter of local custom.

The states embraced within the Southern Appalachian Region rely less on the property tax for the support of state and local government than do the states of the nation as a whole. For example, a government study of 1953 showed that while the states as a whole derived 34 percent of their revenue from the property tax, the seven states into which the Appalachians extend derived a considerably lower percentage from this source, ranging from 28.4 percent in Kentucky to 15.7 percent in Alabama.[19]

The smaller place occupied by the property tax does not necessarily mean that the amount of the property tax is less, only that property is bearing a smaller proportionate part of the total burden. As the range and cost of public services increased, property should not have been expected to bear all the increased load, for property ownership is only one measure of taxpaying ability. But it appears that property owners, at least outside of cities, have succeeded in shifting almost all the added cost to other sources.

In West Virginia, the constitutional limitation on the overall tax rate on property, together with the classification of property, forced a revamping of the State's whole tax structure. Through the years, major reliance for replacement taxes has been upon sales taxes—both general and specific. Property taxes provided only 18 percent of all West Virginia state and local government receipts in 1953 compared to 58 percent in 1932.

Even without the tax limitation, similar developments have been taking place in the other states of the Region. The state continues to collect a property tax only in Alabama and West Virginia; and there the proceeds are returned many-fold in school grants. Six of the seven states impose both corporate and personal income taxes; all except Virginia impose sales taxes. Vast sums are returned to the local units, particularly to counties and school districts, either in the form of shared taxes or grants-in-aid.

The counties have been relieved of responsibility for the construction and maintenance of roads in North Carolina, Virginia, and West Virginia, and of most roads in Kentucky. The upkeep of the secondary roads is still a county responsibility in Tennessee, Georgia and most counties in Alabama, but with the major portion of the cost borne by the state. Of

---

[17] Governor's Commission on State and Local Finance (Charleston, 1954). Twenty-seventh Biennial Report, Tax Commissioner (West Virginia, 1957).

[18] Biennial Report of Department of Tax Research, Raleigh, North Carolina, 1958. Tables 122, 124. Assessment ratio computed from data in Report of North Carolina Committee for the Study of Public School Finance (Raleigh, 1958).

[19] U.S. Department of Commerce, Bureau of the Census, State and Local Government Special Studies, State and Local Government Revenue in 1953. G-ss No. 37, October 27, 1954, p. 18.

course, in all states there is an ever-expanding network of primary roads for which the counties have no responsibility, except in some instances to share the cost of the right-of-way.

Similarly, the counties have been almost completely relieved of the cost of public welfare. Only in North Carolina and Virginia do the counties make any contribution to the support of the federally-aided public assistance programs, and in these states the county contribution is very small. Most counties spend a little money for the relief of those indigents who do not qualify under any of the public assistance categories, though some states even assume part of the cost of this general relief.

The states also share the cost of public health services, agricultural extension work, services to veterans, libraries, courts, and law enforcement. In North Carolina the county jails have been practically emptied, all persons sentenced to 30 days or more being transferred to the state penitentiary or to state operated farms and prison camps. But the area in which there has been the greatest relief is in the support of the public schools. School taxes still represent the heaviest levy on property outside of cities, and sometimes within cities, but these levies provide only a small part of the support, and in the Appalachian counties even less proportionately than in the respective states as a whole.

It must be recognized that many counties in the Southern Appalachians are poor, and that the Region as a whole is relatively low in per capita wealth and income. On the other hand, a little analysis will reveal that many counties are not taxing themselves in any way consistent with their ability. For example, the North Carolina Committee for the Study of Public School Finance found that the local property tax levied for schools in 1956-1957 ranged from 43.4 cents per $100 of equalized valuation in one Appalachian county to 7.6 cents in another. Eighteen of the 22 counties were below the state average of 28.4 cents.[20] Taxable property is only one measure of ability to pay taxes, but it has been, and remains, the only important basis of distributing the local tax burden. Complex formulas have been developed for determining per capita income by counties. It has been computed that in 1954 personal income in North Carolina's Appalachian counties ranged from $445 to $1304 per capita, only one county (Buncombe) being above the state average of $1190. Yet one county with a per capital income of $612 is bearing 16.7 percent of the school costs; another with a

per capita income of $640 is bearing 6.9 percent. A county with a per capita income of $992 is bearing 44.8 percent of the school costs; another with a per capita income of $997 is bearing 28.4 percent.[21] So long as the assessed value of property is used as an index of taxpaying ability, there will be competitive under-assessment. Not only have the rural counties succeeded in distorting the true value of their property, but their dominance in the state legislature has enabled them to shift an increasingly larger part of the total tax load for state and local purposes to income, excise, and sales taxes, particularly consumer taxes that will be paid largely by the urban population.

While no two Appalachian counties even in the same state are exactly alike in sources of revenue or in types of expenditures, those within the same state are dependent generally on the same sources of revenue and broadly support the same activities. However, among the seven states into which the Appalachian Region extends, there are sharp differences both in revenue sources and in objects of expenditure. A consideration of the sources of county revenue by states will illustrate this diversity in county financing.

Alabama. Only five Alabama counties have been included in the Southern Appalachian Region for purposes of this survey. In 1959 the writer visited Alabama's DeKalb County to acquire some understanding of county finances in that state. It turned out that DeKalb was not a representative county in one respect, for it is one of the few counties in the State, and the only one in the Appalachians, in which the state has taken over the maintenance of the secondary roads instead of making a financial grant to the county for this purpose. The year 1958-1959 was the first under state maintenance, the cash grant the previous year being about $120,000. Excluding schools, the county budget in DeKalb County in 1958-1959 was $303,300. The proportional part of this sum which it was estimated would be derived from each of several sources was as follows: property tax, 69.7 percent; courthouse fees and charges, 11.4 percent; state liquor tax, 7.6 percent; privilege taxes, 4.8 percent; and all other sources, 6.5 percent.[22]

Georgia. Twenty of Georgia's 159 counties lie within the Southern Appalachian region. Most of them are relatively poor counties, the 20 in the ag-

[20] Report of the North Carolina Committee for the Study of Public School Finance (Raleigh, 1957), Table 6.
[21] Computed from Report on Public School Finance and county income tabulations.
[22] Compiled by author from county budget.

gregate containing only 6.2 percent of the net taxable property in the state. Georgia's liberal homestead and personal exemptions operate to give the taxpayers in these counties, with many low value properties, relatively more benefit from the exemptions than is enjoyed by taxpayers in the state as a whole. The exempted property in these counties amounts to 35.5 percent of the total assessed value, whereas the average for the state is 29.6 percent.[23] All counties in the area have public utilities, which are assessed by the state. These in 1955 added nearly 36 million dollars to the tax base of these 20 counties. In other words, they accounted for 26 percent of the taxed property. In the state as a whole, utilities represented only 12.4 percent of all taxable property. Since it is unlikely that public utilities constitute a larger part of the true wealth of the Appalachian region than of the rest of the state, one may wonder if other property is not less heavily assessed there than elsewhere.

In Georgia, the state makes large payments to the counties for roads, schools, and public welfare. The 1958 revenues of Rabun County, Georgia, will indicate the relative weight of the several sources from which a total of $216,082 was raised for the county's share of local expenses, school expenses not being included. From the property tax paid by individuals and corporations, 61 percent of the county's revenue would come; from state grants out of the gasoline tax and state funds for road, health and civil defence aid, 23 percent; from U.S. Forest Service, 5.5 percent; and from the sale of gravel, 4.3 percent; leaving only about 4 percent to come from miscellaneous sources.[24]

Kentucky. Kentucky counties rely almost exclusively on the property tax for the support of those functions for which they are still responsible. These do not include any part of the major relief programs, for these are supported entirely from federal and state funds and are state administered. Most roads are now also state maintained.

Except for school taxes, county taxes are light, for for county budgets are small. An examination of the budget estimates[25] of the 32 Appalachian counties for 1958-1959 showed that in four counties the aggregate estimated revenue from local sources (including property tax) was less than $40,000 each, while in seven counties it was more than $200,000. It showed also that the highest estimated revenue of a nonmetropolitan Kentucky county (Pike) that year was eleven times that of the county with the lowest estimated revenue (Elliott).

The aggregate budget estimates for these 32 coun-

ties showed that the property tax would provide about 80 percent of all the revenue to be derived from local sources; the state's return from truck licenses about 11 percent; courthouse business 4 percent; and reimbursement of election costs one percent; leaving 4 percent to come from miscellaneous sources. In most of the counties of the area, the levy required for support of the schools would be at least 50 percent more than that for the regular county budget.

North Carolina. In 1956-1957 the 22 North Carolina counties which lie within the Appalachian region spent about $40,000,000, but this figure is not a measure of the tax load on these counties. The major part of the money for public welfare is derived from federal and state grants-in-aid. As most of the operating cost of the public schools is borne directly by the state, it does not appear on either the revenue or expenditure side of the county budgets. All counties levy some taxes for schools, however, the proceeds being used to provide buildings and to supplement in a modest way the operating funds provided by the state.

In a survey, 1956-1957, of the revenue figures of the 22 Appalachian counties of North Carolina, it was found that in the region as a whole state and federal grants accounted for 42.8 percent of the county income, while local sources provided the remaining 57.2 percent, of which 49.1 percent was derived from the property tax and 8.1 percent from such sources as courthouse charges, TVA payments in lieu of taxes, and a poll tax on males.[26]

The other local sources include, in approximate order of importance, the state-collected tax on intangible personal property, fines and forfeitures, court costs, jail fees, earnings of the clerk of court and register of deeds, payments made by the TVA in lieu of taxes, the two-dollar poll tax on males 21 to 50, payments made in some counties by the U.S. Forest Service, and sometimes other minor items. Among the counties, the portion of revenue derived from local sources ranged from 28.9 percent in Clay County to 76.9 percent in Buncombe County. If the property tax alone is considered, the range was from 25.5 percent in Clay County to 68.1 in Buncombe. These

[23] Computed from Schedule 19, Statistical Report of the Department of Revenue of the State of Georgia for the biennium 1954-56.

[24] Computed by author from Rabun County budget.

[25] On file in office of State Local Finance Officer, Department of Revenue, Frankfort.

[26] Taken from county audits on file in offices of North Carolina Local Government Commission, Raleigh.

amounts and percentages include the tax levies for schools, which the following year accounted for 42 percent of the total.

Tennessee. Tennessee counties are receiving more than 50 percent of their revenue from state and federal sources. Eight of the smallest and most rugged counties receive from 82.2 to 89.4 percent of their county funds from these intergovernmental grants, which means that none of these counties is furnishing as much as 20 percent of its support. In contrast to this situation four of the more urbanized or richer counties receive a relatively small amount of support from outside grants. For example, Hamilton County, in which Chattanooga is situated, derives only 22 percent of its county support from outside grants, thus deriving over three-fourths of its income from local sources. Knox County, containing Knoxville, received only 35 percent of its county revenue from outside, and both Sullivan and Hamblen counties carry a little over half of their county tax load.[27]

Figures show also that the aggregate property tax in this group of 37 Tennessee counties represents about 82 percent of the locally raised revenue, courthouse services and licenses each yielding about seven percent.

Virginia. The 31 Virginia counties which lie within the Southern Appalachian region had revenues, exclusive of school revenues, in 1956-1957 in the amount of some $11,700,000. Of this total, about half was derived from local sources and half from state and federal grants. While outside aid accounts for almost exactly half of the total revenue in the Appalachian counties, in the state as a whole it accounts for only 34.5 percent of the total.

As in other states, the property tax is the principal source of local revenue, but unlike the situation in some other states, it is increasing rather than declining in importance. In these 31 counties collections from the property tax in 1956-1957 accounted for 87.9 percent of all revenue derived from local sources. This is for schools as well as other county purposes.[28]

Next to the grants for the public schools, the largest state grants are to help finance the public assistance programs. There are smaller grants for public health, agricultural extension and libraries. Moreover, in Virginia the state pays all or part of the salary of the county officers. There are no grants for roads, for all secondary as well as primary roads are maintained by the state.

West Virginia. In West Virginia the county and the school district are coterminous, but they are separate taxing units. Forty-three of the State's 55 counties and 43 of its school districts lie within the Appalachian region. As the result of a constitutional amendment adopted in 1932 which placed a ceiling on the overall rate of taxation on property, the property tax occupies a less prominent position in the tax structure of West Virginia than in other state of the region except Alabama. With a maximum combined rate fixed by the constitution, it is necessary to make an allocation among the different taxing units. This is done by statute. To complicate the problem further, West Virginia divides property for purposes of taxation into three classes with differentials in rate. Because of the ceiling on the overall tax rate and the splitting of the rate among several jurisdictions, the amount of property taxes which can be levied by West Virginia counties is decidedly limited. Moreover, there are no other significant sources of revenue. As a result, some services are now provided by the state, others have been sharply curtailed.

Municipal Government

The limitations of space preclude full analysis of municipal government in the region. The few large cities are wrestling with the same problems as other large cities everywhere—traffic control, expansion of utilities, zoning, fringe areas, parking, pay scales, and dearth of revenue. The problems of the smaller cities differ mainly in degree.

The cities and towns of the Southern Appalachians may have to shape their policies and temper their goals to the mores and understanding of an electorate heavily weighted with newcomers from outlying rural areas, whose extreme individualism and naivete make them easy prey to the demagogue. On the credit side, many cities and towns in the Tennessee Valley are the beneficiaries of the industrial upsurge stimulated by the Tennessee Valley Authority.

Unlike the counties, Appalachian cities have followed other cities in adopting improved forms of organization. As of 1958 no less than 64 of them were functioning under the council-manager plan. Many of the young and rapidly growing cities are profiting from the mistakes of older cities and are achieving orderly growth through careful planning and zoning.

[27] Report on the Finances of County Government in Tennessee, Fiscal Year 1957, Bureau of Business and Economic Research, University of Tennessee (Knoxville, 1959).
[28] Report of Auditor of Public Accounts for the Year Ended June 30, 1957 (Richmond, 1957), Exhibit A-I, also Annual Report, 1956-57, Superintendent of Public Instruction, Commonwealth of Virginia (Richmond, 1957).

Oak Ridge is unique in its origin and early history, but it nevertheless demonstrates the results of planning.

Cities in the Southern Appalachians, like cities elsewhere, are likely to be hard pressed for revenue. They must share the property tax with other units, operate often within strict constitutional or statutory rate limitations, and in most instances accept the low valuations placed on property by the counties. Usually the property tax continues to be the largest single source of revenue but no longer does it supply the major part of the revenue. The cities have been less successful than the counties in inducing the state to share with them some of its important taxes, though Tennessee and North Carolina cities seem to have fared a little better in this regard than cities in the other Appalachian states.

Consider the financing of 34 of the larger municipalities of East Tennessee, 21 of which support independent school systems. In 1957, when their aggregate receipts amounted to $43,710,952, a breakdown of their financing showed that they derived 34.7 percent from property taxes, 20.9 percent from state grants for schools, and 13.5 percent from state taxes that were shared with them. The remaining 31 percent of their income was received from several miscellaneous sources.[29]

An examination of the revenue sources of 17 western North Carolina cities and towns, 1957-1958, throws light upon urban revenues in that state. Of their total revenue of $5,821,079, 51.7 percent came from taxes on tangible and intangible property, 32.7 percent from public utility earnings, 6.2 percent from the state gasoline tax, and 3.3 percent from parking meters, leaving the remaining 6 percent to be raised from such excises as occupational license levies and franchise taxes.[30]

West Virginia cities were hard hit by the tax limitation amendment adopted in that state in 1932. The first year their revenues were reduced about 40 percent. While ensuing years have brought some relief, the cities are still severely strained in finding means to support needed services. To help alleviate their plight, the legislature has tried two devices—state aid and optional local taxes in great variety.

The revenue in 1958-1959 for the General Fund of Fort Payne, Alabama, will indicate the limited place occupied by the property tax in the municipal tax structure of that state and the variety of excise taxes which have been imposed as replacements. For its total budget of $199,042 the city expected to raise

23.5 percent from business and automobile licenses, 12.8 percent from utility replacement levy, and 12.3 percent from garbage collection charges, each of these items exceeding the modest 12 percent from property taxes.[31]

The small city of Pikeville, Kentucky, in its estimates for 1958-1959, expected to raise 31.4 percent from property taxes, 27 percent from returns on parking meters and their violations, 19.2 percent from city licenses, 13.8 percent from police court costs, and the small remainder from miscellaneous sources.[32]

Attitudes Toward Local Government[33]

The Appalachian Attitude Survey conducted in the summer of 1958 contained a number of questions directed at securing views on the integrity of local government and willingness to support various local government functions.

An opinion poll is a poor device for measuring the actual existence of integrity in local government, but it is useful for finding out how people feel about their local situations, whether their beliefs are based on fact or fiction. The questions concerning this aspect of political life were straightforward:

Do you feel that a few persons or families really control politics in this county?

Do you think that most of your county elections are honest?

Do you think that most of your county officials are honest?

Not surprisingly, the belief that cliques or family groups control local politics is widespread in the region, but more respondents (44 percent) believed this was *not* the case in their local county than believed it was true (38.5 percent). Two-thirds of the respondents said they thought their county elections were honest, and only 21 percent thought they were not. Sixty-four percent said they thought most of their county officials were honest; 20 percent doubted their honesty. Only 12 to 18 percent of the respondents, disproportionately women, refused to answer the questions on the grounds that they really didn't know.

Strangely enough, it was not in rural counties where

[29] Tennessee Taxpayers' Association, County, City and Town Government in Tennessee, Research Report No. 134 (Nashville, 1959), pp. 61-75.

[30] Compiled from reports filed with North Carolina State Board of Assessment (Raleigh).

[31] Taken from Fort Payne budget for 1958-1959.

[32] Computed from Pikeville budget, 1958-1959.

[33] This section prepared by Thomas R. Ford.

the largest proportion of respondents believed that local government was controlled by cliques or clans, but in metropolitan areas. Metropolitan residents were also slightly more dubious about the honesty of their officials than were rural residents. On the other hand, more than a fourth (25.7 percent) of the rural respondents said they did not think most of their elections were honest compared with 18.2 percent of the metropolitan group. For reasons not readily apparent, respondents in small towns and cities had considerably more confidence in the democracy and integrity of their local governments than did either metropolitan or rural residents.

The reluctance of Appalachian residents to tax themselves for needed public services has already been discussed, and the relevant conclusions drawn from studies of county budgets are supported by attitude survey findings. Survey respondents were asked three questions about eleven different services frequently provided by local governments. The services were road-building and upkeep, public welfare and assistance, keeping of public records and deeds, public health service, police protection, fire protection, sanitary sewage disposal, garbage collection, recreation programs, water supply service, and planning and zoning. The questions asked were:

Which of these public services does your community have?

Which of those which you have would you like to see improved, even though taxes would be increased?

Which of those which you do not have would you like to have provided, even though taxes would be increased?

There was no single service for which a majority of the respondents would hypothetically raise taxes to provide or improve. The importance that can be attached to this is limited because many different local situations were involved, although the same local services could be improved in most counties. However, viewed in totality the data demonstrate impressively the unwillingness of Appalachian residents to tax themselves, even in theory, for needed public services. Road-building and upkeep was the only service for which more than a third (42 percent) of the respondents would vote taxes. Between a third and a fourth said they would vote taxes to provide or improve recreation programs, fire protection, police protection, sanitary sewage disposal, public welfare and assistance, and public health service, in descending order of popularity. Less than a fifth expressed

willingness to raise taxes for any of the other listed services.

Metropolitan residents, probably because they had more and better public services, were generally least willing to have taxes raised for their improvement. Of those who claimed to lack a service, metropolitan residents indicated greater willingness than either rural or small town residents to provide them. Rural residents were least reluctant to support taxes for roads, fire protection, sanitary sewage disposal, and water supply service. Urban residents expressed the greatest willingness to support the remainder.

Because of the variations in the provisions of local services, only limited conclusions can be drawn from the data. Even so, at least two conclusions seem firmly supported. The first, already stated, is that Southern Appalachian residents are generally averse to taxing themselves to provide public services. Whether they differ from any other citizens in this respect is doubtful, but the fact remains that in the Appalachian Region the quality of public services is generally poorer and therefore the need for improvement is greater. The second conclusion is that the general reluctance to bear taxes is lessened when citizens perceive some immediate benefit to themslves. Metropolitan residents, for example, are more willing to raise taxes to provide police protection than to expand the program of the county health department, while the reverse is true of rural residents. The benefits of any tax program must be apparent to the people before they are willing to vote increased taxes, but Southern Appalachian residents appear to have a singularly nearsighted view of the benefits of those public services that must be provided directly from local tax revenues.

Problems and Prospects

In the Southern Appalachian Region there are many small, weak counties that were established to meet conditions that no longer prevail. Formerly they were wholly or largely self-sustaining; now they are highly subsidized by the rest of the state. State-wide financing of services once county-financed has not been accompanied by any appreciable reduction in the county government machinery. If counties are to be retained as administrative districts for schools, roads, welfare, health, and conservation services, they certainly do not need to be retained in such great numbers. There should be many consolidations. Naturally any effort in that direction will be opposed by sentiment, by vested interests, and especially by local politicians. No county can be expected to take the initiative in instituting its own demise; the action must come from the state. But in none of the Appalachian states is the legislature so constituted that it can be expected to act in the public interest. Every county is now assured of a seat in at least one house, and up to the present the small counties have been able to block reapportionment. Thus no movement by state legislatures to bring about county consolidation can be expected until the urban counties, whose taxpayers are being milked to support these small, rural counties, acquire their fair representation. The prospect for county consolidation is therefore not bright.

Short of complete territorial consolidation, there could be functional consolidation and there has been some. There are a few multicounty health districts, library districts, and hospital districts. This process could be carried to the point of optimum size for each type of institution and service, including district jails. Again, there will be resistance, but in this case it will not be so strong.

The most glaring fault in county government is the haphazard and inequitable manner in which property is assessed for taxation. Competitive undervaluation by the counties not only tends to conceal true taxpaying ability in order to get fatter subsidies, but it has driven assessment ratios down to the point where gross inequities within the county are easily obscured. In all the states of the region this evil exists with little concern shown by state authorities. Great improvement could be made by state administrative action, for present laws are generally adequate. In West Virginia, where there is still a small state tax on property, a program has been launched to develop property maps for all counties from aerial photographs. This has been done for individual counties in other states of the region and if done universally could serve as a basis for a sound assessment system.

There are other changes that could contribute to better county government in the Southern Appalachians. The appointment rather than the election of assessors, jailers, superintendents of schools, and tax collectors should improve the quality of these offices. The offices of coroner, constable, and justices of the peace are obsolete and should be abolished. Several of the Appalachian states have already taken this action in respect to the justice of the peace.

Sound fiscal management begins with genuine budgetary control exercised by a budget officer selected on the basis of proved competence. The

situation in most North Carolina counties approaches this ideal. Moreover, the same man often serves also as purchasing agent and supervisor of tax assessing, further integrating and up-grading financial administration. County budgets are reviewed by a state agency in Kentucky, Virginia, and West Virginia, assuring a measure of system and adequacy. Virginia requires accounts to be kept in a uniform manner and annual financial reports are made to the state comptroller. Similar requirements in the other states would permit useful comparisons within and among states. All the states of the Region already require the counties to have an annual or periodic audit either made by the state or in a manner prescribed by the state.

Though perhaps defensible in early days, the fee system of compensating county officials invites abuses and is gradually being abolished. The abolition should be speeded up.

Substantial relief has been given to the counties of North Carolina, Virginia, and West Virginia as a result of the transfer of all secondary roads to the state for maintenance. In the other states of the Region where the aid is in the form of cash grants to the counties, the maximum benefit is rarely received on account of political patronage as well as incompetence. This is not to imply that "politics" does not exist at the state level, but both engineering and administration are much superior.

In this survey, city and town government did not receive critical examination, so any evaluation must be quite general.

To cope with the problems attending physical growth, cities require planning assistance. Lack of earlier planning will long continue to exact penalties, but if future growth can be directed the errors need not be repeated. Few small cities have, or can afford, planning technicians (see Chapter XI). In Tennessee, Alabama, and Kentucky state planning agencies make this assistance available to the cities and towns on a temporary basis at nominal cost. The other states of the Region would do well to provide a similar service.

The financial difficulties of the cities are not to be easily resolved. The demand for more and better services is insistent, while the already overburdened taxpayer pleads for consideration. Obviously, the need is for balance, not just the balance achieved by compromise and political expediency but a balance based on careful analysis. The property tax is not always as high as it appears superficially to be. Often much more revenue could be obtained from it simply by correcting the inequities. In some instances service charges could be adjusted upward. Beyond that, the additional revenue needed may more justifiably come from state-collected, locally-shared taxes than from local sales and excise taxes. Fiscal balance should not be sought solely from additional revenue; the cities must also stretch their expenditure dollars by employing only competent people and the most efficient procedures.

This analysis of local government in the Southern Appalachians reveals some encouraging advances in certain aspects of the public service in the last thirty years and disappointment in others. Better roads, better schools, better health services and more liberal welfare grants exist. But these improvements are, for the most part, financed from outside the region.

County government, on which both urban and rural residents depend, has not manifested a disposition to be provident, energetic, and foresighted. Instead, in many cases, it continues to be wasteful and unimaginative, exercising ingenuity only in dodging its own responsibilities in order to ride on the shoulders of others.

Outside stimulation and aid are justified, but an equally great need in the Southern Appalachians is local leadership, in both government and business, fired by a determination to be more self-reliant.

CHAPTER ELEVEN

Local, State, and Regional Planning

AELRED J. GRAY

THIRTY YEARS AGO THREE MEETINGS were held at the University of Tennessee under the general title "Conference on Companionship of Agriculture and Industry."[1] The major concern of the conference was the declining farm population and income. Participants saw as a solution to the problem the location of small industrial plants in the country where they could draw their employees from the farm population. Income from work in the plants would supplement farm income. As the time of the conferences was a period of economic depression, farms were considered a refuge where the employees of rural industry could sustain themselves when unemployed. Industry was a means of improving agriculture, and cooperation between agriculture and industry was a means of sustaining the agrarian way of life.

Prominent in the discussions was the Jeffersonian view of cities as the breeding places of many of the nation's "social, economic, and political disturbances." The many references to the newly planned town of Kingsport are examples. In all of the discussions the importance of Kingsport as an experiment in creating the kind of sound and healthful environment needed by both city dwellers and industry was overlooked. Instead, the town was seen as a supplement to the agricultural economy, important only for the opportunities it offered to live on the farm and work in the factories of the small town. The Kingsport experiment was a success because it was small in size and did not challenge agricultural power and leadership. All that was needed to hold that power and leadership was more small Kingsports.

These views are still widely held in parts of the Southern Appalachians in spite of the extensive and basic changes which have taken place in population distribution and agricultural-industrial relationships. Industrialization in its modern form is more than additional factories to provide nonfarm jobs for an under-employed and surplus farm population; and it is more than a means of providing additional income to bolster the farm income. Industrialization involves concentration of people, materials, machines, and capital; a reliance on specialization; the mechanization of factories, of farms, of timber and wood production, of mining, of transportation, and of the related services and facilities.[2]

These varied activities and forces characteristic of industrialization are largely responsible for the recent mass growth of urban areas. In turn the urban areas make industrialization possible. Here are the houses, schools, places for recreation, and utilities needed for large concentrations of people; here are the centralized banking, credit, communications and transportation facilities; here are the centers of learning and research, as well as the productivity necessary to finance such activities. Urban areas, by providing these essential

Table 34. *Farm and Nonfarm Population, Southern Appalachian Region, 1930-1960*

Residence	Population (in thousands)			
	1960	1950	1940	1930
Nonfarm	*	4,056	3,165	2,805
Within cities	*	1,561	1,267	1,123
Outside cities	*	2,495	1,893	1,682
Farm	*	1,777	2,244	1,967
Total	5,672	5,833	5,409	4,772

Source: U. S. Census of Population, 1930-1960.
*Not available.

needs, have become the focal centers and the productive organisms of the American economy.

The process of industrialization and urbanization is world-wide, and any technological advance is likely to further the process.[3] The Southern Appalachian Region is no exception to this trend. The population of its agricultural areas has declined while its urban areas have grown in response to the needs of an industrial society. In the short span of twenty-five years since the Companionship Conferences at the University of Tennessee, urban areas have become the focuses of growth in the region rather than supplements to the agricultural economy.

In 1952 a writer who felt that the South perhaps had already become a predominantly urban region wrote that "This is no ordinary fact reflecting merely a regrouping of the Southern people into a new spatial configuration. It is a transcendent fact. Human life and human history are affected by the spaces which exist between people. The instruments by which a rural civilization functions are different from the instruments by which an urban civilization functions. The needs of life are different. The mental and emotional attitudes are different. The resources of communication are different. The opportunities for education are different. The physical requirements for health, transportation, recreation, and housing are different. . . . The problems of social control which affect in turn the requirements of law are different."[4]

Because these changes have been rapid in an area with a long agricultural tradition, the adjustments have been difficult. The future development of the Southern Appalachians may be determined by how well the Region adjusts to these changing conditions.

Population and economic trends suggest that the old urban-rural dichotomy no longer exists. What seems to be emerging is an urban-industrial economy in which both the rural and urban areas have a common stake. This trend is occurring in the Southern Appalachians just as it has been going on in the nation for the past hundred years. Developments since World War II have merely accentuated these trends.

A major difficulty in understanding what is happening to population and settlement trends is that the available data still emphasize the rural as distinct from the urban groups. Census classifications of the population into rural farm, rural nonfarm, and urban groups has become less meaningful as the economic and social influence of cities has spread into wider areas. Even the changes in definition of urban population in the 1950 census did not help materially.

Although a strong agricultural tradition remains in the Southern Appalachian Region, for at least the past thirty years the nonfarm population has consisted of considerably more than half the total population (Table 34). During this period the proportion of nonfarm population increased from 58 percent in 1930 to 70 percent in 1950, and at present may account for more than three-quarters of the total population of the Region.

Most of the nonfarm population—including that classified as "rural nonfarm"—is concentrated in and around cities. In 1950, the 69 urban counties of the Southern Appalachians—counties within the standard metropolitan areas and those with a city of over 5,000 population—contained 65 percent of the Region's total population, 74 percent of the total nonfarm population, and 63 percent of the nonfarm population resid-

The author gratefully acknowledges the important contributions to the study made by Mr. E. David Stoloff. Mr. Stoloff conducted the field survey of local and regional planning agencies in the Southern Appalachians, upon which much of this study is based, and made many helpful suggestions concerning conclusions to be drawn from the survey findings.

[1] Proceedings, First Conference on Companionship of Agriculture and Industry (Knoxville, University of Tennessee, October 21, 1932), 38 pp. mimeo.; Second Conference (April 20, 1933), 70 pp. mimeo.; Third Conference (November 9, 1933), 38 pp. mimeo.

[2] A. J. Gray, "Urbanization: A Fact; A Challenge," *Tennessee Planner*, XVI (April, 1957), 145-55.

[3] Kingsley Davis, "The Origin and Growth of Urbanism in the World," *American Journal of Sociology*, LX (March, 1955), 429-37.

[4] Joseph Ross, "Towards a New Southern Solidarity," *Proceedings*, Sixth Annual Conference, Southern Association of State Planning and Development Agencies, Memphis, Tennessee, October 1952, p. 10.

ing outside the corporate limits of cities. Outside the urban counties, many "rural nonfarm" people are found in coal-mining areas, where concentrations long recognized as urban in nature[5] have remained unincorporated and without municipal services. Nearly a

Table 35. *Changes in Southern Appalachian Farm and Nonfarm Population, 1940 to 1950, with Relative Contributions of Urban and Other Counties*

| | | Population change, 1940 to 1950 | | |
| | | Nonfarm | | |
Area	Farm	Within cities	Outside cities	Total
The region	-467,210	294,155	597,432	424,377
69 urban counties	-200,095	233,625	422,755	456,285
121 other counties	-267,115	60,530	174,677	- 31,908
	Percentage distribution of net change			
69 urban counties	43	79	71	108
121 other counties	57	21	29	- 8

Source: U. S. Census of Population, 1940 and 1950.

quarter of the total population of the Southern Appalachians resided in the six standard metropolitan areas of the Region in both 1950 and 1960. Had Fayette County, West Virginia, remained classified as metropolitan in 1960, the proportion would have exceeded one-fourth.

Moreover, the population growth in the Region during the past several decades was in the 69 urban counties. Between 1940 and 1950 these counties accounted for more than the total growth of the Region, for 79 percent of the population growth within cities, and for 71 percent of the nonfarm growth outside cities. The other 121 counties had an absolute decline in population (see Table 35). By 1960 the number of counties meeting urban criteria had been cut to 65 (Figure 47). The total population of these 65 counties increased by 61,751—about 2 percent—between 1950 and 1960, but the population of the 125 non-urban counties declined by 222,836, or nearly 10 percent.

Table 35 also shows that between 1940 and 1950 in the Region as a whole the city and other nonfarm population actually grew by 891,000—making up for the loss of 467,000 farm people and accounting for the total increase of 424,000 people. In particular, the great increase in "rural nonfarm" population within the urban counties shows that much of the population still classified by the census as rural is increasingly tied to the cities.

This pattern of population change is not much

different from that which has occurred throughout the South. Between 1940 and 1950 the population of the South grew by about 5.2 million, but the nonfarm population—the people living in cities, those in suburban areas adjacent to cities, and those in rural areas who gain their livelihood by nonfarm jobs—made up for the decline in the number of farm people and accounted for the total increase in population. In these 10 years alone the nonfarm population of the South grew by over 9 million people, most of this growth occurring in cities and suburban fringes.

The population decline in the non-urban counties of the Southern Appalachians is also typical of much of the South. In some areas, such as the coal mining sections of West Virginia and eastern Kentucky, the problem is acute, but the nature of the problem is similar to that which is occurring throughout the South.

Similar population readjustments have been going on for a long time in the already heavily industrialized parts of the nation. The State of Massachusetts, for example, was heavily industrialized by 1850. The nonfarm population by 1950 represented 98.8 percent of the total population. Yet between 1950 and 1954 the number of farms declined 22 percent—from 22,205 to 17,316. This process, which has been going on for over 100 years in Massachusetts, is similar to what is occurring today in the Southern Appalachians.

Preliminary population figures for 1960 point to trends which may have even greater significance to the future development of the Region. As pointed out earlier in this study, major growth in the Southern Appalachians between 1940 and 1950 occurred in the sixty-nine urban counties. Between 1950 and 1960 major growth was concentrated in a smaller number of areas principally in the metropolitan counties and the urbanizing Great Valley (see Figure 47). The population decline in the other counties, and particularly in the non-urban counties, is likely to continue.[6]

The trend was already evident by 1950. Figure 48 shows the cities and metropolitan areas in the Southeast. This map suggests that major urban growth is occurring in certain well defined regions.[7] One ex-

[5] U.S. Dept. of Agriculture, *Economic and Social Problems and Conditions of the Southern Appalachians*, Misc. Publ. No. 205 (1935), p. 121.
[6] Kentucky Department of Economic Development, *Eastern Kentucky, Flood Rehabilitation Study*. Interim Report, Frankfort, Kentucky, May 21, 1957, p. 30.
[7] Christopher Tunnard, "America's Super Cities," *Harper's*, CCXIX (August, 1958), 59-65.

THE SOUTHERN APPALACHIANS

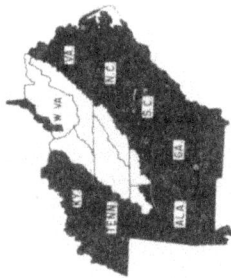

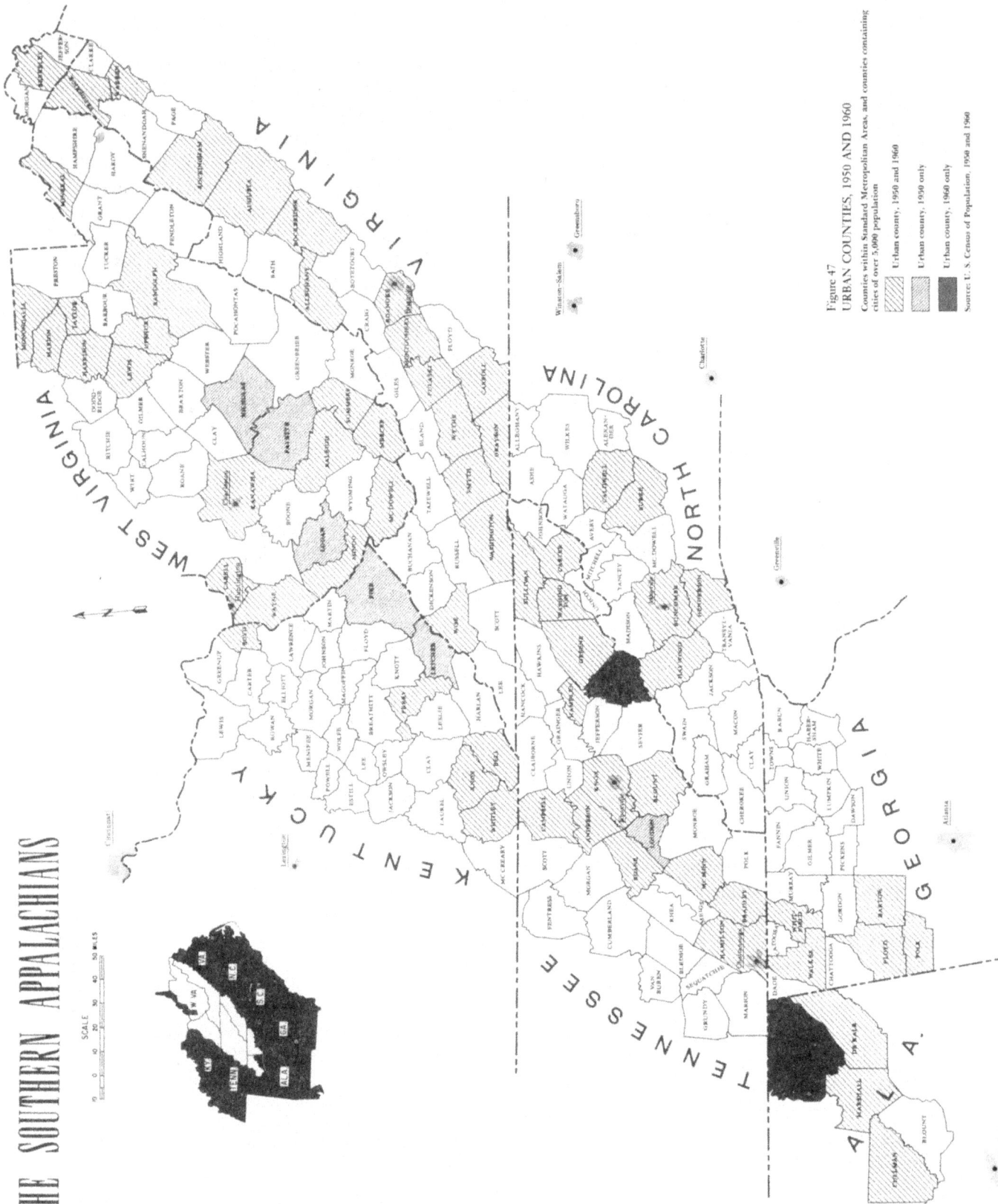

Figure 47
URBAN COUNTIES, 1950 AND 1960
Counties within Standard Metropolitan Areas, and counties containing cities of over 5,000 population

Urban county, 1950 and 1960
Urban county, 1950 only
Urban county, 1960 only

Source: U. S. Census of Population, 1950 and 1960

ample is the Piedmont and includes such cities as North Carolina's Raleigh, Durham, Greensboro, Winston-Salem, High Point, and Charlotte; South Carolina's Spartanburg and Greenville; and Georgia's great urban complex centering on Atlanta.

A similar urban region seems to be emerging in the Southern Appalachians within the Great Valley—the

Lexington, Waynesboro, Staunton, Harrisburg, Winchester, and Martinsburg (see Figure 16). Outside the Great Valley additional growth occurred in the Asheville Basin, the Charleston metropolitan area, and a few of the border counties.

The National System of Interstate and Defense Highways should accentuate the growth of these

Figure 48. *Metropolitan and Urban Places, Southern Appalachian Region and Adjacent Southeastern States, 1950*

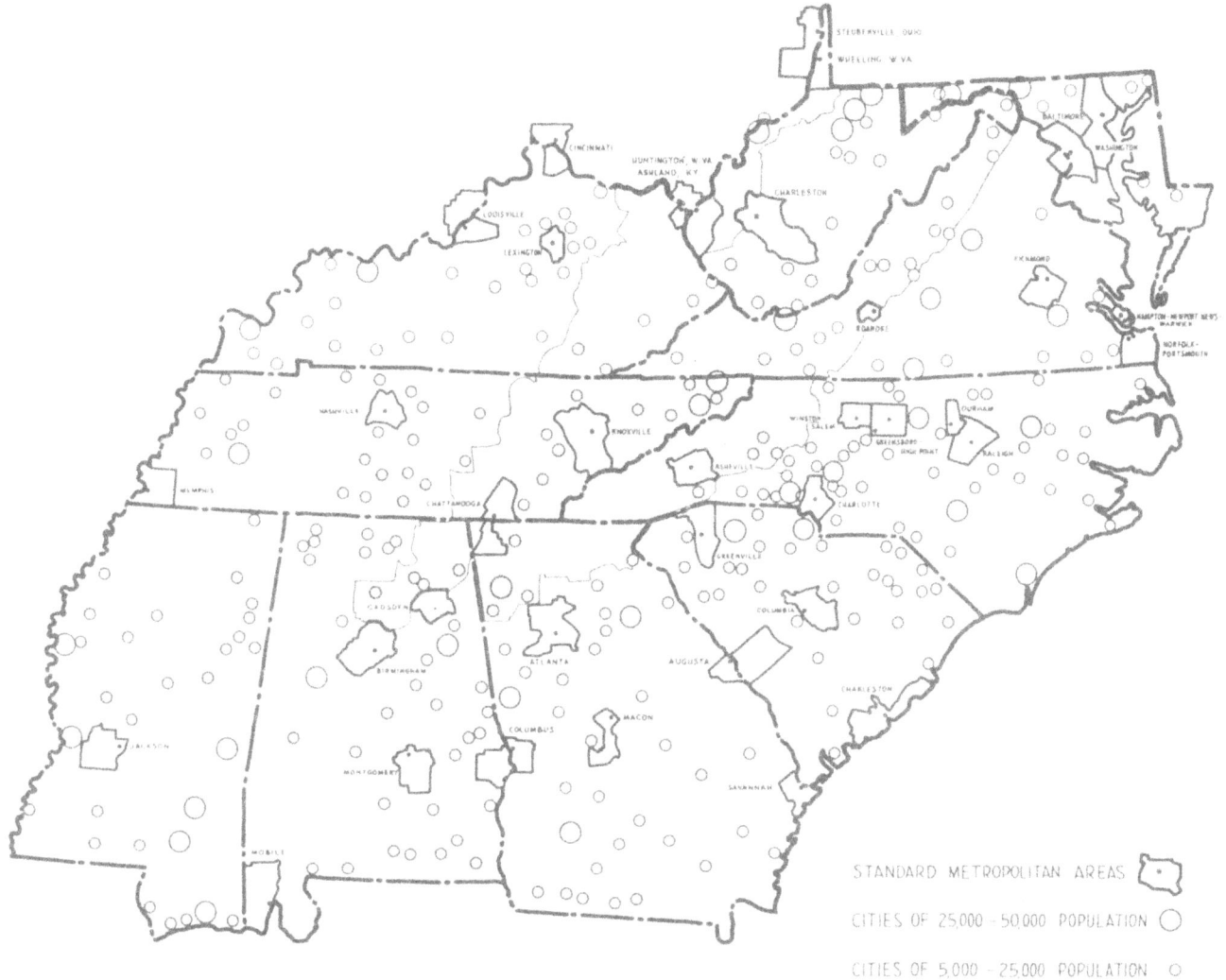

Source: U. S. Census of Population, 1950

area of parallel ridges and valleys located between the Blue Ridge-Smoky Mountains and the Cumberland Plateau. Here growth is centered in a chain of cities and urbanizing areas beginning with Birmingham and Gadsden on the south and extending northeast into the Southern Appalachians through Chattanooga, Knoxville, the Upper East Tennessee area, Roanoke, and the growing cities of the Shenandoah Valley—

urbanizing areas (see Figure 45). This national 41,000-mile system of controlled access highways will connect nearly every major city in the nation. Within the Southern Appalachians the system will tend to unify urban growth in the Great Valley by forming a connecting link between its major cities and other urbanizing areas; in contrast, the system cuts through the Cumberland Plateau and Smoky Mountains, and major benefits will be in the few cities and counties through which it passes.

Recent studies seem to show clearly that for industry "the location of markets tends to exert the dominant locational pull." On the basis of these findings one writer concluded that "If this is as significant as it seems to be, then the great national-

Southern Appalachian Region is coming at a time when the United States is going through what amounts to a revolution in its transportation system.[10] These changes in transportation are altering basic land use patterns within urban areas.

Northern cities grew up at a time when, except for walking or for the use of the horse and buggy,

Figure 49. *Growth of Metropolitan Knoxville, 1800-1960*

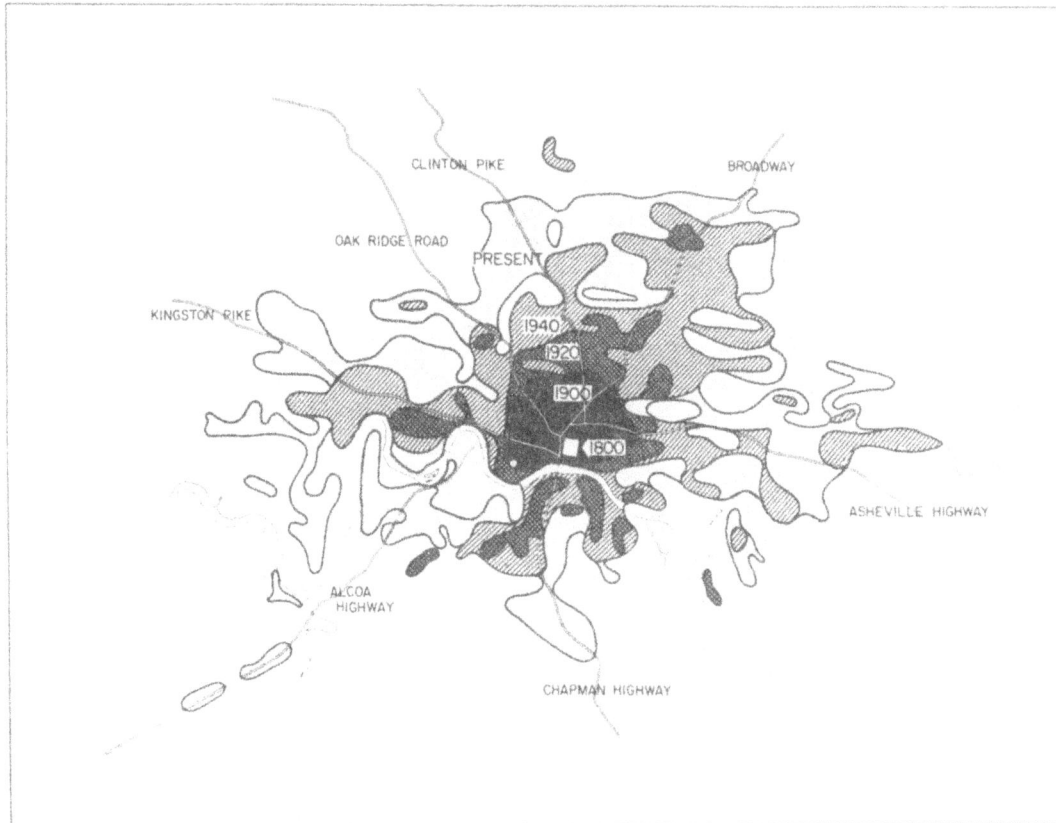

Source: Tennessee Valley Authority

market and regional-market centers might well be the receiving areas for the bulk of American industry, while the more isolated areas might well have difficulty in holding the limited industry they already have."[8]

To the extent that the Interstate Highway System will improve access to national and regional markets it will increase the development possibilities of the metropolitan areas and the Great Valley. These are the areas which have the potential for continuing as a part of the main stream of urban America, and they represent the major hope for the future economic development of the Southern Appalachian Region.[9]

Urban growth in the South as well as in the

transportation facilities held to rigid routes. The horse car, the electric trolley, and the steam locomotive lines are examples. Cities were confined to the limited areas adjacent to these lines and as a result were built as compact centers.

The increased use and flexibility of the automobile,

[8] Harvey S. Perloff, "Lagging Sectors and Regions of the American Economy," *American Economic Review*, L (May, 1960) 226.

[9] Melvin R. Levin, "What Do We Do With Depressed Areas?" *Iowa Business Digest*, XXXI (April, 1960), 1-7.

[10] John T. Howard, "Community Growth—Impact of the Federal Highway Program," *Tennessee Town and City*, IX (July, 1958), 13-18; Marvin J. Barloon, "The Second Transport Revolution," *Harper's*, CCXIV (March, 1957), 37-43.

bus, and truck have had significant effects upon the form and direction of city growth. Millions of acres of formerly inaccessible land adjacent to central cities are now available for residential subdivisions, shopping centers, and industry. As a result cities are no

49 shows how these changes have affected the growth of one metropolitan city within the Southern Appalachian Region—by twenty-year periods how urban growth expanded from the old central city of Knoxville, Tennessee. Since 1900 the population of Knox

Figure 50. *Population Distribution, Crossville, Tennessee, 1958*

Source: Crossville Planning Commission, Special Census, March, 1958

longer the compact centers which developed before the turn of the century. Population densities are relatively low even in the central cities, and by the old standards the area required for cities is out of proportion to the rate of population increase. Figure

County has tripled, but the amount of land in urban uses has increased 12 times.

The same process of outward urban expansion is going on even in the region's smaller cities and towns. Figure 50 shows the distribution of population in and around Crossville, Tennessee, a small incorporated town located on the Cumberland Plateau.[11] In 1958 this city of only 2,100 people had nearly 1,400 additional people living outside the city but within the immediate fringe area.

Actually the influence of cities and at least the beginnings of urbanization have extended miles beyond the limits of the individual cities and their urban fringe. The urbanization process may even extend throughout a county or group of counties.

The tri-county area of Upper East Tennessee is one example. In 1950 this area, made up of Carter, Sullivan, and Washington Counties plus Bristol, Virginia, had a population of 215,000—about 30,000 less than the population of the Chattanooga metropolitan area. Nearly 80 percent of the total population is nonfarm, a proportion comparable to that found in Tennessee's four standard metropolitan areas.

Within this area the major cities—Bristol, Tennessee and Virginia, Kingsport, Johnson City, and Elizabethton—are the centers from which population has expanded. People live in or adjacent to one city and work in another. Industry, such as the Sperry Plant, has moved into the more open country between the cities and draws employees from the whole area. One airport serves the area. Housing, traffic and circulation, utilities, and other problems associated with urban living are common to the individual cities as well as to the area as a whole.[12]

As the states and communities begin to feel the effects of urban growth they face demands for new services and facilities. These in turn require a more formal and elaborate structure for government and administration than is normally needed in rural areas. Because the Region has given little attention to urban problems, it is ill-equipped to meet these demands, and so a whole new set of problems has come into existence.

Basic community services having been neglected for many years, governmental organization and financing are inadequate to the new situation, and the tradition of skilled public service is lacking. While such needed urban services as sewage disposal, water supply, police protection, and recreation programs have been provided at minimum levels for years, large investments and major reorganization will be required to bring these services up to acceptable levels. Some important urban functions, such as library services, adult education programs, and health and welfare services, have been barely acknowledged.

One group of these growth problems is often identi-

fied under the headings of land use, traffic, and housing. The most obvious and serious manifestation of the problem of land use is the general deterioration of the urban environment through the mixing of residential, business, and industrial uses in the older parts of the central city. As blight spreads and land values decline, the areas can no longer support any form of sound and healthful growth. In the suburbs the uncontrolled "urban sprawl" erodes the land by preventing the growth of an orderly pattern of residential neighborhoods, shopping centers, and industrial areas essential to a livable urban environment.

Closely related to land use problems are those presented by the use of the automobile. Except for the paving and repaving of streets, and the installation of parking meters, little has been done to preserve the traffic capacity of existing streets or, more important, to provide an effective circulation system for the mounting numbers of automobiles in everyday use. This situation increases the momentum toward urban sprawl, the fragmentation of shopping services, and the general inconvenience and lack of safe and healthful living conditions for urban residents.

Housing is another of the major problems which must be attacked directly at the community level. Federal aid programs of public housing, slum clearance, and urban renewal are available to the communities of the Region. However, community recognition of slum creation as a continuing process and as symptomatic of a more basic land use problem has not yet occurred. Without aggressive housing and urban renewal programs, slum conditions are likely to grow in the Region's urban areas.

The urban concentrations in the valleys of the coal producing areas are a special case.[13] Here solutions to the serious land use, housing, and even the most basic of environmental health problems will require drastic action. With counties oriented to rural problems and without municipal government or even recognition of the urban character of the concentra-

[11] Crossville Municipal Planning Commission, A *Study of the Population of Crossville and Its Fringe Area,* September 1958, 37 pp.

[12] See the following studies for more detailed accounts of the growth and development of this area: "An Economic Survey of the Tri-Counties Region of Upper East Tennessee," Joint report of the Bristol, Johnson City, Elizabethton, Kingsport, and Sullivan County Planning Commissions; Tennessee State Planning Commission, May, 1956, 77 pp.; A. J. Gray, "Tennessee's Fifth Metropolitan Area," *Elizabethton Star,* June 5, 1955, p. 4A.

[13] Eastern Kentucky Regional Planning Commission, "Program 60, A Decade of Action for Progress in Eastern Kentucky," Hazard, Kentucky, January 1, 1960, p. 9.

tions, direct state action may be necessary if conditions are to be improved.

Local Planning Activities

The demands in urban areas for increased and frequently specialized services and facilities do not grow out of merely an enlarged version of traditional agrarian needs. They are responses to the needs of a whole new social structure. A more complicated system of administration than is needed in rural areas is required to deal with the complex urban problems, involving engineering, finance, law, and social welfare, which now confront the Region.

Planning by some organized body is an essential part of this required administrative change. The agency to which the planning function is assigned is usually a commission or a staff that helps the chief executive of the city or county (such as the mayor, manager, or commission) to bring the services and functions of that governmental unit together into a single unified program. To perform the planning function adequately, the responsible commission or staff should be equipped for fact-gathering and analysis, for plan preparation, and for giving assistance in formulating and coordinating development objectives and programs.[14]

As a part of this study a survey was made in November, 1958, of (1) every city in the Southern Appalachian Region which had a 1950 population in excess of 5,000 and (2) every community of less than 5,000 and every county which, as of the date of the survey, had or was reported to have had an official planning agency. The purpose of the survey was to determine how these cities and counties were discharging the planning function.

In November, 1958, there were 132 local governmental units in the Southern Appalachians with official planning agencies. Although a few were created in the 1930's, the first real growth in the number of official planning agencies came during and immediately following World War II. Most of these agencies were established first within municipalities and appear to be a direct response to the urban growth. The Tennessee Valley Authority joined with the state planning agencies in actively encouraging the organization of the many local planning commissions formed at this time in the Tennessee Valley portion of the Region. In the late 1940's a considerable number of municipalities extended their planning jurisdiction to include both the city and its environs.[15]

The Housing Act of 1954 also provided a major stimulus to the creation of local planning agencies. Nearly half of all existing city planning agencies have been formed since the passage of this act.

By 1954, counties also began to show interest in organizing official planning agencies. Fourteen of the 18 county planning agencies have been created since 1954. This appears to be a response of county government to the growing urban population outside the corporate boundaries of the municipalities.

All cities in the Southern Appalachians with over 10,000 population have official planning agencies. For cities under 10,000 population the proportion with official planning agencies declines with the size of the city. For example, 68 percent of the cities with 5,000-10,000 people, 43 percent with 2,500 to 5,000 people, and only 6 percent with less than 2,500 people have official planning agencies. Only 18 of the 190 counties in the Southern Appalachian Region have planning agencies.

Figure 51 shows the distribution of the 114 cities and 18 counties in the Southern Appalachians which had official planning agencies in 1958. The table with this figure shows the types of planning agencies and their distribution among the portions of states which make up the Region. Note particularly the concentration of these agencies in the rapidly urbanizing Great Valley of East Tennessee and Virginia. The Great Valley, with about 30 percent of the total area of the Southern Appalachians, contains 55 percent of the cities and 83 percent of the counties with planning agencies.

Without exception all of the planning agencies in the Region are organized as commissions. They vary in size from 5 to 15 members. The membership is drawn from many fields, but nearly all commissions have representatives from retail business and from government. Others often included are manufacturing executives, architects, engineers, and real estate men. Education, trades, and labor are rarely represented.

The activities of the city planning commissions appear to fall into four groups, according to the

---

[14] For a more detailed description of the planning function in local government, including its legislative bases, see *Local Planning Administration*, International City Managers' Association, Third Edition, 1959, pp. 1-67.

[15] Although there is considerable variation between states, the enabling legislation in most states permits municipalities to extend their planning jurisdiction, including subdivision control, to the area five miles beyond the corporate limits. For examples, see Section 13-202 of the *Tennessee Code Annotated* and Title 16, Chapter 16, Sections 791 and 797 of the 1940 *Code of Alabama*.

THE SOUTHERN APPALACHIANS

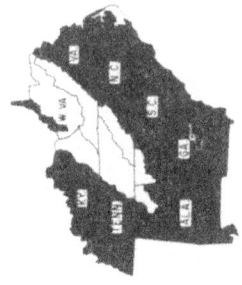

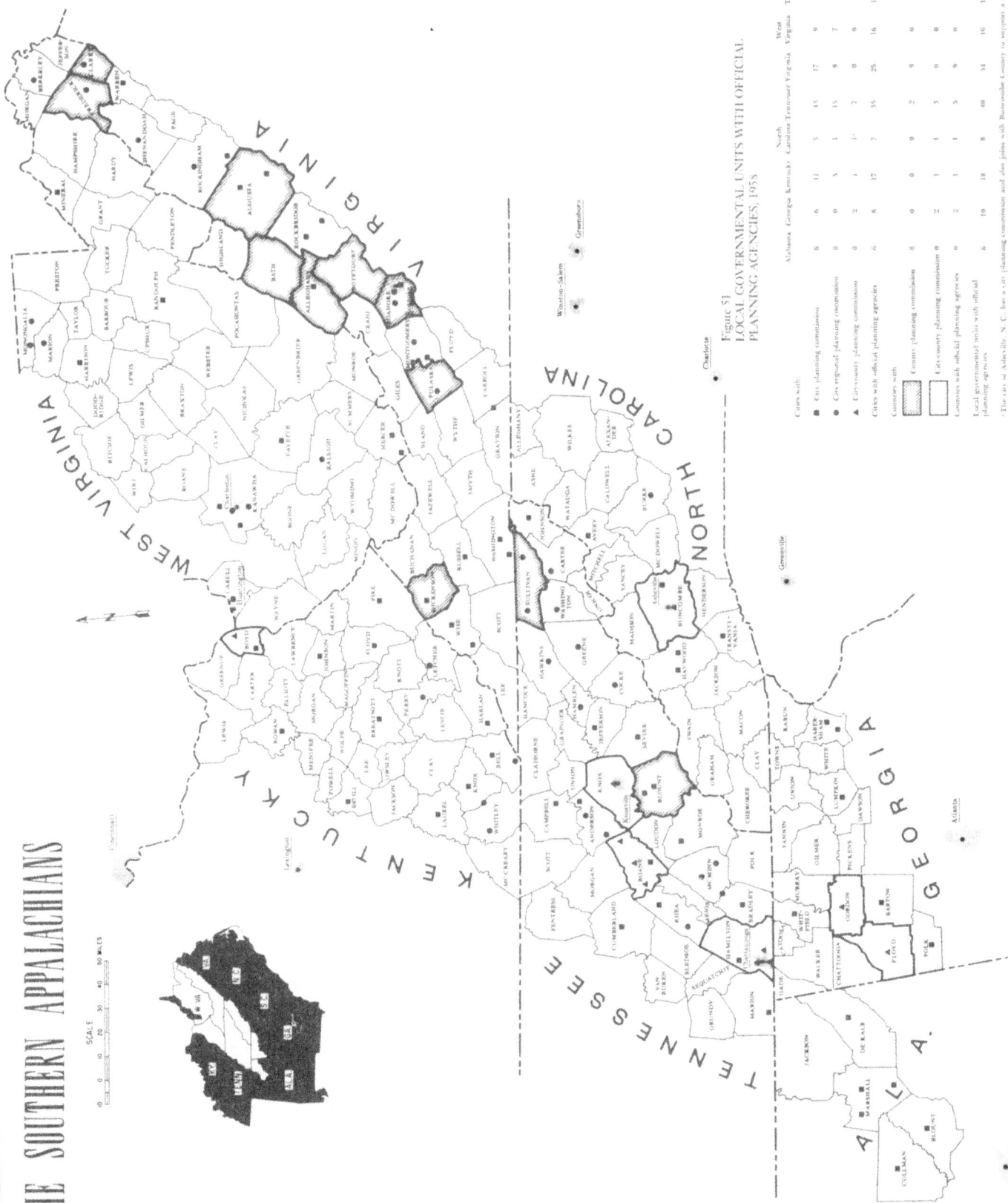

SCALE

10 0 10 20 30 40 50 MILES

WEST VIRGINIA

VIRGINIA

KENTUCKY

TENNESSEE

NORTH CAROLINA

GEORGIA

A L A.

Figure 51
LOCAL GOVERNMENTAL UNITS WITH OFFICIAL
PLANNING AGENCIES, 1958

	Alabama	Georgia	Kentucky	North Carolina	Tennessee	Virginia	West Virginia	Total
Cities with:								
City planning commission	6	6	11	5	13	17	9	67
Co-regional planning commission	0	0	3	1	15	8	7	39
City-county planning commission	0	2	2	1	7	0	0	11
Cities with official planning agencies	6	8	17	7	35	25	16	114
Counties with:								
County planning commission	0	0	0	0	2	2	0	13
City-county planning commission	0	2	1	1	3	0	0	7
Counties each official planning agencies	0	2	1	1	5	9	0	18
Local governmental units with official planning agencies	6	10	18	8	40	34	16	152

The city of Asheville, N.C. has a city planning commission and also joins with Buncombe County to support a county-county planning commission. In this tabulation these two planning agencies are considered as a single agency.

frequency with which the activity is carried on by the commissions. In the first group is zoning, a concern of 84 percent of the commissions. Only about half of these commissions have been concerned with a land-use plan as a basis for their zoning recommenda-

Table 36. *Local Official Planning Agencies, Southern Appalachian Region, November, 1958*

Size of incorporated city or major city in county (1950)	Incorporated cities			Counties with agencies
	Number in Region	Surveyed		
		Number	With agencies	
Under 1,000	259	6	6	1
1,000 to 2,499	152	23	17	3
2,500 to 4,999	66	35	29	1
5,000 to 9,999	47	47	32	4
10,000 to 24,999	17	17	17	3
25,000 to 49,999	7	7	7	2
50,000 or over	6	6	6	4

tions. In a second group are subdivision standards and streets. Fifty-five to 60 percent of the commissions are concerned with this type of activity. In a third group are recreation, housing, and annexation. Thirty to 35 percent of the commissions are concerned with these matters. In the fourth group are schools, utilities, budgets, and finance. Only 15 percent have been concerned with these problems.

The activities of county planning agencies follow the same general pattern except that most of these agencies do not have as varied or active programs as are found in the cities. In fact, two county commissions have not been concerned with any of the activities listed in the survey.

The pertinent enabling legislation of most states charges both city and county planning agencies with responsibility for preparing comprehensive and coordinated recommendations on plans and programs for the full range of development problems facing cities and counties. In actual practice, however, the planning agencies appear to have a predominant concern with zoning and with those functions which have not been the responsibility of other well established and recognized local agencies. For example, most of the communities have well-staffed school and utility boards or agencies, and only a small number of the planning agencies are concerned with these activities.

This tendency seems to indicate that in general the planning agencies have not established effective working relations with operating departments in the specialized fields or with the central administrative organizations of the city and county. It also suggests

that the administrative machinery of both cities and counties may not be adequate to bring all departmental activities together into a single coordinated program.

How to obtain technical planning assistance is a major concern for the small cities and thinly populated counties of the Southern Appalachian Region. Fifty-seven percent of the city commissions (65) have resident staffs, receive continuing planning assistance from the state, or employ consultants. The remaining 43 percent of the city commissions (49) have no technical help or at best receive only occasional consultation from state agencies or from private consultants.

In the counties 39 percent of the commissions (7) have continuous sources of technical help, and the remaining 61 percent (11) are virtually unaided.

There appears to be a direct relationship between the amount of technical assistance available to the commissions and the nature and extent of their programs. This points to the important role of the state in encouraging sound planning and development of urban areas. In Alabama and Tennessee, the two states which have had sustained programs of technical planning assistance to localities, the local planning commission programs are broader in scope and are helping the communities to work on a wider range of problems. Even in Kentucky, where the state program of technical planning assistance did not start until 1952 and did not actually get under way in eastern Kentucky until 1958, the planning commissions in general appear to be starting on broader programs than are the commissions in states where such assistance is not available.

The importance of state action in providing technical planning assistance is illustrated by what appears to have happened in Virginia. This state has had a long-time program designed primarily to assist localities in organizing planning agencies. It has not provided continuing technical planning assistance. The planning commissions, once organized but without technical help, seem to be unable to concern themselves with a broad range of planning activity.

The scope of activities of planning agencies is controlled ultimately by the financial support they receive. Approximately two-thirds of the city planning agencies and slightly less than half of the separate county planning agencies have budgets. As is to be expected, these budgets vary according to the size of the city, averaging about $1,700 for cities under 5,000 population to $29,000 for cities of over 50,000 population.

However, there is a considerable range between individual cities and between the planning agencies of individual states. For example, the range for cities of over 50,000 is from $4,700 in Virginia to $84,000 in Tennessee. It is interesting to note that where

Appalachian Region within this population range. In November, 1958, 29 of these cities had planning agencies and 19 did not. A comparison of these two groups of cities shows that cities with planning agencies are making substantially greater efforts to

Table 37. *Features of Urban Development in Southern Appalachian Cities, November, 1958*

Urban development feature	Number of cities possessing feature		
	Cities with planning agencies (114)	Cities of 5,000-10,000 population (48)	
		With agency (29)	Without agency (19)
Land use plan	52	11	0
Zoning ordinance	84	22	3
Subdivision standards	72	17	3
Subdivision improvements required by subdivider	61	17	4
Subdivision improvement costs shared by city	21	5	3
Workable program	32	9	0
Application for public housing	44	9	4
Application for urban renewal funds	12	2	0
Housing code	16	3	2
Building code	78	22	10
Plumbing code	62	17	6
Electric code	69	20	8
Official recreation agencies	73	19	12
Recreation plan	23	7	2
School plan	45	12	7
Water service plan[a]	22	9	4
Sewerage service plan[a]	21	5	2
Annexation since 1950	62	19	4
Free public library	95	22	15
City-wide park	70	20	10
Auditorium other than in school	30	5	5
Paid fire department	47	11	3
Public nursery schools	3	0	1

[a]For 5 or more years.

cities and counties have a joint planning program, the planning agency has stronger financial support than the separate city or county agencies.

The funds for operating the local planning programs come primarily from local sources, despite recent attention to the matching federal funds available for planning assistance to communities under Section 701 of the Housing Act. The average commission with a budget still receives 70 percent of its money from local sources, with 8 percent coming from state and 22 percent from federal sources.

The evidence gained by the survey suggests that in general those communities with planning agencies are doing a better job of adjusting to problems of urban growth than are the other communities. Since all cities over 10,000 population in the Region have planning agencies, it is necessary to base this appraisal on the survey data for cities of 5,000 to 10,000 population.

The 1950 census showed 48 cities in the Southern

understand and deal with their problems than are those cities without planning agencies. This is illustrated by the greater concern the cities with planning agencies have for standards of subdivision design and the streets and other improvements required for home sites; for building, plumbing, and housing codes to maintain and upgrade housing standards; for recreation programs, for annexation, and for planning essential water and sewerage services.

Although many of these activities are not the direct responsibility of the planning agencies, the agencies seem to represent a part of the positive program of certain communities to provide the machinery for meeting the problems of urban growth. Thus the high correlation between cities with planning agencies and those with positive programs for meeting urban growth problems may be more the result of the aggressive actions of the cities than the existence of the planning agency. In fact, the existence of the planning agency itself is an indication that the community is concerned with its development problems and is trying to find solutions.

The effectiveness of local planning programs is directly related to the effectiveness of local government. To improve the quality of planning which is essential to sound and orderly urban growth, there must be an improvement in the machinery of urban government itself in order that it will be able to cope with the many complex problems characteristic of an urban society. This will require a concerted effort over a long period of time to raise the standards of administrative performance and of community services and facilities. And this in turn involves improved administrative organization, methods, and procedures in order to make effective use of the technical skills required to deal with the problems of urban growth.

Basic to the improvement of planning programs is an examination of enabling legislation. Most of the present legislation provides for the creation of an independent planning commission which will undertake studies leading to the development of a master plan for the community. The theory behind most existing legislation is that the planning commissions should be independent of local government with its political tensions and issues. They would prepare recommendations for consideration of elected and other governmental officials. Liaison between the planning commission and other governmental divisions and offices would be established by cross representation, that is, with the mayor, a member of city council or both serving as ex-officio members of the planning commission.

With the informal structure of government characteristic of rural areas, such organization might be feasible; but in the growing urban areas, and particularly in the large and sprawling metropolitan areas, other arrangements are needed in order that the planning function can be more fully integrated into the governmental machinery. In some parts of the nation planning departments and staffs are set up in the office of mayor and city manager to serve as a central planning unit and to help these officials prepare development plans which can be related to the action programs of the city and to its ability to finance such programs.

Planning at any level of government is not the sole responsibility of a single agency; and if the planning agency is to be effective, its work must be related to the basic policies and programs for city development. This can be illustrated by current zoning practices. Many communities, upon recommendation of their planning commissions, have adopted zoning ordinances which reflect basic policy decisions regarding the use of land within the community. If these policies are to be effective, however, they must be supported by related community policies dealing with land use, the extension of utilities, provision for police and fire protection, for schools, recreation, and the many other services required within the urban community. Failure to supplement zoning requirements with positive policies relating to these other community services and facilities is frequently the basic reason for the breakdown of the zoning ordinance itself.

Moreover, the failure to exercise controls over new development not only affects the physical environment of the city itself but the city's financial structure. For example, some recent studies of residential areas suggest that the location and character of development in relation to available facilities may affect the capital costs of such service facilities as schools, water, sewage, and roads by as much as 100 percent and the annual maintenance and operating costs by as much as 50 percent.[16]

Regional and State Planning

The need for effective planning is not confined to the cities and urbanizing areas. The Southern Appalachian Region as a whole faces serious social and economic problems as the population of a large majority of the counties is drained away and the already weak economies grow weaker. In fact, solutions to many local problems may depend upon how effectively these regional problems are met. To illustrate, attention to traffic and circulation systems within individual communities does not correct the relative isolation of either the Region as a whole or the individual communities within the Region.

A relatively recent development within the Southern Appalachians is the organization of regional planning commissions (see Figure 52). The four regional commissions shown on this map—Western North Carolina, Upper East Tennessee, Eastern Kentucky, and Roanoke Valley—were all created since 1957. For the most part, they are a response to a growing belief that certain groups of counties have common economic and social problems and that these must be solved before adequate solutions can be found to

16 U. S. Housing and Home Finance Agency, *The Cost of Municipal Services in Residential Areas*; by William L. C. Wheaton and M. S. Schussheim. Washington, D. C., Government Printing Office, 1955.

THE SOUTHERN APPALACHIANS

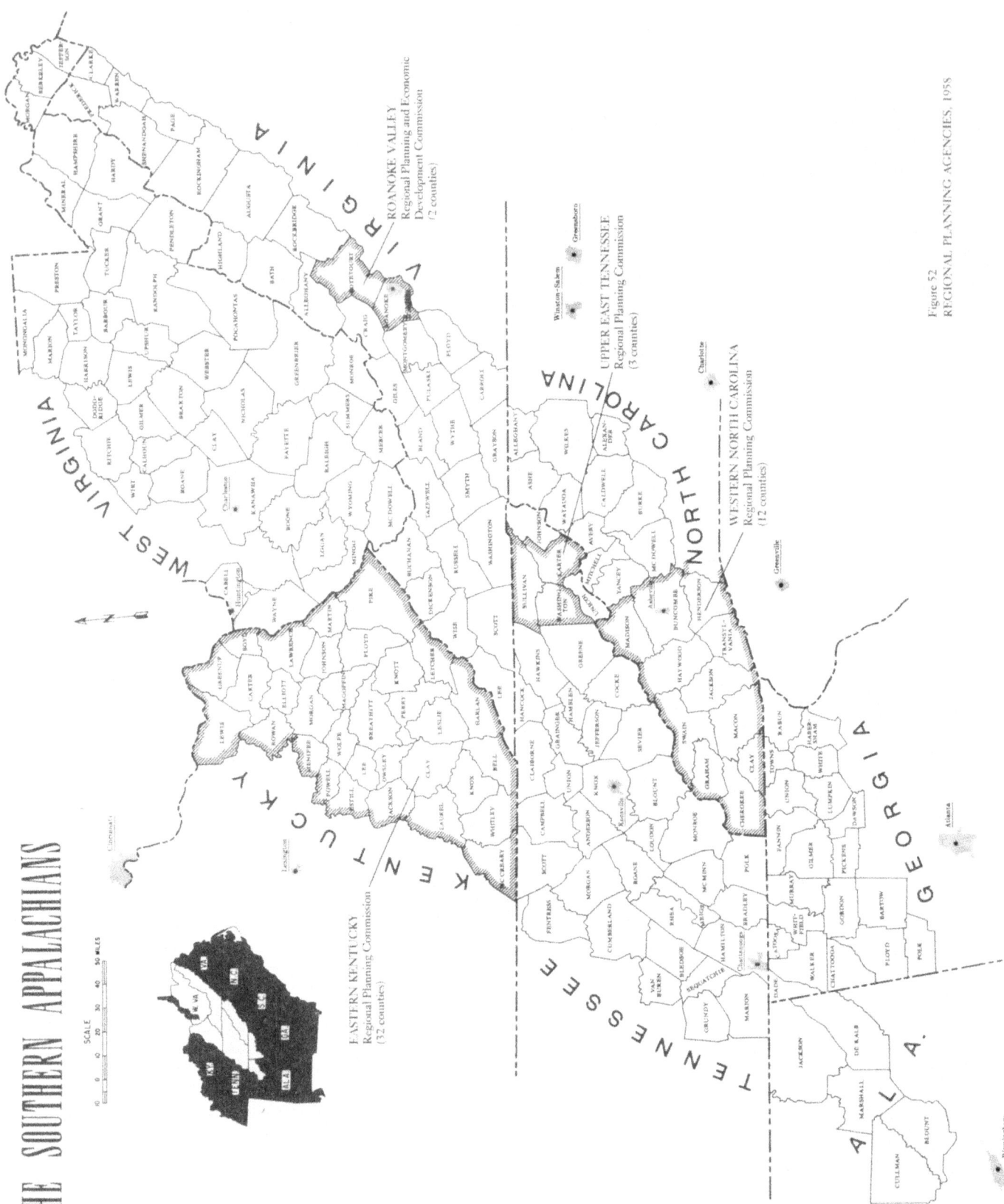

SCALE

10   0   10   20   30   40   50 MILES

EASTERN KENTUCKY
Regional Planning Commission
(32 counties)

ROANOKE VALLEY
Regional Planning and Economic
Development Commission
(2 counties)

UPPER EAST TENNESSEE
Regional Planning Commission
(3 counties)

WESTERN NORTH CAROLINA
Regional Planning Commission
(12 counties)

VIRGINIA

WEST VIRGINIA

KENTUCKY

TENNESSEE

NORTH CAROLINA

GEORGIA

ALA.

Figure 52
REGIONAL PLANNING AGENCIES, 1958

some of the basic problems of the individual cities and counties.

The Western North Carolina Regional Planning Commission has a small resident staff which serves both the commission and the Asheville-Buncombe County Planning Board. It tries to supplement the state program of local planning assistance by providing this kind of assistance to the cities and the 12 counties in the region. In addition, the commission hopes to undertake research programs which can help to solve regional resource problems such as those relating to water, transportation, recreation, and industrial development. At this writing the commission has approved a study of the economy of western North Carolina and the actions required to assure sound growth of the area.

The Upper East Tennessee Regional Planning Commission was formed from representation from the other planning commissions in a three-county area. Technical assistance is provided by the state. Originally this commission was set up with the view of helping to coordinate the activities of the other planning agencies of the Region. It has undertaken one study relating to industrial sites as a first attempt at an approach to the land-use problem in this rapidly developing urban area.

The Eastern Kentucky Regional Planning Commission was formed in an attempt to meet some of the difficult economic problems in 32 Cumberland Plateau counties. Staff for the commission is provided by the Kentucky Department of Economic Development. To date the commission has worked with state operating departments on programs to improve the region, and with specific cities and counties to develop an understanding of what is needed in the region for economic development. The commission has also promoted urban renewal and housing and is attempting to develop the tourist potential.

In 1960 the commission issued a report entitled "Program 60, A Decade of Action for Progress in Eastern Kentucky."[17] This report was "concerned with establishment of the concept and organization for total development action." It proposed certain public improvements such as roads and water control facilities as key elements in providing the region with minimum essential services. Perhaps more important, it gave special attention to institutional arrangements to meet the special problems of the region. This included proposals for the creation of (1) a Federal Regional Development Agency, to provide a "focus" for coordination of development objectives of federal agencies; (2) an Appalachian States Development Authority, to stimulate and coordinate action by the states; and (3) organization of state programs "for the coordination of state government activities around a positive developmental focus."

The Roanoke Valley Regional Planning Commission was originally set up to assist in coordinating the planning and zoning activity in Roanoke County. Jurisdiction of the commission was expanded in January, 1959, to include Botetourt County. The commission has a full-time executive director.

Other areas are considering the formation of regional planning groups. For example, the Coosa Valley Planning and Development Association is encouraging a formal planning organization for 13 counties in northwest Georgia. This organization, to be known as the Northwest Georgia Regional Planning Commission, would have a broad program covering agriculture, industrial development, water resources, recreation, local planning, and governmental affairs. As a basis for commission action it is proposed to start with an intensive program of economic research.

The need for this kind of regional planning was clearly recognized more than 30 years ago. For example, a writer in 1928 noted: "The increase in regional planning agencies, the attention paid to [regional planning] in papers . . . before many organizations . . . , the public recognition of the practical advantages of community cooperation in these days of commuting distances far beyond the boundaries of a single municipality, all point to a future development of planning in this country."[18]

But the problems of organizing effective regional planning, also recognized years ago, are still with us. It is one thing to understand that problems extend across many jurisdictions, but quite another to change the old ways of doing things. "Political boundaries are stubborn facts; popular attachments to symbols are realities—disappointing as their irrationality may be."[19]

Today many people would agree, as did the planners of 30 years ago, that there is a variety of problems whose solutions require actions extending over areas

[17] Eastern Kentucky Regional Planning Commission, "Program 60, A Decade of Action for Progress in Eastern Kentucky," Hazard, Kentucky, January 1, 1960, 60 pp.

[18] Theodora Kimball Hubbard, "Annual Survey of City and Regional Planning in the United States, 1927," *City Planning*, IV (April, 1928), 105.

[19] Marshall E. Dimock, "Political and Administrative Aspects of Regional Planning," in Planning for City, State, Region, and Nation, *Proceedings* of the Joint Conference on Planning, 1936, American Society of Planning Officials, p. 111.

larger than a single local jurisdiction. But has the experience of the past 30 years brought us to a clearer understanding of the methods and procedures for making regional planning effective?

Certainly the present prospects for county consolidation and unification of governmental services are not encouraging—even in the densely populated metropolitan areas where there have been hopes for success (see Chapter X). The regional planning agencies remain as citizen groups with only loose ties to city and county government. In this situation plans, studies, and reports are prepared in the hope that they will be useful to the local governmental units within the planning region. Sooner or later, however, most regional planning agencies have to face the reality that there can be no *official* planning independent of the governmental units which have the power to act on recommendations.

From the experience with planning commissions in the past decade it does not appear that representation by the affected local governmental units on a commission is sufficient by itself to achieve either sustained action by the individual governmental units or unity of action between the several affected governmental units. To add to the complexity of the problem, state and federal agency programs frequently play a major role in regional planning and development.

In that part—roughly half—of the Region which lies within the drainage basin of the Tennessee River, the Tennessee Valley Authority has been working since 1933 with states and localities on many kinds of development problems. Some of the experiences in the Tennessee Valley have a bearing on the problems of regional planning.

In its 1936 report to Congress entitled "Unified Development of the Tennessee River System," TVA proposed a system of multipurpose dams and reservoirs on the Tennessee River to be built for navigation, flood control, and power. The purpose of the report was "to point out those relationships that must necessarily be observed to lead to economical, full, and effective development of the region, and which, if neglected, will result in confusion, waste, inefficiency, and in some cases the permanent loss of great developmental possibilities." A plan for the unified development of the river basin, the report said, "must have in view not only the functions of the Federal Government, but also the proper relating of these functions to the functions of state and local governments, and the activities carried forward under private

initiative, to the end that the best total development may be achieved."[20]

In its application of this policy TVA recognized that in the United States every level of government —federal, state, and local—has some responsibility for regional planning. The problem TVA faced was to find a pattern of working relationships with the state and local governments so that all could work together constructively for the development of the entire valley. TVA did not approach this problem from the point of view of a single regional plan prepared by one central agency. Instead it adopted the dominant American view that planning and action are inseparable and that planning to be effective must be carried out within a framework which will produce action toward agreed-upon objectives.[21]

The planning activity in the Tennessee Valley is carried on through the cooperative relationships between scores of agencies and institutions of the area and involves a continuing effort affecting planning decisions made both by TVA and by state and local agencies. It includes research, inventories of basic resources, and the use of technical contributions of many fields of specialization, such as recreation, agriculture, forestry, and engineering, in appraisal of the potential use of resources and a comprehensive approach to development which recognizes the interdependence of resources.

Specifically the planning activity concerns itself with the broad range of problems dealing with flood damage prevention, transportation, power transmission and distribution, agriculture, forestry, recreation, environmental sanitation, fisheries and wildlife, and industrial development. It is concerned with improving the effectiveness of the planning function within the individual state departments and agencies and works toward the organization and effective operation of overall planning within the individual states.[22]

Efforts to bring together state and local agencies for a comprehensive approach to individual resource development problems such as those relating to recreation or industrial sites have been generally successful. However, the progress toward a comprehen-

---

[20] Tennessee Valley Authority, *Report of the Congress on the Unified Development of the Tennessee River System,* Knoxville, Tennessee, March, 1936, p. 38.

[21] A. J. Gray and Victor Roterus, *The Tennessee Valley, a Case Study.* Washington, D. C., Housing and Home Finance Agency, 1960.

[22] Howard K. Menhinick and Lawrence L. Durisch, "Tennessee Valley Authority: Planning in Operation," *The Town Planning Review,* XXIV (July, 1953), 116-45.

sive program which, for example, relates highways to water supply, land use, and other basic resources, has been slower. In the writer's view this is attributable to inadequate provision for overall planning within state government. Such a state planning program could result in a broad integrated attack on state problems which bring together the specialists in planning for resources, industrial and urban development, capital expenditures, transportation, education, and other important state activities. In fact, effective state planning which concerns itself with overall state development goals to which individual programs are related may well be the key to successful regional planning and development programs.

The Need for State Planning

The experiences in the Tennessee Valley are being duplicated in other areas.[23] Many states are already heavily involved in programs and activities which have a major part in shaping the development of regions within the states. Highways, parks and recreation areas, forest and wildlife reserves, watershed and drainage problems, airports, hospitals, schools, and employment services illustrate the range of the state's concern with regional development. What has been lacking is overall state planning which can help establish development goals (such as purpose of water development as it relates to land use, economic, and other needs) and coordinate the activities of individual state agencies in their application within a particular region. "The state, by reason of its legal authority and its superior financial resources," one writer has said, ". . . must do something more than play the passive role of adopting legislation after the local entities have compromised their difficulties. It must exercise a lead in reaching an acceptable solution."[24]

Another writer observing this problem makes the point that whereas the machinery for regional planning and action presents many difficulties, "the state apparatus is in existence."[25]

The Southern Appalachian states have not given adequate attention to the need for state planning. Although most of them organized state planning agencies in the 1930's, these agencies were abandoned and the responsibility for state planning placed within agencies concerned with industrial development (Figure 53). The industrial development agencies generally have interpreted their state planning responsibility as that of providing technical assistance to local planning agencies.

A review of state planning experience of the past twenty years raises serious questions concerning the ability to discharge the overall state planning function when it is a part of the program of a regular operating department. Planning of departmental activities is essential, but overall state planning is also essential. The recent study of the American Institute of Planners Committee on State Planning, in noting the nationwide trend to place planning within the economic development agencies, observed that once state planning becomes a part of an operating agency with a limited area of activity it seems inevitable that "its ability to function in an overall planning capacity would be weakened or even destroyed."

The report urged the necessity of relating individual state programs—such as highway planning—to broader development goals, and contended that "state planning must be closely associated with the office of the chief executive, for it is there that broad policies and objectives are set and the role of particular departments and agencies is appraised in relation to a total state program."[26]

In two of the Appalachian states some progress has been made in such a redirection of state planning activity. In Tennessee the state planning function has been held intact since the State Planning Commission was created in 1935. Under a recent reorganization the Commission was placed within one of the staff divisions of the office of the Governor. This is a beginning of a sound approach for state planning. In North Carolina a 1957 reorganization established a Department of Administration within the office of the Governor. This department included both the budgeting and planning functions. Unfortunately the planning function has not been activated.

More research and study is needed on ways by which regional planning programs can be made effective. In the absence of regional government,

[23] Elmer Aldrich, "Present Planning by California State Agencies: Do the Pieces Fit?" in *State-Wide Planning*; A selection of patterns from the Sixth and Seventh Annual University of California Conferences on city and regional planning, 1958-1959, Department of City and Regional Planning and University Extension, University of California, pp. 19-25.

[24] Winston W. Crouch, "The Government of a Metropolitan Region," University of Pennsylvania *Law Review*, CV (February, 1957), 488.

[25] Charles M. Haar, "Regionalism and Realism in Land-Use Planning," University of Pennsylvania *Law Review*, CV (February, 1957), 534.

[26] American Institute of Planners, Committee on State Planning, "State Planning: Its Function and Organization," *Journal of the American Institute of Planners*, XXIV (November, 1959), 208.

what basic relationships are needed to secure unified action by the several governmental units involved? What are the implications of these relationships for regional and local development problems. The findings of the survey made as part of this study seem to demonstrate that where the state has undertaken an

Figure 53. *State Planning and Development Agencies, Southern Appalachian States, 1934-1959*

STATE	AGENCY, FUNCTION, AND LEGISLATIVE CHANGES, 1934-1959				
ALABAMA	1935 Alabama State Planning Commission. Broad planning powers.	1943 Alabama State Planning Board. Act amended, changing name and composition of Board; basic functions unchanged. Initiated state-wide local planning assistance.	1955 Alabama State Planning and Industrial Development Board. New agency; retained Div. of Local Planning; expanded industrial activity; state planning curtailed.		
GEORGIA	1937 Georgia Planning Board. Broad planning powers.	1943 Georgia Agricultural and Industrial Development Board. Absorbed and supplemented functions of GPB. Broad powers, but emphasis on advertising and promotion.	1949 Georgia State Department of Commerce. Replaced A&ID Board which was abolished. Program confined to industrial promotion.	1957 State Planning Commission. New agency within Dept. of Commerce charged with research, state planning and local planning assistance; industrial promotion functions of Dept. of Commerce unchanged.	1959 Division of Planning within Dept. of Commerce. Replaced and assumed functions of Georgia State Planning Board. Other dept. functions unchanged.
KENTUCKY	1934 Kentucky Planning Board. Broad planning powers.	1936 Kentucky Planning Board abolished. Functions transferred to Governor's Cabinet.	1948 Kentucky Agricultural and Industrial Development Board. Broad powers, but emphasis on development and promotion.	1952 A&ID Board initiated local planning assistance.	1956 Dept. of Economic Development replaced A&ID Board, which was abolished. Functions include industrial development, mapping, economic research, local planning assistance, and agricultural development.
NORTH CAROLINA	1935 North Carolina Planning Board. Broad planning powers.	1947 NCPB abolished; industrial development functions taken over by Division of Commerce and Industry of Department of Conservation and Development.	1957 Division of Community Planning set up in Department of Conservation and Development; created Department of Administration in the office of Governor with Budget Division and State Planning Division.		
TENNESSEE	1935 Tennessee State Planning Commission. Broad planning powers.	1940 Initiated state-wide local planning assistance.	1953 Agricultural and Industrial Development Board given industrial development functions of State Planning Commission; State Planning Commission retained state planning, research, and local planning assistance functions.	1959 Under general reorganization Tennessee State Planning Commission placed in new Division of Finance and Taxation within office of Governor. Basic planning functions unchanged.	
VIRGINIA	1938 Virginia Planning Board. Broad planning powers.	1944 Initiated state-wide local planning assistance.	1948 Under general governmental reorganization VPB became Division of Planning and Economic Development of Department of Conservation. Basic functions unchanged.	1958 Duties of Division of Planning transferred to Division of Industrial Development. Functions unchanged.	
WEST VIRGINIA	1939 West Virginia Industrial and Publicity Commission. Program confined to industrial promotion.	1944 West Virginia Planning Board. Broad planning powers. Industrial and Publicity Commission continued.	1951 West Virginia Planning Board inactive.	1959 West Virginia Planning Bd. abolished. West Virginia Economic Development Agency created and charged with state planning, local planning assistance, and economic development. West Virginia Industrial & Publicity Commission continued for industrial promotion.	

➤ INDICATES MAJOR ORGANIZATION, FUNCTION, OR LEGISLATIVE CHANGE

the program, organization, staff composition, and financing of the regional planning agencies?

One alternative which needs further investigation is the role of the states in helping to solve some of the regional and local development problems. The findings of the survey made as part of this study seem to demonstrate that where the state has undertaken an aggressive program to help localities they have been better able to cope with these emerging problems of an urban-industrial society.

However, many of the development problems which

were formerly capable of being handled at a local level now far outstrip the resources and jurisdictions of local governmental units. State planning is an essential part of the machinery for responsible state action. It is a basic tool for preparing an overall regional program and for relating the specific state programs to each other for an integrated attack on regional development problems. By assisting communities to perform better the local governmental functions, and by relating state programs to broad regional needs, the state can be an effective force in guiding the future development of the areas within its jurisdiction.

CHAPTER TWELVE

The

Needs

of

Education

ORIN B. GRAFF

DEMOCRACY IS THE SOCIETY IN WHICH the supreme object is the development of the individual. Education in our nation is dedicated to the achievement of our national goal of individual fulfillment, and is concerned with the education of all citizens. No individual's potential should remain undeveloped. The productive contribution of each person is essential to our nation's welfare and continued growth.

In a few of our states about four-fifths of the youth complete four years of high school and one-half enroll in college. But in many states less than half complete high school and less than one-fifth enter college. The Southern Appalachians as a region does no better than the states in this poorest category.

As this chapter will show, the Region has made considerable progress in education since 1935. On the other hand, its progress has been so little when compared with that of the states or the nation as a whole as to merely dramatize its loss of pace.

In 1950, Southern Appalachian residents twenty-five years of age and older were significantly less well educated than the same age group in the nation as a whole (Figure 54). The median school years completed by persons twenty-five and older was 9.3 for the nation and 7.2 for the Region. The regional median was less than the median for any state in the union and less than that for any other economic region in the nation.[1] In a 1958 survey of heads of households in the Region (Table 38), years of schooling averaged 9.3, ranging from 7.4 years for rural respondents to 11.1 for metropolitan respondents. This indicated a noteworthy increase since 1950, but there did not appear to be any narrowing of the gap between the regional and national educational levels.

The low level of education in the Region is associated with and perhaps in part responsible for the low level of the economy. In a study conducted in 1957 for the Joint Economic Committee, it was found that 67 percent of the low-income population of the nation were characterized by a low level of education and showed a high degree of immunity to economic growth.[2]

The problem is not only one of upgrading the educational level in future generations; there is also an immediate and urgent need for adult education. This need is vividly illustrated in a compilation of the percentage of selective service registrants who failed the mental test in 1959. The percentage of registrants failing in the nation was 24.7. The percentage in the seven Southern Appalachian states ranged from 27.1 to 45. The states ranked from 38 to 47 among the 50 states.[3]

Moreover, it cannot be denied that education begets education. The Southern Appalachian attitude survey (see Chapter II) revealed that the people of

Figure 54. *Percentage of Population 25 Years of Age and Over at Specified Educational Levels, Southern Appalachian Region and the United States, 1950*

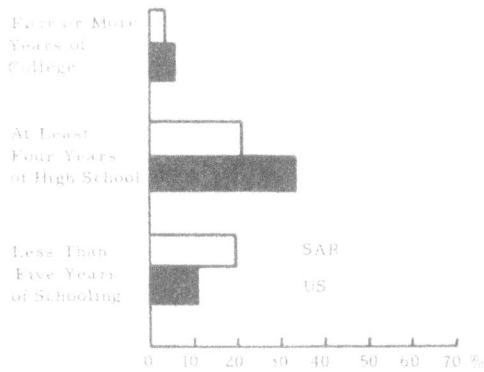

Source:
Ranking of the States (1957); U. S. Census of Population, 1950

the Region were confused about the purposes of education and the educational needs of their own communities. A large majority of them are satisfied with their educational program: they think it is a good one. This satisfaction with an obviously inferior educational program is in large part reflective of an educational level lower than the national average.

The low educational level of the community is related to the lack of holding power of the schools. Although the holding power has improved, it is still alarmingly low. A sample study[4] revealed that high school seniors in the rural systems in 1947 represented about one-fourth of those who were in the sixth grade in 1941, six years prior. Only one-half of the same 1941 sixth graders were in the ninth grade in 1944. The metropolitan systems did somewhat better; about two-thirds of the 1941 sixth grade enrolled in the ninth grade and about 40 percent were retained in the twelfth grade. Between 1953 and 1959, even though improvement was marked, these systems were still losing pupils at the rate of 10 to 20 percent between the sixth and ninth grades and from 44 to 63 percent before high school graduation.

Lack of holding power is a condition of serious proportions throughout the country—one that results in a loss to society and creates a heavy burden in view of the correlation between low income and low education. In 1961 the Kentucky State Department of

Education released figures showing steadily increasing holding power for Kentucky high schools following substantial annual increases in state aid beginning in 1956. Starting in 1956 with 55.5 percent of all ninth grade students completing public high schools, the percentage climbed to 61.4 in 1960. The comparable national average for 1960 was about 60 percent.

Closely allied with the drop-out problem is that of retardation—pupils behind in grade-level attainment. In 1930 there were thirteen counties in the Appalachian region in which 55 percent or more of the fourth grade pupils were older than they should have been for their grade.[5] It was once a common practice in some parts of the Region to keep all children in the first grade for two years. This practice has now been largely discontinued. Although still a serious problem, retardation is not as great now. As indicated in Table 39, 30.7 percent of the rural and 25.8 percent of the metropolitan fourth grade pupils were retarded in 1958. The lower rate of retardation from the eighth to the twelfth grade is explained by the tendency of retarded pupils to quit after the period of compulsory attendance.

To close the gap between Region and nation will demand expansion of school facilities, staff and program. The major effort will need to be concentrated in the areas where population is growing.

From the data on enrollment it is evident that rural elementary enrollments reached a peak in 1950-51, after which they declined slowly but steadily (Figure 55). Rural secondary enrollments increased throughout the school years 1949-50 to 1957-58; it is estimated they will peak in 1960-61 with an index of 157 compared to the 100 base in 1949-50. By 1970-71 the index is expected to decline to 127. Metropolitan counties and city school systems are expected to main-

[1] James S. Brown, *Basic Population Data for the Southern Appalachians* (Social Research Service, University of Kentucky, August, 1958), p. 45.

[2] Robert J. Lampman, *The Low Income Population and Economic Growth*. Study paper No. 12 prepared for the Joint Economic Committee, 86th Congress, 1st Session (Washington, D. C., 1959), p. 29.

[3] National Education Association, *The Case for Federal Support of Education* (Washington, D. C., 1961), p. 8, quoting U. S. Department of the Army, Office of the Surgeon General, "Preinduction and Induction Examination Results, 1959," *Health of the Army*, XV (February, 1960), 1-10, Table 2.

[4] Robert Campbell DeLozier, "Public School Enrollment Prediction for the Southern Appalachian Region." Unpublished M. S. Thesis, The University of Tennessee, August, 1959.

[5] United States Department of Agriculture, *Economic and Social Problems and Conditions of the Southern Appalachians*, Miscellaneous Publication No. 205, Washington, 1935.

tain steady and rapid increases in both elementary and secondary enrollment throughout the projection period, except for a tendency for secondary school enrollment to decline after the school year 1968-69.[6]

School Administration and Financing

The Region has about 1,100 units of local government. This fragmentation contributes to the serious

Table 38. *Years of School Completed by Heads of Households, Their Fathers, and Their Paternal Grandfathers, Southern Appalachian Region, 1958*

	Rural	Urban	Metropolitan	All areas
Respondents	7.4	10.3	11.1	9.3
Fathers	5.9	8.1	8.4	7.2
Grandfathers	5.3	7.5	5.2	5.6

Source: Southern Appalachian Attitude Survey.

organizational and administrative problems of local school systems. Legally the board of education is responsible for the development and maintenance of school policies, but many individual board members have traditionally assumed an executive role. In many counties the board member is still the guardian of schools in his district.

Under the best conditions found in the Region the influence of a well-functioning board of education is limited. The basic limitation is lack of a share in deciding local fiscal matters affecting the educational program. The school board has the right to propose a school budget and, in large measure, to control the expenditures of the budget once it is approved. But school boards in the Region generally have no power to set a tax levy within prescribed legal limits, to force a tax levy in support of an approved budget, or to call for a referendum on a budget proposal slashed by a county court or a city council.

The superintendent of schools should be a professionally trained school executive who serves as executive officer of the board of education. Since he is responsible to the board, he should be hired by the board. The board did exercise this right in 15 of 20 sample systems. All too frequently, however, superintendents of the Region are county politicians rather than professional school administrators. Often they are political opponents of members of their own boards of education and members of other governmental units.

The study of public school finance in the Region was focused on trends and potentialities in public school revenues and expenditures, and the level of

school support for the school years 1939-1940 through 1957-1958. The study confirmed the assumption that the level of public school support in the Region lagged far behind the national average.[7]

The per pupil expenditures for the Region have remained at approximately 50 percent of the national per pupil expenditures (Figure 56). Between 1939-1940 and 1949-1950 the gap was slightly narrowed; the ratio changed from 50.8 percent to 53.9 percent. However, in 1957-1958 the Region's expenditures had dropped to 49.9 percent of the per pupil expenditures for the nation (Figure 56). Over the 18-year period studied, per pupil expenditures were approximately quadrupled, going from $54.01 per pupil in 1939-1940 to $218.14 in 1957-1958. National expenditures were increasing proportionately with a 1957-1958 per pupil expenditure of $437.12. These figures include current and capital expenditures.

The average per pupil expenditure in the Region for current expenses, exclusive of capital outlay, was $48.99 in 1939-1940, $126.00 in 1949-1950, and $203.12 in 1958-1959. The corresponding national figures were $94.64, $216.45, and $341.14.

The 18 Southern Appalachian counties selected for study were divided into four categories: (1) rural school systems with *decreasing* population, (2) rural school systems with *static* population, (3) rural school systems with *increasing* population, and (4) metropolitan school systems. It was assumed that sociological factors such as mobility and fertility would influence trends in school finance. As was anticipated, the more highly industrialized metropolitan systems were doing more than the rural areas. For each $1.00 per pupil spent by the metropolitan systems in 1939-1940, the rural systems with *decreasing* population spent $ .80 per pupil; by 1957-1958, this had increased to $ .95. For these same years the rural systems with *static* population spent $ .60 and $ .73 for each dollar spent by the metropolitan systems, and the rural systems with *increasing* population spent $ .72 and $ .91.

Nationally, the sources of public school revenue have undergone a rather pronounced shift within the past generation. Thirty years ago, about 80 percent of the revenue of public elementary schools came from local governments, about 20 percent from state governments, and less than one percent from the

---

[6] DeLozier, "Public School Enrollment Prediction."

[7] Archie Reece Dykes, "A Study of Public School Finance in the Southern Appalachian Region." Unpublished Ed. D. Thesis, The University of Tennessee, December, 1959.

federal government. Today it is estimated that nearly 4 percent comes from the federal government, about 40 percent from state governments, and only about 56 percent from local governments. There has been a notable increase for the Region's schools in state

Table 39. *Extent of Retardation in Selected School Systems in the Southern Appalachian Region, 1958-1959*

| Location | Grade | Percentage retarded | | | |
		1 year	2 years	3 or 4 years	Total
	4	20.6	6.6	3.5	30.7
Rural	8	24.6	9.9	3.2	37.7
	12	15.9	2.6	1.7	20.2
	4	19.6	5.0	1.2	25.8
Metropolitan	8	19.8	7.5	2.1	29.4
	12	17.4	3.7	2.0	23.1

revenues; the percentage of revenue coming from state sources was 38.6 in 1939, 54.8 in 1949, and 54.7 in 1957. Comparable national figures for these three periods were 30.3 in 1939, 39.8 in 1949, and 39.6 in 1957 (Figure 57). There was little difference in the amount of federal revenue received nationally and that received in the Region. Overall, federal revenues have constituted a very minor portion of school expenditures.

Local revenue in the Region decreased from 60.9 percent of the total in 1939 to 41.9 in 1949 and 41.5 in 1957. Nationally the decline was not as abrupt, going from 67.9 in 1939 to 57.3 in 1949 and 56.4 in 1957. In 1957 the proportion of the educational budget in the Region supplied by local funds was 15 percent less than the national average. It should be borne in mind that total expenditures per child in average daily attendance were approximately half the corresponding national expenditures.

From Table 40 it is apparent that the metropolitan counties came closer to the national average in local self-reliance; however, even here the disparity in 1957 was 9.6 percent.

It may be significant that in 1957 in the rural counties with *static* population, where the per pupil expenditures are smallest, local self-reliance was also the lowest, being more than 30 percent under the average for all classifications.

Since the period studied was one of decreasing local effort in the Southern Appalachians, the question naturally arises "Is the fault a lack of economic ability or lack of initiative and concern for education?" The conclusion reached was that both factors played major roles.

To determine the economic ability of the community to support an adequate educational program two methods were used. The percent that the school revenue was of effective buying income was calculated, and the ratio of revenue per pupil in average daily attendance to the per capita income was also calculated.

Both methods revealed that although dollar expenditures increased more than four-fold during the period 1940 through 1958, overall effort declined. Only the metropolitan counties showed an increased effort. During the eight-year period, 1949 to 1957, rural counties with *increasing* populations showed an increased effort, but did not reach the level of effort exhibited in 1939. It was notable, however, that the gap between the school systems making the least effort and those making the greatest effort decreased during the period.

The total educational effort was broken down to local effort and state effort. This was important for revealing whether state and local efforts tended to complement each other or whether one counteracted the other with resultant loss in total effort. It was observed that local effort declined in each of the four classifications, while state effort declined in the rural counties with *decreasing* population and those with *static* population, but increased in the rural counties with *increasing* population and in the metropolitan counties. Although obvious forward strides were made by states toward equalization as evidenced by a pronounced increase in the proportion of school revenue from state sources, there were still definite disparities among systems in 1957.

The alarming conclusion was that those counties least able to support education were making greater effort than those counties which were most able.

There are many factors which contribute to the lack of adequate financial support for education. That the great majority of the Appalachian residents believe their schools are doing a good job is not surprising, since attitudes reflect experience. Obviously, there had been some improvement of the schools over what the survey respondents had experienced. Inferior educational programs are unlikely to improve with any degree of rapidity until better ways are known and demanded by a community. With the economic level and educational level in the Appalachians proportionately lower than the national average, improvement is next to impossible without such external help as accelerated industrialization and federal aid to education. The attitude survey revealed that, contrary to popular opinion, the residents of the Region would welcome federal assistance for their educational program.

Perhaps the primary factor which inhibits local financial support is the dependence on revenue from

schools from 1918 at which time there were 196,037 such schools.[8]

Consolidation in the Southern Appalachians has likewise progressed rapidly. By 1958 only 27 percent of the Region's elementary schools were one room

Figure 55. *Enrollment Trends and Projections for Southern Appalachian Elementary and High Schools, Metropolitan and Rural Systems, 1948-1949 to 1970-1971*

Enrollment Index

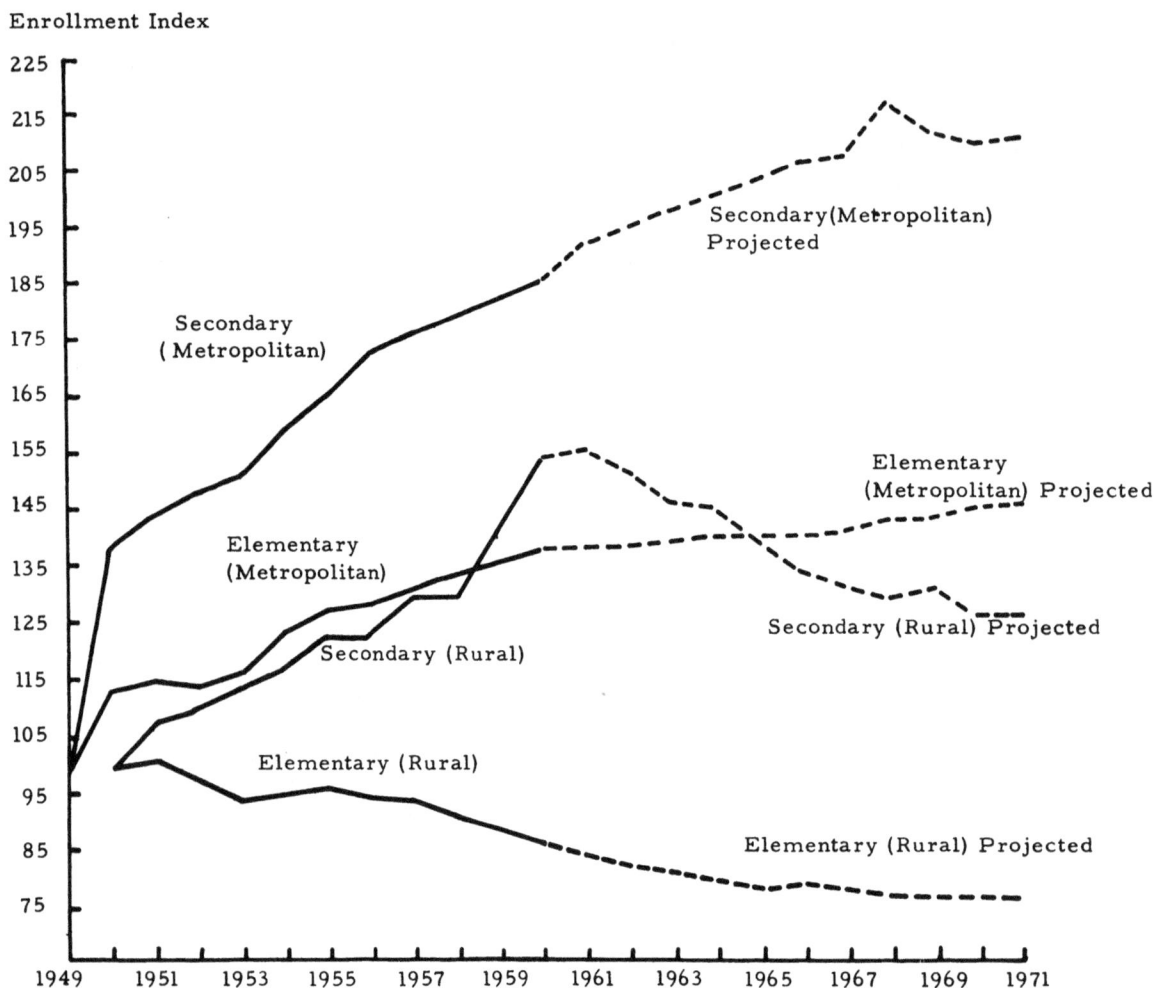

Note: An enrollment index of 100 is used for the metropolitan systems for 1949 and the rural systems for 1950.

property tax. In the rural areas, taxable farms and residential property generally constitute the only source of local revenue.

School Facilities and Transportation

The National Education Association reported that in 1958 there were 23,695 one-teacher public elementary schools still operating in the country. This meant that approximately 25 percent of all public elementary schools were one-teacher schools. Even so, there was an 88 percent decrease in one-teacher

structures. In the twenty-year period 1938 to 1958, the number of elementary schools decreased 39 percent. The abandonment of buildings took place twice as fast during the last decade as during the preceding decade. Figure 58 shows that in 1958, 53 percent of the elementary school buildings had six or more rooms.

During the period studied, there was an increase in

[8] National Education Association Research Division, *One Teacher Schools Today*, Research Monograph 1960-M1, June, 1960, p. 9.

Figure 59. *Per Pupil Expenditures for Capital Outlay in the Public Schools of the United States and of a Sample of Southern Appalachian Counties, 1939-1940, 1949-1950, and 1957-1958*

the number of junior high schools and in the size of the senior high schools. Consolidation in the high schools was not as rapid as in the elementary schools. The size of regional high schools and the availability of enriched program offerings were closely related. The larger schools of all types offered much more in the way of vocational training, shop courses, home

Figure 56. *Per Pupil Expenditures for Public Education, Southern Appalachian Region and United States, 1939-1940, 1949-1950, and 1957-1958*

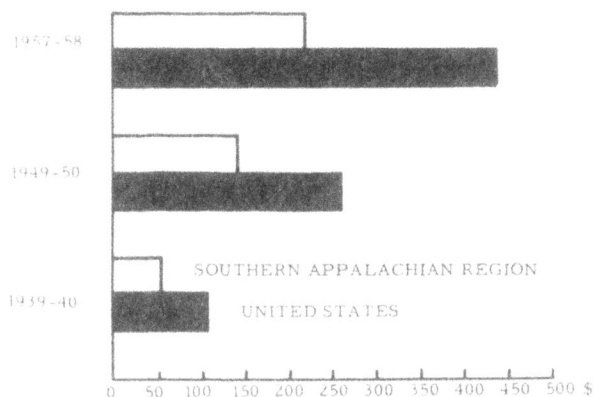

Source: U. S. Bureau of Census, Historical Statistics of the United States; National Education Association, Research Division, Estimates of School Statistics, 1960-61

economics, band and other music activities, hot lunch programs, and indoor physical education facilities. In 1958, at least some of these courses and activities were available to more than twice as many regional pupils as in 1938. It was rare, however, to find a high school in the Region sufficiently comprehensive to meet Dr. Conant's criterion of accommodating the pupils' entire spectrum of abilities.

Overcrowding in the Region became a serious concern by 1948, and the need for more school buildings still exists. Even counties with stable and decreasing population need new buildings because of the increased holding power of the schools, improved enforcement of compulsory attendance laws, and demands for improvement and modernization.

With consolidation came a new problem, that of transportation. In the twenty Southern Appalachian counties sampled, buses transported about 80,000 pupils an average roundtrip distance of thirty-two miles per day. Pupil transportation was a major operation, with costs frequently averaging $30 annually per student transported. However, this cost would not approach the cost of trying to provide quality educational programs in the isolated rural schools, even if such a feat were possible.

It is of interest to note that only a small percentage of participants in the attitude survey thought the school too far away from home. Consolidation seems to be becoming acceptable to Southern Appalachian parents.

In the 20 sample systems, there was a reported need of some $49,000,000 for construction and renovation

Figure 57. *Percentage of Public School Revenues from Federal, State, and Local Sources, Southern Appalachian Region and the United States, 1939-1940, 1949-1950, and 1957-1958*

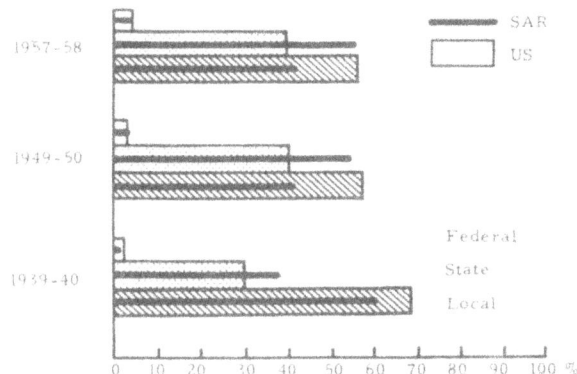

Source: National Education Association, Research Division, Status and Trends: Vital Statistics, Education, and Public Finance (1959) and Estimates of School Statistics, 1960-61

of school buildings. Actual plans underway in 1958 for renovation and new construction totaled $38,000,000.

Although spot year-by-year checks are inadequate for a clear picture of capital expenditure trends, it is accurate enough to portray how far the Region is behind the national outlay for capital expenditures. Figure 59 shows that for the three years studied the difference each succeeding year was increasingly greater until in 1957 the per pupil expenditure nationally for capital outlay was more than six times that of the Southern Appalachians.

The Public School Teaching Staff[9]

The provision of an adequate supply of qualified teaching personnel is a problem of serious import confronting American education in the coming decade. "To meet both growth and replacement needs, we must recruit at least 200,000 new teachers every year for the next ten years."[10] Colleges are producing only 129,000 teachers each year of whom only 95,000

[9] William L. Evernden, "The Professional Status of Teachers in the Southern Appalachian Region." Unpublished Ed. D. Thesis, The University of Tennessee, December, 1959.

[10] The President's Commission on National Goals, *Goals for Americans* (New York, 1960), p. 82.

can be expected to actually take jobs in the teaching profession.[11]

The Southern Appalachian school systems are by no means exempt from these staffing problems. Fifteen of nineteen systems intensively studied had

Table 40. *Percentage Distribution of Public School Revenues by Source in a Sample of Southern Appalachian County School Systems*

Source	Classification of county	1939-40	1949-50	1957-58
Federal	Rural decreasing population	0.6	6.3	2.2
	Rural static population	1.5	4.4	3.8
	Rural increasing population	0.4	2.2	3.8
	Metropolitan	0.4	3.0	3.8
State	Rural decreasing population	67.5	75.2	80.3
	Rural static population	74.3	82.5	85.0
	Rural increasing population	48.8	66.4	63.2
	Metropolitan	31.1	48.7	49.4
Local	Rural decreasing population	31.9	18.5	17.5
	Rural static population	24.2	13.1	11.2
	Rural increasing population	50.8	31.4	33.0
	Metropolitan	68.5	48.3	46.8

difficulty staffing their schools with certified teachers. Fourteen of these fifteen systems had not had a fully certificated teaching staff in any of the previous 10 years. In particularly short supply were teachers qualified in mathematics, the natural sciences, music and band, foreign languages, and primary grade specialization.

Contrary to rather widespread beliefs, today's American school teacher is not typically a young unmarried woman. The typical public school teacher is mature and well-educated, about 43 years of age, has gone to college 4.7 years and has taught for 13 years.[12] Twenty-nine percent of all public school teachers are men.[13] The Southern Appalachian teacher is not very different from the national average. In the study sample, 24 percent were men, 5 percent less than the national average; the average age was 43.3 years, slightly older than the national average; and the average teaching experience was 18.2 years, more than 5 years over the national average. With 3.8 years of college preparation, the Southern Appalachian teacher was almost a year behind the national average.

A teacher shortage invariably imposes a compromise on quality since school systems are forced to employ teachers with inadequate preparation. Of course, certification is no assurance of quality. Many school systems have been obliged through necessity to em-

ploy degree-holding applicants without consideration of scholastic achievement or the quality of the preparatory institution.

Even so, many noncertified teachers have been required. In 1960, there were 93,917 emergency teachers in the nation, some 19,000 more than there were in 1950.[14] In the 12 sample school systems in the Region in 1958, 631 of 3,337 teachers, or approximately 1 in 5, did not have 4 years of college preparation. No comparable national figures are available. The proportion of emergency teachers in the nation that year was 1 in 13;[15] however, this figure includes some who had degrees but were otherwise noncertified, and some who were certified on less than a bachelor's degree. Only 17.5 percent of the Southern Appalachian teachers had graduate training. In 1960, the national average was 25.1 percent.[16]

Despite these current deficiencies, the educational level of the teachers in the Southern Appalachians has shown a significant upward trend. From 1949 to 1958, the percentage increase of staff members with college degrees ranged from 11.2 in Kanawha County, West Virginia, to 42.4 in Pickens County, Georgia. Data from a sample of teachers in the Region indicated that 27.5 percent had earned an average of 8.8 quarter hours of college credit during 1957. This additional college work apparently did not indicate, as a primary concern, efforts to obtain advanced degrees; the mean time since receipt of the last degree was almost 11 years. In addition to formal college work, teachers spent about five hours per month in in-service education activities. Professional reading consumed about 11 hours per month and attendance at professional meetings about 5 hours per month. Membership in teachers' professional organizations was relatively high, especially in the state organizations, and many members were active participants.

Teachers in the Region traveled widely and frequently. Of the 258 teacher-questionnaire respondents, over 80 percent made an average of about 14 trips to places more than 100 miles from home during

[11] National Education Association, *The Case for Federal Support of Education*, p. 10.

[12] "The Status of the American Public-School Teacher," *NEA Research Bulletin*, XXV (February, 1957), 43, 44, 46.

[13] *NEA Research Bulletin*, XXXIX (February, 1961), 28.

[14] National Education Association, Research Division, *Estimates of School Statistics, 1960-61*. Research Report 1960-R15, December, 1960, p. 12.

[15] National Education Association, Research Division, *Estimates of School Statistics, 1958-59*. Research Report, 1958-R6, December, 1958, p. 8.

[16] *NEA Research Bulletin*, XXXIX (February, 1961), 28.

the preceding two years, 60 percent had been in more than 12 states each in the preceding five years, and almost half had traveled outside the confines of the 48 states during their lifetimes.

Perhaps a better indication of professionalization is the pride which members take in being identified with

Table 41. *Teaching Salaries and Family Incomes of 240 Teachers, Southern Appalachian Region, 1958-1959*

Sex of teacher	Mean annual teaching salary	Mean annual family income
Male	$3,967	$5,977
Female	3,610	7,453
Both sexes	3,730	6,888

the profession and recommending its merits to others. Southern Appalachian teachers were asked "Would you advise any of your children to become teachers?" Fewer than half of the respondents (47.7 percent) definitely would recommend teaching as a career, and 22.5 percent definitely would not. Metropolitan teachers were more ready to recommend teaching as a career (55.0 percent) than were rural teachers (45.5 percent). It is significant that the male teachers were more reluctant to recommend teaching than were the females; 28.7 percent of the men and 19.3 percent of the women teachers gave definite negative responses.

The most frequent reasons given for counselling children to become teachers were the personal satisfactions inherent in the life of a teacher and the opportunities to render valuable and needed service. The reasons most frequently given for counselling children against becoming teachers were financial insecurity, the lack of social status, the rigorous nature of the work and its responsibilities, and the low level of public esteem in which teachers were held.

As Figure 60 vividly illustrates, teaching salaries are far below those of other professions. And teachers in the Southern Appalachians are paid considerably less than the national average for teachers. The Southern Appalachian teacher averages $3,730 per year compared to the national average of $4,935 and the southeast average of $3,877.

The salaries of teachers in the Region had shown a marked increase from 1929 to 1958. The dollar increase ranged as high as 458 percent. The purchasing value increase varied from 170 to 278 percent. However, the bases from which these increases were calculated were pitifully low. For example, while the average salary for teachers nationally increased 199 percent in purchasing value between 1930 and 1959, salaries in the State of Alabama increased 278 percent;

but the 1958 average salary in Alabama was still only 73 percent of the national average. And the national average, as has been noted, was far below that of other professions.

Questions regarding family income were incorporated in the study questionnaire. Answers were received from 240 regional teachers, approximately one-third of whom were men. The average family income was almost double the teaching income (Table 41). And the income is almost $1,500 more for families with women teachers than for those with men teachers. Obviously, the husband of a teaching wife is making more money than she. When the husband is the teacher, family income is dangerously low, and if he were the only wage earning member of the family, family support would be marginal indeed.

A steady increase in salaries proportionate to the increase in the national economy is not sufficient to attract qualified teachers; some large increases are essential.

The teachers in the Region are required by state laws to spend from 25 to 35 hours per week in actual classroom and playground teaching. In addition to the regular teaching load, teachers reported another 15 hours per week preparing lessons, grading papers, and other extra school related activities. Teaching is not by any standards a part-time job.

The Educational Program

The states in the Region, through various agencies such as the State Board of Education, the State Department of Education, and the Legislature, establish requirements for high school graduation. With the exception of one state, responsibility for textbook selection rests at the state level, ranging from outright selection to preparing lists of approved texts for local systems to select from. Also, most states exercise some degree of qualitative supervision with respect to the curriculum.

It was the opinion of a vast majority of the superintendents (85 percent) in the sample counties studied that colleges and universities in the region exercised little if any influence on the high school curriculum.[17] A rather heavy influence, however, seems to be the Conant Report, *The American High School Today*. At least one copy was found in 90 percent of the offices visited, and 65 percent indicated that the

[17] Roy L. Cox, "The Curriculum of the Senior High School: A Survey of Offerings, Changes and Current Trends in the Southern Appalachian Region." Unpublished Ed. D. Thesis, The University of Tennessee, March, 1961.

report had been used in some way in their programs.

The use of lay members of the community on committees for selecting textbooks or for determining any other aspect of the school program is rare in the

Figure 58. *Percentage Distribution of Elementary Schools by Number of Rooms, Southern Appalachian Region, 1938 and 1958*

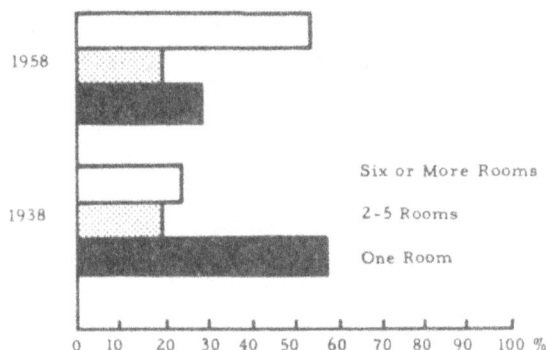

Some few local systems imposed additional requirements, usually science, mathematics and world history.

Twenty-five percent of the superintendents were of the opinion that mathematics should be added to the

Table 42. *Changes in High School Curricula of 20 Southern Appalachian Counties, 1945-1958*

Change	Number of counties reporting
Foreign language program expanded or improved	6
Science and mathematics expanded or made required	4
Vocational agriculture dropped	3
Vocational agriculture added	1
Vocational home economics added or expanded	2
Business programs added or improved	2
Statistics added	2
Industrial arts added	2
Journalism added	1
Guidance program added or improved	5
Three types of diploma introduced	5
Schools for handicapped separately established	2
No changes	3

Region. Overall local needs seemingly have had little influence on the school program.

Table 42 shows curriculum changes in the sample systems since World War II. It is interesting to note that the first four items, those changes most generally made, are related to recommendations of the Conant Report.

A cursory glance at the table indicates a minimal responsiveness to a changing society. No single change was made by more than 30 percent of the sample systems since 1945, and 15 percent had made no changes.

Table 43 represents curriculum offerings which were found in 50 percent or more of the systems reporting. It should be noted that the combination of courses reported does not necessarily represent the typical curriculum in a high school. Only two courses, English and social studies, were offered in all of the systems. About 67 percent of the courses were offered by at least 75 percent of the systems.

The addition of some courses was influenced by the availability of money for their inclusion. For example, the Smith-Hughes Act provided support for vocational agriculture even where opportunities for farming were almost nonexistent. In spite of socioeconomic differences between various sections of the Region, little variation was observable in either basic offerings or graduation requirements.

State requirements for graduation ranged from five to nine courses, usually including English, American history, health education, and physical education.

required list for high school graduation. Fifteen percent were in favor of adding foreign languages. Speech and science were mentioned as desirable additions to current requirements. Health and physical education were listed most frequently as subjects which should be eliminated from the required list.

The attitude survey indicated that more than 90 percent of the citizens in the Region favored compulsory school attendance to the age of sixteen, and only an insignificant minority would not want their children to take advantage of an opportunity to go to college. Opinions about what should comprise the public school curriculum were neither unanimous nor consistent. Ninety-two percent thought that more than the three R's should be taught, but a ranking of 10 subjects by importance displayed inconsistent philosophic orientation. Ranking of the 10 subjects was intended to detect public leanings toward either vocational or liberal education functions of the schools. Science was given top ranking for importance, with foreign languages and music at the "unimportant" end of the continuum. Following science in order of importance were cooking and sewing, driver training, history, typing, agriculture, civics, and automobile mechanics. There appeared to be little consistency in the adjudged importance of either the liberal education or the training functions of the schools.

The inconsistencies of beliefs about what the school program should contain and the limited offerings noted depict a lack of common regional purpose, and a lack of understanding of the role of the public schools.

Higher Education

There are 77 higher education institutions in the Region, 50 four-year colleges and 27 junior colleges.

Figure 59. *Per Pupil Expenditures for Capital Outlay in the Public Schools of the United States and of a Sample of Southern Appalachian Counties, 1839-1940, 1949-1950, and 1957-1958*

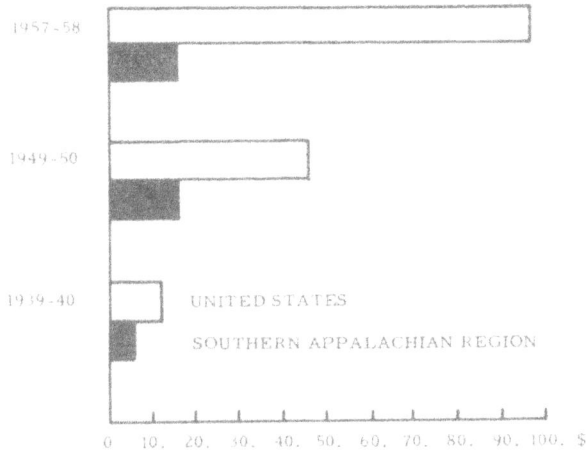

Source: U. S. Bureau of Census, Historical Statistics of the United States; National Education Association, Research Division, Estimates of School Statistics, 1960-61

Seven four-year colleges and six junior colleges were unaccredited by the regional accrediting association in 1958. Table 44 shows the number of institutions by control and accreditation. In the 25-year period from 1933 to 1958 there was an increase of eight in the total number of colleges. Of more significance was the fact that there was an increase of 31 complying with accreditation standards.

All available Southern Appalachian college catalogs published between 1933 and 1958 were reviewed to ascertain changes in institutional purposes and programs.[18] Since the public college purposes were stated in public law, there were few changes in their stated purposes, but many changes were made in programs. Most of the private and church-related colleges changed from liberal arts colleges to "colleges of arts and sciences."

It is generally predicted that college and university enrollments in the nation will double by 1970. The rate of increase in enrollment in the Southern Appalachians will not be as great as the national increase, but the regional institutions face serious problems. By 1968 the rate of increase is estimated conservatively

at 25 percent, an increase of 20,000 bringing the total enrollment to more than 99,000.[19] This increase will place serious demands on these institutions for added facilities and staff.

When compared with the national college enrollment predictions of a 100 percent increase by 1970, the regional predictions of a 25 percent increase from 1958 to 1968 appear to be low. There are several factors which account for the substantially lower predictions. Enrollment in the regional institutions is only some 20 to 25 percent of the total enrollment in the seven states in which the Region is located. Enrollment in these seven states is only 21 to 27 percent of the college-age population, compared to 37 percent for the nation. By 1970, it is expected that the percentage will be only 22 to 32 percent. The increase in enrollment in the seven states between 1961 and 1971 will only be about 43 percent.[20]

An examination of the plans of a sample of 1959 high school seniors for college attendance reveals another reason why predictions for the enrollment increase in the Region are far behind the national predictions and predictions for the seven states. A questionnaire, completed by more than 5,000 high school seniors in the Region in 1959, showed that only 65 percent of their siblings who had enrolled in college attended a college in the Region. An additional 24 percent attended colleges located outside the Region, but within the seven regional states. The remaining 11 percent attended colleges beyond the seven regional states. The 5000 seniors who completed the questionnaire expressed intentions of enrolling in regional and out-of-the-region colleges in the same proportion as had their brothers and sisters.

In the period studied there were no significant shifts in the geographic origin of the students enrolled in the regional colleges. About 80 percent attended colleges in their home states, 24 to 35 percent left their home states to attend other regional colleges. Only about 12 to 13 percent of the regional student population came from states outside the Region and

[18] Robert B. Smawley, "Changes in Purposes and Programs of Colleges and Universities in the Southern Appalachian Region." Unpublished M.S. Thesis, The University of Tennessee, August, 1959.

[19] T. Madison Byar, "A Study of the Student Populations in the Institutions of Higher Education in the Southern Appalachian Region, 1933-1958 (With Estimate of Needs by 1969)." Unpublished Ed.D., Thesis, The University of Tennessee, August, 1959.

[20] Enrollment predictions for the 7 states were furnished by the Southern Regional Education Board, unpublished data, September, 1960.

less than one percent came from outside the United States.

Data on enrollment by sex were available for 46 of the regional colleges. In these colleges the propor-

Figure 60. *Salaries of Teachers in the Southern Appalachian Region, the Southeastern States, and the United States, and Average Earnings in Other Professions, 1958-1959*

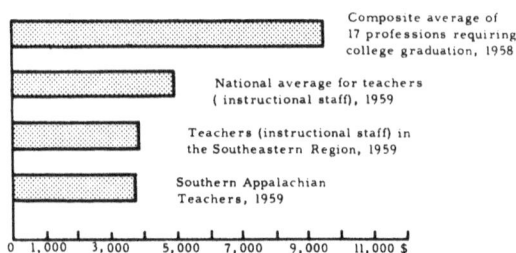

Composite average of 17 professions requiring college graduation, 1958

National average for teachers (instructional staff), 1959

Teachers (instructional staff) in the Southeastern Region, 1959

Southern Appalachian Teachers, 1959

0 1,000 3,000 5,000 7,000 9,000 11,000 $

Source: National Education Association, Research Division, The Case for Federal Support of Education (1961) and Estimates of School Statistics, 1958-59

tion of male students increased from 53.8 percent in 1933 to 59.4 percent in 1958.

The question arises whether these 77 institutions can accommodate 99,000 students by 1968. The task would not be too difficult if there could be coordinated efforts among the institutions for proportionate expansion and coordinated programs to accommodate the wide range of regional needs. Unfortunately, such coordination does not appear to be forthcoming.

Most private and church-related colleges in the Region had plans to limit enrollment at a predetermined size. Unless this trend changes they may enroll as few as 3,000 more students by 1968, and the burden for accommodating student growth in the Region will then rest largely with the public institutions. During the period of the study, student enrollments were tending to shift to the public colleges and universities. During the 1933-1958 period all colleges had increased in enrollment; however, there was a 10 percent shift of student population from private and church-related colleges to public colleges. Public college enrollments increased 220 percent while the average increase of all regional colleges was 177.2 percent. In 1933 public colleges were accommodating 56 percent of the student population; in 1958 this was 66 percent. Comparable figures for the private and church-related colleges were 14 percent and 30 percent in 1933, and 12 percent and 32 percent in 1958, respectively.

Changes in the Region from an agrarian to an industrialized society are making new demands on the institutions of higher education. Although out-migration has held the overall enrollment growth predictions to 25 percent as compared to a prediction of 100 percent growth throughout the nation, new programs are required. And the burden for this expansion will rest with the public institutions.

If students in the Region can find programs in the regional institutions to accommodate their purposes, most probably will attend these regional colleges.

Summary

This study of education in the Region has pointed up major changes and improvements since the 1930's. For example, in 1960 only one of the seven states in which the Region lies fell below the national norm in the percentage of school-age children enrolled in the public elementary and secondary schools. Per pupil expenditures for public education have had a fourfold dollar increase within the past 20 years, and teacher's salaries have been increased in some instances as much as 278 percent in terms of purchasing value. The number of degree-holding teachers has almost tripled. There have been rapid strides in offering more comprehensive programs and providing more adequate facilities for these programs. When comparisons are made with national norms, however, the shocking inadequacy of the Region's educational program becomes evident.

In 1950, only 3.8 percent of the regional population compared with 6.0 percent of the national population twenty-five years of age and over had four or more years of college; only one in five regional adults had finished high school compared with one in three for the nation; and 19.1 percent of the regional population but only 10.8 percent of the national population had less than 5 years of schooling. Approximately 63 percent of the rural public school pupils and 44 percent of the metropolitan pupils are currently dropping out of school between the sixth and twelfth grades.

The amount of money spent for educating a Southern Appalachian pupil in 1958 was only one-half of the national average. Per pupil expenditures for capital outlay in 1957 amounted to less than 16 percent of similar expenditures for the nation. Forty-seven percent of the public elementary schools in the Region in 1958 had five rooms or fewer, and 28 percent were one-room structures. In 1959, the Southern Appalachian teacher was paid about $3,730; this is some $1,200 less than the average for the nation, and some $150 less than the average in the southeastern region.

The programs of most high schools in the Region offer little for the pupil who does not go to college.

Table 43. *High School Courses Offered by 50 Percent or More of 69 Southern Appalachian School Systems, 1958*

Course offerings	Course units
English and foreign languages	4 units of English (no foreign language offered by 30 percent of systems)
Social studies	1 unit of American history required in all systems 1 unit in world history 1 unit in American problems of government 1/2 unit in sociology 1/2 unit in economics
Mathematics	2 units in algebra 1 unit in general mathematics 1 unit in plane geometry 1/2 unit in solid geometry 1/2 unit in trigonometry
Physical sciences	1 unit in general science 1 unit in chemistry 1 unit in physics
Vocational courses	2 units of home economics 4 units of agriculture (no industrial arts offered in typical system)
Business courses	1 unit in bookkeeping 1 unit in shorthand 2 units in typing 1/2 unit in business arithmetic
Fine arts	No arts or crafts available in typical curriculum No orchestra or concert band training in typical curriculum Marching band and vocal music available, but 2 units maximum credit for 4 full years in most systems.

Fewer than 45 percent of a sampling of the 1959 high school seniors planned to go to college, not to mention the 44 to 63 percent of the pupils who had already dropped out of school.

The regional handicaps are not being overcome, but rather are becoming more severe. The breach of inequality between the Region and the nation becomes greater with the forward movement of our country. This is cause for national alarm. The regional leadership can no longer afford to be content to spend even a portion of its time with the re-creation of the past and maintenance of the *status quo*. Nor can the rest of the nation continue to look in the opposite direction. The Region must become more rather than less a part of the national economy. Out-

side ideas and support are required to reverse the trends of a lagging economy with all of its damaging effects. At the heart of the problem is a substandard program of education.

The educational program must be improved to compare favorably with the rest of the country. This will require at least doubling expenditures for educational purposes. Most of these additional funds will need to come from the Federal Government. The regional school systems least able to support education are making the greatest effort. They are educating pupils who will move from the Region, thus returning nothing directly to its economy. The regional states and their local systems are now providing 96 percent of the cost of educating their children, many of whom will move to other states at the time they become productive citizens.

The school programs will need to be made sufficiently comprehensive to hold the non-college bound pupils and to offer vocational training programs to equip youth and adults for an industrialized society. This will require consolidation of high schools to meet Dr. Conant's criterion of a graduating class of 100. Capital expenditures for plant and equipment will need to be increased about tenfold.

Teachers' salaries need to be increased sufficiently to attract qualified teachers from all parts of the country who will bring new ideas to the Region. Salaries are not only lower than the average for the nation but they are under the average for the Southeast, which is lowest of all major geographic subdivisions of the country. Obviously, this appallingly low salary cannot continue to hold those quality teachers native to the Region; teachers outside the Region will be even less inclined to come. It seems important that a concerted effort be made to staff the regional schools with a full complement of teachers, at least some of whom come from other cultural areas of the country. No discredit is meant to the regional teacher, but the injection of new ideas from other cultural areas into the educational program seems highly advisable.

The expressed plans of private and church-related colleges to stop growth at small sizes may portend a decline in the traditional influence of these schools in the Region. Their strategic locations and potential contributions to education, if developed under vigorous modern leadership, could make them a continuing power in the educational life of the people. It would be a great service to the Region if these colleges would reevaluate their purposes and gear their programs and growth to the needs of the Appalachian youth.

The public colleges need also to reevaluate their eager response to public demand for expansion. A

Table 44. *Accreditation of Southern Appalachian Colleges by Type of Control, 1958*

Accreditation[a]	State and local	Church-related	Private
Four-year colleges			
Accredited	19	17	7
Unaccredited	--	5	2
Junior colleges			
Accredited	5	15	1
Unaccredited	--	3	3
Total	24	40	13

[a]All of the accredited colleges in the Region are members of the Southern Association of Colleges and Secondary Schools with the exception of 13 in West Virginia which belong to the North Central Association of Colleges and Secondary Schools.

policy of expansion which is not soundly based on long-range educational needs is certainly as unsound as one of deliberate restriction.

Under present conditions the braking force of tradition in the private and church-related colleges and the opposing force of "public demand" on the public institutions hamper the development of improved college opportunities for all of the people of the Region. Prerequisite to a reevaluation of these programs are comprehensive studies of higher education in the Region and in each of the seven states concerned. Without such studies intelligent decisions on program changes by individual colleges and universities are not possible.

The responsibility for developing programs for reeducating and retraining adults displaced by technological advances must also be accepted by educational leaders in the Region if further wastage of their potential social and economic contribution is to be avoided.

Whether they leave or remain in the Region, the Southern Appalachian people must be adequately prepared for productive roles in an industrial society. If this goal is to be met, higher education in the Region must expand to accommodate growing enrollments and at the same time must accept new functions which extend beyond the usual academic program as currently conceived.

CHAPTER THIRTEEN

Religion

and

the

Churches

EARL D. C. BREWER

THE FIRST SETTLERS IN THE REGION were English, Scotch-Irish, and German, with a sprinkling of French and Highland Scotch. By and large they were nonconformist sectarians in religion, with ties to the early Lollards, Puritans, Separatists, Anabaptists, Presbyterians, and French Huguenots. Most of them or their immediate ancestors had faced persecution in Europe. They came largely from the lower economic groups. Their settlement in the isolation of the Appalachian Highlands reinforced tendencies toward localism and suspicion of centralized authority. Later, evangelical revivals, pushed mostly by Baptists and Methodists, added a New World flavor to Old World nonconformity.[1]

The religious heritage of the Southern Appalachian people has been pictured as "leftwing protestantism." Its characteristics include puritanical behavior patterns, religious individualism, fundamentalism in attitudes toward the Bible and Christian doctrine, little distinction between clergy and laity, sectarian concepts of the church and its mission, revivalism, informality in public worship, and opposition to central authority of state or church. This broad picture of mountain religion has been associated with the prevalence of poorly trained leadership and inadequate budgets and buildings. Under such circumstances, some religious leaders have thought it difficult to carry on programs of worship, religious education, and spiritual service in keeping with present day standards. To what extent is this an adequate description of mountain religion today and what changes are taking place?

Population and church membership data covering the 190 Southern Appalachian counties for 1926 and 1952 were employed in this study.[2] The church membership projections to 1957 were computed on the assumption that the trends in religious membership during the 1926-1952 period would continue to 1957.[3] In view of the limited comparability and reliability of these data, and differences in definitions of church membership, it is necessary to take conclusions based upon them with the proverbial grain of salt.

Membership data by counties for both 1926 and 1952 were available for only eleven denominations. These denominations accounted for four-fifths of the 2.6 million church members in the Southern Appalachian area (Table 45). This left slightly more than half a million members to be distributed among all the other denominations. These same denominations claimed over 70 percent of all church members in the nation, with 25.9 million distributed among other religious bodies. From 1926 to 1957 the Southern

Appalachian population grew about half as rapidly as that of the country. During this period, church membership increased more than twice as rapidly as the population in the mountains and slightly more rapidly than church membership in the United States.

The Southern Baptist churches have the largest membership and are growing more rapidly than any

With some exceptions, metropolitan areas showed a higher proportion of their population in church membership than nonmetropolitan areas.

The counties with less than 30 percent of the population in church membership fell largely in eastern Kentucky and western Virginia with concentration in the northeastern Cumberland Plateau (Figure 61).

Table 45. *Church Membership by Denominations, 1957, and Average Annual Rates of Change, 1926-1957, Southern Appalachian Region and United States*

| Denomination | 1957 Membership | | | | Average annual change rate 1926-57 | |
| | (Thousands) | | Percentage of total | | | |
	SAR	US	SAR	US	SAR	US
Southern Baptist	996	9,556	38.0	10.5	4.4	5.5
Methodist	551	9,660	21.0	10.6	0.9	1.4
Presbyterian, U. S.	122	840	4.7	0.9	1.9	2.8
American Baptist	102	1,712	3.9	1.9	1.8	1.1
Roman Catholic	92	33,230	3.5	36.6	2.2	2.5
Disciples of Christ	86	2,008	3.3	2.2	1.4	1.5
Protestant Episcopal	43	2,780	1.6	3.1	1.6	1.6
United Lutheran	40	2,252	1.5	2.5	2.5	2.7
United Baptists	37	64	1.4	0.1	6.5	7.7
United Presbyterian	26	2,694	1.0	3.0	0.7	1.4
Cumberland Presbyterian	10	101	0.4	0.1	2.9	1.6
Other denominations	516	25,862	19.7	28.5	1.9	1.5
All denominations	2,621	90,759	100.0	100.0	2.3	2.1

Source: U. S. Census of Religious Bodies, 1926; National Council of Churches, Churches and Church Membership in the United States, Series C (1956).

other group except the United Baptists. In fact, more than a third of the church members in the Region are Southern Baptists; in the nation as a whole this is true for the Roman Catholics. Roman Catholics are increasing more rapidly than the population in both the Region and the United States. The Methodists, second largest group in the Region, are growing as rapidly as the population. The Southern Baptists and the Methodists comprise nearly 60 percent of all the church members in the Southern Appalachians but only 21 percent in the country as a whole. The Southern Presbyterians are nearly five times as strong in the Region as in the nation but their growth rate is lower in the Region. Of the denominations listed in Table 45, only the United Presbyterians are growing at a slower rate in the Region than is the population.

In the Southern Appalachian counties a smaller proportion of the people hold church membership than in the country as a whole, but from 1926 to 1957 they were closing this gap by increasing the percentage nearly three times as rapidly as the nation (Table 46). Western North Carolina counties were the "most religious" and eastern Kentucky had the lowest percentage of its population in church membership.

Counties with 50 percent membership and over appeared around the borders of the Region, excepting Kentucky, and in the Appalachian Valleys. The metropolitan areas exercised an obvious influence toward high membership. Counties in the middle group (with 30 to 49 percent of the population in church membership) served generally as buffers be-

[1] John C. Campbell, *The Southern Highlander and His Homeland* (New York: Russell Sage Foundation, 1921), pp. 50-71.

[2] *U.S. Census of Religious Bodies*, 1926; National Council of Churches, *Churches and Church Membership in the United States*, Series C (New York, 1956). The 1926 *Census of Religious Bodies* was based upon data collected from clerks of local churches. In the 1952 study, information on the distribution of church members by counties was obtained from denominational officials. The 1952 study was less complete in coverage of denominations than the earlier one. The most serious omissions from the point of view of this study were the Churches of Christ, Negro churches, and a large number of very small religious groups. See Series A, No. 1 of the National Council study for a discussion of the methodology and its limitations.

[3] Based upon the preliminary work of John C. Belcher, "Number of Inhabitants of the Southern Appalachians, 1900-1957," Southern Appalachian Studies in Cooperation with the University of Georgia (Athens, Georgia, May, 1959), Tables 6-21.

tween high and low density areas, except in West Virginia where they were dominant. In general, counties with lower church membership in 1957 had a larger percentage loss in population from 1950 to 1957 (cf. Figure 12). For example, the counties with

All the churches in randomly selected wards or minor civil divisions within the 21 sample cities and counties were located on maps. From these 585 churches, 240 were randomly chosen for general study without regard to denomination (10 from each city

Table 46. *Percentage of Population in Church Membership, United States and Southern Appalachian Region, 1926-1957*

	Percentage of population in membership		Percentage change
Area	1957	1926	1926-57
United States	53.0	47.1	12.5
Southern Appalachian Region	45.5	34.0	33.8
North Carolina	56.4	43.7	29.1
Tennessee	55.7	38.9	43.2
Georgia	51.2	41.6	23.1
Alabama	48.1	33.0	45.8
Virginia	44.8	38.8	15.5
West Virginia	39.5	30.6	29.1
Kentucky	27.1	19.6	38.3

Source: U. S. Census of Religious Bodies, 1926; U. S. Census of Population, 1920, 1930, and 1950; Bureau of Census Current Population Reports, Series P-25, No. 189; National Council of Churches, Churches and Church Membership in the United States, Series C (1956).

less than 20 percent of the population in church membership had a median decline in population of 8.4 percent while those from 50 to 59 percent had an increase of 0.8 percent in population. This tends to support the observed positive relationship between relative stability of population and church membership.[4] Under conditions of out-migration, however, church membership records are likely to get out of step with population data because people tend to move without changing their church membership. It will be another decade before the impact of the excessive out-migration since 1950 will be fully felt in the membership rolls of churches.

In 1931, field studies of religion were carried on in 17 rural mountain counties, two of which are outside but adjacent to the Region as defined in the present study. An effort was made to locate all the churches in those counties and to hold interviews with the pastors or clerks. The study covered 997 churches.[5]

The 1959 field studies included 10 of the counties studied in 1931, eight other nonmetropolitan counties scattered throughout the Region, three metropolitan cities, and three metropolitan counties outside of the central cities (Figure 62). According to 1956 estimates, a fourth of the Region's population (24.6 percent) was in standard metropolitan areas with three-fourths (75.4 percent) in nonmetropolitan counties. The survey sample respondents were distributed in almost exactly this proportion (24.9 percent metropolitan and 75.1 percent nonmetropolitan).

or county). Finally, 72 churches (three of different denominations from each city or county) were chosen for more detailed study. A total of 96 weeks of field work was carried on during the summer of 1959 in these 72 churches.

The remainder of this chapter is largely based upon information gathered by the field workers in interviews with ministers, lay leaders, church members, and nonmembers (persons not claiming active membership in any local religious organization). This field work produced 240 General Church Schedules, 1078 Religious Survey Schedules, 328 Minister and Lay Leader Schedules, 64 tape recordings of clergy talks, 57 recordings of lay talks, and 61 recordings of group discussions on religious beliefs, plus field notes and miscellaneous data about the 72 sample churches. The Attitude Survey described in Chapter II provided supplementary material.

Religious Attitudes and Beliefs

Values, attitudes, beliefs, and opinions of people are difficult to measure and evaluate. Like motiva-

[4] Harold F. Kaufman in *Mississippi Churches: A Half Century of Change* (Social Science Research Center, Mississippi State University, 1959), pp. 25-26.

[5] The 1931 study of religion in the mountain region was made by the Institute of Social and Religious Research. These publications serve as the "bench mark" for the present work: Elizabeth R. Hooker, *Religion in the Highlands*, New York: Home Missions Council, 1933; U.S.D.A., *Economic and Social Problems and Conditions of the Southern Appalachians*, Misc. Publ. No. 205 (1935), pp. 168-82.

THE SOUTHERN APPALACHIANS

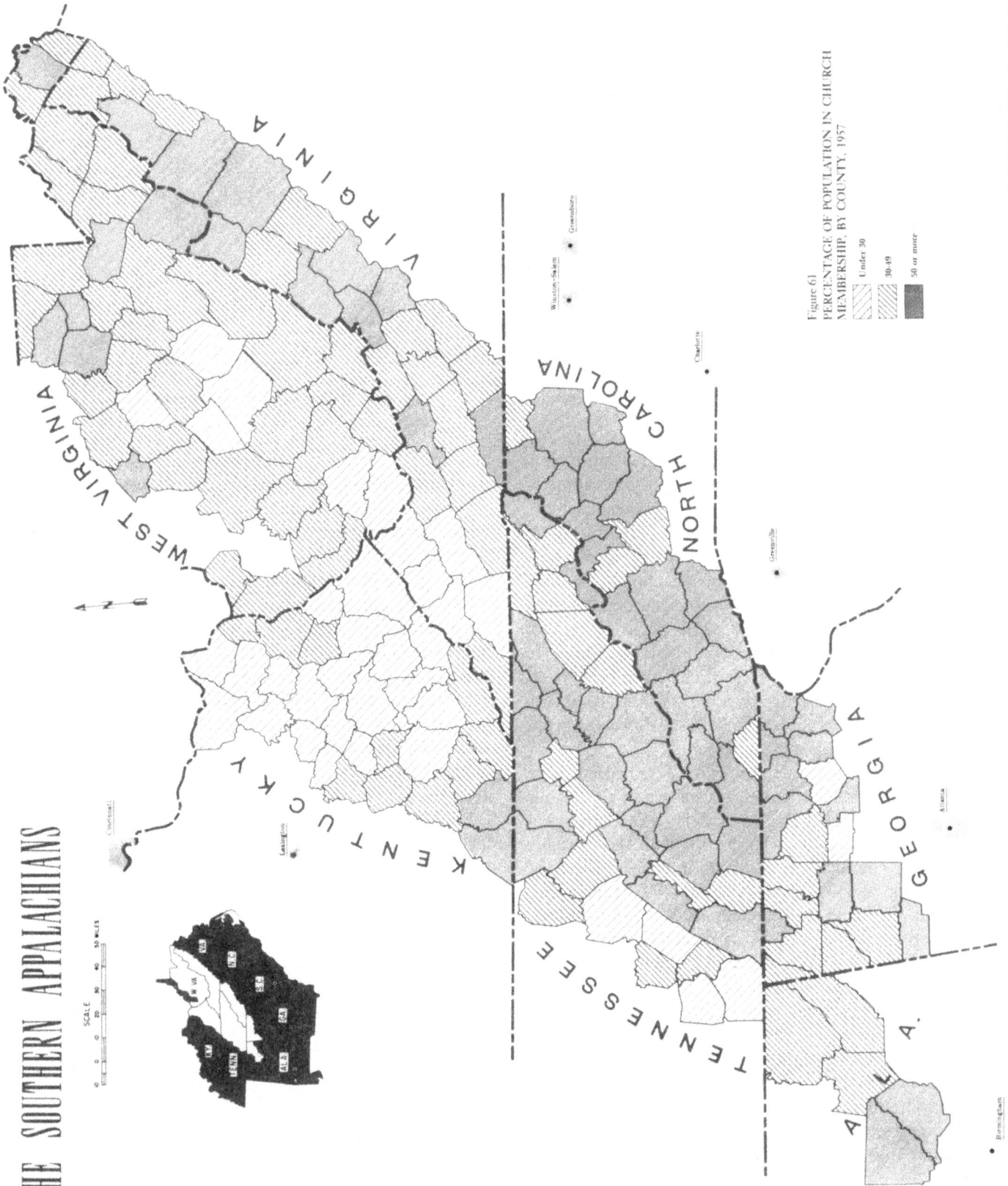

SCALE

Figure 61
PERCENTAGE OF POPULATION IN CHURCH
MEMBERSHIP, BY COUNTY, 1957

Under 30

30-49

50 or more

WEST VIRGINIA

VIRGINIA

VIRGINIA

KENTUCKY

TENNESSEE

NORTH CAROLINA

GEORGIA

A L A.

Charleston

Lexington

Winston-Salem

Greensboro

Charlotte

Greenville

Atlanta

Birmingham

tional forces, they tend to be covert aspects of culture until expressed in verbalized or other forms of behavior. They are evasive—difficult to locate and measure directly—and pervasive—difficult to isolate and identify. This tends to be especially the case with religious attitudes.

It has generally been thought that religious attitudes in the Southern Appalachians were largely fundamentalist, sectarian, puritanical, and conservative. It was possible to test this generalization through the use of the Dynes sect-church attitude scale.[6] Since Dynes had used the scale on a sample of the adult population of Columbus, Ohio, comparisons were possible. The attitude scale consists of 24 statements about religion. Respondents were asked to express agreement, disagreement (with two degrees of intensity) or uncertainty about each item. Item responses were scored from 1 (most sect-type attitude) to 5 (most church-type view). The scale scores for all 24 items would, by construction, range from 24 (extreme sectarianism) to 120 (extreme churchness) with a median of 72. In the Columbus sample, the actual range was from 33 to 103 with a median of 71. In the Southern Appalachian sample, the range was from 28 to 89, with a median of 57. The metropolitan areas in the Southern Appalachians scored higher than the rural areas but below the Columbus sample. The average item score for the Columbus sample was 2.90 compared to 2.37 for the Southern Appalachian sample. In the Columbus sample, 11 of the 24 statements had average scores of 3.0 or above, while there were only three such high scores for the mountain sample. The most church-type score (3.65) for mountain respondents went to this statement: "I think it is more important to live a good life now than to bother about life after death." There was slightly more agreement than disagreement with this statement and this was even more marked in Columbus. This doubtless reflects a declining supernaturalism. Yet, the most sect-type score (1.68) showed agreement with the idea that, "It is more serious to break God's law than to break man's law." Six statements in the attitude scale received extreme sect-type average scores of less than 2.0 in the Appalachians contrasted with only one such item in Columbus. The greatest differences were on two statements. Appalachian respondents agreed that "In church, I think it is better for everybody to join in singing hymns than to listen to the choir sing." The Columbus sample disagreed with this item: "I think a minister should preach without expecting to get

paid for it." The first is an example of the sectarian stress on informality and congregational participation in worship, while the second expresses the sectarian non-professional view of the ministry. In both cases, the attitudes in the Region were much more sectarian than those in Columbus.

The attitude scale not only confirmed the continuation of sectarianism in religion but provided a convenient device for subdividing the respondents into three groups: (1) 363 sect-type or *S* respondents with scale scores under 54; (2) 352 denomination-type or *D* respondents with scores of 54 through 59; and (3) 363 church-type or *C* respondents with scores of 60 and over. All the *S*, *D*, and the majority of the *C* respondents fell below the "normal" constructed median of 72.0 for the scale score. In fact, only around 5 percent of the respondents had scores above 72. This means that the variations observed between *S*, *D*, and *C* respondents were largely differences in degrees of sectarianism and fundamentalism rather than between sect-type and church-type attitudes as measured by the scale.

The attitude scale scores for the leaders and members of the churches were averaged by denominational groupings. The average score for all leaders and members was 56.5 and respondents in the following denominational groupings scored below the average: Church of God 47.2, Advent 50.5, Pentecostal and Holiness 53.0, and Baptist 53.4. These groups scored above the average: Disciples of Christ 57.5, Methodists 59.3, Evangelical United Brethren 60.0, Brethren 62.0, Luthern 63.0, Presbyterian 63.4, Roman Catholic 67.2, Congregational Christian 74.0, and Protestant Episcopal 75.0. The majority of the Attitude Survey (AS) respondents belonged to or preferred churches which scored below the average for all denominations. This is largely due to the fact that the Baptist bodies fell below the average score. Thirty-two of the 60 denominations named as church of preference by AS respondents are classified as small sects (mostly of the Adventist and Perfectionist types) by Clark.[7]

The AS respondents were asked to indicate which of several descriptions most nearly approached their ideas of God. These descriptions and the percentage of total respondents selecting them follow: righteous judge of all men (30.2 percent), loving Heavenly

[6] Russell R. Dynes, "Church-Sect Typology: An Empirical Study" (unpubl. dissertation, Ohio State University, 1954).

[7] E. T. Clark, *The Small Sects in America*, Rev. Ed. (Nashville, 1949), pp. 241-246.

THE SOUTHERN APPALACHIANS

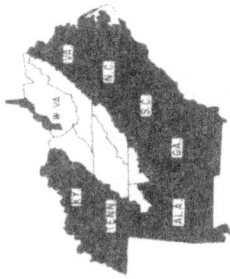

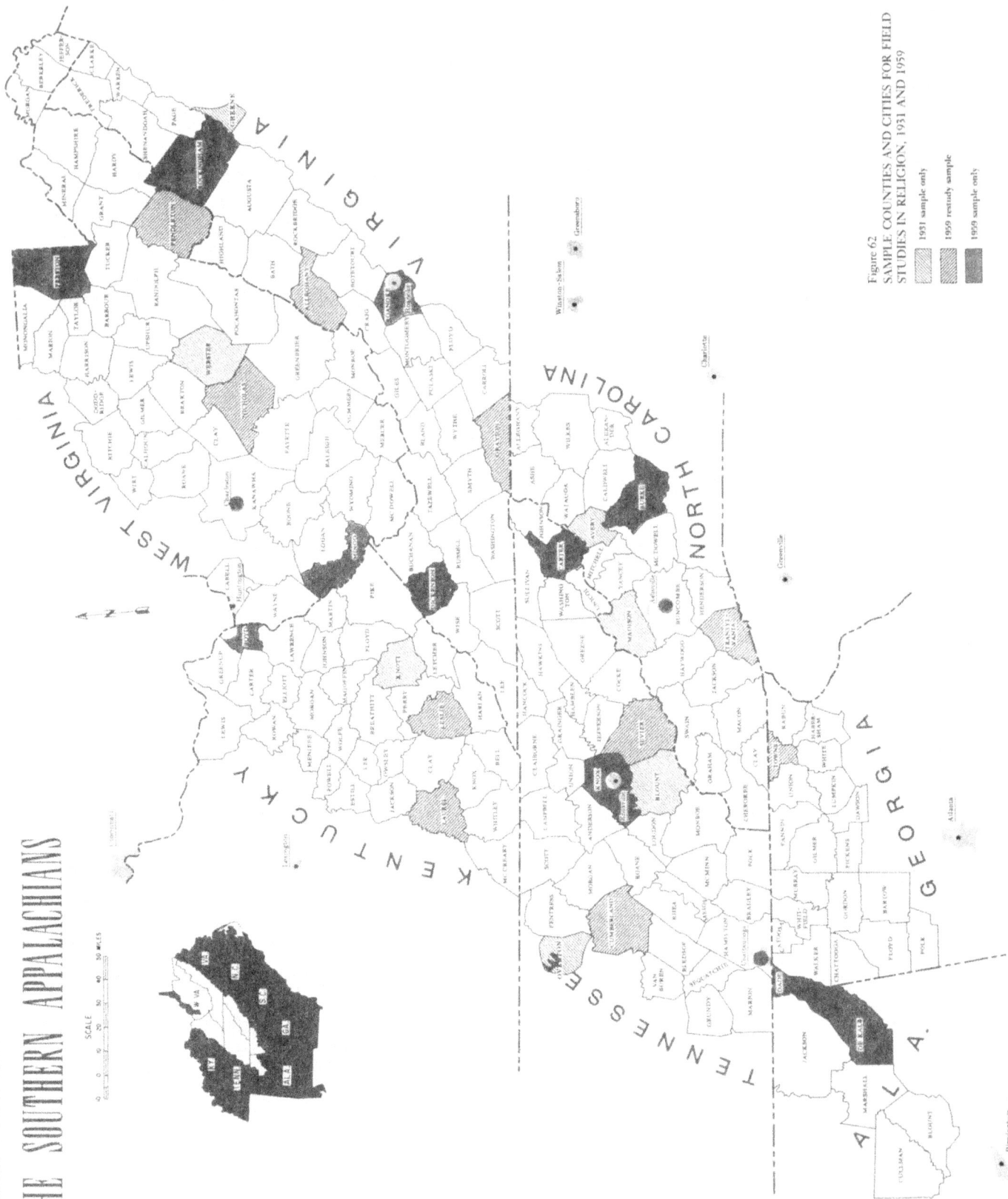

WEST VIRGINIA

VIRGINIA

KENTUCKY

NORTH CAROLINA

TENNESSEE

GEORGIA

ALA.

Figure 62

SAMPLE COUNTIES AND CITIES FOR FIELD
STUDIES IN RELIGION, 1931 AND 1959

1931 sample only

1959 restudy sample

1959 sample only

SCALE
0   10   20   30   40   50 MILES

Father (29.3 percent), creator of the world (10.5 percent), all-seeing eye who watches us (9.0 percent), ideal of truth, beauty and goodness (7.2 percent), God of wrath and judgment (4.2 percent), and the Man Upstairs (1.4 percent). Less than 10 percent

Table 47. *What Do You Think Is Most Important for Religious Salvation? Percentage of RSS Respondents, by Role, Giving Indicated Responses*

Role	Right beliefs	Right feelings	Right deeds	Some-thing else	Don't know
Ministers	60.6	5.6	7.0	26.8	-
Lay leaders	50.3	14.2	17.4	15.3	2.8
Members	41.4	18.3	24.7	11.9	3.7
Nonmembers	34.3	17.8	31.8	9.5	6.6
All roles	42.7	16.2	23.9	13.0	4.2

were unsure about a choice among these ideas. The majority of the respondents chose between the first two descriptions. The first may be thought of as the Old Testament conception of God and the second as coming from the New Testament. By residence areas, rural dwellers largely believed in the Old Testament idea of God while the urban and metropolitan respondents stressed the New Testament notion. Males voted more for the Righteous Judge while females believed in the loving Heavenly Father. The residence and sex differences were significant and consistent. The Old Testament view of God is perhaps more in keeping with the historical background of mountain religion and with traditional rural culture. Clearly, urbanism and women are the agents of change here.

Ideas about salvation usually involve some combination of religious beliefs, emotions or feelings, and activities or deeds. Beliefs were held to be most important for salvation by 42.7 percent of the religious survey (RSS) respondents with 23.9 percent voting for deeds and 16.2 percent for feelings. Six of ten ministers stressed beliefs as most important for salvation and this declined for each of the lay roles to about three of ten for nonmembers (Table 47). All respondents placed least importance upon feelings. This was lowest for ministers (5.6 percent) and highest for members (18.3 percent). Church members (24.7 percent) stressed deeds more than three times as strongly as ministers (7.0 percent). Nearly a third of the nonmembers thought deeds most important in religious salvation. Some of the respondents (13.0 percent) held that "something else," usually some combination of feelings, beliefs, and deeds, was most significant for religious salvation. About twice as many

ministers as others chose this more complicated response. It seems obvious that the stress on "beliefs," even though only a speech reaction, was dominant with little attention to the emotional components of religion. The nearer to the center of the life of the church one stood, the less emphasis was placed on deeds or "works" as important for salvation.

Respondents were asked about the meaning of religious salvation to them personally. Supernatural themes dealing with the eternal life and the right relationships to God were stressed by more than a third of all respondents, by six of ten ministers, and by only two of ten nonmembers. One Presbyterian member called salvation, "belonging to Jesus Christ," while a Church of God Sunday school superintendent declared, "It means a lot to anyone to lay down at night and be in the 'hands of the Master.'" A Methodist member confessed, "For years I went on my own steam but was stricken so that I learned that I had to depend on God." A third of the ministers stressed this right relationship to God with church-type ministers highest (46.3 percent) and sect-type ministers lowest (17.2 percent) while only about half as many laymen placed major emphasis here.

Salvation meant eternal life to a fifth of the respondents. A Baptist preacher expressed the central idea, "It means a home in heaven after this life is over. I don't know how to put it in words." A Church of God pastor called it, "Everlasting life, somewhere in the future. Here, it means we're free from sin; given joy and peace."

The "better life here" view of salvation was stressed by 12.5 percent of all respondents but only by 4.2 percent of the ministers. A Southern Baptist said, "A person gets along better—ends meet better." A Congregational Christian leader stressed, "Greater participation in the community and its welfare." A Roman Catholic lay official declared, "Absolutely necessary to go to church—keeps my boys in line." A Regular Baptist used a pragmatic test, "Salvation helps you out when you go meeting together, mingling with one another, singing, shaking hands."

Salvation was viewed as resulting in a changed personal life by 9.6 percent of the respondents. As expected, ministers placed more than twice as much emphasis here as laymen. A nonmember in a Baptist community put his finger on an important part of this theme, "To be born again and a change of heart." A Church of God young person said, "Before I got saved I didn't care about going to church. Now I love to go. After a man is born again it makes him love people and do things for people that he wouldn't want to do before." A Seventh Day Adventist member put it this way, "It means giving up all worldly things and accepting Christ. It would be by works and faith and love." A Free Pentecost leader declared, "As

Figure 63. *Percentage of Respondents, by Residence, Who Regard Specified Activities as "Always Wrong"*

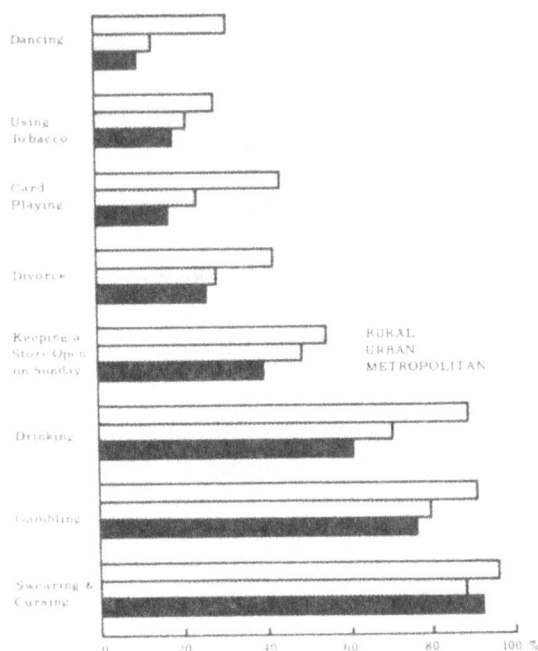

far as my part's concerned, it means practically everything—I was in bondage to Satan and now I am free."

Peace of mind, comfort, joy, and happiness as aspects of salvation were stressed by only 7.5 percent of all respondents. Ministers were even less enthusiastic about this than laymen. Obviously, Appalachian religion has been largely untouched by the "peace of mind" cult of middle class urban America. Man's relationship to his fellows was a minor theme. It appeared as a major stress in only 2.5 percent of the responses, and not at all among ministers.

It was evidently difficult for people to verbalize their ideas about religious salvation with strange interviewers. Thus 20 percent of all respondents answered with "means everything" or some similar phrase, while another 12.8 percent confessed that they did not know or would not talk about it. These inarticulate respondents were lowest among ministers and highest among nonmembers (51.8 percent). A few respondents, mostly nonmembers, frankly admitted that salvation and the church meant nothing to them.

Inquiries into the meaning of death elicited more emotional responses than other belief questions. More people had ideas on the subject and more hostility was aroused here than at any other point in the interview. Over a fifth of the people stressed the fear theme in connection with death. Some of them professed that there should be no fear of death, if one were spiritually prepared. A Baptist member said, "If you're saved, I don't see you should fear. Some people are better off dead than they are here anyway. It's true." Even so, a Missouri Synod Lutheran said, "It is always very sad—I don't care who it is. Death and funerals shake me up. I never have been able to analyze it. It is terrifying to children—we try to shield them. I saw my mother when she died and was hurt by the dirt being turned into the grave. No one can rejoice in death." A Baptist woman leader put it more briefly, "It's awful sad. I just can't hardly take it."

The most dominant belief was that death was a transition marking the end of earthly life and the beginning of eternal or heavenly life. This was stated by around four out of ten respondents while others expressed the same idea, using the "body to dust and spirit to God" formula. A few emphasized the notion that death was merely a sleep until the general resurrection. About ten percent of the respondents viewed death principally as judgment with the "saved" going to heaven and the "lost" to hell, while only half as many declared that death was the end of it all and looked forward to nothing beyond it. Three-fourths of the AS respondents who believed in life after death thought of it as involving punishments or rewards meted out by God. Four of ten such persons believed that treatment in the next life would be based upon the way one lived here, three of ten voted for faith, and the remainder thought it would be a combination of beliefs and type of life.

Beliefs were often stressed as being of greatest importance in achieving religious salvation, yet on the other hand, the kind of life led and deeds done were also frequently cited, as most significant in determining destiny in the next life. This is one illustration of many such inconsistencies in the religious belief system of the Region's people. Such strains and stresses in beliefs are usually found in areas of transition and social change.

The puritanical moral patterns traditionally ascribed to the Region have significance beyond the religious sphere, and many elements of this tradition may seem irrelevant to the major concerns of religion today.

The "unholy trinity" of dancing, drinking, and card playing were viable issues in rural America a century ago. They, and related items in the puritan ethic, remain more important in the Region, perhaps, than in other parts of the country. Yet, a study of the

Church and Bible Knowledge

An attempt to secure a measure of the amount of church and Biblical knowledge possessed by Southern Appalachian residents was seriously handicapped by

Table 48. *Church and Bible Knowledge Scores, RSS Sample*

Role	Church knowledge score[a]			Bible knowledge score[a]				
	Metro-politan	Nonmetro-politan	All areas	New Testament	Old Testament	Metro-politan	Nonmetro-politan	All areas
Ministers	80.4	64.2	68.1	94.1	71.5	87.6	78.9	81.0
Lay leaders	55.1	41.0	44.5	83.1	56.6	72.1	66.2	67.8
Members	35.2	30.3	31.5	76.7	45.9	64.9	56.9	58.9
Nonmembers	8.5	10.8	10.2	47.3	30.5	43.4	35.6	37.5
All roles	34.4	28.9	30.3	69.7	45.6	61.1	53.8	55.8

[a]Church knowledge score is actual number of correct answers to three questions divided by possible number. Bible knowledge score is actual number of correct answers to four questions divided by possible number. A score of 100 would indicate that all persons had answered all questions correctly.

moral profile reveals changes in focus. While everybody may be "agin sin," notions about right and wrong tend to change with the times.

In Figure 63, the stability and shift in traditional morality are reflected in the proportion of AS respondents viewing as always wrong seven pertinent practices. This extreme puritanical view was breaking down for dancing, card playing, divorce, and sabbath observance. It remained most prevalent against drinking, gambling, and swearing and cursing. Card playing has obviously been separated in the Appalachian mind from gambling. Although most did not want the churches to sponsor it, dancing was the least disapproved of the activities. In any case, the rural ethic was more puritan than the urban or metropolitan view. The greatest differences between residential groups appeared for dancing, card playing, and drinking. With respect to these, urban ways are in definite conflict with the traditional patterns.

Although not as decisive as the rural-urban differences, there were important variations in moral attitudes by sex. In general, men tended to support certain features of the puritan ethic more strongly than did women. This was not only true of the most rapidly changing patterns (dancing, card playing, and drinking) but also of divorce, sabbath observance, and using tobacco. Incidentally, women were less opposed than men to birth control practices for married people and to buying on credit. Metropolitan women were definitely leading the way in changing the rigid, rural moral ethic of yesterday. Rural men, with few exceptions, posed as the greatest defenders of the older moral patterns.

the lack of usable standardized tests for this purpose. Such tests would need to be simple enough for persons of all educational levels and general enough to apply to all denominations. In lieu of a standard test, a number of interview questions were designed to meet these criteria, though they may be considered unsatisfactory from other viewpoints.

The church knowledge test was made up of three simple questions: (1) What is the specific denomination of your church? (2) About what would you say was the total annual budget of your church last year? (3) About what would you say is the membership of your church now? For the first question, only the specific denomination, and not the denominational family, was counted as a correct answer. The responses about the budget and the membership were counted as correct if they fell within a range of 15 percent below or above the official church records. The greatest number of correct answers (48.1 percent) were in response to the question regarding the name of the specific denomination of the church, the next highest (29.4 percent) for the size of membership of the church, and the fewest correct answers (13.3 percent) about the amount of the current church budget. The total number of correct answers divided by the total possible number of correct answers to the three questions provided the church knowledge scores shown in Table 48.

The Bible knowledge test was composed of four questions: (1) Would you say that the Ten Commandments are in the Old Testament or the New Testament? (2) How many of the Commandments can you recall? (3) Would you say that the Lord's

Prayer is in the Old Testament or the New Testament? (4) How much of this Prayer can you recall? In asking the second and fourth questions, it was pointed out that the main ideas, rather than the exact words or order, would suffice. With no penalty for guessing, 30.8 percent of the respondents did not locate the Ten Commandments in the Old Testament and 37.4 percent did not know that the Lord's Prayer was to be found in the New Testament. One respondent in eight could not recall any of the Commandments and one in five knew none of the Lord's Prayer. Only four percent recalled all the Commandments while more than half of all respondents could repeat the Lord's Prayer completely from beginning to end.

Bible knowledge scores, shown in Table 48, were computed using the same procedure as for computing church knowledge scores. As tested by these questions, the respondents knew nearly twice as much about the Bible (55.8) as about the church (30.3). They came nearer passing the New Testament test (69.7) than the Old Testament test (45.6) and metropolitan respondents scored higher on both tests than rural dwellers. Ministers had a better knowledge of the church than lay leaders and scored more than twice as high as church members. On the Bible scores, the ministers led, with lay leaders, members, and nonmembers following in that order. In spite of the "Bible belt" stereotype of the rural mountains, metropolitan respondents had higher Bible scores than those in nonmetropolitan areas. Church-type respondents made higher scores than sect-type respondents on both tests and this is perhaps associated with their higher general educational level. New Testament scores were consistently and significantly higher than Old Testament scores. This may be due to the fact that the Lord's Prayer is used in the regular worship services of many churches. Moreover, the Lord's Prayer comprises a compact memory unit, whereas the Ten Commandments are more likely thought of as discrete items, not necessarily hanging together in memory. Nonmembers had the lowest church and Bible scores but, as expected, they knew around four times as much about the Bible as about the churches serving their communities.

In view of the nature of these tests, the variations by religious roles are more significant than the "level" of knowledge reflected. In general, these are in the anticipated directions: the closer to the center of the church's life, the higher the score on church and Bible knowledge. But appropriate educational work would involve increasing the knowledge of ministers as well as laymen.

One of the central tenets of fundamentalism is that "the Bible is God's word and all it says is true." More than two-thirds of all respondents in the AS sample subscribed to this statement. This view was less prevalent in the cities (59.6 percent) than in the country (74.3 percent). Modernists, as represented by those who admit the possibility of error in the Bible, despite its divine inspiration, remained a small minority in the Region, but less than one respondent in 50 admitted to holding agnostic views concerning the Bible.

Local Churches

The church or parish is the religious unit closest to the people. Here persons participate in shared religious experiences through public worship, religious education, fellowship, and service projects. The level of religious development for most people is directly related to the quality of opportunities available in local churches. Denominations interpret religion so differently that it is impossible to designate suitable standards of size of membership, organizational adequacy, physical facilities, and leadership for local churches. Yet, all would agree that such characteristics of local churches are directly linked to the level and nature of the religious culture available to people.

The typical local church of the sectarian type is characterized by small membership, informal services, a simple organizational structure, and limited financial resources. Certainly this was true of the mountain churches studied by Elizabeth Hooker in 1931. The 1959 study included a sample of churches in 10 of the 17 rural counties studied in 1931, making possible direct comparisons that provide some basis for analyzing changes that have taken place. In the following discussion, we shall refer to the churches in these 10 counties as the 1959 rural restudy sample to distinguish them from the total sample which included churches in other areas.

In 1952, there were nearly twice as many churches per 1,000 population in the Southern Appalachians as in the country as a whole. The average size of the membership of mountain churches (167 members) was only a little more than one-third the national average (405 members). In the 1959 field studies, the total sample churches had an average total membership of 161 persons.

Eight out of ten church members in the Region were reported as resident members. This means that they lived within the parish area of the church and could participate in its activities. It should be noted that the 1959 total sample includes 60 churches from the standard metropolitan areas and these city and suburban churches would be expected to differ from

Table 49. *Characteristics of Local Churches, Southern Appalachian Region, 1931 and 1959*

Church characteristics	Percentage of churches		
	Rural study 1931	Rural restudy 1959	Total 1959
Number of resident members			
Under 25	25.6	22.0	19.2
25-49	30.1	34.0	22.9
50-99	29.4	26.0	25.4
100-199	12.8	15.0	19.6
200 & over	2.1	3.0	12.9
Number of organizations other than congregation			
None	16.1	13.0	10.4
1	54.2	32.0	23.8
2	16.7	20.0	16.2
3 or more	13.0	35.0	49.6
Number of rooms			
None (own no building)	10.8	7.0	9.6
1	69.6	38.0	29.6
2-4	13.6	29.0	20.4
5 or more	6.0	7.0	9.6
Size of budget			
No budget	9.5	7.0	6.2
Under $500	78.6	20.0	15.8
$500-$999	7.4	19.0	14.2
$1000 & over	4.5	54.0	63.8

the rural churches. The majority of the rural churches have under 50 resident members and this has changed very little since 1931 (Table 49). Including the cities, one-half of all the churches had fewer than 63 members and less than five percent claimed 500 or more resident members.

The average Sunday school enrollment of 137 persons was 24 fewer than the average total church membership. One-half of all Sunday schools had fewer than 77 members enrolled, with fewer than 54 persons in average attendance during 1959. The median enrollment and attendance were higher for urban Sunday schools (179 enrollment and 100 average attendance) than rural ones (60 enrollment and 45 average attendance). For 1959, one-half of the churches reported an estimated average attendance at services of public worship of fewer than 65 persons and at revival meetings of under 81 persons.

There has been a significant decline in the number of churches with only one organization in addition to the congregation, but the most dramatic change has been in the number of churches with three or more

organizations. Nearly three times as many rural churches had three or more organizations in 1959 as in 1931. Including the cities, nearly half of all the churches studied in 1959 claimed three or more organizations in addition to the congregation. The Sunday school was the most common church organization (appearing in nine of ten churches), and there was little change in this situation. The number of churches with youth organizations more than doubled while those with women's organizations more than trebled over the past 28 years. It appears that the organizing activities of denominational executives have been effective in spite of the very low resident memberships

The tradition of the one-room church was still strong in the Region, but the number of churches with only one room was cut nearly in half from 1931 to 1959 while those with five or more rooms quadrupled. Including those in cities, three of ten churches continued to have only one room while four of ten claimed five or more rooms. The one-room church, as expected, was much more prevalent in the open country and small villages than in the towns and cities. A further reduction in the number of these churches may be expected in the future. There is a fairly close relationship between the number of rooms in the church building and the number of church organizations. Six of ten church buildings were judged to be in good repair while the others ranged from poor to fair in physical condition.

The percentage of rural churches with budgets of $1,000 and over increased twelve times, while those with budgets of less than $500 declined from over three-fourths to one-fifth. In 1959, nearly two-thirds of all the churches had budgets of $1,000 and over. The median budget in 1931 was $259 and it increased five times for the restudy sample and eight times for the total 1959 sample. Yet, only 16.3 percent of the churches, mostly in the cities, reported total budgets in excess of $10,000. Eight out of ten churches not only received no financial assistance from outside sources but contributed (median amount of $182) to the missionary programs of their denominations. This was in keeping with the fact that 96.0 percent of all respondents in the Attitude Survey felt that churches should carry on such missionary work. Even taking into account the declining value of the dollar, these increases in church budgets are significant. In spite of these marked improvements, church budgets remained at an extremely low level and this could only mean inadequate facilities and poor leadership.

It should be noted that nearly a third of the AS respondents were opposed to using systematic methods of church financing.

These local churches characterized by extremely small memberships, tiny budgets, inadequate buildings, and low levels of organizational development cannot supply the variety of opportunities, the necessary facilities, or the trained leadership to cope with the needs of people in modern society. Although significant improvements are under way, these traits are still prevalent in the rural areas. In 1931, 84.5 percent of the churches were in the open country and this was true of 72.0 percent in the 1959 restudy sample. In the total sample for 1959, 21.7 percent of the churches were in urban places of 2,500 population or above, but more than half of all the churches remained in the open country. It is certain that the number of churches in the open country will continue to decline with further out-migration.

In spite of a surplus of small struggling churches, new congregations are being organized in the Region at an accelerated rate. More than half of the total sample churches had been organized since 1900. Around 40 percent of them were started since 1925. If the even higher rate (16.7 percent) of organization since 1950 should continue, this present quarter century would produce more new churches in the mountains than during any previous comparable period. The large number of churches organized between 1925 and 1950 was doubtless influenced by relocations in the T.V.A. area but perhaps more by the emergence of new denominations and the growth of metropolitan areas. Many of these new churches, however, are being established in already overchurched areas of declining population.

Church Functions and Religious Activities

Respondents in the AS sample were asked which of 15 specific functions should be carried on in churches. These activities in descending order of desirability (percentage of "yes" responses) were: (1) Sunday school, (2) prayer meeting, (3) choirs, (4) use of organs in services, (5) weddings, (6) missionary work, (7) singings, (8) revival meetings, (9) church picnics, (10) community improvement programs, (11) church suppers, (12) using pledges to help support the church budget, (13) raising money for preachers, (14) church bazaars, and (15) square dancing. Sunday schools received most "yes" votes (98.6 percent) and square dancing least (19.9 percent). It is perhaps significant of changes in the

image of the church that missionary work ranked ahead of singings and revival meetings. Singings and church picnics were the preferred forms of church-sponsored recreation, with square dancing frowned upon. All activities (11-14) connected with raising money ranked low. The high-ranking functions (1-5) are associated with the traditional image of the church. The community outreach of the church ranked tenth in the field of 15 activities, as would be expected in the sectarian interpretation of religion.

The sectarian character of mountain religion is seen in the overwhelming preference of RSS respondents for baptism by immersion. Two-thirds of all the interviewees preferred immersion, and this was even higher among rural dwellers (70.3 percent) and sect-type respondents (83.5 percent). Baptism by sprinkling or pouring ran a poor second. These methods were preferred by only a tenth of the sect-type respondents but by over a third of those with church-type attitudes.

In general, sect-type groups tend to place less emphasis upon the ritual of the Lord's Supper than do church-type congregations. Forty-four percent of all persons reported no participation in the Lord's Supper during the previous year and this was even higher (47.2 percent) in nonmetropolitan areas. Nine out of ten nonmembers had not been to the Lord's Table in twelve months compared with 27.8 percent of the church members and 14.9 percent of the lay leaders. More church members had neglected the Lord's Supper during the entire year than had celebrated it monthly. This central ritual of Christianity had fallen into disuse or only partial use by the majority of church people in the study. In contrasting participation in baptism and the Lord's Supper, one respondent remarked that "About all we do is dip 'em and drap 'em!" Incidentally, the latter portion of this remark may not refer to the funeral service, although it is the most universally attended religious ritual in the Region. Only 2.4 percent of the RSS sample had never attended a death rite.

The Sunday preaching service or service of worship may be considered the central meeting of the church. There has been a great increase in the number of such services per month. In 1931, less than a tenth of the rural churches had Sunday preaching services four times or more per month. This increased to over half for the 1959 restudy sample, and 69.2 percent for the total. The percentage of churches holding only one Sunday preaching service per month declined from 63.5 in 1931 to only 3.3 in 1959.

This great increase in the frequency of preaching services has apparently been accompanied by a change in the nature of these services of public worship. This change was inferred from a classification of tape-recorded services of public worship using a modifica-

were found about equally in this category. The theological-apologetical sermons appeared almost exclusively in religious groups with church-type scores.

The fact that 28 of the churches had evangelical sermons indicated a dominance of concern with salva-

Table 50. *What Activity of the Past Week Was Most Significant in Your Religious Life? Percentage of RSS Respondents, by Role, Giving Indicated Responses*

Most significant religious activity	Ministers	Lay leaders	Members	Nonmembers	All roles
Private prayer	22.5	32.6	33.4	17.3	27.1
Attending a church service	16.9	27.4	21.1	4.7	17.1
Listening to radio or television	1.4	4.5	9.7	25.6	13.1
Talking about religion	7.1	8.7	6.4	6.7	7.2
Helping the needy	7.0	5.9	7.5	4.2	5.9
Blessing at meals	2.8	5.2	5.3	5.6	5.2
Family prayers	9.9	6.6	4.7	2.5	4.8
Visiting with minister	-	1.4	1.1	0.8	1.0
Other	31.0	4.2	3.6	0.8	4.6
No religious activity or no response	1.4	3.5	7.2	31.8	14.0

tion of Daniels' typology of church services.[8] Each church in which a service was recorded was rated on a sect-church attitude scale. As expected, the more sect-type churches had more informal and demonstrative services, while the more church-type churches leaned toward deliberative and liturgical services. Twenty-eight of the churches (43.8 percent) maintained a pattern of worship characteristic of the Region under frontier conditions. The majority, however, fell into the more formal, preplanned, professionally led services. The deliberative service was dominant. When these services were compared with descriptions of services in the 1931 study, the trend toward formality was unmistakable.

In like manner, McCracken's types of sermons[9] were modified, applied to the sermons in the sample worship services, and related to the sect-church scores. Twelve of the 64 sermons were primarily concerned with ethical issues and showed a rather high sect-church score (60.0). The emphasis, however, was almost entirely upon matters of individual morality. Only in rare instances did social issues appear and not one sermon could be described as primarily oriented toward broadly conceived social concerns. It may be that in actual behavior, members of sect-type religious groups were strongly motivated in personal morality. But from this sample of sermons, it was obvious that the church-type religious groups gave greater emphasis to ethical admonition than did sectarian groups. There does not appear to be any definite pattern of association between the devotional sermon and the scale score. Churches with high and low mean scores

tion, its means and fruits. A further analysis showed that six out of ten of the churches ended the service with an altar call or an exhortation for evangelical zeal on the part of the members. Here, again, methods developed on the frontier have maintained their form. In some of the urban churches, this end-of-service statement was more in terms of an appeal for voluntary choice of church membership. Even so, generally there were references to "confession of Jesus Christ as your Lord and Savior" and stress on the necessity of personal salvation rather than on group affiliation in a community of believers.

Individual participation in religious activities is reported in Table 50. More than a third of the RSS respondents (38.2 percent) were low participators (1-3 activities), four out of ten were middle participators (4-6 activities), and 12.4 percent were high participators (7 or more activities). Seventy of 100 ministers compared to one of 100 nonmembers placed themselves among the high participators. Participation here refers to the number of different types of experiences and not to the frequency of any particular religious activity.

Out of the religious experiences or activities claimed for the week previous to the interview, each respondent was asked to choose the one which had the most significance for his own religious life. Private prayer

[8] V. E. Daniels, "Ritual and Stratification in Chicago Negro Churches," *American Sociological Review*, VII (June, 1942), pp. 352-361.

[9] Robert J. McCracken, *The Making of the Sermon* (New York: Harper & Bros., 1956), pp. 26 ff.

was most significant for lay leaders and church members, but not for ministers, nearly a third of whom mentioned some ministerial function as being most significant for them. Attending church services ranked second for everyone except nonmembers. A fourth

leadership position through four or more; (3) Meetings attended last year—1 for each 50 meetings (roughly a weekly attendance rate); and (4) Money contributed—1 for each $100 contributed through $500 or more (.5 for less than $100). Comparable

Table 51. *Church and Community Participation by Residence and Role, RSS Sample*

	Church participation scores[a]			Community participation scores[a]		
Role	Metropolitan	Nonmetropolitan	All areas	Metropolitan	Nonmetropolitan	All areas
Ministers	18.17	17.80	17.89	3.35	3.71	3.62
Lay leaders	17.94	13.99	14.97	5.82	2.79	3.54
Members	10.92	8.01	8.73	3.47	1.98	2.35
Nonmembers	1.32	0.86	0.97	1.83	1.27	1.42
All roles	10.03	7.90	8.43	3.54	2.11	2.46

[a]For computation of scores, see text.

of the latter said their most important religious experience was listening to religious radio and television programs. Informal "talking about religion" was more important than the traditional patterns of asking the blessing at meals, family prayers, visiting with the minister, and helping the needy. Indeed, only one percent of all respondents looked upon "visiting with the minister" as the most significant religious experience of the previous week. These responses point to a nonclerical conception of religion, with stress upon individualism and informality.

The extreme sect-type interpretation of religion emphasizes a disengagement from the world and a withdrawal into the religious group itself. The church-type interpretation endorses participation in the community and efforts to bring secular institutions in line with religious social theory. In view of the excessive sectarianism already discovered in the religious attitudes of the Region, it would be expected that participation in community affairs would be at a much lower level than participation in church affairs. This expectancy would be strengthened by the method used in choosing respondents since, by definition, two-thirds of them had church memberships and another third held church leadership positions. Identical questions were asked respondents about their participation in church and community activities. These questions dealt with the number of organizations in which memberships were held, number of leadership positions, number of meetings attended during the past year, and the approximate amount of money contributed to the organizations. Composite participation scores were computed by weighting the items as follows: (1) Membership in organizations—1 for each membership; (2) Leadership—3 for each

participation scores were computed for church and community activities. The most important contrast, as seen in Table 51, was between the church and community participation scores. The respondents participated, as expected, between three and four times as much in the church as in the community. This difference held true for all except nonmembers, who participated least in the community (1.43), but engaged even less in church activities (0.97). Church participation was highly differentiated by religious roles, the ministers having a score more than twice as high as members and nearly twenty times as great as nonmembers. Although the difference in community participation was not nearly as great, it was in the same direction. In general, metropolitan respondents participated more in both church and community than rural dwellers. This doubtless reflected the more complex organizational structures in the city. Although there was little difference in church participation, sect-type respondents scored much lower than church-type respondents in community participation.

Six out of ten rural respondents and four out of ten city dwellers did not claim membership in any community organizations. Around a third of all ministers, a half of rural lay leaders, and a fourth of city lay leaders claimed no affiliation with community organizations. Perhaps even more important for the impact of Christian ethics on community affairs, 76.0 percent of city respondents and 84.7 percent of rural respondents reported holding no leadership positions in community organizations. Three of four rural ministers and six of ten city ministers held no formal leadership positions.

These data confirm the general hypothesis about the sectarianism of the Region's religion and its relationship to community well-being and social action. The large number of church leaders in this study who reported no active community involvement cannot but raise questions about the practical influence of local churches on community change and improvement. It was noted in the church activity profile that community improvement programs ranked tenth in a field of 15 items. Yet, 84.5 percent of the AS sample thought the church should engage in such programs. This was slightly higher for rural than metropolitan respondents and for men than women.

Nearly six of ten AS respondents thought that the minister should "stand up and be counted" on public issues facing the community. This was a little higher in the city than the country and for women than men. Yet, when compared with other clerical roles community participation ranked last. Apparently "taking a stand" was associated with the preaching role rather than with working for community improvement in other ways. Most opposition to church leadership in social action came from the upper and the lower classes, although in most cases the majority of each favored church involvement. The middle class group provided the strongest support for church social action. In general, it seems clear that there is much more readiness for change in this field than might have been supposed. With trained and prophetic clerical leadership, a new emphasis on the social witness of the church might find broad lay support in the Region. Such a shift would involve considerable reorientation of present clerical and lay leadership patterns.

Church Leadership

In sectarian religious groups ministers are likely to be "folk preachers" qualified more by having received the call to preach than by educational preparation. In the 1931 study, the characteristics of the Region's ministry were basically sectarian. During the past generation the proportion of churches with nonresident pastors declined significantly from three-fourths to one-half for rural churches and to four out of ten when the metropolitan churches are included.

In 1931, only one church out of 50 had a full-time resident minister, while in the 1959 restudy sample this was one in ten. Pastors living in the community but giving only part time to the work of the church nearly doubled for rural churches. "Part-time" meant that the minister had another occupation, served more than one church, or both. In 1931, 62.5 percent of the rural ministers engaged in other occupations and this

declined to 55.9 percent in the 1959 restudy sample. About 51 percent of the ministers in the total 1959 sample held other jobs. About one-third of these "working" pastors were operatives in mills or mines or were craftsmen, 15 percent were farmers, 16 percent school teachers, 10 percent salesmen and clerical workers, while 10 percent attended school as students. Nearly half of the 1931 pastors served four or more churches and this was 56.0 percent for the 1959 restudy sample. In rural areas, less than one in ten ministers served one church on a resident full-time basis in 1959. The majority of pastors either followed other occupations, served more than one church or both. This, in spite of the fact that two-thirds of the respondents of the AS sample believed that a minister should give full-time to church work.

It would be expected that ministers with the above characteristics would have a low level of formal education. This was indeed the case, although there have been phenomenal improvements in this regard during the past three decades. In 1931, more than eight out of ten rural ministers had less than a college education, and this had been reduced to 48.3 percent by 1959 in the rural restudy counties. Only 43.8 percent of all ministers in 1959 had less than a college education. In the first period, 8.3 percent of the pastors had some or full college training and this nearly trebled by 1959. A greater and more hopeful change may be seen in those with seminary training. A third of the ministers in 1959 claimed seminary training, in contrast to less than one-tenth in 1931. One-half of the rural AS respondents thought that the educational attainments of ministers made no difference or that high school training was sufficient, while a majority of the metropolitan respondents desired full seminary education for their pastors. Yet, four out of ten ministers serving in the Region actually had high school training or less (18.0 percent of these had completed less than eight grades). Under these circumstances, it should not be surprising that religious leadership and motivation in the past have played a minor part in the push for greater educational opportunities. For example, in spite of this low educational level, nearly two-thirds of the 240 ministers reported they had not attended in-service training programs for self-improvement during the preceding year.

Of 70 ministers selected for more detailed interviews, 14.3 percent were not ordained, 47.2 percent had been ordained between the ages of 20 and 30 years, 21.4 percent in their thirties, and 17.1 percent after 40 years of age. Rural ministers were ordained at a much later age than urban pastors.

Salaries received by ministers in 1931 and 1959 were computed in different ways and are not directly comparable. In 1931, the salary included all the income received from churches plus $200 if a rent-free home was provided. In 1959, the salary was the amount paid by the church to the pastor and no amount was added for rent-free homes. Of course, salaries would be somewhat larger for the pastors (52.1 percent) who were furnished homes and for those (48.0 percent) who served more than one church.

There has been a slight increase in the number of churches which provide the minister with no salary, pointing to the persistence of the sectarian conception of the ministry. Half of the churches paid less than $400 to their ministers in 1931 and this median salary increased only to $464 in the 1959 rural restudy sample but was nearly doubled for the total sample ($750). Almost a third (32.1 percent) of the churches in the 1959 study paid their ministers $1,500 or more. The metropolitan churches made a big difference here. In 1959, 7.9 percent of the metropolitan ministers received over $5,000 in salary and half of all metropolitan churches paid $3,687 or more to their pastors.

If a $3,000 salary, plus a rent-free home, may be considered a bare minimum wage, four-fifths of the ministers in the total area received less than this in 1959. Of course, these extremely low incomes were partially offset by the fact that the majority of the ministers worked at other occupations. Improvements in this situation are likely to be slow. More than a third of the AS respondents did not believe that the church should raise money to support the minister, although 88.0 percent of them felt that he should be paid for preaching. This apparent contradiction seems to be another consequence of shifts from a sectarian to a denominational type of religious organization.

The ideas of the proper role of a minister held by AS respondents were in keeping with a sectarian, dissenting tradition. Half said that visiting the sick was the pastor's most important job; about a third voted for preaching. The priestly role (5.8 percent), teacher role (3.5 percent), administrator role (1.0 percent), and community leadership role (0.3 percent) scored low in the estimates. Nearly two-thirds of the AS respondents said that a call to preach was more important for the minister than training, while more than a third thought that he should preach largely from inspiration rather than prepare his sermons.

Clerical and lay leaders have been in their present leadership positions on an average of 5.2 years, although half of them had held office two years or less, and 7.3 percent had been on the job 20 years or more. Metropolitan leaders had a turnover rate almost twice as rapid as those in rural areas. Youth leaders had the shortest and board chairmen the longest tenure. In rural areas, 47.2 percent of the board chairmen and 16.7 percent of the superintendents had held office ten years or more.

More than a half (57.0 percent) of the leaders had attended no in-service training sessions in the previous year to improve their leadership skills. A third of the ministers, over half of the women leaders, and around two-thirds of the other leaders did not participate in training enterprises during the preceding year. Except for the ministers, metropolitan churchmen showed a much better record than nonmetropolitan leaders. The greatest contrast was between city and country Sunday school superintendents. More than three-fourths of the metropolitan superintendents and less than a quarter of those in nonmetropolitan areas had attended a training session during the preceding year. The church leaders who had held their jobs longest and trained least for them were laymen in key positions, such as board chairmen. Four out of ten church leaders had done no reading connected with their work during the previous year. More ministers than laymen and twice as many rural pastors as urban had done some such readings. Among the laymen, the rural board chairmen did least reading and the urban women leaders most. The Sunday school superintendents read more books than other lay leaders and attended more training schools.

Clerical and lay leaders were asked the main reason why they gave time to church work. A somewhat vague "sense of Christian duty" theme was dominant, being claimed as the main reason by around a fourth of the leaders. Other reasons were: "It helps me" (13.1 percent), "For the love or worship of God" (10.0 percent), "It leads others to God" and "It helps others" (4.9 percent each). A third of the ministers were motivated by the "will or call of God," while 38.0 percent of youth leaders stressed the "helps me" theme.

In general, religious leadership in the Region was built on a low level of general education and left much to be desired in terms of current reading and in-service training. As long as four out of ten key church leaders read no books or pamphlets dealing with their church work during an entire year and nearly six out of ten attend no training enterprises to improve themselves in the performance of their church roles, serious questions should be raised about the adequacy of church leadership in the Region.

Missionary and Philanthropic Enterprises

The Southern Appalachian Region has historically been considered home mission territory by major na-

Table 52. *Missionary and Philanthropic Enterprises, Southern Appalachian Region, 1931 and 1959*

Denomination or agency	1959	1931	Reported closed
Adventist bodies	40	8	2
Baptist bodies	121	15	19
Brethren bodies	8	2	1
Church of God bodies	8	-	1
Pentecostal and Holiness bodies	5	1	-
Lutheran bodies	8	3	-
Methodist bodies	89	34	7
Presbyterian bodies	78	68	24
Roman Catholic	98	1	-
Other denominations[a]	39	36	15
Miscellaneous bodies[b]	11	5	1
Other agencies[c]	72	50	13
Total	577	223	83

[a]Disciples of Christ (International), Evangelical United Brethren, Congregational Christian, Protestant Episcopal.
[b]Independent Christian Churches, Society of Friends, Christian and Missionary Alliance, Reformed Church in America.
[c]Independent and nondenominational (Frontier Nursing Service, Y. M. C. A., etc.).

tional denominations and other philanthropic agencies. Missionary enterprises, in addition to churches and Sunday schools, have included schools, rural settlements, health work, handicrafts and farming, orphanages, and other efforts to meet human needs.

In the 1931 study, 223 missionary and philanthropic enterprises were reported by 26 denominations and other agencies (Table 52). There was evidence that 83 of these enterprises had been closed, consolidated, or relocated by 1959. Yet, 577 missionary and philanthropic enterprises, sponsored by 34 agencies, were recorded in 1959. It is not clear whether this large increase in the number of activities represented actual changes in missionary enterprises, differences in methods of collecting the data, shifts in the definition of missionary enterprises, or some combination of these. The Roman Catholic Church increased its missionary units from one to 98, while those of the Southern Baptists increased from 13 to 117. Several of the smaller denominations reported missionary enterprises in 1959 but not in 1931.

An analysis of returns from a questionnaire mailed to the heads of local enterprises indicated growth in the number of mission churches or parishes and of mission workers and a decline in secondary schools and academies. Medical clinics and hospitals increased in number, as did homes for children and the aged. Informal visits and interviews covered 25 enterprises sponsored by various religious and nondenominational groups. They were scattered over the Region and included community centers, orphanages, settlement houses, colleges, mission parishes, schools and academies, and hospitals.

There continue to be new enterprises started, old ones closed, and changes made in services. This is a dynamic, if unstable, field of operations. Most elementary and secondary school services have been taken over by the public school system. The major exception is the increase in the number of Catholic parochial schools. The church-related colleges are dropping their academies and moving toward four-year college programs with appeals for students from outside, as well as inside, the Region. Certain church groups, including the Roman Catholics and Church of God, have appeared as new sponsors of mission enterprises in the Region during the past generation. The former stress on general education and community-center activities among the missions has shifted to specifically religious services, such as mission parishes, Bible colleges, evangelistic efforts, and ministerial training centers.

Summary and Concluding Remarks

Religion in the Southern Appalachians was built upon a dissenting Protestant tradition and it remains dominantly sectarian and fundamentalist today in attitudes and beliefs, in church practice, and in general orientation toward society. The level of religious knowledge, as measured in this study, was extremely low but it was higher for the Bible than for the local church. Responsible participation in community organizations was low for church leaders and members, and even lower for nonmembers. This raises questions about the adequacy of community organizations as such in the area, as well as the relative lack of participation in community affairs of ministers and lay leaders.

There were more churches, smaller churches, and fewer church members in proportion to the Appalachian population than in the total United States. Yet, total church membership was growing more rapidly in the Southern Appalachians than in the country as a whole, moving closer to the national norm. The majority of the Region's ministers had low levels of education, served more than one church, worked at nonchurch jobs, and received low incomes from the churches. The contrasts between metropolitan and nonmetropolitan churches were marked, with larger church buildings and budgets, better trained leaders, and more liberal attitudes characteristic of the cities. Metropolitan churches were moving toward national ideas and ways more rapidly than were rural churches. Metropolitan areas, as centers of communication and organized social dominance, were serving as agents of change in the Region as elsewhere.

The Southern Appalachian Region has remained a large home mission area for major denominations in America. There has been a retreat from the support of primary and secondary educational enterprises and an increase in the more specifically religious enterprises, such as mission churches and workers. A new surge of promotional work on the part of denominations, both from national and regional headquarters, has accelerated the increase in establishment of new churches in an area of declining population already over-churched with undersized congregations. Substandard leadership and programs may be considered one unfortunate result of this competitive organizational activity. Yet, it is precisely in dominantly sect-type religious groups that interchurch cooperation is least likely to occur.

Religion in the Region, especially in the rural areas, seems to be an integral part of the folk culture, passed from generation to generation by word of mouth. This oral tradition, somewhat scrambled in transmission, appears to be largely independent of professional clergy or formal church life. Such folk traditions usually suffer decay and decline during periods of rapid cultural transition such as the present. In this situation, traditional Christianity seems to be responding in two ways. One is the resurgence of the sect-type interpretation of religion, which is most congenial to the traditions of the Region. It is too early

to predict whether this is a forceful revival of fundamentalism and sectism or the dying gasp of a decaying religious heritage. The other is the fresh, if tentative, thrust of religious bodies with church-type views and liturgical patterns. Obviously, this challenge has relatively little support in the older religious culture of the area. Yet, Appalachian traditions are in transition and it remains to be seen whether or not the liturgical churches can furnish the basis for a new integration of religious values.

At the same time, the "in-between" denomination-type bodies, while making a less aggressive organizing effort and exhibiting slower membership growth, may be ideologically best suited to provide leadership in the present social ferment of the Southern Appalachians. Caught between the revival of sectarianism and the resurgence of liturgical churches, these denomination-type groups, although congenial to the present condition of social change, may well be squeezed out. It is certainly too early to predict whether these churches can maintain their own identity and become the foci of a new religious life in the Region.

The rise to prominence of industrial and labor leaders, doctors and lawyers, planners and engineers, school teachers and social workers does not necessarily involve a shift from a distinctly religious to a secular value center for culture. But in the face of present day characteristics of religion and of other aspects of changing society and culture in the Southern Appalachians, prospects for the emergence of a dominantly secular value orientation should not be dismissed lightly by religious leaders.

Christianity can serve as a viable ordering principle only by providing more and better clerical and lay leadership, equipped with broader religious perspective, fuller cultural understanding, more effective organizational abilities, and greater material resources than in the past.

CHAPTER FOURTEEN

Health

and

Health

Services

C. HORACE HAMILTON

THE HEALTH OF ANY COUNTRY OR ANY major region results from many interacting factors. Some of these are common to all people. Other factors are correlated with variations in the broad cultural characteristics of peoples or with regional and local factors which influence the institutions by which health needs are served.

In the United States, variations in health and health services within regions are often greater than variations between regions. Similarly, in the Southern Appalachians, variations in health and health services within state economic areas, and even within counties and communities, are greater than the variations between areas, counties, or communities.

Mortality statistics, being objective and readily available, are widely used as measures of health, but they provide neither a sensitive nor a complete measure of health levels. Deaths per unit (say 1,000) of population do reflect broad differences in health, serious illnesses, health among the aged, and possibly the cumulative effect of poor sanitation, poor health care, poor housing, poor nutrition, and unhealthy living habits; but within homogeneous cultural groups, mortality rates do not vary greatly and certainly do not measure accurately the variations that exist in minor illnesses which cause much misery. Therefore, the data presented here on mortality rates should be interpreted with due regard to their limitations.

General (or crude) death rates, such as all deaths per 1,000 total population, do not provide a suitable basis for comparing the health of one region with another. An area with a young population will tend to have a low crude death rate even though death rates for specific age groups might be comparatively high. This inadequacy may be approximately corrected by computing a weighted average of specific death rates by age. The age-adjusted death rate is suitable for summarizing the health situation in a single measure. Age-adjusted rates in this study have been computed by the indirect method based on the age-specific death rates of the United States population in 1940 and the age distribution of the counties and state economic areas of the Southern Appalachians in 1940 and 1950.[1]

The age-adjusted mortality rate of the Southern Appalachians in 1950 was about the same as that of the United States as a whole: 8.34 deaths per 1,000 population as compared with 8.40 for the United States.[2] The news of the relatively low mortality rate in the Southern Appalachians may come as a surprise to those who have naively assumed that, because of living conditions in the Southern Appalachians, the death rate and associated health conditions were much worse than those in the rest of the nation. It will not come as a surprise, however, to demographers who have analyzed mortality rates in other situations. For

Table 53. *Age-Adjusted Mortality Rates, Southern Appalachian Region and United States, 1940 and 1950*

Area	Mortality rates		Change 1940-50
	1940	1950	
United States	10.8	8.4	-2.4
Southern Appalachian Region	10.8	8.3	-2.5
Metropolitan areas	11.9	8.6	-3.3
Nonmetropolitan areas	10.5	8.2	-2.3

Source: National Office of Vital Statistics; U. S. Bureau of Census.

example, ever since deaths were first tabulated by residence, it has been found that mortality rates in rural areas of the United States were substantially lower than those in urban areas, and the Southern Appalachian area has a higher percentage of rural population than the nation as a whole. However, it is also well known that death rates are decreasing more rapidly in urban areas than in rural areas. Similarly, our analysis of vital statistics shows that death rates in the metropolitan areas of the Southern Appalachians are falling more rapidly than in the nonmetropolitan areas of the Region. On the other hand, between 1940 and 1950 the death rate in the Southern Appalachians declined a little more than that of the nation, as the data in Table 53 show.

The variations in mortality rates from state to state and from region to region in the United States, and among the state economic areas and counties of the Southern Appalachians are not as great as might be expected, considering the variation in social and economic conditions among these residential units. Of the total individual variance in age-adjusted mortality in the Southern Appalachians only 0.38 percent was associated with state economic areas and only 1.02 percent with counties within economic areas. About two-thirds of the counties of the Southern Appalachians have mortality rates within a range of *plus* or *minus* 1.09 deaths per 1,000 of the average of 8.34 for the Region.[3]

If mortality varies little with *space*, it is the more noteworthy that it is decreasing rapidly in *time*. Of the 190 counties and 9 independent cities of the Southern Appalachians, mortality rates decreased between 1940 and 1950 in 173 of the counties and 8 of the cities. No 1940 data were available for one

city, but very likely it too decreased in mortality. The county increases in mortality rates occurred for the most part in counties with very low rates in 1940, and may have been due to either chance fluctuations or underreporting of deaths in 1940. On the other hand, some counties may have been subject to favorable fluctuations or to relative underreporting in 1950. Required reporting of births and deaths may not have been rigidly enforced in some isolated communities. We are sure, at least, that changes in burial customs and in means of communication have improved the reports on deaths as well as on births. In 1940, deaths in such institutions as state hospitals for the feeble-minded and the mentally ill were allocated to counties where the deaths occurred; in 1950 such deaths were allocated, for reporting purposes, back to counties of original residence. This change could have accounted for decreases in mortality reported in seventeen Southern Appalachian counties in which resident institutions are located. The U. S. Public Health Service has no data to show just how much the reallocation affected death rates in these counties.

Heart disease is the prime "killer" in the Southern Appalachians, as it is in the nation. During the three-year period 1954-1956, 34.2 percent of the total number of deaths in the Region were attributed to heart disease as a primary cause, whereas the nation's percentage was 38.5. The lower percentage in the Appalachian Region was due in part to the higher percentage of children in the area. Cancer was the second most prevalent cause of death in the Southern Appalachians, where it was accountable for 13.5 percent of the Region's deaths as compared with the nation's percentage of 15.3. The nation's combined rate for these two diseases was 54.3 percent, over half of the total mortality, while the combined percent for heart disease and cancer in the Region was 47.7, a differential 6.6 percent lower than the nation's rate.

This was counterbalanced by relatively higher regional death rates in other diseases. These diseases included among others influenza and pneumonia, parasitic diseases, and cardiovascular renal diseases (other than heart disease). The regional rate for

[1] Forrest E. Linder and Robert D. Grove, *Vital Statistic Rates in the United States, 1900-1940*, U.S. Dept. of Commerce, Bureau of the Census (1943), 69-71.

[2] Statistics used in this chapter are derived from detailed tabulations in *Health and Health Services in the Southern Appalachians*, North Carolina Agricultural Experiment Station Progress Report RS-35 (Raleigh, 1959), compiled under the direction of C. Horace Hamilton.

[3] *Ibid.*, Table 1 and Figure 1, pp. 1-8.

fatal accidents, including automobile accidents, was higher than in the nation. The mortality rate from diseases of early childhood in the Region exceeded that of the nation. Although the death rate from tuberculosis was decreasing, the regional rate was still

Table 54. *Percentage of Births Occurring in Hospitals and Attended by Midwives, Southern Appalachian Region by States, 1940 and 1956*

Area	In hospital		By midwife	
	1940	1956	1940	1956
Alabama	4.5	86.2	12.0	3.3
Georgia	24.7	94.7	17.4	2.8
Kentucky	5.7	78.5	35.0	10.2
North Carolina	23.9	93.5	20.0	2.1
Tennessee	26.1	92.6	8.9	1.8
Virginia	19.7	89.5	12.6	2.9
West Virginia	17.7	89.5	3.2	1.7
The region	17.9	89.4	14.3	3.2

Source: Vital Statistics of the United States.

50 percent higher than the nation's. The highest regional tuberculosis rates were in Kentucky and Tennessee, the lowest in southwestern North Carolina.

The perinatal mortality rate, based upon the ratio of foetal deaths (stillbirths) plus deaths of infants under 28 days of age, to all births, alive or dead, is considered a more sensitive indicator of the health situation in reproduction than is the infant mortality rate. During the period 1954-1956 the perinatal mortality rate in the Region, 36.7 per 1,000 births, was but slightly higher than the 35.4 in the nation. There is noticeable variation in the perinatal mortality rate within the Southern Appalachian Region. In ten counties the perinatal rate exceeds 50.0 per 1,000 births, while in nine counties the rate is less than 25.0. Counties with very high perinatal mortality are widely scattered over the Region.

The percentage of infants weighing less than 2,500 grams (about 5.5 pounds) is a good index of prematurity and hence of health in early infancy. It was found that 7.7 percent of all births in the Region weighed less than 2,500 grams, the corresponding national percentage being 7.2.

Since 1940, a revolution has occurred in the Southern Appalachians in the care of infants and mothers at childbirth (see Table 54). Between 1940 and 1955 the percentage of infants delivered by physicians in hospitals increased from 17.9 to 89.4; and during the same period the percentage of infants delivered by midwives decreased from 14.3 to 3.2. In the nation, in 1954-1956, 95.4 percent of all infants were delivered in hospitals and 2.9 percent were

delivered by midwives. Midwifery is still a frequent practice in many counties of eastern Kentucky, particularly in areas served by the Frontier Nursing Service, which incidentally has had noteworthy success in reducing infant and maternal mortality. The fourteen counties with highest percentages of midwife deliveries (above 15 percent) are located in eastern Kentucky. In six Kentucky mountain counties the percentage of deliveries by midwives runs over 25 percent: Lee, Lewis, Magoffin, Owsley, McCreary, and Martin. But even in these counties conditions are changing rapidly.

In the field study of 1,466 sample households, conducted by the Southern Appalachian Studies in their area, questions were asked concerning sickness and attitudes toward treatment of the family when ill.

More than half of these people considered themselves "more fortunate than the average" with respect to illness, accident, and death, but rural people seemed less optimistic about their health than did urban people.

Only one respondent out of 20 reported worrying "a great deal" about his health, but more women than men, and more rural than urban and metropolitan women "worry some" about their health. Worrying about one's health may be a symptom of emotional disturbance. It may also reflect feelings of insecurity and of inability to obtain and pay for medical and hospital services. Cancer is more feared by women than by men, and more by urban than by either rural or metropolitan women. Few worry about circulatory diseases which, on the whole, cause more deaths than cancer.

Male respondents indicated a high frequency of diseases of the respiratory system, the highest percentage, 33.5, being reported by rural males. On the other hand, female respondents in all groups reported more infectious and parasitic diseases than did men.

Housing Conditions

Although housing conditions and the availability of certain home facilities are considered to be related to health, high significant correlations between these factors and health indices cannot be found on a county unit basis. Such correlations might show up if it were possible to get accurate data on an individual basis, and also if it were possible to hold various other factors constant. At least, certain housing characteristics make it possible for families to maintain sanitary living conditions conducive to good health.

The national housing census provides some informa-

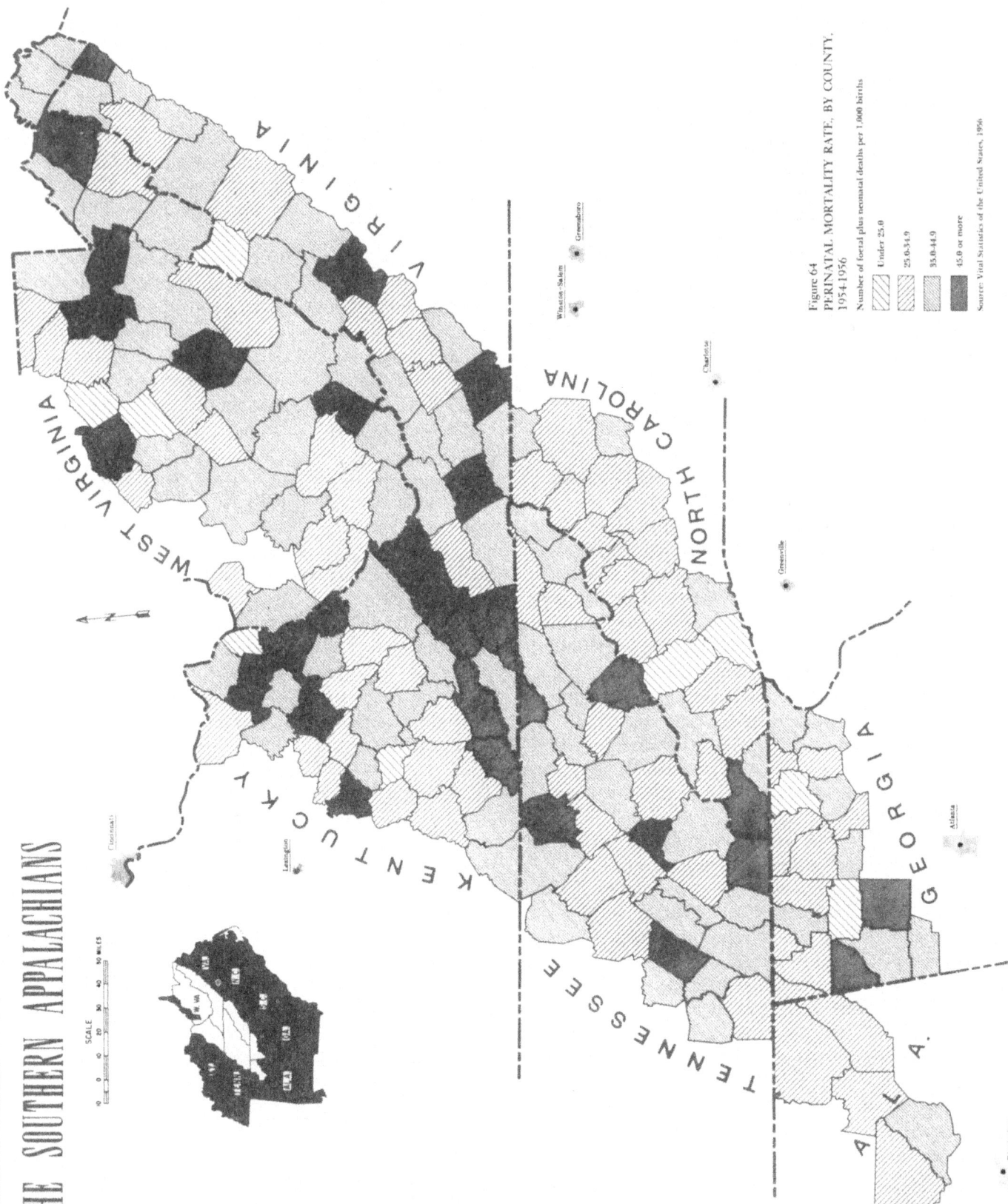

THE SOUTHERN APPALACHIANS

Figure 64
PERINATAL MORTALITY RATE, BY COUNTY,
1954-1956

Number of foetal plus neonatal deaths per 1,000 births

Under 25.0

25.0-34.9

35.0-44.9

45.0 or more

Source: Vital Statistics of the United States, 1956

tion on undesirable living factors. Particularly useful are the statistics on the condition of the house (dilapidated or not dilapidated) and on the adequacy of plumbing facilities, such as flush toilet, running water indoors, hot running water, and bath. Whether

Table 55. *Percentages of Homes Rated as Dilapidated and Lacking Plumbing, Southern Appalachian Region, 1950*

Condition	Metropolitan	Nonmetropolitan	Farm	SAR total
Dilapidated and lacking hot water, private toilet, and bath	11.8	19.8	24.4	17.8
With no piped running water	16.8	46.7	68.6	39.3
With no toilet or privy	1.4	4.3	6.9	3.6
With no kitchen sink	18.9	46.2	63.6	39.2

Source: U. S. Census of Population, 1950.

the house is dilapidated, or inadequately plumbed, or both, it is rated as substandard. Of course it is harder for rural-farm people to provide adequate plumbing utilities, whether they live in Iowa or Georgia, than it is for city residents. The percentage of dilapidated houses and inadequate plumbing facilities is highest in the rural-farm areas in the Southern Appalachians as well as in the nation.[4]

The most recent general statistics available, at this writing, on housing and home facilities by counties are found in the 1950 United States Housing Census.

The percentages of Southern Appalachian homes which were "dilapidated" and which lacked certain modern facilities in 1950 are shown in Table 55.

The housing conditions and facilities in the mountains compare somewhat unfavorably with corresponding conditions in other major regions of the United States (Figure 65). For example, in the United States in 1950, it was found that 8.3 percent of all homes were dilapidated and lacked hot water, private toilet and bath, 8.5 percent did not have running water, 2.1 percent did not have a toilet or privy, and 14.9 percent did not have a kitchen sink. Among the rural farm homes of the nation in 1950, 19.1 percent were dilapidated, 54.6 percent did not have running water, 6.4 percent had no toilet or privy, and 45.2 percent did not have a kitchen sink.

Hospital Services

American medical and health services, public and private, have become highly organized and specialized. Evidence of this is seen in the rapid growth of hospitals and of health personnel, in the increasing expenditures for health services of all kinds, and in the statistics showing use of hospitals, physicians, drugs, and public health services. The general trend in the institutionalization of health services may be seen to some extent in the Southern Appalachians, but many mountain counties do not have hospitals and many others have very small ones.

In 1957 there were 299 hospitals of all types in the 190 counties of the Southern Appalachians. Of these, 125 were established before 1930; 69 from 1930 to 1944; 39 from 1945 to 1949; and 66, or about 22 percent, since 1950. There is a significant relationship between year of establishment and type of control. Of the 125 hospitals established before 1930, 48 are "proprietary," owned and operated by private individuals or corporations; but of the 105 hospitals established since 1945, only 21 are privately controlled.

The most common type of hospital control in the region is the "voluntary nonprofit" type represented by 126 hospitals under the control of nonprofit hospital associations and religious organizations. The second most frequent type of control is "proprietary," 103 hospitals privately owned and operated. This is a much higher percentage than in the nation, for there is a strong trend away from private hospitals in this country. Seventy of the 299 hospitals are controlled by governments: 10 by federal and 60 by state and local governments. One out of every three hospitals in the region established since 1950 is owned and operated by a state or local government agency. This type of control makes it possible to use public funds both for construction and for operation. Public funds are also frequently used for the construction and operation of voluntary nonprofit hospitals—particularly for the medically indigent.

The most common type of hospital is the general short-stay hospital, which provides care for acute illnesses. This is the type of hospital with which the public is best acquainted—and most of our attention will be devoted to it. In addition to the 241 general short-stay hospitals in the region there are 18 short-stay hospitals limited to psychiatric services, tuberculosis, maternity, eye-ear-nose-throat, children, orthopedics, or other specialties. Four short-stay hospitals are actually departments of institutions.

Of the 40 long-stay hospitals, 31 provide service for psychiatric and tuberculosis patients, 4 are general

[4] U.S. Dept. of Commerce, Bureau of the Census, *1956 National Housing Inventory*, I, Part 1, 5-6; Donald J. Bogue, *The Population of the United States* (Glencoe, Illinois, 1959), 718-21.

hospitals under the control of the Veteran's Administration, and the remaining 5 care for orthopedic cases and other types of service for the chronically ill.[5]

Psychiatric and tuberculosis hospitals have about one-half of the beds and provide much more than

Figure 65. *Percentage of Homes Lacking Specified Facilities, Southern Appalachian Region and the United States, 1950*

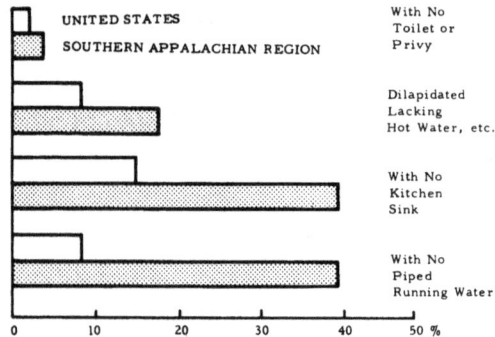

Source: U. S. Census of Population, 1950

half of all days of hospital care. The average length of stay in the 18 psychiatric hospitals is 500 days as compared with 179 days in the tuberculosis hospitals and 123 days in chronic and convalescent hospitals.

In 1957, the 241 general short-stay hospitals of the Region operated at 75.8 percent capacity, admitted 129.7 patients per 1,000 population, and had an average length of stay of 6.9 days at an average expense of $20 per day. These hospitals provided 894 days of hospital care per 1,000 population. Adequate hospitalization involves from 1200 to 1500 days of hospital care per 1,000 people, depending somewhat on the age level of the population. The federal program of hospital construction assumes a "need" of 4.50 general and allied special hospital beds per 1,000 population. The Southern Appalachian Region had 18,631 short-stay general beds, or 3.23 per 1,000 population, and .24 allied special hospital beds per 1,000 —making a total of only 3.47 per 1,000. Thus, according to nationally set goals, the Region had only 77 percent of the beds needed. Another and perhaps more realistic standard by which to judge the adequacy of hospital beds in the Region is the national average, which in 1957 was 3.86 short-term hospital beds per 1,000 population. Many states, however, exceed this average considerably. Another point to keep in mind here is that the national goal of 4.50 beds per 1,000 population was set in 1946-1947; it is very likely obsolete now because of rising per capita incomes, increased use of hospitals for all kinds of

illnesses, and the very great increase in the aged population.

The shortage of hospitals is apparent from Figure 67. Except in unusual circumstances, a county with 10,000 or more population should have a hospital of 20 or more beds. Fifty-eight counties of the Region do not have hospitals of any kind, and 27 of these counties have populations of more than 10,000. Many other counties have hospitals too small for their needs and poorly equipped. Of the counties without hospitals, 16 were in Kentucky, 12 in West Virginia, 11 in Tennessee, 9 in Virginia, 7 in Georgia, and 3 in North Carolina.

The 241 general short-stay hospitals of the Region are located in 171 populated centers, as is shown in Table 56.[6] All centers, except one, above 10,000 in population have hospitals; but over half of the centers of 2,500-4,999 in population do not have hospitals. In some of the centers above 50,000 in population, there are so many hospitals that the average size does not rise above 157 beds, though these centers have from 863 to 940 beds per community. These large centers may have more hospitals than are desirable from the standpoint of efficiency and quality of service.

For both quality and convenience of hospital service, the area of a hospital community is crucial. If communities are too large, people will find hospital service expensive and inconvenient; yet hospital communities must be large enough to include a population sufficient to support a large well-equipped hospital. In most parts of the nation population density (people per square mile) controls the size of hospital communities. As population thins out, hospital communities increase in area but decrease in population. Thus, there seems to be a compromise between hospital size and convenience.[7] In mountainous areas, the additional factor of topography tends to make hospital communities small in both square miles and population, though this tendency is somewhat obscured in the Region by the lack of hospitals in many counties. The metropolitan hospital communities of the Region, with 242 people per square mile, contained only 371 square miles, but 98,538 people per hospital community. On the other hand, the nonmetropolitan communities, with only 56.3 people per square mile,

[5] Guide Issue of *Journal of American Hospital Association, 1958.*

[6] Number of centers and population as reported in U.S. 1950 Census of Population, plus Fountain City, Tennessee.

[7] Commission on Hospital Care, *Hospital Care in the United States* (New York: Commonwealth Foundation, 1947), 271-72.

contained 499 square miles, but only 28,134 people per hospital community.

Percentage occupancy of hospital beds is related to size of hospital community, population density, and size of hospital. The mean annual percent of beds

Hospital Association and the American Medical Society. Of the 81 hospitals with 75 beds or more, all except 4 were accredited; of the 83 hospitals with less than 40 beds, only 5 were accredited; and of the 77 hospitals having 40-74 beds, 45 were accredited.

Table 56. *General Short-Stay Hospitals in the Southern Appalachian Region by Population of Center, 1957*

Population of center	Centers in region	Centers with hospitals	Hospitals	Hospital beds		
				Number	Per hospital	Per community (with a hospital)
Under 1,000	273	29	29	981	34	34
1,000-2,499	287	40	41	1,739	42	43
2,500-4,999	81	36	45	2,402	53	67
5,000-9,999	48	37	52	3,847	74	104
10,000-24,999	17	16	26	2,694	104	168
25,000-49,999	7	7	13	1,636	126	234
50,000-99,999	4	4	23	3,453	150	863
100,000 up	2	2	12	1,879	157	940
All centers	719	171	241	18,631	77	109

Source: Journal of the American Hospital Association, Guide Issue, 1958.

occupied is usually lower in small hospitals than in large hospitals. In the nation as a whole, the normal occupancy rate of a small hospital of about 45 beds is only 56 percent, but about 80 percent for a 300-bed hospital.[8] The average percentage occupancy of short-stay hospitals in the Southern Appalachians was 75.8. However, as Table 57 shows, there is the expected relationship between size of hospital and percentage occupancy. In proportion to expected or normal rates of hospital occupancy most of the hospitals of the Region are overcrowded: 126 general and short-stay special hospitals experienced occupancy rates in 1957 of 10 percent or more above normal standards. Strangely enough also, the crowding (in relation to the normal expected rate) was greatest in the small hospitals. The implication is that small hospitals—located mostly in rural communities—need enlargement more than the large hospitals of urban areas. Some of the areas with small hospitals probably need additional hospitals rather than enlargement of existing ones.

Quality of hospital care, though difficult to measure objectively, is no doubt highly correlated with certain accepted facilities among which the twenty listed in Table 58 were more or less available in the short-stay hospitals of the Region. There is a clear relationship between size of hospital and number of facilities and services offered (Table 57).

In 1957 only 53.9 percent of the Region's general short-stay hospitals were accredited by the Joint Commission on Hospital Accreditation of the American

There seems to be little relationship between type of control and accreditation, if size of hospital remains constant. Over 50 percent of the small hospitals are under private control, but it is because of factors associated with size that they are not accredited.

It is surprising that only 7.1 percent of the Region's hospitals are approved for the training of interns. Obviously, large hospitals can give interns broader experience in medical care, but it is somewhat unfortunate that some method cannot be found to give young doctors experience in small hospitals. More and more the training of physicians is being both carried on in and oriented toward large cities. This practice is no doubt one reason why it is so difficult to get well-trained doctors to locate in the small community.

Only 14.1 percent of the hospitals of the Region have either nursing schools or some affiliation with nursing schools. Obviously, it is impractical for small hospitals to conduct nursing schools, but nursing students do need to gain experience in the small hospital. Some of the larger university schools of nursing are now giving their students training in small hospitals.

In 1957 the 241 general short-stay hospitals reported expenses over $115,000,000. This expenditure represents about $154 per admission or $20 per hospital day. These averages are lower than those of voluntary

[8] C. Horace Hamilton, "The Normal Occupancy Rate in the General Hospital," *Hospitals*, September, 1946; *Hospital Care in the United States*, 278-88.

THE SOUTHERN APPALACHIANS

VIRGINIA

WEST VIRGINIA

KENTUCKY

TENNESSEE

NORTH CAROLINA

GEORGIA

A L A.

Figure 66

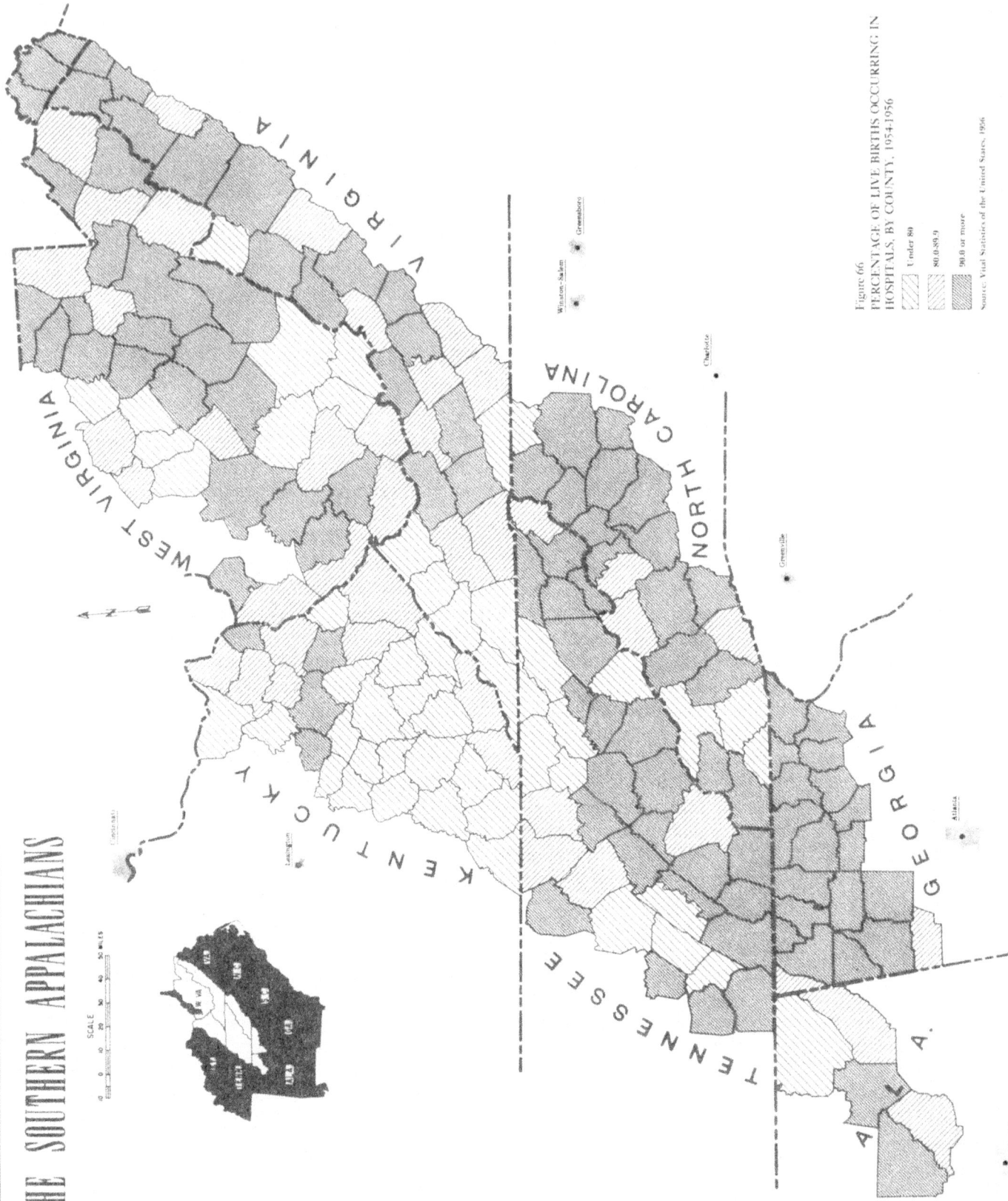

PERCENTAGE OF LIVE BIRTHS OCCURRING IN
HOSPITALS, BY COUNTY, 1954-1956

Under 80

80.0-89.9

90.0 or more

Source: Vital Statistics of the United States, 1956

SCALE
0   10   20   30   40   50 MILES

short-term hospitals in the nation which were about $198 and $25, respectively. Expenses for hospital personnel in the Region amounted to about 54 percent of the total and about $2,400 per hospital employee.

During the period 1948-58, federal aid has been used in the construction of 5,419 general hospital

Table 57. *Percentage Occupancy and Mean Number of Facilities in Short-Stay Hospitals of the Southern Appalachian Region, 1957*

Beds per hospital	Percentage occupancy	Mean number of facilities
Under 40	63.6	11.3
40-74	63.8	12.7
75-124	70.7	14.2
125-199	82.9	17.0
200 up	80.0	18.5
All hospitals	75.8	13.1

Source: Journal of the American Hospital Association, Guide Issue, 1958.

beds, 475 beds for tuberculosis hospitals, 1,259 beds for psychiatric hospitals, 416 beds for chronic patients, and 84 public health centers. Over 1,000 additional new hospital beds have been constructed by the Miners Memorial Hospital Association without federal funds. Possibly a few other beds have been constructed without federal funds. Large areas in eastern Kentucky, southwest Virginia, and southern and eastern West Virginia have constructed very few new hospitals. As of 1958, it was estimated that 7,322 new general short-term hospital beds were needed to bring the Region up to the national standard of 4.5 beds per 1,000 population. Many old hospitals need to be either remodeled or replaced. This would probably involve at least 25 percent of the hospital beds now being used, that is, about four or five thousand beds. More recent and detailed estimates of additional beds needed (both new and replacements) are available in the various Hospital Construction Divisions of the states in the Region.

In the past decade the United Mine Workers of America, by means of their Hospital and Medical Care Fund, supported by a 40 cents per ton levy on coal, have constructed and put into operation a chain of ten hospitals reaching from Beckley, West Virginia, in the northeast to Middlesboro, Kentucky, in the southeast. This 250-mile chain consists of three base or central hospitals located at Beckley and Williamson, West Virginia, and Harlan, Kentucky. These hospitals at the time of their dedication in 1956 had 153 beds at Williamson, 203 at Harlan, and 207 at Beckley. Near Williamson, West Virginia, are two

systems of branch hospitals located at Man, West Virginia, with 87 beds, McDowell and Pikeville, Kentucky, with 62 and 52 beds respectively; and around Harlan are community hospitals at Hazard, Whitesburg, and Middlesboro, Kentucky, and at Wise, Virginia, with 86, 94, 79 and 62 beds respectively.[9]

These hospitals were carefully planned by some of the leading hospital consultants and architects in the nation. They are modern, functional, efficient, well located and equipped to render comprehensive medical care. Altogether the system's hospitals have over 1,000 beds, but they were planned so that they could be expanded to 2,000 beds. Already most of the hospitals are operating to capacity. The system not only operates out-patient departments, nursing schools, and clinics, but also conducts training clinics and seminars for physicians, technicians, and hospital administrators.

The United Mine Workers hospital system represents the application of the principles of both modern business and medical science in the field of health care. Coordination in purchasing and services is similar to that practiced by giant chain stores. Scores of physicians and medical specialists are employed by the hospitals. Although medical services are provided principally for beneficiaries of the United Mine Workers Welfare and Retirement Fund, the general public is also served to the extent that resources permit.[10]

For the year ending June 30, 1958, the Miners Welfare Fund spent $58,135,684.16 for hospital and medical care benefits, provided 1,458,385 days of hospitalization for 85,426 beneficiaries. Medical and surgical services for these hospitalized cases required 1,311,088 visits by physicians. Many additional services, consultations, and outpatient clinics were provided. In 1957 this program of hospitalization and medical care received the Albert Lasker Group Award for outstanding service.[11]

The Medical Profession

The distribution, characteristics, and use of physicians are important measures of the level and quality of health care in any community or region. The 1958 Directory of the American Medical Association lists 4,602 physicians who lived in the Southern Appala-

[9] "UMW's Chain of Ten Hospitals," *Architectural Forum*, CV (November, 1956), 111.

[10] *Arch. Forum*, 112-17.

[11] *Annual Report, June 30, 1958, UMWA Welfare and Retirement Fund*, 8.

THE SOUTHERN APPALACHIANS

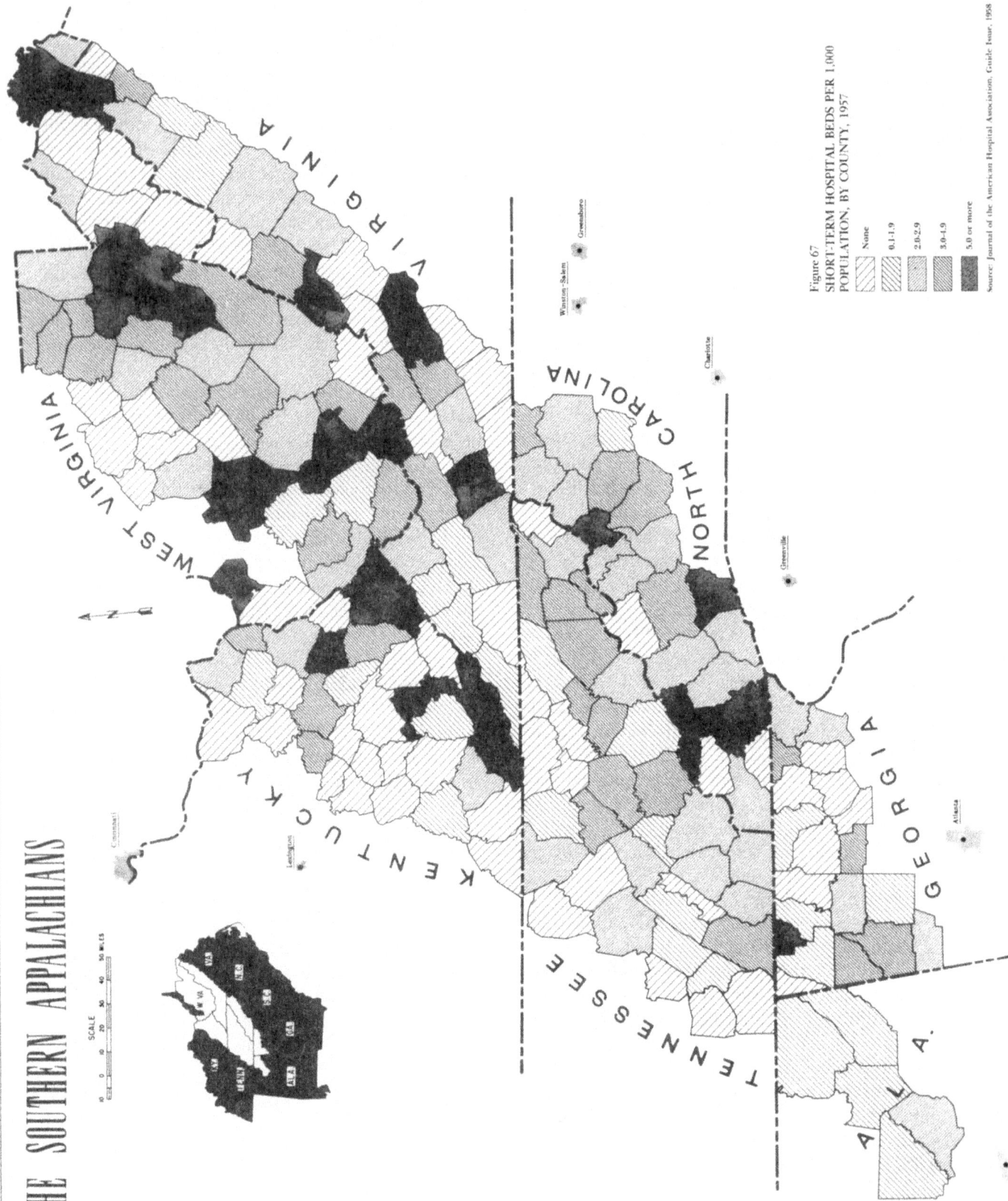

SCALE

10   0   10   20   30   40   50 MILES

N

WEST VIRGINIA

VIRGINIA

KENTUCKY

TENNESSEE

NORTH CAROLINA

GEORGIA

ALA.

Cincinnati

Lexington

Winston-Salem

Greensboro

Charlotte

Greenville

Atlanta

Birmingham

Figure 67

SHORT-TERM HOSPITAL BEDS PER 1,000
POPULATION, BY COUNTY, 1957

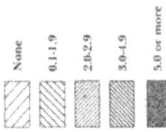

None
0.1-1.9
2.0-2.9
3.0-4.9
5.0 or more

Source: Journal of the American Hospital Association, Guide Issue, 1958

chians in 1957. Only 219 of those listed were either retired or not in active practice. Of the 4,383 physicians in active practice, 3,585 were in private practice on an individual basis, 510 were employed on hospital staffs, 124 were employed in public health, in industry

Table 58. *Services and Facilities of General Short-Stay Hospitals in the Southern Appalachian Region, 1957*

Service or facility	Hospitals offering service	
	Number	Percentage
X-ray diagnostic	239	99.2
Operating room	235	97.5
Obstetrical delivery room	235	97.5
Basal metabolism apparatus	227	94.2
Clinical laboratory	225	93.4
Electrocardiograph	223	92.5
Medical records department	217	90.0
Blue Cross affiliation	215	89.2
Emergency room	213	88.4
Member American Hospital Association	192	79.7
Central sterile supply room	186	77.2
Medical staff library	157	65.1
Outpatient department	149	61.8
Accredited by Joint Commission	130	53.9
Blood bank	130	53.9
Premature nursery	112	46.5
Pharmacy	96	39.8
X-ray, chest, routine on admission	79	32.8
Physical therapy department	76	31.5
Postoperative recovery room	72	29.9
Hospital auxiliary	70	29.0
X-ray therapeutic	67	27.8
Dental department	40	16.6
Nursing school	34	14.1
Radioactive isotope therapy department	24	10.0
Social service department	20	8.3
Electroencephalograph	18	7.5
Approved for internship	17	7.1
Occupational therapy department	13	5.4

Source: Journal of the American Hospital Association, Guide Issue, 1958.

and by insurance companies, 57 were hospital interns, 65 were resident physicians in hospitals, eight were in medical schools, four were in medical administration, and six were in medical research.

The ratio of population to active physicians in the Region was 1,315 people per physician in 1957—1,583 in the nonmetropolitan areas and 870 in the metropolitan areas. However, if all physicians not in private, individual partnership, or group practice are excluded, there were 1,609 people per physician—1,824 in nonmetropolitan and 1,185 in metropolitan areas. In the nation in 1957, according to the American Medical Directory, there were about 803 people per physician.

Figure 70 shows the ratios of population to physicians in the counties of the Southern Appalachians.

Two counties (Dawson, Georgia, and Union, Tennessee) had no active physicians listed, and fourteen counties had only one physician each.

In terms of population per physician, the 190 counties of the Region were distributed as shown in Table 59. In the favored A-group of counties (40.0 percent) there were less than 2,000 people per physician. In the B-group of counties (31.1 percent) there were doubtless many communities with 2,000 to 3,000 people who needed extra physicians. Group C consisted of 28.9 percent of the counties whose resident physician services ranged from none at all to one physician for every 3,000 people. The need for additional physicians in any particular county or community cannot be precisely determined on the basis of county data. For example, a few of the counties in the C-group, like Union and Sevier in Tennessee and Walker in Georgia, are adjacent to metropolitan counties which may have enough doctors to serve them adequately. The county data, however, serve to point out areas which should be more intensively studied by state and local agencies concerned with health services.

It was expected that many small villages under 500 in population would not have resident physicians— and such was the case: 99 populated centers under 500 in population did not have any physicians. On the other hand, 205 physicians were found in 148 villages of comparable size. Although some small centers without physicians may be near larger centers with physicians, it is quite likely that a real shortage of physicians exists in the areas served by many of the towns and villages without physicians. Especially suspect are those places (125 in number) with more than 1,000 population. Surely many of these places need a resident general physician badly. There are 282 centers with only one physician and 52 of these centers are over 1,000 in population.

An illustration of the problem of an insufficient number of physicians is Elliott County, Kentucky. This county, with a population of 6,100, has only one doctor, who lives in Sandy Hook, the county seat, which has a population of about 500. This doctor is greatly overworked. Being the only doctor for miles around, he finds it necessary to work evenings as well as Saturdays and Sundays. He has no time for vacations and has little time to spend with his family. He cares for about 40 calls a day on the average, or more than 14,000 calls a year. Most of these calls are in his office in crowded quarters over a store. He makes home calls only when necessary, and this is

THE SOUTHERN APPALACHIANS

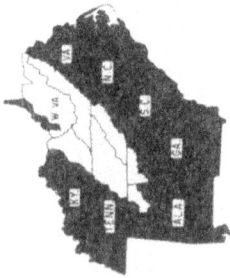

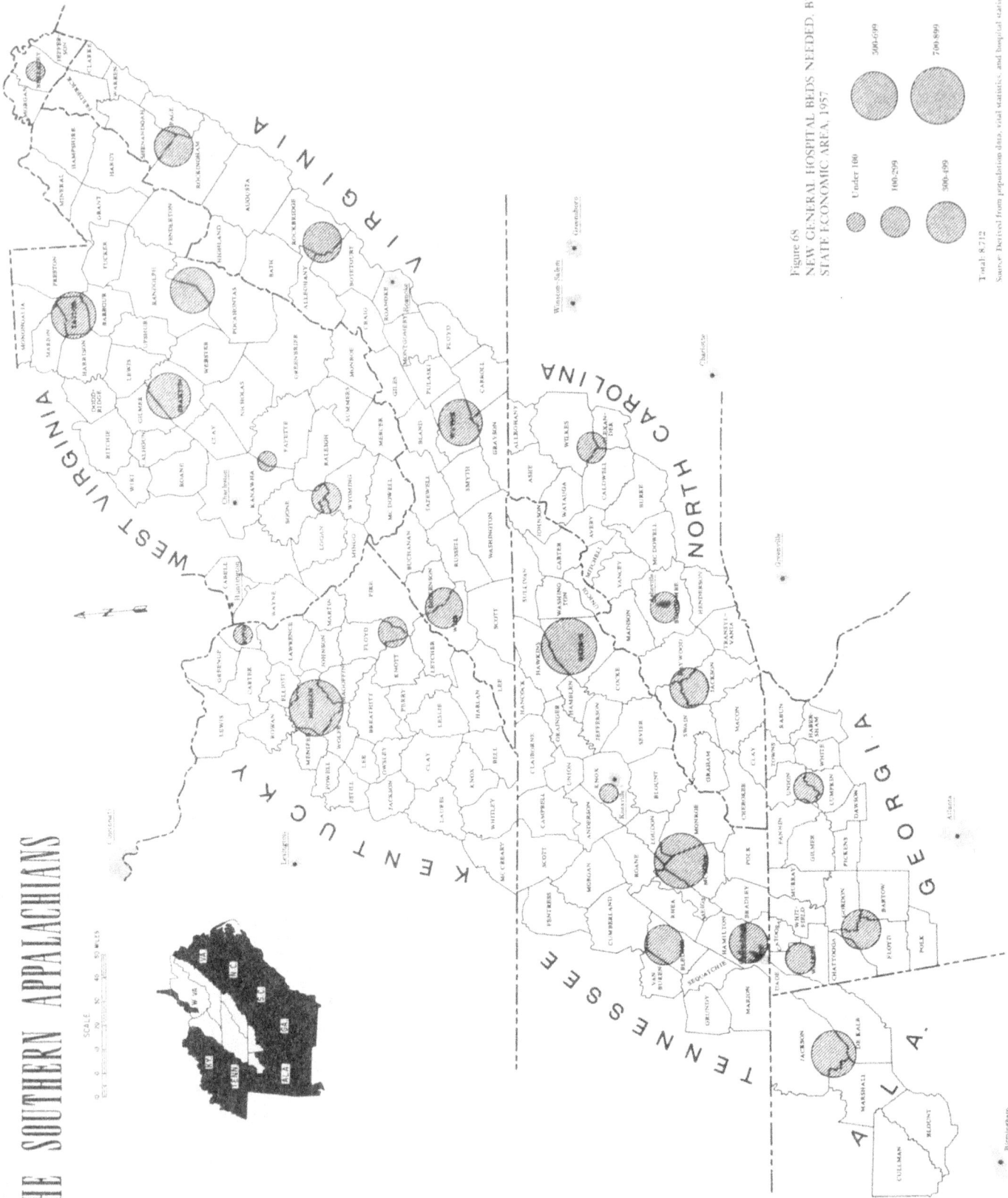

Figure 68
NEW GENERAL HOSPITAL BEDS NEEDED, BY
STATE ECONOMIC AREA, 1957

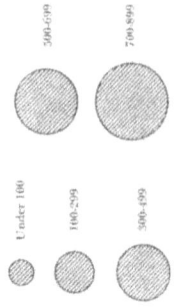

Total: 8,212

Source: Derived from population data, vital statistics, and hospital statistics

about two or three times a day. He does not handle many obstetrical cases because of the time required and because there is no hospital in the county. As a consequence of this situation, many Elliott County people go to centers outside the county for medical

Table 59. *Distribution of Southern Appalachian Counties by Population per Active Physician, 1957*

Population per active physician	Number of counties	Percent of all counties
Group A		
500-999	8	4.2
1,000-1,999	68	35.8
	76	40.0
Group B		
2,000-2,999	59	31.1
Group C		
3,000-3,999	22	11.6
4,000-4,999	10	5.3
5,000-6,999	12	6.3
7,000-9,999	4	2.1
10,000 up[a]	7	3.7
	55	29.0

Source: Directory of the American Medical Association, 1958.

[a]Includes 2 counties with no physicians.

service. Eighty-six percent of Elliott County babies are born in the hospitals of nearby counties.

The shortage of physicians in the small towns of the Region may become worse as the older physicians retire or die. Among the physicians living in villages under 500 in population, 50 percent were above 56.7 years of age and 39 percent were 65 or more years of age. As centers increase in size, the median age of physicians decreases. The youngest doctors were found in cities with 100,000 or more in population, where the median age was only 43.2 years, and only 12.7 percent were 65 or more years of age. Twenty-four percent of the physicians in these large cities were under 35 years of age.

Of the 4,602 Southern Appalachian physicians listed in the 1958 Directory of the American Medical Association, 350 (or 7.6 percent) were 75 or more years of age and 868 (or 18.9 percent) were 65 or more years of age. The median age of all physicians in the Region was 46.2, and 18.8 percent were under 35 years of age. In the nation, the median age of nonfederal physicians was 44.9 years, 21 percent were under 35, and 14 percent were 65 and over.

Among the active physicians in general practice, both the young and the old were overrepresented. Hospital staff members were relatively young, with only 7.5 percent over 65 years of age. Full-time specialists were also relatively young, with only 10.2 percent above 65. Public health physicians and part-

time specialists were relatively old with about 16 percent above 65. And, of course, interns and residents were very young, most of them being under 35 years of age.

A minority of the active physicians were listed as being in general practice. Of the 4,383 active physicians, only 38.7 percent were in general practice while 31.2 percent were full-time specialists; 12.4 percent were part-time specialists; and 11.6 percent were employed by hospitals. For example, the ten hospitals owned and operated by the Miners Welfare Fund employ a considerable number of physicians. By way of comparison, the physicians of the nation as a whole were distributed as follows: general practice, 30.0 percent; full-time specialty, 34.0 percent; part-time specialty, 9.6 percent; employed by hospitals, 7.8 percent (see Figure 72).

Full-time medical specialists are highly concentrated in metropolitan centers. Of the 1,789 metropolitan physicians, 45.6 percent were full-time and 9 percent were part-time specialists; whereas, only 20.2 and 13.5 percent of the 2,873 nonmetropolitan doctors were classified as full-time or part-time specialists respectively (see Figure 73).

Of the 2,395 full-time and part-time specialists, 25.0 percent were in surgery, 16.0 percent in internal medicine, 11.2 percent in obstetrics and gynecology, 7.9 percent in pediatrics, 7.1 percent in otolaryngology, 4.6 percent in radiology and roentgenology, 2.5 percent in ophthalmology, and the remainder were scattered in some 15 other specialties. The corresponding percentages for the nation were: surgery, 28.0; internal medicine, 18.0; obstetrics and gynecology, 13.0; pediatrics, 9.3; otolaryngology, 6.6 percent; radiology and roentgenology, 4.8 percent; and ophthalmology, 4.3 percent.

A measure of quality of specialists' services is certification by one of the national specialty boards. It is not easy to secure certification, for a certain amount of successful experience is required and other strict requirements must be satisfied. Of the 2,395 full-time and part-time specialists in this Region, only 889 or 37.1 percent have been certified by national specialty boards.[12] The corresponding percentage for the nation was 57.2; and 59.8 for the non-Appalachian parts of the seven Southern Appalachian states.

It is most interesting to note that 2,546 or 55.3 percent of the physicians of the region received their medical degrees from schools and colleges located in

[12] *Directory of the American Medical Association*, 1958.

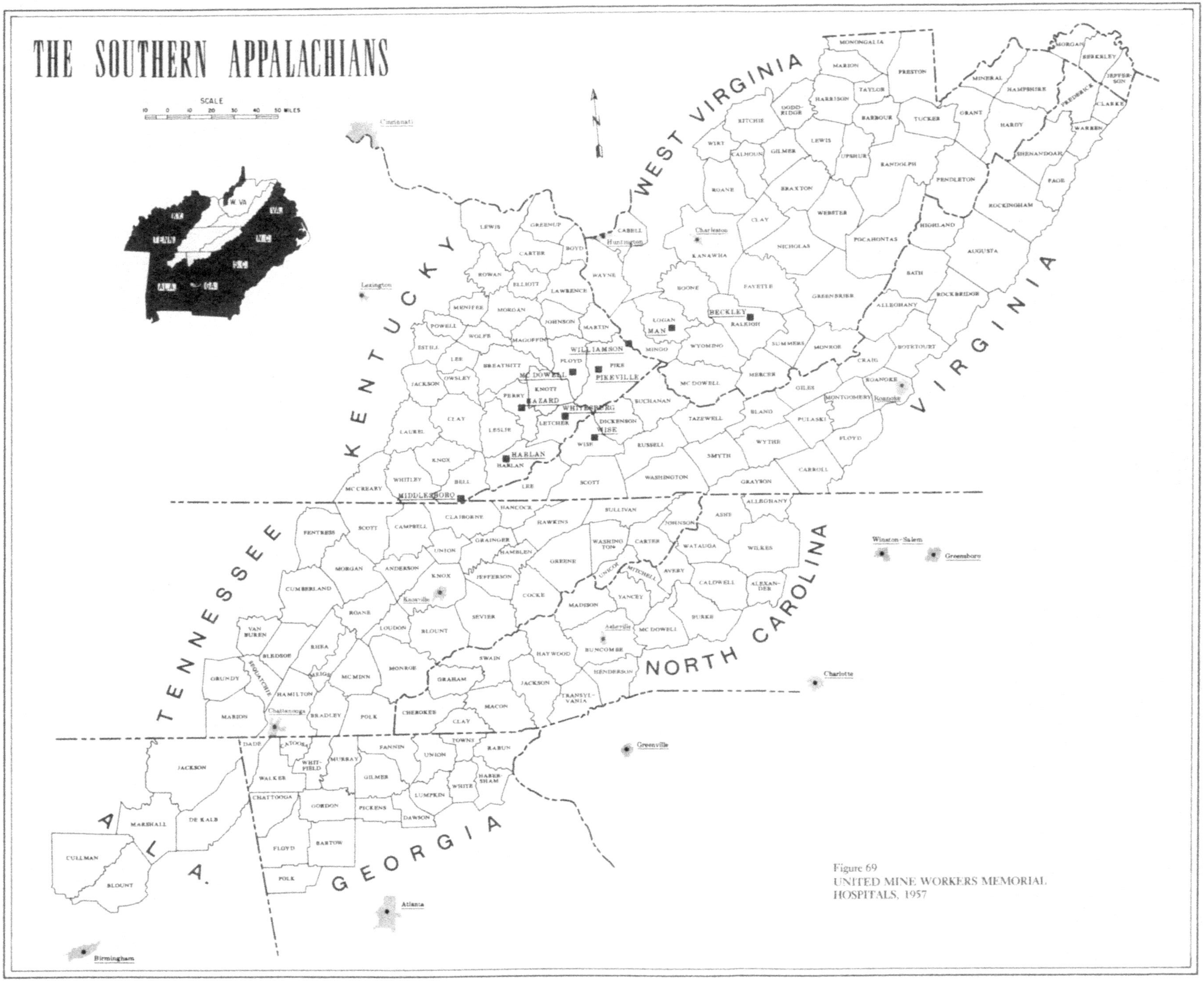

THE SOUTHERN APPALACHIANS

Figure 69
UNITED MINE WORKERS MEMORIAL
HOSPITALS, 1957

the states that include some Appalachian counties. However, certain other well-known medical schools not far removed from the Appalachians have trained a large number of doctors practicing in the Region.

The application of 10-year survival expectancy rates to the present complement of physicians in the

Table 60. *Counties with Only One Active Physician in Private Practice, Southern Appalachian Region, 1957*

State and county	Population
Kentucky	
Elliott	6,100
Jackson	12,500
Menifee	3,900
Owsley	6,400
Powell	7,100
Martin	12,300
North Carolina	
Clay	5,900
Tennessee	
Fentress	14,200
Grundy	11,600
Van Buren	3,700
Virginia	
Bland	6,400
Craig	3,300
West Virginia	
Calhoun	9,400
Wirt	4,900

Source: Directory of the American Medical Association, 1958.

Southern Appalachians indicates that there are now enough physicians in the area to replace, 10 years hence, the physicians 35 years of age and over. This estimate is based on the assumption that there will be no net gain or loss by migration among the physicians. Unfortunately, we have no information on migration rates and direction of migration among physicians. The chances are that there will be migration losses in some age groups and gains in others.

Obviously, the 867 physicians under 35 in 1957 are insufficient to replace the 1,314 physicians between 35 and 44; but the younger group will be constantly replenished by medical schools and possibly by migration. There is no objective basis for determining whether the under 35 group will be replaced. Ten medical schools located in the seven Southern Appalachian states graduate about 750 M.D.'s each year. If the Region gets its normal quota of the graduates from these schools, the replacement will be more than adequate.

Although there appears to be little danger of a decrease in the number of physicians because of aging, retirement, and death, there is evidence that more physicians are needed to raise the level of medical service to standards already reached in many parts

of the nation. "Need," however, is a relative and flexible concept. It is a concept which cannot be defined in terms of wholly objective measures. It is true, of course, that at any particular time, in a particular culture, and in a given economic situation, there is a fixed quantity of medical services to be performed. But medical practice, health values, and economic conditions are in a state of flux.

Ratios of population to physicians and distribution of physicians by counties and size of center, which have already been presented, indicate that many areas have fewer physicians than are needed to serve the people adequately. The differences observed between counties and populated centers cannot be attributed to differences in the need for medical care. Economic conditions and the physical isolation of some areas have a great deal to do with the uneven distribution of physicians in the Region. Isolated rural areas with low per capita incomes will not attract physicians who have been trained in large modern hospitals in urban communities. Nevertheless, the need for medical service does exist in such areas and, in recent years, medical doctors have found that low income rural people do pay their medical bills with surprising promptness.

How many physicians would be "needed" in the Southern Appalachians to bring the ratio of population to physicians down to that of the nation as a whole? The ratio of population to physicians in the United States as a whole in 1958 was about 803. To achieve this ratio, the Southern Appalachians need about 2,500 additional doctors. Possibly this estimate is somewhat high because large specialized medical centers outside the Southern Appalachians require more physicians than do other areas. On the other hand, if it is assumed that there should be at least one physician for each 1,000 people (a minimum standard recognized by many health planning commissions), then the Southern Appalachians would need about 1,650 additional physicians. It is quite obvious that by either of the above standards many more physicians are needed by the people of the Southern Appalachians. Even if enough physicians were obtained for the Region as a whole, there would still remain the problem of intraregional distribution, which should be studied community by community. In those areas already short of young physicians, replacement will be all too slow.

The number of available physicians is not always an adequate measure of their contribution to the health of a community since the utilization of their

THE SOUTHERN APPALACHIANS

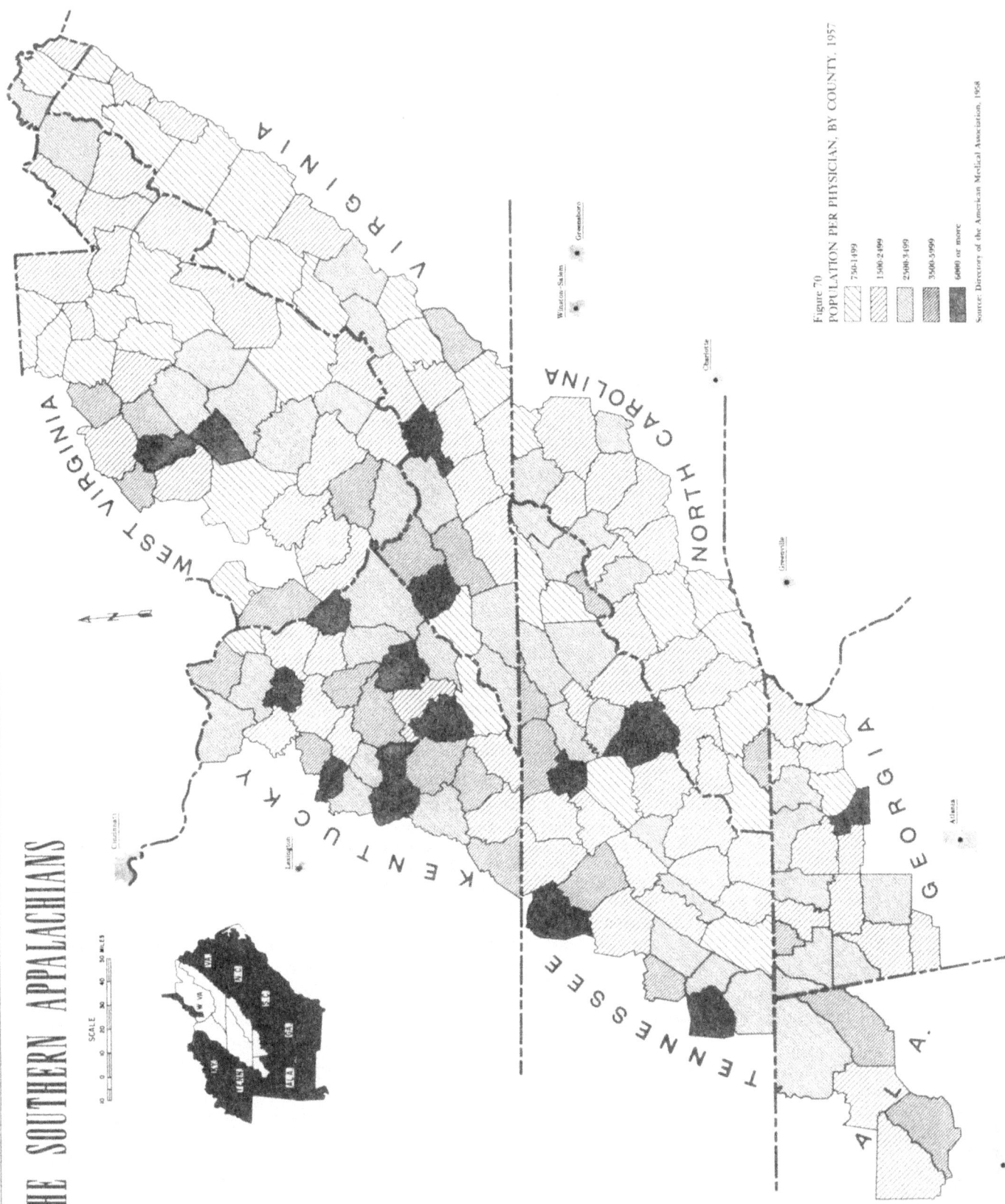

Figure 70
POPULATION PER PHYSICIAN, BY COUNTY, 1957

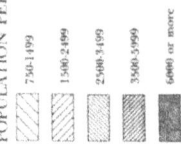

750-1499
1500-2499
2500-3499
3500-5999
6000 or more

Source: Directory of the American Medical Association, 1958

services is influenced by the way in which they are viewed by the people. Obviously, if physician-patient relationships are poor, then to some extent health care will also be poor. If doctors are trusted, if their charges are considered reasonable, if doctors readily

Figure 71. *Median Age of Physicians by Size of Center, Southern Appalachian Region, 1957*

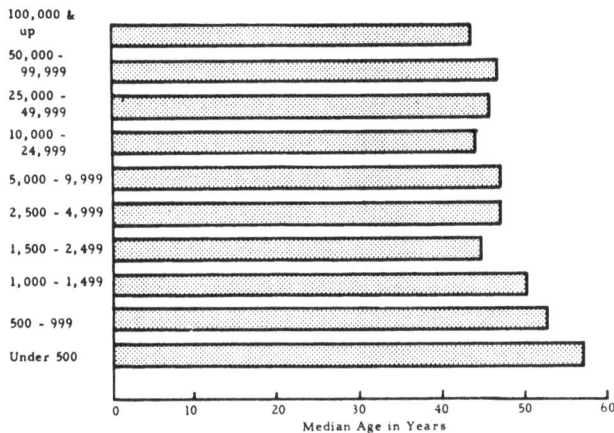

Source: Directory of the American Medical Association, 1958

make calls on patients when needed, and if in other respects the attitudes and relationships between patients and doctors are friendly, then the patients will call the physician when needed and will also cooperate with him in the treatment prescribed. In the field survey, several questions relating to patient-physician relationships were asked. The responses to these questions, in general, reflect rather satisfactory relationships between physicians and patients.

The use of a "family doctor" is considered to be a good practice because it gives the physician an opportunity to learn and make use of family medical history as well as the subtle social and psychological factors involved in illness. In spite of the decline in general practitioners, most families in the Southern Appalachians reported use of a family physician. About 8 of every 10 metropolitan and rural respondents and about 87 percent of urban (nonmetropolitan) respondents reported use of a family physician. Among rural respondents 43.7 percent of the families lived more than 5 miles from the nearest physician; 21.2 percent more than 10 miles; 10.0 percent more than 15 miles; 7.0 percent more than 20 miles; and 3.5 percent lived more than 25 miles. In contrast, over two-thirds of the urban families lived less than one mile, and the remaining less than 5 miles from the nearest physician.

The modern doctor makes few home calls. This

creates problems for those who may be critically ill and live some distance from a doctor. The lack of transportation and communication facilities among poorer families is also a factor. From the doctor's point of view, the choice is one of making the most effective use of his time. He can serve from 10 to 15 patients in his office while making a single trip to an isolated mountain family. To the question: *"Do you have difficulty in getting a doctor to make a call to this locality?"* 24.6 percent of the urban, 31.6 percent of the metropolitan, and 42.1 percent of the rural respondents answered "yes."

It is not surprising that most charges for home calls were reported to be above five dollars per call, even for urban families, and 23.2 percent of the rural respondents reported charges above ten dollars per call. Five and one-half percent of the rural respondents reported charges above twenty dollars per home call. A third of the respondents did not know what a home call would cost—presumably because they had had no recent home calls and probably did not expect to ask the doctor for a home call. One-third of the rural respondents, but only 23 percent of the urban and only 12 percent of the metropolitan respondents, said that they considered home call charges "too high and unreasonable."

The field survey revealed that 9.5 percent of all respondents thought that people around them depended on chiropractors "a great deal," and 32.5 percent "some." This alleged dependence on chiropractors was greater in urban and metropolitan centers than in rural areas. On the contrary, "faith healers" were not considered to be so popular. Only two percent of the respondents said that people around them depended on faith healers "a great deal" and 8.7 percent said "some." Although these data provide only indirect evidence of objective facts, it may be inferred that the norms and values of modern medical science have largely replaced whatever superstitious and unscientific ideas may have existed in the older generation. The decrease in deliveries of infants by untrained midwives is also evidence of this trend.

By all reasonable standards, the level of dental service in the Southern Appalachians is low in comparison with both the dental situation in the nation and other types of health care. According to the 1958 Directory of the American Dental Association, there were only 1,818 dentists in the Southern Appalachians, or 3,171 people per dentist. In contrast, there were 1,679 people per dentist in the United States as a whole. To bring the Appalachian ratio even with that of the nation would require 1,621 additional dentists.

Figure 74 shows the population-dentist ratios for the Southern Appalachians by counties. Eighteen counties have no dentists whatever; 12 counties have

statistics, maternal and child health, sanitation and environmental health, health education, epidemiology and disease control, hygienic laboratory, dental health, hospitals and medical facilities, nutrition, public health nursing, and industrial hygiene. Disease con-

Figure 72. *Nonfederal Physicians by Type of Practice, Southern Appalachian Region and the United States, 1957*

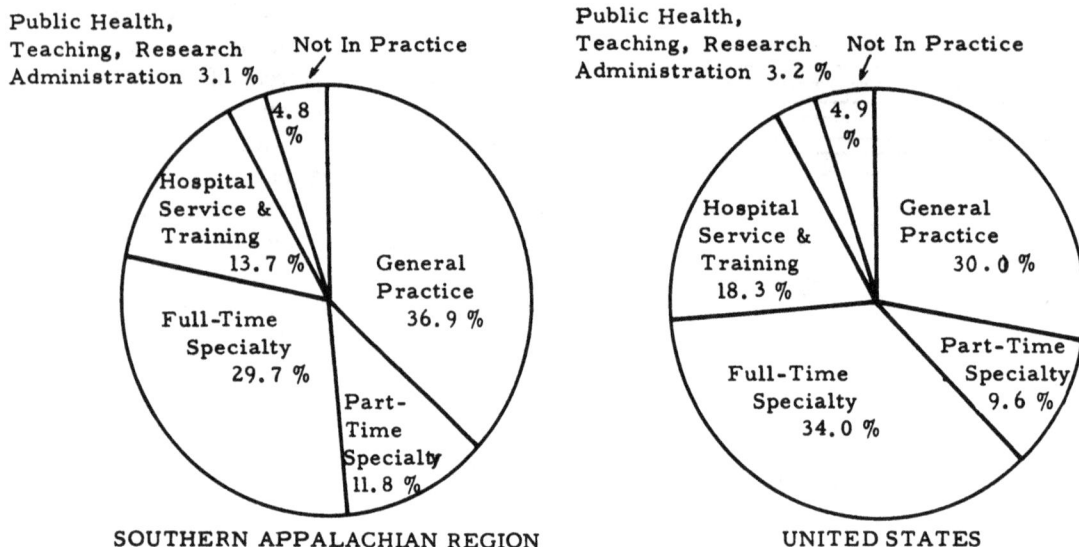

SOUTHERN APPALACHIAN REGION

UNITED STATES

Source: Directory of the American Medical Association, 1958

more than 10,000 people per dentist; 51 have from 5,000 to 9,999 people per dentist and only 2 counties have less than 1,679, the national average per dentist.

The low standard of dental service in the Region is further revealed in the high percentages of extractions as compared with prophylaxis and fillings. Twenty-two and six-tenths percent of the dental visits made were for the purpose of extractions, but only 15.8 percent for fillings and 22.1 percent for periodic check-ups. The percentage of extractions among the rural sample was 33.4 as compared with 14.2 in the metropolitan and 18.5 in the urban sample. Periodic check-ups accounted for 35.7 percent of the metropolitan dental visits, 25.9 percent of the urban, but only 9.3 percent of the rural dental visits. This differential in rural-urban dental service shows the need not only for more dental education but for higher incomes among the rural population. The provision of free dental service financed by local and state taxes should also be given serious consideration.

Public Health Organization

All of the states of the Southern Appalachian Region have public health departments, whose major divisions usually include local health services, vital

trol divisions usually administer several programs such as communicable diseases, tuberculosis, cancer, venereal disease, rabies, diabetes, poliomyelitis, and rheumatic fever.

Local public health organization in the Southern Appalachians leaves much to be desired. Of the 190 counties, 88 have full-time public health departments; 91 counties are served by district health organizations; eight counties are in state or regional health units; and three counties have no public health organization of any kind except a health board with no professional personnel employed.

Of the 88 county health departments, only 22 had, at the time of this survey, full-time M.D. health officers; but 15 additional counties shared the services of a full-time health officer with one or more counties. The remaining 51 counties either had no health officer at all or had only a part-time health officer who spent most of his time in private practice. Several of these 51 counties had funds for health officers but the positions were temporarily vacant.

Of the 91 counties in district health units, 34 were in districts which did not have a full-time M.D. health officer at the time of the survey. Many counties of the Region have populations too small to support a full scale local health department, but even if a county is served by a district department, it should have a small health center with at least a public health nurse and frequently a sanitarian.

Local health departments have more public health nurses than any other class of professional health per-

fifteen in Kentucky, nineteen in North Carolina, twenty-one in Tennessee, ten in Virginia and one in West Virginia.

Per capita expenditures for public health work in the Southern Appalachians during the fiscal year 1957-1958 amounted to only 97 cents, less than half of

Figure 73. *Nonfederal Physicians by Type of Practice, Southern Appalachian Region, Metropolitan and Nonmetropolitan Areas, 1957*

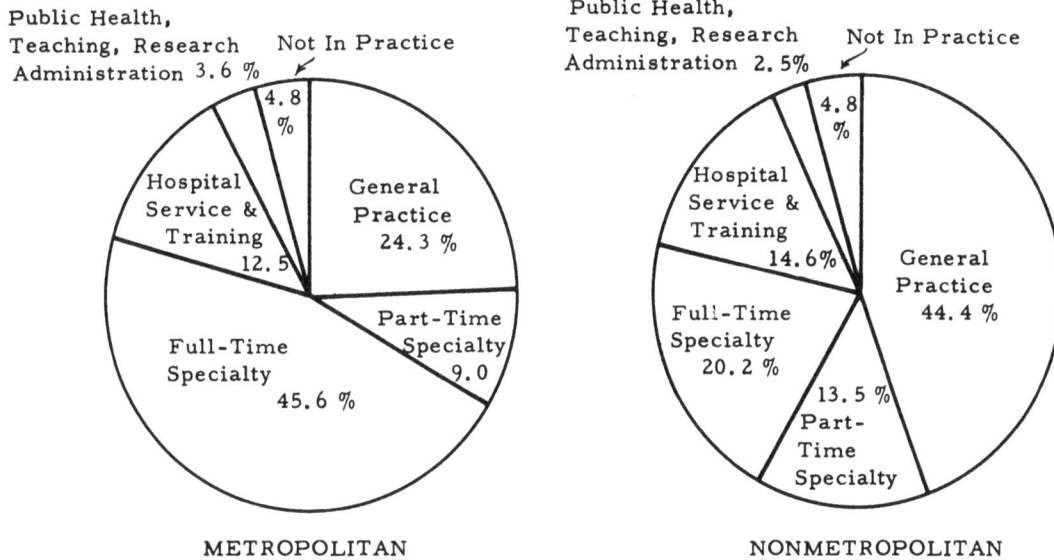

METROPOLITAN   NONMETROPOLITAN

Source: Directory of the American Medical Association, 1958

sonnel. The number of public health nurses may be used as a sort of minimal index of local health organization. There should be, we are told by competent public health authorities, at least one public health nurse for each 5,000 people. However, we find only 375 public health nurses in the Region, or 15,373 people per nurse. Thus, in order to have one nurse for each 5,000 people, 778 additional public health nurses are needed.

Authorities also state that one public health sanitarian is needed for each 15,000 people. Yet, we find only 174 sanitarians in the Region which amounts to a ratio of 33,060 people per sanitarian. Over 200 additional public health sanitarians are needed.

A fully staffed local health department should of course have a secretary. No estimate of the need for additional secretaries has been made, but, needless to say, the health department secretary is an important person in the organization.

During the period 1948-1958, local health centers were constructed in 79 Southern Appalachian counties with the aid of federal funds. Three of these modern health centers were built in Alabama, ten in Georgia,

what is needed for a reasonably good public health program. The metropolitan counties spent $1.22 per capita and the nonmetropolitan spent $.88 per capita in local public health work, the expenditures varying considerably by county, state and region. The per capita expenditures for local public health work in the Appalachians ranged from $.62 in Alabama to $1.42 in North Carolina; and the percent of funds from local sources ranged from 28.5 in Virginia to 72.5 in North Carolina (Table 61).

In the field survey, several questions were asked concerning the public health service. The results, in general, indicated that the public was well informed concerning the existence of public health departments in their counties and of the services which these departments are rendering.

The entire population of a county is benefited either directly or indirectly by a well-staffed, active local public health department. However, only 27 percent of the survey respondents said that they had made use of one or more public health services during the year before the survey. More rural than urban people (30 percent as compared with 24 percent)

THE SOUTHERN APPALACHIANS

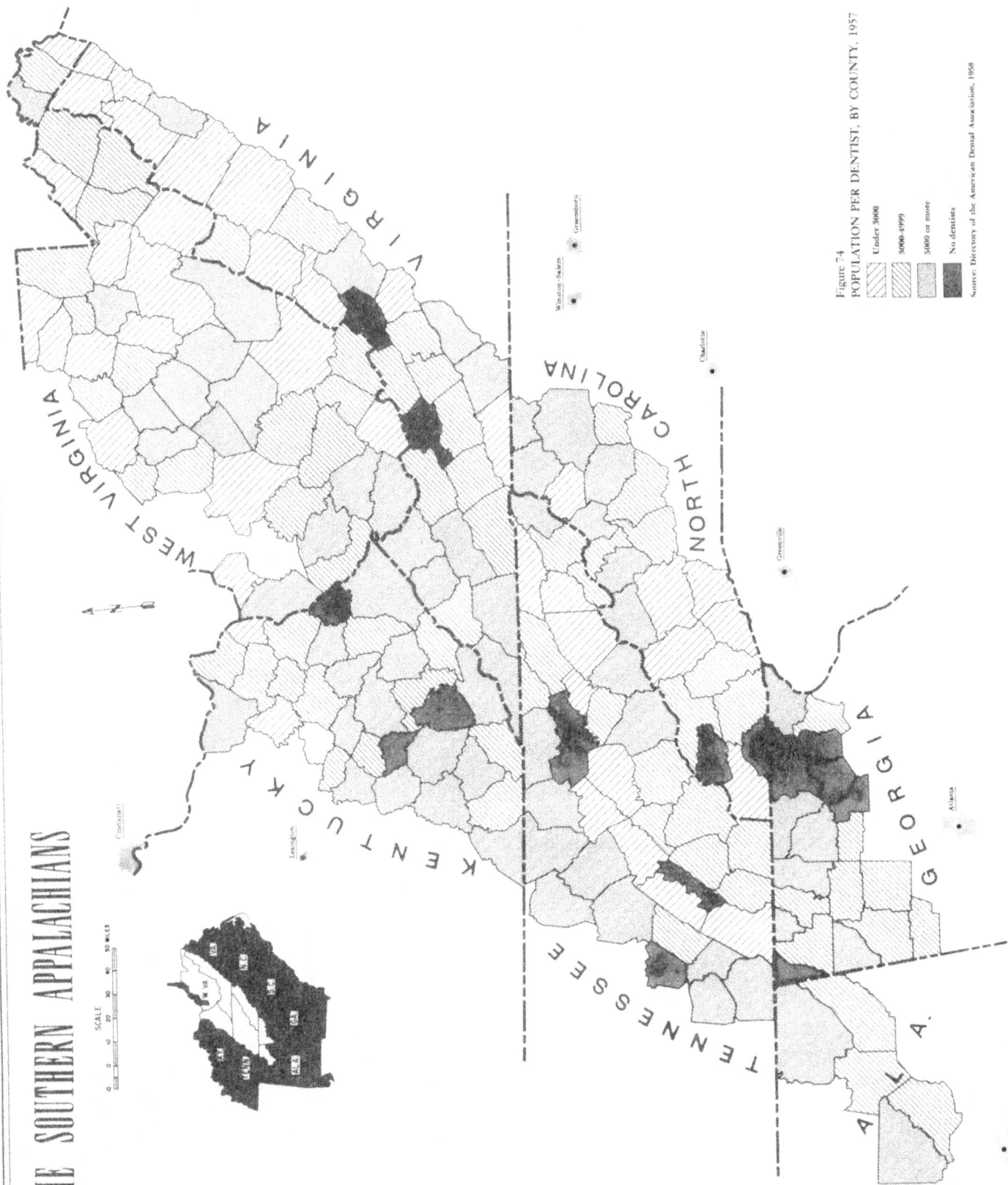

Figure 74
POPULATION PER DENTIST, BY COUNTY, 1957

Under 3000
3000-4999
5000 or more
No dentists

Source: Directory of the American Dental Association, 1958

said that they had used public health services during the past year.

Annual reports of local public health departments and visits to a small sample of departments reveal the great volume and variety of public health services

Table 61. *Expenditures for Public Health Services, Southern Appalachian Region, by States, 1957-1958*

State	Per capita expenditures	Percent from local sources
Alabama	$0.62	59.3
Georgia	1.14	52.1
Kentucky	0.87	35.0
North Carolina	1.42	72.5
Tennessee	0.88	58.7
Virginia	1.04	28.5
West Virginia	0.88	49.6

Source: U. S. Public Health Service, Directory of Local Health Units, 1958.

rendered. An excellent illustration is afforded by the Pike County, Kentucky, Health Department. This county of about 85,000 population, located in a coal mining section of eastern Kentucky, has a modern two-story health center, and a staff of fifteen including a full-time health officer, five nurses, three sanitarians, four clerks, one x-ray technician, and a maintenance worker. The annual budget of this department during the fiscal year 1958-1959 was $77,039, about half of which came from county taxes and the remainder from state and federal sources.

A typical day in the work of the Pike County Health Department reveals it to be as active as a bee-hive during the productive season. For example, on the day that this writer visited the county, a mental health clinic was being held with the help of two state medical specialists in mental health. More than thirty people, effectively recruited by the public health officer, attended this meeting. Many were children brought to the clinic by their mothers.

During the day staff members were reporting on a survey in progress to determine how many people of various ages in the county had received polio shots —considered to be a serious health problem all over the Region at the time. For example, one survey worker, reporting on his visits to 72 families in the Hurricane Creek School District, had found 76 of 170 children, and 137 of 147 parents without any protection against polio. Such information was being used by the health department as a means of educating the public on the subject and of obtaining funds with which to purchase additional vaccine and employ additional nurses to give the shots.

During 1958 the Pike County Health Department

reported (among other things) the activities listed in Table 62. Although this report is from only one outstanding health department in a large county, many other departments reported a similar variety of activities. On the other hand, these and other necessary health services are not being provided in many counties where public health is poorly supported and poorly organized.

The Frontier Nursing Service, organized in Leslie County, eastern Kentucky, about 1925 under the leadership of Mrs. Mary Breckinridge, has developed into an effective voluntary health service for isolated mountain people in Leslie County and adjoining areas of eastern Kentucky. It is supported entirely by philanthropy and its reputation is national and even worldwide. The Service gives bedside nursing care to the sick, care to women in childbirth and to young children, and does preventive health work in twelve nursing districts at eight nursing centers.

An unusual and outstanding activity of the Frontier Nursing Service is a six-month training course in midwifery for graduate nurses. Its graduates are working in many states and foreign countries. Locally the Frontier Nursing Service gives free medical, hospital, and social service care to over 5,000 children a year. During the period 1925-1955, over 10,000 registered midwifery cases were handled by this agency, and 7,500 of these were home deliveries.

The present personnel and facilities now include: a small hospital of 25 beds and 12 bassinets at Hyden, on a spur of Thousandsticks Mountain, Kentucky, a physician who is the medical director, a hospital superintendent, hospital nurses, and volunteer workers as well as 8 nursing stations in isolated areas staffed with approximately 16 district nurses, living quarters for nurses, facilities for elementary home food production, and a number of jeeps and horses for transportation on all sorts of roads and mountain trails.

Fees for prenatal care and delivery are reasonable. No fees are charged those who are unable to pay, but usually $40 is charged for a home delivery. Hospital deliveries are advised in difficult cases and no extra charge is made, but $75 is charged for normal deliveries in the hospital if the family so elects. Children are provided with free hospital care in any case.

The annual budget of the Frontier Nursing Service is something like $220,000. The work of this private agency is correlated with public health activities at the state and county levels, and the home demonstration agent is called on to advise mothers in proper

THE SOUTHERN APPALACHIANS

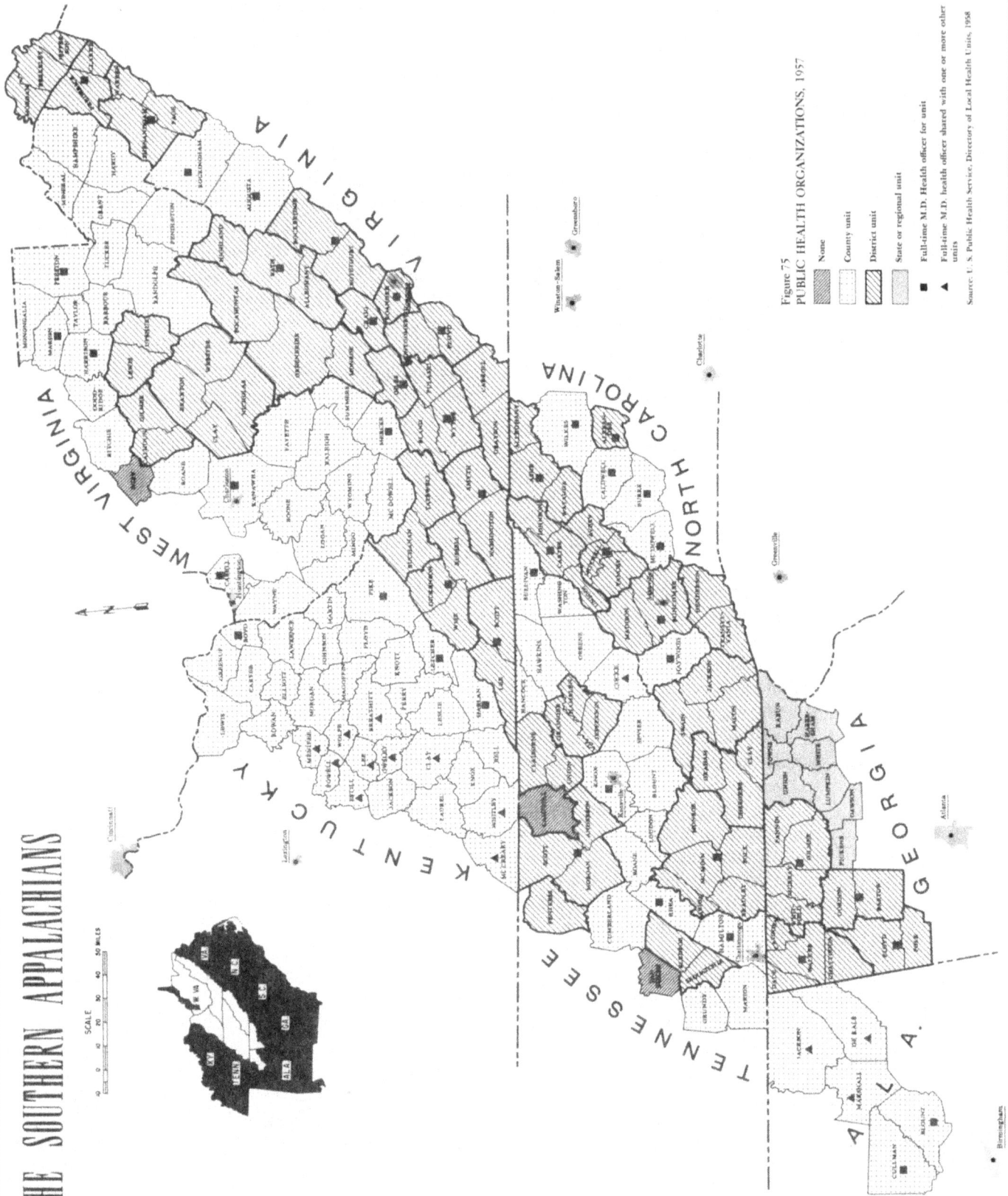

Figure 75
PUBLIC HEALTH ORGANIZATIONS, 1957

None
County unit
District unit
State or regional unit

■ Full-time M.D. Health officer for unit

▲ Full-time M.D. health officer shared with one or more other units

Source: U. S. Public Health Service, Directory of Local Health Units, 1958

nutritional practices for themselves and members of their families.[13]

Health Insurance

With the increase in hospital care and the commercialization of medical care in general, the problem

Table 62. *Activities of Pike County, Kentucky, Health Department, 1958*

Service	Times performed
Immunizations	38,441
Sanitary inspections of public places	566
Water tests	831
Diabetic urine tests	2,146
Venereal disease treatments	165
Crippled children examined	144
Vision tests	157
Nuisance control cases	119
Food handling classes taught (attendance 141)	6
Dogs quarantined	77
Dogs immunized	832
Health education lectures (attendance 27,296)	609
Children examined	2,421
X-rays	1,814
Rabies treatments	177
Hearing tests	253
Heart and suspected heart cases examined	40
Dental inspections	1,153
Field visits (community medical needs)	2,055
Field visits (community sanitation control)	1,537

of paying for the cost of health care has become increasingly serious for low income families.

Following a growing practice in the nation, the people of the Southern Appalachians have turned to health insurance as a means of cushioning the shock of medical and hospital expenses. About three out of every four families surveyed in the Region in 1958 reported that they were carrying some sort of health insurance. The percentage of rural families reporting health insurance coverage was only 63.4 as compared with 81.4 for the nonmetropolitan urban and 87.0 for the metropolitan. Over 90 percent of the Region's families with insurance said that they were satisfied with it, but more of the rural than the urban families reported some dissatisfaction. About a fourth of the families reported having dropped health insurance at some time. Reasons most frequently given for dropping health insurance were dissatisfaction with payments and financial difficulties.

Blue Cross and Blue Shield Service plans which serve the Southern Appalachians report that coverage runs (by state) up to 24 percent, but in some areas the percentage is much lower. Obviously a lot of "commercial" health insurance is sold in the area on an individual basis.

Although voluntary health insurance is growing and is gradually being improved, there is much yet to be desired. Low income families are least likely to be covered and the typical individual policy is severely limited in coverage and can be cancelled by the company.[14] At least one state, however (North Carolina), has passed legislation limiting the right of companies to cancel health insurance.

Catastrophic, or major medical insurance, is just now beginning to be sold on a group basis in the Region. It is not yet available to individuals, especially to those above 65 years of age. Unionized mine workers in the Region are, of course, rather fully protected by the United Mine Workers Welfare and Retirement Fund and by the associated hospitals. Unless private medical care institutions and voluntary insurance do a much better job of helping low income families pay for adequate medical care, a public program modeled after the Mine Workers plan may be the answer. The UMW program of comprehensive medical services for all workers regardless of income is excellent, but it serves only a single industry and, in recent years, unemployment in the coal mines has forced the system to curtail benefits for unemployed miners. A public system largely supported through the social security system, but supplemented with taxes to take care of people not covered by social security, seems to this writer to be the ultimate and the best solution to the problem faced by the great majority of low-income mountain people as well as low-income people everywhere.

Such a publicly supported system can and will, I think, evolve over the years. In its development it will be possible to retain the best features of our present system including our voluntary nonprofit hospitals, private medical practice, free choice of physician, local controls, and so on. Unless we can develop a better medical care system than we have, there seems to be little that can be done for most of the low-income people of the Southern Appala-

---

[13] Mary Breckinridge, *Wide Neighborhoods: a Story of the Frontier Nursing Service* (New York, 1952), 169-181, 185-190, 209-220, 253-261, 303-313, 345-357; *Thirty Years Onward: Frontier Nursing Service, 1925-1955*, Frontier Nursing Service, 1955.

[14] Recent studies by the Health Information Foundation and the United States Public Health Service provide a great deal of information showing that voluntary health insurance is failing to reach low income people, rural people, and the aged. See particularly Odin W. Anderson, Patricia Collette, and Jacob Feldman, *Health Insurance Benefits for Personal Health Services*, Health Information Foundation, Research Series 15, 1960.

chians. We have depended on haphazard philanthropy long enough.

A Summary Evaluation

The major findings of this study of health and health services in the Southern Appalachians may be summarized as follows.

As measured by the general mortality and perinatal mortality rates, the health of the people of the Region, on the average, is about the same as in the nation. Although the perinatal rate is still slightly higher in the Region, a revolution has taken place during the past twenty years in the types of medical care and hospitalization of mothers and infants during the natal and prenatal periods. From 1939-1941 to 1954-1956 the percentage of infants delivered by physicians in hospitals more than quadrupled so that at the end of this period nine out of ten babies were delivered in hospitals. Midwife deliveries during the same period declined from 14.3 to 3.2 percent of all live births.

Tuberculosis, with a death rate 50 percent higher than in the nation as a whole, remains a serious problem in the Region. Other diseases having higher than normal death rates in the Region are influenza, pneumonia, parasitic diseases, cardiovascular-renal diseases, and diseases of early childhood. Fatal accidents were also found to be more frequent in the Region.

Modern health services and institutions have increased rapidly in the Region during the past 25 years and are still improving. However, the Region still lags behind the nation in this respect, and backward areas of the mountains are in great need of physicians, dentists, hospitals, and public health services. There is a need for six to eight thousand additional hospital beds and for the replacement of several thousand obsolete beds. Fifty-eight of the 190 counties studied have no hospitals, and twenty-seven of these counties have more than 10,000 population.

Many of the existing hospitals are small, poorly equipped, understaffed, and crowded. Only 54 percent of the Region's hospitals have been accredited by the Joint Commission on Accreditation. It is necessary to have many small hospitals in the rural parts of the Region if the people are to be conveniently served, but it does not follow that small hospitals are doomed to be poorly equipped, poorly managed, and thus render low quality care. Fortunately, many new small hospitals, well-equipped and well-managed, have been constructed in recent years with the help of federal and union funds.

There is a general shortage of physicians in the Region, and the shortage is particularly acute in rural areas. The fact that smaller towns tend to have older physicians indicates that many more small towns may be without doctors within a few years.

The relative shortage of dentists in the Southern Appalachians is even more serious. In order to bring the area up to the national average, more than 1600 additional dentists are needed. Programs of dental education and preventive services are also badly needed. However, the full benefits of dental education can be derived only if accompanied by rising family incomes and increasing public support for preventive dental work.

Although many new public health centers have recently been constructed, the general level of public health organization falls far short of reasonably good standards. Only a fourth of the county health departments had full-time health officers, and a third of the counties in district health units lacked the services of full-time district health officers. Furthermore, there is a serious shortage of public health nurses and sanitarians. The Southern Appalachian people are aware of their public health departments and services, but they spend annually only 97 cents per capita in their support, nearly half of which comes from state and federal sources.

Hospitalization, surgery, and other medical services in the Southern Appalachians, as in the nation, are being increasingly supported by health insurance, prepayment plans, and welfare funds. The United Mine Workers Welfare and Retirement Fund and the chain of ten hospitals supported by the Fund represent not only an outstanding development in the Region but in the nation as well. Its very success throws into bold relief the plight of thousands of low income mountain families who are not employed in mining. More than a third of the rural families have no health insurance of any kind, and most of these are in low-income classes.

In spite of the deficiencies listed above, the Southern Appalachian area, as a whole, is following the nation in the improvement of its health and health services. Mortality rates have dropped; the numbers of physicians and dentists have increased; many new hospitals have been constructed; public health organization has grown; the financing of personal health services through voluntary health insurance is expanding; better roads have made it possible for rural people of the area to have easier and quicker access to physicians, hospitals, and public health services; the development of communication and the improvement of public education have taken health out of the realm of fear and superstition and have greatly stimulated the people's interest in the scientific approach to medicine. Perhaps most important is that the health progress in the Southern Appalachians evidences the hard and enthusiastic work of hundreds of local and state leaders in health affairs. This leadership is the prime resource on which we must depend for continued development and coordination of health institutions and services.

Although past achievements in health and health services in the Southern Appalachians are considerable, this study has revealed grave problems and serious deficiencies. The questions to be considered are: How can these deficiencies be overcome? How can more physicians be attracted to those isolated areas in greatest need? How can the needed hospital facilities be obtained? How can public health organizations be expanded and strengthened? And what sort of health insurance can be developed for the low income families, especially rural families, who do not now carry insurance? Finally, how can the working relationships between public, private, and voluntary health agencies and services be improved?

The successful achievement of a health program will depend to a large extent on the solution of the basic economic problems of the area. Help from outside the area must be considered as a definite and realistic approach. Federal monies for hospital construction and for public health services are already important outside contributions, but there are other opportunities for both public and private agencies.

A first step in an expanded health program is getting the facts about health and health services, collected and analyzed in a scientific manner, to the people as a means of interesting and motivating them. This present study is only a starter. A continuous flow of new, specialized local surveys is needed to keep the pot boiling and to serve as a guide for new programs. Each state in the Region should have its own health survey and research activity. Present activities along these lines are entirely too restricted.

At the local level, well planned and directed "self-surveys" on critical and important health conditions and problems are needed not only to provide the information needed for action programs but also as a means of motivating people for action. At district and state levels research is needed to determine extent and nature of poor health and the social and economic obstacles to effective prevention and treatment of dis-

ease, to evaluate health programs, to assess health attitudes, to discover effective forms and areas of community organization in health services, and to determine the need for different types of health personnel and institutions.

A second step is the expansion and intensification of health education—covering not only the technical and medical aspects of health but also such social and economic aspects as the organization of health services; factors in the utilization and cost of health services; and use of prepayment plans, health insurance, and public funds in paying for medical care. This needed educational activity should be participated in by both health and nonhealth agencies—public, voluntary, and private. The medical profession should support and participate in these activities. The primary responsibility for spearheading an intensified health education program rests with the public health services of the various states, which should employ both local and state health educators for the task. All of the states of the Southern Appalachians have too few health educators, a situation that is due partly to lack of funds and partly to lack of interest on the part of the public and its leadership.

A third step is the development of regional, state, and local lay organizations to support health programs, institutions, and services. We need an organization in the health field comparable in scope and power to the PTA's in the field of public education.

Fourth, the medical and dental professions should become more active in supporting public health activities, the building of hospitals and nursing homes, and in health education. Unfortunately, some physicians in the Southern Appalachians are still actively opposing the expansion of public health services.

Fifth, more state and federal financial aid must be provided for the support of public health programs in low-income counties and communities. Also there should be some sort of public financial incentive provided to encourage physicians and dentists to practice in low-income areas. A more drastic solution would be the employment of physicians and dentists by the public health service to practice in areas where there are serious shortages of medical and dental personnel.

A better system of financing personal medical service would go a long way toward bringing more hospitals to the area. Coordination of small hospitals with larger hospitals on a regional basis is the best way to insure high quality care. However, this kind of hospital system can only be developed under government supervision and with government support.

Finally, it is recommended that both lay and professional leaders in the Southern Appalachians give more attention to the development of health insurance plans for low-income families, particularly those in rural areas who do not have an opportunity to get group health insurance by virtue of being employed in business and industry. Health insurance for the aged, a most critical need, should be promoted and supported vigorously. Voluntary health insurance has failed miserably to meet the needs of these marginal population groups—rural, low income, and the aged. Attention must now be given to the possibility of more active participation of government in the health insurance field.

CHAPTER FIFTEEN

Social

Problems

and Welfare

Services

WILLIAM E. COLE

A DESCRIPTION OF THE SOCIAL PROBLEMS in the Southern Appalachians must be largely subjective, for on many relevant topics only state data are available. When county data exist, they are often most fragmentary and incomplete for the problem areas with which we are here chiefly concerned. Low income, the most familiar of the Region's problems and the chief source of many of the conditions to be discussed in this chapter, can be rather thoroughly documented, however. Income levels in the Appalachian counties are not only below those of the nation but, as a rule, are below those of the states in which these counties lie (see Figure 13).

In 1959 the per capita income for the nation was $1,700, yet, usually, only in the urban counties of the Appalachian area did per capita income exceed $1,400. In most of the rural counties the per capita income is 10 to 50 percent below national averages.

The largest single group of counties where per capita income is less than $1,000 annually is found east and west of the Virginia-Kentucky border and extending southwest through the Cumberland Plateau in Tennessee to the Alabama line. A similar group of counties is found along the North Carolina-Tennessee border and ranging south into northeast Georgia. Along the Virginia-Tennessee border is another group of Appalachian counties with per capita incomes of less than $1,000.

A study of per capita personal income by counties in Tennessee for 1958 revealed median incomes of $513 in Hancock County; $705 in Johnson; $754 in Campbell, and $730 in Van Buren, as compared with $1,439 for the state as a whole; $1,722 in industrialized Sullivan County, which joins mountainous, rural Johnson County; $2,370 in Anderson County; $1,560 in urban Knox County, and $2,026 in urban Hamilton County. On the whole, incomes were higher in the East Tennessee Valley counties than in the mountainous counties which fringe the Valley.[1] Anderson County is exceptional because of Oak Ridge.

Even family incomes in the Appalachians are often lower than the nation's per capita income. For instance, a study of family incomes in thirty-five Upper Tennessee Valley counties revealed a median income of all families and unrelated individuals of $1,296 for the area in 1950. The median family income in Anderson County was $3,220, four times the $790 median income of nearby, rural Hancock County. The median income of the upper fifth of the thirty-five counties was almost three times that of the lowest fifth, or $2,777 as compared to $932.[2]

The above income data are indicative of the severe problem of low income in the more rural Appalachian counties which contributes to the inability of people to solve their other problems.

The Appalachian Region has a low rate of labor force participation. Around 48 percent of the population was in the labor force in 1950 in contrast to 58 percent for the nation. Of the area's women, aged 14 and over, only one in five was in the labor force, as contrasted to one in three for the nation.[3] Contributory to the low rate of participation in the labor force is the low educational level, which is about two years below the national median (see Figure 54).

Other data indicate that income maintenance is a critical problem, with social and welfare implications, in many Appalachian communities. Chronic unemployment is most severe in the coal mining regions of Kentucky, Virginia, and West Virginia. Cutbacks in railroad employment and mechanization of mines create problems of income maintenance in some areas, as does seasonal employment in agriculture, in some tourist centers, and in some coal mining areas. Probably one out of six workers is jobless or has only part-time employment.

While the part-time worker may receive unemployment compensation for a period of twenty-two weeks, many family heads work at jobs not covered by unemployment compensation. Many of the Southern Appalachian counties are welfare deserts as far as funds for emergency welfare needs are concerned. For example, in many family situations which result in income losses, neither parent is eligible for public assistance, and local funds are not available for rent, clothing, fuel, or medical expenses.

While it is true that higher incomes and greater security in income maintenance do not solve the critical social problems of an area, especially such problems as crime, juvenile delinquency, and family disorganization, a higher level of income in the Appalachians is needed to make the people more adequate to cope with everyday needs, meet emergencies, and to enable communities to tackle many of the social problems which are solvable, in part at least, at the local level. Lack of local resources frequently handicaps participation in some state and national welfare programs which might bring trained help and financial resources to the community.

The physical settings in which the people of the region live are, in general, bad. About 80 percent of the houses in one fourth of the counties are dilapidated, according to the census of 1950. A dwelling was reported as dilapidated "when it had serious deficiencies, was run down or neglected, or was of inadequate original construction, so that it did not provide adequate shelter or protection against the elements or endangered the safety of the occupants."[4] Generally speaking, the best housing is in urban counties, the counties adjacent to counties containing cities of 10,000 or more, and counties in which new industrial developments have taken place requiring new housing. Counties along main highways have better housing than hill counties off main highways. On the whole housing is better in Virginia and West Virginia counties than in Tennessee and Kentucky counties. In Kentucky, Tennessee, and Virginia the worst housing is found in the coal mining counties and in those counties depending heavily upon agriculture and timber industries for employment.

The urban counties have the highest percentage of dwelling units which are not dilapidated and which have hot running water, bath, and private toilet. The United States average for such facilities was 63.1 percent in 1950. Only six counties in the study area reached 60 percent, and 84 fell below 20 percent. It is assumed that the situation improved between 1950 and 1960, but the housing situation in the Appalachians is critical and is more of a rural than an urban problem. Fantastic lows were reached in some counties. For instance, only 2.1 percent of the dwelling units in 1950 in Wolfe County, Kentucky, had the facilities mentioned above, and for Owsley County, Kentucky, the percentage was 2.4. At the other extreme, 66.0 percent of the dwelling units in Boyd County, Kentucky, were undilapidated and had hot running water, private toilet, and bath. Hancock County, Tennessee, showed 2.8 percent of its dwelling units with hot running water, bath, and toilet. Not far away was Anderson County, Tennessee, containing Oak Ridge, where 67.3 percent of the dwelling units have modern conveniences. Similar extremes exist in other states. Much of existing older housing is of wood and has reached a stage of critical deterioration.

[1] C. Ormond Corry and Staff, *Estimates of Personal Income in Tennessee By County, 1950-1958* (Knoxville: Bureau of Business and Economic Research, The University of Tennessee, July, 1960), pp. 8-10.

[2] Tennessee Valley Authority, *Income Levels in the Upper Tennessee Valley: A Comparative Analysis* (Knoxville, 1957), p. 5.

[3] *Basic Population Data for the Southern Appalachians.* University of Kentucky, Social Research Service, p. 53.

[4] U. S. Bureau of the Census, *U. S. Census of Housing, 1950,* Vol. I, *General Characteristics* (Washington, D. C., 1953), p. xviii.

In the poorer counties maintenance has not been good. Much company-owned housing is not well maintained. The sources of loans for rural housing have not been as adequate as for improved urban housing, and the interest rates are higher. Even much

which respect is lacking for public property both by youth and adults in the Region is very great.

Physical handicaps result in a great deal of dependency and limited earning capacity in the Region. Adult crippling is to be expected where many are

Table 63. *Crime Rates per 100,000 Inhabitants for Indicated Offenses, United States and Southern Appalachian States, 1959*

Area	Murder and non-negligent manslaughter	Forcible rape	Robbery	Aggravated assault	Burglary	Larceny	
						$50 and over	Auto theft
United States	4.8	8.3	40.3	67.3	385.9	227.0	162.3
Metropolitan areas	4.6	9.8	57.0	81.7	474.2	291.0	221.5
Other cities	3.6	3.7	15.2	45.1	328.4	172.1	104.9
Rural areas	6.2	7.1	11.6	43.0	192.1	93.9	42.8
Alabama	12.9	8.3	25.1	91.3	321.9	174.7	96.4
Georgia	13.4	10.6	26.5	101.7	351.2	162.7	141.7
Kentucky	5.3	6.8	28.3	45.4	341.9	185.2	139.2
North Carolina	8.9	8.2	14.9	182.2	254.2	113.1	71.4
Tennessee	7.0	6.6	26.9	56.2	437.8	151.4	135.7
Virginia	8.8	7.3	26.8	104.2	311.1	184.6	125.6
West Virginia	4.4	6.0	12.9	31.5	225.1	101.8	75.3

Source: Federal Bureau of Investigation, Crime in the United States, Uniform Crime Reports, 1959.

of the new housing is shoddy because most rural counties and many cities have inadequate subdivision controls and building codes. Thus in a region that is urbanizing at a fair rate of speed, acute planning and land-use problems are arising.

The availability of rural electricity has been a strong factor in the improvement of rural housing. Power facilitates the pumping of water, improved lighting and heating, makes possible electrical appliances, and, from all observations, is an important factor in home improvement. Also, through the efforts of the Rural Electrification Administration, telephone services have been made available to some remote communities. The availability of electricity to rural churches and schools has been a factor in the improvement of institutional facilities and programs in many communities.

Travel in the Appalachian area and a perusal of the church, educational, governmental, and planning sections of this volume will show that the physical state of community institutional facilities in a large percentage of communities is substandard. Probably the schools are least substandard, especially in communities where consolidation has been possible. Churches are often drab, poorly equipped, and uninviting. In many county seat towns public buildings, especially county court houses, are a disgrace. Jail conditions are so bad that most county jails are not used for Federal prisoners. Even where excellent public buildings exist, adequate custodial care seems to be a problem. In passing, we may say that the degree to

employed in agriculture, mining, timbering, woodworking, and quarrying. As a result of the high accident rates of these occupations, and the toll taken by accidents on the highways, a backlog of handicapped persons has grown up in the mountain areas. Hospital, surgical, and medical facilities have in the past been inadequate and often unavailable, and it has been a common practice in isolated communities to protect and shelter the handicapped, especially children, in the home. As a result, there is still a substantial number of handicapped people in the Region, many of whom have only recently been "discovered."

It was not possible to survey the extent of adult crime in the Region, since rural areas are not completely covered by state data or by the *Uniform Crime Reports* of the Federal Bureau of Investigation. In the seven states containing Southern Appalachian counties, murder and manslaughter rates are generally higher than in the nation as a whole (Table 63). Assault rates also are higher, except in Tennessee and West Virginia. Burglary, robbery, larceny, and auto theft are less frequent in the Appalachian states than in the nation. The favorable position of West Virginia in comparison with the other states and the nation leads one to suspect incomplete reporting from that state.

In an examination of state trial dockets in a number of counties and cities of the Region, the investigator was most impressed by the frequency of offenses involving violence and those associated with the use of alcohol. For example, on two trial dockets selected at random the number of persons cited for drunken driving and for possessing, transporting, or manufacturing whiskey was greater than the number cited for all other offenses combined. The most common offense besides these was felonious assault. Surprisingly, law enforcement officers reported that beer was a more prevalent intoxicant than "hard liquor," although some sheriffs remarked that oldtimers in the mountains felt it was their right to make whiskey and use it as they wished.

The situation with respect to statistics for juvenile offenses is little better than that for adult crime. In many of the counties there is no uniform reporting of juvenile offenses by the county judges or even (in some cases) by the special juvenile judges. Only in the last year has Tennessee begun to obtain anything like reliable data on juvenile offenses from counties. There, the chairman of the county court may now hold a juvenile docket where there are no special juvenile courts.

An examination of juvenile dockets did not indicate any great difference between juvenile offenses in the mountain counties and those in the urban counties within the region. The usual offenses are prolonged truancy from school, driving without a license, driving while intoxicated, violation of game laws (less common in cities), disorderly conduct or lewdness (in the case of girls), incorrigibility, and malicious mischief.

The metropolitan counties, of course, have special juvenile court laws, or else they operate special juvenile courts under permissive state laws. These courts as a rule are fairly well supplied with probation officers. It is in the rural counties where a particularly critical need exists. By legislation during 1960 Tennessee established a state-wide system of juvenile probation officers who are located in the various grand divisions of the state. They work with county judges, law enforcement officers, welfare workers, and others in handling of juvenile cases and in preventing juvenile offenses.

A serious problem in some Appalachian rural counties is the objection of church people to programs that might reduce juvenile delinquency, such as dances or other recreational activities in school buildings on Friday or Saturday nights. As one teenager put it: "There is nothing to do in my community but to park and neck." Yet many of these counties have excellent natural resources for recreational facilities. Even many well churched, well schooled, and economically adequate communities do little in the way of community-wide recreational planning for their children, although

many youth service groups function in the Region. Also, a customary pattern of discipline and control in the rural parts of the Region is to supervise children through the elementary school period and then release them rather suddenly from the rigid supervision to which they have been accustomed. Thus many teenagers suddenly find themselves with more freedom than they can wisely use.

Public Welfare Legislation and Effort

As the nation was settled, the new colonies and states used England's Elizabethan Poor Laws as their models for welfare legislation. Virginia, North Carolina, and to a lesser extent Tennessee, Kentucky, West Virginia, Georgia, and Alabama modeled their Poor Laws after Elizabethan principles as interpreted by some of the middle Atlantic and New England states. For example, Tennessee had a law on its statute books dating from a North Carolina law of 1762 which allowed the county court to bind out orphans as apprentices. Until about 1777, relief for the poor in North Carolina was administered by the church through vestrymen. In the new order inaugurated by the Revolution, the law was revised to provide that freemen of the counties would elect seven freeholders as overseers of the poor. This body was empowered to levy taxes for the support of the poor. In 1785 North Carolina enacted a new statute allowing counties to levy taxes for purposes of building houses for the poor. These came to be known as "poorhouses" or "almshouses," and some exist even today. In 1797 Tennessee passed a law assigning local responsibility for the poor and naming residence requirements, both of which were Elizabethan principles. The residence requirements were from a North Carolina Act of 1777. It is interesting to note that most counties, as well as states, still enforce residence requirements for assistance, usually because local authorities do not have adequate welfare funds to take care of needy newcomers.

Other early welfare legislation in the Appalachian states granted certain exemptions to paupers, such as homestead exemptions and exemptions from seizure for debt, and gave county courts power to make allowances to the poor or construct almshouses for them. Thus there grew up in the Appalachian states a type of local or county welfare assistance which could take either the form of almshouse care or outdoor relief. Even in this century it has been common practice for the members of the county governing body to handle the "pauper grant" in their local district.

At the turn of the century most counties in the Appalachian area had a county "poorhouse" or "poor farm." They also maintained some form of "pauper" relief allocated to needy persons who lived in their own homes or with relatives. Sometimes these grants were as low as $1.25 a month, and they were often administered by the district member of the county governing body. Frequently he would keep the grant and supply the pauper with bacon, meal, and flour from his own supply, thus supplying him with the amount of the grant "in kind," "cash money" being hard to come by.

In 1937, eighty-one of Tennessee's ninety-five counties operated poor farms. By 1960, only thirty-seven counties had such facilities, twelve of which were Appalachian counties. During the decade 1950 to 1960, six counties abandoned their almshouses, eighteen sold them to citizens for private use, eight sold or leased their almshouses to private operators as homes for the aged, and one county converted its institution to other use.

As of November, 1960, in the one hundred North Carolina counties there remained twenty-five "county homes," housing 1,200 persons. Some of these homes are in the Appalachian area. North Carolina has made substantial progress in recent years in the development of a program of domiciliary homes licensed by the State Board of Public Welfare and in providing homemaker services.[5] There are now some 450 such homes in the state. In some cases the county home was greatly improved in terms of physical structure and was leased for private operation. The poorer homes were closed entirely. By and large the twenty-five remaining homes, some of which were visited by the writer, appear to be rather adequate institutions.

In September, 1935, after the passage of the Social Security Act, Alabama had sixty-one almshouses with a population of 1,413, of whom 62 percent were over 65 years of age. The fact that federal funds were available for assistance outside institutions to those over 65 was an incentive to close the almshouses. County welfare departments worked closely with county governing bodies to develop substitute plans for the care of residents in the county institutions. As a result of these efforts, seven almshouses were closed in 1935, thirty-two in 1936, and eleven in 1937. As of November, 1960, only two such institutions remained. These are in populous counties. A move is currently under way to close one of the two remaining institutions and to convert the other into a nursing home.

Kentucky in 1960 could not provide information on the number of county homes in operation. State welfare officials did, however, indicate that about twenty-five counties have leased former county homes to private individuals who now operate them as personal care or nursing homes. Other counties have closed their almshouses or are using private personal care homes for the indigent who must have some form of home or institutional care.

The last county almshouse in Virginia was closed in December, 1958. At the turn of the century Virginia had almshouses in ninety-eight of its one hundred counties. By 1928 the number had been reduced to forty-two, a result of concerted effort at that time to organize district homes for the indigent. As a result of 1946-1948 legislation to promote better standards of care in both public and private welfare institutions for the aged and infirm, the number of county almshouses dropped to nine in 1950. Most of these were discontinued in 1954 when all homes for the aged, both public and private, were made subject to license by the State Board of Welfare and Institutions.

The 1950 edition of the West Virginia Blue Book listed twenty-five counties as having a superintendent of "County Infirmary"; the 1959 edition lists only sixteen. Actually, only three infirmaries were in operation in November, 1960.

The county "poorhouse," while being gradually eliminated from the Appalachian states, is still present to an uncomfortable degree. By and large, such institutions, where they are not under state supervision, are dumping places for the feeble-minded, the homeless senile, the mildly mentally defective, and persons otherwise inadequate, defective, or deficient, who cannot be cared for by qualifying for one of the public assistance categories.[6] One Appalachian county almshouse, selected at random, was established in 1923 on a farm acquired at a cost of $35,000. The county has no "paupers" who receive monthly out-of-institution grants. The salary of the keeper is $1,200 annually and he receives his housing, and apparently food for his family, from the farm. There are at

[5] North Carolina State Board of Public Welfare, *Homemaker Services for the Aged in North Carolina*, Information Bulletin No. 30 (Raleigh, n.d.).

[6] William E. Cole and Russell R. Dynes, "Homes for the Homeless in Tennessee," *The University of Tennessee Record*, Extension Series, Vol. 27, No. 4 (Knoxville: 1951). See also, William E. Cole, "Almshouse Policies and Almshouse Care of the Indigent in Tennessee," *The University of Tennessee Record*, Extension Series, Vol. 14, No. 2 (Knoxville: July, 1938). Also correspondence and other materials from the state commissioners of welfare of the Appalachian states.

THE SOUTHERN APPALACHIANS

SCALE

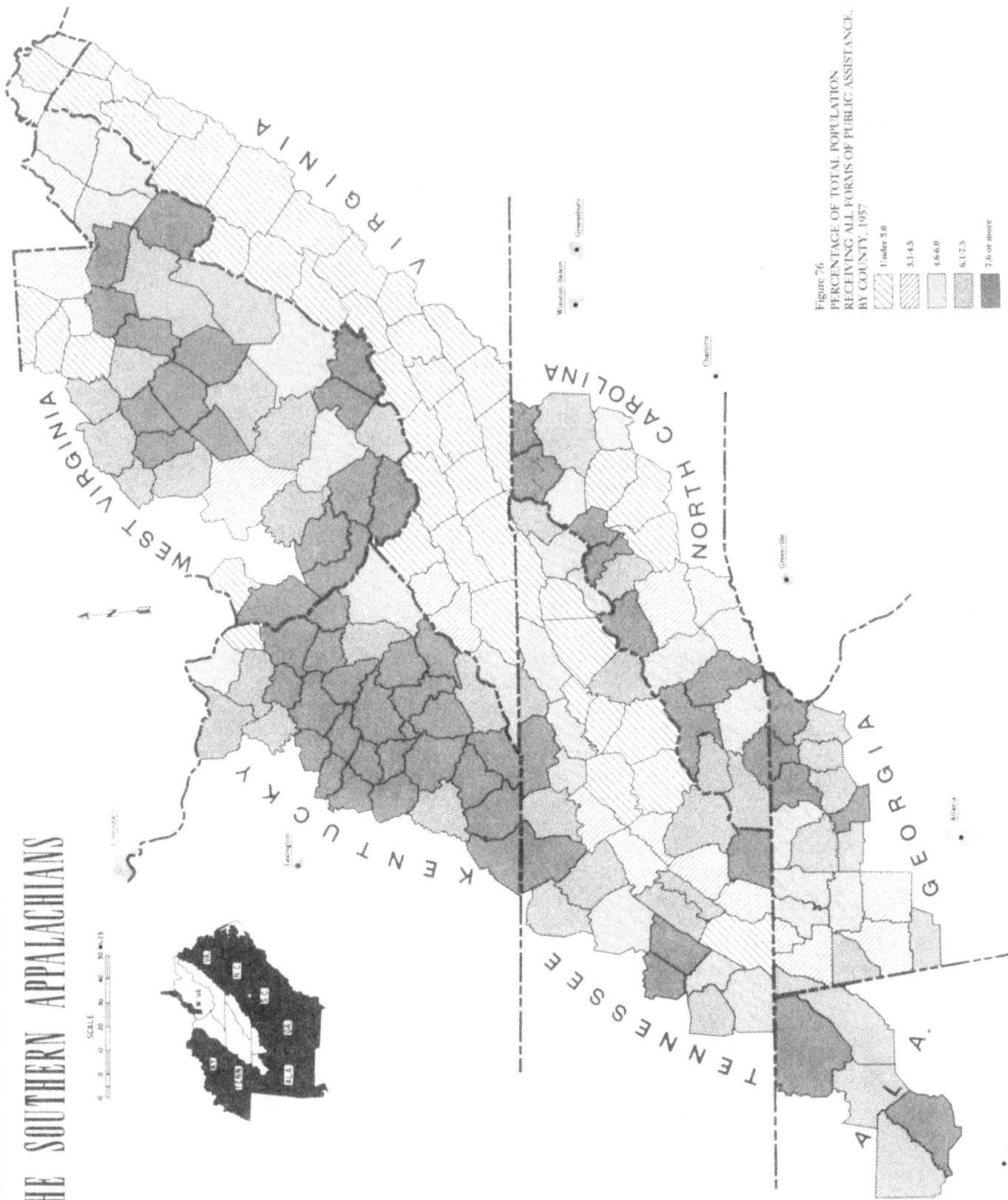

Figure 76
PERCENTAGE OF TOTAL POPULATION
RECEIVING ALL FORMS OF PUBLIC ASSISTANCE,
BY COUNTY, 1957

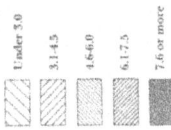

Under 3.0
3.1-4.5
4.6-6.0
6.1-7.5
7.6 or more

WEST VIRGINIA

VIRGINIA

KENTUCKY

TENNESSEE

NORTH CAROLINA

GEORGIA

A L A.

Cincinnati

Lexington

Winston-Salem
Greensboro

Charlotte

Greenville

Atlanta

Birmingham

present four inmates, and all cost of care is paid by the county. The total amount appropriated for the "county home" is $2,200 a year. Supervision is by the County Home Committee appointed by the county court.

Most counties today provide some form of local welfare aid, subject to need and residential requirements. This is usually in the form of institutional care, grocery orders, surplus commodities, or a small cash stipend made by the county governing body to people who live at home. Residence of six months or a year is usually required. Most counties in the Appalachian area appear to spend from 1 to 3 percent of their tax monies for "welfare purposes."

In the State of Kentucky as of July, 1958, 2,730 individuals were receiving some form of welfare assistance from twenty-nine Appalachian counties out of annual appropriations of $274,000, in addition to a distribution of surplus commodities by local units which, in July, 1958, reached 100,000 persons. Appropriations ranged from a high of $51,600 in the case of Harlan County for hospitals, charities, and corrections, through appropriations of $33,900 in Pike County; $30,450 in Boyd; $20,672 in Bell; $20,000 in Floyd, to $111 in Jackson; $100 in Wolfe, to zero appropriations in Elliott, McCreary, and Owsley. Laurel County's 1958-1959 welfare appropriation was distributed as follows: general home relief, $3,000; aid to the blind, $950; hospital care, $800; county burials, $450; idiot claims, $250; and other forms of care, $200.

In time the Appalachian state governments entered the welfare field with North Carolina and Virginia taking an early lead. However, it was not until the depression of the 1930's and the passage of the Social Security Act that state departments of welfare were established in the Appalachian states to administer the public assistance programs made possible by the Social Security Act and subsequent revisions and additions to it.

In 1957, 284,859 persons in the Appalachian counties were receiving public assistance payments under these programs. This was 4.9 percent of the estimated population of the Region. The percentage has not varied greatly in recent years. As the map (Figure 76) shows, there is considerable variation from county to county, ranging from Virginia's low county (.8) to Alabama's low (6.6), and from Virginia's high county (5.3) to Kentucky's high (15.1).

Public assistance rates are highest in the poorer mountain counties in contrast to lower rates in the fertile valley and prosperous urban counties, especially the metropolitan counties. The heaviest concentration of assistance is in the mountain counties of West Virginia and Kentucky and in the Cumberland and Blue Ridge Mountain counties of Tennessee, Alabama, and Georgia. The low total assistance rates in Virginia may be due in large measure to the more conservative policy which Virginia has in granting public assistance.

Probably the most accepted and least controversial form of public assistance is Old Age Assistance. In 1957, 86,456 persons—1.5 percent of the population—were receiving such assistance in the Region (Figure 77). Rates ranged from under 0.5 percent in nine counties of Virginia and one of West Virginia to over 3.1 percent in a group of West Virginia, Alabama, and Georgia counties. A high rate of 6.3 percent was reached in one of the Kentucky counties and 5.4 percent in a West Virginia county. On the other hand, such urbanized counties as Sullivan and Hamblen in Tennessee had rates of 0.9 and 0.8 percent, respectively.

The average monthly payments in Appalachian counties ranged from $24.56 to $45.98, and were generally lower than the average payments in the seven states, presumably because of lower living costs in the rural counties. In some states, however, payments are remarkably uniform, indicating a tendency to pay the maximum permitted by state and federal funds available, and/or the lack of good case work to determine need. Local welfare offices that put most emphasis upon case work seem to have the greatest variation in Old Age Assistance grants between clients. In counties where certification is a very routine matter recipients in the same general area seem to receive about the same amounts. More investment in trained case workers would conceivably save the states' public assistance monies. Some states increased their average payments between 1957 and 1959 but the general trend was for payments to be fairly stable from year to year.

Unfortunately, most studies of persons receiving various forms of public assistance in the Appalachian states deal with statewide totals or samples and do not contain county data; nevertheless, they are indicative of situations in the Appalachian study area. A Kentucky survey of Old Age Assistance made in 1956 shows, for example, that 59 percent of the recipients of O. A. A. were women, and that 64 percent had no spouse (or no spouse present). About 24 percent were bedridden, chairfast, or otherwise

THE SOUTHERN APPALACHIANS

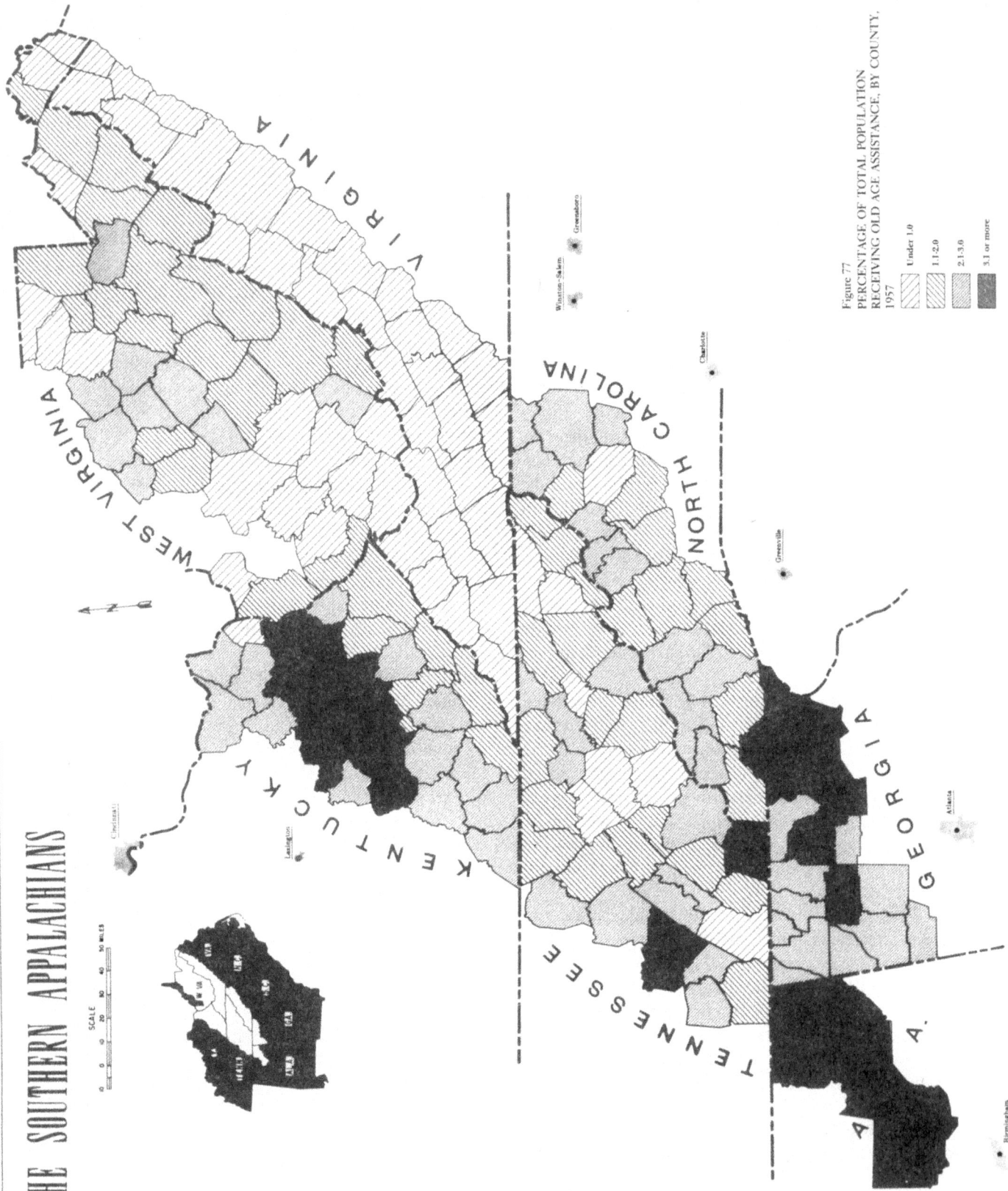

SCALE

0   10   20   40   60   80 MILES

VIRGINIA

VIRGINIA

WEST VIRGINIA

KENTUCKY

NORTH CAROLINA

TENNESSEE

GEORGIA

A. A.

Cincinnati

Lexington

Birmingham

Atlanta

Greenville

Charlotte

Winston-Salem
Greensboro

Figure 77
PERCENTAGE OF TOTAL POPULATION
RECEIVING OLD AGE ASSISTANCE, BY COUNTY.
1957

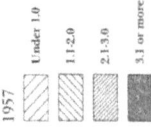

Under 1.0

1.1-2.0

2.1-3.0

3.1 or more

housebound, but 76 percent were capable of outside activity without help.[7] More than half (53 percent) were 75 or older, and less than one in five (19 percent) were under 70.

One of the most constructive provisions in the public assistance program is Aid to Dependent Children, a major objective of which is to keep families together and children in school. In 1957, 175,531 children and adults were in families receiving Aid to Dependent Children. This was equivalent to 3 percent of the Region's population. Rates tend to be high in the coal mining sections and in the more mountainous counties (Figure 78). Virginia rates are somewhat lower than those of other states. In Tennessee, rates are lowest in the East Tennessee Valley counties and highest in the Cumberland Plateau and Blue Ridge Mountain counties. The rates are generally lower in urban than in non-urban counties. Average monthly payments in 1957 varied from around $100 per family downward to $35 per family, and from $25 per person down to $17 per person. In 1959, the lowest Appalachian state averaged $35 per family for A. D. C. and the highest $94. The state with the highest average payment per individual paid $24 and the lowest $9, a change in this instance from an average payment of $22 in 1958. Rather abrupt changes in A. D. C. payments are made in keeping with the amount of funds a state has. In most of the states about 20 percent of the cost of the A. D. C. program is borne by the state, 70 percent by the Federal government, and 10 percent by the counties.

About 33 percent of families receiving A. D. C. assistance are one-child families; 40 percent are families with two and three children, and 27 percent have more than three children. A study of families receiving Aid to Dependent Children in Kentucky revealed that the father was incapacitated in 45 percent of the cases, dead in 14 percent, divorced or separated from the mother in 9 percent, was not married to the mother in 16 percent, and was in a correctional institution in 5 percent. Other conditions existed in the remainder of the families.[8]

A state-wide study of families in North Carolina receiving A. D. C. aid revealed that almost two-thirds of the families who had been receiving such aid over a period of time had become self-supporting, most of them because of increased earnings. Also notable was the fact that scholarship recognition awards had been received by 10 percent of the children of A. D. C. families who had attended North Carolina public high schools.[9]

In 1957, 4,896 persons in Appalachian counties were receiving Aid to the Blind. Monthly payments averaged slightly more than $50 in the counties with the highest payments, and were less than $35 in the counties with the lowest payments. Other state services are active in counseling and vocational training of the blind.

More recent in origin is Aid to the Permanently and Totally Disabled. The number covered by this program is not large but it fills an important gap in the assistance programs by giving a form of assistance to the disabled who cannot qualify in other assistance categories. Grants usually ranged from $35 to $55 in the Appalachian counties. Only fragmentary data are available on the condition of people receiving Aid to the Disabled. Among the more frequent disabling factors among such recipients are mental deficiency, diseases of the central nervous system, infectious and parasitic diseases, hypertension, cardiac conditions, and arthritis.

Vocational Rehabilitation Services—another joint state-federal program—provides surgical treatment, physical rehabilitation, and occupational training for the handicapped and, to a lesser degree, follows them up on their jobs after they are employed.

In addition to the assistance categories mentioned above, all states in the area administer fairly small amounts of general assistance, the purposes of which are indicated in a statement from the Roanoke County (Virginia) Department of Public Welfare: "General Relief serves many a purpose when no category is available. It is particularly useful to pay for doctors, x-rays, prescriptions, out-patient clinic care. When a family's credit is gone and the pantry is bare, General Relief is useful to prevent hunger."[10]

Since the Appalachian people are usually applauded for their individuality, self-sufficiency, and resourcefulness, the extent to which public assistance is viewed with favor in the Appalachian area is rather surprising (see Chapter II). The aspect of the public assistance which stirs up the most controversy, objections, and publicity in both rural and urban counties is the

[7] Kentucky Department of Economic Security, "Characteristics of Needy OAA Recipients in Kentucky," *Statistical Journal of Economic Security in Kentucky*, May, 1958.

[8] Kentucky Department of Economic Security, "Characteristics of Families Receiving ADC," *Statistical Journal of Economic Security in Kentucky*, April, 1956.

[9] North Carolina State Board of Public Welfare, *Families Receiving Aid to Dependent Children in North Carolina* (Raleigh, August, 1949).

[10] Virginia Department of Welfare and Institutions, *Virginia Welfare Bulletin*, XXXVIII (July, 1960), 6-7.

THE SOUTHERN APPALACHIANS

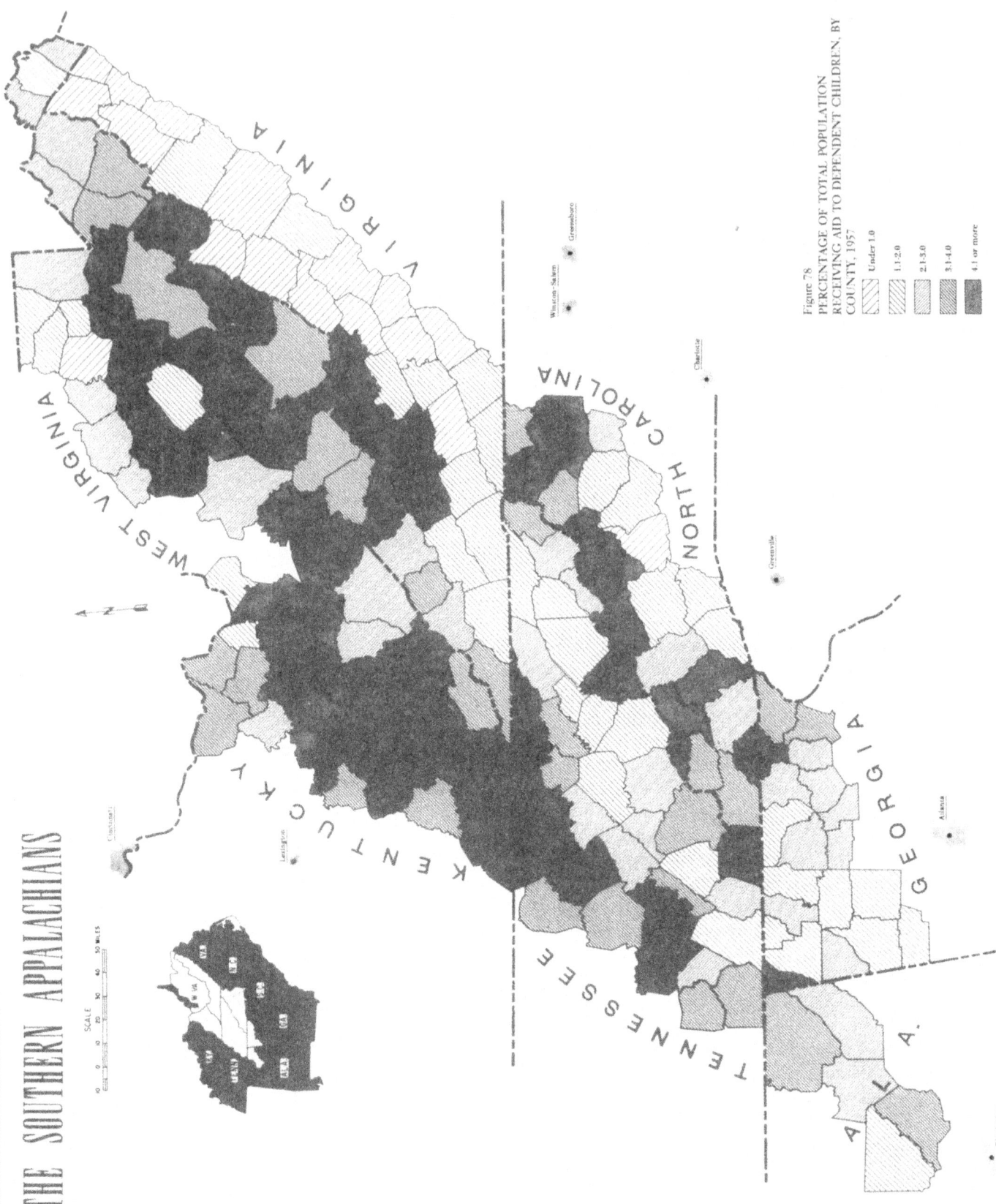

Figure 78

PERCENTAGE OF TOTAL POPULATION
RECEIVING AID TO DEPENDENT CHILDREN, BY
COUNTY, 1957

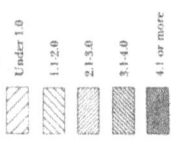

Under 1.0
1.1-2.0
2.1-3.0
3.1-4.0
4.1 or more

SCALE
0   10   20   30   40   50 MILES

WEST VIRGINIA

VIRGINIA

KENTUCKY

TENNESSEE

NORTH CAROLINA

GEORGIA

A L A.

Cincinnati

Lexington

Winston-Salem

Greensboro

Charlotte

Greenville

Atlanta

Birmingham

A. D. C. assistance to children born out of wedlock. Church leaders often bring pressure to bear upon legislators and welfare officials either to have "illegitimate" children barred from public grants or at least to limit the number of grants to unwed mothers. Local criticism is particularly sharp when unwed mothers already on A. D. C. rolls receive assistance for a new child born out of wedlock. It is somewhat surprising, therefore, to learn that, of the 1,466 respondents in the attitude survey, about two-thirds (64.3 percent) said that they believed an unwed mother should receive welfare payments, if needed, to support her child. Only 14.1 percent opposed such aid; 18.8 said it should be given in "some cases," and 2.9 percent made no response to this question. In the metropolitan areas the percentage of respondents who believed an unwed mother in need should not receive assistance payments was 7.1, whereas in the rural areas the percentage was 17.4, the higher figure apparently reflecting a degree of rural moral conservatism. No question was asked relating to how many illegitimate children in a family should receive A. D. C. assistance. The reason for pressure to limit the number of assistance grants to children of unwed mothers is that such assistance is believed to encourage mothers to have additional children.

In a Tennessee study made in 1955, the author found that about 5 percent of all children born in Tennessee were born out of wedlock, and that 8 percent of the children mothers had when they came on the A. D. C. rolls had been born out of wedlock. However, since the mothers had been on A. D. C. rolls, only about 3 percent of their new children had been born out of wedlock. A study made in North Carolina in 1957 reported that 2 percent of white births and 23 percent of non-white births were reported as illegitimate. A sample study of 75,000 children receiving assistance showed that 62,000 had been born in wedlock and 13,000 out of wedlock. Among white children in the state who were born out of wedlock, 9.3 percent received Aid to Dependent Children, while among non-white children born out of wedlock, 8.8 received aid. Of all white children born in wedlock, 2.5 percent received aid, while of all non-white children born in wedlock 6.8 percent received aid.[11]

The above data would seem to indicate that in these states public assistance to unwed mothers has not increased the number of illegitimate births, and that a high percentage of illegitimate children are not on assistance rolls.

Private Welfare Organizations

The development of county public assistance to the needy was accompanied by the growth of private welfare agencies, organized as a result of church effort and the effort of private non-church related charities.

Several dozen community welfare projects within the Appalachian study area are supported by church or other private groups. Some of the community projects started as schools, at a time when isolated areas did not have adequate schools; many of these centers have kept up their health and welfare activities after their school work has been made a part of the county public school system. While many services formerly provided by these agencies are now provided from public sources, the flexibility and diversity of the welfare efforts of such agencies have left them with plenty to do. Among the well-known community projects in the Region are Pitman Center in Sevier County, Tennessee; the Konnarock, Virginia, Community Project; the Church of Christ School, Hazel Green, Wolfe County, Kentucky; the Frontier Nursing Service, Wendover, Kentucky; and the church-sponsored school and hospital projects at Banner Elk, North Carolina.

The most universal county-based private welfare activity in the Appalachian area is that of the American Red Cross. The Red Cross raises modest sums of money in rural counties, often under $250, but large sums in urban counties, sometimes $50,000 or more. Red Cross aid is returned to the people of the county mostly during periods of emergency. In some communities the resources of the local Red Cross are tapped to meet acute family emergencies.

The larger Appalachian cities have United Fund or Community Chest campaigns and organizations. Some of these in their annual fund drives raise a million dollars in funds and may support as many as thirty agencies. In the metropolitan cities and in some smaller cities, Councils of Community Services have been developed for the coordination of the work of welfare agencies, especially United Fund agencies.

The Save the Children Federation has school sponsorship programs in thirty-six counties within the Southern Appalachian Region and in twenty-one counties just outside it. The Federation also maintains a used clothing project in many of the mountain counties. In addition to the clothing sold, the S. C. F.

---

[11] For a summary of the study see Gareth D. Thorne, "Births Out of Wedlock," *Tennessee Public Welfare Record*, August, 1960, pp. 206-212.

area consultants provided schools during the year 1959-1960 with 59,000 pounds of free clothing, and shoes. To its sponsored schools, S. C. F. makes a small grant-in-aid as a means of stimulating each school community to develop a self-help program.

Agricultural extension services, the Carolina Power Company, the Georgia Power Company, and other agencies have developed self-help programs in certain communities, similar to those of the S. C. F. communities. Some private colleges like Berea in Kentucky and Hiwassee in Tennessee have long sponsored community development programs.

Special mention should also be made of the hospital and associated services made available through the United Mine Workers of America Welfare and Retirement Fund to miners and their families. When the U. M. W. Fund came into existence there was a big backlog of crippled miners in the Appalachian area, many of whom could not work. One miner, injured in a slate fall, had spent thirteen years at home in bed, completely helpless. Both of his legs had been amputated and his body was a mass of bed sores when he was found by a U. M. W. representative. He received physical treatment in a U. M. W. hospital, was sent to an eastern rehabilitation center, and was finally put to work at a useful occupation. Many such people have been rehabilitated. The work of the U. M. W. in rehabilitating the physically handicapped has been a stimulus to the development of other rehabilitation services (see Chapter XIV).

Improvement of Welfare Services

Appalachian counties contain a minimum of three or four welfare agencies in the smaller rural counties to more than one hundred agencies in the metropolitan counties. In the smaller counties there is usually a welfare committee of the county governing body, a local office of the state department of public welfare, and a county unit of the Red Cross. These are the most common welfare agencies, exclusive of some welfare efforts of PTA groups. In one urban county there were eighteen agencies concerned solely with giving protective services to children, and twenty-eight agencies and services having to do with other kinds of welfare services.

Probably the most critical deficiency in local public and private welfare administration in the study area is the lack of coordination of welfare services outside the metropolitan counties, where there are Councils of Community Services. This lack of coordination results in duplication of fund drives, some duplication of service, and much duplication of expense, even in communities where welfare services and resources are inadequate. Agency personnel and boards are frequently ill informed about available local, state, and national welfare services. One practice that has worked well in some Appalachian counties has been the development of county welfare committees that act in an advisory capacity to the county office of the state welfare department. Such committees should be made up of persons with wide experience who know welfare needs and resources, both developed and potential, of the county and its communities. These committees, however, are not an adequate substitute for a social services or welfare council, with a paid director, working on a county-wide basis.

There is also critical need for more counseling to the assistance applicant and the recipient of assistance. Too many people in the Region have come to depend upon welfare departments for permanent assistance. More effort needs to be devoted to the rehabilitation of welfare recipients and development among parents and adult children of more personal responsibility for the care of dependents. For this effort, better qualified case workers, with greater freedom from political ties and pressures, will be needed. It is not unusual to find social workers with a case load of three hundred or more public assistance clients. With the heavy case loads carried by most social workers, it is impossible for them to do more than routine investigation, or to review case loads more than once a year. Smaller case loads, handled by well-qualified workers, would save money and improve services.

Outside of recreational and character building agencies, adoption and foster home placement of children, spotty family counseling programs, and the probationing of juvenile offenders, preventive social agency programs in most local communities are hard to find.

It is hard for the public to see that the most productive effort in welfare in the long run is the type of program which prevents problems from developing. Disease and accident prevention and adequate prenatal, natal, and post-natal care are preferable to having to care for the crippled and physically handicapped. Locating and treating pre-delinquency is more productive of desirable social habits than the custodial care and remedial treatment of delinquents or criminals. Investments in recreation, education, and religious activities for children and youth are, in the long run, more productive for a society than similar efforts with adults. The Appalachian social services critically need more emphasis on prevention.

Folk Arts in Transition

*T*HE TENDENCY *of traditionalistic societies to resist change is perhaps more than matched by the tendency of modern societies to deprecate traditional beliefs and practices as unprogressive and obsolete. Yet, even if we use the progressive's criterion of functionalism, there is much to be found of value in the culture of yesteryear. Certainly this has proved to be the case in the preservation of the folk arts and crafts of the Southern Appalachian people.*

"The traditional folk arts may well find their last refuge between the covers of a few books," write W. D. Weatherford and Wilma Dykeman in their analysis of regional literature. But if this is to be so, at least they are to be preserved in a form that can continue to give pleasure and enlightenment in the future as in the past. And the mountain culture has provided both a rich store of the raw materials of life and no few creative artists who could capture them in literature of enduring value.

Whatever the future of mountain folk arts, it is still too early to write their obituary. This is clearly indicated in the persistence of square dances and singing games which, as Frank H. Smith has observed in his essay, are enjoying a revival of interest in many localities. Convinced of their intrinsic worth, he offers several recommendations for preserving their vitality in our contemporary culture.

The renaissance of mountain crafts has already occurred, and the story of their decline and revival is recounted in the chapter by Bernice A.

Stevens. So successful has been their reemergence as a functional part of the regional culture and economy that they have attracted foreign competition in the form of spurious craft objects, and have aroused local enthusiasm as a major means of raising regional income. Miss Stevens deplores the former development as a threat to the reputation of genuine mountain crafts and cautions handicraft partisans that "crafts are not a quick answer to all financial needs of depressed mountain areas."

CHAPTER SIXTEEN

Literature

since

1900

W. D. WEATHERFORD

WILMA DYKEMAN

A CONTEMPORARY POET HAS SAID, "Literature is news that stays news."[1] A contemparary American judge has offered the opinion that "literature exists for the sake of the people—to refresh the weary, to console the sad, to hearten the dull and downcast, to increase man's interest in the world, his joy of living, and his sympathy in all sorts and conditions of man."[2]

There are, of course, other more profound definitions, but these two suggest an approach to consideration of the literature of the Southern Appalachian mountains as it fits the purposes of these studies. (1) Is there a significant literature of the mountains? (2) Has it recorded the "news" of the sort of people who settled and now inhabit this region, the fundamental changes that have been taking place in their lives during the last quarter-century, and their attitudes and needs as they experience these changes? (3) And has this recording been accomplished with an artistry of style, a universality of understanding that will make these events of yesterday and today "stay news"? (4) Finally, if this literature exists, and if it is of merit, is there any way by which its power to refresh, console, extend interest, increase joy and enlarge sympathy may be implemented?

The answer to the first question is simply yes, and its proof is implicit, we believe, in the discussions of the other questions. Answer to the second question is predicated on a conviction that the literature of the mountains may provide both outside observers and native participants with a depth of understanding that the breadth of a sociological survey cannot, and does not seek to, achieve.

The third question involves evaluation of mountain writing. That wise Frenchman, Montaigne, once said, "To judge of things high and mighty, there is need of a mind of the same scope. Otherwise we attribute to them the pettiness that is our own. A straight arrow always appears crooked in the water. It isn't the fact that you see it that counts, but how you see it."[3]

We have held this thought in mind while choosing which author, and sometimes which book of that author, would best illustrate the point at hand. Certain facts or aspects of the Region's life may have been dealt with in several books by several different authors. Since we are more interested in evaluating a representative selection than in enumerating a lengthy collection of books, we have tried to select those which seemed to us to render mountain life with the greatest accuracy, clarity and artistry.

Perhaps this is also the proper place to mention the matter of cause and effect. Jesse Stuart, the Kentucky hill poet-novelist has asked, "Should it matter where a man is born—a shack, a cottage or a palace? Does his environment make him or does his blood tell? This is an old question and we'll not debate it here. The only thing is, I pray that it really doesn't matter."[4]

How many of the men and women we mention here are writers because they were born in the mountains? Or in spite of it? These are matters that have confounded the critics for centuries. The more valid evaluation perhaps concerns the accuracy—or, in a more philosophical realm, the truth—with which the writer records the segment of mountain life he has chosen to interpret, and the artistic success of his completed work. Emerson wrote, in a discussion of history, that "Time dissipates to shining ether the solid angularity of facts. No anchor, no cable, no fences avail to keep a fact a fact."

It is this "ether" which we seek here to penetrate and partially describe. A Kentucky artist, Elizabeth Madox Roberts, has understood this and suggested it in one of her early poems:

Men will be telling their joys, or be singing
Their loves, and the earth be renewed in the giving.
The tales of their fathers retelling, and looking
In prayer to their God. And softly the cradles be
    rocking.

Men will be speaking together to tell
Of the wars, and be asking, and leaving
Their labors to hear. And the hearing be grieving.[5]

Of the speaking and the hearing, "the tales retelling" since 1900, we shall concern ourselves in this chapter.

Because they were frontiersmen so early and so long, one of the first and firmest traditions of the Southern Appalachians included a folk literature. The peoples of early Appalachia were made up primarily from two streams of immigrants. First, the Scotch-Irish landing in the Delaware Bay moved westward through Southern Pennsylvania to the section of Harper's Ferry where they divided, some going on west into West Virginia, Ohio, and further, the other group crossing the Potomac and going down the Shenandoah Valley, into the Holston River country of East Tennessee, from there spreading out into North Georgia, North Alabama, and Kentucky. The second wave of migration was from the Scotch Highlands. This wave of people landed at Wilming-

ton, Charleston, and Port Royal, and moved up the Great Pee Dee, the Neuse, and the Cape Fear Rivers into the mountains of North Carolina, and over into the "western waters" of Tennessee and Kentucky, merging with the Scotch-Irish trek into the same country. Of course some English, some Germans, and some Dutch also came into the area, but the dominating strain was Scotch.

Their characteristics have been summarized as including an economy, perhaps parsimony, of words; an insuperable dislike to wear their hearts on their sleeves; a quiet and undemonstrative deportment which may have great firmness and determination behind it; a dour countenance which may cover a genial disposition; much conviction, wariness, and reserve; and a decided faculty for the practical side of life.

This was the popular view of the mountaineer and —as is the case with most generalizations—it was partly true, partly false, and greatly over-simplified. For instance, although many of the old ballads would support this portrait of gloom and fatalism, many of the "liar's bench tales" and local stories we can classify only as folk history reveal a deep "belly-laugh" sense of humor, a sense of the ridiculous that would suggest these were also relaxed, sociable people, at least with their own kind. They wedded music to tale-telling and perpetuated a distinctive form.

In one of her many authentic children's books about the Southern Appalachians and its people, the Tennessee writer, May Justus, has a little girl respond to one of the ballads, " 'That,' Honey Jane declared when the song was done, 'is almost as good as a story.'

" 'It is a story,' Father replied. 'All the old ballads are stories which have been handed down from far-off times, generation after generation.' "[6]

The accumulated wisdom of many ancestors, the colorful words and phrases and similes of folk language, are part of the heritage of this century's mountain literature. Almost totally overwhelmed, in many parts of the region, by the onslaughts of radio and television, the traditional folk arts may well find

[1] Ezra Pound, *How to Read*, 1931.

[2] Judge M. T. Manton, "Dissenting Opinion in United States vs. One Book Entitled *Ulysses*," 1934.

[3] Quoted in Philo N. Buck, Jr., *Literary Criticism* (New York, 1930), p. 177.

[4] Jesse Stuart, *Beyond Dark Hills* (New York, 1938), p. 26.

[5] Elizabeth Madox Roberts, *Song in the Meadow* (New York, 1940), p. 11.

[6] May Justus, *Honey Jane* (New York, 1938), p. 13.

their last refuge between the covers of a few books.

Some straightforward collections of this "spoken literature" have been made by mountain writers. During the depression years five writers gathered some of the tall yarns told on Tennessee courthouse lawns or around pot-bellied stoves in country stores, and called their book *God Bless The Devil!* James R. Aswell, writing an introduction, made this observation:

"Liars' Bench tales are intended solely to amuse the teller and his listeners, but sociologists and students of psychology could find in them a depth of unintended meaning. At the Liars' Bench a man is relaxed; he gives his mind the reins and lets it wander where it will. Because his words will not be weighed, judged, and held against his morals or character, his stories are more apt to reveal what he really thinks about life and death, religion, and his fellow men than does his public attitude toward these things."[7]

Fifteen years later, when Leonard W. Roberts published a collection of Kentucky tales entitled *South from Hell-fer-Sartin,* he pointed out changes which were overtaking this form of culture.

"After World War I the way of life in the Kentucky Hills quickly changed. The growing industrial demand for coal coupled with the improvement of the automobile brought more and better roads. With the highways came the electric lines, and with electricity came the radio. In boom times thousands of men and women traveled over the new roads to the industrial centers; laid off in slack times, these homesick people came back to their valleys with new ideas of how to live. . . .

"The significance of these changes for the folklorist is tremendous. The old ways of entertainment have been almost forgotten. The haunting tunes of the folk songs have given way to whining hillbilly music, and the barn dance has replaced party games. People no longer gather for an evening of storytelling. . . . If the general reader finds pleasure in these old stories and gains some insight into a way of life that is now vanishing from our country, I shall feel amply repaid for collecting them."[8]

In two distinguished collections, Richard Chase has preserved *The Jack Tales* and *Grandfather Tales* that are familiar in the hills. They record as faithfully as possible the way these stories sound when they are spoken by the human voice rather than the way they look when they are read on the printed page, and this is as it should be, for such a record also reflects something of the character of the people who spun these stories out of their individual and collective, real or imagined experiences.

Modern novelists and poets of the mountains have drawn on this rich source of inspiration in both story and style. One, North Carolinian Robert K. Marshall, has told how he searched out the foundations for his half legendary, half realistic novel, *Little Squire Jim:* "When it came time to write my first novel I returned to the hills of my birth, and by foot and by car I went into the mountains, gathering materials. I renewed old cousinships (one claimed to be a twenty-second cousin!). I revived old political acquaintances of my father and uncles. I went wherever my story carried me. And as I listened to these folk talk, I tried to snare not only the words and rhythms of their speech but also the pulse of their blood, the beat of their hearts, the light in their eyes as they talked of things close to them."[9]

No writer of the mountains has captured more faithfully the distinctive idiom of the people than James Still. In three books—a volume of poetry, *Hounds on the Mountain,* one novel *River of Earth,* and a collection of short stories, *On Troublesome Creek*—he has created minor classics of mountain literature. In one story from the latter volume three sentences chosen at random suggest the flavor of Still's writing, and the living language he has captured in print: "[She] says she washes clothes so clean you'd swear dogwoods bloomed around the house on Monday. Says she can trash air' man ever she did see hoeing a corn row."

And: "[Jumpup Holler] hit's so far backside o' nowhere folks have to use possums for yard dogs and owls for roosters."[10]

Perhaps no single novel of the mountains has drawn deeper on the legendary folk qualities of speech and character, the brooding atmosphere and terror of the old ballads, than Mildred Haun's *The Hawk's Done Gone.* For many generations life in the mountains was confined by geographical boundaries and this confinement often made both the life and the folk literature which grew out of everyday existence intensive and introspective, and at the extreme, re-

---

[7] James R. Aswell, et al., *God Bless the Devil!* (Chapel Hill, 1940).

[8] Leonard W. Roberts, *South from Hell-fer-Sartin* (Lexington, Kentucky, 1955).

[9] Robert K. Marshall, *Little Squire Jim* (New York, 1949), quote from dust jacket.

[10] James Still, *On Troublesome Creek* (New York, 1941), pp. 154, 169.

pressed and retrospective. It is this dark extreme that Miss Haun brings to awesome life in her story of several generations of a family in a remote corner of East Tennessee. Superstition holds their daily routine in an iron grip as tight as the poverty and ignorance that circumscribe the horizons of their future. Yet there is also love, pity, an occasional flash of nobility. The commonplace and the weird meet and merge in this extraordinary book. For example there is the passage in which a midwife watches as the father kills his daughter, Cordia, who has borne an illegitimate baby. Together the midwife and father make a coffin for the girl. The old woman recounts the gruesome details in completely realistic fashion.

"When we got the coffin done we didn't even stuff it and put a lining in it. We piled some quilts in it and laid Cordia on them. I did wash Cordia and wrap her up in a new quilt. But we had to break her knees to get her legs down into the coffin.

"And the baby, it kept on living. Mos, he just picked it up and put it on in. I stood and watched him. Stood stone-still and watched him. We nailed the lid down. It was about chicken crow then. I had to stay there in the room while Mos went to dig a grave. And the baby alive."[11]

A ballad is by its very nature the creation of many people. There is one poet of the north Georgia hills, however, who has managed to create ballads whose beauty and authentic quality is undeniable. They may help to prove that the blare of the synthetic and the lure of the commercialized folkways has not yet completely stilled the voice of individual inspiration. *Ballad of the Bones, Bow Down in Jericho,* and *A Song of Joy* combine many of the qualities of the Old Testament Bible with a personal quality of fresh testimony to the mystery and majesty of life. The concluding verses of the title poem in his first book will suggest the pure ballad quality of his work.

Ezekiel,
Behold the blood
Of My sons that fall
In the world's dark wood!

Now prophesy
To the troubled host
Whose bones are dry,
Whose hope is lost;

In the battle's shock,
In the ways they grope,

I am their Rock,
I am their Hope!

Their blood I see,
I hear their groans,
Yea, and I am He
That raised the bones![12]

Here, then, is something of the religious quality brought by the settlers into the mountains. It was a fundamentalist religion, and its deepest internal tensions, as reflected in the churches up to the present day, have often grown out of the opposite attitudes of resignation versus resolution.

Certainly many of the novels describing life of the pioneers have dramatized the resolution of those men and women who came first, remained stronger than the wilderness, and never let go of their grip on hope and courage. Elizabeth Madox Roberts' novel, *The Great Meadow,* is the most triumphant achievement of this group of novels. More recently, the boys' stories of William O. Steele, of Chattanooga, have recorded this aspect with a rare combination of faithfulness to history and craftsmanship in writing.

When confronted with the twin eternals enclosing life, however—birth and death—and some of the enigmas between—pestilence, disease, corruption—mountain people have often relied on resignation rather than resolution. Many of the most forceful passages in mountain literature show the cost, the waste, resulting from this attitude. Jesse Stuart, in a short story, "Fern," tells of the death of a girl by that name who was "sick all her life with consumption." When the narrator and his brother find the delicate girl deserted and dead, the boy says, "I tried to lift Fern. Her body was still. Her blue eyes stared sightless from their dark sockets. They was set still as a picture under glass. I couldn't lift Fern. Maybe I was scared. No, she was stuck to the bed. I hated to uncover Fern. But I was curious to see if she was tied in the bed. The slats of the bed had stuck into her thin body. The bed tick had rotted where she laid on it without attention. Maggots were working around the slats.

" 'No wonder she died,' I cried out to the empty house, 'no wonder Fern died. She died from the want of attention.' "[13]

[11] Mildred Haun, *The Hawk's Done Gone* (Indianapolis, 1940).
[12] Byron Herbert Reece, *Ballad of the Bones and Other Poems* (New York, 1946).
[13] Jesse Stuart, *Men of the Mountains* (New York, 1941), p. 201.

In an unforgettable scene of neglect and slow death, Harriette Arnow in her novel, *Hunter's Horn*, tells of the girl Lureenic, deserted by her husband. "This woman smiling at the fire was no more than the ghost of the old Lureenic who had laughed and cried and loved and hated, cursed Rans every time a child was born, then laughed at her pains when she heard the first cry of her child.

"Sue Annie put a little wormseed in the sulphur and molasses. 'You'll be all right—you'll git along. You'll hear frum Rans an you'll last a long time yit.'

"Lureenie smiled, almost gaily. 'Me, I don't want to last a long time. I think I'd ruther go out like a cedar bush in a brush fire than wear out slow like a doorsill.' "

The night her baby is born, Keg Head, Lureenie's father-in-law, will not fetch a doctor—Sue Annie, the midwife, will do well enough, he says—although he and the other men drinking coffee around the fire are shaken by the girl's agony.

"Lureenie now seemed to have lost most of her reason—she screamed and cried and begged to die in a voice hoarse and dry. She wouldn't bear down to her pains any more, or maybe it was just one long pain—Sue Annie couldn't tell. The listeners by the hearth were restless and Keg Head went outside to pray."[14]

When Lureenie finally dies, Keg Head mourns his own luck and the neighbor's criticism, with "that fool Sue Annie claiming a doctor could have saved her, but God's will was God's will."

The mysteries of life and death as experienced in the institution of the church have been burned into mountain consciousness and conscience early. Jesse Stuart, who embraces all the experiences of mountain life in his zestful, vivid writing, recalls "the cold winter night when my father and my mother wrestled with the Devil. Five Baptists participated in the preaching. I think the Devil was completely whipped that night and had he been there they would have hanged him to the ceiling and filled him full of holes. Anyway there were many powerful threats made against him that night. I was scared—my sister and I sat on the back seat and wondered what it was all about. But my father and mother wrestled the Devil. They won. The next day a hole was chopped in the ice. They were baptized. 'It must be done soon,' said one of the ministers. 'It is high time we were whipping the Devil.' "[15]

And James Still, in his novel, *River of Earth*, shows the child narrator at a midsummer church meeting.

"The preacher raised a finger. He plunged it into the Bible, his eyes roving the benches. When the text was spread before him on the printed page he looked to see what the Lord had chosen. He began to read. I knew then where his mouth was in the beard growth. 'The sea saw it and fled: Jordan was driven back. The mountains skipped like rams, and the little hills like lambs. Tremble, thou earth. . . .' He snapped the book to. He leaned over the pulpit. 'I was borned in a ridge-pocket,' he said. 'I never seed the sun-ball withouten heisting my chin. My eyes were sot upon the hills from the beginning. Till I come on the Word in this good Book, I used to think a mountain was the standingest object in the sight o' God. Hit says here they go skipping and hopping like sheep, a-rising and a-falling. These hills are jist durt waves, washing through eternity. My brethren, they hain't a valley so low but what hit'll rise agin. They hain't a hill standing so proud but hit'll sink to the low ground o' sorrow. Oh, my children, where air we going on this mighty river of earth, a-borning, begetting, and a-dying—the living and the dead riding the waters? Where air it sweeping us?' "[16]

Such a passage suggests one of the distinctive virtues of contemporary mountain literature as opposed to that of an earlier day: it has grown from within the Region. Mountain life had the misfortune of being represented for many years by authors from outside the Region—by missionaries, Northern teachers, junketing newspapermen, or even by such able storytellers as O. Henry. What one critic has said of one of O. Henry's stories, about a feud in the Southern Appalachians, might be said of many of these writers: "He knew that Northern readers of John Fox, Jr. would accept his story as plausible if not authentic."[17]

In his study, *The American Novel*, Carl Van Doren said that "besides the rich planters and their slaves one other class of human beings in the South especially attracted the attention of the local colorists: the mountaineers. . . . Here again formulas sprang up and so stifled the free growth of observation that, though a multitude of stories was written about the mountain people, almost all of them may be resolved into themes as few in number as those which

[14] Harriette Arnow, *Hunter's Horn* (New York, 1949), p. 392.
[15] Jesse Stuart, *Beyond Dark Hills* (New York, 1938), p. 29.
[16] James Still, *River of Earth* (New York, 1940), p. 76.
[17] Jay B. Hubbell, *The South In American Literature* (Durham, N.C., 1954), p. 842.

succeeded nearer Tidewater. . . . The mountain people, inarticulate themselves, were almost uniformly seen from the outside and consequently studied in their surface peculiarities more often than in their deeper traits of character. And, having once entered the realm of legend, they continued to be known by the half-dozen distinguishing features which in legend are always enough for any type."[18]

Jean Thomas, who has done much to put on record some of the unique aspects of Kentucky life, challenged this inclination to "type" her people. "The mountain people of Kentucky already have an established place in literature: they have represented themselves, and have been represented, and misrepresented, by others. I could wax indignant on the matter of misrepresentation; indeed, one purpose of this book is to show the mountain people as they are rather than as romantic fiction would sometimes have them: proud, aloof, liberty-loving people, on the one hand; degraded poor-white trash on the other. The truth, of course, lies between, as it always does, and the truth, at present, is changing as rapidly as the colors on a distant wooded hill in September twilight."[19]

Perhaps one reason for the "typing" of the people in many early books on the mountains was the overwhelming impact on authors of the natural world. Even as understanding a novelist as Charles Egbert Craddock (Mary N. Murfree), who wrote both before and after the turn of the century, in such books as *The Prophet Of the Great Smoky Mountains, In the Tennessee Mountains* and a dozen others, often creates characters who are less individual than the mountain summits she describes. Indeed, "describes" may be the key word to her flaw, and that of a host of similar writers, who describe characters as they do scenery, as picturesque, rather than letting them grow and reveal themselves through the conflicts and processes of life. Craddock loved nature so much that at the least appeal she turned aside from the main story to fill in every detail of the scenic background.

With the rise of an indigenous literature, nature has assumed both a larger and a lesser role. The latter has meant that literary description is no longer acceptable as a substitute for meaningful insight. Pathetic fallacies and purple prose have fallen by the wayside as native writers revealed the larger influences of the mountains, of the natural world, on the people who live therein.

As an indiscriminate "love" of nature may become a literary pitfall, so a complete yielding to its lures

may also become a man's nemesis. In her *Hunter's Horn*, Harriette Arnow has given us the story of such a man and his downfall. Nunnely Ballew is obsessed with the idea that he is destined to catch the red fox, King Devil, which is the scourge of the countryside. To that end he neglects his farm, starves his family, allows his place to fall to ruin, and wakes up too late to recover what he has lost. It is a sad, grim story, and yet Nunn Ballew is touched by something of the same fire that drove Ahab after the great white whale. Thus, experiences of mountain life are translated into universal terms.

Such terms include Jesse Stuart's celebrations of his native soil, which would be understood by all people everywhere who have lived next to and by the hardness—and goodness—of the earth. "My hills have given me bread," he says. "They have put song in my heart to sing. They have made my brain thirst for knowledge so much that I went beyond my own dark hills to get book knowledge. But I got an earthly degree at home from my own dark soil. I got a degree about birds, cornfields, trees, wildflowers, log shacks, my own people, valleys and rivers and mists in the valleys."[20]

A strong sense of place infuses many other mountain novels, Henry Giles' *Harbin's Ridge*; the children's books of Billy C. Clark and Rebecca Caudill Ayars; and *Homeplace*, written by a husband-and-wife team whose single pen name is Maristan Chapman. Bess, one of their characters, says, "A homeplace is like that. Hit wraps a person around; hit's where things happen to a person."[21]

In a more subtle way and dealing with a more difficult milieu, perhaps, James Agee's *A Death In the Family* is one of the remarkable and moving novels of this region. Agee, born and reared through early childhood in Knoxville, Tennessee, wrote in a variety of fields—poetry, movies, social and artistic criticism, fiction—but his last and probably best book, published posthumously, the novel mentioned above, returned to the town of Knoxville for its setting and to the middleclass families of his childhood for its characters. These are mountain people once-removed from the mountains, now dwellers on concrete, just beginning to be standardized by their neighbors and urban ways, but still aware of the land

[18] Carl Van Doren, *The American Novel: 1789-1939* (New York, 1940), p. 206.

[19] Jean Thomas, *Big Sandy* (New York, 1940), p. 4.

[20] Jesse Stuart, *Head O' W-Hollow* (New York, 1936), p. 339.

[21] Maristan Chapman, *Homeplace* (New York, 1929).

around them, the hold of family ties, the meaning of gentleness and religious faith, and all this is reflected in the response of a young boy to the death in the family.

A vivid and poetic, albeit realistic, sense of place also permeates the work of a young West Virginia author, Mary Lee Settle. *O Beulah Land* and *Know Nothing* are the first two of a series of novels she plans to write on the history of West Virginia from frontier days to the present. They augur well for the future, for this young native of Charleston, West Virginia, possesses a rare talent for absorbing the facts of history and seeing them, not with the hindsight of the historian, but with the immediacy of those contemporaries living the events of the past. Thus her work provides that third dimension that excellent fiction has always brought to historic fact: it permits readers to know what happened and believe it happened and also to feel with the happening. Rich characterization and a skillful narrative style distinguish Miss Settle's writing. West Virginia may well have found in her its finest chronicler, although she is wise enough to know that, for every artist, any region begins in the human heart.

Awareness of the beauty and treachery of nature, the grandeur of the mountains that can lift man to nobility or reduce him to inconsequence, and of the balance between the natural and manmade world, has also been reflected in some of the region's nonfiction. Wilma Dykeman's *The French Broad*, a study of the Western North Carolina and Eastern Tennessee country drained by that river, would be an example. In her first chapter, the author says, "The French Broad is a river and a watershed and a way of life where day-before-yesterday and day-after-tomorrow exist in odd and fascinating harmony. There is the same coexistence of past and present within the people. It helps explain how they may be at once so maddening and so charming, wrong about so many things and yet fundamentally right so often."[22]

And in her closing chapter, she says, "You cannot know this river by simply sitting on the level banks of its lower body or by striking out on any straight road up its course; you must judge the 'lay of the land' and follow a wandering path that will take 'rounders' on its sources high in the mountains. Likewise, to know its people you cannot adopt quick attitudes or secondhand generalities, a frontal approach forespells failure in any friendship; you must take 'rounders' here, too, and find your way by easy conversation into their sources of character and life.

As each odd characteristic little branch finally drains the fullness of its stream into the French Broad, so each individual person finally pours the ripeness of his personality into the region where he dwells. There is no one creek, there is no one person, representative of the river of this region. But there are a few of the little creeks and little people whose lives and words bespeak with special force some particular feature of the French Broad." And the bulk of this book is made up of the history and folklore and fact of the little streams and the "little" people who have made the Region "above all, a country of rich and varied life."

Just as reaction to natural surroundings may result in a curse or a blessing, depending on the person involved, so reaction to the chief characteristics of mountain life, as reflected in its literature, may vary. Economic poverty, one of the persistently predominant aspects of life in the Southern Appalachians, may provide a challenge to residents or artists of the Region. On the other hand, it may serve to reinforce a mental, spiritual and cultural wasteland. Self-sufficiency, inspired by great need, may start as a virtue and end as a vice—or a vise, holding itself in an unwarranted and fruitless isolationism, impeding the growth of good schools, progressive churches, adequate medical care, improved roads, new industries and an efficient political arrangement. Pride that is a virtue may also be a handicap-fostering withdrawal from a competitive world, breeding frustration and violence. These truths have provided themes for most of the outstanding books in the mountains today, many of which have already been mentioned.

In Jean Ritchie's autobiographical *Singing Family of the Cumberlands*, both the simplicity and complexity of life in a family of fourteen children in the hills is meaningful and real. The drudgery and reward of hard physical labor are described in one illustrative passage:

"I began my work in the fields as a water-carrier, but by the time I was ten I was an all-day worker taking my own row with my hoe. I felt mighty important and grown-up those first few days, but then the shine was gone; and it was just a tired back bending over the green rows that had no end, grubby fingers reaching down without the eyes seeing to thin out the hill, leaving the two strongest stalks to grow. It was the clinking sound that came too

---

[22] Wilma Dykeman, *The French Broad* (New York, 1955).

often of hoes fighting the millions of rocks; Dad's tired swearing at the old mule and Mom's weary fussing at him for it . . . it was the heaven in the cool shade at the end of the round, the ecstasy in a gourd-ful of spring water, the foolery in a snatch of song."[23]

The sense of close family ties is one of the most fundamental facts of mountain character. Harry Harrison Kroll, in his novel *Darker Grows The Valley*, shows the strength of family ties that are cherished down through generations from pioneer patriarch through granddaughters of the mid-twentieth century. Mr. Kroll has also demonstrated that this pride of family may be distorted into a destructive force. *Their Ancient Grudge*, the story of the Kentucky Mountains' famous Hatfield-McCoy feud, shows Devil Anse Hatfield, wicked and cruel, nevertheless following a perverted sense of honor in killing those he believes to be enemies of his clan.

Because of the frequent paradoxes in mountain life, its literature is likewise paradoxical. At its best it is both poetic and realistic, tough and tender, objective and subjective. As Professor Harlan Hatcher pointed out in discussing Elizabeth Madox Roberts' fine first novel, *The Time of Man*, published in 1926: "Its success was arresting because of the poetic mood she had created out of materials that were starkly realistic. She wrote of a family of poor whites from the hill regions of Kentucky and showed them moving about in their shiftless poverty, drifting, sinking no roots in any one place. Ellen Chesser, the center of the novel, was, however, endowed by her creator with a soul and a confused sense of beauty. It was precisely this feeling for beauty that gave the novel its distinction. For it conveyed not so much the harsh, external realities of Ellen's life with her poor farm-hand husband (although it did that too), but rather an imaginative world created by the poetic mood of the author and made to seem more real than pure objectivity."[24]

A reality "made to seem more real than pure objectivity"—this, of course, embodies the artistry of style and universality of understanding mentioned in question three on the purposes of this discussion. As we consider some of the changes in mountain life and how they have been interpreted by our writers, let us keep in mind this evaluation of style and appeal.

Of some of the changes wrought in the mountains by depression and war, relief and pensions, one of the most entertaining examples is Jesse Stuart's *Taps For Private Tussie*. Here are the individualists turned parasite. War brought a new peace to such people—

a truce with the threat of starvation. Hard work, determination to "get ahead," or at least survive, may be the rule in the mountains, but the Tussies are the exception that prove it.

When Grandpa Press Tussie receives word that his son, Kim, has been killed in World War II, the tribe is plunged into an orgy of grief. When Vittie, Kim's widow, receives his insurance money, they plunge into an orgy of spending. After all, the charity food never had been good, but it was better than working! The cycle from cabin to big house to hovel runs its course and Kim finally returns from war, very much alive. His body had been falsely identified by his brother, Mott, who wanted to marry Vittie himself. The deeper family responsibilities and all sense of individual dignity are shown in the Tussies as gone to seed. But the tone of Stuart's writing is so extravagant and so filled with a simple sort of folk humor that the story is similar to several novels of world literature, Gogol's *Dead Souls*, for instance, where the indolent and the rascally try to outwit the sober workers for civilization.

The changes wrought by improved roads and communications have not always been welcomed by the mountain writers, who understand that the physical improvements are nothing in themselves, it is the use to be made of them that is important. James Still, in a poem, "White Highways," has written,

I have gone out to the roads that go up and down
In smooth white lines, stoneless and hard;
I have seen distances shortened between two points,
The hills pushed back and bridges thrust across
The shallow river's span.
To the broad highways, and back again I have come
To the creek-bed roads and narrow winding trails
Worn into ruts by hoofs and steady feet;
I have come back to the long way around,
The far between, the slow arrival.
Here is my pleasure most where I have lived
And called my home.[25]

Another mountain poet, George Scarbrough, has stated much the same belief in a poem, "The Source Is Anywhere."

The others have gone searching,
Screaming for their find

[23] Jean Ritchie, *Singing Family Of the Cumberlands* (New York, 1955), p. 75.

[24] Harlan Hatcher, *Creating the Modern American Novel* (New York, 1935), p. 250.

[25] James Still, *Hounds on The Mountain* (New York, 1937), p. 45.

With one mind.
But I wait here for a miracle
Beside the brook.

. . . . .

I wait at any point along the brink
For what they seek to come to me.[26]

Many have gone out to the highways, gone searching, and not returned. *Call Home the Heart* and *A
Stone Came Rolling* were two of the earliest mountain novels to tell of the migration of people seeking a better way to make a living outside the hills.
Written by Fielding Burke, the nom de plume of
Olive Tilford Dargan who also wrote, under her own
name, one of the distinctive books on the mountains,
Highland Annals, these novels deal with the new mill
towns of the South and the mountain men and
women who go to work in them, and particularly a
girl named Ishma Waycaster. Ishma, a North Carolina hill-born girl, struggles into a larger understanding of life as she fights for daily bread in the textile
mills without sacrificing her personal dignity and
strength.

The forces of progress have brought their problems
to the ways of mountain life. In Harry Harrison
Kroll's story of five generations of the Clinch family,
near Cumberland Gap, his final conflict within the
family involves their response to the coming of the
Tennessee Valley Authority, and the fact that they
will have to let their bottom lands go for a dam.
"Old WPA TVA CCC PDQ Roosevelt and his
forty thieves! It's a sin and a crime to drown out our
valley. . . . They'll pay me worth the money for this
old house. Yah—but I have lived here all my life,
my father was born here, my grandpaw hewed out
the cove and cleared the land and broke the dirt.
My life and blood is in this soil. The ghosts of my
kin haunt the long cracks in my house. Where is
the worth the money TVA will pay for that?"[27]

These are very real conflicts and experiences taking
place in the mountains and it is well they are depicted in the literature. There are reflections on the
new and terrible vistas opened by the discovery of the
atom bomb. It might be wished that everyone could
react with the sanity and courage of "Old Op," the
central figure in Jesse Stuart's novel, *The Good
Spirit of Laurel Ridge*. When a pair of distant cousins, fresh from the neuroses of city life, come to
Laurel Ridge and Old Op's domain, they bring him
word of the new world of science. Alf and his wife
Julia tell Old Op:

"I couldn't take it any longer. One of these days
planes will cross the Atlantic and Pacific with atom
bombs and wipe out our industrial cities and airfields.
The only safe places in America will be the mountains
and the rough spots where nobody lives. The safe
places will be spots like Laurel Ridge!' "

" 'What's all this ye're a-talkin' about?' Op said,
staring at the intruders. 'I never heard tell of the
adam bumb!' "

And after their explanation, he tells them, " 'I-
gollies, I've never heard a thing about all these bombs,
saucers, and pizen dust.' " He looked suspiciously at
Alf. Then he said, " 'But I'm not runnin' from
nothin!' "[28]

This is personal courage. It typifies something at
once unique and universal in mountain character.

Often more discouraging than the vision of the
world's ending with a bang, however, is the gnawing
dread that one's personal world will end with a whimp-
er. Such is the fear wrought by one of the biggest
changes taking place in this mountain region, the
decay of one of its most important industries, one
of its ways-of-life: coal mining.

No one has described the toll of being a coal
miner, or in a miner's family, better than James
Still. In his *River of Earth* he tells of one spring when
the father is out of work.

"There was no abundance of food and we ate all
that was set before us, with never a crumb left.
Father told us the mines were closed in the headwaters of the Kentucky River and there was hunger
in the camps. We believed that we fared well, and
did not complain.

"Father's face was thin as a saw blade. It seemed
he had grown taller, towering over us. His muscles
were bunched on his arms, blue-veined and not
soft-cushioned now with flesh. He went hunting,
searching through the sedge coves and swampy hollows, never wasting a shot. We ate squirrel and
rabbit, broiled over hot coals, for there was not a
smidgen of grease left in the stone jar. . . .

"We had come through to spring, but Mother was
the leanest of us all, and the baby cried in the night
when there was no milk. Mother ate a little more
now than the rest of us, for the baby's sake, eating
as though for shame while we were not there to see,

[26] George Scarbrough, *Summer So-Called* (New York,
1956), p. 36.
[27] Harry Harrison Kroll, *Darker Grows the Valley* (Indianapolis, 1947), p. 382.
[28] Jesse Stuart, *The Good Spirit of Laurel Ridge* (New
York, 1953), pp. 94-95.

fearing we might not understand, that we might think her taking more than her share."[29]

Still is too excellent a writer to emphasize only one aspect of life, however. Although poverty shapes the lives of most of the people in his stories, and although their actions are often circumscribed by lack of "schooling" and by an innate shyness, there are also flashes of humor, moments of quiet triumph and tenderness, universal love and hate, that lift his novels from the "problem" level to the realm of art.

This same concern for character first and situation and problem second, lifts Harriette Arnow's *The Dollmaker* from a novelized account of migration to industrial centers and makes it, instead, the memorable portrait of a woman and a group of people who are trying to adapt to a strange environment and new customs.

Gertie Nevels, the dollmaker, is a woman cast in the heroic mold. She covets above everything else a little farm all her own where she can be independent and rear her five children in peace and in that sense of security which she believes comes only of life on a farm. Clovis, her husband, is a mechanical tinkerer, and he yearns for the city where he hopes to make big money. When he fails to pass his Army examination, he goes on to Detroit, joining the migrant horde of mountain people who are traveling that path each year. In a particularly effective scene, Mrs. Arnow describes the women gathering at the little mountain post office after all their men have gone to the war or to the manufacturing plants in northern cities. "They were like people huddled together in a wild storm, looking out, looking up, wondering what next the wind will take or the lightning strike."[30]

When Gertie follows her husband to Detroit, the flimsy house in which she has to live is so small that her big body is constantly knocking against a shelf or a door. The alley in which she lives has a veritable melting-pot population with numerous quarreling, fighting children. When the plants shut down, there is no pay and none of the natural bounty of the earth to fall back on. In the midst of all this, Gertie holds to her principles, though Clovis compromises by making cheap tool-shaped dolls and crucifixes. Gertie cherishes the hand carved work. This is a stark picture of the life of mountain people caught in unfamiliar urban surroundings, unprepared for the risks that are part of life in industrial centers no less than in agricultural work. Mrs. Arnow compels us to share Gertie's sense of loss for what has been left behind, her uncertainty about what their search means.

This sense of loss and pursuit of the search is characteristic of the most important writer born and reared in the mountains: Thomas Wolfe. The fact that he might be called an American writer first, a mountain writer second, and a Southern writer third, would perhaps make him more typical than not of mountain writers. Yet he towers above all the rest the way Mt. Mitchell, near his home town of Asheville, North Carolina, towers above all the other mountain peaks of eastern America.

In Wolfe most of the paradoxes of mountain character—indeed, of human nature itself—are met and compounded: the pride and the suspicion, the self-pity and the compassion, the tenderness and the brutality; and one critic has called him "the most romantic of our realists."[31] This same man has said, "He is the creature of his heredity and environmental conditions that determine him to violence and frustration. I find here the artistic justification for the otherwise disproportionate attention given by Wolfe to his childhood. He wishes to show that his hero was given in childhood the bent that doomed him to so much suffering and disillusion, as well as the bent for artistic creation by which he triumphed in the end over evil and disorder. . . . We have many tales of the uncles and aunts and grandparents on his mother's side—sunk in poverty, violence, superstition, pride and ignorance. Even as a boy he realizes that this is the same stock, and that he is of them by his mother's blood."[32]

With the passion of one who has loved his native region, Wolfe recorded some of the changes—for the worse—that refashioned its appearance and its character. In a collection of short stories called *The Hills Beyond*, Thomas Wolfe wrote about his native town, which he calls Zebulon, and the western North Carolina countryside. "Some changes had occurred in Zebulon in those years, but for the most part these were tragic ones. The great mountain slopes and forests of the section had been ruinously detimbered; the farm-soil on hillsides had eroded and washed down; high up, upon the hills, one saw the raw scars of old mica pits, the dump heaps of deserted mines. Some vast destructive 'Suck' had been at work here;

[29] James Still, *River of Earth* (New York, 1940), p. 12-13.
[30] Harriette Arnow, *The Dollmaker* (New York, 1954).
[31] Joseph Warren Beach, *American Fiction 1920-1940* (New York, 1941), p. 215.
[32] *Ibid.*, p. 184.

and a visitor, had he returned after one hundred years, would have been compelled to note the ruin of the change. It was evident that a huge compulsive greed had been at work: the whole region had been sucked and gutted, milked dry, denuded of its rich primeval treasures; something blind and ruthless had been here, grasped and gone.

". . . True, the hills were left—with these deteriorations; and all around, far-flung in their great barricades, the immense wild grandeur of the mountain wall, the great Blue Ridge across which they had come long, long ago; and which had held them from the world."[33]

His first novel, *Look Homeward, Angel*, Wolfe called "a story of the buried life." It was the buried life of eager, dreaming Eugene Gant, of his big, lusty, loving and brawling family, and of the little North Carolina mountain town of Altamont where they lived. Altamont was either a village-becoming-town or a town-becoming city, no one was sure, but the "progressive" citizens were eager to bury their rural backgrounds under a patina of metropolitan sophistication. The tensions between this new elite and the old mountain individualism helped create some of Wolfe's finest humorous passages.

The superstitions of the mountain folk, their enjoyment of the snows that sweep down in winter from the dark and distant and beckoning northland, the magic of all the other seasons in the Southern Appalachians, and the drama of times and people that are now part of history, are included in the tremendous outpouring of Wolfe's novels and short stories.

In a story called "Men of Old Catawba," Wolfe described aspects of the history of his native state: "The real history of Old Catawba is not essentially a history of wars or rebellions; it is not a history of democracy or plutocracy or any form of government; it is not a history of business men, puritans, knaves, fools, saints, or heroes; it is not a history of culture or barbarism.

"The real history of Old Catawba is a history of solitude, of the wilderness, and of the eternal earth, it is the history of millions of men living and dying alone in the wilderness . . . who have listened to the earth and known her million tongues, whose lives were given to the earth, whose bones and flesh are recompacted with the earth, the immense and terrible earth that makes no answer."[34]

Maxwell Geismar has written of the influence of his mountain heritage on Wolfe's writing. "Just as Wolfe came to settle here [in New York], so, too,

for all his earlier exasperation, it was his continuing bond with his first home and with the hill people themselves . . . that helped him equally to preserve a sort of balance on the pavements of the metropolis. . . . There was, in these hill people with their involved family histories and their back-country rituals, their abundant hospitality and their endless talking, their mountain laughter and their clinging legends of sin and bloodshed, a strain that probably came closest, among all our rich regional strains, to what we have labeled the 'Russian' soul: I mean, of course, merely the human soul, though at once more deeply enslaved and freer, a soul, as it were, in fetters and in ecstasy. And there is also a mountain mixture here that is not so noticeable in the Mississippi deltas or in the Georgia pinelands—of primitive myth *and* equalitarian enlightenment; of voodoo and the bill of rights. . . . The relationship of the writer and his people concerned Wolfe as it had not always concerned the aesthetic rebels of the 1920's and as it would not always concern the social revolutionaries of the 1930's. You might almost say, in fact, that in Wolfe's work the American people came back into the American novel."[35]

Another literary critic, Floyd C. Watkins, in his study, *Thomas Wolfe's Characters*, has emphasized that "No author has ever better represented the primitive and simple tales of the Southern Mountaineer."[36]

Discussing one short story, "The Return of the Prodigal," about a mountain murder Wolfe witnessed when he came back to the hills of North Carolina in the summer of 1937, Watkins points out that "the account here is almost as bare and stark as it would have been if Hemingway had written it. Every movement is casual; a good part is told in dialogue, saturated with the understatement of mountain men. . . . No flood of the rhetoric of *Look Homeward, Angel* could have made killing so nauseous and awesome, nor could the lyricism have been as appropriate a vehicle for the content. Wolfe was learning to describe mountain men in the simple terms of their own lives and speech."[37]

Consider the story "Chickamauga," successful "as

[33] Thomas Wolfe, *The Hills Beyond* (New York, 1941).
[34] Thomas Wolfe, *From Death to Morning* (New York, 1935), pp. 204-205.
[35] *The Portable Thomas Wolfe*, edited and with an introduction by Maxwell Geismar (New York, 1946), pp. 19-22.
[36] Floyd C. Watkins, *Thomas Wolfe's Characters* (Norman, Okla., 1957), p. 83.
[37] *Ibid.*, pp. 135-36.

much because it is a story about a mountaineer as because it is a story of a battle in the Civil War," and some of narrator old John Pentland's salty recollections: "You could see the nurses and the stretcher-bearers movin' through the woods, and each side huntin' fer hits dead. You could see them movin' in the smoke an' flames, an' you could see the dead men layin' there as thick as wheat, with their corpselike faces an' black powder on their lips, an' a little bit of moonlight comin' through the trees, and all of hit more like a nightmare out of hell than anything I ever knowed before.' "

Wolfe's roots are in the mountain soil but his vision includes the world. He is at once the most specific and the most universal of mountain writers. Wolfe, the mountain boy, the American singer, the lost and seeking man, has spoken not only to other mountain people, or to American readers, but to men everywhere. That excellent Englishman, J. B. Priestly, concluded his recent monumental study, *Literature and the Western Man*, with a discussion of Wolfe. Among other things, he said, "The truth is that, once his limitations are accepted, Wolfe is one of the most satisfying and rewarding of all these American novelists. It is not only that his scene is big, as indeed it is, but that he explores the scene with a wonderful eye and ear, with astonishing thoroughness, often taking us to a great depth. Because he invented so little, shaped and cut so little, drove himself so hard while he was writing, he was able to give life, down to the last flicker or whisper, to an amazing range of scenes . . . he remains one of the few major *young* writers of this age, a giant of the morning; and everything about him, faulty and over-youthful, candid and vital and endearing, belongs essentially to an America that is itself still a giant of the morning. And indeed any America that shrugs him away, forgetting what he did and tried to do, will be smaller, older, closer to death."[38]

A regional literature that can include in its achievement the universality of Thomas Wolfe has cause for pride in the past and hope for the future.

Much of the world's significant literature has come out of a time in which basic changes were taking place, when old folkways were in conflict with new patterns, accepted beliefs were challenged by new conditions. Such a period now grips the Southern Appalachian area and offers opportunity for writing that springs from regional sources but is also in the mainstream of a great literary tradition.

At the optimum, people of the Southern Appalachians and their literature might contribute to America the wisdom of a balance between making a living and making a life.

To implement the use of the literary heritage that is already in existence in the mountains, and to enlarge it by the encouragement of new literary efforts, is one of the challenges facing educators, social workers, religious and civic leaders throughout the region. Perhaps the single element most necessary to this renaissance, however, is one most difficult to achieve: a new attitude on the part of these leaders themselves, and on the part of the majority of mountain people, toward literature. Literature is not some esoteric ritual practiced by a small coterie and enjoyed by a few of the initiated. It is not separate from life. At its best, literature is as small and specific as a tear shed by one of James Still's "chaps;" it is as large and rhetorical as Wolfe's imprisoned cry for "a stone, a leaf, an unfound door." It is a staff of life, made of the stuff of life, and without it a man or a people wither and perish.

38 J. B. Priestly, *Literature and Western Man* (New York, 1960), pp. 439-40.

CHAPTER SEVENTEEN

Dances

and

Singing

Games

FRANK H. SMITH

EACH REGION OF THE UNITED STATES has its distinctive folk heritage, but in many regions a number of separate folk cultures are competing for survival. This is not the case in the Southern Appalachian Mountains, since its people are predominantly of British origin. The affinity of Appalachian square dancing and singing games to their British parentage is striking. This may be illustrated by an experience of Cecil J. Sharp, then director of the English Folk Dance and Song Society, who first visited the Region in 1916. When he saw mountain square dancing at Pine Mountain, Kentucky, "We realized at once that we had stumbled upon a most interesting form of the English Country dance," he wrote, "which, so far as we know, had not been hitherto recorded, and a dance, moreover, of great aesthetic value."[1]

From the collections of English singing games by Sharp and Lady Gomme, it is evident that children of English villages and Appalachian rural communities could easily join in such games as London Bridge, Nuts in May, Green Gravel, Old Roger, A-Hunting We Will Go, and Poor Mary Sits A-Weeping. (In the mountains, Poor Mary has become Little Sally Ann.)

It is now generally recognized that many of the Appalachian dances and singing games are survivals of rituals or ceremonies whose origins are lost in antiquity. For example, Sharp observed that the well-known figure, " 'The Basket' was an adaptation to the dance of a children's singing game, 'Draw A Pail of Water,' which is a dramatic representation of several incidents connected with the ceremony of well-worship."[2]

Many of the pioneers who left England, Scotland, and Northern Ireland and settled finally in the Southern Appalachian Mountains brought with them not only their folk culture, but likewise the Puritan attitude toward worldly pleasures. Joseph Strutt records, in *The Sports and Pastimes of the People of England*, how James I "... did justly, in our progresse through Lancashire, rebuke some puritanes and precise persons, in prohibiting and unlawfully punishing our good people for using their lawfull recreations and honest exercises on Sundays and other holy dayes, after the afternoone sermon or service. It is our will, that at the end of divine service, our good people be not disturbed, letted, or discouraged, from any lawful recreation, such as dancing, either for men or women; archery for men, leaping, vaulting, or any other such harmless recreation; nor for having of

May-games, whitson-ales, and morris daunces, and the setting up of May-poles, and other sports therewith used."[3]

In the New World, however, there was no monarch to countermand the actions of "puritanes and precise persons" and so down to the present day we find that certain religious groups and individuals have exercised a powerful ban against fiddle-playing and dancing. Nevertheless, the traditions of dance music, dances, songs, tales, and singing games have displayed remarkable vitality.

The dances and singing games, like other phases of folk culture, have come down to us by oral tradition. In former days, dances in the Southern Appalachians were customarily held in the home, as they sometimes are even today. The neighbors would gather, perhaps for a friendly visit, or maybe for a "working"—an occasion when neighbors would gather at a certain home to help the family at some special task; and when work was done the frolic would follow and would go on until the early hours. An old person will boast: "Many a time I've danced all night." In seeking information for the present study a number of older persons were consulted who had attended workings. The occasions were bean-stringing, sorghum making, house-raising, quilting, log-rolling, corn-hoeing, and cornhusking.

A peculiar characteristic of Appalachian square dancing is that usually it is done in a circle with no set number of couples, whereas, in other regions of the United States, a square dance is in a square, formed by four couples. To those not familiar with square dancing, it should be explained that an Appalachian square dance is not a single dance like the Virginia Reel, but is a succession of figures which are danced, not in any prescribed order, but combined at the discretion of the caller.

Cecil Sharp, when he witnessed Appalachian square dancing in Kentucky, heard the expression "run a set." As a consequence, he later referred to the dance as "Running Set," a term which led to considerable confusion and misunderstanding. The "Running Set" is part of the Appalachian square dance.

One cannot be sure why the Appalachian square dance is done in a circle, but a possible explanation might be that, with no hall or auditorium to dance in, it was natural to use an average size room in a home for the dancing area and, in order to accommodate all who came to the frolic, to form a circle around the room.

The first mountain square dance attended by the writer was in a home at Peachtree, North Carolina, about thirty years ago. Before the dance the furniture was carried out and stacked on the porch; the musicians took a position in a doorway; all who wanted to dance circled up around the room. The caller and his girl then would lead off with each new figure by dancing it with the first couple to their right, and then, in turn, with each remaining couple. Other dancers remained inactive, simply waiting in their places; but presently the second couple and later each of the other couples made the rounds dancing the same figure. The circle soon became too large: the next step was to take the furniture out of an adjoining bedroom, where a second circle with its own caller went into action. The musicians simply stayed in their original place. The music was perfectly adequate for the two groups of dancers.

It is now customary in the Appalachian square dance for all the couples to dance at the same time. To accomplish this, the caller, when the circle has been formed, may say: "Couple up four, in the middle of the floor," whereupon each alternate couple will move inside the circle and, facing the couple on the right, will join hands with them. Each group of two couples will then dance the figure called. At this point "Do Si Do" may or may not be danced at the direction of the caller before he says, "And on to the next," which indicates that the inside couple will move on to the next outside couple. In addition to the figures such as "Mountaineer Loop" and "Ocean Wave" danced by two couples, a number of interesting figures like the "Basket" and "The Wagon Wheel" are executed by all the dancers.

It is difficult to determine how widespread mountain square dancing actually is today in the mountain region. In an attempt to obtain additional information on this point, and to check on the extent to which other types of dancing are used, a questionnaire was sent to 220 county superintendents of education in and near the study area. Of these, 110 were returned. In 70 counties it was reported that, apart from schools and school-sponsored events, mountain square dances were sponsored by a wide variety of organizations, among which civic clubs and veterans' organizations took the lead. Among the sponsoring organizations were the Trail Riders Club,

[1] Cecil J. Sharp and Maud Karpeles, *The Country Dance Book, Part V* (London, 1918), p. 7.

[2] Sharp and Karpeles, p. 11.

[3] Joseph Strutt, *The Sports and Pastimes of the People of England* (London, 1838), p. lvi.

Veterans of Foreign Wars, American Legion, Lions Club, Department of Recreation, Fair Association, a restaurant, church groups, scouts, recreation center, P.T.A., Fire Department, Youth Association, Travelers Club, Junior Chamber of Commerce, Supper Club, State Park, square dance clubs, and 4-H clubs.

It was reported in 55 counties that at least some dancing was taught in high schools and elementary schools, but in only 29 counties was such instruction the general rule. In 73 counties mountain square dancing was part of the students' extra curricular recreation.

Square dancing in the mountains is not always in good repute. This is due to religious objection to dancing and to the fact that drinking and disorder sometimes occur at square dances.

The singing games of the Southern Appalachian Mountains are in two categories. One is the children's singing game, like "Old Roger" and "London Bridge," which contains an element of "play-acting" besides the rhythmical movements and the song; the other is the "play party" game for older youth and adults. Many of the latter are done in the same formation as the Virginia Reel. Among these may be mentioned "Cedar Swamp," "Bow Belinda," "Charlie," and "Going to Boston." Some others, like "Skip to Ma Lou," "Old Dan Tucker," and "Jump Josie," are danced in a circle.

To illustrate a children's singing game and to draw attention to a parallel with an English one, here is a version of "Little Sally Ann."

> Little Sally Ann, sitting in the sand,
> Weeping, crying for her man.
> Rise, Sally rise! Wipe your eyes!
> Turn to the east, turn to the west,
> Turn to the one you love the best!

In the center of a circle, a child kneels and covers face with hands. Children stand facing the center and sing. When the words of song indicate, the child in center rises. With her eyes still closed and her right arm outstretched and finger pointed, she slowly turns to the right as they sing. The child at whom she is pointing, when the song is finished, takes her place.[4]

The English game, "Poor Mary Sits A-Weeping," contains essentially the same situation. The children in the circle sing to the child in the center:

> Poor Mary sits a-weeping,
> A-weeping, a-weeping.

> Poor Mary sits a-weeping
> On a bright and summer's day.

> Pray tell me what you're weeping for
> You're weeping for, you're weeping for,
> Pray tell me what you're weeping for
> On a bright and summer's day.

Mary answers that she is weeping for a lover. She is then invited to stand up and choose one, which she does, whereupon the children sing:

> Now you're married, you must be good
> And make your husband chop the wood;
> Chop it thin and bring it in
> And kiss him over and over again.

And Poor Mary does just that.[5]

In order to obtain some information about the use of children's singing games in the Appalachian region, a questionnaire was sent to 655 elementary teachers in De Kalb County, Alabama; Rabun County, Georgia; Harlan and Lee Counties, Kentucky; Avery County, North Carolina; Cumberland County and the city of Knoxville, Tennessee; Dickenson County, Virginia; and Fayette County, West Virginia. In the 219 questionnaires returned it was reported that singing games were played in 94 percent of the schools. In 84 percent of these, the children were said to have their own singing games tradition; and two out of three respondents said the children selected their own song leader. The games were played both in the classroom (especially on rainy days) and on the playground. Most of the teachers (58 percent) taught singing games, and occasionally an outside person such as a recreation leader would do so.

While 150 different singing games were listed as played by the children, actually the use of a number of old favorites was very marked. The ten most popular, each mentioned by more than 50 teachers, are given below in the order of children's preference:

1. The Farmer in the Dell
2. London Bridge
3. In and Out the Window
4. Skip to Ma Lou
5. The Bear Went Over the Mountain
6. Green Gravel
7. Bluebird
8. Jolly Miller
9. Oats and Beans
10. Old Dan Tucker

[4] Marion H. Skean, *Circle Left* (Homeplace, Kentucky, 1938), p. 11. Copyright material reproduced through the courtesy of Homeplace, Ary, Kentucky.

[5] Alice B. Gomme and Cecil J. Sharp, *Children's Singing Games*, Set III (London, 1923), pp. 18-19. Copyright material reproduced courtesy of Novello and Company, Ltd.

Two-thirds of the teachers reported that interest in the singing games on the part of the children declines when they reach about the fifth or sixth grade. Then competitive games, current dance fads, and adult dancing are likely to appear desirable. The dancing interest, however, is usually much more prevalent among the girls.

A generation or more ago in the mountains, interest in play party games was a natural outcome of enjoyment of the children's singing games. There is no hard and fast distinction between the two, but the play party games were associated with courting and grown-up sociability.

Mr. and Mrs. L. L. McDowell say of the play party game, "It seems to have grown out of unending conflict between the natural desire to dance and be merry and the stern religious prohibition of all worldly pleasures."[6] When young people were forbidden to dance, and when fiddle music was frowned upon, a simple song might in favorable circumstances be used as a disguise for what soon in actual fact became a dance. What could be more natural on the part of young people than to sing traditional songs and make up their own rhymes, and along with the singing to slip in a few mountain square dance figures or a little of the Virginia Reel?

It has been the observation of the writer that during the last fifteen or twenty years the popularity of the play party games has declined sharply in the mountain communities and schools. On this point, a questionnaire was sent to 31 persons who for many years have been in positions of leadership in the use of folk arts. Of the 21 persons who returned the questionnaires, 12 were born in the mountains and the others have lived and worked in the area for periods averaging 30 years. Twenty persons said play party games were in common use in their communities a generation ago; 16 reported that little attention is paid to them today. There was general agreement that a decrease in religious objection to dancing, the availability of dance records, and, to a degree, a general decline in the old customs are principal reasons for the falling off of interest in the play party games. There was also strong agreement that the play party games have great inherent social and cultural values and that carefully thought-out efforts should be made for their revival. One leader, who could speak with the added authority of a mountain native and mother, wrote: "Nothing makes a group feel closer and more friendly than sharing in relaxing games with the informal

words and rhythm of the play party games. We need to keep them alive just as much as we need to keep the history of our country before our school children. Through them we can understand the culture of the people from whom we have gotten the games, and can have a greater appreciation of the folk who settled here before our day."

The decline of interest in the play party games is in itself a small thing, but often small changes put us on the track of greater ones. The isolation of mountain life was broken down chiefly by the automobile. It is now easy for most people in the mountains to go to the county seat. On Saturday afternoons the small mountain towns are thronged; many mountain residents buy goods there instead of at the neighborhood store. The movie houses offer pictures which feature people, places, and behavior decidedly unlike those the audience has known at home. The drug stores have their juke boxes, and outside of town are roadhouses. The country folk, besides seeking a wider selection of goods in the stores, perhaps at lower prices than the country store can offer, engage in a great deal of socializing. People meet and talk on the street. They go together to a restaurant or a drug store; a wider circle of social acquaintances is thereby secured.

The changes which consolidation of schools brings into the lives of the children are profound. The journey by bus is a new experience, as are improved buildings and facilities, the larger classes, the school movies, new courses such as science and home economics in rooms containing laboratory equipment and the latest models of stoves and refrigerators, the sports program (especially basketball), the stimulation of "school spirit," school parties with a tendency to social sophistication. When to these altered conditions we add the significant effects of radio and television, the impact on the old customs is far-reaching indeed. And so it is not difficult to understand that the play party games may well appear to be rather old-fashioned to the new generation of young people.

People sometimes look back nostalgically to an earlier era of mountain life in the belief that the folk arts were not then in a state of change. But even when oral tradition provided the sole means for passing on the folk culture, changes were constantly being introduced. Sometimes it was because a portion of a folk dance or a phrase of music had

---

[6] Lucien L. and Flora Lassiter McDowell, *Folk Dances of Tennessee* (Ann Arbor, 1938), p. 4.

been forgotten and was replaced by an improvisation. Or a creative folk artist might introduce a change which met with community approval. Whatever the reason, the fact remains that many versions of folk dances, songs, tales, and the like frequently exist in the same region as evidence of changes that have taken place in the original. In this sense it might be said that the status of the form of the folk arts has always been precarious.

Less use is made nowadays of oral tradition. The folk songs and dances are often taught in school, and many are recorded in books. There are obvious advantages in the publication of folk arts. It provides assurance that the materials will be preserved and makes it possible for others outside the region to make use of them. On the other hand, it is difficult to record the exact character and spirit of the folk culture from which the materials are drawn. Consequently, dependence upon books alone is likely to result in serious misconceptions.

There can be no doubt that the influence of social forces has tended to bring about changes in the folk arts, yet the fact remains that an astonishing variety of active dance and song traditions survive in the United States. Illustrations of this may be found in the program of the National Folk Festival, of the festivals held at St. Paul, Minnesota, and of those sponsored by the Folk Dance Federation of California. Despite the inevitable changes that occur, it does seem that both the form and the spirit of the folk arts are capable of survival.

While social changes in the life of mountain communities endanger the old folk customs, it is nevertheless true that in some respects a revival of interest is taking place. Opportunities for the utilization of the various phases of folk culture are becoming more numerous. This is apparent in a listing of the situations in which Appalachian square dances and, in a lesser degree, play party games are being used as a part of a wider folk dance program. Included are physical education and other classes in college, the programs of extra-curricular organizations in college, assembly programs in high schools and elementary schools, activity group and club programs in high schools, P.T.A. programs, 4-H clubs, church socials, conferences, festivals, fairs, pot luck suppers, May Day programs, dances sponsored by civic bodies, dance schools, and recreation institutes.

Although in many parts of the study area folk culture is languishing, except as regards the children's singing games, many significant things are being done. The developments described below are only a few of those found in the mountains today. They have sometimes been aided by extension workers from educational institutions. Almost all of them operate exclusively in the mountains. Two exceptions to this are The Kentucky Folk Festival and the Christmas Country Dance School, both of which include individuals and groups from other states. The singling out of certain events and organizations is done simply to provide examples of how the traditional folk arts can be used to enrich mountain life today.

In 1934, the folk festival was proposed as a way to stimulate the employment of folk culture as material for a wider recreational movement in the mountains, and the first one was held in May of the following year at Berea College. From it regional festivals and an adult section have sprung. And when the University of Kentucky became interested in sponsoring a folk festival on a state basis, the Mountain Folk Festival was regarded as a suitable model.

The Mountain Folk Festival belongs to the groups who attend it. Their leaders choose the programs and place of meeting. It has been customary to elect a folk arts leader who is on the staff at Berea College to the chairmanship of the Festival, because the Berea campus is thought of as a desirable home.

The Mountain Folk Festival and the regional festivals have two purposes: the use and preservation of traditional dances, songs, fiddle tunes, tales and the like, and the fun of non-competitive recreation. Visitors who come to observe the Festival often expect to see awards made to the best dancers. When the beautiful dancing of the whole group is combined, this idea of singling out individuals seems to be out of place. The competitive element, of course, is easily awakened, and the festival leaders realize the need for emulation of the best dancers. Thus, striving for good standards involves a limited use of comparisons, if not of competition. A basic aim is to stress the social side of group dancing along with the cultivation of grace and courtesy, an enjoyment of lovely dance tunes, and the skillful employment of the body in dance design.

The Kentucky Folk Festival, sponsored by the University of Kentucky, is a large, well-organized festival, in which a wide selection of dance traditions is employed. The participants are chiefly adults, although separate programs have been arranged for elementary school children. Besides those coming from all sections of Kentucky, many individuals and groups are attracted from Ohio and Indiana. The general character of the festival is non-competitive; included in the program are folk songs, tales, and handicrafts.

Two other festivals of a somewhat different kind, which for many years have attracted wide interest, are held in Asheville, North Carolina. The Mountain Dance and Folk Festival under the leadership of Bascom Lamar Lunsford, and the Youth Jamboree, guided by Hubert Hayes, are semicommercial enterprises which feature Appalachian square dancing and folk singing. Since the programs are held only at night on the stage of the Asheville City Auditorium, it is not possible for the groups to enjoy the sociability of dancing together. These two festivals provide a focal point for the activities of a large number of groups. The recognition given to these festivals has undoubtedly affected the attitude of the public in western North Carolina in various ways: a wealth of indigenous material has been brought to light; the dancing has received favorable publicity; rural churches have become more friendly; and some of the square dance groups have given programs for civic and business organizations. All this brings rural and urban communities and schools closer together.

The Youth Jamboree has had a remarkable influence in both secondary and elementary schools. It has stimulated the use of mountain square dancing in clubs and physical education classes, and in this has received much support from P.T.A. groups and civic clubs.

Significant work in the study and preservation of mountain folk culture has been done at Homeplace, a community center located a few miles from Hazard, Kentucky. Homeplace was among the social service enterprises initiated in the mountains a generation ago by E. O. Robinson, a wealthy lumber merchant who possessed large land holdings in Eastern Kentucky. The community center was originally organized and is still directed by Lula M. Hale, of Knott County, Kentucky. Miss Hale and her associates incorporated native dancing and play party games, under local leadership, in their program. This led to the collecting of very valuable folk material from Perry, Breathitt, and Wolfe Counties, and to the publication of *Circle Left* by Marion H. Skean, who was a traveling librarian on the Homeplace staff.

The University of Kentucky, with its wide resources, has shown a constructive interest in Appalachian folk culture. This is apparent in its spon-

sorship of the Kentucky Folk Festival and of a Recreation Institute; in the discriminative and skillful use of mountain dances in various programs of the Agricultural Extension Service; and in the considerable use made of folk and square dancing by the Department of Physical Education.

Berea College is the home of the Mountain Folk Festival and the Christmas Country Dance School. Since 1937 the college has employed a staff member who has been assigned the task of teaching folk arts on the campus and throughout the mountains. A student organization known as The Country Dancers has for over 20 years furnished leadership for campus dance groups, and has represented Berea College with artistically attractive programs of folk and square dancing in many parts of the United States. The Centennial Year of 1955 saw the production at Berea's Indian Fort Theatre of "Wilderness Road," Paul Green's drama, which was played for four summers and drew audiences from throughout the United States. The drama was based on regional history and made ample use of folk tunes and mountain dancing. Among the books published as part of the Berea Centennial, were *Wake Up and Sing*, by Gladys Jameson, and *The Appalachian Square Dance*, by Frank H. Smith. A number of records of folk music by Berea students were also released in conjunction with the Centennial, including recordings for dance groups of mountain square dance airs and English and Danish folk dance tunes.

The John C. Campbell Folk School in Western North Carolina was founded by Olive Dame Campbell, who was instrumental in arranging Cecil Sharp's important visits to the Appalachian Mountains. Mrs. Campbell was the widow of John C. Campbell (author of *The Southern Highlander and His Homeland*), who had believed that Scandinavian folk schools might in some helpful way be adapted to conditions in the mountains. Mrs. Campbell and Marguerite Butler Bidstrup, having studied in the Scandinavian countries, worked out a program which, with frequent changes, has contributed in many ways to the revival of folk culture, especially in Appalachian music and handicrafts. The Folk School, a remarkable social and educational center, is well known for the use of Danish folk dances and singing games.

The Hindman Settlement School, founded by May Stone and Katherine Pettit, already displayed a keen appreciation of the mountain culture when Cecil Sharp visited Hindman in 1917. Some years later under the leadership of the Director, Elizabeth Watts, and Marie Marvel, a county-wide program of folk arts was established in remote schools, some of which could be reached only by jeep, on horseback, or on foot. The present director, Raymond K. McLain, is keenly interested in the folk arts program; his influence as a musician and regional leader is far-reaching.

This writer went out into the mountains in 1933 as an itinerant recreation and folk arts leader under the sponsorship of the Council (then the Conference) of Southern Mountain Workers. Since that time, the Council, under the guidance of Helen Dingman and others, has accomplished a great deal in the development of a folk arts program. Smith College has cooperated in the extension work of the Council.

The Country Dance Society of America is an outcome of Cecil Sharp's work in the United States. Beginning as the American Branch of the English Folk Dance and Song Society, it has undergone an interesting evolution through the years, but has always maintained the close ties which Sharp established with the Southern Appalachian Region. The director, May Gadd, has served as consultant to the Mountain Folk Festival and has taught in the Christmas Country Dance School at Berea since its founding in 1938. Many leaders in the area have attended the Society's summer camp at Long Pond, Massachusetts, and acquired there understanding and techniques needed to enhance their own contribution to the development of a richer folk arts program in the mountains.

Partly as a consequence of the folk festivals, many varied dance traditions are coming into the mountain area. This is especially apparent in the selection of material in physical education classes in colleges, and in physical education and health manuals for the high schools and elementary schools, which tend to stress a wide variety of European dances and square dances from various regions of the United States. The recreation program at Fontana Dam, North Carolina, has apparently seen an invasion of the Western Square. The Christmas Country Dance School at Berea College for over twenty years has taught English and Danish dances, Middle Western and New England square dances, and New England contra dances, in addition to Appalachian square, children's singing games, and play party games. The same sort of selection has characterized the courses of the John C. Campbell Folk School.

This trend certainly gives rise to a number of questions about the authenticity of dances, the suitability of certain dances to the Appalachian region, and the number of dance traditions that may possibly be assimilated in a manner worthy of reputable institutions. A dance or a singing game is not merely a thing of casual interest. It is an expression of a certain culture, and can best be appreciated with a background of knowledge and understanding of the country or region of its origin.

In America, more than in most countries, a sharing of folk arts is possible. The Appalachian Square Dance was one of the main influences in the development of Western Square. English, Danish, and other dances have enriched the use of folk culture by people in the mountains. It was to be expected that in this sharing some problems would arise. To be successfully assimilated, dances should be authentic and suited to the cultural background of the people in a region. The depth and complexity of each dance tradition obviously will place limits upon the variety of dances in the program of any reputable dance group.

When Cecil Sharp saw mountain dancing at Pine Mountain, the sole accompaniment was rhythmical clapping of the hands and patting of the foot. When he was at Hyden, the music was played on a fiddle; at Hindman on the fiddle and banjo. The widespread use now made of records for dancing has certain limitations, but it does enable more persons to dance who would otherwise be unable to do so. If the recordings have been made by musicians with wide experience in playing for dance groups under excellent leadership, the results may be satisfactory. Singing games, of course, do not need an instrumental accompaniment, although books on the subject usually do contain the musical notation.

In 80 percent of the counties, in which school instruction in traditional dancing was reported, and in 66 percent of those reporting instruction in children's singing games, instruction was said to be in a physical education program. The programs of colleges where most teachers of the area are educated are, therefore, an important factor in the preservation of these traditions. The suitability of a college for the transmission of folk culture, which is the antithesis of the academic, may well be questioned. But certainly any concern for the humanities would bring an institution close to the area of folk culture, and the importance of traditional dancing in the culture of a nation could hardly be open to question.

To get some facts from the colleges about their

use of traditional dance, especially mountain square dancing and singing games, a questionnaire was sent to 73 colleges in the states with which the study is concerned. Of these, 54 were returned. Thirty-four colleges reported that traditional dancing was taught as an academic subject. Mountain square dancing was taught in 16 of these, other square dancing in 28, folk dancing in 31, and singing games in 12. With two exceptions, traditional dancing and modern social dancing (which were usually combined) were taught by physical education teachers. The lack of awareness of the depth and artistic potentialities of traditional dance seems apparent in the fact that in 21 colleges only one semester hour of instruction was given. It is inconceivable that mastery of dance technique or more than a glimpse of traditional dance background could be gained in that amount of time. Yet the questionnaire respondents frequently stated that, in addition to other kinds of dancing, folk dancing of "all" or "various" nationalities were taught. Actually in one semester hour no real understanding of the dances of one nation would be possible.

One firm conclusion to be drawn from the survey findings is that few colleges in the region now offer programs from which a student can gain both a mastery of the art of folk dancing and an understanding of its cultural significance. On the basis of information received from the questionnaires it would appear that only three colleges in the area of the study offer a program of dance instruction that could be considered adequate to equip their graduates to teach folk dancing.

Nevertheless, much has been accomplished in the use of the Appalachian square dance, singing games, and other suitable dance material in certain areas and in the programs of some colleges, schools, and social organizations. From the activities described above, it is evident that the revival of interest in the folk arts which has taken place in recent years in the United States has been reflected in a greater appreciation of these arts in the mountains. There is considerable evidence of the increasing recognition of the true worth of mountain folk culture.

The basic need at the present time is for more adequate leadership. In addition to the training in traditional dancing available in the physical education departments of the college and universities, a number of folk arts and dance schools such as the Christmas Country Dance School at Berea College and the short courses at the John C. Campbell Fall School—to mention only two—offer the kind of leadership training that is needed. These and many other training opportunities are listed regularly in *Mountain Life and Work*, quarterly magazine published at Berea by the Council of the Southern Mountains.

We have seen that traditional dance instruction and its social and recreational use in the schools rests chiefly with the physical education director, aided and encouraged by the principal. The physical education director, however, often is too engrossed in trying to coach a winning basketball team to give much thought to the broad educational aims of an intelligent physical education program. A new approach is needed which will take into consideration social and artistic as well as purely athletic ideals. The wholesome enjoyment of square dancing, folk dancing, singing games and other rhythmic activities may be shared by the entire student body; school principals, teachers, and parents have often commented to the writer on the value of such activities in cultivating friendliness, poise, and good discipline. Such a program can, at the same time, help to preserve a valuable part of our cultural heritage.

CHAPTER EIGHTEEN

The

Revival

of

Handicrafts

BERNICE A. STEVENS

IN A PRIMITIVE SOCIETY, SURVIVAL depends upon what one's hands can make of the materials in his environment. Personal dignity is based upon independent achievement. A man looks upon the work of his hands—his tools, his household goods—and takes pride in their utilitarian beauty. Here lies the foundation of a culture.

In a more sophisticated society, man's fundamental need to create with his hands persists, even when the practical necessity for such creation is gone. The craft revival that has swept this country in recent years is an expression of that hunger for personal achievement. The man who makes a useful or beautiful object with his own hands has a kinship with all who have done the same, in all times, in all places.

The craft revival began earlier in Southern Appalachia than in other parts of this country for the same reason that the pioneer crafts had a longer life here— economic necessity. The revival was built upon a foundation of old crafts that had never completely died out in the area. Many of these were renewed, and new crafts were added.

The word *crafts* can be interpreted in many ways, but the skills discussed in this chapter are those accepted for membership in the Southern Highland Handicraft Guild, for many years the most potent force in the mountains for preserving and developing good craft work.

Many crafts, both traditional and contemporary, are concerned with textile production and decoration: weaving, spinning, vegetable dyeing, hooking, braiding, quilting, knotting and fringing, stitchery (creative embroidery), block printing, stenciling, and silk-screen printing. Greeting-cards and prints are also block-printed, stenciled, or silk screened.

Wood working, traditional in the forest-rich mountains, includes cabinet work, furniture making, and the fashioning of musical instruments such as the mountain dulcimer, as well as the turning, carving, and whittling of tools, utensils, and purely decorative objects. Wood sculpture is also included.

Ceramics, in the mountain area, consists chiefly of making functional pots, though a few ceramists work in both practical pottery and ceramic sculpture.

Basketry seems, from time to time, in some danger of dying out, especially the old-style mountain baskets, but every effort is being made to encourage their production. The Cherokees continue to produce a superior product. Baskets in this area are made chiefly of oak and hickory splits, honeysuckle vines, and river cane.

Corn shucks are used for making everything from dolls to chair seats. Shucks and cane are not only still used in seating the traditional mountain chair; they have been successfully adapted to contemporary handmade furniture. Shuckery is a popular craft among farm women. Brooms have always been made from broomcorn, sedge, and even oak splits and twigs. Today, although many mountain women still prefer handmade brooms for house work, most of the brooms made in the area are of the decorative hearthbroom variety. Such native materials as seed, pods, nuts, and cones (called "woods pretties" by the mountain women) are fashioned into wall and table decorations. Toy-making is traditional in the mountains, and employs such varying materials as corn shucks, corn stalks, wood, cloth, straw, and clay.

Metal work ranges from wrought-ironwork to silver or gold jewelry, and includes work in pewter, brass, and copper. Some metal sculpture is done. Silversmithing is rare. Mineral-rich mountains, especially in North Carolina, have made the region a natural center for "rock-hounds," and, hence, for lapidary work.

Because of the presence of certain minerals and other raw materials necessary to the production of glass, several glass companies, specializing in hand-blown objects, are located in West Virginia. There are a few workers in stained glass, slumped glass, and other decorative uses of the material.

Leather work, once a necessity for the mountaineer who had to have harness for his horses and mules as well as shoes for his family, is now a relatively minor craft. Other crafts practiced by a very few individuals or groups are candle and soap-making, and crafts involving plastics. The latter is in its infancy in this area.

There are several types of craftsmen in the highlands today. The rapidly-vanishing pioneer type, who still lives in a secluded area, and makes, from necessity and long habit, many of the things he needs, probably does not think of himself as a craftsman. He is not widely represented in this survey, but his presence is well known to the author, and he is considered in the conclusions drawn from this study.

Then there are those highlanders who, since the revival of crafts, have discovered the economic value of their forefathers' skills, and have continued or renewed them. Some, learning their craft at home, have changed the original product very little. Others, with training in schools, colleges, or craft centers, are making an improved product related to what their ancestors made. Still others are producing sophisticated and contemporary articles. The craftsman, counterpart of the European artisan, who works for or in a craft center making articles designed by another, is usually a native highlander.

Increasingly important to the area is the in-migrant, usually a designer-craftsman, who may have brought his craft with him, or may have learned it when he found himself located in a craft-conscious area.

The craft world of Southern Appalachia today has a firm foundation in the crafts of the past. Pioneer crafts, in the mountains as in other parts of the country, started with the building and furnishing of the pioneer home. Whatever was needed, someone had to make by hand. Even pottery, metal and leather goods often had to be fashioned by the mountain farmer or by some member of a small community.

But crafts were more than an economic necessity in pioneer life. The kind of coverlet a woman wove, the kind of tools a man worked with, and what he did with them, had much to do with the respect in which a family was held by the neighbors. A girl who had well-woven "kivers" in the family chest and knew how to weave jeans could look forward to a good marriage with a man who could build a tight cabin and make a good trencher. A "quiltin' bee" or a "house raisin'" were among life's great social occasions. The exchange of weaving drafts and quilt patterns in a community, the habit of making for the old or the unfortunate what they could not make for themselves, the teaching of traditional skills to children, were everyday activities. Crafts were a social force.

But pioneer days passed. By the latter half of the nineteenth century, factories, mills, and growing cities gradually released most American homes from the necessity of being self-sufficient. In most of the country, handweaving died out with the Civil War. Other crafts followed into near-extinction, in the Appalachians as well as in the rest of the country. Even in the hidden coves of the mountains, in spite of scarcity of money and poor communications, looms fell into disuse, and household equipment was cheaply bought, not lovingly made. Although hand-woven and hand-made objects were still in use in mountain homes, few were being produced. By 1900, though there were still, far back in the mountains, a few people living as primitive a life as they had before the Civil War, crafts were dying.

In the last decade of the nineteenth century, however, interest in crafts began to revive, largely through the efforts of outsiders, who came to the mountains for a vacation or a stint of teaching, fell in love with the highland area, and stayed to devote their lives to its people. Interest in crafts became apparent in several places in the mountain area almost simultaneously.

Mr. Allen Eaton relates: "The first effort to revive the handicrafts of the highlands of which there is any clear account was in the fall of 1893 when Dr. William Goodell Frost began his long 'extension' tours in the mountains and at once noted the attractive homespun bedcoverings in many cabins."[1] Dr. Frost bought some of these "kiverlids" and discovered that there was a market for them in the north. This discovery initiated at Berea College the custom of bartering such handmade objects for the "book-learnin'" that many of the mountain people so desperately wanted for their children. It was the beginning, too, of the famous Berea Fireside Industries.

Berea saw a great revival of craft work in the next ten years. The students themselves were taught crafts, and, through them, earned much of their tuition. But also the women of the area were taught to spin and weave. Many of them resurrected old spinning wheels and looms from shed and attic and added appreciably to the family income.

Similar projects developed in other parts of the mountain area. Miss Frances L. Goodrich, a social worker for the Presbyterian Women's Board of Home Missions, searched out women in the Asheville area who could still weave, helped locate old drafts, and established a weaving center.[2] Thus started the Allanstand Cottage Industries that developed into a craft center and market. In 1931 Miss Goodrich gave Allanstand to the Southern Highland Handicraft Guild. As a Guild shop, it does a thriving business for craftsmen in downtown Asheville today.

Wilmer Stone established one of the early weaving centers at Saluda, North Carolina. At Penland, Lucy Morgan developed a weaving center which is now the nationally-known Penland School of Handicrafts. Clementine Douglas' weaving center, the Spinning Wheel, in Asheville, is now a retail shop selling fine crafts. Thus, the revival of interest in crafts grew, sparked by the efforts of a few scattered, dedicated people who were interested in good, basic craft work.

There were other interesting highlights in the handicraft movement in the early years of the century: A Berea coverlet won a medal at the Paris Exposition in 1900. In 1912 John C. Campbell organized the Conference of Southern Mountain Workers, which, though not primarily interested in crafts, was destined to play an important part in their progress. Mrs. Woodrow Wilson, in 1913, planned the Mountain Room of the White House, and personally chose the mountain-woven rugs, coverlets, and upholstery materials that went into it.[3]

In 1917, the Smith-Hughes Act was passed, giving financial aid to industrial arts teaching. In some areas of the Highlands, funds from this act were used in training craftsmen, particularly weavers, to produce marketable goods. These funds helped to establish several craft centers, some of which are still active, although Smith-Hughes funds are not at present being used for this type of training. An appreciative audience was gradually developing for mountain crafts, and their market was expanding. Craft production often made the difference in a family between a bare existence and a fair degree of comfort; between having the children grow up illiterate, and sending them to school or even college. Weaving and other crafts brought beauty and color and purpose into drab existences, and particularly into the home of many a woman who, marrying early, spent her entire life within a few miles of her birthplace.

Meantime, at meetings of the Council of Southern Mountain Workers, craft-interested people naturally came together to discuss their problems, and it was from these discussions that there grew the idea of a separate organization for the promotion of crafts.

In 1929 the organization meeting of the Southern Highland Handicraft Guild was held at Clementine Douglas' center, the Spinning Wheel, Asheville.[4] At this meeting, besides Miss Douglas, were Frances Goodrich of Allanstand; Mrs. John C. Campbell of the John C. Campbell Folk School of Brasstown, North Carolina; Dr. Mary Sloop, of Crossnore; Lucy Morgan of Penland; Wilmer Stone (later Viner) of the Weave Shop in Saluda; Evelyn Bishop of Pi Beta Phi School in Gatlinburg, Tennessee; Helen Dingman of Berea; and Allen Eaton of the Russell Sage Foundation in New York.

With the formation of the Guild, individual centers could save time and effort by pooling their knowledge and resources. They could establish workable standards and give better help in designing, producing, and

[1] Allen H. Eaton, *Handicrafts of the Southern Highlands* (New York, 1937), 60.
[2] Frances L. Goodrich, *Mountain Homespun* (New Haven, 1931).
[3] Eaton, pp. 241, 66, 108.
[4] Eaton, p. 242.

marketing craft work. The Guild was dedicated to helping the mountain people to help themselves through crafts.

In 1935 a similar organization, the Southern Highlanders, was formed under the sponsorship of the T. V. A.[5] The emphasis of this organization was chiefly on marketing the wares of craftsmen, and it dealt with small craft-type industries more than with individuals. The work of the two groups was much the same, however, and in 1949 the two merged into one organization, retaining the name of the Guild. All member of the Highlanders became members of the Guild, and the three sales shops then maintained by the Highlanders became Guild shops.

Crafts flourished under the auspices of such organizations, and interest was further stimulated by the publication in 1937 of Allen Eaton's *Handicrafts of the Southern Highlands*, with Doris Ullman's fine photographic illustrations—a classic which is now regrettably out of print.

The depression of the thirties spurred the craft movement on, for when there was no other work to be found, home crafts could be followed. Churches and other organizations helped to sell mountain crafts.

But the Second World War dealt crafts a triple blow: It took away the young men, many of them never again to return to the mountains; it took away thousands of families to cities where work in war plants was plentiful and well paid; and for those who remained at home, it stopped the tourist trade as completely as it stopped the flow of raw material needed by the craftsmen.

At this seemingly inopportune time the Guild made a survey of mountain craftsmen, hoping to encourage them to continue working at their crafts, and to plan bigger and better things for the postwar years. This survey was conducted by Marian Heard, of the Related Arts Department of the College of Home Economics, University of Tennessee, under the combined auspices of the Guild and the Southern Highlanders, and with the financial support of the General Education Board of the Rockefeller Foundation. The study, completed in 1945, included a five-year plan for education in the crafts, to be carried on by the Guild and financed by the Foundation.[6] This program, which ended in 1950, was a great force in the development of crafts in the area. It concentrated on locating craftsmen and helping them with design, technique, production, and marketing problems.

The years after the war saw a fabulous increase in tourism and consequently an ever-increasing demand for mountain crafts. The results of this were contradictory. Many shops sprang up that handled the cheapest kind of foreign and domestic souvenir items, usually machine-made, selling their wares under the name of mountain crafts. This seriously damaged the reputation of the area's craftsmen. At the same time, the Guild and other discriminating groups and individuals opened shops that carried the best in mountain crafts, thus spreading the Highlands' reputation for fine work.

In July 1948, the Guild held the first Craftsmen's Fair in Gatlinburg. Here craftsmen from eight states demonstrated their crafts, and exhibited and sold their wares. At least one fair has been held every year since then, either in Gatlinburg or in Asheville, and the Fairs have done much to establish the reputation and integrity of mountain crafts.

In 1958 the Guild published a small booklet called *Crafts in the Southern Highlands*, with text by Emma Weaver in collaboration with a group of Guild members. This attractive booklet, based upon Allen Eaton's book of 1937, pictures crafts as they are in the mountains today.

Today, crafts are firmly entrenched in the mountain area. To many tourists, one of the most interesting things about highland crafts is that here traditional crafts live at peace with the contemporary and experimental, in mutual respect and admiration.

Craft development in this area is partly due to a national—rather, an international—trend back to the satisfactions of doing things by hand. But it is also due in large part to the unceasing efforts of such organizations as the Southern Highland Handicraft Guild. This does not mean that all good craftsmen in the area are affiliated with the Guild, but it does mean that Guild membership is a sign of competence, and that what the Guild attempts to do is representative of the area's best efforts for crafts.

To become a member of the Guild, a craftsman or a group of craftsmen must successfully submit work to a jury of standards. The Guild consists at present of 274 individual members with a wide range of crafts represented, and 52 center members. An individual member is a designer-craftsman, designing and executing his own work. A center is a group of craftsmen working together. As each center is organized on its own plan, each one is unique.

[5] Eaton, p. 251.
[6] Marian Heard, "Survey on Crafts in the Southern Appalachians" (unpublished report to General Education Board of the Rockefeller Foundation, 1945).

Centers vary in size from two members to well over two hundred. Work may be done entirely at the center itself, or it may be done in the homes of the workers. A center may be solely for the teaching of crafts, as is the Summer School of Crafts at Cherokee, North Carolina, or it may be strictly a production center, like the Blenko Glass Company of Milton, West Virginia. Some centers are both educational and production organizations. For instance, the John C. Campbell Folk School at Brasstown, North Carolina, teaches woodcarving, weaving, and other crafts; it is also a craft production center. In some centers each member may do both designing and construction. Others resemble European craft centers, with one or several designers directing the work of artisans. The designers are usually individual Guild members.

One of the largest and most interesting of the craft centers is the Qualla Arts and Crafts Mutual in Cherokee, for which approximately 200 Indian craftsmen produce baskets, weaving, pottery, and woodwork. This center is a true cooperative owned by the Cherokees. It has its own beautiful sales shop.

The Guild maintains five shops in which only members' work is sold. Outside the shop managers and their helpers, and one stenographer, the Guild's permanent staff consists of a director and a director of education. Throughout its history, the Guild has worked to maintain high craft standards, to preserve the best of the traditional, and to encourage the contemporary and the creative.

The present educational program of the Guild, started in 1959 with a full-time education director, has three objectives: to help Guild members solve their problems in design, production, and marketing; to help non-Guild members to get advice and training in these same things, preparing them for membership if they so desire; and to educate the public to an appreciation of fine crafts. To these ends, the education program sponsors workshops and conferences, often using experts in various craft fields from the Guild's own membership; provides speakers; stages exhibits of craft work; and maintains a library of craft books and slides.

Since 1948, the Guild has held a Craftsman's Fair every July, either in Asheville or in Gatlinburg. In 1960 and 1961, two fairs were held each year: one in Asheville in July; one in Gatlinburg in October.

At a typical Craftsman's Fair, the visitor is met at the entrance to the auditorium by a scene from the past. Before a log cabin, a bonneted woman stands over an enormous black dyepot, stirring its contents, and occasionally lifting out a hank of wool of some bright but muted hue, the product of natural or "vegetable" dyes. Perhaps a blacksmith is at his forge nearby, beating strips of iron into andirons, or a woodworker at a long-obsolete boom-and-treadle lathe shapes a table leg.

Inside, the visitor comes first into the quiet of the exhibit room. Here contemporary and traditional crafts are displayed side by side. Every effort is made in these exhibits to demonstrate to the visitors how crafts can make a home or a costume more beautiful and can contribute to the graciousness of living.

In another area of the fair are the demonstrators—the spinners of wool and flax, the hookers and weavers of both traditional and contemporary designs. The woodcarver and the sculptor may be found next to the maker of corn-shuck or straw dolls. Of the potters of the area, one is a member of a family of potters, and the business is in its fourth generation. Another is a young man fresh from college and craft training. A maker of exquisite marquetry, trained in Europe, works within several feet of a mountain-born man who is hollowing out a wooden bowl with chisel and mallet, or polishing the waxed walnut of a dulcimer, or, with nothing more than a pocket-knife, whittling a small animal figure from a piece of holly. Across the way, an enamelist draws a red-hot copper tray from a kiln, and the visitor watches it cool into sparkling color.

The Fair often includes visiting exhibits from other areas. It usually includes also folk singing or folk dancing or both, as well as talks on various phases of craft work. For many years, Mr. Allen Eaton was the featured speaker on crafts of the area.

The Fair gives the whole picture: the range of crafts from traditional to contemporary, the range of craftsmen from native mountaineer with generations of mountain ancestors to the newly-come craftsman from New York or Cincinnati, looking for a peaceful life of work among fellow enthusiasts. The standard of work is high.

Many of the Craftsmen count on the contacts made at the Fair, as well as the on-the-spot sales, for a large part of the year's business. Many also count on the beauty of the fair and the association with other craftsmen for re-creation and inspiration in their own work.

At the fairs, and at the five shops maintained by the Guild, as well as at other good shops in the area, the tourist may buy quality crafts. In other shops, so-called crafts are sold, many of them actually

THE SOUTHERN APPALACHIANS

Figure 79
DISTRIBUTION OF INDIVIDUAL AND CENTER
MEMBERS OF SOUTHERN HIGHLAND
HANDICRAFT GUILD, 1959

Number of members in county:

1-20

21-50

50 or more

■ Member center

factory-made and/or from parts of the world where labor is very cheap. The consequent confusion in the minds of the potential customers usually is great. The Guild is making a conscientious effort to meet the demand for inexpensive souvenirs by stressing the production of low-priced high-quality items.

The survey that formed the basis for this chapter produced some interesting and often surprising facts that contribute to the complete picture of highland crafts. During this survey, the author contacted over a thousand individual craftsmen and sent out 949 questionnaires. Of this number, 348, or 36.7 percent, were returned with answers more or less complete. This number includes only an occasional example of the man, deep in a mountain cove, who still makes his own tools, or the woman on an upland farm who never bought a broom. There are probably several thousand such people in the area.

Approximately the same percentage of the fifty centers that were contacted returned questionnaires; these were chiefly Guild centers.

There are many craft centers besides Guild centers scattered through the area. Most of them are concerned with weaving. Mountain women get weaving materials from these centers, weave specified articles at home or at the center for a specified wage, usually the minimum, and return the articles to the center. Often the woven articles are collected at the homes of the weavers, and materials are brought to them. This type of work is convenient for women with small children.

Other crafts have led to the establishment of small industries. The making of tufted bedspreads and related articles, once a handicraft in the area, has been largely taken over by small factories, and there is little if any handwork involved. The same is true of leather work. An occasional industry of this kind employs a good designer and produces an acceptable product, but for the most part the work ranges from mediocre to unacceptable, by Guild standards, in design and workmanship.

Of the seven states covered by this survey, Tennessee and North Carolina account for over 70 percent of the craft production (Figure 79). Although there are many craftsmen scattered throughout these states, the chief areas of concentration are around the big tourist sections: Gatlinburg in Tennessee and Asheville in North Carolina. Both the presence of tourists, and the fact that there were early craft centers in these regions account for this concentration.

In Kentucky, the stronghold of crafts is still around Berea. In 1946 the state of Kentucky granted funds for the promotion of craft work in the state. A Kentucky Craft Guild was formed, and plans were made for searching out native craftsmen and arranging for both craft teaching and the marketing of craft products. Through the courtesy of the L. & N. Railroad, two railroad cars were converted into an art and craft exhibit hall and a craft workshop. This train is touring Kentucky, stopping at small towns where people can not only see the exhibit but can get some craft instruction.

Craftsmen in the highlands still evidently prefer country living. Approximately half those who responded to the questionnaires lived in open country. Only 11 percent of highland craftsmen lived in cities of over 25,000 population.

Only thirty-five workers reported that they earned their entire living through crafts. There were almost three times as many women working in crafts as men, and almost half the women were housewives. Fourteen percent of the total number were teachers. The others were scattered widely among various occupations.

Strangely enough, while over 15 percent of the craft workers reported their ages as over 65, very few called themselves "retired." The inference is that people interested in crafts just don't retire. The people of the highlands who devote their time to crafts are, for the most part, mature people, the median age being in the 46 to 55 bracket, and only six out of the 348 being twenty-five years old or under.

Over half of the craftsmen reported having lived in the area all their lives. In this survey, at least, inmigrants did not outnumber native craftsmen. Fifty-seven percent stated that both their parents were mountain people, and over 50 percent reported that all four of their grandparents were from the mountains. Over 36 percent reported that their parents did some form of craft work, and over 21 percent remembered that their grandparents were engaged in handicrafts.

In view of the nativity of the craftsmen, it is especially interesting to note their educational level: 21 percent were college graduates, with many of these having credit past their degrees; another 20 percent had some college work to their credit; over 17 percent had less than a high school education. Barely 10 percent had less than an eighth grade education.

A third of the total 348 craftsmen reported some craft training within the previous five years. Many of these gave workshops at colleges, universities, craft schools, or craft agencies as the place of their training.

Only 20 percent of the craftsmen concerned sold their products regularly, but over 60 percent reported they would like to sell more than they did. However, only a little more than 25 percent checked "markets" as one of their chief difficulties; 50 percent checked "time for work," and less than 10 percent checked "money." Almost 60 percent expressed a desire for more training, which indicates that the craftsmen themselves feel that the need for training is important. Both this need and the need for time to work far outweigh the desire to sell.

Thirty-seven percent of the 348 respondents were members of the Guild, and another 24 percent said they would like to be. A gratifying 77 percent said they were happier at craft work than at any other kind.

Many craftsmen do more than one kind of craft work. Many crafts are done by comparatively few people. But today, as in the early years of the craft revival, by far the most popular craft is weaving.

In attempting to arrive at some estimate of the economic value of crafts to the area, the researcher is handicapped by the fact that no thorough studies have been made on the subject. The Southern Highland Handicraft Guild, in a survey of its own members, made in 1957 and included in the booklet *Crafts in the Southern Highlands*, estimated that approximately one million dollars was paid into the hands of mountain craftsmen for Guild-approved work during the year 1956.

In the present survey, only 189 craftsmen answered the questions concerning actual earnings. These earnings totaled approximately $129,450, or an average of $648.92. Using this average to project the earnings of the 949 craftsmen contacted would give a possible total of $649,989. This average may be far too high, but, on the other hand, the number of craftsmen contacted is much lower than the number actually working in the mountain area.

Other findings that might help the reader to arrive at some conclusions concerning the economic value of crafts are these:

Thirteen center members of the Guild gave information on earnings. These centers ranged from two to 200 workers each, and from $40 to well over $1,750,000 in gross sales per year. Since there are many centers both in and outside the Guild, and since many reported gross sales of over $40,000, it would seem that the centers themselves probably net at least a million dollars a year.

In the Guild centers there are about a thousand workers, only about half of them full-time workers. For these 500, at the minimum wage, the earnings per year would be in the neighborhood of another million. If we again make use of the average of $684.92, the other 500 workers in craft centers, people who work part-time and, many of them, in their homes, might earn as much as $342,460. Again, this average may be much too high. Skilled craftsmen and designers in craft centers, full-time and part-time craft teachers scattered through the area's schools, missions, colleges, and centers might total $50,000 in earnings. Guild personnel, including sales people and incidental workers, earned over $37,000 in 1958, and that total exceeded $40,000 by 1960.

There are at least as many non-Guild craftsmen and craft centers in the area as there are Guild craftsmen and centers. There are many more craft shops in the non-Guild category. Earnings can be figured accordingly.

These scattered figures are not conclusive, and any effort to convert them to an estimate of the dollar-and-cents value of crafts could lead only to argument. This author considers that the important thing is not the actual money value of crafts for any one year. The important thing is that crafts have an ever-growing economic value, definitely related to tourism and in-migration, and that that value can continue to grow, along with the cultural value of crafts.

These further points may be added as an indication of the growth of interest in and money spent for highland crafts: Until 1961, no Craftsman's Fair had ever reached 13,000 in attendance. Yet in 1960, the first year that two fairs were held, those two totalled 24,000. In 1961, the total rose to over 26,000, with 14,500 visitors to the autumn fair alone. Gross receipts for the two 1960 fairs were well over $75,000.

At the close of the autumn fair of 1961, the *Gatlinburg Press* estimated that the fair had brought $250,000 to the motel and hotel owners and other businesses of the town. One merchant added, "And it gave us a million dollars' worth of publicity all over the country."

In spite of this cheerful picture, crafts are still not a road to riches either for the individual craftsman or for the Guild. The money that reaches the craftsman from shops and fairs is scattered among many. Craft work is painstaking and slow, and many craftsmen estimate that their actual hourly wage is very low. The bulk of the Guild's receipts, after craftsmen are paid, goes for salaries of personnel, for staging the next fair, for maintaining the shops, and for financing the expanding Education Program. Certainly few craftsmen are in craft work in the hope of great monetary gains. As Allen Eaton has said, "All the satisfactions . . . are not subject to measurement,"[7] and it is a relief to turn from the economic value of crafts to the personal ones.

Personal values are the ones most often stressed by the individual craftsman. These values have to do with the social, recreational, educational, cultural, and therapeutic aspects of crafts. Association with other craftsmen, learning to appreciate both the traditional and the contemporary in crafts other than their own, finding relaxation and happiness in craft work—these are important. Crafts are used as therapy to an ever-increasing extent in practically all hospitals of the area, rated high by doctors and nurses in preventive and curative treatment for both physical and mental ills.

But the greatest personal value of crafts is that the craftsman who makes a beautiful thing that others pause to admire—perhaps to buy—gains stature as an individual. He is one who creates with his hands, and as such he knows a kinship with all other craftsmen and with the great creative forces of nature.

The Appalachian craftsman, as depicted by the 348 respondents of the present survey, emerges as a composite personality: the native and the in-migrant, the traditional and the contemporary, the family-trained craftsman and the college-trained one. He is becoming more aware of markets and of the value of his work. His technical and design standards are higher each year. He is at last forsaking his retirement and beginning to gain regional, national, and international recognition. But he remains a product of the mountains. The danger to the mountain craftsman is not that he will change but that he may lose his individuality. Unless he understands his own cultural heritage and does all he can to develop its possibilities, the mountain area will eventually cease to make a unique contribution to our national culture.

Education in the meaning of fine crafts is the answer for both producer and consumer, but education must start with the mountain people themselves. The present is a difficult time to evaluate crafts in education, since they are in a state of flux, but these points are true as of 1961:

Most public schools of the area are not teaching crafts either as a practical subject or as a cultural foundation for pride in a mountain heritage, although there are exceptions to this. A course of study of the

crafts, music, dances and literature of the area would be an excellent thing both in the public schools and in colleges and universities of the Region.

Until recently, little craft teaching was done in the colleges and universities, with such notable exceptions as Berea and the University of Tennessee. The University of Tennessee, for example, has had a Related Arts Department in the College of Home Economics for almost thirty years. Since 1946, the University and the Pi Beta Phi School in Gatlinburg have collaborated on an excellent summer school of crafts held each year at Pi Beta Phi.

Now more and more colleges and universities in and near the Southern Appalachians are adding craft courses, and any statement that is true today of their offerings will be proved obsolete by tomorrow's catalogues. Few, however, are stressing crafts as a part of the culture of the area.

There are many opportunities for craft education in the area. Well-trained young highlanders, understanding the mountain people, could do much in teaching crafts and their appreciation in public schools, in centers, in home demonstration clubs, at college level, and with such organizations as the Guild.

Many of the centers that started in the early days of the craft revival have slowly disintegrated. The Craft Education program of the Guild is revitalizing some of these. With some financial help and much help from craft-trained teachers, many more could be reinstated as centers where both children and adults might learn crafts.

The possibilities of the recreational values of crafts have barely been touched. A few mountain resorts have hired craft teachers to instruct their guests, but very little has been done with this in comparison with what could be done. The recreational and economic values of crafts are being increasingly recognized in geriatrics, as well as in the therapeutic applications already mentioned. In these fields trained teachers will be increasingly in demand.

In the meantime a definite and comprehensive plan for craft education in the mountain area is of primary importance. The Guild's education program strives to meet the heavy demands made upon it by schools, centers, individuals, and communities who call for help in setting up a craft program or teaching groups of interested people. The Education Director answers these calls in person or employs one or more of the Guild-member experts in various crafts. Help

---

[7] P. 110.

given by the Guild may take the form of an illustrated talk, a small exhibit, a personal conference, or a short workshop. A much more efficient program could be carried on if financial aid were available. With sufficient resources, a definite program could be set up for exploring the economic possibilities of crafts within selected areas, studying existing craft work, interested workers, and available materials in the region, as well as possible markets and need for economic aid. Much research could be done on the possible uses of such commonplace materials as cornshuck, as well as in such relatively new materials as plastics. Craft centers might be established with trained personnel responsible for quality of items produced and for their marketing. Such programs could be of value in some economically distressed areas. Tourist areas would have excellent potentialities.

Such educational ventures could well be handled under the guidance of the Guild with its years of experience in handling just such vital problems as a new center would be sure to face. This program, well administered, would help greatly to maintain the quality of the crafts offered for sale in shops, to encourage craft groups in progressive steps, and to aid in improving the training of young craftsmen who wish to become leaders in regional craft development.

Such an extensive program is entirely beyond the Guild's financial powers, however. Only if outside funds become available can such a program be planned.

Crafts now, as in pioneer times, are an important part of life in the Southern Appalachians. They still bring beauty, color, and purpose, as well as much-needed dollars, into the lives of mountain craftsmen. In such projects as the Craftsman's Fair, the Southern Highlander stands before the world as the product of a unique and developing culture.

Many interested and well-meaning people misunderstand the character of crafts. Crafts are not a quick answer to all financial needs of depressed mountain areas. A craft is not learned in six easy lessons and its products sold cheaply and without effort. Education, whether of the old father-to-son variety or the contemporary college or workshop kind, is essential. Only craft work of high quality can contribute to the cultural or financial well-being of the mountain area.

With intelligent planning and timely financial aid for a comprehensive educational program, crafts could become a more vital factor in the cultural, social, and economic life of the Southern Appalachian Region.

CHAPTER NINETEEN

The Region's Future:

A National

Challenge

RUPERT B. VANCE

OVER TWENTY-FIVE YEARS AGO, AN earlier survey of the Southern Appalachians concluded that the basic problems of the Region grew out of "maladjustments of land use and in relation of population to land." Little has occurred in the intervening years to suggest that this diagnosis was incorrect. Glancing through the chapters of this report, though, the reader will find that sweeping changes have taken place in the Southern Appalachians during the past three decades. In general, these changes reflect the efforts of the people of the Region to achieve the living standards of the more prosperous areas of the nation. Until recently the efforts have been largely those of individuals and communities, uncoordinated and lacking any common regional objective. Nevertheless, they have resulted in a better, though by no means completely satisfactory, adjustment of population and resources.

As our studies of population and migration have shown, the net movement of nearly two million persons out of the Region between 1940 and 1960 has arrested the increase of population. With the movement of young adults from the Region, birth rates have declined drastically in most rural counties. Fewer now live in rural areas dependent upon subsistence agriculture and mining; more live in metropolitan areas that offer a greater variety of economic opportunities. The metropolitan areas of the Region, like those elsewhere in the nation, have enjoyed a relative prosperity.

As population growth has tended to stabilize, there has been notable improvement in the utilization of resources. Since 1939, manufacturing production and employment have increased more rapidly in the Region than in the nation (Figure 40). Mining and agriculture have not kept pace, but fewer people now depend upon them for their livelihood. As a consequence, per capita income has increased above and beyond the effect of inflation on the wage level in practically all mountain counties.

The benefits derived from the improved balance of population and resources have been supplemented by unprecedented aid from outside the Region. Construction of new roads and highways and betterment of existing ones have made most areas accessible. Schools have been improved; more students attend them and for longer periods; and increasing numbers of graduates go on to colleges and universities. Health conditions, at least to the extent that they are reflected in mortality rates, are on a par with those of the nation (Table 56). Many new hospitals and public health centers have been constructed, and public health services have been substantially strengthened and extended. Programs of public assistance to the needy and dependent, while still inadequate to the task, are immeasurably more effective in the provision of relief and rehabilitation services than those of thirty years ago.

With the improvement of community institutions and the establishment of better transportation and communication links, there have been substantial changes in the values and aspirations of the people of the Region. As our attitude survey data (analyzed in Chapter II) have shown, the traditional outlook of passive resignation is rapidly disappearing. Like other Americans, the people of the Region want the material comforts and social services that only an advanced economy can support. If they cannot get them in the Region, they will seek them elsewhere, but increasingly efforts are being made to secure such benefits in the Southern Appalachians.

In listing the many beneficial changes that have occurred in the Southern Appalachians since the earlier survey we have deliberately sought to combat any impression that the Region is a stagnant enclave. Yet, let no one be deceived: the problems that prompted our new survey are not solved, nor are they well on the way toward solution. Much of the satisfaction to be gained from the changes we have cited evaporates under the stress of national comparisons. If population in the Region has declined since 1950, it still remains nearly a fifth greater than in the 1930's when removing some of the population was considered imperative for the "fundamental alleviation of the conditions of life" in the mountains.[1] The migration of young adults has served to lower the birth rate of the Region, but the number of children under five years of age per 1,000 women aged 15-49 is still over 500 in 47 of the 190 counties, as compared with the national ratio of 408. Despite the movement of more than a million persons out of the Region during the single decade 1950-1960, unemployment and underemployment remain critical in areas of mining and subsistence agriculture.

The apparent prosperity of the metropolitan areas of the Region, as compared with the rural areas, must be reassessed when they are compared with other metropolitan areas of the nation. Not a single one had a growth rate during the 1950-1960 decade as high as the national average rate for metropolitan areas, and out-migration exceeded in-migration in all except one, Roanoke. To the extent that the attraction of new people is an indication of economic growth, even the most prosperous parts of the Southern Appalachians fared poorly.

Similarly, the relative gain in manufacturing industry must be weighed against the fact that on a per capita basis the Region still lags far behind the remainder of the nation with regard to number of manufacturing establishments, value added by manufacture, and employment in manufacturing. Moreover, manufacturing activity actually declined in some parts of the Region (Figures 42, 43). Average annual wages in the Region's manufacturing were only 80 percent of the national average wage in 1958. Low agricultural income, layoffs from union mines and low wages in nonunion mines, general unemployment and underemployment have served to keep the general level of income below the national level even though the difference is not quite so great as it was thirty years ago.

There is little prospect of a substantial rise in mining employment even if the market for coal improves, for, as Gibbard has pointed out, continued mechanization of mining operations is inevitable. Most farms in the Region are not commercially competitive. Possibly half of the people, certainly a third, could leave Appalachians farms without appreciably lowering farm production. Except in a few areas the terrain will not permit farms to be as large, as mechanized, and as scientifically managed as the highly specialized farms of other regions. Where subsistence farming is dominant (Figure 34) even the application of the latest and best agricultural practices will not adequately sustain the population at its present density. It is extremely fallacious to expect relief in Appalachian agriculture without a continued heavy out-movement of farm population.

The consequences of institutional erosion from years of poverty are not quickly remedied. Schools may be improved, but it is less easy to repair the educational damage already inflicted. Nearly a fifth of the regional population 25 years of age and over had less than five years schooling in 1950 and, as Brown and Hillery have pointed out, migration tends to be selective of the better educated, thus slowing the rise in educational level in the Region. Obsolescent and inefficient modes of local government organization and operation persist to retard rather than promote economic and social development. And reluctance of

[1] *Economic and Social Problems and Conditions of the Southern Appalachians*, U.S. Department of Agriculture, Miscellaneous Publication No. 205 (1935), p. 5.

communities to revitalize their tax systems has remained a formidable obstacle to institutional improvements that are both needed and desired.

New Approaches to Old Problems

By 1960 it was evident that both the Federal Government and the states were prepared to mobilize their efforts in behalf of regional and area planning. Gradually a suggestion of overall strategy for action began to emerge.

Governors of Appalachian states had already proposed that appropriate agencies should develop plans for the Region. The Conference of Governors on Underdeveloped Areas of the Appalachians first met in May, 1960, on the call of Governor J. Millard Tawes of Maryland, for consideration of a report on the economic conditions and problems of the Appalachian portions of eleven states.[2] Meeting again at Lexington, Kentucky, during the same year, the Conference agreed that the states represented should continue their voluntary association, and that the group would devote itself to state and federal promotion of increased highway facilities, development of water resources, and related programs.

In the 1960 presidential campaign, public attention was focused on the problems of the Appalachian Region. Two contenders for the Democratic nomination, Senator Hubert Humphrey of Minnesota and Senator John F. Kennedy of Massachusetts, waged a stiff running battle for the convention vote of West Virginia. Both candidates were shocked by conditions they found in the mountain areas, especially by those in the mining camps; and both promised relief, if elected. Reporters following the campaign sent out reams of publicity; national television programs were focussed on the Appalachians; and the Governor of West Virginia felt called upon to discuss the state's situation over a national television hookup.

The new administration solidly backed its pledges and on May 21, 1961, President John F. Kennedy signed the Area Redevelopment Act. The stated purpose of the measure was to help "stranded" rural and urban communities throughout the nation to overcome chronic unemployment.

The Area Redevelopment program comprehends three related proposals. One is a $200-million loan program for the purchase or development of land and facilities for commercial or industrial use; these funds are available to qualified public or private applicants in two types of redevelopment area. Another $100 million in loans is available to state or local govern-

ments or other community organizations for the provision or improvement of public facilities such as water systems, sewage disposal plants, and similar projects, where such public facilities will improve the prospects for industrial and commercial development. A fund of $75 million is provided for grants to communities unable to finance such loans. A smaller grant fund is provided to support surveys, fact-finding, and consultation required to initiate industrial development. The third program provides funds to assist local or state agencies in setting up occupational and industrial training programs to retrain workers whose skills are obsolescent. Under this program, subsistence payments are available to jobless workers receiving training. To carry out the provisions of the act, the Area Redevelopment Administration was established in the Department of Commerce,[3] and William L. Batt, Jr., was appointed administrator by President Kennedy.

In order to extend its study and action to the wider and deeper problems of the Appalachian Region, the Area Redevelopment Administration is working closely with the Conference of Appalachian Governors. At the request of the latter body, the ARA has employed a planner in its Washington office whose function is to develop basic programs of natural and human resource development in such areas as highways, vocational training, water, minerals, and recreation. His office is designed to work closely with the principals and staff of the Conference of Appalachian Governors and, through them, with the increasing number of state and local efforts.

Much of eastern Kentucky, all of West Virginia, and other sections of the Southern Appalachian Region have been designated redevelopment areas under provisions of the Area Redevelopment Act and the standards established by the ARA (Figure 80). Although it is as yet too early to evaluate the effectiveness of the redevelopment program, it obviously offers a fresh approach to some of the economic problems of the Region. It is less obvious, perhaps, that its provisions will benefit most those areas that have a good potential for industrial or commercial development. Clearly not all portions of the Region possess such a potential, and for the people of some areas a different approach would seem to be indicated.

[2] Maryland Department of Economic Development, *The Appalachian Region* (Annapolis, 1960).

[3] Public Law 87-27, 87th Congress, S. 1, May 1, 1961; *Area Redevelopment Act. Report of the Committee on Banking and Currency.* House of Representatives, 87th Congress, March 22, 1961.

THE SOUTHERN APPALACHIANS

Figure 80)
REDEVELOPMENT AREAS, FEBRUARY 12, 1962

Areas of persistent unemployment

Rural redevelopment areas

Development project approved

Source: Area Redevelopment Administration

SCALE
10 0 10 20 30 40 50 MILES

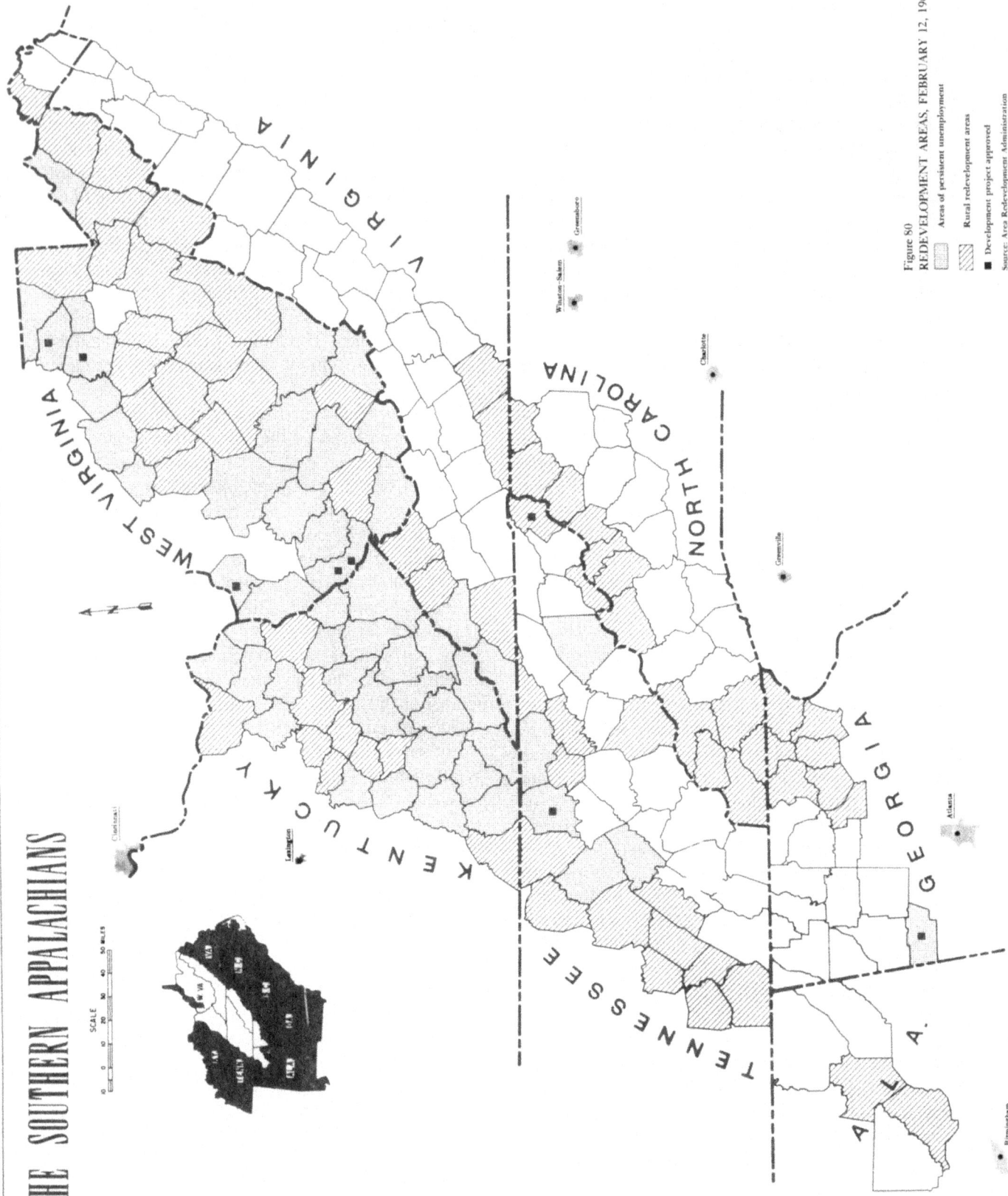

WEST VIRGINIA

VIRGINIA

KENTUCKY

TENNESSEE

NORTH CAROLINA

GEORGIA

ALA.

Chattanooga

Lexington

Winston-Salem

Greensboro

Charlotte

Greenville

Atlanta

Birmingham

Area and Human Development: A Dual Strategy

The tendency heretofore has been to speak of the Appalachians as an undeveloped area, the implied assumption being that a high stage of development is a natural order to be achieved in all American regions. But if a given area is undeveloped, it is realistic to ask what resources for development exist within that area. Two answers are possible. The first and most obvious is that here are physical resources to be developed, and this answer implies that the need must be met by industrialization. But it is obvious that physical resources are not equal for all regions, and that some areas are more likely than others to benefit from the further industrialization of the national economy. A second answer, equally realistic, points to the population as human resources to be developed.

We have thus to consider on the one hand the potential for area development; on the other, the potential for human development. While the two must be seen as related and overlapping problems, they are not entirely congruent. Populations are not tied to specific localities. If it is shown that certain localities have little potential for development, there is no need within the national context for human resources so placed either to be lost or left to deteriorate. Where the necessary basis for area development is not present, we need to concentrate on development of the human potential—a development which in some communities of the Appalachians will involve preparing large numbers of the population for jobs to be found only outside the Region. In most of the Region's coal camps and areas of subsistence agriculture, low priority must be given to area development and high priority to development of the human resources.

If the national program of the Area Redevelopment Administration is clearly addressed to the first consideration—that of resource development—it is equally clear that development of the population as a resource potential is left largely to state and local leadership. Here is found the basis of the conflict between area development and human development as we have viewed it. To expect the Region's community leaders to devote themselves to preparing their youth so that youth will be better able to migrate is to expect them to undercut the resources base on which both community agencies and businesses feed. What banker, what real estate owner, what school administrator wishes to aid in the depopulation of his community and thus weaken the basis of his business and of the community's social institutions? Local leadership would naturally prefer to be able to check all migration out of the area and to make use of human resources at home. To do so, however, would almost immediately stop the trend toward increased income and lead to the piling up of poverty.

The balance between area development and the development of human resources thus poses the major problem in the strategy of redevelopment. The goal of overall planning should be to achieve a high level of living by dealing with both the resource and population factors in balance—not with one or the other alone.

The Strategy of Area Development

With administrative machinery at hand, and with seed capital in sight, we have come to the point where the alternatives in regard to subareas must be examined. To say that not all the areas considered underdeveloped are capable of economic growth even with subsidy is not necessarily a criticism of the Area Redevelopment Act. But a critical problem in the administration of ARA will be to develop criteria that will distinguish between areas which can be expected to respond to redevelopment and those which cannot. Certain areas, it may be pointed out, will classify themselves by seeking only grants rather than industrial loans.

Certain guiding principles for area development are already quite clear. First, area development must take place within the context of national economic development. It can be expected to expand as the national economy expands. It will contract or cease to expand when the national economy faces recession or plateau. Second, it must be based on the economic potential of the region and its resources, not simply the economic needs—or wishes—of the local population. Thus, the first priorities will, of necessity, go to those metropolitan areas that are in trouble. They have facilities, leadership, manpower pools, and credit. Having once tasted economic expansion, they are anxious to get underway again. The coal industry may have contracted in their hinterlands, but the metropolis remains the best configuration in which to place new or auxiliary industry. As payrolls are generated, the larger community reemerges as an important market area, thus helping to underwrite its own recovery. Moreover the stakes are greater in the metropolis. These centers once offered hope of employment to surrounding areas; if their "surplus labor" is forced out, it will add appreciably to the nation's unemployment ratios.[4] Only if the Region's metropolitan areas are able to compete successfully with the growing cities of the Southeast and the nation can they be expected to attract their share of the migrants who will continue to move from the Region's rural areas. Brown and Hillery have demonstrated that migrants tend to move short distances, and to stay within their own states; yet in the accelerated outmovement of the past decade, Southern Appalachian cities have lost population. The inference is strong that these cities have been unable to offer the Region's people the economic opportunities which they have therefore sought elsewhere.

The movement of people from the Region's distressed areas toward cities outside the Region will doubtless continue, and of course it is not in itself undesirable. But it is urged by many of the Region's leaders that the difficult adjustment problems raised by this migration would be less severe if the Region's own cities, closer in culture as well as in geography, could absorb more of the migrant population. In view of the migration patterns observed by Brown and Hillery, it seems very likely that population from the Region's disadvantaged areas would gravitate toward these cities if the cities were able to provide the economic opportunities which the people seek. This point of view was expressed recently by community leaders in Ashland, Kentucky, in their formulation of plans for the redevelopment of metropolitan Boyd County:

"In addition to the characteristics which are normally those of a metropolitan center in any region, . . . Boyd County, with its existing and potential capacity for industry and service activities, represents the only area of such clear and present capacity within the Eastern Kentucky region. The communities of this region, in the main, have a past dependence largely upon mining and marginal or limited agriculture and face a current status of economic depression. . . . This situation—Boyd County with a growing industrial might and a clear potential in a region which industry and immediate potential for industry is so completely limited—imposes upon Boyd County both a unique responsibility and an unusual opportunity. . . . In Boyd *must* be located much of the large industry to serve as a market for regional resources; to process those resources; to serve as basic industry for satellite service plants; and to provide jobs for many members of the regional labor pool in early stages of the region's future economic development process."

For these reasons, they conclude, the redevelopment of Boyd County must be seen not only in the contexts of the county's own industrial development and its role in the development of the tri-state Huntington-Ashland area: it must also be considered in the light of Boyd County's situation as "the much needed and, in many ways, exclusive Regional Center for the utilization of resources, the provision of an industrial base and new jobs in Eastern Kentucky."[5]

The "little economies" prevalent in the Region operate under different principles.[6] Here industries most likely to succeed will be those devoted to supplying local markets. For example, a community of very small size and income base can be expected to support its own county newspaper. Other businesses— bakeries, dairies, etc.—which once could be supported by small communities, can survive in the era of truck transportation only by competing successfully over wider areas. When an Appalachian community undertakes to support an industry, its sponsors should satisfy themselves that the industry is truly competitive. Possessed of transportation, of good labor supply, good management, and adequate organizations—and this is not always given nor easy of achievement—some local industries in the Region can expect to reach markets sufficiently wide for success. Local markets, however, cannot offer the great potential of national markets. Economic potential, therefore, and not simply the economic needs of the local population, must guide the plans. If there is little likelihood that an industry—including agriculture—can compete in the national market without prolonged subsidy, it should not be encouraged simply because the need is evident, the area is depressed, and the people want industry. In America, the people everywhere want industry.

In attempting to raise the level of living, forced development must be geared to resource potential and population growth geared to resource development. Developmental levels should be exploited to the full natural potential, but these levels should not

[4] *Guiding Metropolitan Growth* (New York: Committee on Economic Development, 1960); *Manpower Requirements and Training Needs of the Wheeling-Steubenville Metropolitan Area* (Charleston: West Virginia Department of Employment Security, 1958).

[5] Boyd County Area Program Council, "Overall Economic Development Program" (Submitted to the Administrator, Area Redevelopment Administration, September 1, 1961), pp. 19-21.

[6] Donald R. Gilmore, *Developing the Little Economies. A Survey of Area Development Programs in the United States* (New York: Committee on Economic Development, 1958); V. F. Gegan and S. H. Thompson, "Worker Mobility in a Labor Surplus Area," *Monthly Labor Review*, December, 1957.

be artificially raised by long-range deficit financing unless certain counties wish to repeat the experience of the coal plateaus and artificially create their own crisis of over-expansion. Instead, population should be adjusted to the level which can be adequately supported by the resources of the area. An adequate level of income, measured by national standards, is a major test of adjustment. Without some such guiding principle as this, forced industrial development in the Southern Appalachian Region—or anywhere else—is headed for disaster.[7]

Another possible source of error in planning for area development is the tendency to place an unrealistic dependence on developments which, even if successful, will be limited in their effects on the most disadvantaged areas. In some parts of the Region tourism contributes substantially to the economy, and it may be possible to increase this contribution both in existing tourist centers and in some new ones. Resort facilities, which have a long history in the mountains, may expect some expansion, and the Region may have increasing attraction as a retirement area. But the employment potential of such developments is limited; they cannot be expected to support large numbers of untrained workers in heavily overpopulated areas. Moreover, the large capital investments required for the development of profitable tourist facilities are not likely to be available in underdeveloped communities. In his study of the Region's tourist industry, Morris has pointed out areas of spectacular scenery, accessible by modern highways, which have little or no tourist trade; tourists do not visit these areas because they do not offer the transient accommodations, restaurants, and recreational facilities which the modern tourist demands. Such facilities are most likely to be developed in those areas which already have a sound economic base—where capital for investment, administrative machinery for sound planning and regulation, and labor trained for service activities are available. Here again the influence of the cities will be felt. If the Region's cities prosper, the potential attractions of rural areas accessible to these cities may be developed.

Similarly, the native handicrafts which have contributed to the attractions and to the commercial life of some of the Region's major tourist centers cannot be expected to produce prosperity in distressed areas where no such trade exists. Miss Stevens has shown in her survey that the income of individual craftsmen is low, and that even in the areas of greatest activity handicrafts are for most workers a secondary or part-time occupation. Moreover, only by maintenance of high standards can the native crafts retain their present reputation for excellence and command the relatively high prices which must be paid for handwork if it is to be even a supplemental source of income for the worker. The high degree of skill required to produce such work is not attainable by all and is attainable by none without proper instruction and devoted study. As Miss Stevens has wisely suggested, the craft movement should be encouraged as a valuable expression of the Region's culture, not as a palliative for its economic ills.

The potential of area development in the Southern Appalachians has certainly not been fully exploited up to now. More industries will be developed, but some will fail. While the criterion should be the development of industry where it is economically feasible, results will not be final until trials are run. Many areas that have been neglected for lack of capital, for lack of enterprising leaders, will now have their chance.

Certain developments should be fostered on the basis of the higher per capita income of a sparser population. Thus mining will continue in Kentucky and West Virginia; it remains a resource to be developed with fewer people, receiving higher incomes and living in better communities. Unmet crisis need not continue forever. These areas can begin a new cycle of development if they begin on the basis of sparser settlement and higher average income. Certainly the closing out of mining operations that prolong poverty and hold out no hope of reestablishing a thriving industry can be set as a short range goal. The old days in mining will never return. Mechanization has seen to that, and the sooner the level at which these areas can support the industry is realized, the better it will be for them.

One need not approve of all the policies of the United Mine Workers to recognize the realism of the UMW's policy in regard to the displacement of miners. John L. Lewis never opposed the mechanization of coal mining; he only contended that miners' wages must remain at national levels. Only through the application of such a policy is the eventual raising of the economic level of mining areas to national standards likely to be achieved. The problem of displaced miners is a serious one, but its existence should not blind us to the fact that the alternative policy of

[7] Harvey S. Perloff, Edgar S. Dunn, Jr., Eric E. Lompard, and Richard F. Muth, *Regions, Resources and Economic Growth* (Baltimore: The Johns Hopkins Press, 1961).

providing employment for many miners at substandard wages can only perpetuate poverty. Since the terrain of most mining areas is too rugged to invite other industries, economic stabilization at an acceptably high level can be achieved only by the migration of the unemployed.[8] If fewer sons of miners can expect to enter the occupation of their fathers, the implication is inescapable: miners should have fewer children, and most of them must be prepared to seek their livelihood elsewhere. Failure to take into account this basic fact will reduce any remedies to the unemployment situation to mere temporary palliatives.

The analogy with forestry in the Appalachians is explicit. The Appalachians are a natural region for growing trees. With virgin stands cut out and the introduction of the portable power saw, it is obvious that forestry can sustain a relatively small population. Much of this employment should be in the maintenance of Federal and state forests. But whether in public or private employ, this population should be expected to function at a high level of living. At present, however, much of the industry in the Southern Appalachians is characterized by low wages and temporary work. As Gibbard has said: "The great social need in forestry is to increase its impact on the levels of living of the people; the route to this end is better forestry practices."

The Strategy of Human Resources Development

In planning for the development of the Region's human resources, the goal should be to provide the people with opportunities to develop their full social and economic potential, whether they remain in the Region or leave it.

Certainly the development of the oncoming generation should be geared to the nation's future rather than to the Region's past or present. No young person now growing up in the Southern Appalachians should be brought up to wring a livelihood from subsistence farming. If these young people, with their inherent abilities, cannot be transferred to industrial or commercial employment within the area, they should be frankly encouraged in the expectation that at the appropriate time they will migrate and seek a normal American future in a community able to provide such a future. As our survey of education has amply documented, a great proportion of the schools serving these youth are grossly inadequate when measured against any national standard. It is not unreasonable to use national standards to evaluate the quality of education in the Region, for its youth must compete in a national market for job opportunities.

The provision of good basic education is a fundamental requirement if the regenerative cycle of poverty is to be broken. Few would disagree with Graff's contention that a substandard educational program is at the heart of the Region's problem. But Graff has also shown that where the needs are greatest and most urgent the financial resources of the communities are least adequate to meet them; and in such communities the potential leadership has often been drained away by migration. The provision of fewer, larger, and better equipped schools; better teachers and school administrators; and more adequate programs will call for a drastic increase in school revenues. Already the seven Southern Appalachian states carry a larger proportion of school expenses than do state governments in the nation as a whole (Figure 57). Surely the fact that so much of whatever training the Region's youth is to receive will be used elsewhere will justify a much broader base of financial support for their education.

Vocational training should be viewed as a supplement to, rather than a substitute for, sound basic education. In a rapidly changing technology, specialized technical skills can quickly become obsolescent and, as has been so clearly illustrated in the case of displaced coal miners, retraining of workers lacking an educational foundation poses a difficult problem. In any case, vocational training and retraining must be fitted to the market needs of an industrial society, both national and regional. The major vocational program available in the Region—and in many communities the only one—is in agriculture, which is taught under Smith-Hughes funds even where farming opportunities are almost nonexistent. Once regarded as well adapted to rural communities, these programs are now under fire because few young people can or should go into agriculture. Since we have in this program an existing structure for the assistance of local school systems, the possibility of revising the program's content to provide a greater variety of training should be examined. Training in the service occupations is greatly needed. Known shortages exist of nurses, secretaries, and teachers. We would do well to reexamine not only the existing Smith-Hughes program but the old programs of the N.Y.A. and C.C.C.

[8] Cf. Harold A. Gibbard, *Habitat, Economy, Society, A Form of Reference Applied to the Southern Appalachian Coal Country.* Mimeographed. From the author, University of West Virginia.

developed in the depression of the 1930's. Job place-ment, counseling, and arrangements for relocation should be integrally related to training programs.

While training for service occupations might well be carried on in rural school systems under an adapta-tion of the program used in the past for the teaching of agriculture, vocational training for the industrial complex is best carried on in large employment centers. In industrial cities vocational training can make use of the facilities of public education and private industry. Among the most successful are the apprenticeship programs in which the industries exer-cise selection and the student feels an immediate relation to the learning process as a job. Even a well-equipped consolidated school in a rural community could hardly expect to provide comparable training.

The Area Redevelopment Act contains provision for retraining of unemployed or underemployed work-ers in defined redevelopment areas. Already in prog-ress in one of the Region's cities (Huntington, West Virginia), such training programs may prove of con-siderable value in relieving local imbalances of labor supply and demand. But at best this is only a remedial measure. What is needed is a preventive program which will keep the oncoming generation from adding to the numbers of willing but unemployable workers both within the Region and elsewhere. In the coal mining and marginal farming areas of the Southern Appalachians, such a program will begin with a frank recognition of the limited prospects for local employ-ment; it will provide the youth of these areas with the knowledge of occupational opportunities else-where; and it will instruct them in the basic skills needed to participate in a modern industrial society and in the exercise of good citizenship in urban communities. In this connection Graff's suggestion that a large number of teachers from outside the Region should be recruited for the Region's public schools deserves attention. Certainly contact with such teachers would be a valuable stimulus for the Region's youth, especially for those who will later seek their futures in cities outside the Region. Per-haps even more effective would be teachers native to the Region but trained in institutions elsewhere. Not only prospective teachers, but other talented young people should be made aware of the opportunities for higher education and specialized training outside the Region, and aided where necessary to take advantage of them. Such contact with the national society and with other regional cultures will not only aid those who make use of their training elsewhere but will be

of inestimable value in terms of community leadership through those who return to their native Region.

The general improvement in public education and the more specialized efforts to deal with local problems through education which are recommended here are beyond the capacity of regional resources. Not only are the financial resources of distressed areas wholly inadequate to the necessary tasks, but, as was stressed earlier, local leadership cannot be expected to make financial sacrifices for the training of young people whose social and economic contributions will ulti-mately be for the benefit of other communities. The participation of the federal government, and of other agencies both public and private outside the Region, will be necessary if the crisis is to be met. Whether the training these young people receive is used within the Region or outside it, no expenditure for the development of human resources can be counted as lost.

One final consideration with regard to the human resources of the Region deserves our attention. If people should no longer rear their children to go into subsistence farming; if only one-sixth to one-tenth of the males growing to adulthood in mining camps can expect to find employment in the mines; if large contingents of mountain youth must migrate to strange cities to engage in new trades and crafts; if those who remain will face difficult periods of adjust-ment in relation to new industries which may or may not survive; if the rate at which the regional labor force replaces itself or is *disemployed* exceeds the rate at which its members are *re-employed* or migrate out-ward; if the Region's problem is thus self-renewing—a certain drastic conclusion is inevitable. It may be that the people of depressed areas can no longer allow themselves the luxury that the American people are now enjoying in the midst of the new prosperity —that is the enjoyment of the "baby boom." In a comparable though more perilous situation the Irish population responded to famine by postponing mar-riage, by sharply reducing their birth rate, and by migrating to America.

An experiment conducted in the coal mining county of Logan, West Virginia, during the depression of the 1930's, served to indicate a way whereby popula-tion growth might be checked. Over 13,000 rural non-farm wives, 32 percent of the women aged 15-44 in the county, were reached by a volunteer contraceptive service, frankly set up by private philanthropy as a social experiment in the control of fertility. This group of rural women had been responsible for over

50 percent of the county's births in the period 1936-1938. About a third of the Negro wives and a half of the white wives had sought to limit fertility before they were contacted by the public health nurse, but their inefficient use of methods at hand had meant a reduction of only 10 to 15 percent in birth rates. After admission to the contraceptive service, their birth rate fell 41 percent—a decline which would have reduced the county's fertility by 20 percent, if extended to all rural nonfarm wives. After two years, however, only 36 percent of the women were still using the prescribed methods.[9]

The support of the Logan county program indicates its acceptance by the families who need it most—those who are too poor to have their own family physicians and too isolated to know of acceptable means of planned parenthood. It was shown that the cost of such service can be greatly reduced if it is integrated with county public health services.

Family limitation is not sufficient by itself to enable such a region to attain economic equality with the nation. Used in conjunction with redevelopment and migration, an effective program should enable young couples to marry at a normal age and to postpone having their families until they are established. Population growth thus checked is less likely to outrun economic growth and thus endanger the whole range of redevelopment plans.

A Priority Schedule for the Next Generation

It would be well to develop a sense of urgency about the problems of the Appalachian area and its people and to set up a "statute of limitations" as it were, with a schedule of priorities. The Appalachian problem has been with us this long, we believe, because it was self-renewing. To be explicit, population growth has proceeded at a more rapid rate than new employment opportunities have been provided and migration has drained off the surplus. And the institutions of the Region, geared to an economy of poverty, not only have failed to solve the problems of poverty but have often contributed to their perpetuation. The schools, for example, have failed to provide the youth with the knowledge and skills required for high income employment, thus severely restricting the development of an economy that could support better schools. Local government agencies, operating in an atmosphere of poverty in which any expenditures beyond the bare functional minimum are regarded as luxuries, are unable or unwilling to make capital investments needed for economic growth. How long a period

should be allotted to carry through on a program and when should we be able to determine that the Appalachian problem is no longer self-generating?

The answer suggested is one generation. This is implicit in the provision of the Area Redevelopment Act that no industrial or commercial development loan, including extensions and renewals, shall exceed twenty-five years. Certainly this seems long enough to separate the industries that will prosper from those that will fail. In 30 years the "lost generation of mountaineers," those too old to adjust and too set in their ways to change, will be over 70 and passing off the stage. Realistically, most of this group must be written off so far as any major economic contribution is concerned and special provision as necessary should be made for their welfare in the form of public assistance. But public assistance must not be perpetuated as a way of life in the areas where dependence upon it has become so widespread (Figure 76).

For the oncoming youth, a period of twenty years will be required to realize the full benefits of efforts devoted to the improvement of education, the provision of vocational training, and guided migration. Because of the slow pace at which our institutions change, two decades of concerted effort probably will be needed to bring about substantial reforms in the methods of community organization and action to deal with social and economic problems. Particularly is this likely to be the case where current constitutional and legislative provisions perpetuate obsolescent structures and practices of local government units. During this period systematic retirement of submarginal land should be effected through public purchase of subsistence farms to which families in the area cling to their own detriment.

A final ten-year period should be devoted to a "mopping-up" operation that will consist of concentrated attacks on remaining problems and the determination that conditions leading to the regeneration of poverty have been eliminated. The mountains have suffered from a kind of fatalism in the past; they must not become victims of over-optimism in the future.

Research furnishes the scientific basis for planning and development. Accordingly, one value of the suggested priority schedule is that we will have three census periods in which to measure the progress of

[9] Gilbert W. Beebe, *Contraception and Fertility in the Southern Appalachians* (Baltimore: The Williams and Wilkins Co., 1942).

the program. Analyses of the censuses of agriculture, business, and manufactures should enable us in 1970 to gauge the movement out of low-level agriculture and the success of manufacturing and commercial enterprises in areas expected to benefit from the Area Redevelopment Act. Data from the population censuses of 1970 and 1980 should be analyzed to determine the progress of out-migration and fertility control, changes in the employment structure, and the extent to which the gaps between regional and national levels of education and income have been closed. Examination at these check-points of other pertinent statistics such as school consolidation and enrollments, local government finances, number of public relief beneficiaries, and the like should serve to identify remaining problems and problem areas. On the basis of these findings, programs should be revised as necessary to focus on the most critical problems, and efforts should be redoubled to eliminate self-renewing problem conditions where they still persist. Where spot areas of poverty are disclosed in 1980, intensive campaigns should be organized as part of the mopping-up operation to eliminate them before the program is closed out at the end of a thirty-year period. Much of this can be accomplished under vigorous state leadership.

Not all the responsibility for success or failure falls on the people of the Region, for the consequences of success or failure are not limited to the Region.[10] The implications of the failure of the richest nation in the world to eliminate or alleviate the Region's poverty within three decades are not likely to be overlooked by those underdeveloped nations of the world seeking to solve their own problems of poverty under conditions far less advantageous. But if the nation is organized and prepared to furnish the cooperation the people and communities of the Region need, they are prepared to share the national destiny, for better or for worse.

[10] Cf. *Economic Growth in the United States—Its Past and Future* (New York: Committee on Economic Development, 1958).

Contributors

RUPERT B. VANCE, research consultant for these studies, is Kenan professor of sociology and research professor in the Institute for Research in Social Science at the University of North Carolina. He is the author of *Human Factors in Cotton Culture* (1929) and *Human Geography of the South* (1932); coauthor of *All These People: The Nation's Human Resources in the South* (1945), *New Farms for Old* (1946), and *Exploring the South* (1949); and coeditor and contributor to *The Urban South* (1954).

THOMAS R. FORD, director of research for the Southern Appalachian Studies and editor of the present volume, is professor of sociology at the University of Kentucky. He is the author of *Man and Land in Peru* (1955).

JOHN C. BELCHER, sociologist at the University of Georgia, is the author of *Mississippi's People* (1950) and *A Short Scale for Measuring Farm Family Level of Living* (1952), and editor of *Georgia Today: Facts and Trends* (1960). Throughout his training and experience he has had a primary interest in population phenomena.

JAMES S. BROWN, a recognized authority on the Southern Appalachian family, is now directing a research project, sponsored by the National Institute of Mental Health, on the adjustment of mountain migrants to urban life. GEORGE A. HILLERY, JR., a specialist in the fields of demography and community, is a member of the Department of Sociology of the University of Kentucky.

ROSCOE GIFFIN has lectured and written on the problems of Appalachian newcomers in northern cities for the Mayors' Friendly Relations Committee of Greater Cincinnati, the Welfare Council of Metropolitan Chicago, and the Chicago Commission on Human Relations. Since 1960 he has been on leave from Berea College to serve as director of the Economics of Disarmament Program of the American Friends Service Committee.

ROY E. PROCTOR, formerly research and extension economist in Kentucky, since 1946 has been professor of agricultural economics at the University of Georgia. T. KELLEY WHITE is an instructor in the Department of Agricultural Economics at North Carolina State College.

HAROLD A. GIBBARD is professor and chairman of the Department of Sociology at West Virginia

University. His publications include contributions to *Patterns for Modern Living* (1949), *Fundamentals of Sociology* (1950), and *Essays in Social Sciences* (1958).

CHARLES L. QUITTMEYER has conducted research for the Advisory Council on the Virginia Economy, the Virginia Travel Council, and the Bureau of Population and Economic Research of the University of Virginia. He is now senior scientist for Technical Operations, Inc., at Fort Monroe, Virginia. LORIN A. THOMPSON has served as director of the Virginia Population Study for the Virginia State Planning Board, and as director of research for the Regional Department of Economic Security, Cincinnati, Ohio. Since 1944 he has been director of the Bureau of Population and Economic Research of the University of Virginia.

JOHN W. MORRIS has made recreational studies in the Ozarks and the Arkansas River basin for the National Park Service. Professor of geography at the University of Oklahoma, he is coauthor of *World Geography* (1958) and editor of a series of state geographies.

PAUL W. WAGER, professor of political science at the University of North Carolina, is the author of *County Government and Administration in North Carolina* (1928), *North Carolina—the State and Its Government* (1947), and editor of *County Government across the Nation* (1950).

AELRED J. GRAY, community planner with the Tennessee Valley Authority, has served as planning technician with the Alabama State Planning Commission. He directed the Rhode Island Hurricane Rehabilitation Study (1955) and was consultant to a similar study in North Carolina and to the Eastern Kentucky Flood Study (1957).

ORIN B. GRAFF has served in the public schools of Ohio and Tennessee as classroom teacher, principal, and superintendent. Since 1945 he has been professor of education and head of the Department of School Administration and Supervision in the College of Education of the University of Tennessee.

EARL D. C. BREWER has served as pastor of churches in Louisiana and North Carolina, and as secretary of the Board of Education of the Western North Carolina Conference of the Methodist Church. Now professor of sociology in the Candler School of Theology, Emory University, he is the author of *The Church at the Crossroads* (1947) and a contributing editor of *Review of Religious Research*.

C. HORACE HAMILTON, distinguished professor of rural sociology at North Carolina State College, has served on the Broughton Hospital and Medical Care Commission, and as director of sociological research for the National Commission on Hospital Care. He is now a member of the National Committee on Vital and Health Statistics.

WILLIAM E. COLE is the author of *Urban Society* (1958) and coauthor of *Tennessee Citizen* (1958) and *Southern Citizenship Problems* (1960). He has served as chairman of the advisory committee of the Tennessee Department of Welfare and as president of the Knoxville Council of Community Services. Mr. Cole is professor and head of the Department of Sociology at the University of Tennessee.

W. D. WEATHERFORD, director of administration of the Southern Appalachian Studies, has been a member of the Berea College Board of Trustees for forty-seven years. He is the author of *The Negro from Africa to America* (1924) and *Pioneers of Destiny* (1955), editor of *Religion in the Appalachian Mountains* (1955), and coauthor with Earl D. C. Brewer of *Life and Religion in Southern Appalachia* (1962), a report of the religious survey conducted by Southern Appalachian Studies. WILMA DYKEMAN is coauthor of *Neither Black Nor White*, winner of the Hillman Award in 1958, *Seeds of Southern Change: The Life of Will Alexander* (1962), and author of *The French Broad* (1955) in the Rivers of America Series. Her forthcoming novel, *The Tall Woman* (1962), is a story of the Southern Appalachians a century ago.

FRANK H. SMITH, author of *The Appalachian Square Dance* (1955), has served as chairman of the Mountain Folk Festival, Berea, Kentucky, director of the Christmas Country Dance School, Berea, and as vice president of the national Country Dance Society. Now retired from the Berea College staff, he is still engaged in the study and teaching of folk arts.

BERNICE A. STEVENS is director of education for the Southern Highland Handicraft Guild, Gatlinburg, Tennessee, and a regional representative of American Craftsmen's Council. A craftsman as well as a teacher, she has exhibited her jewelry in national and regional shows.

Index

www.ingramcontent.com/pod-product-compliance
Lightning Source LLC
Chambersburg PA
CBHW080230270326
41926CB00020B/4191